"Where do you go to hear hip jazz in Houston or down-and-dirty blues in Philadelphia? If the joint is jumping—or has ever jumped—it's in the **Jazz and Blues Lover's Guide to the U.S.**"

—*The Boston Globe Magazine*

"[T]his is an entertaining must-read for music-loving travelers or for those who want to travel through the then and now of jazz and blues."

—*New Orleans Times-Picayune*

"Jazz . . . is an acquired taste, yet Christiane Bird engages us right off."

—*The Washington Post*

"The **Jazz and Blues Lover's Guide to the U.S.** is the best work of its kind I have ever seen. Christiane Bird knows and loves her subject. She's obviously done her background research, but more importantly, she's been to the places she writes about and manages to convey what it's like to be in a Mississippi Delta juke joint or an East St. Louis biker's bar. This is a great travel guide, but it should also be viewed as an important historical resource, since so much of the material about landmarks, local history, the clubs, and the people who run them has never appeared in any other book."

—Jim O'Neal, founding editor of *Living Blues* magazine

"Gives jazz lovers 'Landmarks and Legends' that could form the basis for walking tours in many United States cities."

—*The New York Times*

"Dig it!"

—*Playboy*

ALSO BY CHRISTIANE BIRD

*Neither East Nor West: One Woman's Journey Through the
Islamic Republic of Iran*

New York Handbook

New York City Handbook

Below the Line: Living Poor in America (co-author)

THIRD EDITION

DA CAPO JAZZ AND BLUES LOVER'S GUIDE TO THE U.S.

*With More than **900** Hot Clubs,*
Cool Joints, Landmarks, and Legends,
from Boogie-Woogie to Bop and Beyond

CHRISTIANE BIRD

DA CAPO PRESS

Designed by Jeffrey P. Williams
Set in 8.5-point Bookman by Perseus Publishing Services

A CIP catalog record for this book is available from the Library of
Congress.

ISBN 0–306–81034–4
First Da Capo Press edition 2001

Published by Da Capo Press
A Member of the Perseus Books Group
http://www.dacapopress.com

Da Capo Press books are available at special discounts for bulk pur-
chases in the U.S. by corporations, institutions, and other organizations. For more information, please contact the Special Markets
Department at the Perseus Books Group, 11 Cambridge Center,
Cambridge, MA 02142, or call (617) 252-5298.

1 2 3 4 5 6 7 8 9—05 04 03 02 01

Contents

Acknowledgments

FIRST AND FOREMOST, I would like to thank the thirty-odd writers and researchers who contributed to this book. Many went far out of their way to provide me with current, well-written, and evocative updates; their names can be found in their respective chapters and on the "About the Contributors" page. Also, I would like to thank the dozens of people who contributed to the earlier versions of this book, and Jim Dilts in Baltimore, Joe Jennings in Atlanta, Don Marquis in New Orleans, Michael Frank in Chicago, Lou Dare in Kansas City, Lee Hildebrand in San Francisco, and John Morthland in Austin —all of whom helped me with one research question or another this time around.

A special thanks, too, to my editor Andrea Schulz and her assistant Jane Snyder, both of whom did so much to help pull together all the many pieces of this book, and to my agent, Neeti Madan of Sterling Lord Literistic.

Preface to the Third Edition

MORE THAN TEN YEARS AGO, I had the good fortune to travel around the country in search of jazz and blues clubs, historical sites, and anecdotal history. That solo—and to me, extraordinary—journey resulted in the first edition of this book, published in 1991 and revised in 1994.

This time around, I took a different approach, by using expert contributors in each city to update their respective chapters. The book that I wrote a decade ago is still here, but it's now laced with both more current information and a multitude of voices interjecting with passion and authority about a subject they know and love best. This seems only appropriate; jazz and blues itself is also a community effort.

Receiving the contributions was both exciting and surprising. To my delight, most of the venues that I wrote about seven or ten years ago are still in existence, and many of those that are not have been replaced with equivalent venues. With the possible exception of San Francisco, which suffered an overall loss in its number of full-time jazz clubs (though not in its blues venues, which are flourishing), and Kansas City, which lost too many neighborhood joints, I can't think of a single city covered by this guide that seems to have fewer clubs now than it had in 1991 or 1994—and most have more. Los Angeles, especially, is bursting with new serious jazz venues, while usually pricey New York now offers a significant number of more affordable clubs. The already healthy St. Louis and Chicago blues scenes have become livelier than ever, while Austin boasts several new swing-jazz lounges and Miami has added a few unusual venues—including a jazz gallery—to its roster.

Much of this activity is undoubtedly due to the strong state of the economy. However, I'd like to think that a growing appreciation for the music has something to do with it as well.

—*Christiane Bird*
New York City, 2001

INTRODUCTION TO THE FIRST EDITION

I WISH I COULD SAY THAT after four months spent traveling around the country compiling information for this book, I had discovered dozens upon dozens of hitherto unknown jazz and blues clubs; that deep in the bowels of Atlanta or Indianapolis were holes-in-the-wall that rocked until dawn; or that way down on some back alley in Houston or Los Angeles were juke joints packed with mind-blowing musicians the likes of which the world had never heard. This, of course, is not exactly the case—the golden era of jazz and blues is over (at least for now). But in some ways, the truth is almost as exciting, and certainly as interesting, for in every major American city—even those with no commercial jazz or blues club, and a general population that could care less about either—the music is being kept very much alive, sometimes through small African-American neighborhood clubs, sometimes through sophisticated concert series, sometimes through enthusiastic restaurateurs. There is a tremendous number of talented musicians out there and—among a limited audience at least—a tremendous enthusiasm for the music.

To bemoan the condition of jazz and blues in this country (despite what seems to be a current renaissance of interest) has become commonplace, and with good reason. Jazz and blues is America's most original art form, and yet it's woefully neglected by the mainstream. Many people barely know who Duke Ellington or Charlie Parker are, let alone Charlie Christian or Sonny Boy Williamson (I or II), or newer stars such as Lester Bowie or David Murray. The Europeans and the Japanese, who flock to jazz and blues concerts by the thousands, may appreciate the music's enormous beauty and complexity, but in general, we Americans do not. One of the saddest things about working on this book—and there were many sad things, as the history of jazz and blues is in many ways the history of the oppression of blacks in America—lay in realizing how many talented musicians have no place to play. I can think of no city that has "enough" clubs, especially for the younger or lesser-known player.

Some of this may be inevitable. There's always been something underground about jazz and blues anyway, and perhaps that's the way it always will be, even should be. Art of all types seems to need a certain amount of neglect to grow. But in the jazz and blues world, even artists who have come into their own rarely receive full-scale recognition, and many musicians working today have a hard time making a living.

Most major cities have two basic types of clubs, those that bring in national talent, and those that feature local players. The national clubs have the best musicians, the best acoustics, and the best sight lines; but the local clubs, though much more erratic, are often more atmospheric and more fun.

Local clubs are like families. Everyone knows everyone else, and people stop by to gossip, play cards, and watch television, as well as to drink and hear music. This is especially true in the poorer communities, where there is almost always a club or two that never advertises and is generally unknown to the rest of the city but that has been offering music at least once a week for 10, 20, even 30 years. It was in little joints such as these that jazz and blues was born, and even today, there's a certain magic about the neighborhood place. Never mind that it's often built of cement blocks or located in an isolated part of town, never mind that its talent is usually unknown (and sometimes deservedly so). On a Friday or Saturday night, when the notes start to circle and soar, these places are the musical centers of the universe.

Among club owners on both the local and the national level, rich and poor, black and white, I found a predictable mix. Some were running their establishments for the love of the music, some were operating purely as efficient businessmen (these were the majority), and some were looking to make a quick buck (though this seldom works for long in the jazz-blues world, where there's not that much money to begin with). Usually, though not always, it was surprisingly easy to tell which was which simply by walking into a place. There's a certain indescribable feeling about a good club, whether its decor is upscale or down. Good times, good spirits, good sounds seem to vibrate off the walls, even in the daytime, when all that's tangibly evident is the smell of last night's beer.

As a white woman exploring an art form that is predominantly black, I was constantly aware of the slippery, cumbersome issue of race. For all the strides that have been taken in civil rights over the past three decades, very few music venues in this country are truly integrated. Every establishment that I visited was either white, or it was black, and though many did have a somewhat mixed audience, there was often depressingly little real interaction between the races.

This black/white dichotomy seems especially true in the blues world, where most clubs are either trendy air-conditioned white establishments charging $10 to $20 a head, or poor cement-floored black juke joints with no cover charge. Jazz venues are usually more mixed, but the upscale African-American clubs attract even fewer whites—sometimes deliberately so—than do the poor juke joints. R&B is yet another story. There's still a "chitlin circuit" out there, featuring such stars as Tyrone Davis and Denise LaSalle, and these audiences are almost always 99 percent black.

And then there's the thorny question of the relationship between jazz and blues. Most people acknowledge that blues predates jazz and that the two forms borrow frequently from each other, but beyond that all agreement ends. Many see the two sounds as totally different and totally incompatible. Today's young white blues fans often dismiss jazz as sophisticated cocktail chatter, while many jazz musicians still equate bluesmen with raw and unsophisticated country folk. Club owners even say that the crowds' drinking habits differ. Blues fans drink beer; jazz fans drink hard liquor. Blues fans drink a lot; jazz fans sip. This kind of thinking gets extended even further by audiences who describe jazz as *only* the sounds of the 1920s and '30s, or *only* those that are post-bebop.

Part of the problem is that jazz is a complicated music that requires listening. Appreciating it takes time and effort, and since few people take that time or effort, or even get exposed to the music in the first place, it often gets left by the wayside, or else stuck in definitions and settings so formal that it scares people off. Blues, being more accessible, has a somewhat easier time of it, yet many white audiences still have no real idea of where it comes from. I think of the strange irony of one enthusiastic club owner who told me in one proud breath that he featured "nothing but the blues," and then, in another, whispered that I ought to skip the next stop on my list because it was, "you know, *black*."

Despite such muddled thinking, and our still ugly, much-segregated world, jazz and blues have probably done more to further integration than any other single art or entertainment form. One of the most wonderful things about the music is how it has brought together so many different people from so many different worlds—if not always physically, at least spiritually. I spent many amazing nights traveling from poor juke joints to plush hotel lounges to pretty yuppie-buppie clubs;

and on some level, the audiences were always the same. The club business may be extremely volatile, susceptible to everything from social whim to changes in the drinking laws, but the appeal of the music itself is stable and timeless. A song or riff heard in a black club today will be heard in a white club tomorrow, just as it was heard in the Cotton Club in the '20s or on 52nd Street in the '40s.

Many of the smaller clubs located in run-down districts are managed by women, usually motherly or grandmotherly sorts striving to provide something "nice for the neighborhood," and it is largely their care, I think, that makes the poorer places, often impeccably kept, so appealing. They're not only entertainment centers, they're also living rooms, and homes. Usually all gray and nondescript on the outside, looking more like storage sheds than anything else, they are all explosive beauty on the inside, alive with more color, sight, and sound than can be found in a dozen more upscale clubs put together. A woman dressed in high, high heels and a sequined skirt hugs the arm of a man dressed in a white three-piece suit with an elegant hat. A middle-aged stud with sunglasses dances next to a grandfather with a cane dances next to a young gyrating woman in a red slinky dress. Meanwhile, a tuxedoed musician with diamonds on his fingers and gel in his hair moans out the blues; and chicken wings and pig-ear sandwiches are for sale behind the bar. It's all a very private, self-contained world completely apart from mainstream American life, a world that despite its poverty seems rich and warm and real and makes the late twentieth century, with its constant emphasis on materialism and success, seem even more vapid than usual.

But as warm and real and exciting as the smaller, poorer clubs are, they're also far too easy to romanticize. As an outsider, I had the option of leaving when I was ready, of going back to a plusher, more open world; for many of the neighborhood people I met, their Friday or Saturday nights were it, the high point of their week. They'd just spent their extra cash and tomorrow would be another day.

As a single, middle-class woman visiting clubs in poorer neighborhoods, I never had any trouble and only once or twice encountered a hostile remark. Instead, most people were extremely gracious and hospitable. Interested that I was interested, they were pleased and proud to show off their clubs and their music. I must also quickly add that although on any given night I may have been the only out-of-towner in the crowd, I am hardly the only middle-class person "foolish" enough to venture into run-down districts. In every major city, there exists a hard-core group of musicians, deejays, critics, and music enthusiasts who make regular forays to the "wrong side of town" to catch those hot jam sessions that can somehow never quite be duplicated at the commercial clubs. It was, in fact, this group who directed me to many of the clubs I visited, and always, there had been many other out-of-towners there before me. I was especially struck by this in Mississippi, when in some tiny, hole-in-the-wall joint, looking for all the world as if it had never had *any* visitor of *any* kind, the owner would bring out a scrapbook filled with pictures and letters from Norwegians, Japanese, Germans, and Swedes, all of whom had passed through his place in earlier years.

As for the more established, nationally known clubs, many have long and proud histories. Often started up by jazz and blues fanatics while they were still in their early twenties (Joe Segal of the Jazz Showcase in Chicago, the late Max Gordon of the Village Vanguard in New York, Clifford Antone of Antone's in Austin), they've played an important role in bringing top musicians to the attention of the general public. Max Gordon was one of the first to present everyone from Dinah Washington to Sonny Rollins, while Clifford Antone has helped launch the careers of innumerable Texas bluesmen, including the late Stevie Ray Vaughan, his brother Jimmie Vaughan, and Angela Strehli.

Like the local clubs, the national clubs have a regular clientele, and it often includes well-known musicians who hang out in the joints after their gigs elsewhere are done. Nowadays, too, the nationally known spots attract numerous foreigners, who seem to come straight from the airport to the clubs and then, suffering from jet lag, fall asleep during the second set.

But clubs and live music are only part of the story. Today's music was shaped by yesterday's musicians, and one of the joys of working on this project lay in seeing the very direct connections that exist between the present and the past, reality and legend. To see the hospital where Bessie Smith died, the house where John Coltrane lived as a young man, the building where Charlie Parker first played with Dizzy Gillespie, the graveyard where Howlin' Wolf is buried—all this contributes to a vivid picture of the music and its culture as an integral part of the American scene.

Back in the days before desegregation, nearly all American cities had one main drag that was the black community's business and entertainment center. Sometimes these streets were big and elaborate affairs, like Seventh Avenue in Harlem or 47th Street in Chicago; sometimes they were tiny and rather rural—Nelson Street in Greenville, Mississippi, East 11th Street in Austin, Texas; but always, they housed important theaters and nightclubs bursting with sound. Even today, when you mention U Street in Washington, D.C., Pennsylvania Avenue in Baltimore, Decatur or Auburn Avenue in Atlanta, Beale Street in Memphis, Elm Street (Deep Ellum) in Dallas, or Hastings Street in Detroit, someone's eyes will light up.

All of those once-splendid avenues are gone now, replaced by abandoned lots and boarded-up buildings. Most fell into decline in the early 1960s with urban renewal, the building of the super-highways (which often cut through the heart of African-American neighborhoods), desegregation, and the advent of rock. Urban renewal not only destroyed the fabric of black neighborhood life by demolishing old familiar buildings and replacing them with cold edifices, but also cut jazz and blues to the quick by removing the grass-roots clubs where both children and adults first learned about the music. In addition, when African Americans were finally allowed to frequent the white clubs, many formerly successful black businessmen who had been catering exclusively to black customers went bankrupt as their clients went elsewhere.

Traveling through these poor neighborhoods by day, when there's no live music or liquor to help smooth the rawness, is even sadder than it is by night. In terms of pure acreage alone, the amount of devastated urban landscape in this country is appalling. It's one thing to live in a big city such as New York, and to be vaguely aware of Harlem or the South Bronx, perhaps occasionally venturing to a specific address therein, and quite another to drive through mile after mile after mile after mile—will it never end?—of East St. Louis, South Dallas, the South and West sides of Chicago, the Mississippi Delta, Watts, southwest Atlanta, parts of northwest Washington, east Kansas City, Detroit. Boarded-up building follows boarded-up building, empty lot follows empty lot, and how anyone or anything can emerge from this ravaged land with any sense of self or soul intact—let alone an artistic vision—is truly remarkable.

Only a few historic jazz and blues landmarks are left, and visiting them is an emotional thing, even for one who wasn't around back then. To see the old Minton's in New York, the old Cherry Blossom in Kansas City, or the old Cosmopolitan Club in St. Louis, after all the stories and all the songs—once such hotbeds, now such shells—"That, my love," said bass player Keter Betts, as he helped me locate some of Washington, D.C.'s, old U Street sites, "is like seeing a long-ago love. You see them again years later, and . . ." He shrugged. "Nothing."

Some cities, most notably Memphis, are trying to bring back their rich musical past by revitalizing historic clubs and neighborhoods. Others, most notably Kansas City, have created all sorts of music commissions, boards, and societies to help preserve the music. So far, none of these schemes seems to be working terribly well: hanging on to heritage is a tricky thing. Bygone eras cannot be recreated, and sometimes the stamp of approval destroys the very thing that it is trying to preserve. (The same could be said of this book, which by directing readers to out-of-the-way places could help to dilute the very atmosphere that makes those places special.)

On the other hand, recognition is necessary for survival. Without it, much of the richness of jazz and blues history could be lost forever. Throughout my travels, I met numerous people who are desperately working against time to interview dying generations of jazz and blues artists, or to otherwise preserve and promote the music. Many are toiling unofficially, without pay or promise of publication.

In the jazz and blues world, people are always scraping, always just getting by. There's never enough money, never enough manpower, never enough popular interest. Nonetheless, in this same world, people are always dreaming. Most operate completely outside the mainstream, where strokes of serendipitous fortune are hard to come by (few poor neighborhood clubs are going to be "discovered," few jazz or blues musicians are going to "make it") but they believe too passionately in what they are doing to let this bother them.

Just where is jazz and blues going? I'm really not scholar or critic enough to say. All I know is that the music is out there, and will always be out there.

It's time to give it its due.

—*Christiane Bird*
New York City, 1990

HOW TO USE THIS BOOK

EACH CHAPTER IN THIS BOOK is divided into two sections: one that briefly covers the history of jazz and blues in that city and mentions a few music landmarks, and one that covers the current music scene. Neither category pretends to be definitive, but is a sort of musical potpourri compiled from my own experience, the experiences of this edition's contributors, and information given to me by local experts.

The main danger in writing a book like this is high club turnover. Places come and go at an alarming rate, and by the time this guide is published, some of the establishments listed herein will be no more. On the other hand, for every club that dies a quick death, there are many others that have been around for decades (predicting which clubs are which is next to impossible; ironically, it is often the smallest, poorest club that lasts the longest). It is therefore imperative to call all clubs before visiting, or in the case of the Delta juke joints that have no phone, to stop by in the afternoon. Throughout the listings, I have also included information on when music is offered, what kind of music is offered, cover charges, food, etc. This has been included as a general guideline, rather than for strict informational purposes and should be checked in advance. CALL, CALL, CALL.

The section called "Sources," which lists local publications, etc., that give day-to-day music listings, will help you orient yourself in the jazz and blues scene of each city (see also "National Sources," below). At the end of each chapter, the sections "Radio" and "Record Stores" contain specific information on jazz/blues programming and the best places to buy the music.

Especially for the smaller cities, I have mentioned numerous places that aren't, strictly speaking, clubs, or even regular music venues. Some of these are primarily restaurants; others just offer live entertainment once or twice a week. I have felt it important to include these spots, however, as they are often local institutions that have been the mainstays of their respective jazz and blues communities for years and years. I have also used the terms "local" and "national" musicians rather loosely, and more as a way of indicating whether a club books touring talent or not than as a way of measuring the quality of its music. Many cities are home to "local" musicians who are nationally or even internationally known.

Not all of the clubs in the following pages are for everyone. Some are extremely informal; some are extremely expensive. Still others are located in rough neighborhoods, and should be visited with caution. If you do venture into a rough neighborhood, it's a good idea to arrive early so that you can park near the door. Also, inquire about parking or cab service when you call. Surprisingly enough, some of the tiniest and most unassuming of clubs—Checkerboard's on Chicago's South Side, Eli's Mile High Club in West Oakland—have become so well known that they now offer security parking. Others, located in neglected neighborhoods in major cities are happy to call cabs for their patrons.

As for the sites mentioned under "Landmarks and Legends," many are abandoned buildings that will be of interest only to a handful of fans, or to the armchair traveler. Others are private homes, and the privacy of their residents should be respected.

Key

Dollar signs are used throughout the book to indicate cover charges and other prices:

$ = inexpensive ($1–$6)
$$ = moderate ($7–$15)
$$$ = expensive ($16–$25)
$$$$ = very expensive ($26 and above)

National Sources

Three top national magazines covering the jazz scene are *Jazz Times* (8737 Colesville Rd., Fifth Fl., Silver Spring, Md. 20910–3921; 301–588–4114), *Down Beat* (102 N. Haven Rd., Elmhurst, Ill. 60126–2970; 630–941–2030, www.downbeat. com), and *Jazziz* (2650 N. Military Trail, Suite 140, Fountain Square II, Boca Raton, Fl. 33431; 561–893–6868). *Jazz Times* publishes a jazz-and-blues club guide every year, usually in their September issue.

Living Blues (P.O. Box 1848, 301 Hill Hall, University, Miss. 38677; www.LivingBluesOnline.com), a bimonthly magazine available by mail only, does an excellent job of covering blues nationwide and includes information on clubs, festivals, and other special events. *Living Blues* also puts out a biannual national blues directory listing club addresses, blues society addresses, booking agents, festivals, and more ($35).

National Public Radio hosts a jazz web site, www.npr-jazz.org, with listings of NPR jazz stations around the country, reviews of CDs and books, links to other major jazz sites, and events listings for a few cities such as New York, Chicago, and Seattle. The site www.jazzusa.com publishes a monthly on-line 'zine with lively articles and CD reviews, and has links to other jazz sites.

DA CAPO JAZZ AND BLUES LOVER'S GUIDE TO THE U.S.

The Preservation Hall Jazz Bands have
been a New Orleans staple since the 1960s.

Jazz Club Collection, LSM

NEW ORLEANS

Updated by the staff of *OffBeat*

> One of my pleasantest memories as a kid growing up in New Orleans was how a bunch of us kids, playing, would suddenly hear sounds. It was like a phenomenon, like the Aurora Borealis—maybe. The sounds of men playing would be so clear, but we wouldn't be sure where they were coming from. So we'd start trotting, start running—"It's this way!", "It's that way!"—And, sometimes, after running for a while, you'd find you'd be nowhere near that music. But that music could come on you any time like that. The city was full of the sounds of music. . . .
>
> — *Danny Barker in* Hear Me Talkin' to Ya

The list of New Orleans jazz, blues, and R&B greats is tremendously impressive, beginning with Buddy Bolden, King Oliver, Jelly Roll Morton, Sidney Bechet, Johnny Dodds, and Louis Armstrong, and continuing in more recent times with Professor Longhair, Fats Domino, Dr. John, Allen Toussaint, the Marsalis family, Irma Thomas, and Harry Connick, Jr. In between are scores of other internationally renowned artists playing in a wide variety of styles.

As far as music historians can tell, jazz was first heard on the streets of New Orleans in the late 1800s. A strong African influence (see Congo Square, page 20), combined with Creole and Anglo elements, led to the development of the new sound, which was played in the open air by the city's countless brass bands. Parades, picnics, "lawn parties," and especially funerals—to an early New Orleanian, all called for music.

In 1898, the city's notorious Storyville district was created, and suddenly there were hundreds of jobs for all kinds of musicians. Classically educated Creole musicians, representing the cream of black society, mixed with uneducated musicians playing a more raw, more emotional sound, and "jass," as it was then called, evolved yet further.

Storyville was closed in 1917, the same year a group of white New Orleans musicians, the Original Dixieland Jazz Band, recorded the first jazz record. In 1918, Louis Armstrong began testing his chops by playing on the Streckfus riverboats that plowed the Mississippi, but by 1922 he was gone, up to Chicago to join King Oliver's band.

During the 1920s and '30s, Milneburg on Lake Pontchartrain, 10 miles from downtown New Orleans, was one of the best places in the city to hear jazz. Back then, the shoreline was lined with hundreds of fishing camps built out onto piers over the water, where the town's citizens would come for the weekend, bringing with them food, friends, and private jazz bands. On any given weekend, there might be as many as 50 or 60 jazz groups playing up and down the docks. "We'd hire Papa Celestin's band for thirty-five dollars for the weekend and bring the cook," said jazz historian Al Rose, who lived through those days. "We'd buy a two-hundred-pound green turtle. The Creole word for turtle, 'cawein,' also means picnic, and we'd get on a railroad train that took us to the lake. The train had an empty car on it for the drunks coming back, and they'd be loaded on like cordwood."

The late 1940s, '50s, and '60s brought with them a new urban sound, best represented by the blues and R&B music of such masters as Fats Domino, Professor Longhair, Huey "Piano" Smith, Dr. John, and Irma Thomas. Though less known for its blues than for its jazz, New Orleans has always had a strong blues sensibility, as can be heard in its gospel choirs and honking saxes.

In the 1980s, jazz in New Orleans went through another renaissance, this one led by trumpet player Wynton Marsalis. Along with Wynton came his brothers Branford on sax and Delfeayo on trombone, trumpeter Terence Blanchard, saxophonist Donald Harrison, pianist Harry Connick, Jr., the Dirty Dozen Brass Band, the ReBirth Brass Band, and others.

Sources

OffBeat (504–944–4300, www.offbeat.com) is an excellent free music guide, written especially for out-of-towners; club listings are updated daily on their Web site. *Gambit* (504–486–5900), a free weekly, also has listings, as does the Friday section of the *Times-Picayune* (504–826–3464).

OffBeat also publishes the *Louisiana Music Directory* ($35), which includes extensive listings of bands, musicians, booking agents, record labels, clubs, and festivals in Louisiana. Another good source for general music info is the Louisiana Music Factory (210 Decatur St., 504–596–1094, www.louisianamusic factory.com), a record store.

For general maps and other information, contact the Greater New Orleans Tourist and Convention Commission, 1520 Sugar Bowl Dr., 504–566–5011, or stop by the Tourist Information Center at 529 Ann St. in the French Quarter. Good general city Web sites are www.insideneworleans.com, www.nolalive.com, and www.neworleans.citysearch.com.

A Note on Neighborhoods

New Orleans is a city deeply rooted in its past. Nothing seems to change here, not the old French Quarter, not the fine Creole cooking, not the love of good times. Tourists may come and go by the thousands, but New Orleans never changes.

"Uptown" New Orleans means anything west of Canal Street, while "Downtown" includes, among other neighborhoods, the historic French Quarter. The Garden District, located Uptown, is an elite nineteenth-century residential neighborhood; Faubourg Marigny, near the French Quarter, is a young, nontourist area known for its avant-garde theaters, art galleries, and music clubs. Tremé, also near the French Quarter, is one of the oldest African-American neighborhoods in the city.

Traffic in the French Quarter is often heavy, but otherwise, driving in New Orleans is relatively painless.

Landmarks and Legends

In and Around the French Quarter

(The following sites can be viewed on foot. The route below begins at the northwestern end of the Quarter, proceeds east and south, and then circles back around to the Uptown side of Canal Street.)

Storyville, once bounded by Basin, Robertson, St. Louis, and Iberville streets.

Storyville, the notorious red-light district whose reputation has taken on mythic proportions over the years, was once located adjacent to the French Quarter, just north of Basin Street. Today, the 16-block area is occupied by the Iberville housing projects and it is marked by an historical plaque on the Basin Street traffic island, near Iberville Street.

Created on January 1, 1898, Storyville was an urban planning experiment designed to stop the spread of whorehouses throughout the city. But much to the chagrin of the city alderman, Sidney Story, for whom it was named, it quickly evolved into virtually a self-contained kingdom of vice. It even had its own mayor, state legislator Tom Anderson, who was also its foremost pimp.

The streets of Storyville were lined with huge, ornate brothels, cabarets, honky-tonks, gambling dens, and dance halls. At one time there were over 2,000 prostitutes working the District, as it was called, and typical prices ranged from as high as $50 in the brothel-mansions, of which there were 30 to 40, to as little as 50 cents in the "cribs," small rooms with doors facing the streets for seductive posturing.

The District provided musicians with a wealth of employment opportunities. All the dance halls needed bands, and all of the major whorehouses had their own steady "professor" or house piano player. Jelly Roll Morton, Tony Jackson, Clarence Williams, and King Oliver were among the hundreds of musicians who once played Storyville.

In 1917, the Secretary of the Navy decreed that the vices of Storyville constituted a threat to America's military forces and shut the District down. Some of its madams moved to the French Quarter, and some of its musicians moved north in a migration that had already begun before 1917.

In addition to this official Storyville, which employed whites, blacks, and octoroons, there was also an unofficial Black Storyville, located just uptown of Canal. Louis Armstrong grew up in Black Storyville.

Lulu White's Saloon, NW corner of Bienville and Basin streets.

Lulu White was the most famous madam of Storyville, and Mahogany Hall was the most notorious brothel, with a mirrored parlor that alone was estimated to have cost $30,000. Among the many things White, the aunt of composer Spencer Williams, was famed for were the diamond rings she wore on all her fingers, including her thumbs. She also employed some of the finest piano players in the city, including Jelly Roll Morton and Tony Jackson.

Mahogany Hall is gone now, replaced by a parking garage, but Lulu White's Saloon, a windowless brick building on the corner of Bienville and Basin streets that was once attached to the hall, still stands. The building once had a third floor (torn off by a storm not too long ago) and that's where the legendary "Blue Book," a guide to the ladies of Storyville, was published. It listed its subjects by name, address, and color, with the 1915 edition including nine octoroons, 254 blacks, and 464 whites. The publication also contained advertisements; a sample read:

"Of all the landladies of the Tenderloin, there are few better known or admired than Grace Lloyd. Grace, as she is commonly called by all who know her, is a woman of very rare attainments and comes of that good old English stock from across the waters.

"Grace is regarded as an all-round jolly good fellow, saying nothing about her beauty. She regards life as life and not as a money-making space of time."[1]

Old Storyville Cribs, Bienville between Basin and Crozat streets.

Of all the hundreds of "cribs" that once existed in Storyville, these are the only ones still standing. According to jazz historian Al Rose, each one of the six compartments in the small two-story building would be rented out to different women for $3 per eight hours, thereby allowing landlords to earn what was then a substantial $12 a day.

Frank Early's Saloon, SW corner of Bienville and Crozat streets.

A wonderful old wooden building with shutters and a rickety second-floor balcony, Early's Saloon is now a convenience store for the Iberville projects. Tony Jackson, flamboyant and homosexual and one of the best piano players in the District, was playing here when he wrote the song "Pretty Baby." It was written about another man.

Not far away, at Hula Mae's Laundry, 838–40 N. Rampart St., is a plaque commemorating the site of the **J&M Recording Studio**, a legendary spot run by Cosmo Matassa. Everyone from traditional jazz musicians to R&B greats Fats Domino and Little Richard recorded here in the 1950s and 1960s.

Louis Armstrong Park

Though it boasts a gaudy new arch marking its entrance, and will one day be home to the Jazz National Historical Park (see below), the Louis Armstrong Park today stands sadly deserted and run-down. Once, however, this whole area (torn down in the 1950s) housed dozens of important jazz spots—San Jacinto Hall, the Gypsy Tea Room, Economy Hall, the Frolic, Globe Hall.

Louis Armstrong's solemn statue now stands in a shallow pool to the right of the entrance. The Municipal Auditorium, the Theatre for the Performing Arts, Beauregard Square, Perseverance Hall, and the studios of WWOZ radio are also located here, but the park is no place for a lazy afternoon stroll. It is unpatrolled and should be visited with caution.

Congo Square, now Beauregard Square, in Armstrong Park.

In the left-hand corner of the park, near the entrance, is a square lined with dark shiny bricks arranged in dizzying circles. Nowadays the square is usually completely silent, swept clean by the wind, but somehow, as you stand listening, you can almost hear and see it all again . . . the drums, the dancing, the horns, the chanting—the endless lines of people swilling and swirling—the parades, the masks, the mysteries of *voodoo*. . . .

Congo Square is the place before the place, the actual spot where, many experts believe, jazz was born. Back in the 1800s the square was the Sunday-afternoon gathering place for African slaves and one of the only spots in the New World where blacks could legally play and dance to the complex polyrhythms of Africa (drum playing was against the law in most parts of the United States, as slave owners felt it led to rioting). Through the performances at the square, the African sounds were not only preserved but also gotten out into the open where they could both influence and be influenced by European music (i.e., become jazz).

Perseverance Hall, NE corner of Armstrong Park.

Perseverance Hall, with its imposing Greek Revival facade, is the oldest Masonic Temple in Louisiana, dating back to 1820. During its early years it was both a meeting place for the Masonic Lodge and a sort of civic center for the "free men and women of color" who lived in the nearby Tremé district.

Later the hall was known for its dances. The crowds were white but the bands were black, and the Captains Streckfus, riverboat captains who hired jazzmen to play on their steamboats, would come here looking for players. Buddy Bolden and Kid Rena were among the musicians who played the hall.

The New Orleans Jazz Club Collections, Louisiana State Museum, United States Mint, 400 Esplanade Ave., 504–568–6968 or 504–568–8215, http://lsm.crt.state.la.us.

Started in 1961 by the New Orleans Jazz Club, the collections have had a variety of homes over the years, finally moving into the old United States Mint building as part of the Louisiana State Museum in 1983. The exhibits, which cover one wing of the museum, are large and well presented, with plenty of blown-up photos and memorabilia. Sidney Bechet's soprano sax is here; so are Baby Dodds's drumsticks and Papa Jack Laine's cowbell. One whole case is devoted to Armstrong: highlights are the cornet he learned to play on in the Municipal Boys' Home in 1913 and the bugle he played at home, also in 1913. Another case contains the cuff links Bix Beiderbecke wore shortly before his death, and his handkerchief. These were donated to the museum by Hoagy Carmichael, with a note saying, "You may launder the handkerchief if you wish, but perhaps it is better to display it in its present state of age."

Added to the museum in 1993 was a letter of admiration written by Harry Connick, Jr., age ten, to Eubie Blake, age 84. Other recent additions include an exhibit on the Marsalis family, and another on the history of New Orleans women in jazz.

Open: T–Su, 10 A.M.–5 P.M. *Admission:* $.

New Orleans Jazz National Historic Park, 916 N. Peters St., 504–589–4841, www.nps.gov/neor.

One of the newest units of the National Park system, the New Orleans Jazz National Historic Park is temporarily housed in this visitor/orientation center. Inside, find a cluster of three changing exhibits on such topics as "Riverboats and Jazz," the "Louis Armstrong Centennial," or Bunk Johnson, as well as a performance stage where about a dozen afternoon jazz concerts are presented every month. Among those who have performed here are Chris Clifton & His All-Stars, Bob French's Original Tuxedo Band, Henry Butler, and David Torkanowsky. Lectures, kids programs, a CD/book shop, and an events information kiosk are also integral parts of the center.

The jazz park, which focuses on traditional jazz (covering 1895–1930), has big plans in the works. Within the next two to three years, it hopes to move to Louis Armstrong Park (see above), where it will eventually occupy a total of four buildings. One, to be shared with WWOZ radio, will house an expanded visitors center; another, a dance hall and performance space; a third, a resource center; and a fourth, administration services.

Hours: W-Su, 9 A.M.–5 P.M. *Free.*

Odd Fellows Masonic Hall, 1116 Perdido St. near S. Rampart St., and **Eagle Saloon,** 401 S. Rampart St.

On the second floor of this long, gray building, whose entrance was once through 1116 Perdido, was the Masonic Hall, a popular dance site. The legendary Buddy Bolden was a regular here from 1900 to 1906, as was a floorwalker named Bob Foots, who wore size 14 shoes and carried a nightstick. Beneath the hall was the Eagle Saloon (401 Perdido), from which Frankie Dusen's Eagle Band took its name.

It was in front of the Odd Fellows one Labor Day that Louis Armstrong first heard Sidney Bechet play. All the musicians were working in parades that day, but somehow Bechet had fallen between the cracks. Then Henry Allen, Red Allen's father, spotted him standing near the hall and immediately put him to work. "Bechet joined the band," writes Armstrong in his autobiography *Satchmo,* "and he made the whole parade, blowing like crazy. . . . I followed him all that day.

There was not a cornet player in New Orleans who was like him. What feeling! What soul! Every other player in the city had to give it to him."

Jane Alley, between Loyola and S. Rampart streets, directly opposite City Hall.

Jane Alley, the one-block street where Louis Armstrong was born, supposedly on the Fourth of July, 1900 (though music historians have since established that his true date of birth was August 4, 1901), is now part of an empty lot marked CENTRAL PARKING SYSTEM. On the north side of the lot is a brick wall, over the top of which you'll see a tree, where Armstrong's house once stood (it was torn down in 1964).

In Louis's day the area was known as Black Storyville, or "the Battlefield," and it was a tough part of town, crowded, writes Armstrong in *Satchmo,* with "gamblers, hustlers, cheap pimps, thieves, prostitutes and lots of children." At the age of 12 or 13, Armstrong fired a pistol during a New Year's Eve celebration and was hauled off to jail by a policeman. Two days later, he was sentenced to the Colored Waifs' Home for Boys. All was not lost, however, because he joined the home's brass band and was quickly made its leader.

Colored Knights of Pythian, 234 Loyola St., near Perdido.

This boxy green office building stands on the former site of the Colored Knights of Pythian, a major black success story of its day. Housed in the organization's 13-story headquarters were offices, a theater, dance hall, movie house, and roof garden. The place enthralled a young Louis Armstrong, who played there both as a member of the Colored Waif's orchestra and, years later, as a professional musician performing in the roof garden.

Red Onion, 762 S. Rampart St. at Julia.

Back in the 1910s and '20s, the then-seedy Red Onion, now a well-kept office building, was a mecca for black and white musicians alike. Jelly Roll Morton, Louis Armstrong, Johnny Dodds, and Sidney Bechet all played here; later, in New York in 1924, Louis recorded with several groups called the Red Onion Jazz Babies, one of which included Sidney Bechet. Johnny Dodds also recorded a tune called "Red Onion Blues."

Downtown

(These sites are best toured by car. The following route begins near the Quarter, and proceeds north and then east, crossing a bridge into the Ninth Ward.)

Jack Laine's home, 2401–2405 Chartres St. at Mandeville.

Laine, one of the first white jazz musicians, lived in this big house, complete with a balcony and, today at least, orange trees out front. Laine was a popular bandleader who sometimes had as many as four jobs in one day and is said to have had the first ragtime marching band in the city.

Italian Hall, 1020 Esplanade Ave., near N. Rampart St.

A handsome mauve-and-white building with lions at its door, the Italian (now condominiums) was a popular dance hall during the 1920s. The first racially mixed recording in the South was made here when a white clarinetist sat in with a black band called the Jones and Collins Astoria Hot Eight.

Sidney Bechet's Home, 1507 Marais St., near St. Bernard.

Bechet, the Creole clarinetist and soprano saxophonist who would later go on to become a national celebrity in France (Nice has a statue dedicated to him), grew up in this small, somewhat dilapidated wooden house with the big front porch. As a young boy, Bechet began playing with his brother's Silver Bells Band, but even back then he knew he wanted a different sound. "I could see there was other bands who were doing more to advance ragtime, playing it with a better feeling," he writes in his autobiography, *Treat It Gentle.* "I'd listen and I'd get the feeling terrible strong that I wanted to play how they were playing." Before long, young Bechet, then only about 10, formed his first band, the seven-piece Young Olympia Band, with trumpet player Buddy Petit. The young men had considerable success, playing many kinds of engagements—balls, banquets, and parades—all over the city.

The Alley, off Claiborne Ave., near St. Bernard St.

Just west of the Circle Mart located at the southwest corner of Claiborne and St. Bernard is an extremely narrow alleyway. Back in the 1910s, before unions, this tiny space was usually jammed with musicians looking for work. A prospective employer would come here and shout out what he wanted—a drummer, a trumpet player, a piano player; $4 for the night— and would often conduct an audition right on the spot.

Edward Boatner's home, 2139 Ursulines Ave., at Galvez.

This large, two-story building with columns and a gate was once home to Detroit preacher and composer Edward Boatner, who wrote not only the religious classic "He's Got the Whole World in His Hands" but also the jazz classic "When the Saints Go Marching In." According to jazz historian Al Rose, "Saints" was first published in a Baptist hymnal in 1916 and it was Louis Armstrong who first turned it into a jazz hit in 1936. Boatner's son was the jazz saxophonist Sonny Stitt.

Jelly Roll Morton's home, 1441–1443 Frenchmen St., at Robertson.

This very attractive house, built in the traditional mid-nineteenth-century Creole style, was the boyhood home of composer and piano player Jelly Roll Morton (Ferdinand La Menthe). Born into a well-educated family, Morton learned to play a number of instruments as a child, eventually settling on the piano.

In *Mister Jelly Roll,* by Alan Lomax, Ferdinand states that he was first exposed to music at the age of six months. A "sporting woman" to whom his godmother had "loaned" him was arrested and thrown into jail, along with her young charge. "The inmates were singing and making a lot of noise . . ." says Jelly Roll, "and, as long as they would sing, it would keep the baby happy."

Fats Domino's home, NW corner, Caffin Ave. and Marais St.

Antoine Domino grew up in this working-class neighborhood in the lower Ninth Ward, located just beyond the Industrial Canal, and even after making it big, he vowed he'd never leave. The house where he now lives, just a few streets away from his boyhood home, surely stands out, though: it is three times bigger than anything else in sight, a tan-brick 1950s-style residence with a peaked roof, pink and yellow trim, a white wrought-iron fence with pink and green roses, and surveillance cameras.

Inside, rumor has it, there are crystal chandeliers, four ivory dominos set into the tile of a white marble floor, and closets filled with hundreds of wonderful suits in all colors of the rainbow. Fats's favorite room is said to be the kitchen, for he loves to cook, and even when he travels, packs hotplates and cooking gear along with his clothes and musical equipment.

Uptown

(The following route, best toured by car, begins at Constance Street and proceeds as far north as La Salle Street and as far west as Webster.)

Nick LaRocca's home, 2216 Constance St. near Philip.

LaRocca, the leader of and cornet player for the Original Dixieland Jazz Band (the group that made the first jazz recording in 1917), had a musical staff imprinted on his front door. The notes, still there today, spell out the beginning of the jazz classic, "Tiger Rag."

Professor Longhair's home, 1740 Terpsichore St. near Baronne.

The house is brown, wooden, and typically New Orleans, this last abode of the Professor, who lived here for only a short period prior to his death. That period was one of the few happy ones of his life.

Fess's story is an all-too-familiar one. Born Henry Roeland Byrd in 1918, he grew up haunting the clubs of Rampart Street and did some recording for Atlantic in the early 1950s. Nothing really took off, though, and Fess sank into a long and impoverished obscurity until 1970, when a British blues journalist, Mike Leadbitter, found him sweeping out the floor of a record shop. After this, a New Orleans promoter, Quint Davis, set about resuscitating his career. "He was in a totally depreciated state physically . . . " Davis once said. "When he sat down, he couldn't get up. When he did stand up, his knee would rattle around until it set into a groove so he could walk. He had a vitamin deficiency, he had no teeth, no digestion, and he couldn't go to the bathroom."[2]

One of Davis's first moves was to book the Professor into the New Orleans Jazz and Heritage Festival (an event that Davis had helped launch), and from then on, Fess's luck began to change. He began playing at local clubs and international festivals, released two albums and became part owner of the club Tipitina's (see "Clubs, etc.," page 40).

In 1980, shortly after moving to this house, Fess was on the brink of national stardom. His concerts were attracting more and more attention; he was scheduled to be taped for a television documentary; and his already sold-out album, *Crawfish Fiesta,* was about to be released. But it was not to be. On the morning of January 30, the Professor died in his sleep. He is buried beneath a piano-shaped tombstone in the Mt. Olivet Cemetery in Gentilly, a suburb of Orleans Parish.

Dew Drop Inn Café and Bar, 2836 La Salle St., near Washington.

In the 1940s and '50s, the Dew Drop Inn was the most famous African-American nightclub in New Orleans. Known for its R&B talent, it featured everyone from national names like Big Joe Turner, Little Richard, and Dinah Washington to local up-and-comers like Guitar Slim, Charles Neville, and Allen Toussaint. Big-name entertainers—Duke Ellington, Ray Charles, Ella Fitzgerald—also stopped in whenever they were in town.

Basin Street was once lined with innumerable dens of iniquity, from whose windows poured "jass."

Jazz Club Collection, LSM

According to *Up From the Cradle of Jazz* by Berry, Foose, and Jones, the club was started by chance by a barber named Frank Painia, who began selling refreshments out of his shop when city workers building a nearby housing project needed a place to buy lunch. The shop eventually grew into a restaurant, which grew into a nightclub.

Because it was the late '40s and the Dew Drop was an African-American club, it was against the law for whites to enter. As word about the Dew Drop spread, however, whites began frequenting the club, with owner Painia welcoming everyone. This led to periodic raids. One case in 1952, involving white movie star Zachary Scott, made the papers, and as late as 1964, Painia, who was still being harassed, filed suit in federal court to challenge the constitutionality of the law. The passage of the Civil Rights Act by Congress that same year made the case moot and it was dropped.

The original Dew Drop closed down in 1972, following the death of Frank Painia, and for years the place lived on only in memories and in the words of the song "Jumpin' at the Dew Drop" by Ivory Joe Hunter: "Jumping at the Dew Drop, meet you down there/Jumping at the Dew Drop, really send you/They swing and they boogie and they groove some, too/If you don't enjoy, there's something wrong with you." Recently, however, the place has reopened as a neighborhood bar and occasionally sponsors special music events.

Buddy Bolden's home, 2309 First St., just off La Salle St.

Of all the figures in jazz history, Buddy Bolden is the most elusive. One of the first jazzmen—some say *the* first—and idolized by musicians and audiences all over the city, he is shrouded in legend. They say that he could memorize music instantly; that the ladies followed him wherever he went; that he drank heavily; that he was never slow to pick a fight.

Some things, however, are known to be fact: Bolden did blow a mean cornet, he did die in a mental institution, and he did live at 2309 First from 1887 to 1906. In fact, he used to sit on the front steps of this small yellow house with the red trim and play jazz duets with Harry Shields, a white clarinet player who lived down the street.

By the time Bolden went insane in 1906–07, he had left this house and moved in with his mother and sister at 2302 First. As he became increasingly violent and incoherent, his family, not knowing what else to do, called the police. They placed him first in a common jail cell, then in the Jackson State Hospital for the insane, where he died, oblivious to his surroundings, nearly 20 years later.

Other Nearby Sites

New Orleans Fairgrounds, near Gentilly Blvd. and Esplanade Ave., not far from City Park (5 min. N of Quarter).

The premier music festival in the United States takes place every late April on the grassy grounds of the New Orleans race track (see "Major Festivals," page 458). Now ten days in length, the extravaganza presents more than 7,000 musicians playing jazz, blues, R&B, gospel, zydeco, Cajun, Afro-Caribbean, ragtime, folk, country-and-western, Latin, and more. The event is also known for its food—boiled crawfish, jambalaya, gumbo, etc.—and its crowds, a total of about 450,000 at last count.

The first forerunner of today's New Orleans Jazz & Heritage Festival took place in May 1968, as part of the 250th birthday celebration of the city. Back then, the events were free and held downtown on Canal Street and in what is now Armstrong Park. Louis Armstrong, Dave Brubeck, Duke Ellington, Pete Fountain, and Woody Allen (who flew in from filming *Bananas*) were among the headliners.

Marsalis Motel, corner of Shrewsbury and River roads (25 min. W of French Quarter).

Ellis Marsalis, Sr., father of Ellis Marsalis, Jr., and grandfather of Wynton, Branford, and Delfeayo, once ran a motel out of this one-story brown building in a residential area of Jefferson Parish. Ellis Sr. was an influential local businessman who did much to promote civil rights in New Orleans, but he reportedly was none too happy when his son, Ellis Jr., began running a jazz club out of the family motel in the 1950s. Ellis Jr. has since served as a mentor and role model to dozens of today's New Orleans musicians.

Lake Pontchartrain and **Milneburg Lighthouse** (10 min. N of Quarter).

Many visitors to New Orleans never make it out to the lake, and that's a shame because it's a beautiful sight (even though the lake is polluted), a pale blue expanse stretching as far as the eye can see. Fishermen sit along its edges, casting their lines; sailboats tack gently in the wind, their bright sails billowing in the breeze.

During the early years of jazz, the lake resounded with music. First there was the West End, where from the late 1890s to 1910 or so public concerts were held in large outdoor bandstands. Then there was Spanish Fort, which was basically an amusement park with entertainment stages. Finally, on the eastern end of the lake, there was Milneburg, a mind-boggling place where 50 to 60 top-quality bands played up and down the docks.

All of that is gone now, replaced by landfill and the University of New Orleans, but the names of two of the lake's three main resorts, Milneburg and West End, remain as a sort of legacy, along with the Milneburg Lighthouse. Spanish Fort is no more.

A scenic lakeshore drive follows the shoreline between West End and Milneburg.

CLUBS, ETC.

New Orleans has a live music scene that is as active, vital, and enduring as any place in the world. The music clubs are very diverse in nature and many, if not most, book many different genres of music, often making it difficult to classify a venue specifically as a "blues club" or "jazz club." The general level of musicianship is unparalleled in New Orleans to the extent that it is impossible for a mediocre musician to make it as a professional.

However, Bourbon Street, once a mecca for jazz fans, now has very few good jazz spots. Rather, it has metamorphosed into a wasteland, lined with sex shows, souvenir shops, and third-rate music clubs, all of which loudly hawk their wares to the drove of tourists who stroll, drinks in hand, from one amusement to another. Bourbon Street is not filled with mediocre musicians, but it does deliver a steady diet of unin-spired music to visitors who don't know any better and don't care. At its best, the street feels like a seedy carnival filled with characters; at its worst, it's a cheap, exploitative tourist trap.

To find good jazz and blues in New Orleans, as elsewhere in the country, you have to look. Most of what you'll hear here is New Orleans–style jazz, in both its traditional and contem-porary forms, but modern jazz can also be found, especially at the city's top jazz club, **Snug Harbor**, which hosts much national talent. Touring blues acts are most frequently booked into **Tipitina's** and **House of Blues**.

For the most part, music clubs in New Orleans do not charge significant cover charges. Alcohol likewise is relatively inexpensive and is consumed in quantities that tend to shock the uninitiated. As a general rule, most performers play mul-tiple sets and, true to local custom, are known for taking somewhat lengthy breaks between sets.

New Orleans has a plethora of great musicians—some well known, others more obscure. Whatever its faults, the city has always nurtured young musical talents, allowing them to grow up at the feet of the masters—often at a startlingly young age—and served as a mecca for aspiring musicians from all over the world.

Among the many, many jazz artists to watch out for are (in alphabetical order) James Andrews, Rebecca Barry, Germaine Bazzle, Terence Blanchard, John Boutte, Wendell Brunious, Henry Butler, Thais Clark, Davell Crawford, Tony Dagradi, Jeremy Davenport, Phil DeGruy, Lance Ellis, George French, Bob French, Victor Goines, Tim Green, Roland Guerin, Donald Harrison, Clarence Johnson III, Leroy Jones, Kidd Jordan, Marlon Jordan, Clyde Kerr, Tim Laughlin, John Mahoney, Jack Maheu, Phillip Manuel, Delfeayo Marsalis, Ellis Marsalis, Jason Marsalis, Steve Masakowski, Irvin Mayfield, Charlie Miller, Roderick Paulin, Nicholas Payton, Walter Payton, Pfister Sisters, Shannon Powell, Kermit Ruffins, Wardell Quezergue, Michael Ray, Herlin Riley, Bill Solley & Kim Prevost, Sista Teedy, David Torkanowsky, Eric Traub, Rick Trolsen, Don Vappie, Johnny Vidacovich, and Rob Wagner.

Among the jazz bands to watch out for are (also in alpha-betical order) the Algiers Brass Band, Astral Project, Cool-bone, Egg Yolk Jubilee, Los Hombres Calientes, Lil Rascals Brass Band, Naked on the Floor, Newbirth Brass Band, New Orleans Nightcrawlers, Olympia Brass Band, Pinstripe Jazz Band, ReBirth Brass Band, Quintology, Soul Rebels Brass band, Tremè Brass Band, and Tuba Fats and his Chosen Few.

Blues artists well worth seeking out include Brint Anderson, Tab Benoit, Spencer Bohren, Clarence "Gatemouth"

Since 1961, Preservation Hall has been smoking with New Orleans trad jazz.

Courtesy Preservation Hall

Brown, Henry Butler, John Carey, Willie Cole, John Fohl, Andy Forest, G. G. Shinn, Smokey Greenwell, Henry Grey, Corey Harris, Kenny Holladay, Wallace Johnson, Mathilda Jones, Luther Kent, Chris Thomas King, Earl King, Bryan Lee, Nelson Lunding, Jeremy Lyons, J. Monque D, John Mooney, Raful Neal, Paula & the Pontiacs, Coco Robicheaux, Rockin Jake, Jumpin Johnny Sansone, Mem Shannon, Tabby Thomas, Chris Vincent, Walter "Wolfman" Washington, and Kipori Woods.

New Orleans is a late-night town, with many bars and clubs staying open until 4 or 5 A.M. on the weekends. Live music generally starts at about 10 P.M. and stops at 2 A.M.

Personal Favorites

Best-known New Orleans clubs: *Preservation Hall, Tipitina's*
Best modern jazz club: *Snug Harbor*
Best sound in a blues club: *House of Blues*
Best traditional jazz club: *Palm Court*
Best atmosphere: *Funky Butt*
Most fun: *Donna's, Mid-City Lanes Rock 'n' Bowl*
Best neighborhood joint: *Vaughan's*

FOR JAZZ

In and Around the French Quarter

Preservation Hall, 726 St. Peter St., 504–523–8939, www.preservationhall.com.

Preservation Hall has contributed much to New Orleans's music history. In 1961, when it was founded by Allan and Sandra Jaffe, there was no place in the whole city of New Orleans in which to hear authentic jazz played by its originators. Oh, sure, there was *jazz*, in fact there was lots of *jazz*, all up and down Bourbon Street, but most of it was young and most of it was white.

Preservation Hall (which many skeptics predicted would die an early death) and the Jaffes, through much personal sacrifice, changed all that. They gave the older traditional African-American jazzmen—Kid Thomas, Punch Miller, George Lewis, Willie and Percy Humphrey—a forum in which to play; and before long, the place began attracting national attention. The Jaffes' next step was to book their bands out of town, and eventually they developed a highly successful touring schedule placing three Preservation Hall bands on the road at the same time.

Today, Allan Jaffe's work is being carried on by his son Ben, and while you may be turned off by the hordes of unsophisticated tourists consistently lined up to get into the place, the music is generally first-rate. Top players here these days include band leaders Wendell Brunious and Leroy Jones, who have established themselves as twenty-first century masters of classic jazz.

Preservation Hall is tiny and has no climate control. The seating is limited to few battered wooden benches and patrons are often forced to stand or sit on the floor. But it's all worth it when the music begins.

Music: nightly, starting at 8 P.M. *Cover*: $.

Donna's Bar & Grill, 800 N. Rampart St., 504–596–6914, www.donnasbarandgrill.com.

The brass band headquarters of New Orleans, this institution features brass band and traditional jazz five nights a week. On the edge of the French Quarter across from Louis Armstrong Park, Donna's is a favorite hangout for music lovers and musicians. On Monday nights, George and Bob French lead their traditional jam session with some of the city's finest musicians; free food is served after the first set. Thursdays through the weekend, such great acts as Tuba Fats and his Chosen Few, Leroy Jones, and Steve Walker and Friends perform.

True to its no-frills atmosphere, Donna's also serves up great barbecue rendered with skill by Donna's husband Charlie, who spent many years as a dining car chef on the Amtrak "City of New Orleans" train. Parking can be a problem; if coming from the French Quarter, a cab is recommended.

Music: Th-M. *Cover:* $. *Food:* barbecue.

The ladies of Storyville once hawked their wares from "cribs" facing the street.

Funky Butt, 714 N. Rampart St., 504–558–0872, www. funkybutt.com.

One of the best places in New Orleans for modern jazz, this dark atmospheric club has a genuine historic feel despite the fact that it has only presented music for a few years. The upstairs room features a wonderfully sounding grand piano and a perfect view of Armstrong Park and Congo Square. Downstairs, there's a cozy, stylish bar, which on slower mid-week nights is sometimes used for performances.

A favorite haunt of musicians and other denizens of the night, the Funky Butt often features such internationally known local talent as Astral Project, Delfeayo Marsalis, Jason Marsalis, Quintology, and Have Soul Will Travel. As at Donna's, parking can be a problem; if coming from the French Quarter, a cab is recommended.

Music: W-Su. *Cover*: $-$$.

Storyville District, 125 Bourbon St., 504–410–1000, www.thestoryvilledistrict.com.

The only music club on Bourbon Street that is not a tourist trap, Storyville is a joint-partnership venture between Quint Davis, the man primarily responsible for creating the New Orleans Jazz and Heritage Festival, and Ralph Brennan, one of New Orleans' most successful restaurateurs. Multiple rooms and stages in this historic building feature first-class sound and lighting, and the music usually starts quite early—

around 6 P.M. Gregory Davis, founding member of the Dirty Dozen Brass Band, books the place with an unusual mix of traditional and modern jazz bands. On the menu is top-notch New Orleans fare, including much Creole cuisine.

Music: nightly. *Cover*: none, except during special events. *Food*: New Orleans, Creole.

Palm Court Jazz Café, 1204 Decatur St. 504–525–0200.

Nina Buck, wife of George, founder of Jazzology (the world's oldest independent jazz record label), GHB, and other record labels, opened this winsomely pretty restaurant in 1989 and it's been a local favorite ever since. One of the best places in New Orleans to dine while listening to music, the Palm Court is housed in a high-ceilinged room complete with lace curtains and slowly spinning fans. The music begins each evening at 8 P.M. and if you're not interested in eating, you can catch the music from the bar for the price of a drink. First-rate local musicians such as Lionel Ferbos, Thais Clark, Lucien Barbarin, and Ernie Elly usually perform, though well-known out-of-towners such as Jay McShann are featured on occasion. The Creole food is both delicious and reasonably priced; George Buck's records are for sale in back.

Music: W-Su. *Cover/minimum*: $. *Food*: Creole. Reservations recommended.

Tin Roof Café, 532 Frenchmen St., 504–948–3100.

Not far from the Palm Court is this charming Frenchmen Street spot, now known for its classic jazz. Large photos of the old masters taken from the famed Eddie Condon's in New York—long defunct—reflect a bygone era. Owner Jack Maheu is an excellent musician who leads a rotating house band nightly. A variety of top local talent is also showcased here.

Music: W-Su. *Cover*: $.

El Matador, 504 Esplanade Ave., at Decatur, 504–569–8361.

Housed in the old United States Mint building at the edge of the Quarter, the Matador offers a wide variety of music, along with a very mixed crowd of locals and hip tourists. On Sunday nights, there's a traditional jazz jam and on Wednesdays, the Soul Rebels Brass Band plays. The club features an incredible circular bar that alone is worth a trip.

Music: nightly. *Cover*: none-$.

Snug Harbor, 626 Frenchmen St. (Faubourg Marigny), 504–949–0696, www.snugjazz.com.

The premier venue for modern jazz in New Orleans, spacious Snug Harbor consistently brings in the best of the old masters and international stars, as well as top local talent, some of whom are internationally known in their own right. Dinner is served in the brick-walled front room, by big picture windows, while the music takes place out back in an intimate, high-ceilinged space rimmed with a balcony. The sound system is close to perfect, and there's also a friendly bar area up front. Friday nights often feature pianist Ellis Marsalis. Charmaine Neville is also a regular.

Music: nightly. *Cover*: $$. *Food*: Creole, New Orleans, etc.

Sweet Lorraine's, 1931 St. Claude St., 504–945–9654, www. sweetlorrainesjazzclub.com.

The newest modern jazz spot in the city, located just outside the Quarter, Sweet Lorraine's has a sleek and spacious feel to it that's unusual in this town of cozy, atmospheric clubs. Top New Orleans talent appears here regularly, including such highly esteemed performers such as Nicholas Payton, Clarence Johnson III, and Clyde Kerr, Jr.; the crowd tends to be well-dressed and sophisticated. When it first opened, Sweet Lorraine's got rebuked for its occasional poor sound, but that problem has since been corrected.

Music: Th-Su. *Cover*: $-$$.

Pete Fountain's, New Orleans Hilton, 2 Poydras St., 504–561–0500.

The famous jazz clarinetist, who used to run his own place on Bourbon Street, now has a jazz club on the third level of the Hilton Hotel. The new place—all brown and deep red decor—is a snazzy reproduction of the old. Fountain's shows, which seat 500, are enjoyable but tightly controlled and no bargain. He starts each night at 10 and ends at 11:15 sharp.

Music: Tu, F-S. *Cover:* $$$. Reservations required.

Also

Café Brasil (Frenchmen St., at Chartres, 504–947–9386), a hip, eclectic club best known for its Brazilian and world music, sometimes offers jazz in the early evenings. **Fritzel's** (733 Bourbon St., 504–561–0432), a casual, comfortable bar, located somewhat off the tourist track, also offers worthwhile jazz, usually on the weekends.

Elsewhere in the City

Circle Bar, 1032 St. Charles Ave., at Lee Circle, 504–588–2616.

Once a skid-row dive, the Circle Bar is now decidedly hip, with a cool crowd of 20- and 30-somethings usually filling it to capacity. Music of the most eclectic variety imaginable is presented, but keep an especially close eye out for Rob Wagner & Kevin O'Day, Roger Lewis & Friends, and Egg Yolk Jubilee. Happy hours on Fridays are hosted by Phil DeGruy, a solo guitarist of phenomenal ability and great wit.

Music: M-Sa. *Cover*: none.

Joe's Cozy Corner, 1532 Ursulines, at Robertson (Tremé, 5 min. from Quarter), 504–561–9216.

A friendly neighborhood club run by Joe Glasper and his family, Joe's is long, neat, and compact, with a bar in the front room and music in the back. Pictures and photographs hang from the walls, and pink tablecloths drape the tables.

Live music is usually featured only on Sunday nights, and often courtesy of Kermit Ruffins and/or the ReBirth Brass Band. These great musicians play elsewhere in the city, of course, but this cozy neighborhood club is a great spot in which to catch them.

Music: Su. *Cover*: none.

Columns Hotel, 3811 St. Charles Ave. (10 min. from the Quarter), 504–899–9308.

Built in 1881 and on the National Register of Historic Places, the Columns is one of those lovely Southern mansions with big white pillars and enormous spreading trees out front. Over the past decade or so, it has also developed a reputation for presenting jazz, currently usually compliments of John Rankin (Tuesdays) and Chip Wilson (Wednesdays). The music setting is magnificent: a pale blue-and-pink ballroom with 20-foot-high ceilings and marble fireplaces. On Fridays, a salsa band is featured, and on Sundays, there's a jazz brunch.

Music: Tu, W, F, Su brunch. *Cover*: $. *Food*: Cajun, Continental; available in the Patio Tea Room across the hall.

The Red Room, 2040 St. Charles Ave., 504–528–9759.

This beautiful upscale club, trendy to the max, was formerly located in Paris's Eiffel Tower. Moved to New Orleans over a decade ago, it has since evolved into a music-oriented club that features jazz several times a week. Come when Kermit Ruffins or Jeremy Davenport are playing. Note: This is one of the few jazz venues in New Orleans with a dress code. Cover charges are tolerable, but drink prices are high by local standards.

Music: W-Su *Cover*: $-$$. *Food*: Traditional American with European influences.

Vaughan's Lounge, 800 Lesseps, 504–947–5562.

A neighborhood bar in the up-and-coming, formerly working-class Bywater area (below the French Quarter and Marigny), Vaughan's only features music one night a week, but what a night it is. Kermit Ruffins, the jazz artist who most single-handedly embodies this city's essence, appears here every Thursday night. Free red beans and rice is served at midnight. The neighborhood is not as bad as some people make it out to be, but those unfamiliar with the area may wish to take a cab; the club is about a five-minute ride from the French Quarter.

Music: Th. *Cover*: $.

Zeitgeist, 1724 Oretha Castle Haley Blvd., 504–525–2767 or 504–525–6246.

Zeigeist, a huge loft-like performance space adjacent to Barrister's art gallery, has become the home for experimental, avant-garde, and free jazz in New Orleans. Regulars include such cutting-edge performers as Jonathan Freilich, Rob Wagner, Rob Cambre, and that dean of free jazz in the city—Kidd Jordan. The venue is ultra-modern and brand new, but is located in Central City, a rough area just three blocks off St. Charles Avenue. However, it's an easy cab ride to here from anywhere in town and secure, on-premises parking is available.

Music: several nights weekly. *Cover*: $-$$.

Sandbar, University of New Orleans campus at the Cove (on shore of Lake Pontchartrain, near corner of Elysian Fields Ave. and Leon C. Simon Dr.; 15 min. from Quarter), 504–286–6381.

A small and unassuming pub with low lighting, cork walls, and excellent acoustics, the Sandbar showcases students enrolled in the university's jazz studies program, as well as faculty members and visiting professionals. Unfortunately, however, the venue no longer offers a consistent music schedule; call for information.

Music: about once a month. *Cover*: $.

Also

Although the **Maple Leaf** (8316 Oak St., 504–866–9359) is not primarily a jazz venue, the ReBirth Brass Band puts on a lively house party here every Tuesday night. **Kemp's** (2720 La Salle St., bet. Washington and Fourth Sts., 504–891–2738), a neighborhood bar in a rough area, often hosts the ReBirth Brass Band on Thursday nights. Not far from Kemp's is the

Dew Drop Inn (2836 La Salle St., near Washington, 504–895–9303), an historic spot (see "Landmarks and Legends," page 26) that offers music during special events such as the New Orleans Jazz & Heritage fest.

The **Old Point**, a neighborhood bar located across the Mississippi River in Algiers Point, usually presents jazz about once a week (see "For Blues," below). **Andrew Jaeger's House of Seafood** (522 Conti St., 504–522–4964, www.andrew-jaegers.com) hosts quality jazz acts such as trumpeter Charlie Miller, pianist Fred Staehle, and vocalist Ellen Smith.

Unlike "cigar bars" in other cities, **Dos Jefes Uptown Cigar Bar** (5535 Tchoupitoulas St., 504–891–8500) has a mellow vibe and the music is often quite good. Look for Tony Green & Gypsy Jazz, Rebecca Barry, Leigh Harris, and Rick Trolsen. Thursday night is bebop night.

Believe it or not, **Harrah's Casino** (512 S. Peters St., at Canal, 800–427–7247) presents excellent jazz performers several times a day in their various bars. There is no cover but the place can be very noisy.

Jazz Brunch

The jazz brunch was supposedly originated by Ella Brennan of the famous Brennan restaurant family. Since then, the idea has spread all over the city, and although the music is usually only pleasant background sound, the food—this being New Orleans—is always first-rate. Some of the more popular spots are listed here.

The Commander's Palace (1403 Washington Ave., 504–899–8221), in the Garden District, is an amazing bright aqua Victorian mansion and 1920s bordello turned restaurant. Run by the Brennan family. Jazz brunches Sa–Su. $$$. Reservations recommended, jackets required on Sundays.

Arnaud's (813 Bienville St., 504–523–5433), one of the most famous fine Creole restaurants in the French Quarter, serves a Sunday brunch accompanied by a jazz trio. Brunch $$$. Reservations recommended.

Mr. B's (201 Royal St., 504–523–2078), one of New Orleans's "best kept secrets," is also run by the Brennan family. Brunch on Sundays often features jazz trios. $$$. Reservations recommended.

La Gauloise in the Meridien Hotel (614 Canal St., 504–527–6712) is a "true" French restaurant with a Sunday buffet jazz brunch. $$$. Reservations recommended.

Other restaurants offering jazz brunches include the medieval-like **Court of Two Sisters** (613 Royal St., 504–

522–7261), **Kabby's** in the Hilton (2 Poydras St., 504–561–0500), and **The River Bend Grill** in the Wyndham (100 Iberville St., 504–566–7006).

FOR BLUES

In and Around the French Quarter

House of Blues/The Parish, 225 Decatur St., 504–529–2583, www.hob.com.

When the House of Blues landed in New Orleans in the mid-'90s, it significantly altered the city's club scene. Prior to that time, there had been no large, upscale music venue with first-class sound and lighting that consistently booked touring talent. The famed Tipitina's (see below), a big bare-bones club, could be counted on for presenting some national acts, but lesser-known musicians had to make do with various local dives.

House of Blues is in many ways the antithesis of a local music club. With a crowd capacity of 1,000, it is expensively decorated with a huge collection of folk art, and it charges substantial covers and drink prices. Tourists usually comprise the majority of the audience, and the place has a palpable "corporate" feel that rubs the wrong way. Still, this is the only place in the city that consistently schedules great talent in deluxe surroundings.

Alas, little of that talent is blues. Despite its moniker, the club only offers blues in its main room a few times a month. You'll have more luck hearing 12-bar sounds in the Parish, a small room located off to one side. Many fine local musicians play here, including John Mooney and Kipori Woods.

Sundays feature a popular gospel brunch showcasing some of the city's many superb gospel groups and choirs.

Music: nightly, Su brunch. *Cover*: $$-$$$$. *Food*: Southern, New Orleans.

Tipitina's French Quarter, 233 N. Peters St., 504–566–7095, www.tipitinas.com.

An outpost of the famed New Orleans' club located on Napoleon Avenue (see "Elsewhere in the City," below), Tip's French Quarter caters mostly to the tourist crowd. Still, the place books many of the same fine local bands as the Uptown original, and is worth a stop if you're staying in the Quarter.

Music: Th-Sa, some blues. *Cover*: $-$$.

El Matador, 504 Esplanade Ave., at Decatur, 504–569–8361.

The Matador (also listed under "For Jazz," above) presents as much blues as it does jazz, along with an eclectic range of other live music. One of New Orleans' very finest blues acts, Jeremy Lyons and the Deltabilly Boys, plays here every Tuesday night, when enormous glasses of sangria are also served up, at $2.00 a glass. Mathilda Jones, an old-fashioned blues mama, appears on Fridays. Check out the back court-yard during the breaks for a little taste of French Quarter charm.

Music: nightly. *Cover*: none–$.

Margaritaville Café, 1104 Decatur St., 504–592–2565, www.margaritaville.com/neworleans.

Jimmy Buffett's joint is very much a tourist-oriented club, but it isn't a tourist trap, and even the locals have come to appreciate the variety of free music it offers. Jeremy Lyons frequently plays, as do Kenny Holladay and Coco Robicheaux. There is a smaller bar in the front and a large room in the back where music is presented. One nice feature is that the club's music begins in the afternoon and continues through the evening, making it easy to catch an act here before head-ing out to hear late-night fare elsewhere.

Music: nightly. *Cover*: none. *Food*: Gulf Coast–Caribbean, pastas, salads.

Vic's Kangaroo Café, 636 Tchoupitoulas St. (1¹/₂ blocks from Poydras and the Quarter), 504–424–4329 or G'DAY.

Located in the Warehouse District, home to many art gal-leries and newly minted condos, Vic's is a little bit of the Land Down Under transported to New Orleans. A hopping joint on a busy corner, the place—long and narrow, with a bar to one side, a step-up stage to the other—is usually packed with a young, enthusiastic crowd. Australian flags, stuffed koala bears, and pictures of kangaroos seem to be everywhere.

Local blues acts are featured regularly on the weekends, when Australian owner Vic himself has the tendency to join his customers for a few rounds. On the menu are good Australian wines and bar food, including "dog's eye" (meat pie) and "snap roll" (sausage roll), as well as an excellent selection of beers.

Music: F-Sa. *No cover*. *Food*: Australian, etc.

Elsewhere in the City

Tipitina's, 501 Napoleon Ave. (Uptown, 15 min. from Quarter), 504–891–8477, www.tipitinas.com.

Named after the song by Professor Longhair, Tipitina's was founded in 1977 by a group of New Orleanians who saw a need for a large music hall featuring all kinds of sound—blues, R&B, rock, jazz, reggae, Cajun, alternative. Professor Longhair, a close friend of the group's, was in the midst of his comeback then, and there was no place in New Orleans for him—or anyone like him—to play. There was also no place for the city's many different ethnic populations to mix.

After much searching, the group found its current cavernous location (previously a livery, bordello, boxing gym, bar room, and meeting place for the Ku Klux Klan), and almost immediately the place took off. It became home base for the Neville Brothers, the Radiators, and Dr. John, not to mention Professor Longhair himself, who as part owner played here several times a month while he was still alive.

Most major blues acts have passed through Tipitina's, where they play on a big black stage, surrounded by balconies, while the crowd dances the southern nights away. Makers of the film *The Big Easy* even came here, hoping to catch some of the club's magic on celluloid, but Tip's was temporarily closed at the time and so the movie—rumors to the contrary—was actually shot at a nearby dance hall.

Because Tipitina's was the only large music club in town for so many years, it long got away with the fact that it was run down, lacked adequate air conditioning, and suffered from indifferent sound. The arrival of the state-of-the art House of Blues in the mid-'90s almost put Tips out of business, but since then the club, under new ownership, has remedied many of its former problems and entered the modern era. Nonetheless, Tipitina's has never really recovered its status as the premier music club of New Orleans and now books more first-rate local talent than it does touring acts. A small park dedicated to Fess has been added to the grounds outside the club, but Tips is no longer a hangout in any way, shape, or form, as it closes as soon as the last note rings out.

Music: Tu–Su, some blues and R&B. *Cover*: $-$$.

Mid-City Lanes Rock 'n' Bowl, 4133 S. Carrollton Ave. (Uptown, 15 min. from Quarter), 482–3133, www.rockandbowl. com.

Built in 1941, this creaky old 18-lane bowling alley is one of the hottest and weirdest, not to mention most fun, blues joints in the city. Where else can you listen to the honks, riffs, howls, and blues of the likes of Snooks Eaglin, the Iguanas, Ernie K-Doe, or Tab Benoit while picking up a 7–10 split?

Even so, the history behind the place is even stranger. It all began back in 1988, when owner John Blancher, then in his mid-thirties, went on a pilgrimage to the city of Medjugorje, in what was then Yugoslavia, with the hopes of seeing an apparition of the Virgin Mary (reports of such apparitions were in the news at the time). He had no such luck, but while there placed a wish in a mountainside altar asking that he find something that his whole family could get involved in. One week later, back in New Orleans, someone asked him if he wanted to buy a bowling alley.

Blancher, who'd worked as a teacher, insurance agent, and caterer, but never as anything remotely resembling a bowling alley owner, gamely put in his bid, and three months later, Mid-City was his. Today, he can be found working most nights alongside his wife, Deborah, his parents, his sister, and his kids.

There are two music stages upstairs, as well as a huge newer music room on the first floor, and occasionally, the club operates all three stages at the same time. Another unique feature is the club's two long murals, one of which is considered to be something of a local masterpiece. Stretching for at least 50 feet, it was painted by musician/artist Tony Green, and depicts a surreal '60s–era Canal Street scene populated with local characters, Keith Richards, Brian Jones, and Bob Dylan.

Mid-City is hardly strictly a blues club, but blues is usually featured several times a week. On Tuesdays, there's a blues jam, and on Wednesdays and Thursdays, zydeco bands perform.

Music: Tu-Sa, much blues. *Cover*: $-$$.

Maple Leaf, 8316 Oak St., 504–866–9359 or LEAF.

A cherished Uptown institution, the Maple Leaf consistently books excellent local blues acts, as well as much Cajun and zydeco—for which historically it is best known. Possessing true, laid-back New Orleans charm, the "Leaf" features antique pressed-tin ceilings, an extensive offering of local beers, and a lush candlelit back patio that is perfect for getting away from the crowd. Best known these days for its raucous Tuesday nights with the ReBirth Brass Band, the club also offers great blues two to three times a week. Regulars include John Mooney, Joe Krown, and Nelson Lunding, while Saturdays are often reserved for Walter "Wolfman" Washington and the Roadmasters. The Maple Leaf also is home to the Krewe of O.A.K., a Mardi Gras organization that convenes in steamy August to parade in a depraved fashion from bar to bar in this neighborhood. The music at the Maple Leaf often lasts until 2:00 A.M. or later, making it a good last stop.

Music: nightly, much blues. *Cover*: $.

Old Point Bar, 545 Patterson, Algiers Point, 504–364–0950.

Located in Algiers Point, directly across the Mississippi River from the French Quarter, the Old Point has been a neighborhood watering hole for over 100 years. Only recently, however, has it begun presenting live music. Blues are usually booked at least once a week—as is jazz—and the music is consistently good. The blues band Tyrone and the Mindbenders are regulars and well worth seeking out. In between sets, music fans often congregate on the levee across the street to get a wonderful view of the New Orleans skyline by night. You can get to the Old Point via the Canal Street Ferry, but be forewarned that the last ferry crosses at midnight.

Music: most nights, some blues. *Cover*: $.

Other Venues and Special Events

On any given Saturday or Sunday, the streets of the French Quarter, especially Jackson Square and Royal Street, are bursting with music. Up to 35 groups—some jazz, some folk, some blues—perform. Some of it is quite good, but much of it is mediocre-to-awful.

Street music has such a history in New Orleans, beginning with its early marching brass bands and funeral processions, that it's hard to believe it was ever frowned upon. Yet from the 1930s to the '70s, the streets of the city were almost musically dormant, so much so that when, in 1973, trumpet player Scotty Hill (then newly returned from San Francisco, where street music was everywhere) started playing on a local corner, he was arrested.

Eventually, of course, the case was resolved, permits were issued, and a new era of New Orleans street music began. Hill still plays the streets on occasion with his six-piece traditional French Market Jazz Band. (Watch for a Scottish-looking guy dressed in plaid). Also, be sure to keep an eye out for the talented high school–age brass bands who usually play Jackson Square.

The *Creole Queen* (504–524–0814), leaving from the Poydras Street Wharf near Riverwalk, offers a jazz dinner cruise every evening. The *Steamboat Natchez* (504–586–8777), which leaves from the Toulouse Street Wharf behind Jackson Brewery, offers day and nighttime Dixieland cruises.

Photographer Johnny Donnels, who runs a gallery at 634 St. Peters St. (504–525–6438), specializes in jazz and New Orleans photography.

In addition to the world-famous **New Orleans Jazz and Heritage Festival** (see "Major Festivals," page 458), the three-day **French Quarter Festival** (504–522–5730) is held every April, and the **Tomato Festival** (504–290–7000), featuring brass bands and Caribbean music, is held in early June.

Radio

WWOZ/90.7 FM (504–568–1238). Premier station for New Orleans sounds. Noncommercial.
WWNO/89.9 FM (504–286–7000). NPR affiliate, run by the University of New Orleans. Jazz late nights; blues, M nights.
WTUL/91.5 FM (504–865–5887). Student-run station, affiliated with Tulane University. Some jazz and/or blues daily.

Record Stores

The **Louisiana Music Factory** (210 Decatur, 504–586–1094) specializes in Louisiana music. **Tower Records** (Jackson Brewery, 408 N. Peters St., at Decatur St., 504–529–4411) and **Warehouse Music** (231 N. Carrollton Ave., 504–484–7200, or 5300 Tchoupitoulas, 504–891–4026) also offer a good selection of local artists; the **Palm Court Jazz Record Center** (Palm Court Café, 1204 Decatur St., 504–525–0200) offers much in the way of traditional jazz. Other stores include **Jim Russell Rare Records** (1837 Magazine St., 504–522–2602), which specializes in New Orleans and hard-to-find artists; **Record Ron's** (1129 Decatur St., 504–524–9444) and **Record Ron's Stuff** (239 Chartres St., 504–522–2239), carrying new, used, and rare records, tapes, and CDs.

MEMPHIS

Updated by David Nelson with Scott Barretta

Of all the cities in the United States, none is closer to the blues than Memphis, Tennessee. From the early 1900s on, blues musicians from all over the South and especially the Mississippi Delta came here to seek their fortunes after leaving small poverty-ridden homes in farming and plantation communities. W. C. Handy, Bukka White, Furry Lewis, Memphis Slim, Memphis Minnie, Big Joe Williams, Riley "B. B." King, Bobby "Blue" Bland—they all came here, some to stay for good, others to begin a journey that would eventually take them around the world.

The central gathering spot for blues musicians in Memphis was Beale Street (see "Landmarks and Legends," page 46). Here, they could play for tips on street corners, or—if they were lucky—perform in local theaters and clubs. From 1912 to 1918, W. C. Handy published the first commercial blues music from an office on Beale; by the 1920s, nationally known artists such as Ma Rainey and Bessie Smith were coming to town specifically to perform in theaters on Beale.

As the century progressed and the music world became more complex, so did the Memphis sound. In 1949, Sam Phillips opened a studio on Union Avenue, where he would record not only such blues greats as Howlin' Wolf and Ike Turner, but also the King of Rock-and-Roll, Elvis Presley. In the early 1950s, B. B. King and Bobby "Blue" Bland helped to urbanize the traditional blues sound by using gospel and jazz elements. In 1960, Stax Records began recording the R&B and soul sounds of Rufus and Carla Thomas, Booker T. and the MG's, Otis Redding, and Isaac Hayes.

Memphis also has a lesser-known but important jazz history. Alberta Hunter was born here in 1895, and Jimmie Lunceford, who is buried in the city's Elmwood Cemetery, taught at a high school in the city for years. Other nationally known jazz musicians who have come out of Memphis include a long line of piano players, among them Lil Hardin (who later married Louis Armstrong), Phineas Newborn, Jr., Donald Brown, and James Williams; drummer Jimmy Crawford; trumpet players Booker Little and Marvin Stamm; multi-instrumentalist Frank Strozier; saxophonists George Coleman, Hank Crawford, and Sonny Criss; and guitarist Calvin Newborn.

Sources

The best music source is *The Memphis Flyer* (901–521–9000; www.memphisflyer.com), a free weekly with excellent listings. Other sources include the "Playbook" section of the Friday edition of *The Commercial Appeal* (901–529–2211; www. gomemphis. com) and the eclectic website www.memphis-mojo.com ("Spreading the Butter of Memphis Music Across the World Biscuit").

WEVL/90 FM frequently announces music happenings around town. Kreature Comforts' *Lowlife Guide to Memphis* ($), available at the Center for Southern Folklore (see "Landmarks and Legends," p. 50) and Shangri-La Records (see "Record Stores," page 65), is a quirky, irreverent guide to such essential attractions as the sites where Jim Jarmusch's

Mystery Train was filmed and the barbershop where Elvis got his hair cut.

For maps and other general information, contact the Memphis Visitor Information Center (340 Beale St., 901–576–8171), or the Memphis Convention & Visitors Bureau (47 Union Ave., 901–543–5300, www.memphistravel.com).

A Note on the Neighborhoods

Sitting on the bluffs overlooking the Mississippi River, Memphis is a sprawling, fan-shaped city with a population of about 600,000. Downtown, where Beale Street and most of the city's oldest buildings are located, is situated on the edge of the river. Through its center runs Third Street, which becomes the legendary Highway 61 south of the city. In the last decade, downtown Memphis has taken off, revitalized by the renovation of the city's old warehouse district and the addition of a ballpark for the Memphis Redbirds, a AAA baseball franchise.

Midtown is located about 15 minutes east of downtown, and then the city fans out to its suburbs, East Memphis and Germantown. Pinch is a 12-block district just north of downtown, and Whitehaven (once exactly what its name implies, but now a mixed neighborhood) is located 20 to 30 minutes south of the city. Many of Memphis' older African-American neighborhoods, where figures such as Alberta Hunter and B. B. King once lived, have disappeared, victims of urban renewal.

Getting around Memphis is easy, although a car is essential if you're planning on leaving the downtown.

Landmarks and Legends

(With the exception of the old WDIA building, the old Stax Recording site, and Graceland, all of the locations below are within walking distance of downtown, although Sun Studio and the Mallory-Neely house, both east of downtown, are a hike.)

Beale Street

> If Beale Street could talk
> If Beale Street could talk
> Married men would have to take
> their beds and walk
> Except one or two
> Who never drink booze

And the blind man on the corner
Who sings the Beale Street Blues . . .
—*W. C. Handy, "Beale Street Blues"*

By the early 1900s, Beale Street was the African-American capital of both Memphis and the Mid-South. A bustling street lined with everything from stores to banks, it was nonetheless best known for its nightlife: theaters, taverns, nightclubs, and bordellos. For many of the blacks in the area, almost all of whom lived in abject poverty, Beale Street was *their* street, an unreal world to which they could escape, if only for an evening. Whites were rarely even allowed on Beale after dark.

W. C. Handy arrived on Beale in the early 1910s, and he was followed by everyone from Bukka White and Furry Lewis to Arnold "Gatemouth" Moore and Albert King. During the 1940s, a band called the "Beale Streeters" was formed by B. B. King, Bobby "Blue" Bland, Johnny Ace, Rosco Gordon, Willie Nix, and others.

Bluesmen were not the only musicians to roam Beale. Jug bands were once an institution in what is now Handy Park, while in the 1920s and '30s, jazz and swing dominated the clubs. The "zoot suit," that emblem of the jazz and gangster era, was also invented here, by Louis Lettes, a Beale Street tailor. Its long jacket was originally designed not for fashion, but for practicality—to keep the suitpants from wearing out.

Part of the reason that Beale Street was so wide open to everything from gambling to prostitution was politics. Under Memphis' then mayor, E. H. "Boss" Crump, anything could—and often did—go down. In the first decade of the century, Memphis was the murder capital of the country, with 556 homicides per annum, most of them involving African Americans. In the 1950s, however, bad publicity caused the mayor to clamp down on all forms of vice, and many Beale Street establishments were closed for good.

It was the beginning of the end for Beale. One by one the remaining legitimate businesses moved elsewhere, and by the 1960s, after the Civil Rights movement provided new opportunities for blacks in other parts of town, the old Beale Street was completely gone.

Today, the entire area is a National Historic District filled with restaurants, clubs, and shops.

W. C. Handy's Home, 352 Beale St., 901–552–1556 or 901–527–3427.

W. C. Handy lived in this simple shotgun house in the early 1900s. Here Handy wrote many of his most famous works—

"Yellow Dog Blues," "Beale Street Blues," "Ole Miss Blues"—and raised six children before moving to New York to start his own publishing company.

Today, copies of Handy's sheet music lie strewn about the one-room museum (moved here from its original location at 659 Jenette Pl.), along with an old rocking chair, a piano, and plenty of photos.

Open: Summer: Tu-Sa, 10 A.M.–5 P.M.; Winter: Tu-Sa, 11 A.M.–4 P.M. *Admission:* $

The Monarch Club, 340 Beale St.

Also known as the "Castle of Missing Men" because gunshot victims killed here could be quickly disposed of at the undertaker's place out back, the Monarch was nonetheless one of the classiest joints on Beale. Mirrored walls decorated its lobby and there were black-cushioned seats built into its walls.

Palace Theater, 318 Beale St. (NE Corner of Hernando St.).

Now demolished, the Palace was once one of the most important places on Beale for aspiring young blues musicians. A Wednesday night amateur show, hosted first by deejay-schoolteacher/newspaper columnist Nat Williams and then by blues veteran Rufus Thomas, gave many musicians—B. B. King, Johnny Ace, and Bobby "Blue" Bland among them—their first shot at stardom. Rufus was especially partial to B. B., whom he allowed to come back time after time so that the young man could earn the one-dollar prize that would keep him fed.

PeeWee's, 315 Beale St.

PeeWee's was once a favorite hangout among blues artists because the proprietors, two Italians, were always willing to take messages over the phone from promoters and anyone else booking musicians. Many of the bluesmen checked in here daily for messages and while they were waiting for work, rolled dice in the backroom.

W. C. Handy wrote the first commercially successful blues—"Mr. Crump's Blues," later retitled "Memphis Blues"—at Pee-Wee's. The song was originally meant to be a campaign tune for mayoral candidate E. H. "Boss" Crump.

Mitchell's Hotel, 207 Beale St.

From the 1940s to the 1960s, Andrew "Sunbeam" Mitchell and his wife, Ernestine, ran a hotel and upstairs club in this gray building. Sunbeam was a sort of godfather to the struggling bluesmen, giving them a bed when they were homeless, a bowl of chili when they were hungry, and a place to jam after the other clubs had closed. He also encouraged younger musicians by buying them instruments and, during the Civil Rights era, made his hotel available for meetings and rallies.

Over the years, Sunbeam ran a number of clubs on Beale, including the Club Handy, the Domino Lounge, the Flamingo Room, and the Hippodrome. The list of blues, soul, R&B, and jazz artists who passed through them is enormous, including Count Basie, Lionel Hampton, Johnny Ace, and Bobby "Blue" Bland. When B. B. King was just starting out and needed a manager, Sunbeam was on hand; when Little Richard couldn't get work during the 1950s, Sunbeam hired him to wipe down tables to keep him near the music.

Sunbeam, who died in 1989, managed clubs up to the end, his last being the still-operating New Club Paradise (see "Clubs, etc.," page 61).

Handy Park, NW corner of Beale and Hernando streets.

Located across the street from the old Mitchell's, this small bench-lined park, once a marketplace, was created in 1931. W. C. Handy came down from New York to be on hand for its dedication, and a statue of him was added in 1960, two years after his death.

For years, the park was a primary gathering place for country bluesmen arriving from the Delta, and even today, it continues to draw blues musicians like guitarists Uncle Ben and Fred Sanders, as well as gospel singers and cadres of teenaged drummers and breakdancers. It remains to see how the park's atmosphere will be changed by an ongoing renovation project that includes the addition of a permanent stage.

A. Schwab's Dry Goods Store, 163 Beale St., 901–523–9782.

The oldest continuously operating business on Beale, A. Schwab's, founded in 1876, is the kind of place that isn't supposed to exist anymore. Sprawled over three stories, with creaky wooden floors and even creakier wooden staircases, it's jammed full of all the essentials and nonessentials of life. "If you can't find it at Schwab's, you're better off without it" is the store's motto, and it's one that's hard to refute. Ketchup bottles sit next to magic potions sit next to 99–cent ties sit next to a pair of size–74 blue jeans. Meanwhile, overhead, swings a bunch of gloves bearing an uncanny resemblance to a bunch of grapes.

On Schwab's second floor is an old-fashioned record player spinning out the blues: Bessie Smith, Muddy Waters, B. B. King. Schwab's, it turns out, may have been the first business in the country to sponsor a blues radio program; called "Bluestown," it was aired for an African-American audience from 1943 to 1947 by WHBQ. In those years, the radio station had few records of its own, so Schwab's graciously lent them a varying selection, 25 at a time.

For many years, Schwab's was also one of the only places in town where blues records were sold. Back then, nobody knew the names of recordings—they just referred to songs by their number on the local jukebox, a confusing matter since jukebox numbers were hardly interchangeable.

"We sold those records three for a dollar, right next to the nightgowns," says Mr. Schwab, a talkative, ruddy-faced man with twinkling eyes who's usually roaming about in a green apron. "We played them there, too, and sometimes the crowd got so big, nobody would do any shopping. That's when we'd put on a spiritual record—that weeded out the listeners from the buyers in a hurry."

Open: M-Sa, 9 A.M.–5 P.M.

Center for Southern Folklore, 119 S. Main St., 901–525–3655, www.southernfolklore.com.

Recently relocated from Beale Street to downtown's Peabody Place, the center is a wonderful not-for-profit institution that has been documenting the grass-roots culture of the South through films, records, oral histories, books, and festivals for almost three decades. In addition to exhibits on Memphis music and a folk art gallery, the new location includes a café serving Southern-style food, a coffee and beer bar, a cybercafe, and a media area for film screenings. Best of all, the center remains a haven for live blues, featuring regular performances from pianist Mose Vinson, singer Di Anne Price, and downhome Memphis groups like the Fieldstones and the Daddy Mack Blues Band.

Open: Su-W, 11 A.M.–7 P.M. Th-Sa, 11 a.m.–11 P.M. *Admission:* $ for some events.

Memphis Rock 'n' Soul Museum, 145 Lt. George W. Lee Ave., 901–543–0800, www.memphisrocknsoul.org.

Opened in April of 2000, the Memphis Rock 'n' Soul Museum is housed on the second floor of the city's new Gibson Guitar factory, located a half-block south of the intersection of Beale and Third Street. The centerpiece of the museum is the Smithsonian Institution's "Rock 'n' Soul: Social Crossroads" exhibition, which explores the creation of Memphis soul and early rock-and-roll. The exhibit, which includes video and audio clips as well as instruments, clothes, rare records, memorabilia, and photos, is divided into six galleries, including "Rural Music," "Arriving in Memphis," and "Music and Social Change—Civil Rights and Soul Culture." Among the artifacts on display are the piano on which Ike Turner learned to play boogie woogie and B. B. King's original "Lucille," a 1960 Gibson ES–335 guitar.

Open: Su-Th, 10 A.M.–6 P.M., F-Sa, 10 A.M.–8 P.M. *Admission:* $.

The National Civil Rights Museum, 450 Mulberry St., 901–521–9699, www.civilrightsmuseum.org.

Following S. Main from downtown to W. Huling St., then turning left for one block, takes you to the National Civil Rights Museum. Dedicated in 1991, the museum is located in the former Lorraine Motel, where Dr. Martin Luther King, Jr., was assassinated on April 4, 1968. In addition to exhibits on Dr. King, the museum includes displays on the March on Washington, the Montgomery bus boycott, student sit-ins and freedom rides, the 1968 Memphis sanitation workers' strike, and other key events in the Civil Rights Movement.

Open: M, W, F, 9 A.M.–5 P.M., Th 9 A.M.–8 P.M., Su 1 P.M.–5 P.M. *Admission:* $.

The Peabody, 149 Union Ave., 901–529–4000.

For nearly 70 years, the Peabody has been Memphis's most elegant hotel, a luxurious establishment frequented by the elite of the South that is on the National Register of Historic Places. It is perhaps best known for its marching ducks, who descend from their penthouse on the roof every morning to swim and play in the lobby fountain all day, and for historian David Cohn's comment, "The Mississippi Delta begins in the lobby of the Peabody Hotel and ends on Catfish Row in Vicksburg."

During the 1930s and '40s, the Peabody was also known for its big band sounds. A national CBS radio program was broadcast by local station WREC from the swish Skyway ballroom, where for as little as $5 young white audiences could hear such stars as Paul Whiteman, Tommy Dorsey, and Harry James. An interesting aside: the man who set up the remote hookup for CBS was Sam Phillips, later the founder of Sun Studio.

Several early blues musicians (Speckled Red, Tommy Johnson, Willie Brown) were recorded at the Peabody, thanks to field units sent out by various record companies, and later, in 1969, a performance at the hotel marked a turning point in B. B. King's career. Up until then, B. B., like most African-American artists, had been performing primarily on the chitlin circuit, a loose connection of black nightclubs scattered across the country. Then, after his hit "The Thrill Is Gone," he was invited to showcase at the Peabody for a group of social chairmen from college campuses. He was an instant success and college concerts quickly became a staple in his schedule.

The Memorabilia Room, situated on the second floor of the hotel, documents some of its history. Items on display include programs from the Skyway and a copy of "Rhapsody in Blue" autographed by George Gershwin for W. C. Handy.

WDIA/1070 AM, 112 Union Ave., 901–529–4300.

In February 1999, WDIA, the nation's first all-black format radio station, celebrated its fiftieth anniversary. It's still on the air 24 hours a day with talk, news, and a mix of oldies, blues, and gospel.

Many a famous blues deejay has come through WDIA, including Nat D. Williams, A. C. Williams, the Reverend "Gatemouth" Moore, Robert "Honeyboy" Thomas, Theo "Bless My Bones" Wade, B. B. King, and Rufus Thomas. WDIA is also known as the "Goodwill Station." Over the years, it has helped find lost children, cats, and dogs; gotten help for people whose homes have burned, bused the handicapped, and built a center for African-American children from broken homes. WDIA has a small museum documenting these and other events.

Open: By appointment. *Admission:* free.

Stax Recording Studios, 926 McLemore Ave., now a vacant lot.

The old Stax Building (large and white with a huge orange arrow on its side), demolished in late 1989, was to have been rebuilt inside the Pyramid, a museum in downtown Memphis. Those plans seem to be on indefinite hold, however. Meanwhile, souvenir bricks from the old studio are on sale at Shangri-La Records (see "Record Stores," page 65).

Stax Records, established by Jim Stewart and Estelle Axton in 1960, made a major contribution to the world of soul and R&B. During the sixties, it recorded everyone from Otis Redding and Rufus Thomas to Sam and Dave and Booker T. and the MG's.

Sun Recording Studio, 706 Union Ave., 901–521–0664. www.sunstudio.com.

Sam Phillips, probably best known for discovering Elvis Presley, first rented this modest space—now a museum—in 1949. Phillips, who was working as a sound engineer for local radio station WREC, had been listening to black musicians for years and was determined to record them. "I thought it was vital music," he tells writer Robert Palmer in *Deep Blues*, "and although my first love was radio, my second was the freedom we tried to give the people, black and white, to express their very complex personalities, personalities these people didn't know existed in the fifties."

Some of the blues artists Phillips recorded include Howlin' Wolf, Muddy Waters, Ike Turner, Little Milton, B. B. King, James Cotton, Junior Parker, and Walter Horton. Rufus Thomas's "Bear Cat" was Sun's first hit, and "Rocket 88," believed by some to be the first rock-and-roll song ever, was recorded here by Ike Turner, Jackie Brenston, and others in 1951.

In the early days, anyone could walk into Sun and cut a record for a mere $4. One of the musicians who did so in 1954 was 18-year-old Elvis Presley, who subsequently remained with Phillips for approximately one year before switching to the bigger RCA Victor label. Other white artists recorded by Sun included Johnny Cash, Carl Perkins, Roy Orbison, Conway Twitty, and Jerry Lee Lewis.

Today, Sun Studios is a modest one-room museum. A tour guide gives a brief history of the place (complete with cuts from songs) and then leaves visitors alone to examine the pictures on the wall, the mobile recording unit near the door, and the WHGU mike used the first time one of Presley's songs ("That's All Right, Mama") was aired.

Sam Phillips still lives outside Memphis, and there's a recording facility down the street run by his sons. It's also possible to record in the original Sun Studios, which has been equipped with state-of-the-art tracks.

Open: daily, 10 A.M.–6 P.M., tours every hour on the half hour. *Admission:* $.

Mallory-Neely House, 652 Adams Ave. (midtown), 901–523–1484.

W. C. Handy used to play for parties given by a Mrs. Frances Neely in this historically preserved 25-room Italian-style Victorian home, located on Memphis's "Millionaire's Row." He and other African-American musicians played in a small room in the back, where they could be heard but not seen. Many years later, when Handy was famous and living in New York, he sent Mrs. Neely a letter consoling her for a broken leg, and the letter is now on display in the mansion turned museum.

Open: Tu-Sa, 10 A.M.–4 P.M.; Su, 1–4 P.M. Closed Jan.–March. *Admission:* $.

Old WDIA Building, 2267 Central Ave.

Before WDIA moved to Union Avenue it was housed in this nondescript tan-brick building, and it was here that Riley "B. B." King came in 1948, having heard of the new African-

American station and hoping it would give him a break. Station owner Bert Ferguson listened to the young man, decided he was unpolished but "wholesome," and gave him a job as the "Pepticon Boy." It was Riley's job to advertise a new health tonic ("Pepticon, Pepticon, sure is good / You can get it anywhere in your neighborhood") during a 10-minute spot for which he could sing and play anything he liked. On weekends he was required to drive around town and play from the top of a Pepticon truck while someone sold the tonic out the back. There was no pay involved in any of this, but Riley was allowed to advertise a gig he then had in West Memphis.

Riley's popularity grew steadily, and the station soon gave him a new full-fledged show. They also gave him a new name, "Beale Street Blues Boy," soon shortened to "Blues Boy King" and finally to "B. B." King.

Graceland, 3734 Elvis Presley Blvd. (Whitehaven), 901–332–3322 or 800–238–2000, www.elvis-presley.com.

The home of the King of Rock-and-Roll is bigger and more tourist-oriented than ever, with packed vans leaving for the mansion every few minutes, an ultrasophisticated car museum, and umpteen souvenir shops. Everything from the King's favorite sequined costumes to his half dozen Harley Davidsons are on display, while everything from velveteen portraits of Elvis to Graceland dinnerware is for sale. It's all fascinating, somehow, and well worth the steep ticket price. More people visit Graceland than any other private home in the United States except the White House.

Elvis was deeply influenced by the blues. Many of his early hits were blues songs that he'd first heard performed by black artists—songs for which he received millions while the originators received next to nothing (Arthur "Big Boy" Crudup's "That's All Right, Mama," for example).

As a young man, Presley spent much time on Beale Street, listening, watching, talking. While there, he met deejay and emcee Nat Williams and badgered him into letting him perform along with the black contestants at amateur night at the Palace Theater. "We had a lot of fun with him," Nat Williams tells Margaret McKee and Fred Chisenhall in *Beale Black and Blue*. "Elvis Presley on Beale Street when he first started was a favorite man. When they saw him coming out, the audience always gave him as much recognition as they gave any musician—black. He had a way of singing the blues that was distinctive. He could sing 'em not necessarily like a Negro, but he didn't sing 'em altogether like a typical white musician. . . . Always he had that certain humanness about him that Negroes like to put in their songs."

Open: daily, 9 A.M.–5 P.M. *Admission:* adults, $$-$$$, children, $-$$ (depending on tour chosen).

Also

Albert King, the "Godfather of the Blues" (and no relation to B. B.), who died in December 1992, is buried just over the river from Memphis in the Paradise Gardens cemetery, Edmondson, Arkansas (870–735–2552). Following King's funeral services, which were held in Memphis, the hearse took a short detour down Beale Street, led by the Memphis Horns playing "When the Saints Go Marching In."

Blues legend Furry Lewis, who died in 1981, is buried in the Hollywood Cemetery, 2012 Hernando Road (901–774–0260), on the outskirts of Memphis. Fans raised the money for his impressive headstone, inscribed with a guitar, in 1983.

A leisurely drive south into Mississippi on U.S. Highway 51 (Elvis Presley Blvd.) takes you eventually to the Oak Grove M. B. church near Nesbit; in the Greenview Memorial Gardens north of the church is the tombstone of Memphis blues and jug band favorite Gus Cannon.

CLUBS, ETC.

Memphis is steadily trying to recapture the magic of its musical past. New clubs, festivals, and music projects seem to be conceptualized almost monthly. Unfortunately, though, much of this activity, well intentioned though it is, has a hollow feel. Things are too sanitized, too sanctified, and everyone seems to be trying too hard.

This is not to minimize the Memphis scene. There are a number of fine musicians performing around town regularly. The present can never be the past, however, and it pays to venture beyond the commercial Beale Street area to some of the lesser-known clubs such as **Wild Bill's** or the **North End**.

Some of the blues and R&B talent that can be heard in Memphis today includes veteran bluesmen Mose Vinson and Big Lucky Carter, the latest incarnations of longtime bands the Fieldstones and the Hollywood All Stars, vocalists Ruby Wilson and James Govan, and R&B entertainers Bill Coday and Toni Green. Some of the jazz figures include guitarist Calvin Newborn, saxophonist Jim Spake, pianist Marvell Thomas (the son of Rufus Thomas), and vocalists Joyce Cobb and Di Anne Price.

Blues in Memphis can usually be heard a healthy seven days a week, especially during the spring and summer, when Beale Street flourishes and outdoor festivals and concerts abound. The jazz scene is much more confined, with the only truly rich day for the music being Sundays.

Generally speaking, bars and clubs in Memphis stay open until 2 A.M., but some, like **Blues City Café/Band Box**, have late licenses that allow them to operate until 3 A.M. and beyond.

Personal Choices

Best upscale blues club: *B. B. King's*
Best late-night blues clubs: *Blues City Café, The Black Diamond*
Best juke joint: *Wild Bill's*
Best jazz spot: *Huey's Midtown*
Most atmospheric jazz bar: *Mallard's*

FOR JAZZ

The North End, 346 N. Main St. (Pinch district), 901–526–0319.

Tucked away from mainstream Memphis, the North End is a tiny gem of a place that features both jazz and Delta blues. The red-brick building is old and feels it, with creaking wooden floors, exposed brick walls, and dark green oilcloth tablecloths. Lots of old signs hang from the walls: DRINK COCA-COLA, GRAPETTE SODA, PAUL BEAR BRYANT BLVD., while the menu ranges from wild rice blended with everything imaginable (mushrooms, chicken, cheddar cheese) to tamales and stuffed potatoes.

The group Front Line Jazz is here on Sundays.

Music: W-Su, jazz and some blues. *Cover:* $. *Food:* sandwiches, etc.

Huey's, 1927 Madison Ave., (midtown), 901–726–4372.

Huey's is a big friendly place with a solid, beer-soaked bar, booths with red-and-white-checkered tablecloths, and thousands of toothpicks stuck in the ceiling. Classic blues and jazz vocalist Di Anne Price and Her Boyfriends are a Sunday afternoon staple, and guitarist Calvin Newborn & the Newborn Trauma Center are also sometimes featured at the club.

Huey's Downtown (77 S. Second St., 901–527–2700) is more likely to present contemporary blues (including national acts) while three suburban locations—**Huey's East** (2858

Hickory Hill, 901–375–4373), **Huey's Collierville** (2130 W. Poplar, 901–854–4455), and **Huey's Cordova** (1771 Germantown Pkwy., 901–754–3885)—offer a mix of jazz and blues by local groups.

Music: Su. No cover. *Food:* American.

King's Palace Café, 162 Beale St., 901–521–1851.

King's Palace is the most promising bet for jazz on Beale Street, though the club also offers solid blues acts on a regular basis. One of the most comfortable and least hectic venues on Beale, King's Palace is divided into two sections, a main room that resembles an English pub and a smaller music room with an elevated stage.

Music: W-Su. *Cover:* $

Mallard's, Peabody Hotel, 149 Union Ave. (downtown), 901–529–4140.

Everything from rock to blues and R&B has been featured at this beautiful Old World bar, done up in heavy dark wood

Alberta Hunter made a triumphant homecoming appearance at the Orpheum in 1978.

and engraved glass. The Peabody also features a jazz brunch in its Skyway Room.

Music: F-Sa, occasional weekdays. *No cover.*

Also

The Beale Street club **Blues City** (see "For Blues," below) features jazz regularly, as do two of Memphis's coffeehouses—**Java Cabana** (2170 Young Ave., 901–272–7210) and **Java, Juice & Jazz** (1423 Elvis Presley Blvd., 901–774–3004)—and the lounge of midtown's **French Quarter Suites** hotel (2144 Madison Ave., 901–728–4000). Jazz can also be heard occasionally on the weekends at **Automatic Slim's** (83 S. Second St., 901–525–7948), an airy Southwestern-looking restaurant (though its menu is mixed) lined with works of art.

FOR BLUES

B. B. King's Blues Club & Restaurant, 143 Beale St., 901–524-KING.

B. B. was 20 years old with $2.50 in his pocket when he arrived on Beale in 1946 to make a name for himself, and 65 years old with over 50 albums to his credit when he returned in 1991 to open this large and friendly, two-storied club, always rocking with fine sounds. Purists may object to the club's well-scrubbed and somewhat touristic atmosphere, but it's done a lot to bring much-needed business to Beale and give the whole Historic District a more permanent feel.

Ruby Wilson, a big-throated Dallas schoolteacher who came to Beale Street when it reopened to pursue her lifelong dream of becoming a singer, is a regular here, as are guitarists Jimmy King (the adopted grandson of Albert King) and Preston Shannon. National acts are regularly booked, and B. B. plays the club several times a year.

Featured items on the club's menu include an Itta Bena salad, *blues*berry cheesecake, a Lucille burger, and a King steak. The club also has a souvenir shop.

Music: Tu-Su. *Cover:* $; more for national acts. *Food:* American, Southern.

Blues City Café/Band Box, 138–140 Beale St., 901–526–3637.

Located directly across from B. B.'s, Blues City has such a grungy, low-down comfortable feel that it's no wonder it's one of the best spots on the street for late-night blues. One side of the club is a simple café serving catfish, steak, tamales, ribs, and the like; the other is a bar and music room where the brick walls seem to lean in at odd angles and tiny Christmas lights twinkle up near ceiling fans. The club is home to a spirited house band, the Blues City All Stars, and on a typical night all kinds of players are likely to show up, including the young and handsome Jimmy King—gold tooth flashing—who plays his guitar upside down and left-handed like his namesake. National artists such as John Hammond and Mose Allison are also booked on a regular basis.

Following Albert King's death, Blues City held an all-day memorial tribute to raise money for his tombstone. Over $5,000 was raised, $3,000 from the Splash Casino in Tunica, Mississippi.

Music: nightly. *Cover:* $; more for national acts. *Food:* Southern.

The Black Diamond, 153 Beale St., 901–521–0800.

The narrow and dimly lit Black Diamond is not the most attractive room on Beale, but its no-frills approach to the blues makes it a haven for those who enjoy real-deal music in less-touristy surroundings. The club hosts songwriters' evenings led by Memphian Keith Sykes as well as the regular events of the Beale Street Blues Society.

Music: nightly. *Cover:* $.

Rum Boogie Café, 182 Beale St., 901–528–0150.

Whoever designed this two-level place, connected by an iron circular staircase, did one terrific job—there are guitars donated by big-name artists (the late Stevie Ray Vaughan, The Radiators, Kenny Loggins) hanging from the ceiling, and rusting signs from Highway 61 and Stax hanging from the walls.

The Rum Boogie features music seven nights a week, usually compliments of house band James Govan & the Boogie Blues Band, and the club is always packed with a young crowd drinking, dancing, listening, and eating. Booker T. and the MG's and Bon Jovi are among those who have put in surprise appearances over the years.

Music: nightly. *Cover:* $. Food: *American.*

Blues Hall, 184 Beale St., 901–528–0150.

Adjacent to the Rum Boogie—and covered by the same admission price—is a small dusty hall filled with a hodgepodge of mismatched tables and chairs. There are no fancy guitars hanging from the ceiling here, just an old battered guitar case with the words FURRY LEWIS in thick, white-paint brushstrokes.

Blues Hall tries to be Memphis's answer to Preservation Hall in New Orleans by booking artists who tend to play roots blues. The hall also provides a sometimes welcome relief from

The popular Rum Boogie features house band James Govan and the Boogie Blues Band.

the craziness next door: the mood is quiet and the audience listens well.

Music: F-Sa. *Cover:* $. *No food.*

Marmalade, 153 E. Calhoun St. (downtown), 901–522–8800.

R&B is the staple here, along with first-rate Southern-style cooking. The place is large and rambling, with a bit of a homey rec-room feel, perhaps because of the college pennants pinned to one wall and the game boards in the backroom. Pictures of Memphis artists—B. B. King, Alberta Hunter, Phineas Newborn—hang in the hall, and a wide-screen TV provides entertainment before the music starts.

Music: F-Su. *Cover:* $. *Food:* Southern.

Ernestine's and Hazel's, 531 S. Main St., at Calhoun, 901–523–9722.

Ernestine Mitchell, wife of Sunbeam (see Mitchell's Hotel, page 48), and her sister Hazel (who passed shortly after Sunbeam) opened this scruffy lunch counter on the edge of

downtown back in 1967, and it's since become a neighborhood institution. "Neck bones, beets, chitlins, ham hocks,
buffalo fish, any kind of peas, beans, all kinds, meatloaf,
cornbread . . ." answers Ernestine, a heavy-set woman who
seems half asleep but is undoubtedly not missing a beat,
when asked what she serves.

Ernestine's regularly offers live blues and R&B, most often
on Friday nights.

Music: F. *Cover:* $. *Food:* Soul.

Elsewhere in Memphis

Wild Bill's, 1580 Vollintine (north of midtown), 901-726-
5473.

With its packed-in crowd and an atmosphere that's rowdy
in all the right ways, this neighborhood café and club has
established itself as Memphis's premier juke joint. The cold
beer is sold in quart bottles and the regular band is the
Hollywood All Stars, a Memphis institution since the
mid-1970s. Another familiar face at Wild Bill's is Big Lucky
Carter, an elderly guitarist and singer who, despite his age, is
one of the freshest songwriters in contemporary blues.

Music: F-Su. *Cover:* $. *Food:* Soul.

George's #2 Blues Club, 2160 E. Person (between midtown
and East Memphis, near Defense Depot), 901-278-4730.

With the legendary Fieldstones on the bandstand, smoke-
filled Green's Lounge on E. Person was the juke joint of choice
in Memphis for many years, and patrons were devastated
when it burned down in 1999. George Stout, who's been running clubs in the city for more than 30 years, has picked up
the slack by opening George's #2 just down the street from the
old Green's location. Stout claims his place is nicer than
Green's, but he admits that it still qualifies as "a hole in the
wall." The latest incarnation of the Fieldstones, fronted by
vocalist and guitarist Will Roy Sanders, has been performing
on weekends.

Music: weekends. *Cover:* $.

New Club Paradise, 645 Georgia Ave. (10 min. S. of downtown), 901-947-7144.

A huge club with a somewhat rough reputation, the New
Club Paradise was the last Memphis establishment owned by
the late Sunbeam Mitchell (see Mitchell's Hotel, page 48).
Open only when major blues and R&B acts such as Marvin
Sease or Denise LaSalle are booked, the Paradise, its façade
alive with graffiti'd color, is housed in a converted bowling

alley that's part of a run-down shopping center near the Foote Homes Housing Project.

Music: occasional weekend nights. *Tickets:* $$-$$$.

The Hi-Tone, 1913 Poplar Ave. (midtown), 901–278-TONE, www.hi-tonecafe.com.

This roots rock club, which has booked everyone from rockabilly guitar hero Link Wray to country singer/songwriter Iris DeMent, sometimes features local blues groups like the Fieldstones as well as the occasional national blues act. Posters on the walls pay homage to juvenile delinquency, 1950s style, while 21st century "hoods" can hustle pool at the club's two tables. A small dance floor in front of the stage is often packed, but tables are also available for more reserved members of the audience.

Music: nightly. *Cover:* $-$$.

Also

The Center for Southern Folklore (see "Landmarks and Legends," page 50) is one of the best spots to hear authentic Memphis blues. **Huey's Downtown** and **King's Palace Café** (see "For Jazz," pages 56–57) regularly offer blues. Several of the city's college-oriented rock clubs also book the occasional blues act, especially **Newby's** (539 S. Highland Ave., 901–452–8408, www.newbysbar.com) and the **Young Avenue Deli** (2119 Young Ave., 901–278–0034).

Other Venues

The Reverend Al Green has a ministry at the **Full Gospel Tabernacle** (787 Hale Rd., 901–396–9192) in Whitehaven, and when he shows up, there's nothing quite like hearing that huge soul voice shake down this evil world. The only trouble is, there's no telling when he'll appear, and since he took over the church almost 20 years ago, the congregation has dwindled. Sometimes there seem to be almost as many tourists and curiosity seekers in the church as bona fide members.

Even without the reverend, the modern, octagonal tabernacle is worth visiting. Its choir, though small by gospel standards, has a full, powerful sound and is accompanied by drums, a piano, and tambourines. Services start at 11 A.M.

Built in the late 1920s for vaudeville and movies, the **Orpheum Theater** (203 S. Main St., at Beale, 901–525–7800), has been restored to the tune of $5 million, and is a glittering palace complete with immense chandeliers, ornate tapestries, and triple balconies. Once host to everyone from Harry Houdini to John Philip Sousa, it now features cultural events ranging from the opera to the annual W. C. Handy Blues Awards.

Alberta Hunter, who spent a tough, poor childhood in some of Memphis's meanest neighborhoods (so much so that she ran away to Chicago at the age of 16), made a triumphant return to her hometown in 1978. Her performance at the Orpheum attracted over 2,000 people, many of whom were shocked when the spirited lady, instead of mouthing the expected gracious remarks, blasted the South for its still apparent racist attitudes.

One of the best barbecue places in town (look for the building with the smoking chimney) is the **Cozy Corner Restaurant** (745 N. Parkway, 901–527–9158), which also features great jazz and blues in the form of tapes played over a loudspeaker (and occasional live music). Owner Raymond Robinson has cassettes of everyone from Louis to Dinah.

Special Events

Producer Irwin Scheft and the **Jazz Foundation of Memphis** (901–725–1528) sponsor approximately eight jazz concerts a year at different locations, featuring national artists. Watch the local papers for listings.

Blues artists Taj Mahal, Mudcat, and Beverly Watkins join forces in Memphis.

Photo by Euphus Ruth © Delta Images

Every May, the entire blues world descends on Memphis for a four-day conference and celebration that culminates in the **W. C. Handy Awards**, a national blues awards show. Begun in 1980, the program, sponsored by the Blues Foundation (49 Union Ave., 901–527-BLUE, www.blues.org), gives out W. C. Handy Awards to performers in approximately 20 categories.

During the week of the conference, all the major clubs in Memphis present special performances of the blues. The three-hour ceremony itself features live acts and is open to the public. General admission tickets are limited; advance reservations highly recommended. The foundation also sponsors **BluesFirst**, a two-day conference and festival held in February, which includes a talent competition, the International Blues Challenge, and the annual "Keeping the Blues Alive" Awards for industry promoters, clubs, and societies.

Bluestock (901–526–4280, www.bluestock.org), held on Beale Street in November, is another "blues industry" event that features showcases, conference sessions, and a music festival designed to spotlight up-and-coming artists as well as nationally known performers. Wristband tickets allow the general public to club-hop on Beale until the wee hours during the festival. The Beale Street clubs periodically join forces to present wristband events at other times during the year.

The annual **Beale Street Music Festival**, a three-day bash held on the riverfront in Tom Lee Park in early May, features a blues tent with local and national acts and two main stages featuring rock, R&B, and blues headliners. A more low-key atmosphere prevails at the **Memphis Music and Heritage Festival**, which emphasizes blues, jazz, and rockabilly, and is put on by the Center for Southern Folklore (see page 50). A local writer calls that event "the best-kept secret in the country for regional Southern music." Call the center for details, as the festival has changed dates and locations several times in recent years.

"Blues on the Bluff" is a series of fund-raising concerts held by WEVL in July and August on the meadow outside the National Ornamental Metal Museum (374 W. California Ave., 901–774–6380). The concerts offer spectacular views of the Mississippi River.

Radio Stations

WEVL/90 FM (901–528–1990). Jazz and blues daily. Of special note: "Cap'n Pete's Blues Cruise," "Memphis Beat" with Wally Hall, both F nights.

WDIA/1070 AM (901–529–4300). Blues all day Sa.

WSMS/92 FM (901-678-3692). Student-run jazz station connected with the University of Memphis.

Record Stores

Shangri-La Records (1916 Madison Ave., 901-274-1916, www.shangri.com) is the place to go for Memphis music and has a mail-order catalogue. **Poplar Tunes** (308 Poplar St., 901-525-6348) also has a good selection of Memphis artists. **Boss Ugly Bob's Tapes and Records** (726 E. McLemore Ave., 901-774-6400) specializes in R&B and has a good selection of blues and jazz.

Other Nearby Locations

Juke joints and fife-and-drum picnics in north Mississippi

For years, a Sunday evening excursion to guitarist Junior Kimbrough's world-famous juke joint in Chulahoma, Mississippi, was essential for any hardcore blues enthusiast visiting Memphis. After Junior died in 1998, his sons—drummer Kinney and multi-instrumentalist David—kept the place running until April 6, 2000, when it burned to the ground in a mysterious early morning fire. The good vibes and distinctive "cotton patch" blues that made Kimbrough's club so attractive live on, however—most recently in a cavernous multi-purpose center in rural Tate County. The place lacks the charm and intimacy of Junior's, but the freewheeling dancing inspired by the music of the Soul Blues Boys makes up for the lack of atmosphere. Barbecue and other refreshments are sold. For the latest information, call Tim Davis at Betty Davis' Grocery (662-252-7144) or Tommy Davis at the Chulahoma Grocery (662-564-2206).

Another attractive blues pilgrimage is a visit to nonagenarian Othar Turner's annual fife-and-drum picnic in Tate County, Mississippi. Held the weekend before Labor Day weekend, the party on Turner's farm features goat barbecue, dancing, and the mesmerizing sounds of fife-and-drum music, an archaic tradition once prevalent among African Americans in the rural South. Area bluesmen are also liable to show up and perform at Othar's—guests in recent years have included R. L. Burnside and T-Model Ford. For information and directions, try the folks at Shangri-La Records (see "Record Stores," above) or call the Delta Blues Museum (601-624-4461).

Oxford, Mississippi, an hour-and-a-half's drive southeast of Memphis via U.S. 78 and Miss. 7, is home to *Living Blues* magazine, published by the University of Mississippi, and the blues-oriented Fat Possum Records label, famous for its recordings of Kimbrough and Burnside. **Proud Larry's** (211 S. Lamar, 662–236–0050), a typical college town bar featuring pizza, pasta, and burgers, is the most likely spot in Oxford for good live blues.

The West Tennessee Delta Heritage Center, 121 Sunnyhill Cove, Brownsville, Tenn., 901–779–9000, www.westtnheritage.com.

An hour's drive east of Memphis off Exit 56 on Interstate 40 is the West Tennessee Delta Heritage Center, which includes an exhibit devoted to area blues musicians, notably guitarist Sleepy John Estes, mandolinist Yank Rachell, and vocalist Tina Turner (who was born Anna Mae Bullock in nearby Nutbush in 1938). Country singer Eddy Arnold (from Madisonville) and rockabilly pioneer Carl Perkins (from Jackson) are also honored. Estes' former home in Brownsville has been relocated to the grounds of the museum. Brownsville also holds an annual blues festival in late September/early October that features both local and national acts. For details, contact the Brownsville-Haywood County Chamber of Commerce (901–772–2193).

Museum hours: M-Sa, 9 A.M.–5 P.M., Su 1–5 P.M. *Free.*

W. C. Handy's Home and Museum, 620 W. College St. (downtown), Florence, Ala., 256–760–6434.

Located approximately 125 miles southeast of Memphis in the town of Florence, Alabama, is the log cabin where W. C. Handy was born in 1873. The son of a Methodist minister, W. C. lived here until he was 19, attending the local school (where he also taught for a time) and playing the organ in his father's church. His father did not approve of his son's interest in music and, when W. C. came home with a guitar one day, demanded that he turn it in for a dictionary.

The log cabin is furnished with period pieces, and adjacent to it is a museum filled with Handy memorabilia, such as the piano on which he wrote "St. Louis Blues," his trumpet, schoolbooks, family albums, and awards. Especially interesting is the Braille sheet music that Handy used during the last 15 years of his life, after losing his sight.

A weeklong W. C. Handy festival featuring concerts, art exhibits, and more is sponsored by the Music Preservation Society in Florence every August (P.O. Box 1827, Florence, Ala. 35631; 256–766–7642). Started up by bass player Willie Ruff about 20 years ago, the festival presents a multitude of musical events (jazz, blues, gospel), and 80 percent of the concerts are free. Roberta Flack, the Manhattan Transfer, and

Dizzy Gillespie have all played the fest, and there's even music in the church where Handy's father and grandfather once preached, the Greater St. Paul AME.

Open: Tu-Sa, 10 A.M.–4 P.M. *Admission:* $.

THE MISSISSIPPI DELTA

Updated by David Nelson with Scott Barretta

The Mississippi Delta is generally believed to be the place where the blues originated. A wedge-shaped region of land lying in northern Mississippi between the Mississippi and Yazoo rivers, it has spawned an enormous number of musicians, many of whom now have international reputations.

Some scholars pinpoint Dockery Farms near Cleveland as the actual birthplace of the blues.[1] From this area came such early musicians as Charley Patton, Tommy Johnson, and Willie Brown. Later, musicians could be heard in tiny juke joints throughout the region: Muddy Waters in Clarksdale; Sonny Boy Williamson* in Helena, Arkansas; Son House and Robert Johnson in Robinsonville; and dozens upon dozens of others. Even a partial list of the Delta's bluesmen is overwhelming in its musical importance: Howlin' Wolf (Chester Burnett), James Cotton, Willie Dixon, Memphis Minnie, Pinetop Perkins, David "Honeyboy" Edwards, John Lee Hooker, Mississippi John Hurt, Albert King, B. B. King, Jimmy Reed, Robert Lockwood, Jr.

The conditions that gave birth to the blues—poverty, racism, and inhumane working situations—led many musicians to leave the state as soon as they could. Most traveled North, heading first to Memphis and then to urban centers such as Chicago, St. Louis, and Detroit. Nonetheless, the blues hardly vanished from the Mississippi countryside, and even today—though much diminished in scope—the music can still be heard in a number of juke joints in a number of towns, its raw hypnotic sound reaching deep into the night.

---

*The Sonny Boy Williamson referred to throughout this chapter is Rice Miller, also sometimes referred to as Sonny Boy Williamson II to distinguish him from John Lee "Sonny Boy" Williamson.

Sources

The best center for blues information throughout the Delta is the **Delta Blues Museum** in Clarksdale (1 Blues Alley, 662–627–6820). Posters and flyers advertising chitlin circuit venues, juke joints, and small festivals are often placed on telephone poles.

For maps and other information, contact the local Chambers of Commerce.

A Note on Mississippi

Something surprising has happened in Mississippi. After decades of ignoring—virtually denying—the existence of that "devil's music," the blues, the state now acknowledges its importance. In Clarksdale and Cleveland, the Chambers of Commerce put out maps pinpointing blues sites. In Greenville, local entrepreneurs promote "blues breakfasts" and "blues happy hours" during the Delta Blues festival. In Moorhead, a state historic plaque marks the spot where the "Southern crosses the Dog" (see Tutwiler, page 80).

It is uncertain how much of Mississippi's changing attitude is due purely to economics. This is a poor state, and blues fans bring in much-needed tourist dollars. But the Mississippi of the 2000s is not the Mississippi of the 1960s. Racially and economically, things are changing around here—due in part at least to the influx of casinos and related development along the Mississippi River, which has altered the once-sleepy atmosphere of the Delta.

The casinos have also brought mixed blessings for the blues. While some of the casinos occasionally book national blues acts and local groups, the lure of 24-hour gambling and alcohol sales has taken business away from the Delta's juke joints.

Strikingly, however, an increasing number of Mississippi's younger African Americans seem to be getting into the blues, especially the R&B–flavored variety of entertainers like Marvin Sease, Lynn White, and Clarksdale's own O. B. Buchana—just a few of the names you're likely to find on showbills taped to telephone poles here. Through the efforts of grassroots blues teacher Johnnie Billington in Lambert and the educational programs offered by the Delta Blues Museum, young musicians are also being mentored in more traditional blues styles.

Juke Joints

Visiting juke joints takes time and patience. Most feature live music only once a week, on Friday or Saturday nights or Sunday afternoons, and there are no set times for performances. Also, since the juke joint scene is in constant flux and many places don't have phones, it's hard to find out what's happening in advance.

One way around this is to stop by the juke joints in the afternoon. Many are hard to find, anyway, and it helps to scout them out during daylight hours. In all likelihood, someone will be around then to answer questions, and if they're not featuring music that night, they'll be able to direct you to some place that is.

Most juke joints are poor, simple, windowless affairs, built of cement or tin. There are usually a few rickety tables, a makeshift bandstand, a large dance floor, and Christmas-tree lights and ornaments to brighten the place up. Sometimes there's a nominal $2–$3 cover; and beer and soda and setups (i.e., cups and ice for hard liquor, which must be brought in) are for sale.

Artists to watch for in the Clarksdale/Helena area include Big Jack Johnson (when he's home—he spends much time on the road), his nephew Super Chikan, Sam Carr, Robert "Bilbo" Walker (on his regular visits from California), Wesley Jefferson, J. B. & the Midnighters, Dr. Mike & the Interns, and John Weston. In the Greenville area, there's T-Model Ford, Abie "Boogaloo" Ames, John Horton, Eddie Cusic, and Willie Foster.

HIGHWAY 61

WELCOME TO MISSISSIPPI reads the sign with the huge magnolias, and almost immediately, the hills give way to a flat green land stretching fine as a wire beneath the Southern sun. Already there's the sound of a freight train far in the distance, while cotton fields appear to the left and the right.

Driving south from Memphis to Clarksdale on Highway 61—once the black man's and woman's lifeline to the North—can be a strange, lonely experience, although there's much more traffic on the four-lane highway now since the casinos came in. The ache of the blues seems to hover in the air as the familiar names flash past: Walls, where Memphis Minnie was born; Robinsonville, where Robert Johnson grew up; Tunica, where James Cotton was born; Lula, where Charley Patton and Robert Nighthawk once lived.

For all the apparent lushness of the fields and the glitter of Tunica's casinos and hotels, the towns en route remain small and poor. All is quiet and peaceful, though it's a peace that one senses can be easily snapped.

Truckstops and convenience stores selling fried catfish appear from time to time, along with strange farm vehicles looking like giant flies. Reminders of the blues are everywhere. The old Highway 61 parallels the new and is lined with miles of rusting red Illinois Central railroad cars. Crossroads, often marked with official highway signs, appear out of nowhere, and in the evening, driving beneath a midnight-blue sky gradually turning black, it's easy to imagine the Devil lounging against a tree somewhere, waiting.

I went down to the crossroads, fell down on my knees,
I went down to the crossroads, fell down on my knees,
Ask the Lord above for mercy, say boy, if you please.
Mmm . . . standing at the crossroads I tried to flag a ride
Mmm . . . standing at the crossroads I tried to flag a ride
Ain't nobody seem to know me, everybody pass me by.
—*Robert Johnson, "Crossroads Blues"*

ROBINSONVILLE

At one end of town are a few big homes, surrounded by cypress trees. At the other end are small, rickety buildings, their roofs held up by spindly sticks of wood. In between is a simple post office building, its American flag hanging limp, and a huge nightclub called the Hollywood. Behind everything, overwhelming the day, are the cicadas, their harsh chirping voices canceling out words and thought.

Robert Johnson, one of the most enigmatic of blues singers, spent much time in and around Robinsonville. He grew up on plantations located nearby and may have gone to school in Commerce, the next town over. He started playing the jukes as a young man and, according to fellow musician Son House, was reasonably good on the harmonica and a disaster on the guitar. "Such a racket you never heard," Son House once said. "It'd make people mad, you know."

Johnson left Robinsonville at about 20, only to return a year later. Son House recounts their reunion:

"He spoke, and I said, 'Well boy, you still got a guitar, huh? What do you do with that thing? You can't do nothing with it.' He said, 'Well, I'll tell you what.' I said, 'What?' He said, 'Let me have your seat a minute . . . So he sat down there and

finally got started. And man! He was so good! When he fin-
ished, all our mouths were standing open. I said, 'Well, ain't
that fast!' He's gone now."[2]

Johnson, according to Son and others, was gone in more
ways than one. There was only one way he could have learned
the guitar so quickly—by selling his soul to the Devil waiting
by the crossroads.

CLARKSDALE

From the '30s on through the '40s and '50s, Clarksdale was a
major blues town. John Lee Hooker was born here, and so
were Ike Turner, Little Junior Parker, and Sam Cooke. Robert
Nighthawk, Bukka White, "Gatemouth" Moore, Eddie Boyd,
Son House, and Charley Patton all once lived in the area, and
Muddy Waters, who moved here at a young age, may have gotten his nick-name from going fishing on Fridays (getting
"muddy") and selling his catch on Saturdays at the town's
then-legendary fish fries.

Martin Luther King, Jr., Drive (formerly known as Fourth
Street), a short street on the other side of the tracks, is the
main drag of black Clarksdale. Most of the blues joints were
located here, and several are still situated nearby. The street
itself, however, has seen better days. Crack has been a problem for more than a decade.

Otherwise, Clarksdale is a quiet, low-slung town of one-
and two-story buildings. Small shops and banks line the
downtown streets, and traffic lights (despite the fact that
there's very little traffic) seem to be everywhere.

Clarksdale sponsors an annual blues festival that grows
larger with each succeeding year, and its Delta Blues Museum
has moved into exciting new quarters. But the city's blues
scene has also lost some of its most notable attractions—and
people—in recent years. Legendary WROX deejay Early Wright
and barber/bluesman Wade Walton, who occasionally played
music at his shop at 317 Issaquena Ave., have both passed
away. (A museum devoted to Wright and the history of WROX
is under construction at 257 Delta Ave.) Jim O'Neal, who cut
albums for his influential Rooster Blues Records label from a
backroom studio at his record store, the Stackhouse/Delta
Record Mart (232 Sunflower Ave.), has moved to Kansas City,
leaving Clarksdale blues musicians without their main hangout and blues tourists without what was always the best
source of information on the jukes. Margaret's Blue Diamond
Lounge, once one of the Delta's most popular jukes, closed
down permanently in 1994 after an ice storm damaged its
roof beyond repair. And the remains of the cabin where

Muddy Waters once lived on the Stovall Plantation outside
town were bought and carted off by the House of Blues nightclub chain (though the house will apparently return to
Clarksdale in the future, perhaps for reassembly at the Delta
Blues Museum).

Sources

The Delta Blues Museum (see below) is the best source for
blues info. The Coahoma County Chamber of Commerce (1540
De Soto St., at Highway 49S, 662–627–7337, www.clarksdale.
com) puts out a free map pinpointing blues sites.

Landmarks and Legends

Delta Blues Museum, 1 Blues Alley, 662–627–6820, www.
deltabluesmuseum.org.

Formerly housed in cozy quarters in Clarksdale's Carnegie
Library, the Delta Blues Museum has recently made a long
anticipated move into the newly restored Illinois Central Freight
Depot, an expansive brick building built in 1918. Interactive,
multi-media exhibits and regular concerts are planned for the
new museum, which is adjacent to the stage for the Sunflower
River Blues and Gospel Festival. Among the many fascinating
bits of memorabilia in the museum's collection are an early
microphone from WROX radio (used by Ike Turner), a Sonny
Boy King Biscuit flour bag, the huge charred sign from the store
at Three Forks behind which Robert Johnson reportedly died
(see "Quito," page 86), skull sculptures by Son Thomas, one of
B. B.'s "Lucilles," a bottle-top slide donated by Bonnie Raitt,
and a harmonica signed by James Cotton.

The museum's archives of printed materials remain in the
Carnegie Public Library (114 Delta Ave., 662–624–4461).

Museum hours: M-Sa, 9 A.M.–5 P.M., Su 1–5 P.M. *Admission*: $.

Delta Blues Education Fund, 662–627–4070, www.bluesed.
org.

"It's better to put a guitar in a child's hand than a gun" is
the motto of the Delta Blues Education Fund, founded in
1992 and directed by Clarksdale blues musician and
Mississippi River guide John Ruskey. In addition to coordi-
nating educational programming with the Delta Blues
Museum, the Fund is active in training young blues musicians at the grassroots level through the work of "Mr.
Johnnie" Billington, whose former students (including
Ruskey) now form the backbone of Clarksdale's current blues
scene. Billington welcomes visitors at his classes and week-

end performances (see "Clubs, etc.," page 75), while Ruskey offers canoeing and kayaking expeditions on the Lower Mississippi through his Quapaw Canoe Company (291 Sunflower Ave., 662–627–4070, www.island63.com).

W. C. Handy's home, Issaquena St., near Third St.

Handy lived in Clarksdale from 1903 to 1905. His house once stood on the site later occupied by former bluesman Wade Walton's barber shop, and a plaque out front commemorates the spot: "In Clarksdale, Handy was influenced by Delta Blues which he collected and later published. . . ."

Riverside Hotel, 615 Sunflower Ave., 662–624–2694.

September 26, 1937: A car crashes into a truck parked alongside Highway 61. One of the passengers, a woman, is severely injured; her arm is nearly severed. Bleeding profusely, she is rushed to a nearby hospital, but it is too late, and she is dead before morning.

The woman is Bessie Smith, about whose death so much controversy once raged. An early article, written by John Hammond in *Down Beat*, stated that Bessie bled to death while waiting for treatment at a white hospital, and despite Hammond's later retraction (his apology stated that he'd been writing primarily on hearsay), white liberals reading the story became enraged and turned her death into a cause celebre that refused to die. As late as 1960, Edward Albee was writing a play about it.

All this was doubly ironic, both because Hammond frequently denounced much real racial injustice that most liberals conveniently ignored, and because later evidence showed that Bessie was not taken to a white hospital, but to a black one: the G. T. Thomas Hospital located at 615 Sunflower Avenue, Clarksdale.

Today, the Thomas Hospital has become the Riverside Hotel, a modest establishment of some 25 rooms, and Bessie Smith is far from the only blues artist connected with it. During the '40s, shortly after it had become a hotel, a whole host of musicians—Sonny Boy Williamson, Robert Nighthawk, Kansas City Red, Jackie Brenston, and others—called this place home.

Also connected with the hotel is Ike Turner, who was born and bred in Clarksdale. According to the Riverside's late proprietor, Mrs. Z. L. Hill, who owned the hotel from the '40s through the '90s, "When he was old enough and thought he was a man—he wasn't, but he thought he was—he quit school and came to the hotel and got him a room."

Before long, Ike also got him a band, with Jackie Brenston, and one of the songs that the group both wrote and rehearsed while staying at the Riverside was "Rocket 88" (see Sun Studio, page 52). Mrs. Hill was in on the tune from the very beginning, and she sewed little ROCKET 88 badges onto the band members' ties before sending them on their way to the recording studio. "They were the prettiest things," she once said.

Mrs. Hill's son "Rat" now operates the hotel.

Bell Grove Baptist Church, 831 Garfield St. (just S of Highway 61), 662–624–2920.

One of Muddy Waters's cousins, the Reverend Willie Morganfield, still preaches at this big brick church with the square white steeple. Morganfield is an impressive and inspiring preacher, and is also a recording artist in his own right, with numerous records and tapes to his name.

Morning worship: Su, 11 A.M. *Prayer meeting*: W, 6:30 P.M.

CLUBS, ETC.

South End Disco (a.k.a. **Red's**), 395 Sunflower Ave. at MLK., 662–627–3166 or 662–627–1367.

Red Peyton has been running this scruffy brick blues club, with its big cylindrical barbecue smoker outside the front door, for the past 30 years now. Inside, the club boasts a hodgepodge of mismatched tables and chairs, a pool table lit by blue lights, and a small disco ball. Big Jack Johnson occasionally performs here when he's in town, and the place is always packed on Friday and Saturday nights, whether there's live music or not.

Smitty's Red Top Lounge, 377 Yazoo Ave., 662–627–4421.

Smitty's is a dark windowless room. Stuff is stored in the corners and the floors are uneven. None of this matters when the band begins to play, but the music is extremely sporadic— call ahead.

During the club's heyday, Frank Frost and the Jelly Roll Kings once posed for an album cover here, and the place was written up in a Swedish magazine.

The Millennium Club, 352 Delta Ave. (adjacent to the Delta Blues Museum), 662–624–2129.

This increasingly popular juke sometimes features Super Chikan, Willie Foster, or the John Horton Band. Good barbecue served from behind the bar is an added attraction in this roomy, high-ceilinged space, which also includes a poolroom in back.

Mr. Johnnie's Place, 717 Darby St., Lambert, 662–326–5934.

Blues guitarist Johnnie Billington runs his blues workshops for Clarksdale-area youth out of this no-frills room in the nearby town of Lambert. Billington, who used to work as a mechanic for the Mississippi school system, wants to pass the blues heritage on to the next generation, as well as give the kids somewhere to go besides the streets. He's a strict teacher, though, who tolerates no fooling around. "I want kids who'll stick through it," he says.

Billington conducts his apprenticeship classes every weekday afternoon (except Wednesdays) from 4 P.M.–6 P.M. Public performances are often held on Friday and Saturday nights at the same location. Visitors are welcome at both the classes and performances, but call ahead to verify the schedule.

Born about 35 miles east of Clarksdale, Billington, who's usually nattily dressed in a white shirt and tie, has an unusual theory about the blues. "The Delta blues comes from the birds," he says. "Each bird had a different sound and they would be beeping each other. The blues comes from that."

Also

Blues Shangrila at the Crossroads (224 Sunflower Ave.) and **Sarah's Kitchen** (208 Sunflower Ave.) are other Clarksdale jukes worth checking out. The **Pastime Lounge** (426 DeSoto Ave.) and the **VFW** on Highway 49S at the edge of town are more upscale venues that occasionally feature live blues.

Every August, the Sunflower River Blues Association (P.O. Box 1562, Clarksdale, MS 38614; www.sunflowerfest.org) puts on a two-day **Sunflower River Blues and Gospel Festival** featuring music, workshops, lectures, and films. Despite the Delta's often stifling August heat, the festival, with its laidback atmosphere and focus on Mississippi artists, is one of the best and most enjoyable blues events in the country.

Record Stores

The **Sunflower River Trading Company** (252 Delta Ave., 662–624–9389, www.sunflowertrading.com) offers videos and recordings of local blues artists, as well as Mississippi gifts, books, and Delta artwork.

Radio

WROX/1450 AM (662–627–7343). Blues, M–F nights.
WWUN/101.7 FM (662–627–1113). Blues, M nights.
WQMA/1520 AM (662–326–8642). Daily, 6 A.M.–6 P.M.

HELENA, ARKANSAS

Located across the Mississippi from Clarksdale, Helena was a thriving wide-open port town during the '30s and '40s. The main street, Cherry, which paralleled the levee, had dozens of white saloons, while Elm Street, running just behind, had dozens of black. Bluesmen from all over—Johnny Shines, Robert Johnson, Howlin' Wolf, Sunnyland Slim, and Roosevelt Sykes (born in Helena)—congregated here by the dozens, knowing they could get work. Roosevelt Sykes wrote a song called "West Helena Blues" and Memphis Minnie sang about "Reachin' Pete," an unpopular policeman who patrolled Cherry Street.

"Most everywhere you'd go back then, you'd step into them blues," says one longtime Helena resident.

Today, Helena is a sad little place trying to get its feet back on firm economic ground. Cherry is still the main street—and it's lined with some wonderful pre-World War I buildings, but many stand abandoned. Except, that is, during the week of the annual **King Biscuit Blues Festival** (www.kingbiscuit-fest.org), when the town comes alive and several usually empty storefronts are transformed into temporary juke joints.

One of the best blues festivals around, the King Biscuit Blues Festival is held every October (see "Major Festivals," page 458) in honor of Sonny Boy Williamson. Williamson was the town's most famous resident, and those who knew him still talk about him with amazement.

Sources

For blues information, visit Blues Corner (see "Record Stores," page 79). For maps and general information, contact the Phillips County Chamber of Commerce (111 Hickory Hill, 870–338–8327) or the Tourist Information Center (Highway 49 bypass, 870–338–7602).

Landmarks and Legends

KFFA Radio, 1360 Radio Drive, 870–338–8361, www.king-biscuit.com.

In the annals of blues history, there's nothing quite like KFFA's "King Biscuit Time," which over the 28 years it was broadcast live probably had more impact on the blues than any other radio program.

It all started back in 1941, when the station's owner was approached by Sonny Boy Williamson (then known as Rice

Miller) and Robert Lockwood, Jr., who sold him on the then novel idea of playing on the air in return for the chance to advertise their gigs. The owner agreed and they lined up a sponsor, Interstate Grocer Co., distributor of King Biscuit Flour.

The show, broadcast Mondays through Fridays from 12:15 P.M. to 12:30 P.M. (later 12:15 P.M. to 12:45 P.M.), was an instant success, almost immediately expanding to include other musicians such as Pinetop Perkins, James "Peck" Curtis, and Houston Stackhouse. Sonny Boy's picture was plastered onto cornmeal bags, sales soared, and the show went on the road, playing from the back of Interstate's delivery trucks.

Other businesses, impressed with King Biscuit's profits, soon followed suit, hiring blues singers to advertise a wide range of products. Before long, too, radio shows dedicated exclusively to the blues (nonexistent before then) started up around the country.

Williamson left KFFA intermittently throughout his career but remained affiliated with it all his life. He was not an easy man to work with. "He was a mean SOB," says Sonny Payne, the announcer who broadcast thousands of Sonny Boy's shows. "Twice a month we had to get him out of the clink. He'd been taken advantage of so many times, he started fighting back. That's what got him in trouble all the time."

"King Biscuit Time" switched from a live to a record format in 1969, and the show went off the air completely in 1980. Revived again in 1986, it is now running in its old time slot, with its old announcer, Sonny Payne. Nowadays, however, the show, which won the prestigious Peabody Award in 1992, is being broadcast out of the Delta Cultural Center (below).

Meanwhile, KFFA, basically a country music station that has moved several times over the years, is currently housed in this small building surrounded by tall grasses on the outskirts of town. A rusting Interstate truck with the KING BISCUIT FLOUR logo sits outside its front door, and souvenirs such as KFFA mugs and bumper stickers are on sale inside.

Open: M–F, 8 A.M.–5 P.M.

Delta Cultural Center, 95 Missouri St. (at the end Cherry St. by the river), 870–338–8919.

Dedicated to the heritage of the Arkansas River Delta, this well-conceived nonprofit center, housed in a renovated 1912 train station, includes exhibits on everything from the Civil War to the Mississippi River. Near the back of the museum is a small display featuring some of the blues, gospel, and country artists who have come out of the state (including Johnny

Cash, Al Green, and Conway Twitty) and a room with a rough wooden floor from which "King Biscuit Time" is broadcast. Visitors are welcome to listen in on the broadcast, which takes place every weekday at 12:15 P.M.

Adjacent to the center, on the wall at the Mississippi River levee, is a mural on Helena's musical tradition painted by local artist Larry Spakes. The center also has an education complex at 137 Cherry St., which offers programs for children and art exhibits.

Open: M-Sa, 10 A.M.–5 P.M.; Su, 1–5 P.M. *Admission:* free.

Helena National Bank Building, 302 Cherry St.

KFFA was broadcast from the fifth floor of this, the tallest building in Helena, during the mid-sixties. On May 25, 1965, Williamson failed to show up for work, and Sonny Payne sent Peck Curtis out to find him. "When he got back," says Payne, "We had already started the show. 'Mr. Sonny,' Peck says to me, 'Sonny Boy's dead.' 'Dead?,' I said, 'you joshing me?' 'No sir.' 'Get on in there and let's play.' That's all I said."

Gist's Music Company, 307 Cherry St., 870–338–8441.

Gist's is a huge barn of a place, with the wooden floors, hanging fans, and dusty smell of another era. Harmonicas fill the old glass cases, guitars hang from the walls, and a bell tinkles every time someone steps over the well-worn threshold.

Proprietor Mr. Morse Gist, called "Mr. Guitar" by his customers, is a tall quiet-spoken man. He once owned the building where Williamson lived and died, and sold the musician and his band their instruments and guitar strings.

"It would take Sonny Boy a long time to buy a harmonica," says Mr. Gist, "and one time he stormed back in, wanting to return one he'd bought that morning. Now he knew that wasn't allowed, it wasn't sanitary, and I got angry, he got angry, it was hot. Finally, I grabbed another harmonica off the shelf and told him never to come back. I threw the old harmonica away, but later I took it back out and put it in the back drawer. I needed something to remind me not to get angry. Darned if some museum people didn't come by a few years back and ask me for it."

Open: M–Sa, 10 A.M.–5 P.M.

Interstate Grocer Company, Walnut Street between Missouri and Phillips streets.

Located three blocks from Sonny Boy's boarding house, Interstate Grocer had introduced King Biscuit Flour two years before the founding of KFFA. The product was doing well, but not that well, and the owner, Max Moore, jumped at the chance to sign up the "King Biscuit Entertainers."

Today, another distributor, Helena Wholesale, sells Sonny Boy meal throughout Arkansas and Mississippi.

Sonny Boy Williamson's Boarding House, 427 1/2 Elm St. at the corner of Pecan St., now an empty lot.

A large brick building once stood on this site that over the years housed a chicken-processing plant, an auto-repair shop, and, upstairs on the second level, a half dozen "rooms" available for rent (they were actually more like cubicles built of two-by-four's). Sonny Boy Williamson first came here in 1941, and even though he would be gone for years at a time, recording up North or touring in Europe, the landlord always kept his room intact.

In 1964, Sonny Boy returned to Helena one last time. Though virtually unknown in the United States, he was a star in Europe. He'd been the hit of several blues festivals and had recorded with The Yardbirds and Eric Clapton, among others. The Helena townspeople were therefore surprised to see him back in town, resuming his old duties at KFFA. The explanation that he gave them was that he'd come home to die. "We're like elephants," he said. "We knows." Eight months later he was dead.

No. 427 1/2 was still standing until late 1989, when it was severely damaged by lightning and high winds, and was torn down. The Sonny Boy Blues Society (P.O. Box 237, Helena, AR 72342) salvaged many of the original bricks, and they hope one day to erect a museum on the site.

Record Stores

This Little Pig Antiques and Gifts, and **Blues Corner**, 105 Cherry St., 870–338–3501.

Bubba Sullivan of the Sonny Boy Blues Society runs a first-rate blues record shop in a large room next to his wife's sprawling antique store. Sullivan, a lifelong blues enthusiast who turned to the record business when he lost his farm a few years ago, is one of the few people in town—black or white—who really appreciates its music history, and he's constantly struggling to get it more recognition. In addition to being a motherlode of Delta blues recordings, Blues Corner is a hang-out for area musicians.

Open: M–Sa, 9 A.M.–6 P.M., Su, 1–5 P.M.

Radio

KFFA/1360 AM (870–338–8361). "King Biscuit Time" with Sonny Payne, M–F, 12:15–12:45 P.M.

FRIAR'S POINT

Between Clarksdale and Helena is Friar's Point, Mississippi, once the Coahoma County seat and the site of the ferry crossing, which was the only way to cross the Mississippi before the mid-1950s. More than one blues musician on his way to a gig screeched onto a soon-to-depart ferry in the nick of time; and Eddie Condon's jazz tune "Friar's Point Shuffle" was named after this place.

Today, Friar's Point is a forsaken little town with a few nice homes, a few not-so-nice homes, and an historic museum featuring, rather surprisingly, artifacts of Native Americans.

MERIGOLD

South of Clarksdale and Merigold on Highway 61 is the Rushing Winery, founded by the Rushing family. Three generations ago, in the 1920s, Tom Rushing was the town's deputy sheriff, and was the subject of "Tom Rushen Blues" (a misspelling of "Rushing"), recorded by Charley Patton: "When you get in trouble, it's no use to screamin' and cryin'/When you get in trouble, it's no use to screamin' and cryin'/Tom Rushen will take you back to the prison house flyin'."

The major blues attraction in Merigold today is **Po' Monkey's Lounge**, a country juke house that features a fashion "strip" show on Monday nights and music on Thursdays—usually records, but occasionally a live band. To reach Po' Monkey's from Highway 61 heading south, turn right at the blinking light (the only traffic light in Merigold) and go approximately three quarters of a mile to a fork in the road. Turn left at the fork (the road will turn to gravel) and Po' Monkey's is a little over a mile on the left. Owner Po' Monkey lives on site.

TUTWILER

Right through the middle of Tutwiler cut the railroad tracks. A tight line of brick buildings line either side, but the town feels empty, almost abandoned, even at high noon on a hot summer's day, and it's easy to imagine how eerie the place must seem at night.

W. C. Handy was sitting in the old Tutwiler railroad depot (no longer standing, although the foundation is still visible), waiting for a train that was nine hours late on that fateful night in 1903 when he first heard the blues. "A lean, loose-

The Queen of Hearts in
Jackson is as known for its
barbecue as for its blues.

jointed Negro had commenced plunking a guitar beside me
while I slept," Handy writes in his autobiography, *Father of the
Blues.* "His clothes were rags; his feet peeked out of his shoes.
His face had on it some of the sadness of the ages. As he
played, he pressed a knife on the strings of the guitar. . . . The
effect was unforgettable."

   One of the phrases that the man repeated three times was
"Goin' where the Southern cross the Dog." Handy asked what
it meant and the man explained that he was headed to

Moorhead, farther south, where the tracks of the Southern Railroad cross the Yellow Dog, a local name for the Yazoo and Mississippi Valley Railroad.

This was the first documentation of the blues and the slide guitar. As far as music historians can ascertain, blues did not exist much before 1900.

Sonny Boy Williamson's grave, cemetery, Whitfield Church, just outside Tutwiler. Heading south, take Highway 49W $^{7}/_{10}$ mile to a paved road on right. Go about $^{1}/_{2}$ mile, then turn left. Go another $1^{1}/_{2}$ miles, past houses and fields, and watch for the abandoned church on right.

Sonny Boy's gravestone is impressively large, unusual for a blues musician's (their graves are usually unmarked), but depending on the season, it can be extremely difficult to find as it's often covered over with brambles and vegetation. Look for the gleam of harmonicas—offerings left by earlier passersby—that surround the stone.

Parchman Penitentiary, Highway 49W between Tutwiler and Drew.

Before there were blues there were work songs, call-and-response chants used to coordinate groups of workers. Work songs were common among railroad workers and at penitentiaries, where prison gangs would sing while cutting wood or hoeing cotton.

Many bluesmen found themselves in Parchman at some point in their careers, and the penitentiary has been celebrated in a number of songs, including Bukka White's "Parchman Farm Blues." According to one legend, White was involved in a bar fight in which someone was killed. Rather than face charges, he fled to Chicago. He landed a recording session with Lester Melrose and was sitting in front of a microphone, singing, when the sheriff's deputies from Mississippi arrived, arrested him, and took him back to Parchman. His time here was not a total waste, however. While at the prison, he was recorded by Alan Lomax, who came to Parchman in 1939 to gather material for the Archive of American Folk Song in the Library of Congress.

Parchman is still operating as a state penitentiary today. Signs on either side of the institution say "Emergency Stopping Only Next Two Miles" but the prison itself—surrounded by dry, dusty fields—is located rather near the highway, where a red-and-white railroad crossing stick is raised and lowered to admit visitors, volunteer or otherwise.

DREW

Howlin' Wolf used to play in Drew's central square, while Charlie Patton, Tommy Johnson, and other musicians often gathered here to talk, swap stories, and sing the blues.

Today, the small town is home to the **Music Mart** (161 N. Main St., 662–745–6576), a record store owned by Drew native Marvin Flemmons, which carries a good selection of R&B and some blues. Flemmons grew up listening to the big bands, playing in his own high school band, and spinning records for local events, but it wasn't until he was listening to the radio one day in 1972 that he learned that the number one song of that year, "I'll Take You There," was by a group from his hometown, the Staple Singers. "I thought, 'How can they be from Drew?,'" he says.

Today, Flemmons organizes the one-day **Staples Park Festival,** featuring Pops Staples and local blues musicians, the first Saturday of June. The festival is scheduled to coincide with the **B. B. King Homecoming Concert,** held in Indianola the Friday night before.

CLEVELAND

While leading his orchestra at a dance in Cleveland in 1905, W. C. Handy learned that he needed to update his sound when he was unable to perform "blues" requests from the audience. "My enlightenment came in Cleveland," he later wrote. "That night an American composer was born." A historical marker in front of the Bolivar County Courthouse commemorates Handy's life-changing experience in this Delta cotton town.

Today, Cleveland is home to Delta State University (whose sports teams are nicknamed the "Fightin' Okra"). A Mississippi Delta Blues Hall of Fame is currently in the works; artifacts are temporarily housed in the university's Charles W. Capps Archives and Museum (662–846–4780).

Sources

The Cleveland-Bolivar County Chamber of Commerce (800–295–7473) publishes a flyer that lists blues sites.

CLUBS, ETC.

Airport Grocery, Bishop Rd., 662–843–4817.

Greenville bluesman Willie Foster, whose business cards identify him as "a harmonica parader with soul," cut a live album at this rustic restaurant and bar. On the menu are steaks, burgers, and barbecue, and live blues on Friday nights.

DOCKERY

Dockery Farms, Highway 8 between Cleveland and Ruleville.

In his book *Deep Blues*, music critic Robert Palmer writes that Dockery's—a huge plantation that's a town unto itself—may have been the actual place where the Delta blues originated. Charley Patton, one of the earliest bluesmen, once lived here, as did his teacher, a man named Henry Sloan, about whom almost nothing is known, but who was playing the blues as far back as 1897.

Patton lived in the Dockery area most all his life, attracting a coterie of imitators, and many of his songs reflect his life there. "Pea Vine Blues," for example, was written about the railroad, nicknamed the "Pea Vine" because of its circuitous route, that Dockery's men built in the late 1920s. Two of Patton's most famous students were Son House and Howlin' Wolf, and the first song the Wolf ever played was "Hitch Up My Pony, Saddle Up My Black Mare," Patton's showpiece.

INDIANOLA

The road leading into Indianola, once home to both B. B. King and Albert King (no relation), is a pretty one, long and winding. It follows the banks of a wide, dark river on whose surface float dozens of ducks.

Indianola's downtown consists of a small park and short main street. Though the town has yet to really acknowledge its best-known sons, there are two concessions to their fame: a B. B. King Street, and B. B.'s half-forgotten handprints, stamped into the cement sidewalk on the southwest corner of Second and Church streets. The location is an interesting one: a little farther on, just over the tracks, is the poor, black section of town, but this corner falls—just barely—within the boundaries of middle-class "respectability."

Unlike many musicians, B. B. King has never forgotten his hometown. He returns to Indianola every June to give a free concert in Fletcher Park (and elsewhere in the state) and a paying one in his old haunt, the Club Ebony. He also sponsors a local baseball team, the B. B. Kings.

Sources

The Chamber of Commerce (662–887–4454) is located at 104 E. Percy St.

Dockery's, once home to Charlie Patton, may be the actual place where the blues were born.

CLUBS, ETC.

Club Ebony, 404 Hannah St., 662–887–9915.

The Club Ebony used to be Jones' Night Spot, and it was here that a young B. B. King first heard Sonny Boy Williamson, Robert "Junior" Lockwood, and Louis Jordan, among many others. Some years later, B. B. met his second wife, Sue Carol Hall, here while playing a gig of his own. Hall's mother, Miss Ruby, managed the place back then.

B. B. still does an annual show here, in this cozy, handsome club, and the place occasionally features other touring blues acts.

MOORHEAD

Like many of the towns in the center of the Delta, Moorhead has a different feel from the towns farther north. Things are greener and lusher here, and catfish farms—neat little man-made tracks of water—abound.

Moorhead is a simple one-street town, and right through its middle run the tracks of the Southern and the Dog (see Tutwiler, page 80), around whose gleaming, pragmatic lines so much lore has arisen. An historical marker marks the juncture.

CLUBS, ETC.

Cotton Inn, Olive Street (Highway 3), downtown, across from the gas station.

T-Model Ford has been known to take to the stage of this small, dark, unmarked joint with its painted pink walls. The place is rough-looking even for the Delta—the cement floors are uneven, the light bulbs are exposed, and the seats are cracked—but that's because it's been around forever. For decades, people working the fields picking cotton used to come here to celebrate on the weekends. Said bluesman John Price, once a regular here, "A man worked five days a week, he want to come in and kick up his legs."

QUITO (about 4 miles south of Itta Bena on Highway 7)

The how, where, and why of Robert Johnson's death continues to fascinate. Some say he was stabbed, some say he was poisoned, some say he died on all fours, barking like a dog,

> You may bury my body, ooh, down by the highway side,
> So my evil spirit can get a Greyhound bus and ride.

The mystery surrounding the bluesman's death has resulted in the erection of two different markers, one in Quito, the other near Morgan City. Both purport to indicate Johnson's gravesite.

Quito's **Robert Johnson tombstone** stands near the Payne Chapel M. B. Church (on Highway 7 south from Itta Bena, turn right onto a dirt road marked "Leflore Co. #512 West"; the church is a few hundred yards down on the right and the tombstone is to the left of the church in the back of a small cemetery abutting a field). It was donated by an Atlanta rock group, appropriately called the Tombstones, who'd read about the supposed burial site, as identified by an ex-girl-friend of Johnson's in *Living Blues* (No. 94). The stone was erected in late February 1991.

Johnson reportedly died behind the **Three Forks Store.** No one seems to be quite certain where that site was either, but some believe that it was the brown building at the bridge in Quito (on the right just before reaching the Payne Chapel), moved here from a mile or so farther down the road sometime after Johnson's death.

MORGAN CITY

The **Robert Johnson Memorial Monument** at the Mt. Zion M. B. Church (heading north on Highway 7 from Morgan City, turn right onto Leflore Co. #511, toward the National Wildlife Refuge; the church is on the left) is an impressive affair, with inscriptions on all four sides. Funds for the memorial, dedicated on April 20, 1991, were donated by Columbia Records, thanks to the efforts of organizer Skip Henderson. Columbia, which also paid off the church's debts (again thanks to Henderson), was to have erected Johnson's tombstone as well, but when the stone was delivered, a deacon at the church refused to accept it because one already stood in Quito.

To make things even more confusing, the Zion Church *is* Johnson's official burial site, according to his death certificate. *But,* writes blues expert Jim O'Neal, a number of people, including Honeyboy Edwards, have said that Johnson's sister had Robert's body moved to another cemetery (the Payne Chapel's?).

Whatever the truth may be, the Mt. Zion church itself stands simple, lovely, and serene, a small white clapboard building with a cross on top overlooking lush green fields.

HOLLY RIDGE

Charley Patton's grave is located in the tiny, dusty one-street town of Holly Ridge, just off Highway 82 between Leland and Indianola. Coming off the highway, turn left onto the main street and look for the New Jerusalem M. B. Church (on the left), where Patton once performed religious songs back in the 1930s. The church's graveyard is located two lots farther down, also on the left, opposite the last house in town, and Patton's grave is near the back. It went unmarked until July 20, 1991, when funds for a headstone—complete with an inscribed guitar and photo—were raised, mainly by Creedance Clearwater great John Fogerty, through the efforts of Skip Henderson.

Behind the graveyard, empty fields stretch out, dotted with abandoned railroad cars.

LELAND

Leland, ten miles east of Greenville at the intersection of Highways 82 and 61, was home to the late folk artist and bluesman James "Son" Thomas. The small town is bustling (by Delta standards, anyway) with blues activity these days, with an annual **Highway 61 Blues Festival** happening the first weekend in June, a Highway 61 Blues Mural on display on 3rd Street (between Broad and Main), and a Highway 61 Blues Museum scheduled to open in 2001 in the old Temple Theater on Broad Street.

CLUBS, ETC.

The Bourbon Mall, 105 Dean Rd., 662–686–4389.

The Bourbon Mall is not a shopping center or a liquor store but rather an old grocery in an almost deserted country community, now converted into a restaurant that serves excellent steaks and Southern food. Live blues—often courtesy of guitarist Eddie Cusic—is usually offered on Friday and Saturday nights, but call first to confirm.

Lillo's Restaurant, Hwy 82 E., 662–686–4401.

This family-run place, around since 1948, hosts Doc & the Three B's featuring pianist Boogaloo Ames on Thursday nights. Sometimes, the band performs on the weekends as well.

GREENVILLE

Greenville, population 50,000, is one of the few cities in the Delta. It's also Mississippi's largest river port and is home to many manufacturing, towboat, and barge-construction companies—as well as to a number of new, glitzy riverside casinos.

Nelson Street has traditionally been the town's blues street, renowned not only in Greenville but also elsewhere in the Delta. "When you're on Nelson Street on a Saturday night, you're as deep in the blues as you can get," Jim O'Neal once wrote.

At one time, the music could be heard everywhere along Nelson—in the cafes, in the liquor stores and bars—but today, **Perry's Flowing Fountain** is the street's only real blues club, and it features live music only occasionally. Nelson Street's notorious drug problems haven't helped matters any either.

MACE (Mississippi Action for Community Education), a nonprofit organization founded by civil rights activists in 1967, puts on the city's **Mississippi Delta Blues and Heritage Festival** (MACE, 119 S. Theobold St., 662–335–3523, www.deltablues.org) every September. The fest draws up to 30,000 music fans to a large field south of town, where they feast on blues, R&B, soul, catfish, barbecue, and giant smoked turkey legs.

Sources

The Chamber of Commerce (662–378–3141) is located at 915 Washington Ave.

CLUBS, ETC.

Perry's Flowing Fountain, 816 Nelson St., 662–335–9836.

Perry Payton has died, but the Flowing Fountain lives on. Neat and cozy, the club is filled with rows of tables and chairs, dozens of tiny Christmas lights, and a bright mural on the wall depicting a purple-clad lady in a fountain. One side of the club is "Annie Mae's Café," which is mentioned in a Little Milton song (this was once his hangout and he still stops by occasionally when he's in town). A deejay spins on the weekends, and there's occasional live blues.

At one time, Payton, a mortician by day, knew all the big names—Ray Charles, B. B. King, Little Junior Parker, Howlin' Wolf—because he used to book them into the Elks Club for $300 when they were first coming up.

One Block East, 240 Washington Ave., 662–332–3800.

Popular with a younger crowd, One Block East doesn't offer much in the way of blues atmosphere, but the club does

Whether it's a jukebox or a live band, there's always lots of dancing at Lucille's Café.

Photo by Euphus Ruth © Delta Images

regularly feature bluesman John Horton on Thursday nights. Live blues is occasionally offered on the weekends as well.

Also

Lucille's Café (Watson Rd. in the Darlove community) is a neighborhood café with good barbecue, a pool table, a jukebox, and—sometimes—Sunday night blues, compliments of John Horton. **Old River Coffee House** (139 S. Walnut St., 662–335–7580) occasionally has blues on the weekend.

Radio

WESY/1580 AM (662–378–9405). Some blues.

VICKSBURG

Best known as the site of the battle that turned the tide of the Civil War, Vicksburg, which marks the end of the Delta, has its own surprising share of jazz and blues history. African-American brass bands were common in the city as far back as the 1880s, and from 1953 to 1973, one of the Mid-South's most popular bands, the Red Tops, headed by drummer

Walter Osborne, was based here. Vicksburg, which was also the hometown of Willie Dixon, even has a rather tenuous claim to being the site where the word "jazz" originated: in 1924, the *Vicksburg Evening Post* quoted a *New York Times* critic as saying that the word was coined to refer to a black drummer named Chaz (short for Charles) Washington who was known for his syncopated beat.

And then, there was the Blue Room. Ah, the Blue Room! Mention that name in Vicksburg and eyes will light up. From 1937 to 1972, the Blue Room, located at the corner of Clay and Mulberry streets, was one of the best clubs around, featuring the finest that jazz and blues had to offer: Louis Armstrong, Dinah Washington, Louis Jordan, Count Basie, and many more.

It was the club's owner, Tom Wince, however, who really made the place unforgettable. The legends that surround him are endless: half black, half Jewish, he had 13 wives, one child by each; his bronzed baby shoes were his most prized possession and they hung in his club; he owned a huge diamond ring, reaching to his knuckle, that he kept wrapped in tissue paper in his pocket, ready to be taken out upon request; he drove a pink Lincoln with leopard-skin upholstery; he allowed whites into his club only on special occasions; he didn't allow visiting from one club table to another, as he felt it led to fighting.

Tom Wince's flamboyance didn't end with his death in 1972, either. His grave in the city cemetery (where part of the movie *Mississippi Burning* was filmed) is an amazing affair—a huge star, flanked by two urns, bearing the epitaph: "An internationally known night club owner who established and operated the famous Blue Room Night Club."

JACKSON

Technically speaking, Jackson, the state capital, is too far south and east to be located in the Delta. Nonetheless, it's played an important role in Delta blues history. During the late 1920s and '30s, H. C. Speir, a Jackson music store owner, was a talent scout for all the major record companies and was responsible for getting many of the early Mississippi bluesmen—Charley Patton, Tommy Johnson, Skip James, and Robert Johnson, among them—recorded. Later, in the 1950s, Lillian McMurry, who owned a furniture store and record shop, launched the Trumpet label, and Johnny Vincent launched Ace. Nowadays, Malaco Records (3023 W. Northside Dr.), a major contemporary blues and R&B label, is headquartered here.

McMurry's store was located on Farish Street, which was and is the main artery of the city's African-American community (although some white store owners, such as McMurry, also had businesses here). During the '20s and '30s, the street also housed the second-story Crystal Palace (538 N. Farish), a jazz club that brought in all the big acts of the day. Right across the street from the Crystal was the Alamo Theater, now marked with a neon sign, where Otis Spann won a talent concert at the age of eight.

Blues researcher and writer Gayle Dean Wardlow is currently in the process of establishing a Farish Street Blues Museum (405 N. Farish St., 601–944–0000).

Sources

The local paper, the *Clarion-Ledger* (601–961–7000, www.clarionledger.com) and the alternative *Planet Weekly* (601–355–1491) do a good job of listing music events. The Chamber of Commerce (662–948–7575) is located at 201 S. President St., and Rand-McNally city maps are available in local convenience stores.

Landmarks and Legends

Trumpet Records, 309 N. Farish St.

In 1950, Lillian McMurry, who ran a furniture and record store out of this gray building near the intersection of Amity Street, founded Trumpet Records. One of the first artists she wanted to record was Sonny Boy Williamson, whom she had heard over KFFA radio. She and her brother and a friend set out to comb the Delta to locate Williamson, but no one would tell them where he was. Finally McMurry realized that the two white men were hindering rather than helping her cause. As Mike Rowe relates in *Chicago Blues,* she went into the next shack alone, introducing herself as a record company owner, "and this lady grinned and said, 'Why, come right in, Mrs. McMurry, he's right in the back room.'"

CLUBS, ETC.

The Subway Lounge, 619 W. Pearl St.

Rotating vocalists—all of them good—add to the freewheeling nature of this after-hours club, one of the city's oldest (it was a venerated jazz venue before switching to blues). Located "across the tracks" in the basement of an old hotel, the Subway has an integrated atmosphere, both in the audience and on the bandstand; that's rare for Jackson. The space is intimate, funky, and crowded, with patrons going up and down the stairs to buy beer from a makeshift store outside. Things don't really get going until after midnight, and the music often lasts until 4 A.M. Veteran guitarist and vocalist King Edward is a regular attraction.

Music: F, Sa. *Cover:* $

Hal & Mal's, 200 S. Commerce St., 601–948–0888.

Located near the railroad tracks downtown, this long brick building houses a large and friendly commercial club that features both local and national talent. Rock-and-roll is the focus, but all sorts of other music—blues, jazz, folk, country—can also be heard. B. B. King, Tyrone Davis, and Lionel Hampton have played here.

Music: F-Sa. *Cover:* $-$$. *Food:* American, soul.

Also

George St. Grocery (416 George St., 601–969–3573), which caters to college students and young professionals, offers blues fairly regularly. The **Living Room Coffee House** (301 W. Capitol, 601–354–9259) and **Seven All Arts Café** (110 Westley Ave., 601–966–2150) are places to hear local jazz musicians.

Jackson also hosts a number of festivals, including the one-day **Zoo Blues** fest (601–352–2582) in April, the **Farish Street Festival** (601–960–1557) over Labor Day weekend, and the two-day **Jubilee Jam** (601–960–1557), held in May.

Radio

WJSU/88.5 FM (601–968–2140). Affiliated with Jackson State. Jazz and some blues daily.
WMPR/90.1 FM (601–956–0212). Affiliated with Tougaloo College. Excellent blues shows daily.

ATLANTA

Updated by Eugene Holley, Jr.

For a major city with a large African-American population, Atlanta, surprisingly, has never had a particularly strong jazz history. Probably the best-known names to come out of here were composer/arranger Duke Pearson and pianist/composer Mary Lou Williams, who was born here before moving to Pittsburgh as a young child. Others include saxophonists George Adams and Marion Brown, singer-pianist Perry Bradford, pianist Eddie Heywood, trombonist J. C. Higgenbotham, and in more recent years, the Harper Brothers. Fletcher Henderson is also associated with the city—he studied chemistry at Atlanta University before pursuing a music career.

Among the local groups, the Peachtree Strutters, playing an early New Orleans style, were a popular band in Atlanta for years and years. And the music departments of two schools, Clark-Atlanta University and Spelman College, led by James Patterson and Joe Jennings respectively, boast excellent ensembles that have performed with the likes of Dizzy Gillespie and Wynton Marsalis.

Blues played a prominent role in Atlanta in the first half of the century. Back then, the city served as a communications center connecting the South with the Northeast, and numerous record labels, including Columbia and Okeh, set up field recording units here. The hub of the city's blues activity was Decatur Street, once home to Blind Willie McTell, Peg Leg Howell, and Georgia Tom Dorsey. Bessie Smith also spent much time in Atlanta in the early part of her career.

Sources

The best sources for music listings are *Creative Loafing* (404–688–5623, web.cln.com/) and the Friday and Saturday editions of the *Atlanta Journal-Constitution* (404–526–5151, www.accessatlanta.com/partners/ajc/).

For maps and other information, contact the Atlanta Convention and Visitors Bureau, 233 Peachtree St., NE, Suite 100; 404–521–6600, www.acvb.com.

A Note on the Neighborhoods

Atlanta is a sprawling metropolis made up of a small downtown, a few major streets, and a multitude of suburbs. Buckhead is an affluent neighborhood located to the north; Virginia–Highland (centering around Virginia and Highland streets) is a young, trendy area in an older part of town to the east. Five Points, so named because five streets converge here, is another entertainment district near the downtown, while Little Five Points is a more eclectic entertainment area somewhat south of downtown. The Underground is a Rouse Company development whose entire basement floor (Kenny's Alley) is devoted to music clubs. Patrons here shop from one sound to another as if they were shopping for clothes, but some of the music is actually quite good. Southwest Atlanta is home to a large African-American community.

Since many of Atlanta's clubs and historic sites are located in or near the downtown, it is possible to navigate the city by taxi. If you are driving, traffic is usually light, and parking spaces plentiful.

Landmarks and Legends

(With the exception of the Waluhaje Club and La Carrousel, all of the sites below are near the downtown and can be toured on foot.)

Auburn Avenue, from Peachtree Street east.

Nearly two miles long, Auburn Avenue was the heart of Atlanta's African-American commercial district from the turn of the century to the 1960s. The nation's oldest black daily, the *Atlanta Daily World*, was founded here in 1928, and Martin Luther King, Jr., was born here in 1929. In 1957, *Fortune* magazine called the avenue "the richest Negro street in the world."

Some of the establishments located along Auburn in days gone by include the Gate City Colored School (the first public school for blacks in Atlanta) and the European Hotel (the first hotel for blacks). Auburn never acquired the nightlife reputation of nearby Decatur Street, but two important theater-nightclubs, the Royal Peacock and the Top Hat Club, were located here in the 1950s.

The avenue, which begins in the heart of Atlanta's downtown, went into a steep decline following the Civil Rights riots of the '60s, but the area has since been somewhat revitalized. The Martin Luther King, Jr., Historic District, which includes King's grave and a small museum, is located on the far eastern end of the avenue. For a leader of such magnitude, the museum is much too small and haphazardly put together, but at least it's there.

Royal Peacock, 186 Auburn Ave.

The Royal Peacock was opened in 1949 by a Ms. Carrie Cunningham and quickly became the social and cultural center of Auburn Avenue. Nat "King" Cole, Lucky Millinder, Cab Calloway, Sam Cooke, and many others performed here; Little Richard got one of his first big breaks here.

The Royal Peacock reopened in the early 1990s, but has since closed down again. Outside, however, the original marquee and neon theater sign are still in place.

WERD, 330 Auburn Ave.

No longer in business, but once located in a mustard-colored building that now houses Atlanta's Southern Christian Leadership Conference, WERD was the first African-American-owned radio station in the country, founded by Jesse B. Blayton in 1947. The station's sign still hangs out front.

The APEX Museum (African-American Panoramic Experience), 135 Auburn Ave., 404–521–2739.

A sophisticated, well-lit museum dedicated to African-American history and culture, the APEX changes its exhibits from month to month, but always on view are historical photos and a short film describing the history of the area. The exceptional film *Sweet Auburn Avenue,* narrated by Cicely Tyson and Julian Bond, is alone well worth the visit; a $25 million expansion project is in the works, to be completed in 2003.

Open: T–Sa, 10 A.M.–5 P.M. *Admission:* $.

Decatur Street, Near Peachtree Street

During the early 1900s, the downtown end of Decatur Street (where Georgia State University is now located) was the heart of Atlanta's black nightlife, filled with saloons, pool halls, taverns, and theaters. The street was also overrun with gangsters, both black and white, and a "normal" Saturday night brought with it at least six "razor operations."[1]

Before World War I, Decatur was famous for its blues piano players. Later, it became filled with musicians from all over Georgia, Alabama, and the Carolinas, many of whom played the lighter sound of the Piedmont blues. One of these new arrivals was Blind Willie McTell, whose name later became synonymous with Atlanta blues. Blind Willie—who could be heard on the streets of the city as late as the early '60s—was fiercely independent, breaking record contracts whenever he felt like it.

Another famous Decatur Street bluesman was Peg Leg Howell. Peg Leg turned to blues in 1916 after his brother-in-law shot him in the leg and he had to give up farming. One of the first Atlanta musicians to be recorded, Peg Leg usually worked the streets with other musicians where, according to Giles Oakley in *The Devil's Music,* "they generated a wailing excitement, singing together with extrovertedly exaggerated voices."

Decatur Street was home to two major theaters, the "81" and the "91," named after their respective street numbers (and since replaced by the university's auditorium). The "81"

Blind Willie's is named after
Atlanta's best-known bluesman,
Blind Willie McTell.

was the larger and more prestigious of the two. Georgia Tom Dorsey worked there as a boy, selling soda pop, and Bessie Smith was "practically raised" in its backyard.

Film actor Leigh Whipper remembered Bessie from those early days back in 1913: "She was just a teenager and she obviously didn't know she was the artist she was. She didn't know how to dress—she just sang in her street clothes—but she was such a natural that she could wreck anybody's show."[2]

By 1924, Bessie, returning to the "81" after a national tour, was not only fashionable but famous. People lined up three abreast to buy tickets to her shows and a special performance was put on for whites only. This was common practice at the time—whites might adore black artists, even purchase their albums, but when it came to seeing them in concert, the musicians were still booked almost exclusively into all-black theaters, which usually reserved a night or two for an all-white audience.

Underground Atlanta, Martin Luther King, Jr., Dr. and Peachtree Street

Today's Underground is a vast shopping and entertainment complex in downtown Atlanta. Opened in 1989, to the tune of $142 million, it is yet another Rouse Company project, complete with the usual cute boutiques and pricey restaurants.

What makes the Underground unique, however, is that it is built on the historic city viaducts that were constructed between 1893 and the 1940s to route street traffic over congested railroad lines. Back then, merchants located on the lower levels promptly moved their stores up to the street to be near traffic, and left abandoned buildings behind. Some of these buildings became homes for the city's poorer folk; others became prostitution houses or blues bars.

In "Preachin' the Blues" Bessie Smith describes those days: "Down in Atlanta, G.A. / Under the viaduct every day / Drinkin' corn and hollerin' hooray / Pianos playing 'til the break o' day."

Despite the celebratory words of Bessie's song, the underground must have been a horrible place, cold in the winter, hot in the summer, dirty, airless, rat-infested. It's hard to get a true feeling for all of that in today's squeaky-clean Underground, but at the nearby Mitchell Street viaduct (which is actually the one referred to in Bessie's song), conditions back then are all too easy to imagine. The place, now a parking lot located near the junction of Martin Luther King, Jr., Drive and Butler Street, is ugly, cavernous, and threatening—not an area to wander around alone in late at night.

The Waluhaje, West Lake Ave., on the left, heading from Simpson Street (it's the only large building in the area).

This red-brick building, looking stern and institutional behind a pillared fence, was once a luxury hotel housing the Waluhaje Club. During the '50s, clubs and fraternities held dances here, and famous performers such as Dinah Washington, Tony Bennett, and Ella Fitzgerald were regulars.

Dizzy Gillespie played the Waluhaje in December 1956 shortly after making an enormously successful State Department tour to Africa, the Near East, the Middle East, and Asia. The date was an important one to both him and other African-American musicians, as he explains in his autobiography *To Be or Not to Bop.* "This was still a mixed band with a black leader playing in Georgia where whites were still struggling to hold on to segregation. One of the reasons we'd been sent around the world was to offset reports of racial prejudice in the United States, so I figured now we had a chance to give the doctor some medicine. . . . We opened at the black-owned Waluhaje, a beautiful new luxury apartment and entertainment complex in Atlanta, and, of course, a lot of whites there wanted to come to see us and they did, with no segregation."

La Carrousel, at Paschal's Motor Hotel and Restaurant, 830 Martin Luther King, Jr., Dr. SW (Southwest Atlanta, 10 min. from downtown), 404–577–3150.

La Carrousel, located in an African-American commercial district, is one of the oldest still-operating clubs in Atlanta. A big long room filled with low tables and red swivel chairs, it's lined with oil paintings of the circus: Emmett Kelly, the big top, a merry-go-round. Two painted horses greet guests at the door, and the bar itself is a mock carousel, twinkling with red lights.

At one time, La Carrousel was *the* jazz room in Atlanta, attracting music fans of all ages and races. Ramsey Lewis, Dizzy Gillespie, Jimmy Smith, Count Basie, Cannonball Adderley, Billy Taylor, and the Modern Jazz Quartet are among the many who once played here. Today, however, alas, things aren't what they used to be. La Carrousel is now mostly a bar, only offering jazz on rare occasions.

Things aren't what they used to be at the Paschal Motor Hotel, connected to La Carrousel by a skyway, either. An ineffable sadness seems to hang over the place, perhaps because, back in the '60s, the hotel and its restaurant was a place of such hope. Martin Luther King, Jr., Ralph Abernathy, and Andrew Young were regulars here; the Selma march was planned from here; Robert Kennedy, following King's assassination and before his own, set up an office here.

Today, all that fervor and expectation are gone, long gone. The halls at the hotel are dim and half empty, smelling of stale air and tired lives. Voices echo down from the restaurant; newspaper odes to the past are mounted on the wall. . . .

Paschal's, their words read, is a rags-to-riches tale. Opened in 1947 by two brothers who came from a tiny Georgian town, it started out as a chicken shack. Back then, a full meal cost a mere 52 cents, and before long, the place became so popular that it expanded into a restaurant. Next came the hotel and La Carrousel.

CLUBS, ETC.

Although Atlanta has no jazz club that books national talent on a regular basis, it does have a few clubs that offer satisfying nights of swing. Tops on the list are **Churchill Grounds**, **Dante's Down the Hatch,** and the **Sambuca Jazz Café**. (To hear national jazz talent, visit the city during its three fine summer music festivals: the **Atlanta Jazz Festival**, the **Montreux-Atlanta Music Festival,** and the biennial **National**

Black Arts Festival.) Blueswise, Atlanta fares somewhat better, with two strong club venues: **Blind Willie's**, which concentrates on root blues, and **Blues Harbor**, which leans more toward national touring acts.

Some of the local jazz talent to watch for includes saxophonist Joe Jennings and his band Life Force; piano players Ojeda Penn, Dan Mattrazzo, Gary Motley, and Bill Anschell; keyboard player Mose Davis; alto player James Hudson; tenor players Howard Nicholson and Kebbi Williams; trumpeter and pianist Danny Harper; drummers Eric Vaughn and Woody Williams; guitar player Jacques Lesure; and jazz singers Audrey Shakir, Bernadine Mitchell, Crystal Fox, Debra Brown and Freddy Cole (brother of Nat King Cole). Blues players include Luther "Houserocker" Johnson, Lotsa Poppa, Sandra Hall, Chicago Bob Nelson, and Francene Reid.

Most bars and clubs in Atlanta stay open until two A.M. (three A.M. on Fridays).

Personal Choices

Best jazz hang: *Churchill's*
Oldest jazz club: *Dante's Down the Hatch*
Best restaurant-jazz club: *Sambuca Jazz Cafe*
Best blues club: *Blind Willie's*

FOR JAZZ

Dante's Down the Hatch, 3380 Peachtree Rd., NE (Buckhead), 404–266–1600, www.dantesdownthehatch.com; and **Dante's Down the Hatch**, Underground Atlanta, 404–577–1800.

Think of a quirky cross between bop and the *Bounty* sailing ship and you'll come up with this one-of-a-kind jazz venue: a mock 18th-century vessel landlocked in the city's Buckhead district. Thanks to Atlanta's mercurial jazz club history, this operation, named for its owner, Dante Stephenson, is the oldest club in the city, operating since 1970. Adorned with all types of seafaring artifacts, including portholes, wooden booths, fishnets, and anchors spread out over 13 levels, the club can entertain up to 400 patrons. Mainstream jazz by top local musicians is presented on the lower deck, while national names such as Max Roach and Keith Jarrett have also performed here.

Dante's sister club in Underground Atlanta is a smaller version of its older sibling, and offers much the same in the way of jazz. Both clubs feature a menu published in 70 languages; everything from gourmet cheeses and fondues to Chinese dumplings is served.

Music: nightly. *Cover/minimum*: $$-$$$$. *Food*: American/international. Reservations recommended.

Sambuca Jazz Café-Buckhead, 3102 Piedmont Rd., 404–237–5299, ww.sambucajazzcafe.com.

One of a national chain headquartered in Dallas, this club is an upbeat, multi-colored venue located in trendy Buckhead. Contemporary smooth jazz is on the agenda here, with national acts such as Grover Washington, Jr., Rick Braun, and Jonathan Butler performing from time to time. Local favorites include Rita Graham, the Jacques Lesure Quartet, and the World Mambo Session.

Music: nightly. *Cover/minimum*: $$-$$$$. *Food*: American. Reservations recommended.

Churchill Grounds, 660 Peachtree St., NE, 404–256–3942, www.churchillgrounds.com.

With its 1920s décor, Havana ambiance, and candlelit tables, this venue is the best mainstream jazz hang in the city. Among the regulars here is local favorite Jerry Fields' Vecinos del Mundo, a group that once shared the stage with the late Tito Puente.

Music: nightly. *Cover/minimum*: $$-$$$$. *Food*: American. Reservations recommended.

Café 290, 290 Hildebrand Rd. (Sandy Springs, 20 min. N of downtown), 404–256–3942.

Located in the Balcony Shopping Center on the outskirts of town, Café 290, with its low ceilings, flickering candles, and suburban feel, offers local jazz ranging from traditional to bop. Come on a Sunday night, when jazz jam sessions showcasing up to 40 musicians are featured.

Music: nightly. *Cover/minimum*: none on weekdays, $$ on weekends. *Food*: American.

Also

The **Ying Yang Music Cafe** (64 3rd St., NW, 404–607–0682) is the best place in the metro area in which to hear hip-hop/acid jazz, usually compliments of DJ Kemit; the spoken word/poetry is also featured here. Yuppies and buppies frequent the retro, Euro-chic **Martini Club** (1140 Crescent Ave., NE, 404–873–0794), where jazz can be heard Tuesdays through Saturdays. For those looking for Latin grooves, check out the **Havana Club** (247 Buckhead Ave., 404–869–8484).

FOR BLUES

Blind Willie's, 828 N. Highland Ave. (Virginia–Highland), 404–873–2583.

Small and friendly, with an exposed brick wall, a great blues jukebox, a neon sign of a guitar-playing crocodile, and high revolving fans, Blind Willie's concentrates on roots blues. A poster of Blind Willie McTell, the club's namesake (see Decatur Street, "Landmarks and Legends," page 96), hangs to one side, and Mardi Gras beads are draped over the bar.

Once a hardware store, the club features a mix of local and national talent. Atlanta-based favorites such as Luther "Houserocker" Johnson and Billy Wright are regulars here, while national acts such as Lonnie Mack, Taj Mahal, and Johnny Copeland pass through on occasion.

Music: nightly. *Cover:* $$.

Blues Harbor, 2293-B Peachtree Rd. (Buckhead), 404–605–0661.

Located in a building with large windows overlooking a creek, Blues Harbor is one fancy blues bar, equipped with blue-and-white Laura Ashley–type curtains, lots of nice posters—even a carpet on the floor. Well, at least the chairs are mismatched.

But don't let appearances fool you. The bands here rock hard; among those who have played the club recently are Roomful of Blues, Mack "Guitar" Murphy, and Johnny Rouse.

Food is also an important part of the club, and the place is famous for its "Blues Plate Special," lobster and prime rib.

Music: nightly. *Cover:* $–$$. *Food:* American.

Other Venues and Special Events

Jazz in Atlanta gets its largest exposure through three major festivals. The season kicks off on Memorial Day weekend with the **Atlanta Jazz Festival** and concludes on Labor Day weekend with the **Montreux-Atlanta Festival** (for both events: 404–817–6815, www.atlantafestivals.com). Both festivals have their main stage in midtown's Piedmont Park, while also sponsoring performances and jam sessions in other venues around town. The Atlanta Jazz Festival, founded in 1973, has presented a wide range of jazz stars including Herbie Hancock, Regina Carter, Steve Turre, and Cassandra Wilson. The Montreux-Atlanta fest, in contrast, highlights blues, gospel, and world music artists as well as jazz musicians; past performers have included ex-Prince percussionist Sheila E, Shemekia Copeland, Hugh Masakela, Al Jarreau, and David Sanborn.

Another high-profile event is the **National Black Arts Festival** (404–730–0177, www.nbaf.com), held every even-numbered year in late July and early August. The fest focuses on the Afro-centric arts of the black diaspora, and presents music, theater, dance, poetry, literature, the visual arts, and film. Past performers have included Wynton Marsalis, Abbey Lincoln, Max Roach, and Ali Farka Toure.

National jazz stars can sometimes be heard at the **Fox Theater** (660 Peachtree St., 404–880–2100), a lavish 1929 former Shriners temple whose architecture is half Moorish, half Egyptian. The classic **Spivey Hall** at Clayton State College and University (5900 N. Lee St., 770–961–3683, www.spiveyhall.org/), just south of Atlanta, produces a fine jazz series.

Radio

WCLK/91.9FM (404–880–8273, www.wclk.com). Known as "The Jazz of the City" since 1974, affiliated with NPR and Clark-Atlanta University. Much jazz, smooth jazz, and gospel, with real jazz broadcast weekdays 10 A.M.–2 P.M. and 6 P.M.–5 A.M. Blues and reggae weekends.

WRFG/89.3 FM (404–523–3471). Blues, M-F mornings; W, Th evenings. Of special note: "True Blues," Th evenings with Eric King.

WOKS/1340 AM (706–576–3565). Much blues daily.

Records

The unassuming **Wax & Facts** (432 Moreland Ave. NE, 404–525–1679), located in Virginia-Highland, is the best out-of-print one-stop for used and rare, jazz and blues, CDs and LPs.

Elsewhere in Georgia

Gertrude "Ma" Rainey's Home, 805 Fifth Ave., Columbus, Ga.

The "Mother of the Blues" lived in this small two-story row house 90 miles south of Atlanta for the last five years of her life. For years, the house stood unoccupied and in dilapidated condition, but in 1992, thanks largely to the efforts of the Columbus African-American Heritage Preservation Society and the City of Columbus, the home's exterior was restored to the tune of $76,000. The house is now on the National Register of Historic Places and used as offices by local businesses.

Once a performer with the Rabbit Foot Minstrels, Ma Rainey cut numerous best-selling blues records, and, legend has it, kidnapped Bessie Smith and taught her how to sing the blues. (Many dismiss this story as apocryphal; others say that Ma and Bessie were lovers.) By the time she returned to Columbus, the city of her birth, Rainey had stopped performing, but she kept her hand in the entertainment business by owning and operating two theaters in nearby Rome. Nonetheless, when she died in 1939 at the age of 53, her death certificate listed her occupation as "housekeeper."

Fletcher Henderson's Home, 1016 Andrew St., Cuthbert, Ga.

Approximately 120 miles south of Atlanta is the house where Fletcher Henderson and his brother Horace, also a jazz musician, grew up. A one-story Victorian dwelling, the house was built in 1888 and was the home of Professor Fletcher Hamilton Henderson, Sr., a leading black educator, until his death in 1943.

While living here, both Fletcher and Horace attended the school where their father taught, and studied piano. Fletcher then moved to New York, where he led the house orchestra at the Roseland Ballroom. Horace moved to Ohio, where he formed his own ensemble, which was noted, back then, for its progressive sound.

MIAMI/FORT LAUDERDALE

Updated by Pedro Acevedo

Miami has produced only a handful of nationally recognized jazz and blues artists over the years, but from the 1930s through the '60s, the city had an active and sophisticated jazz scene, catering largely to the tourist trade. Overtown Square in the African-American section of town was once renowned for its glittering black-and-tan clubs featuring artists such as Nat "King" Cole, Louis Armstrong, and Lena Horne. Meanwhile, over in lily-white Miami Beach, many of the posh hotels had showrooms presenting black entertainers and Las Vegas stars. The "Jackie Gleason Show" in particular, taped at the Miami Beach Auditorium (now Jackie Gleason Theater) in the 1960s, brought in many of the biggest jazz names of the day.

After the 1960s, Miami went into hibernation until the 1990s, when Miami Beach reemerged as a hot spot for nightlife. Most of this renaissance has revolved around dance clubs and restaurants, but it has also improved the jazz scene, by drawing talented jazz performers, mainly from New York City, down to this corner of the world.

The distinct Latin flavor of Miami has also attracted many Latin jazz artists. Trumpeter Arturo Sandoval, pianist Gonzalo Rubalcaba, flutist Nestor Torres, and Carlos Averhoff—one of the founding members of the legendary Cuban jazz band Irakere (along with Sandoval, Paquito D'Rivera and Chucho Valdez)—all have residences here. Several major Latin record labels, including Sonny and BMG Latin, are headquartered in the city as well.

Some of the musicians born in South Florida include drummer Panama Francis, bassist Jimmy Garrison, saxophonist George Kelly, and trumpeter Blue Mitchell. Musicians born in other parts of the state—Fats Navarro in Key West, the Adderley brothers in Tampa—once spent much time in the city, as did, and does, Ira Sullivan, the great trumpet player who's lived here for decades now.

Sources

New Times Miami (305–571–7500, www.miaminewtimes.com) and *New Times* Broward/Palm Beach (954–618–2831) free weeklies, have excellent listings. Other sources are the Friday editions of the *Miami Herald* (305–350–2000,www.herald.com/hurricane) and the Fort Lauderdale *Sun Sentinel* (954–761–4000). *City Link* (954–356–4943), another free Fort Lauderdale weekly, also has listings.

The Greater Miami Convention & Visitors Bureau is located at 701 Brickell Ave., Suite 2700, 305–539–3000 or 800–283–2707, www.tropicoolmiami.com. The Greater Fort Lauderdale Convention & Visitors Bureau is at 200 E. Las Olas Blvd., Suite 1500, 954–765–4400 or 800–22-SUNNY, www.sunny.org.

A Note on the Neighborhoods

Eleven million tourists fly south to Miami each year, many of them heading for the sun-and-fun communities of Miami Beach (including South Beach), Coral Gables, and Coconut Grove. South Beach, 15 minutes from downtown, is filled with luscious pastel-colored Art Deco buildings, most of them renovated and housing trendy restaurants, boutiques, and clubs. Coral Gables, 15 minutes southwest of downtown, was the nation's first planned city, and it's a moneyed land filled with fine hotels and restaurants. Coconut Grove, also to the southwest, is billed as Miami's "Bohemia," but it's usually packed with tourists on the make.

Carol City, 20 minutes north of downtown, is home to a large African-American community as well as to recent immigrants from the Caribbean. Fort Lauderdale, a mecca for tourists from the North, is approximately 40 minutes north of Miami; Hollywood is located between Miami and Fort Lauderdale.

Landmarks and Legends

Overtown Square, N.W. Second St. bet. Sixth and Tenth Streets.

Originally settled by workers for the Flagler railroad system, Overtown, adjacent to the downtown, was once the largest and most vibrant African-American community in Miami. Through its heart ran Avenue G (now Second Avenue), which was also known as "Little Broadway" or the "Great Black Way." Lined with jazz clubs, hotels, and theaters of all sorts, it attracted both blacks and whites and actively courted the tourists from up North with promises of "exotic" foods and entertainment.

The tallest building in Overtown was the Mary Elizabeth Hotel (now torn down), which hosted everyone from Supreme Court Justice Thurgood Marshall to Adam Clayton Powell. Many of the black artists who were then performing on Miami Beach but were not allowed to overnight there also stayed at the Mary Elizabeth. Other important Overtown spots included the Lyric Theater, one of the most elegant theaters in town; the Harlem Square Club, where Sam Cooke recorded his memorable album; and the Sir John Hotel, in whose basement was the Knight Beat club, run by Clyde Killens.

As was the case with many other early African-American communities, Overtown was destroyed in the process of "urban renewal" and the construction of expressways. Now, however, the area, which is filled with abandoned buildings, is being revitalized. The 16,500-seat Miami Arena was built here about ten years back and a Historic Overtown Folklife Village, highlighting black history, is in the works. The Folklife Village will include studio spaces for the performing arts.

Lyric Theater, N.W. Second Ave. and Ninth St.

The Lyric, built in 1913 by a wealthy black businessman, may have been the first legitimate theater in Overtown. Once described as "possibly the most beautiful and costly playhouse owned by colored people in all the Southland," it presented all the greats, including Count Basie, Lena Horne, Ella Fitzgerald, and Nat King Cole. Converted into a church around 1960, it stood vacant for a few years in the '80s and '90s, but was restored to its former grandeur in 2000.

CLUBS, ETC.

With its large Latin population, Miami is a melting pot of sounds. There's lots of reggae, lots of salsa, lots of dance music—all of which has its effect on jazz. The city is also home to the University of Miami, which has one of the most respected jazz programs in the country.

Downtown Miami has little to offer in the way of nightlife, most clubs and restaurants being located in Miami Beach, Coconut Grove, Coral Gables, and Fort Lauderdale. The majority of these cater to a tourist clientele.

Though the Miami area has no steady club venue for national touring jazz acts, the city does have a large number of fine restaurants and clubs that present first-rate, locally based talent. Foremost among these are **Café Nostalgia** (in Miami Beach), the **Globe** (in Coral Gables), **O'Hara's Pub** (in Fort Lauderdale), and the **Sushi Blues Café** (in Hollywood). **Tobacco Road** and **Alligator Alley** bring in national blues acts on a regular basis.

Some of the many top-caliber jazz musicians playing in the Miami/Fort Lauderdale area today include trumpet players Ira Sullivan and Pete Minger; pianists Dr. Lonnie Smith and Arthur Hanlon; saxmen Kenny Millions, Gary Campbell, Carlos Averhoff, and Ed Calle; jazz and blues vocalists Toni Bishop and Valerie Tyson; blues guitarist Joey Gilmore, and Caribbean jazz steel drummer Othello. Saxophonist Mo Morgen and his group Mo Jazz, after playing at their own celebrated jazz club (alas, now closed) for many years, still perform around town at various venues.

Most jazz clubs close around 2 A.M., but clubs on South Beach often keep on going until 5 A.M., or even later.

Personal Choices

Best jazz club: *O'Hara's, The Globe*
Best Latin jazz club: *Café Nostalgia*
Best blues clubs: *Tobacco Road*

FOR JAZZ

Jazid, 1342 Washington Ave., Miami Beach, 305–672–9372.

Smack in the middle of the vertiginous South Beach club scene is Jazid, *the* place to unwind after a night of partying. A watering hole with a dozen or so candle-lit tables crammed near a tiny stage, the club is half classic jazz room, half hip American Riviera.

But don't be fooled by Jazid's discreet, almost unassuming appearance. Its stage has hosted everything from Delta blues to funk and progressive jazz. On any given night, you can hear anyone from drummer Bobby Thomas (formerly with Joe Sawinul's Syndicate) jamming with his protégé Felix Pastorius (son of the legendary bassist Jacko Pastorius) to the silky Caesar's Jade.

The club's lack of space is a great way to meet other music lovers; table sharing is a must here. But if the claustrophobic, and sometimes noisy, downstairs gets to you, you can escape to a roomier lounge upstairs.

Music: nightly. *No cover.*

Upstairs at the Van Dyke, 846 Lincoln Rd., Miami Beach, 305–534–3600.

Looking for some after-dinner drinks and some good music? Van Dyke is your place. Ideally located in the heart of Lincoln Road, a boulevard lined with shops and some of the best restaurants in town, Van Dyke features jazz seven nights a week in an elegant setting. Its wood paneling and cast-iron furniture provide a somewhat European feel that is complemented by continental cuisine served in both the downstairs restaurant and upstairs jazz lounge.

Yet the main action is on stage. The house band, led by Don Wilner, is a tag team of local talent. There's also a regular diet of Brazilian and Latin jazz, while musicians such as Fred Hersh or Mose Allison play from time to time.

Music: nightly. *Cover:* $-$$. *Food:* Continental.

Café Nostalgia, 432 41ˢᵗ Street, Miami Beach, 305–695–8555.

Perhaps the best place in Miami for Latin jazz, Café Nostalgia was founded in 1995 in Little Havana by owner Pepe Horta, but moved to Miami Beach in 1999. As its name implies, its main theme is nostalgia, nostalgia for the homeland—Cuba. Memorabilia and old pictures of famous Cuban musicians adorn its walls.

But even if the theme is "Old Cuba," it's a new crop of musicians from the island, many of them recent arrivals, who really bring the place to life. Led by Omar Hernandez, the Café

Nostalgia Band melts Afro-Cuban rhythms with funk and jazz in a way that makes it hard not to get up and dance. Such contagious music has prompted celebrities like U2's Bono, Spanish heartthrob Enrique Iglesias, and other glitterari to sit in and jam on occasion.

Music: W-Sa. *Cover*: $$.

The Globe, 377 Alhambra Circle, Coral Gables, 305–445–3555.

Sometimes credited with the awakening of sleepy Coral Gables, the Globe Cafe moonlights as a nightclub on Fridays and a jazz club on Saturdays. Small and cozy, the cafe packs just a dozen tables inside in an L-shaped room and a few outside on the sidewalk.

Although jazz happens here only on Saturdays, the Globe brings in top talent from all over South Florida. Ira Sullivan, Arthur Hanlon, and Carlos Averhoff are among those who have played there. The club's music and the relaxed ambiance make it a favorite among locals.

Music: Sa. *No cover*. *Food*: Continental, American.

Meza Fine Art and Gallery Café, 275 Giralda Ave., Coral Gables, 305–461–2723.

When Andrea Meza opened her gallery in Coral Gables, she never envisioned it as also encompassing a restaurant and music club. But things grew naturally, as first she began inviting musicians in to perform and then started offering food and drink. The result: a beautiful gallery café featuring jazz and Latin music.

Music: Tu-W, F-Sa. *Cover*: $$. *Food*: Continental.

O'Hara's Pub, 722 E. Las Olas Blvd., Fort Lauderdale; 954–524–1764; and **O'Hara's Hollywood**, 1903 Hollywood Blvd., Hollywood; 954–925–2555.

About a decade ago, Kitty Ryan decided to open a jazz club in downtown Fort Lauderdale, which back then resembled a ghost town. Luckily for her, however, things quickly turned around, with the little pub on now-chic East Las Olas Boulevard becoming a near-overnight success.

The cozy but elegant wood-paneled room with mirrors all around is now one of the best jazz spots in the area. Among the regulars are Doctor Lonnie Smith and Melton Mustafa. Various featured performers also sit in with the house band a couple nights a week.

Ryan's concept has worked so well that she opened a second O'Hara's in downtown Hollywood a few years back. It features many of the same performers as the first, but is more casual, with a black-and-white tiled floor and cast-iron tables and chairs. Both clubs also have outdoor seating areas.

Music: nightly, Su afternoons. *No cover. Food:* sandwiches, pizza, salads, etc.

Sushi Blues Café, 1836 Young Circle, Hollywood, 954–929–9560, www.sushiblues.com.

In yet another odd musical combination, this tiny sushi spot, known to have excellent food, offers up much jazz and blues, usually compliments of Kenny Millions and friends, who include bluesman Dave Morgan and Mick Taylor, of Rolling Stones' fame. Millions, who is a world-renowned "avant-garde scholar of the saxophone," with 30 recordings to his credit, owns the club along with his wife, Junko, who is also the restaurant's cook. The club is all wood and tile, with seats for about 50 customers, and lots of posters from Millions's tours on the walls.

Music: W–Su. *No cover:* $. *Food:* sushi, etc.

One Night Stan's, 2333 Hollywood Blvd., Hollywood, 954–929–1566, www.onenightstans.com.

One day about a dozen years ago, saxman Stan Waldman got tired of constantly tracking down gigs. So he decided to open a club of his own, and One Night Stan's was born. An unpretentious, dimly lit room, the club usually features a mix of aspiring local musicians and seasoned veterans. There's even a weekly night for college students to play with the Jerry Fischer 16-piece big band. Blues lovers can join in on Sundays for the open blues jam.

Music: Th-Su. *Cover*: $. *Food*: burgers and pizza.

Also

Some very good local jazz is featured nightly at the **Club Java Music Café** (9651 Westview Dr., Coral Springs, 954–346–3178). **Champagne's Restaurant and Jazz Lounge** (1060 NE 79th St., Miami, 305–754–6036), offers jazz Thursday through Sunday, often compliments of the Mo Jazz Quartet. **Doc Dammer's Saloon Bar and Grill** in the posh Omni Colonnade Hotel (180 Aragon Ave., Coral Gables, 305–441–2600) is a good place to catch jazz on Friday and Saturday nights. Jazz can also be heard at some of the blues clubs mentioned below, including **Satchmo's Blues Bar, Tobacco Road,** and **Club M**.

FOR BLUES

Tobacco Road, 626 S. Miami Ave. (near downtown), Miami, 305–374–1198.

At about 90 years old, Tobacco Road's liquor license is the oldest in Miami. Even better, the long, narrow (it's only 24 feet wide) club—built of Dade County pine—is a first-rate blues joint, one of the best in the country. IKO-IKO is its house band, and a whole host of national talent, including the late Albert Collins, B. B. King, Taj Mahal, and Charlie Musselwhite, have passed through its doors. Current regulars include Todd Thompson and August Campbell, and every Wednesday there's a popular jazz jam.

The current incarnation of Tobacco Road was started up about a dozen years ago by Kevin Rusk and Patrick Gleber, two young men then not long graduated from college (Rusk has since moved on to work in the ale brewing business). At the time, everyone thought they were crazy: the club and its neighborhood had fallen on dirty, drug-infested times. But the two ignored public opinion—first cleaning the place up, then serving food, then adding music—and today the club is usually packed with a young, urban crowd. A few years ago the city even named the street running along outside Tobacco Road.

The club is laden with stories. At one time, rumor has it, Al Capone hung out here, and upstairs there's a fake bookshelf built for hiding booze during Prohibition. Also upstairs—reached by climbing a circular staircase lined in red—is the **McClain Cabaret,** named after the half sister of Bessie Smith, Miami resident, "Diamond Teeth" Mary McClain.

Music: nightly. *Cover:* $–$$. *Food:* burgers, etc.

Satchmo Blues Bar and Grill, 60 Merrick Way, Coral Gables, 305–774–1883, www.miamiblues.com.

When owner Harald Neuweg opened Satchmo in 1999, he was hoping to draw in the "suits" that prowl downtown Coral Gables by day. That's why you see a proliferation of Dockers and Gap wear here by night. There's plenty of seating indoors, as well as a number of sidewalk tables. The décor is a mix of sports bar and music room with both TV sets and posters of jazz and blues greats adorning the walls. Nonetheless, good music happens here.

Known to pack in about 2,000 people during happy hour on Fridays, this is one of the few venues in South Florida with a stage big enough to host big bands (jazz, swing, blues), which usually perform once a week. Local talent, including some Latin jazz with Oriente and blues with Joey Gilmore, complete the rest of the week. Occasionally, national touring acts perform.

Music: nightly. *Cover*: none-$. *Food*: American.

Alligator Alley, 2079 University Dr., Sunrise (15 min. W of Fort Lauderdale), 954–742–6874, www.alligatoralley-florida. com.

Although a relative newcomer to the music scene, this club is already drawing some very good reviews from music lovers. It's also the only club in South Florida with a steady flow of national acts. The 10,000-square-foot club has featured a cavalcade of big names since it opened, including Gato Barbieri, Levon Helm, Leon Russell, Little Feat, and Billy Preston. The big hall is all decked out in a celebration of South Florida's swamp and Seminole Indian cultures, while a more intimate lounge nearby offers solo piano players.

Music: nightly. *Cover*: $-$$$$. *Food*: Southern cuisine.

Also

Club M (2037 Hollywood Blvd., 954–925–8396) is a smallish neighborhood joint, housed in one of the oldest buildings in town, that offers blues and occasional jazz on most Fridays, Saturdays, and Tuesdays. **Power Studios** (3701 NE Second Ave., Miami, 305–576–1336), in the Miami Design District just five minutes from downtown Miami, offers a very eclectic lineup—rock, blues, jazz, Haitian, and Afro-Cuban folk.

Blues can also be heard at some of the jazz clubs mentioned above, including **Jazid**, **O'Hara's Pub**, **Sushi Blues Café**, and **One Night Stan's**.

Other Venues and Special Events

The **Hollywood Jazz Festival** (954–921–3404), held in November in Young Circle Park, has drawn a number of top-quality acts in recent years, including Jack De Johnette, Gonzalo Rubalcaba, and John Patitucci.

The weekend-long **Sound Advice Blues Fest** (954–761–5984), held in November at Fort Lauderdale Stadium, is one of the largest music festivals in the area. Every year, dozens of local and national acts perform on three stages.

The **SunTrust Sunday Jazz Brunch** (954–761–5985) takes place every first Sunday of the month along Riverwalk, a bricked walkway that runs through downtown Fort Lauderdale, along the New River. Several stages are set up, and all kinds of local and regional musicians are presented, along with gourmet foods offered by area restaurants.

Now over ten years old, **Festival Miami** is a month-long event featuring classical, chamber, and jazz music that's put on every fall by the University of Miami School of Music (305–284–4940). About 25 concerts are presented, most at the Maurice Gusman Concert Hall on the University of Miami Campus, Coral Gables. The University also presents numerous jazz concerts by students and faculty throughout the year. Some are free and outdoors, others are held in Gusman Hall, and all are open to the public.

National acts also sometimes come through the **Gusman Center for the Performing Arts** (174 E. Flagler St., 305–374–2444), and the **James L. Knight International Center** (400 S.E. Second Ave., 305–372–0929 or 305–372–4633).

Radio

WLRN/91.3 FM (305–995–1717 or 305–995–2236). NPR affiliate, licensed by Dade County school system. Much jazz daily.
WDNA/88.9 FM (305–662–8889). Public access station with much jazz, 7 A.M. to midnight, some Latin and blues.
WLVE/93.9 FM (305–654–9494). Contemporary jazz.
WTMI/93.1 FM (305–856–9393). Jazz and blues, midnight to early morning, Tu–Sa.

Record Stores

The best store for jazz and blues in the area is **Blue Notes Warehouse** (2299 N.E. 164th St., North Miami Beach, 305–354–4563), run by the knowledgeable Bob Perry.

Back in the late 1930s, Count Basie packed
them into 52nd Street's Famous Door.

Frank Driggs Collection

NEW YORK

New York has been the international center of jazz for so long that it's hard to believe things were ever otherwise. But compared to New Orleans and Chicago, New York came relatively late to jazz. Although there were stride piano players in the city in the late 1910s and early 1920s, and the Original Dixieland Jazz Band played to packed houses at Reisenweber's Restaurant in 1917, it was only in the late 1920s—largely because of the growing importance of its radio and recording industries—that New York began attracting large numbers of musicians.

New York's first major jazz center was Harlem, which already by the mid-1920s was filled with clubs, theaters, dance halls, and speakeasies, all exploding with sound. Many were located along Seventh Avenue in the 130s and Lenox Avenue in the 140s. Chick Webb was playing for thousands of "happy feet" at the Savoy Ballroom, while Count Basie, then known as "Bill," was lying on the floor of the Lincoln Theater, trying to learn how Fats Waller worked the organ pedals. Some blues could be found, too, at theaters such as the Apollo and the Alhambra, but New York never was—or is—much of a blues town.

As exciting though all this activity was, however, it was nothing compared to the 1930s, when New York, along with the rest of the country, witnessed an unprecedented rise in the popularity of jazz. As the big band era began in earnest, crowds black and white flocked to dance halls and ballrooms all over the city to hear the then new swing sounds of bands led by Fletcher Henderson, Lionel Hampton, Paul Whiteman, Benny Goodman, Tommy Dorsey, and many others. "Battles of the bands," in which two competitive big bands were pitted against each other on opposite sides of a huge dance floor, became commonplace, with many of the best-known groups showcasing top vocalists such as Ella Fitzgerald and Billie Holiday.

In the 1940s, Harlem again became hot as Minton's and Monroe's, two tiny clubs known for their jam sessions, gave birth to modern jazz through the experimentations of Charlie Parker, Dizzy Gillespie, Thelonious Monk, Kenny Clarke, and others. Their new bebop sound spread quickly, igniting audiences throughout the city, and soon, 52nd Street, whose Prohibition-era speakeasies had turned into jazz clubs, became the new center for the new music. The Onyx, the Three Deuces, and the Famous Door were among "the Street's" most famous clubs; then, on nearby Broadway, there was Birdland, named after Charlie Parker, and the Royal

Roost, reputedly the first modern sit-down jazz club. Prior to the 1940s, jazz had been played mostly for the dancing.

Fifty-second Street began to decline in the early 1950s, as the old jazz clubs turned into strip joints and the music's center moved downtown once again, this time to Greenwich Village. Clubs such as Café Society, the Five Spot, Café Bohemia, and the Village Vanguard, which had already been thriving in the 1940s, began featuring musicians like Miles Davis, John Coltrane, Charles Mingus, Ornette Coleman, and Sonny Rollins. Audiences queued up round the block to hear the hottest new talents, and New York garnered the reputation of being the only real city in the country where top-caliber music could be heard in dozens of top-caliber clubs every night of the week.

And so it remains to this day.

Sources

The city's two best music sources are the free weekly *Village Voice* (212–475–3300; www.villagevoice.com), the granddaddy of alternative papers, where all the major clubs advertise and the critics highlight a few choice acts each week; and *Time Out New York* (212–539–4444; www.timeoutny.com), which does an excellent job of covering nightlife, with a phenomenal listings section. Another free weekly, *New York Press* (212–244–2282; www.nypress.com), also contains a solid music calendar.

The *New Yorker* magazine (212–286–5400; www.newyorker.com) presents a good, selective, critical listing of clubs, and *New York* magazine (212–508–0700; www.nymag.com) presents a selective, not so critical, listing. The *New York Daily News* (212–210–2100; www.nydailynews.com) has music listings on Friday and Sunday; *The New York Times* (212–556–1234; www.nytimes.com) has listings on Sunday, and its critics make extensive music recommendations on Friday. The *New York Post* (212–930–8000; www.nypost.com) has listings on Friday.

Another good source is *Hot House* (19 Whippoorwill Ln., Rockaway Tnpk., NJ 07866; 973–627–5349), a free jazz nightlife guide that's available in many clubs.

The Jazz Foundation of America (212–245–3999) is a nonprofit organization that assists jazz and blues musicians in need. The foundation runs a Jazzline at 212–479–7888 that highlights some of the smaller and often overlooked jazz and blues events in the city, along with some major clubs. The New York Blues Society hosts a Web site at www.NYBluesSociety.org and a hotline at 212–726-BLUE.

For maps and other general information, stop into the New York Convention & Visitors Bureau at 810 Seventh Ave. (bet.

52nd and 53rd Sts.), 212–484–1200 or 800-NYC-VISIT; www.
nycvisit.com. The center is open 365 days a year, Mon.-Fri.
8:30 A.M.–6 p.m., Sat.-Sun. 9 A.M.–5 P.M.

General online guides to New York City that include club
listings are CitySearch NY, www.citysearchnyc.com, and New
York Sidewalk, www.newyork.sidewalk.com.

A Note on Neighborhoods

Despite its enormous size, New York is an easy city to navigate. Fifth Avenue divides the city into the East and West
sides, and except in Greenwich Village and a few other areas,
streets are laid out in numbered grids. The even-numbered
streets run east, the odds, west. The even-numbered avenues
run north, the odds, south.

Harlem, the city's historic African-American neighborhood,
is located in northwest Manhattan, above W. 110th Street.
Greenwich Village, the fabled Bohemian district now usually
filled with tourists, is to the southwest, between West 14th
and Houston streets. As used here, "Downtown" refers to
addresses below 23rd Street, and "Midtown" to addresses
between 23rd and 57th Streets. The Upper West Side, known for
its performing arts, lies above West 57th Street, and the
Upper East Side is a well-heeled area above East 57th Street.

New York's public transportation system is excellent, and
all of the spots listed below can be reached via subway, bus,
or taxi. Driving should be avoided, as street parking is difficult to find and lot parking, expensive.

Landmarks and Legends

Harlem and Upper Manhattan

The following sites are all located within walking distance of
each other. As outlined below, the tour starts at 142nd Street
and Malcolm X Boulevard/Lenox Avenue (both names are
used for this end of Sixth Avenue), heads west to Adam
Clayton Powell, Jr., Blvd. (Seventh Avenue), and then north
to 156th Street before circling back downtown to 118th
Street. (See also "Tours," page 171.)

Cotton Club, 644 Malcolm X Blvd./Lenox Ave., at 142nd
Street.

This most famous of the big three Harlem Renaissance night
clubs (the other two were Connie's Inn and Smalls' Paradise)
was torn down in the 1950s to make way for a housing project.
The plush club, which once catered to a whites-only, cream-of-
society and gangster crowd, was Duke Ellington's home base

for four years and Cab Calloway's for three. All the other top entertainers of the day—Louis Armstrong, Ethel Waters, and Ivie Anderson, among them—also performed here.

The Cotton Club started as the Club Deluxe, owned by former heavyweight boxing champion Jack Johnson. Owney Madden's gang took the place over in 1922, hiring Andy Preer's Cotton Club Syncopators and "high-yaller" chorus girls, who had to be under 21 and at least 5 feet 6 inches tall. In 1927, Preer died and Madden recruited Ellington up from Philadelphia, demanding that he break his contract there. "Be big," Madden's henchman allegedly told Ellington's boss, "or you'll be dead."[1]

Duke Ellington then was still an unknown, but before long his name became a household word. He and his Jungle Band, as they were called, were broadcast on radio stations across the country, and the nightclub became a "must" stop for every out-of-towner visiting New York.

The Cotton Club moved from Lenox Avenue to West 48th Street in 1936, following the Harlem race riots. The new location lacked the magic of the old, however, and closed a few years later.

Savoy Ballroom, 596 Malcolm X Blvd./Lenox Ave., near 140th Street.

Now demolished (a brick complex of one-story shops marks the spot), the second-story Savoy once covered an entire city block and featured a large dance floor, two bandstands, and a retractable stage. In the 1920s and '30s, it was the most popular dance hall in Harlem, accommodating crowds of up to five thousand.

Drummer and bandleader Chick Webb, with his star singer, Ella Fitzgerald, was the acknowledged "King of the Savoy," and any visiting band had to take up battle against him, playing on the other bandstand at the opposite end of the hall. These "battles of the bands" attracted tremendous crowds, and once when Fletcher Henderson and Chick Webb (representing New York) were pitted against King Oliver and Fess Williams (representing Chicago), the riot squad had to be called in. Another famous battle took place during the Swing Era when Benny Goodman took on Chick Webb. Goodman was then at the height of his career, but the crowd cheered loudest for Webb.

Billie Holiday's first New York apartment, 108 W. 139th St., near Malcolm X Blvd./Lenox Avenue.

Billie Holiday and her mother moved into a railroad apartment in this solid five-story building shortly after Billie arrived in New York. The Depression was then on and Billie walked

Seventh Avenue every day trying to find work. Finally, she was auditioned as a dancer by the manager of a small club called Pods' and Jerry's (168 W. 132 St.), but when he found out that she only knew two dance steps, he angrily tried to throw her out. The piano player took pity. "Girl, can you sing?" he asked. "Sure I can sing," she said, "What good is that?"

Holiday quickly found out. The piano player started in on "Trav'lin' All Alone," and by the end of the song, the young singer had a new job. That job led to other jobs, which led to a review by music critic John Hammond and a debut at the Apollo.

As Billie settled into her new life, so did her mother, Sadie, who took up her favorite occupation—cooking. Before long, Holiday writes in *Lady Sings the Blues*, their apartment became known as "a combination YMCA, boardinghouse for broke musicians, soup kitchen for anyone with a hard-luck story, community center, and after-after-hours joint where a couple of bucks would get you a shot of whiskey and the most fabulous fried-chicken breakfast, lunch, or dinner anywhere in town."

Schomburg Center, 515 Malcolm X. Blvd./Lenox Ave., at 135th St., 212–491–2200.

The Schomburg Center for Research in Black Culture is a world-renowned institution founded by Arthur A. Schomburg, a Puerto Rican of African descent who as a child was told that the Negro had no history. Scholars come from all over the world to consult the extensive collection of this branch of the New York Public Library, housed in a modern brick-and-glass building; some of the library's most impressive holdings are in jazz history.

For the general sightseer, however, the center's most interesting attraction is its adjacent exhibit area, where a wide array of changing exhibits—some concerning music—is presented. The Schomburg also features jazz concerts about once a month, along with the occasional jazz lecture or film. In the back is an excellent book and gift shop.

Hours: M-W, noon–8 P.M.; F-Sa, 1–6 P.M.; Su 1–5 P.M. *Exhibits*: free. *Music*: $-$$.

Lincoln Theater, 58 W. 135th St., near Malcolm X Blvd./Lenox Ave.

The Lincoln, opened in 1915, was one of Harlem's earliest theaters, and unlike many other uptown venues, it catered to an African-American audience from the very beginning. Fats Waller was the theater's house organist for years,

pounding out tunes to accompany silent films, and a young
Bill Basie used to come in from his home in Red Bank, New
Jersey, to watch the more established musician play. Fats
got used to seeing Basie, and before long, the future Count
was literally lying at the maestro's feet, watching how he
used the pedals.

The Lincoln is now a church.

Liberation Book Shop, 421 Malcolm X Blvd./Lenox Ave., at
131st St., 212–281–4615.

This most famed of Harlem bookstores, once a 125th Street
landmark, has a good collection of books on jazz and blues, to
say nothing of one of the largest selections of African-
American, African, and Caribbean books in New York.
Founded by Lewis Michaux, the store has been a favorite
gathering spot for intellectuals for decades. Malcolm X once
bought much of his reading matter here.

Open: Tu-F, 3–7 P.M.; Sa noon–4 P.M.

Smalls' Paradise, one of the big
three Harlem Renaissance clubs,
was still going strong in the '40s.

Frank Driggs Collection

Harlem YMCA, 180 W. 135th St., bet. Malcolm X and Adam Clayton Powell Blvds.

The Harlem YMCA was an important gathering spot for artists, writers, jazz musicians, and other entertainers during the Harlem Renaissance. Writers Langston Hughes and Ralph Ellison lived here temporarily, and Paul Robeson began his acting career here.

Smalls' Paradise, 2294 1/2 Adam Clayton Powell (Seventh Ave.) Blvd., at W. 135th Street.

Opened in 1925 and closed in 1986, Smalls' Paradise was originally a long basement room capable of holding 1,500. During Prohibition it attracted a large downtown crowd and was famous for its Sunday morning breakfast dances, which featured customers in glittering evening dress and waiters doing the Charleston while balancing trays of bootleg liquor. (Unlike the Cotton Club, Smalls' did admit blacks, but prices were so high that most were unable to afford it.) Later, during both the Depression and the war years, Smalls' continued to function as a smaller music spot, drawing everyone from Duke Ellington to Benny Goodman; in the '60s, it became "Big Wilt's" in honor of its new owner, basketball player Wilt Chamberlain.

Ed Smalls, the original owner, was a former elevator operator who had previously run the Sugar Cane Club (2212 Fifth Ave. at 135th Street), the first Harlem club to attract a large white crowd. Today, Smalls' is a boarded-up building.

Abyssinian Baptist Church, 132 W. 138th St., near Adam Clayton Powell Blvd., 212–862–7474.

Charlie Parker's funeral was held at the Abyssinian. Fats Waller's father was a minister here.

The Gothic and Tudor structure, with its marble pulpit and stained-glass windows, was opened in 1924, but the church itself dates back to 1808, when a few members of the First Baptist Church, then located on Gold Street, refused to accept that church's racially segregated seating policy and broke off to form their own congregation.

Two of the church's most famous leaders were the Adam Clayton Powells—Sr. and Jr. The flamboyant Powell Jr. was also the first black U.S. congressman from an Eastern state, and he did much to empower the black community before being charged with misconduct and failing to win reelection. The church houses a small memorial room honoring both the Powells.

The Reverend Dr. Calvin Butts is the Abyssinian's current pastor, and he continues the church's activist tradition. Services, complete with gospel music, are held Sunday at 9

A.M. and 11 A.M. Visitors are welcome; arrive early to get a seat.

Renaissance Ballroom and Casino, 150 W. 138th St.

Right next door to the Abyssinian is a two-story red-brick building that was once the Renaissance, a ballroom offering gambling, dancing, and cabaret acts from the 1920s through the early '50s. Among the jazz musicians who performed here were Chick Webb, Lester Young (then playing in Al Sears's big band), and Fletcher Henderson, who packed the place in 1925, just after a highly successful tour of New England.

Striver's Row, 138th and 139th Streets, between Adam Clayton Powell Blvd. and Frederick Douglass Blvd. (Eighth Ave.).

The King Model houses, built by developer David King in 1891, are two of the most stunning blocks in Harlem. Three different sets of architects designed the development, with the most impressive row, the northernmost one, done by McKim, Mead & White. Both blocks (which acquired their nickname when they became the preferred address of ambitious African Americans) are immaculately kept, with service alleys running behind and flower boxes out front. Among the jazz and blues musicians who've resided here were W. C. Handy, Eubie Blake, and Fletcher Henderson.

Currently in the works is the Striver's Center Development Project, which will be centered just south of Striver's Row, along 134th, 135th, and 136th Sts. between Adam Clayton Powell Blvd. and St. Nicholas Ave. Hopes are that the development will eventually include restaurants, boutiques, art galleries, and jazz clubs.

James P. Johnson's Residence, 267 W. 140th St. near Frederick Douglass Blvd.

In the early 1920s, the great stride piano player James P. Johnson moved into his sister's apartment in this now boarded-up building. A friend introduced J. P. to Fats Waller, then just a youngster, and Fats became Johnson's star pupil. The two of them often worked together in J. P.'s home on two pianos, and Johnson's sister became Fats's surrogate mother (his own had recently died), buying him his first pair of long pants.

"It was one big headache for me," May Wright Johnson says in *Hear Me Talkin' to Ya,* edited by Nat Shapiro and Nat Hentoff. "Fats was seventeen . . . and [he] would bang on our piano till all hours of the night—sometimes to two, three, four o'clock in the morning. I would say to him, 'Now go on home, or haven't you got a home.'"

Our Lady of Lourdes Church, 472 W. 142nd St., bet. Convent and Amsterdam Avenues.

In the 1950s, pianist Mary Lou Williams, depressed and dispirited, left music for a period of about three years. Turning to religion, she spent most of her days in Our Lady of Lourdes, meditating and talking to the needy. "I became a kind of fanatic for a while," she tells Whitney Balliett in *American Musicians: 56 Portraits in Jazz.* "I'd live on apples and water for nine days at a time. I stopped smoking. I shut myself up here like a monk. Father Woods got worried and he told me, 'Mary, you're an artist. You belong at the piano and writing music. It's *my* business to help people through the church and your business to help people through music.' He got me playing again."

Mary Lou Williams's Apartment, 63 Hamilton Terrace.

Williams lived just down the street from the church in this handsome apartment building. In the '40s, musicians such as Thelonious Monk, Dizzy Gillespie, and Charlie Parker stopped by—day or night—to try out their new ideas on her. In the '60s, Williams devoted much of her time to launching a foundation for helping musicians down on their luck.

Dinah Washington's apartment, Bowery Bank Building, 345 W. 145th St.

Dinah Washington moved into this big boxy Harlem landmark in early 1963. Most of her biggest hits, including "What a Difference a Day Makes," were recorded while she was living here, in a twelfth-floor penthouse. "It was a gorgeous place," says Lorraine Gordon of the Village Vanguard, "like the inside of a jukebox."

"A" Train, 145th Street near St. Nicholas Ave. (among other stops).

The "A" Train subway line had just been built when Billy Strayhorn wrote the composition that Duke Ellington made famous. New, fast, and strong, it was the quickest way to get to Harlem.

Duke Ellington's Apartment, 935 St. Nicholas Ave., near West 156th St.

Although born in Washington, D.C., the Duke spent 22 years of his life, 1939 to 1961, in Apartment 4A of this handsome Harlem Gothic apartment building that's now a National Historic Landmark. While living here, he wrote many of his most famous compositions, performed at the Cotton Club, and premiered his controversial "Black, Brown and Beige," which he called a "tone parallel to the history of the American Negro," at Carnegie Hall.

Living with the Duke during this time was Beatrice Ellis, more often known as Evie Ellington, even though the two never officially married. They were still together when they moved downtown in the 1960s, but by that time they were seeing little of each other, as Ellington was constantly on the road and Evie had become reclusive.

Monroe's Uptown House, 198 W. 134th St., corner of Adam Clayton Powell Blvd.

An important spawning ground for modern jazz (see Minton's Playhouse, page 129), Monroe's was opened by Clark Monroe in the 1930s. Billie Holiday sang here for three months in early 1937, and Charlie Parker played a central role in the club's cutting contests. On one legendary night, just before coming to Monroe's, Parker was jamming at a chili parlor up the street between 139th and 140th. "I was working over 'Cherokee,'" he said later, "and, as I did, I found that by using the higher intervals of a chord as a melody line and backing them with appropriately related changes, I could play the thing I'd been hearing. It came alive."[2]

Today, the former Monroe's is a deli.

Lafayette Theater, 2227 Adam Clayton Powell Blvd. at 132nd St.

In the 1920s, the Lafayette, now a church, was one of two major theaters in Harlem (see Lincoln Theater, page 120). Located on the entertainment esplanade that was then Seventh Avenue, it hosted all the major talent of the day, including Duke Ellington, who made his first New York appearance here in 1923 as a member of Wilbur Sweatman's band, and Fats Waller—until he got fired, that is. An item in the New York *Age* on October 1, 1927, reported: "Fats Waller, who has been playing the organ at the Lafayette Theatre, was paid a visit by his wife one afternoon. She sat on the same stool with Fats as he was playing. The management objected. Words. Fats quit there and then."[3]

The Lafayette was twice as big as the Lincoln, and was best-known for its impressive variety shows and revues. *Shuffle Along* by Noble Sissle and Eubie Blake, the first major African-American review to make it to Broadway, was first produced at the theater in 1913; and it was followed by the *Plantation Revue* with Florence Mills, *The Chocolate Dandies*, also by Sissle and Blake, and Lew Leslie's *Blackbirds*.

Connie's Inn, 2221 Adam Clayton Powell Blvd., at 131st St.

Located right next door to the Lafayette was Connie's Inn. Originally called the Shuffle Inn in honor of the Sissle-Blake production, the swank basement club was opened in 1923 by

two men in the delicatessen business, Connie and George
Immerman (they had once hired Fats Waller as a delivery boy).
Connie's Inn featured many major performers, including
Fletcher Henderson, Zutty Singleton, Billie Holiday, and Louis
Armstrong, who performed here in a show called "Hot
Chocolates," written by Fats Waller and Andy Razaf.

One of the more infamous events in New York's gangland
history took place right outside Connie's. "Mad Dog" Vincent
Coll, wanted by both the mob and the law, kidnapped George
"Big Frenchy" DeMange and George Immerman late one night
and held them for ransom. Eventually, his demands were
met, the two were released, and a gala celebration was held at
the club. Later, "Mad Dog" was gunned down in a 23rd Street
phone booth by Dutch Schultz's gang.

Connie's wasn't the only hot spot at 131st and Seventh,
once known as "The Corner." There were also the Band Box,
the Barbeque, the Hoofers' Club, and more. "This wasn't just
one more of them busy street crossings, with a poolroom for
a hangout. Uh, uh," writes Mezz Mezzrow in *Really the Blues.*
"On The Corner in Harlem you stood with your jaws swinging
wide open while all there is to this crazy world, the whole fran-
tic works, strutted by."

The Tree of Hope, a famous Harlem talisman, once stood
outside Connie's. Back then, legend had it that to rub the
tree's bark brought luck, and many a musician stopped by,
hoping for his or her big break. Later, when Seventh Avenue
was widened, Bill "Bojangles" Robinson had the tree trans-
planted to the median strip that now runs down the parkway.
His nearby plaque reads: "You wanted a tree of hope and here
it is. Best Wishes."

Today, Connie's Inn is a discount store, and the Tree of
Hope is gone, marked only by a dilapidated purple wooden
monument that looks like half a tree. Directly across from
Connie's is the site of Reid's Cleaners, Tuxedos for Hire, a
shop that made costumes for the Apollo entertainers for
decades. Reid's shut down in the 1990s, but its sign is still
visible.

Alhambra Theater, 2110 Adam Clayton Powell Blvd., at
126th St.

It was to the Alhambra that the future record producer and
jazz critic John Hammond, then 16, slipped away one evening
to hear his first blues singer, Bessie Smith. He told his family
that he was going out to practice music with friends. Across
the street from the theater, at number 2120, once stood the
Alhambra Grill, where Billie Holiday sang before moving on to
the Hot-Cha Bar and Grill, at 134th and Seventh, where

Ralph Cooper of the Apollo discovered her. Holiday also head-lined at the Alhambra in the early 1930s.

The Alhambra is now an office building for the Department of Motor Vehicles.

Hotel Theresa, 2090 Adam Clayton Powell Blvd., at 125th St.

The Theresa, once Harlem's largest and most famous hotel, is now an office building. A beautiful white-brick edifice that glistens in the sun, it played host to everyone from singer Lena Horne and guitarist Jimi Hendrix to boxer Joe Louis and Cuban leader Fidel Castro. Lester Young lived here until Billie Holiday invited him to move in with her and her mother; bandleader Andy Kirk managed the place in the late 1950s.

Cab Calloway's band also frequented the Theresa, and they stayed here one week while playing the State Theatre in Hartford, Connecticut, located about three hours away. Dizzy Gillespie, Jonah Jones, Cozy Cole, and Milt Hinton were all members of the band back then; they had a habit of throwing spitballs at each other when the Cab wasn't around. They were doing exactly that, while waiting for the State Theatre concert to start, when a spitball landed, *plunk*, right in the spotlight. Cab was furious, and after the show he accused Dizzy (Jonah Jones was actually the culprit), who in response drew a knife and cut the bandleader in the thigh. Cab fired Diz on the spot, and Diz took the bus home. But when the band pulled up to the Theresa that night, the trumpet player was there to meet it, and he and Cab sheepishly made up.

Apollo Theatre, 253 W. 125th St., 212–749–5838.

Perhaps the single most important landmark in the history of African-American music, the Apollo has hosted nearly every major jazz or blues artist to come along. Bessie Smith, Ella Fitzgerald, Billie Holiday, Duke Ellington, Louis Armstrong, Count Basie, Lil Armstrong, Fats Waller, Pearl Bailey, Ray Charles, and James Brown all played the Apollo, and the list could go on and on. It is said that when a teenage Elvis Presley first came to New York, the one place he wanted to see was the Apollo. The same was later said of the Beatles.

Originally built in 1913, the Apollo was once Hurtig & Seamon's New Burlesque Theatre, known for presenting vaudeville to a Harlem that was then predominantly white. Back in those days, the best seats in the house cost a whopping $1.65. Frank Schiffman and Leo Brecher took the place over in 1935, by which time the neighborhood's racial mix had shifted to predominantly black.

Under its new management, the two-balconied theater, capable of seating two thousand, soon became especially famous for its Amateur Nights, in which new talent was presented to a highly critical audience that either applauded or booed the performers off the stage. Sarah Vaughan and Billy Eckstine made their New York debuts that way, as did Ella Fitzgerald (who was hired by Chick Webb that very night) and Billie Holiday.

Not all major entertainers had such positive experiences at the Apollo. Alberta Hunter opened on December 6, 1946, for what was to be a one-week engagement, but the show was abruptly "closed out," much to her hurt feelings. Lena Horne had a similar experience—the audience drove her offstage by throwing pennies at her.

Closed down in the late 1970s, the Apollo was completely refurbished in the early 1980s and run by a non-profit institution for years. Internal squabbling and a lawsuit led to the neglect of the state-owned theater, however, which as of this writing is in dire need of repairs—the seats are torn, the ceiling is peeling, and the carpet is dirty and pock-marked with cigarette burns. But Time Warner recently gained control of the theater's board and has ambitious plans to completely refurbish the place in 2001. On the drawing board: hopes to turn the Apollo into a major cultural center that would stretch from the vacant lot just west of the Apollo to the Victoria, an abandoned movie theater several doors to the east.

Despite the Apollo's current well-worn condition, it still presents its famed amateur night every Wednesday, as well as occasional concerts. In the lobby is a small exhibit on the theater's early history.

Baby Grand, 319 W. 125th St., near St. Nicholas Ave.

Across the street from the glistening new Magic Johnson multi-plex, complete with its own Disney Store and Old Navy shop, is the site of the old Baby Grand. Once a stylish club, now a stationary and party goods shop, the Baby Grand was one of the last of the Harlem clubs to go, closing its doors for good only in 1989. For 42 years the cabaret had been home to musicians such as Jimmy Butts and Joe Turner, as well as comedians such as Manhattan Paul and Nipsey Russell. In 1988, Ruth Brown taped a birthday show here for national television.

2040 Adam Clayton Powell Blvd. (Seventh Ave.), near 122th St.

Now part of a larger residential building, 2040 Seventh was once an apartment house filled with musicians. Dizzy Gillespie and his wife lived here shortly after they were married, and so did Billy Eckstine and his wife. The two musicians became close friends, and according to Eckstine, Dizzy was constantly studying, working out chord progressions and countermelodies on an old piano. Other residents living at number 2040 at that time or shortly thereafter included Erroll Garner, Clyde Hart, Buck Clayton, Harry Edison, and Don Byas.

Dewey Square, Adam Clayton Powell Blvd. and 118th St.

A small triangular park with the old Dewey Square Hotel (now a residential building) located on the north side, Dewey Square is where Charlie Parker developed his famous number of the same name. Today the park is called A. Philip Randolph Triangle.

Minton's Playhouse, Cecil Hotel, 210 W. 118th St. 212-864-5281.

One of the greatest revolutions in jazz, the birth of bebop, was spawned in this neighborhood club run by onetime bandleader Teddy Hill in the Cecil Hotel. In 1941, Hill hired a house band that included Thelonious Monk and Kenny Clarke, and soon the small, dark place was packed every night with talent eager to jam. Dizzy Gillespie, Charlie Parker, Charlie Christian, Max Roach, and Tadd Dameron were among the regulars; Monday nights, the traditional night off for musicians, brought big band talent such as Teddy Wilson and Roy Eldridge as well.

The Minton sessions—spontaneous, informal and often after-hours—gave the musicians a chance to explore new ideas, such as the flatted fifth. Everyone sat in at Minton's, including some who had no business doing so, and for them, the insiders would play their new complex ideas, forcing the incompetents off the stage.

According to Oran "Hot Lips" Page in *Hear Me Talkin' to Ya,* the word "bop" was coined at the club by Fats Waller. Often, when the younger musicians were fooling around trying out some of their new bop runs, Fats would shout at them, "Stop that crazy boppin' and a-stoppin' and play that jive like the rest of us guys."

Today, the renovated Cecil Hotel houses apartments for the elderly, while in the old Minton's—now on the National Register of Historic Places—stretches a magnificent mural depicting four musicians, two of which have been identified as Tony Scott and Charlie Christian. For years, plans have been in the works to reopen the historic club. But the project, backed by Robert DeNiro and his restaurateur partner Drew Nieporent, is currently stalled, due to investors wary of signing onto this $3.1 million project in the heart of Harlem.

Upper West Side

(The four sites below are spread over a 50-block area, but they could be walked on a nice day.)

George Gershwin's Home, 316 W. 103rd St., near Riverside Dr.

George Gershwin, the composer whose work had such an enormous impact on jazz, once lived (1925–31) in this small stone house near the Hudson River. He and his family had originally moved here so that he could have more privacy in which to work, but things didn't work out quite that way. When his friend S. N. Behrman came to visit one day in the late '20s, he found a group of strange young men playing billiards on the first floor and another group lounging on the second. Behrman finally found George's brother, Ira, and asked who the men were. Ira had no idea. "There's a bunch of fellows from down the street who've taken to dropping in here every night for a game," he said.[4]

The Gershwin building is marked with a plaque honoring the two brothers, who "created many memorable works here," and the awning out front reads GERSHWIN HOUSE.

Billie Holiday's last New York apartment, 26 W. 87th St.

The last year of Billie Holiday's life was sad and lonely. Her health was poor, her career was at a low point, and days would go by without her seeing anyone. Says fellow singer Annie Ross in *Billie's Blues* by John Chilton: "She sat alone watching television night after night. She sat in an armchair puffing away at a marihuana 'joint' . . . just staring at the screen, shuffling the pages of the papers, making sure that she had planned her viewing schedule in such a way so that she didn't miss a single cartoon film."

On May 31, 1959, Billie collapsed and sank into a coma. Luckily, a friend was present, and he immediately rushed her to the hospital, where her case was diagnosed as "drug addiction and alcoholism." A few rough days passed and she was just beginning to recover when the police burst into her room, allegedly found a small envelope of heroin, and posted a guard outside her door. (Some, pointing out that the singer was too sick to leave her bed, said that the drugs had been planted; others believed that a well-wisher had brought them by.) Billie's books, flowers, and radio were confiscated, and she was "mugged" and fingerprinted while still in bed.

Meanwhile, her physical condition deteriorated. Cirrhosis of the liver and a serious kidney ailment were now diagnosed; a few weeks later, on the morning of July 17, she died. She was buried in St. Raymond's Cemetery in the Bronx, beside her mother.

Miles Davis's apartment, 312 W. 77th St.

Davis moved into this handsome red townhouse, a former Russian Orthodox church that he had extensively remodeled, in the early '60s. In the basement he installed a gym and a music room where he could rehearse without disturbing anyone, and out back there was a garden. With him at first were his wife, Frances Taylor, and their children, but their marriage fell apart, as did Davis's subsequent marriage to Betty Mabry.

Davis recorded many important albums, including *Miles Smiles, In a Silent Way,* and *Bitches Brew,* while living at number 312. Nineteen sixty-nine and '70 were particularly productive years, and by 1971 Davis was not only making about $400,000 annually but had also been voted Jazzman of the Year by *Down Beat* magazine.

Nonetheless, by 1975, owing to health problems, disillusionment with the music industry, and an extensive cocaine habit, Miles's life had fallen apart. "From 1975 until early 1980 I didn't pick up my horn," he says in his autobiography, *Miles.* "For over four years, didn't pick it up once. I would walk by and look at it, then think about trying to play. But after a while I didn't even do that. . . . Mostly during those four or five years that I was out of music, I just took a lot of cocaine (about $500 a day at one point) and fucked all the women I could get into my house."

Eventually, through the help of George Butler at Columbia Records, Davis pulled himself out of his depression and drug habit and back into the world of music. He sold the house at number 312 in the early '80s when he and Cicely Tyson started living together.

Thelonious Monk's apartment, 243 W. 63rd St.

For most of his life, Thelonious Sphere Monk lived in this red-brick building, part of a vibrant apartment complex behind Lincoln Center. A gentle, introverted, and eccentric man, Monk was long regarded by critics and club owners as unpredictable and unemployable, and was one of the last of the modern jazz pioneers to receive recognition.

Monk was a private man who seldom visited others and, upon answering the phone, often said, "Monk's not home." He spent most of his days playing and writing, and—despite periodic hospitalizations for mental illness—living a remarkably stable life with his family and wife, Nellie.

From 1951 to '57, Monk's cabaret card—this card was then a prerequisite for a musician working in New York—was taken from him when he was found sitting with a friend in a car that contained narcotics. Monk could have cleared himself by informing on his friend, who owned the dope, but he refused. He also refused to work outside New York or outside music, and spent those six years just barely surviving on scant income from rare recording dates.

In 1976, six years before his death, Monk withdrew from public performing. He is buried in Ferncliff Cemetery in Hartsdale, New York.

Upper East Side

Ellington Statue, Central Park, Fifth Ave. and 110th St.

In 1994, a 20-foot-high statue of Duke Ellington was erected at this northeast corner of Central Park by the Duke Ellington Memorial Fund, an organization spearheaded by Bobby Short. The statue's design, by Los Angeles artist Robert Graham, was unveiled to the public in 1990, and it met with considerable controversy. Sexist and tacky is what then New York *Daily News* columnist Bob Herbert called the statue, which shows nine nude women (supposedly the Muses) standing with a baby grand piano and an elegantly dressed Duke Ellington on their heads.

Stanhope Hotel, 995 Fifth Ave., across from the Metropolitan Museum of Art at 82nd St., 212–288–5800.

On the night of March 12, 1955, Charlie Parker died in the hotel apartment of the Baronness "Nica" de Koenigswarter while watching jugglers on the "Tommy Dorsey Show." The Baroness, who was a friend and patron of many jazz musicians, had called a doctor upon Bird's arrival three days earlier, and he had warned her that the musician could die at any time. No attempt was made to move Parker, however, and none of his friends or wives were notified, although Bird did call his mother in Kansas City, who begged him to come home and not die in a hospital.

Parker was only 34 when he died, but his death certificate estimated his age to be 53. Drugs and alcohol had so ravaged his body that he seemed much older. A great deal of controversy also surrounded his death. The tabloids had a heyday with the fact that he had died in the Baronness's apartment, and there was an ugly tug-of-war between his wives over where he should be buried.

John Hammond's home, 9 E. 91st St.

John Hammond, the record producer and writer who was responsible for discovering, recording, and promoting so many major musicians (Billie Holiday, Count Basie, Bessie

Smith, Benny Goodman, Benny Carter, Teddy Wilson, Charlie Christian, and, later, Aretha Franklin, Bob Dylan, and Bruce Springsteen, to name but a few) grew up in this luxurious six-story mansion. The son of a wealthy lawyer and a Vanderbilt, Hammond, born in 1910, could have chosen an easy and pampered life. Instead, he discovered jazz and blues—listening to early records when he was 8, slipping away from prep school to hear Bessie Smith in Harlem at 16—and spent a lifetime doing everything within his power to further the music. Hammond was also an ardent civil rights activist, covering the Scottsboro trial for the *Nation;* fighting for the rights of miners in Harlan County, West Virginia; and serving as an early board member of the NAACP.

Midtown

(The following tour starts at West 58th Street and Eighth Avenue and proceeds south down the West Side, before cutting over to the East Side and heading north again.)

Reisenweber's Restaurant, W. 58th St. and Eighth Ave., S.W. corner, just south of Columbus Circle.

Though no longer standing, Reisenweber's was the spot where the Original Dixieland Jazz Band appeared in 1917, a sensational event that is generally credited with ushering jazz into New York. Shortly after appearing here, the ODJB, a New Orleans band led by cornet player Nick LaRocca, made the very first jazz recordings ever, cutting "Livery Stable Blues" and the "Original Dixieland One-Step" on February 26, 1917, at the Victor Studios.

Carnegie Hall, 154 W. 57th St., at Seventh Ave., 212–247–7800.

New York's premier concert auditorium, built in 1891 in an Italian Renaissance design, has been featuring jazz ever since the musical form emerged. James Reese Europe, the country's first African-American bandleader, who used jazz elements at times, organized events here from 1912 to 1914, and in 1928, jazz pianists James P. Johnson and Fats Waller played a tribute to W. C. Handy. Then there was the historic "From Spirituals to Swing" concert organized by John Hammond in memory of Bessie Smith on December 23, 1938. Backed by *New Masses,* a Marxist publication (and a supporter that Hammond had some doubts about), the event was the first major concert produced in New York for an integrated audience. Hammond traveled all over the country collecting talent for the show, and among the many who played that night were Sidney Bechet, Meade "Lux" Lewis, Albert Ammons, Big Joe Turner,

Big Bill Broonzy, the Mitchell's Christian Singers, the Kansas City Six (including Buck Clayton and Lester Young), and the Basie band. Benny Goodman also gave a highly acclaimed concert performance in 1938, and a released recording of the event brought to him a wide audience.

Other historic concerts followed. Norman Granz used the hall for his "Jazz at the Philharmonic" concerts between 1949 and 1953; and Duke Ellington presented his suite "Black, Brown, and Beige" in 1943. Charlie Parker played the hall in the late '40s, and Miles Davis and the Gil Evans orchestra performed here in 1961. Major jazz talent is still being presented by Carnegie Hall, and the JVC Jazz Festival sponsors events here every summer.

Park Central Hotel (now the Park Central New York Hotel), 870 Seventh Ave., near W. 55th St., 212–247–8000.

In 1928, the Ben Pollack band, which then included an all-star cast of Jack Teagarden, Benny Goodman, and Jimmy McPartland, opened at the Park Central, which was once known for its big bands. The reviews were ecstatic and every night the hotel was packed with audiences eager to see the hot new group. Nonetheless, there was a lot of friction in the band. McPartland kept skipping rehearsals, and an ambitious Goodman—according to Pollack—kept taking too many solos.

Finally, tempers snapped. McPartland appeared on stage one night without garters, and his socks slipped down around his ankles. Pollack scolded him after the show, saying that wrinkled socks didn't look good on stage, and McPartland flew into a rage, quitting on the spot. Goodman, hearing the shouting, quit a moment later.

To add insult to injury, when Pollack stopped by the Park Central the next season to talk about his contract, he learned that Goodman and McPartland had already offered the hotel the entire band, *sans* Pollack, at a bargain price. Pollack eventually got the gig back and hired new men, but his band never regained its old popularity.

Fifty-Second Street, between Fifth and Sixth Avenues.

Back in the 1930s and '40s, more great musicians congregated on this one small block than any place else in the world, before or since. Art Tatum, Billie Holiday, Coleman Hawkins, Oran "Hot Lips" Page, Roy Eldridge, Teddy Wilson, Fats Waller, Erroll Garner, Mary Lou Williams, Dizzy Gillespie, Charlie Parker, Miles Davis, Sarah Vaughan, Count Basie, Woody Herman, Charlie Barnet, Buddy Rich, Dave Tough, George Shearing—all were here.

Fifty-second Street's magic began just after Prohibition, when New York's jazz center began shifting from Harlem to downtown. "The Street" at that time was lined with dark and smoky speakeasies, all housed in dilapidated brownstones with tiny vestibules, long bars, pressed-tin ceilings, and water-stained walls. The street's real heyday came about 10 years later, however, with the arrival of modern jazz (see Minton's, "Landmarks and Legends," page 129).

The music on 52nd Street ranged from New Orleans and Chicago jazz to bebop and early cool, and the musicians moved from one club to another with an ease that seems incredible today. In a single night, for the price of a few drinks, one could hear the same musician playing in three or four different clubs with three or four different bands.

The first music club to open on the Street was the Onyx, later dubbed the "Cradle of Swing." Then there was the Famous Door, named for the door inscribed with autographs of the famous that sat on a small platform near the bar; the long-running Hickory House, located on the next block, between Sixth and Seventh avenues, where Art Tatum often played during intermission; the Downbeat, a regular gig for Dizzy Gillespie; Kelly's Stable, where Coleman Hawkins recorded his famous 1939 "Body and Soul"; the Three Deuces, where Erroll Garner and Charlie Parker were regulars; and Jimmy Ryan's, known for its Dixieland.

The street began to decline after World War II, when its jazz clubs turned into striptease bars and clip joints. Today, all the old brownstones (with the exception of the 21 Club) have been torn down, to be replaced by towering glass-sheathed buildings. The only reminders of the past are the street signs that read SWING STREET (52nd St. between Fifth and Sixth avenues) and W. C. HANDY PLACE (52nd St. between Sixth and Seventh avenues). There are also small sidewalk plaques on the 52nd Street side of the CBS Building at Sixth Avenue honoring some of the jazz greats.

Ed Sullivan Theater, 1697 Broadway, near 53rd St.

Ed Sullivan, a former sports columnist, began broadcasting his famous variety show, which quickly became a sort of arbiter of popular taste, from here in 1949. B. B. King, like Elvis Presley and the Beatles before him, played the theater. With him on the bill on October 18, 1970, were the Carpenters. (Benny Goodman also played the venue, when it was known as the Billy Rose Casino.) The theater is now home to the "David Letterman Show," and has been extensively restored.

Roseland Ballroom, 239 W. 52nd St.

This Roseland Ballroom, opened in 1956, has been home to some jazz greats—Count Basie, among others—but it was the old, now destroyed Roseland at 1658 Broadway near 51st Street that had the legendary past. One of the largest ballrooms in New York from the '20s through the '40s, it was lavishly decorated and known throughout the country for its hot jazz and dancing. Fletcher Henderson's band (which included Louis Armstrong for a time, as well as Billie Holiday's father, who wanted nothing to do with either her or her mother) played a long and important residency there, while Jean Goldkette's band with Bix Beiderbecke performed at the ballroom in the late '20s.

Men never hurt for dancing partners at Roseland, where the "taxi" dance may have originated. Patrons rode up to the ballroom in cabs and bought rolls of 10-cent tickets that allowed them to dance with the hostesses, whose income depended on the tickets they collected. Roseland was also a segregated hall. No African Americans were admitted in the audience and even Latinos were discouraged.

Ballroom dancing was still featured at Roseland well into the 1990s, slipped in during the afternoons between the hard-hitting rap, hip-hop, funk, and rock concerts that continue to take place at night. On a typical afternoon, a few older couples would dance beneath the domed ceiling dotted with lights, while singles in their sixties and seventies sat on little red chairs, watching. One older woman would wring her hands; an older man, stunningly dressed in black with patent leather shoes and striped socks, would adjust an enormous red carnation in his lapel. Today, however, ballroom dancing at Roseland is no more.

Birdland, 1674 Broadway, near 52nd St.

Now a deli and convenience store, Birdland was once located in the basement of this stolid building. Named after Charlie Parker, who opened the club in December 1949, it was an important center for bop.

Like the Royal Roost (then located at 1580 Broadway at 47th St., now the site of the Ramada Renaissance Hotel), which was the first sit-down club for jazz, Birdland had tables on the dance floor, bleachers for those who wanted to pay only the cover charge, and a milk bar for nondrinkers. Unlike the Royal Roost, it also had parakeets in bird cages (who were soon killed off by the air conditioning and smoke), its own radio wire and booth, manned by the renowned disc jockey Symphony Sid Torin, and a midget emcee named Pee Wee Marquette.

It was in front of Birdland one night that Miles Davis, then working the club, was badly beaten by two cops who challenged his right to "loiter" on the street. Miles, who would later need five stitches, was then taken to jail, where he was charged with disorderly conduct. A crowd of supporters gathered in protest, and the incident was covered by newspapers around the world. The charges were eventually dropped.

Charlie Parker, then suffering badly from drug addiction, also had his share of troubles here. One night he arrived at the club in pajamas, having just snuck out of a hospital where he was taking a cure. Another evening he fired the entire string section backing him, and then later that night, despondent, tried to commit suicide by swallowing iodine. He also had a bitter argument on stage with band member Bud Powell, causing Charles Mingus, who was also in the band, to step up to the mike and say, "Ladies and Gentlemen, I am not responsible for what happens on the bandstand. This is not jazz."[5]

Eventually, sadly enough, Parker was banned from the club that bore his name.

Metropole, 725 Seventh Ave., near 48th St.

The Metropole featured afternoon and evening jazz through the 1950s and '60s. Writes trumpet player Buck Clayton in his autobiography, *Buck Clayton's Jazz World,* "The bandstand was behind the bar. It was only about four feet wide and many cats would fall off of the bandstand and down into the bar below if they were too tipsy. It was a long bar and as one group would finish their set the other group would come up. . . . We called the whole show 'Wall to Wall Jazz.' . . . You'd see about fourteen or fifteen musicians elevated on the stand behind the bartender and all swinging away on the closing number."

Scott Joplin's Boardinghouse, 252 W. 47th St.

From 1911 to 1915, Scott Joplin and his wife, Lottie, ran a boardinghouse out of this small residential building just down the street from the Hotel Edison, where many of Ellington's sidemen would later stay. (The boardinghouse was later moved to 133 W. 138th and then to 163 W. 131st St.)

Joplin had a difficult time of it in New York. His classic piano rags were selling poorly, he was quarreling with his publisher, and no one was interested in publishing his opera, *Treemonisha.* Finally he published the 230-page score himself, and for a period, it looked as if the Lafayette Theater might produce it, but nothing ever came of it.

Dispirited, Joplin went through long periods of depression and began playing badly. Often he had trouble remembering his most popular compositions. There was no private studio at the boardinghouse—just a piano in the front parlor—and he would become acutely embarrassed whenever his playing slipped.

In 1917 Joplin was admitted to Ward's Island for mental trouble, and three days later he was dead. He was buried in St. Michael's Cemetery in Astoria, Queens (72–02 Astoria Blvd., East Elmhurst, 718–278–3240). The grave went unmarked until 1974, when a simple plaque reading SCOTT JOPLIN, AMERICAN COMPOSER was laid.

Whitby Apartments, 325 W. 45th St.

Now a coop apartment building, the Whitby was once the home of Gil Evans, composer, pianist, and arranger, who lived here throughout the '50s and '60s. Evans did much of his finest work with Miles Davis while living in this building, including the albums *Miles Ahead, Porgy and Bess,* and *Sketches of Spain.*

Blue Room, Lincoln Hotel, 700 Eighth Ave., at 44th St.

Now the middle-brow Milford Plaza, this solid brown-brick building was once the Lincoln Hotel, where the Blue Room nightclub was housed. Count Basie played here in the 1940s, and Billie Holiday—then with the Artie Shaw band—was given the backdoor treatment here in 1938. "Gee, it's funny," she told Bill Chase of the *Amsterdam News* the following year, "we were really a big hit all over the South and never ran into the color question until we opened at the Lincoln Hotel here in New York City. I was billed next to Artie himself, but was never allowed to visit the bar or the dining room, as did the other members of the band. Not only was I made to enter and leave the hotel through the kitchen but had to remain alone in a little dark room all evening until I was called. . . ."[6]

Town Hall, 123 W. 43rd St. bet. Sixth and Seventh Aves., 212–840–2824.

Opened in 1921 as a public meetinghouse, Town Hall was the site of Bird's last public concert, held on October 30, 1954. According to his producer and biographer, Robert Reisner, the musician played magnificently throughout, despite the fact that the concert—owing to limited advertising—was poorly attended.

Town Hall began featuring jazz concerts in the early 1940s, when Dixieland jazz master Eddie Condon organized a regular series of jam sessions, featuring such artists as Oran "Hot Lips" Page, Pee Wee Russell, and Zutty Singleton. The sessions were informal—the musicians lounged, smoked, and whispered to each other on stage—which was unusual at the time, and they met with great critical acclaim.

Today, the hall is still known for its jazz concerts.

Chez Josephine, 414 W. 42nd St., near Ninth Ave., 212–594–1925.

This charming, upscale French bistro is run by Jean-Claude Baker, the oldest of entertainer Josephine Baker's 13 adopted "Rainbow Tribe" children. Downstairs, find an excellent French menu (average entrée $15), lots of red velvet, and a lively piano player; upstairs, find a small museum honoring Baker and other pre-1930 entertainers, such as Florence Mills. The collection includes some 500 music programs, pieces of sheet music, photos and other artifacts, and over 500 hours of audio tape.

Museum hours: Tu–Sa, 2–5 P.M.

Aeolian Hall, 33 W. 42nd St., near Sixth Ave.

Now completely absorbed by the CUNY Graduate Center (only a few elevator doors, old walls, and ceiling details are left), Aeolian Hall was the site of the "First American Jazz Concert" presented by Paul Whiteman on February 12, 1924. Whiteman had set out to prove to the world that jazz has as much validity as classical music, a notion that many dismissed as "Whiteman's Folly" until they heard the concert's twenty-second selection, "Rhapsody in Blue," performed on the piano by its composer, George Gershwin.

Hotel Pennsylvania, 401 Seventh Ave., near 33rd St.

The Hotel Pennsylvania was once a popular spot for all the major swing bands. Glenn Miller's signature song, "Pennsylvania 6–5000" (still the hotel's phone number), was named after the place.

Hotel Roosevelt, Madison Ave. and 45th St.

In 1934, the Benny Goodman Orchestra played its first dance-hall engagement at the Roosevelt. The event was a disaster. The Roosevelt was Guy Lombardo's home base, and the waiters kept motioning to Goodman to tone it down. Some even requested a transfer to another room, and the customers sent caustic notes to the band.

Waldorf Astoria, Park Ave. at E. 49th St.

There was a time when the Waldorf was known for its jazz. Many major big bands, including those led by Benny Goodman and violinist Leo Reisman, played the Waldorf's Empire Room during the '30s and '40s, and Charlie Parker and Sidney Bechet performed for a youth conference sponsored by the hotel in 1949.

Louis Armstrong gave his last concert at the Waldorf in 1971. Then already in poor health, he insisted on playing despite the warnings of his doctor, who later reported that the following incident had taken place at his office two weeks earlier:

"'Louie,' [I said,] 'you could drop dead while you're performing.' He said, 'Doc, that's all right, I don't care.' . . . And he sat there for a moment sort of removed and went through the motions of blowing that horn. 'I've got bookings arranged and the people are waiting for me.'"[7]

Armstrong went through with the concert (which got lousy reviews), and then checked into Beth Israel Medical Center, as he had promised his family and doctor. He died a few months later.

Downtown

(The following route, which can be toured on foot, begins in the East Village, on Second Avenue near 10th Street, and proceeds east and then south before heading west to Greenwich Village.)

Stuyvesant Casino, 140 Second Ave.

Now a Ukrainian hall and restaurant, the Stuyvesant was once known for its dancing and jazz. New Orleans musician Bunk Johnson made his New York debut here in 1945; and others who played the hall included Sidney Bechet, Art Hodes, Henry "Red" Allen, and Buck Clayton.

The Stuyvesant and its music were also the objects of some controversy. When Bunk was brought up from New Orleans, bebop was in its infancy on 52nd Street, and many writers and critics, unable to understand the new sound, heralded Johnson's group with fulsome reviews, calling them the only band left playing "true jazz." Naturally, this did not sit well with the newer players.

Charlie Parker's Apartment, 151 Ave. B, bet. Ninth and Tenth streets.

In 1951, Bird moved downtown into a solid four-story white stone building looking out onto Tompkins Square Park. With him were his girlfriend, Chan, and her daughter, Kim. "I like the people around here," he said once to his biographer Robert Reisner. "They don't give you no hype."

The apartment, large and comfortable, was filled with castoff furniture and Kim's toys, including a five-foot rabbit that Parker had given her. While here, the musician kept his life middle-class and respectable, greeting Chan's relatives in a suit and tie, and taking walks with Kim in the park. Later, Chan said that if it hadn't been for his talent, race, and drug addiction, Charlie could have lived out his days on Avenue B as a "happy square."[8]

The city renamed this block "Charlie Parker Place" in 1993.

Five Spot, 2 St. Marks Pl. (SE corner of Third Ave.).

It was at the Five Spot, originally located at 5 Cooper Square, that Thelonious Monk finally became recognized in the late 1950s. A shadowy figure up until then, known mostly as the eccentric who'd written "'Round About Midnight," he brought with him to the club a quartet that included John Coltrane. Their impact was enormous, and before long, the club was packed every night. "Trane was the perfect saxophonist for Monk's music because of the space that Monk always used," says Miles Davis in *Miles.* "Trane could fill up all that space with all them chords and sounds he was playing then."

From the beginning, the Five Spot was known for its serious commitment to music. Before Monk, there had been Cecil Taylor; after him came Ornette Coleman, who made a controversial New York debut at the club, and Eric Dolphy, who gave some of his most inspired performances there. Charles Mingus, who destroyed his $2,000 bass in anger at two hecklers one night, was also associated with the Five Spot.

No. 2 St. Mark's place now houses a pizza joint.

Charles Mingus's loft, 5 Great Jones St., near Lafayette St.

Mingus, his nerves frayed through career disappointments and personal problems, lived at this address for a turbulent period in 1966. While here, he worked at the Village Gate, where he threw a drum at Herbie Mann and wore a little but very real pistol (a Derringer with two bullets in it) around his neck as a charm.

On November 22, 1966, Mingus was evicted from his loft-apartment for alleged nonpayment of rent. The event was documented in the film *Mingus* by Tom Reichman, in which Mingus gives a long and bitter soliloquy and fires his shotgun at the ceiling.

Number 5 now houses a storefront on the first floor, with living quarters up above.

The Cookery, 21 University Pl. at E. Eighth St.

Alberta Hunter, who had entered show business at the age of 16 and had had more than her share of ups and downs, suddenly quit music, without fanfare, in the mid-1950s. For the next 20 years she worked as a nurse at the Goldwater Hospital on Roosevelt Island. This was *after* going back to school for both her high school diploma and her nursing diploma, which she received at 62, having lied about her age to get into the program.

Then, in 1977, through a mutual friend, Hunter came to the attention of Barney Josephson, (see Café Society, below) who was running a restaurant-club called The Cookery. Josephson booked Hunter, and before long, at age 82, she was in the midst of a tremendous comeback.

The Cookery building now houses a barbecue joint.

Bradley's, 70 University Pl., near 12th St.

From the 1970s to the 1990s, Bradley's was the city's premier piano-bass room. A dark and den-like place, it was first run by the beloved Bradley Cunningham and later by his equally beloved wife Wendy. All the top piano and bass players played at Bradley's, with Tommy Flanagan, Hank Jones, Dave McKenna, and Charles Mingus having a particularly strong affiliation. Musicians often hung out at Bradley's after their gigs elsewhere were done, and the music usually lasted until 4 A.M.

Bradley's closed down in the mid-1990s, but its wonderful piano, once owned by Paul Desmond, has since found a new home in the Jazz Gallery (see "For Jazz," below).

Café Society (Downtown), 2 Sheridan Sq. (where Barrow St. runs into W. Fourth St., now the Ridiculous Theatrical Co.)

Opened in 1939 by Barney Josephson, then a 36-year-old former shoe manufacturer, Café Society was one of the first truly integrated clubs downtown. Whites and blacks could sit and dance together—a courageous innovation for the time—and anyone who made a racial slur was immediately asked to leave.

Billie Holiday opened the L-shaped basement club, lined with quirky murals, and the engagement marked the turning point of her career. It was also here that her song "Strange Fruit" was born. The song came out of a poem written by poet Lewis Allen, whom Billie first met at the club.

Lena Horne followed Billie, and then there was Sarah Vaughan, Mildred Bailey, Joe Turner, Josh White, Big Bill Broonzy, Teddy Wilson, Art Tatum, James P. Johnson, Lester Young, Django Reinhardt, and many more. Fletcher Henderson played his last gig here in 1950.

Josephson opened a second Café Society Uptown (128 E. 58th St.) in 1940. Both clubs closed down in 1950.

Café Bohemia, 15 Barrow St., near Fourth St.

Now a local watering hole, the Café Bohemia opened in 1955 with Oscar Pettiford as musical director. Saxophonist Cannonball Adderley, then a 26-year-old high school teacher up from Florida, made a New York debut here that same year that launched his career.

"Great night!," said Cannonball's brother Nat in a 1984 interview with Phil Schaap of WKCR radio. "We'd just come into town because my brother was going to do some work at NYU. He was gonna get his master's. And we went down, the first night, to Café Bohemia. . . . Oscar Pettiford was playing. . . . Charlie Rouse was there as well, he recognized Cannonball from Florida and one thing led to another. Cannon sailed through the first couple of tunes and then I went up and played and two nights later, we had a job. . . ."

Nick's, 170 W. 10th St. at Seventh Ave. S.

One of the earliest spots in the Village for jazz, Nick's (now the Riviera Café) was a Dixieland haunt during the '30s. The club's resident band, led by Bobby Hackett, featured Eddie Condon, Pee Wee Russell and Zutty Singleton. Sidney Bechet also put in numerous appearances, as did Meade "Lux" Lewis, Muggsy Spanier, and Wild Bill Davison.

Electric Lady Studios, 52 W. Eighth St., near Sixth Ave.

In early 1970, Jimi Hendrix completed his splendid Electric Lady Studios, shaped like a giant guitar, built into a row of four-story brownstones. He wanted the studios to be as beautiful physically as the music that would be created within, and so outfitted the place with state-of-the-art equipment, curving passageways, a giant multicolor space mural, and walls of white carpet that reflected muted lights.

Hendrix recorded some 600 hours of tapes at the studios, but died on September 18, 1970 (from inhalation of vomit following barbiturate intoxication), before anything was released. Later, the Jimi Hendrix Estate hired an independent producer to put together albums from the raw, unedited tapes. The results didn't measure up to Hendrix's earlier work and ignited much controversy, largely because of the producer's decision to erase tracks featuring the original sidemen and replace them with Los Angeles studio musicians.

Before the Electric Lady Studios were created, 52 Eighth St. housed the Generation, a music club where Hendrix, B. B. King, and Buddy Guy played on the night that Martin Luther King, Jr., was killed. Today, alas, the building's ground floor is no longer rounded like a guitar, but there's still a shiny Electric Lady plaque at the door.

Village Gate, 158–180 Bleecker St., at Thompson St.

Now home to a sterile CVS pharmacy, this building once housed the Village Gate, a sprawling multi-level club that was a famed New York institution from the late 1960s to the early 1990s. With three shows often running simultaneously, the Gate featured everything from cabaret and revues to blues and Latin music, but was best known for its jazz.

Run by impresario Art D'Lugoff, the Gate boasted a list of great performers that was long and mean: Miles Davis, Horace Silver, Dizzy Gillespie, Dexter Gordon, Charles Mingus, Albert King, Memphis Slim, John Lee Hooker. Over 60 albums were recorded in the club's main basement room—a dark and cavernous space, with a bombed-out feel—and B. B. King gave one of his first performance before a white audience there, in 1968. In 1979, Monk made his last night-club appearance at the Gate, and Red Garland was lifted off the stage once by two men in blue (he was being sued for alimony). The Gate also hosted a legendary Monday-night "Salsa Meets Jazz" series that ran for over 20 years. Originally emceed by Symphony Sid Torin, the sessions showcased everyone from Willie Colon to Tito Puente.

Elsewhere in the City

Louis Armstrong's home, 34–56 107th St., Corona, Queens.
The great Satchmo lived in this attractive red-brick building with beautiful gardens out back from the early 1940s until his death in 1971. It was his longest stay in one abode, and tales are often told of how he used to sit on the front steps with his trumpet and entertain the neighborhood kids, some of whom came by with horns of their own. Lots of musicians also stopped by, and then there'd be the private jam sessions, especially on the Fourth of July (Armstrong's alleged birthday), when Louis would throw giant parties in the backyard.

The Corona house was actually bought by Louis's wife, Lucille. Upon their marriage, he had told her that he did not want a home, that he was content to live in hotels, but she went ahead and bought one anyway and he grew to like it, holing up here whenever he was off the road and refusing to move even after the neighborhood had deteriorated.

Today, the Armstrong house is on the National Register of Historic Places and under the management of Queens College. All of Armstrong's belongings except for his furniture have been removed—many to the Louis Armstrong Archives (see below). For close to a decade, plans have been in the works to turn the house into a museum; current target date for the grand opening is 2002.

Louis Armstrong Archives, Rosenthal Library, Queen's College, 65–30 Kissena Blvd., 718–997–6670, www.satchmo.com.

Now housed in the Rosenthal Library of Queens College are many of Armstrong's personal belongings, including 12 linear feet of personal papers and writings, 82 scrapbooks, 650 homemade tapes, and dozens of hand-decorated tape boxes. The archives stage two temporary, well-presented Armstrong exhibits every year. Topics in the past have included "Satch and Duke: Louis Armstrong and Duke Ellington," "Pops Off-Stage: Louis's Home-Recorded Tapes," "Eye of the Beholder: The Iconography of Louis Armstrong," and exhibits on Louis' wife, Lucille, and his manager, Joe Glaser.

Open: M-F, 10 A.M.–5 P.M. by appointment. *Free.*

Flushing Cemetery, 163–06 46th Ave., Corona, Queens, 718–359–0100.

Satchmo is buried in this cemetery, located not far from his former home. On his tombstone, on which his epitaph is etched in gold, is a sculpture of a trumpet draped in cloth.

Jazzmen Johnny Hodges, Charlie Shavers, and Dizzy Gillespie are all buried here as well, Dizzy in a family plot where his name remains unmarked on the tombstone, as per the request of his family. After a private ceremony for the late great trumpet player (who died in 1993), held at St. Peter's Lutheran Church in Manhattan, a 14-car cortege drove along 52nd Street and up Broadway, past the sites of Birdland and the Royal Roost, and then on up into Harlem, past the site of Minton's Playhouse and the Apollo Theatre.

Open: daily, 8 A.M.–4:30 P.M.

Woodlawn Cemetery, Webster Ave. and 233rd St., the Bronx, 718–920–0500.

Duke Ellington, W. C. Handy, Joseph "King" Oliver, and Miles Davis are all buried in Woodlawn Cemetery, an idyllic park that's recognized as one of the most beautiful cemeteries in the world. Dating back to Civil War days, it's built on rolling hills with lots of shady trees and a shimmering sky-blue lake.

Ellington's grave is located in a corner plot, beneath a large tree, while Miles is buried less than 10 yards away, beneath a shiny black granite stone that reads IN MEMORY OF SIR MILES DAVIS. Handy's grave, with its lyre design, is also impressive, and all three sites are marked on the cemetery map.

Oliver was not so fortunate. Once "King" of the Chicago jazz scene, he died poverty-stricken and alone and is buried in an unmarked grave in the Salvia section. In 1927, Oliver—who had all of Chicago eating out of his hand—turned down an offer to headline at the Cotton Club in New York. (Duke Ellington took the job, which sprung him into stardom.) It proved to be a fatal mistake. By 1928, he was having a hard time finding work, and following the Depression, he lost his band. By the mid-1930s he was running a fruit stand in Savannah, Georgia. Later, he took a job as a janitor in a pool hall, but although he worked from early morning until midnight, he couldn't earn enough money to care for his worsening health. In one heartbreaking letter to his sister, who lived in the Bronx, he wrote that he had finally saved $1.60 and was coming to New York. He only made it in a casket.

Open: daily, 9 A.M.–4:30 P.M.

Williamsburg Bridge, near Delancey St.

One of three suspension bridges that span the East River, linking Manhattan with Brooklyn, the Williamsburg was Sonny Rollins's private retreat from 1959 to 1961, when he withdrew from a successful career to further explore the world of music. "I found it's a superb place to practice," he tells writer Whitney Balliett in *Dinosaurs in the Morning.* "Night or day. You're up over the whole world. You can look down on the whole scene. There is the skyline, the water, the harbor. . . . It makes you think."

CLUBS, ETC.

For an out-of-towner, the jazz scene in New York can come as a shock. Prices at the better-known clubs are often extremely high ($15–35, plus a two-drink minimum) and the clubs, small and crowded. The quality of the music is almost always superb, but because many of the famed places have become so formal, a certain energy sometimes seems to be missing. Good hangout-type places must be sought out, and making a spontaneous stop is often impossible in a city that's become more and more dependent on reservations.

However, on the brighter side, jazz in New York is thriving. A surprising number of smaller and less expensive clubs, often attracting younger audiences, have opened in the last few years, along with several more upscale venues featuring national and international talent. Jazz at Lincoln Center has grown from a relatively small arm of Lincoln Center into an enormous program that will soon be moving into a home of its own (see "Other Venues and Special Events"), and more Harlem clubs are in operation now than at any other time in recent history.

On any given night in New York, there's so much talent to choose from that it's hard to know where to go first. Below, find a few guidelines. Generally speaking, music in the city stops at 2 A.M. Many clubs have set showtimes each night; call for information.

THE QUINTESSENTIALS: The **Village Vanguard**, the oldest jazz club in New York; the **Blue Note**, the city's premier jazz supper club, known for mainstream acts; **Sweet Basil**, good for both straight-ahead and avant-garde jazz; the **Jazz Standard**, one of the most enjoyable of the newer upscale clubs; **Birdland**, especially known for its many fine big bands; the **Knitting Factory** and **Tonic**, meccas for jazz on the cutting edge; **Small's**, the only club in the city with jazz until dawn; **Red Blazer Hideaway** and **Swing 46**, known for traditional jazz; the **Bottom Line**, known for eclectic acts; **St. Nick's** and the **Lenox Lounge**, the best of the Harlem clubs; and **Up Over Jazz Café**, the best jazz room in Brooklyn.

THE BARGAINS: The **Zinc Bar, Village Underground, Small's, Jazz Gallery, Cornelia Street Café**, and **Arthur's Tavern** in Greenwich Village; **Tonic** on the Lower East Side; **Kavehaz** in Soho; **Detour** and the **Nuyorican Poets Café** in the East Village; **Cajun** in Chelsea; **Red Blazer Hideaway, Swing 46,** the **Jazz Foundation Jazz Jam**, and **Metropolitan Cafe** in Midtown; **Smoke** and **Cleopatra's Needle** on the Upper West Side; **St. Nick's** and **Showman's** in Harlem; and **Up Over Jazz Café** in Brooklyn.

FOR BRUNCH: **Sweet Basil, Blue Note, Cajun, Makor, Tonic** (klezmer music), the **Cotton Club** (gospel), and the **BAM Café** (gospel).

FOR DANCING: **Red Blazer Hideaway, Swing 46**, the **Cotton Club, Chicago B.L.U.E.S.,** and events sponsored by the **New York Swing Society**.

FOR BLUES: For a city of its size, New York has very little in the way of blues clubs. The only spots with blues most nights are **CHICAGO B.L.U.E.S.**, which books both national and regional talent, and **Terra Blues,** which books mostly local and regional talent. **Tribeca Blues** offers blues three or four nights a week. The **B. B. King's Blues Club & Grill** is an enjoyable venue but books much less blues than its name implies.

ONE-NIGHT STANDS: A number of clubs feature weekly events that draw enthused audiences of regulars. On Mondays: the Sugar Hill Quartet and vocalists' jam at **St. Nick's,** the Roy Campbell jazz jam at the **Lenox Lounge**, Roy

Affif and guitar jazz at the **Zinc Bar,** Les Paul at **Iridium**, the **Jazz Foundation Jazz Jam**, and Woody Allen at the **Café Carlyle**. On Tuesdays: Dave Kolker and blues loosely defined at the **Baggot Inn**. On Wednesdays: Ray Vega and Latin jazz at **Kavehaz**. On Thursdays: the Mingus Big Band at **Fez Under Time Café** and Chris Washburne and the Syotos band playing Latin music at the **Nuyorican Poets Café**. On Sundays: the Chico O'Farrill Big Band at **Birdland**.

FOR JAZZ

Greenwich Village

Village Vanguard, 178 Seventh Ave. S. at 11th St., 212–255–4037, www.villagevanguard.net.

A narrow staircase leads down, down into a dark wedge-shaped room filled with rickety tables. Along the walls, at odd angles, hang fading pictures of the greats—Thelonious Monk, Gerry Mulligan, Dexter Gordon—while up front is a crowded stage with a few battered chairs and a big piano.

Welcome to the private musical world of the Village Vanguard—still the best jazz club in New York. For sixty-odd years, this tiny club, once run by the legendary, now deceased jazz impresario Max Gordon, has seen them all come and go. There was Miles Davis—"He was always tough," Gordon once said. "Always full of his own juice"; John Coltrane—"A very shy man, very much involved with his work"; Charles Mingus—"One time he was looking for an advance and I didn't have it. He ripped the front door off the hinges and threw it down the stairs." There was also Dinah Washington, who insisted on performing in a big blond wig, and Sonny Rollins, who simply disappeared one night after playing a superb first set and never came back.

Gordon, born in Lithuania, moved to New York from Oregon in 1926, planning to attend Columbia Law School. Instead, six weeks later, he was down in the Village, where, he later said, he'd been headed ever since setting foot in New York.

The Vanguard, opened in 1934, started out as a simple hangout for writers and artists, but Gordon soon began booking such then unknown talent as Leadbelly, Josh White, the Weavers, Lenny Bruce, Eartha Kitt, Woody Guthrie, Woody Allen, and Burl Ives. Later, in the mid-fifties, he started specializing in jazz, and since then virtually every major musician has played here, from Thelonious Monk to Chick Corea.

Today, the Vanguard is the oldest jazz club in New York, and it's always filled with a mix of jazz-loving New Yorkers, tourists from the heartland, and enthusiastic foreigners, who sometimes come here right off the plane. Now operated by Gordan's wife, Lorraine, who's long had input into the place (she was responsible for Monk's first booking here), it still features all the greats, from Clark Terry and Lou Donaldson to Geri Allen and Cyrus Chestnut. Cutting-edge sounds are seldom heard at the Vanguard, however; the emphasis is on jazz of the '40s and '50s. Meanwhile, the Vanguard Jazz Orchestra (formerly the Mel Lewis Big Band) has been jamming at the Vanguard every Monday night for close to 30 years.

Music: nightly. *Cover/minimum:* $$$. Reservations recommended.

The Blue Note, 131 W. Third St. near Sixth Ave., 212–475–8592, www.bluenote.net.

Much of the time, the Blue Note, New York's premier jazz supper club, is an annoying place: commercial, expensive, crowded. Sometimes, though, the atmosphere is just right. This is most likely to occur at a late show during the week, when the crowd level is down and the intimacy level is up.

The Blue Note, a large rectangular place all done up in glitzy blues with mirrors (there's even a souvenir room upstairs), is known for its upscale mainstream sounds. Many of the biggest names in jazz have played here, including Chick Corea, Dave Brubeck, the Modern Jazz Quartet, Lionel Hampton, Nancy Wilson, Ray Brown, and Max Roach, along with newer stars such as Kevin Mahogany and Nicholas Payton. Mondays are often reserved for up-and-coming talents, and Sundays feature a jazz brunch.

A well-kept secret is the club's after-hour jam sessions, usually run by Charles Blenzig & Friends, which begin after the last set on Fridays and Saturdays, and last until 4 A.M. There's no additional cover for patrons already in house; $ for newcomers.

The Blue Note operates two sister clubs in Japan and one in Los Angeles, and is co-owner of the new B. B. King Blues Club & Grill in Midtown (see "For Blues," below). The club also broadcasts live shows on the Internet and has its own record label, Half Note Records.

Music: nightly. *Cover/minimum:* $$$–$$$$, Tu–Su; $$, M; $, after-hours. *Food:* American. Reservations recommended.

Sweet Basil, 88 Seventh Ave. S. between Grove and Bleecker Sts., 212–242–1785, www.sweetbasil.com.

One of the most wonderful things about Sweet Basil is that it's not predictable. One night the sounds will be straight-ahead, the next night things will be more experimental—Dewey Redman, Pharoah Sanders, Hammiet Bluiett, and the

Jason Lindner Big Band are among the many top names who have recently played here. The club also hosts more foreign jazz musicians (especially from Japan) than any other joint in town, and on the weekends, there are jazz brunches featuring the Ilhan Ersahin Quartet (Sa) and Chuck Folds & Friends (Su) for no cover.

Another wonderful thing about Sweet Basil is that it's a good, comfortable place, intimate but not too intimate, crowded but not too crowded, with lots of light-colored pine and brick. Jazz photos hang from the walls; candles flicker on the tables. There's a small bar near the back, and a section built out onto the street for diners.

Started up 30 years ago as a natural foods restaurant whose owner soon added jazz to the menu, Sweet Basil's is now under Japanese ownership. Numerous albums have been recorded here, and Gil Evans, during the last five years of his life, led his orchestra here every Monday night. Those sessions were legendary, with the rock star Sting, who'd recorded with Evans, so taken with the master that he often came down to listen and occasionally sit in. Nowadays, Monday nights are devoted to the Spirit of Life Ensemble, a 17-piece Afro-Cuban jazz orchestra.

Music: Tu–Su. *Cover/minimum:* $$$, nights; $ for brunch. *Food:* continental. Reservations recommended.

Small's, 183 W. 10th St., near Seventh Ave., 212–929–7565, www.smallsjazz.com.

The music starts at about 10 P.M. and often lasts until dawn at this small, subterranean, candlelit club usually overflowing with young musicians. There's no real stage, just a performance area cleared around a battered baby-grand, along with a clutch of small tables, benches lining exposed brick walls, and a bar where only water, ice tea, lemonade, and coffee are served. Guests wishing to consume alcohol must bring their own.

Since starting up in 1994, Small's has become something of a Village institution. The only place in the city where jazz can be heard eight hours or more a day, it 's both a kind of school for up-and-coming musicians and late-night hang for addicted jazz fans. Scheduled musicians play in the earlier hours of the evening and morning, while jam sessions open to all begin at around 3:30 A.M. The $10 cover is good for all night.

Music: nightly, 10 P.M.-dawn. *Cover:* $$.

Arthur's Tavern, 57 Grove St., near Seventh Ave., 212–675–6879.

Housed in a building dating back to the early 1800s, Arthur's has been a jazz joint since the 1940s. Tiny and dark, with a beaten-up wooden bar and lots of Christmas-tree lights, it once saw the likes of Charlie Parker and Wild Bill Davison on its stage. Nowadays the place is home to various Dixieland bands and to the Grove Street Stompers, a traditional band that's played here since 1961.

The Stompers, who play on Monday nights, are an enthusiastic six-piece band of both professional and "avocational musicians" (one's a commercial artist, another's in finance) led by piano player Bill Dunham (in real estate). The band's players have changed over the years, but the gig hasn't, and it's the longest-running same club, same night, same band act in the city.

Music: nightly. *No cover.*

55 Bar, 55 Christopher St. near Seventh Ave., 212–929–9883.

Two doors down from what was once the Lion's Head, a famed hang-out for writers (now a generic bar), is the 55 Bar, an old dive that dates back to Prohibition. Regulars at this tiny hole-in-the-wall that's reached by descending three well-worn steps include guitarist Mike Stern and drummer Jim Mason. One of the bar's trademarks is its free popcorn, and its jazz jukebox, filled with old classics, is the best in town.

Music: nightly. *Cover/minimum:* $-$$.

Village Underground, 130 W. Third St., near Sixth Ave., 212–777–7745.

Located directly across from the Blue Note, this newcomer has promise. A long, spare, rectangular room that's both no-frills and hip-elegant, it sports a glittering bar along one wall, with many simple booths and wooden tables scattered around. A basement space with a brightly painted sarcophagus at its entrance, the club books a wide variety of music. Mark Whitfield and his jazz band are regulars (with luminaries such as Chico Freeman sometimes sitting in) and on Thursdays, there's blues. Sundays are singer-songwriter nights.

Music: nightly. *Cover:* $.

Zinc Bar, 90 W. Houston St., bet. La Guardia Pl. and Thompson St., 212–477–8337.

This tiny basement space, located at the bottom of a steep set of stairs, is *the* place in which to hear guitar jazz in the city, thanks to the Ron Affif Trio, who plays here most Mondays. The group often showcases special guests, and star guitarists such as George Benson have been known to stop by. Other nights are devoted to Brazilian jazz, world music, and jazz vocalists. Get here early, as the place fills up fast.

Music: nightly. *Cover:* $-$$.

The Bottom Line, 15 W. Fourth St., at Mercer St., 212–228–6300, www.bottomlinecabaret.com.

Known for its eclectic booking, the Bottom Line is a big, comfortable Village institution, filled with a crowded sea of tables. The range of talent that has performed here is mind-boggling: Dr. John opened the place in 1974 with Stevie Wonder sitting in late that night to jam; Bruce Springsteen, then just on the cusp of fame, played a legendary five-night stand in 1975; and Dolly Parton was at the club in 1977, in a concert that drew both Andy Warhol and John Belushi. Then, too, there's been Patti Smith, Lou Reed, the Talking Heads, Graham Parker, Elvis Costello, Prince, and Suzanne Vega; and Miles Davis, B. B. King, Muddy Waters, George Benson, Grover Washington Jr., John Mayall, and Robert Cray. Nowadays, the club features jazz and blues only a few times a month.

Music: most nights, some jazz/blues. *Cover:* $$–$$$. *Food:* burgers, pizza, etc. Reservations recommended on weekends.

Knickerbocker Café, 33 University Pl., at Ninth St., 212–228–8490.

A place for the "novice jazz listener" is the way management bills this historic restaurant with its heavy mahogany bar, brass railings, Hirschfeld drawings, and 28-ounce Porterhouse steaks, and that seems a fair assessment, although some top people, usually in the form of piano-bass duos, can be caught here. Harry Connick, Jr., played here for two years for no cover before going on to win fame and fortune at the Algonquin Hotel.

Music: W–Sa. *Cover:* $. *Food:* American.

Also

Poetry readings, new writings, new theater, and much jazz come to the long white-brick-walled basement of the **Cornelia Street Café** (29 Cornelia St., bet. Bleecker St. and Sixth Ave., 212–989–9319, www.corneliastcafe.com) most every night of the week. Now over 20 years old, the café features a little bit of many things, including vocalists, bebop, and Latin jazz. The food here (contemporary American) is also quite good.

Gonzalez y Gonzalez (625 Broadway, bet. Bleecker and Houston Sts., 212–473–8787) may be a rather ordinary-looking Mexican restaurant, but some top-notch Latin bands appear here W–Su. Most play pure salsa, but occasionally, jazz sounds have been known to sneak in.

Jazz artists influenced by hip-hop sometimes play at **The Cooler** (416 W. 14th St., bet. Ninth Ave. and Washington St.,

212–229–0785), a club housed in a former meat locker in the Meatpacking District on the western edge of Greenwich Village. **Fat Cat** (75 Christopher St., at Seventh Ave., 212–675–6056) is a large, basement-level pool hall with jazz most nights, 10 P.M.–4 A.M., often courtesy of the bands that play Small's (see above). The **Corner Bistro** (331 W. 4th St., at Jane St. and Eighth Ave., 212–242–9502) is a dark pub with creaky wooden booths, some of the best burgers in the city, and an excellent jazz jukebox.

Elsewhere Downtown

The Knitting Factory, 74 Leonard St., bet. Broadway and Church St., 212–219–3006, www.knittingfactory.com.

Back when it opened in 1987, the Knitting Factory was considered to be just another quirky downtown music venue—albeit always a highly interesting one. Now, it's meta-morphosed into KnitMedia, a mega-entertainment conglomer-ate encompassing clubs in New York, Hollywood, and Berlin; music festivals and conferences; record labels and Web sites, and a nationally syndicated radio show. Nonetheless, the New York club has never lost its hip, iconoclastic, avant-garde edge, and remains one of the best places in the city in which to hear cutting-edge jazz and alternative music. Among the many names affiliated with the place over the years are John Zorn (who now plays mostly at Tonic, below), Bill Frisell, Don Byron, James "Blood" Ulmer, the Lounge Lizards, Wayne Horvitz, Doug Douglas, Steve Lacy, Elliott Sharp, Vernon Reid, Sonic Youth, and Skeleton Key.

Housed in its own narrow-ish building in once-industrial Tribeca, the Knitting Factory offers three floors of music. Larger acts play on the main stage on the ground floor—a medium-sized room, sometimes set up with chairs, with a bal-cony up above—while lesser known acts appear in three inti-mate rooms in the basement and subbasement. All the stages feature state-of-the-art sound systems and are flanked by small bars, while near the entrance is a bar-only room with KnitMedia CDs for sale. On any given night, three, four, or even more musical events take place at the club; usually, each has a separate cover fee ranging from $5 to $20.

Music: nightly. *Cover*: $-$$$.

Tonic, 107 Norfolk St., bet. Delancey and Rivington Sts., 212–358–7501, www.tonicnyc.com.

Cavernous and raw, eclectic and downtown, Tonic also presents jazz that is experimental and cutting edge, but in a much less commercially developed venue. Each month a different artist—John Zorn, Arto Lindsay, Ikue Mori, Susie Ibarra—creates his or her own series, bringing in various groups to perform before a discerning audience of hipsters. Among those who've appeared here recently are the Either/Orchestra, Lonnie Plaxico, Ken Vandermark, Cecil Taylor, and Marty Ehrlich. Surprise celebrities such as Laurie Anderson and Yoko Ono also occasionally show up.

The club's huge main room is very dark, with only a few lights, a high stage framed by a red curtain, a motley collection of tables and chairs, and a metal bar that looks like it belongs in an industrial kitchen. Downstairs is tucked a cozier bar where deejays and electronic music are featured; to one side here loom large wooden wine vats because before Tonic was Tonic, the building housed the Kedem Kosher Winery.

On Sundays, Tonic offers a klezmer brunch. Adjoining the main music room is Soft Skull Shortwave, a bookshop selling CDs and music books, many published by alternative presses. *Music*: W-Su. *Cover*: $$.

Fez Under Time Café, 380 Lafayette St., at Great Jones St., 212–533–2680, www.feznyc.com.

One of the most unusual jazz events in the city, the gathering of the Mingus Big Band, takes place every Thursday in a basement club located deep inside the Time Café. For one of those odd, inexplicable reasons, the weekly concert (now over eight years in this venue) had became a hip downtown happening, a place to see and be seen, whether a person has ever heard of Charles Mingus or not. The 16-piece band, playing the bluesy, rambling, sometimes cacophonous, and often astonishing music of the late composer puts on a good show, and though those at the door can be snooty, even downright rude, the room is casual and comfortable. Often in attendance is Sue Mingus, the musician's fourth wife, who first assembled the big band in 1991.

Note: The Charles Mingus Orchestra, a more classically arranged version of the big band, plays Friday nights in the Granite Room at City Hall, an upscale restaurant in the Financial District (131 Duane St., 212–227–7777).

Music: Th. *Cover*: $$$. *Food:* upscale pizza, burgers, simple contemporary entrees. Reservations recommended.

S.O.B.'s, 204 Varick St., at Houston St., 212–243–4940, www.sobs.com.

What began as a Brazilian nightclub ("Sounds of Brazil") has since become a multiethnic sort of place that emphasizes "tropical music" (African, Caribbean, reggae, Latin, hip hop). Jazz can also be heard at this stylish club-restaurant outfitted with straw huts, bamboo, and fake palm trees; it ranges from Latin (Eddie Palmieri, Gato Barbieri) to South African (Hugh Masekela) to American (Gil Scott-Heron). Most of the bands are dance-oriented, and there's a small dance floor that's almost always packed with beautiful bodies. On "La Tropica Monday" nights, a salsa band performs; free salsa dance lessons are offered before the show.

Music: M–Sa. *Cover/minimum:* $$$-$$$$. *Food:* "Tropical." Reservations for dinner only.

The Jazz Gallery, 290 Hudson St., near Spring St., 212–242–1063.

Former social anthropologist Dale Fitzgerald opened this second-story jazz gallery in 1995 on the premise that jazz is more than just music—it's an entire culture, encompassing many other arts. Now chartered as a museum, the gallery presents many first-rate exhibits—including the recent Smithsonian show, "Seeing Jazz"—serves as a classroom for New York University's jazz programs, and presents live jazz anywhere from one to four times a week.

The intimate gallery is long and thin, with a grand piano at one end, glasses of wine for sale at the other, and many rows of metal folding chairs in between. The piano once belonged to Paul Desmond and was bequeathed to the gallery—temporarily at least—after the demise of Bradley's (see "Landmarks and Legends," page 142). Another piano, this one once owned by Carmen McCrae, is in back.

Roy Hargrove was the first jazz artist to play the gallery and has played here many times since, along with Randy Weston, Chucho Valdez, and John Hicks. The gallery also sponsors several on-going series, including "Heartsong" (jazz vocalists), "Jazz Cubano," and "Strings that Swing" (jazz and guitar duos). Cover charges are surprisingly reasonable.

Music: varies. *Cover:* $$.

Kavehaz, 123 Mercer St., bet. Prince and Spring Sts., 212–343–0612, www.kavehaz.com.

Hungarian for "Coffee House," Kavehaz is a large, friendly cafe/lounge filled with overstuffed sofas and armchairs, tables and chairs. To one side is a small bar and pastry case, to another, a wide informal stage. Many of the musicians who play here are young and/or up-and-coming, but on Wednesdays, the great trumpet player Ray Vega—who played with Tito Puente before his death—takes to the stage.

Somewhat European in feel, Kavehaz serves a mix of exotic coffees, desserts, alcoholic beverages, and light entrees. The cafe/lounge is also an art gallery, with exhibits that change every month.

Music: nightly. *Cover/minimum:* $$.

Nuyorican Poets Café, 236 E. Third St., bet. Aves. B and C, 212–505–8183, www.nuyorican.org.

A long-time center for the spoken word—and best known for its poetry slams—the Nuyorican Poets' Café is also home to the longest-running Latin jazz session in the city. It happens every Thursday night, compliments of Chris Washburne and the Syotos band, featuring Ray Vega on trumpet and Bobby Sanabria on bongos and percussion. Now in its sixth year, the swinging, smoking event packs an appreciative crowd of regulars into this spare, high-ceilinged space, with its long worn bar, exposed brick walls, and simple tables and chairs. Every Sunday, too, a different Afro-Cuban band performs, making the Poets' Café Manhattan's premier venue for Latin jazz.

Note: The great trumpet player Lee Morgan was fatally shot just down the block from the Nuyorican Cafe, at 242 E. Third St., now a plumbing and heating supply store.

Music: Th, Su. *Cover*: $.

Detour, 349 E. 13th St., at First Ave., 212–533–6212.

This tiny neighborhood bar, with its cheery neon beer signs and single strand of Christmas-tree lights, is a popular East Village hang that's known for its jazz. Every night of the week, favorite local players appear on a crowded makeshift stage, while on Sundays, drummer Mike Magilligan hosts the "Jazz Spot," featuring various special guests.

Music: nightly. *Cover/minimum*: $.

Joe's Pub, 425 Lafayette St., bet. E. Fourth St. and Astor Pl., 212–539–8777, www.joespub.com.

Tucked into one end of the grand, imposing building now known as the Joseph Papp Public Theater is classy Joe's Pub. It is housed in a 19th-century edifice that was once home to the Astor Library and evidence of those stately days seem to be everywhere—in the pub's high ceilings, in its towering indoor columns, even in its muted orange lighting and comfortable black leather chairs.

An imaginative variety of jazz and blues artists usually perform at the pub four or five times a month, along with a wide variety of other musicians. Among those who have played here recently are vocalist/comedian Kurt Elling, South African jazzman Abudullah Ibrahim, jazz vocalist Patricia Barber, Brazilian jazzman Ze Luis, and Mali bluesman Boubacar Traore. The pub also features a "Piano + Series" that showcases some jazz and New Orleans R&B, along with pop, classical, and experimental.

Music: varies. *Cover*: $$-$$$. *Food*: contemporary American.

Steve Wilson blows away the
night at the Jazz Standard.

Courtesy Jazz Standard

Cajun, 129 Eighth Ave., at 16th St., 212–691–6174.

Traditional jazz and Dixieland bring the regulars back again and again at this brightly lit, boisterous place with the red-checked tablecloths, long wooden bar, and no cover charge (though an entrée or its equivalent must be ordered if sitting at a table). The quality of the music varies from night to night; come when clarinetist Joe Muranyi, banjo player Eddy Davis, or stride piano player Chuck Folds play.

Music: nightly, Su brunch. *No cover; minimum at tables.*
Food: Cajun.

Also

Though primarily a rock club, the long, dark **Mercury Lounge** (217 E. Houston St., near Essex St., 212–260–4700), featuring an antique wooden bar and excellent sound system, hosts the occasional hip jazz act. Housed in the sleek, pricey SoHo Grand Hotel is the equally sleek and pricey **Caviarteria** (310 W. Broadway, bet. Canal and Grand Sts., 212–925–5515), a restaurant/lounge that offers jazz on some weekday nights. The comfortable **C-Note** (157 Ave. C, at 10th St., 212–677–8142), a modern bar/lounge, often hosts jazz bands on Sunday afternoons. The big, stylish, high-ceilinged **Metronome** (915

Broadway, at 21st St, 212–505–7400) offers tasty Mediterranean food, big-band dancing, and some jazz.

Midtown

The Jazz Standard, 116 E. 27th St., bet. Park and Lexington Aves., 212–576–2232, www.jazzstandard.com.

Off the beaten jazz and tourist tracks is the expansive Jazz Standard, one of the city's most enjoyable jazz rooms. The sound system is superb, the staff exceedingly friendly, the ambience elegant yet laid-back, and the food, first-rate. All the top venerable names in jazz—Billy Higgins, David Newman, Harold Lands—play here, along with such younger stars as Jason Moran, Greg Osby, and Eric Reed. Latin jazz is featured on occasion, and a big band—courtesy of the likes of Maria Schneider—often plays on Monday nights.

Also one of the largest jazz clubs in town, the Jazz Standard is a maroon-and-deep-green basement space with muted cylindrical lights. The stage is at one end—with a piano picked out by MJQ pianist John Lewis—a small bar at the other, and lots of tables and chairs in between. Upstairs from the club is a fine-dining restaurant where lesser-known combos perform; often featured on drums here is the club/restaurant's owner, James Polsky.

Music: nightly. *Cover*: $$$-$$$$. *Food*: New American.

Birdland, 315 W. 44th St., bet. Eighth and Ninth Aves., 212–581–3080, www.birdlandjazz.com.

Once located in crowded quarters on the Upper West Side, Birdland has since stretched out to occupy this large, sophisticated, Theater District club/restaurant filled with white tablecloths, flickering candles, and discreet black-and-white photos on gray walls. The tables are arranged on three slightly rising tiers, while near the entrance is the bar, outlined around the top with a thin red neon line. Sight lines are excellent.

Birdland presents a regular line-up of some of the best big bands in the city. Not to be missed is Chico O'Farrill's Afro-Cuban Jazz Big Band, playing on Sunday nights, followed by the Toshiko Akiyoshi Jazz Orchestra featuring Lew Tabackin on Mondays, and the Duke Ellington Orchestra on Tuesdays. Wednesdays and some early evenings (Tu, W, F, 5:30–7:30 P.M.) are usually devoted to lesser-known artists (Friday's Lou Anderson All-American Big Band is especially worth catching), while Thursdays through Sundays feature top names. Among those who have performed here recently are Stanley Jordan, Christian McBride, Wallace Roney, and Andrew Hill.

Music: nightly. *Cover/minimum*: $$-$$$$. *Food*: Contemporary American.

Jazz Foundation Jazz Jam, 322 W. 48th St., bet. Eighth and Ninth Aves., 212–245–3999, www.jazzfoundation.org.

In the heart of the Theater District is the musicians' Local 802, housed in an ordinary office building. Ever Monday night, however, the not-so-ordinary happens here—a free jazz jam that usually attracts more musicians than fans. Sometimes the performing talent is top notch, sometimes it's only fair, but either way, the weekly sessions are always lively, friendly, and interesting, with jazz artists exchanging both musical ideas and shoptalk.

The jams take place on the building's ground floor, in an institutional-looking room filled with fluorescent lights, an American flag, and rows of metal folding chairs. There's a sign-up list in back, a high stage up front. Among the better-known musicians who've played here are Monty Alexander, Billy Taylor, Benny Powell, Harold Mayburn, and Irene Reid.

The sessions are sponsored by the Jazz Foundation of America, a non-profit institution that helps out musicians in need, with funding from the Mary Flagler Cary Foundation. The jazz foundation was founded in 1989 by Herbert Storfer, Billy Taylor, and Ann Ruckert, and anyone can join for a basic membership fee of $25. The money goes directly towards aiding musicians.

Music: M, 7:30–10 P.M. *No cover.*

Swing 46, 349 W. 46th St., bet. Eighth and Ninth Ave., 212–262–9554, www.swing46.com,

One of the best places in the city for traditional jazz, Swing 46 is a well-lit, old-fashioned, drinking-man–friendly type of place that presents mostly big bands playing swing and jazz. Come when George Gee and His Make Believe Orchestra perform—featured are recent Grammy nominee Carla Cook and soloists Lance Bryant and Cleave Guyton. Free dance lessons are offered every night at 9:15 P.M., and on Tuesdays in the early evening, there's a "jazz piano jam."

Music: nightly. *Cover/minimum*: $$. *Food*: American.

Red Blazer Hideaway, 32 W. 37th St., bet. Fifth and Sixth Aves., 212–947–6428.

Another haven for traditional jazz, the Red Blazer also presents much big-band swing, along with some Dixieland. San Rubin's Big Band has been playing the club in one or another of its various incarnations for years and years; other regulars include Sam Ulano (now over 80) and his Jazz Band, the Felix Swing Band, the Alan Russell Big Jazz Band, Simon Wettenhall's Oceanic Dixieland Band, and Bob Cantwell's Dixie & Swing Band.

Music: M-Sa. *Cover/minimum:* $$. *Food*: Italian, continental. Reservations recommended.

Also

Midtown is the place to catch the best cabaret in the city. The **Oak Room** at the Algonquin Hotel (59 W. 44th St., tel. 212–840–6800) is a gracious, elegant spot where jazz-influenced singers occasionally perform. On Friday and Saturday nights, the **Carnegie Club** at Carnegie Bar and Books (156 W. 56th St., 212–957–9676), presents everything from Frank Sinatra impersonators to big bands. The **Firebird Café** (365 W. 46th St., 212–586–0244), a posh Russian restaurant in the heart of the Theater District, often features jazz duos and vocalists.

Big bands with names such as the Flipped Fedoras and Crescent City Maulers perform most Friday and Saturday nights at **The Supper Club** (240 W. 47th St., 212–921–1940), a sleek 1940s–style club all done up in blue.

Upper East Side

Café Carlyle and **Bemelmans Bar**, Hotel Carlyle, Madison Ave. at 76th St., 212–744–1600.

High society's favorite jazzman Bobby Short has been playing at the posh Café Carlyle for over 30 years now, making two appearances annually, one in the spring, one in the fall. At other times, other classic cabaret acts such as Eartha Kitt perform, while on Mondays, Eddy Davis and His New Orleans Jazz Band blow Dixieland away. Featured during the jazz band's first set is Woody Allen on clarinet—come early to get a good seat.

The Carlyle is an elegant, intimate, cocoonlike place with pink tablecloths, low red lights, ever-so-discreet waiters and ever-so-high prices. Delicate Vertes murals that evoke bygone splendours line the walls, while just across the hall is Bemelmans Bar, a similarly outfitted place usually featuring solo piano artists.

Music: Tu–Sa. *Cover:* $$$$ ($ for Bemelman's Bar). *Food:* bistro continental. Reservations required.

Also

The **Metropolitan Café** (959 First Ave., bet. 52nd and 53rd St., 212–759–5600) is a steakhouse with some first-rate jazz, often compliments of studio musicians, on Tuesdays and Sundays; expect to see many other jazz musicians in the audience.

Upper West Side

Iridium, 48 W. 63rd St., 212–582–2121, www.iridiumjazzclub. com.

It's been compared to the land of Dr. Seuss, this upscale basement club kitty corner to Lincoln Center, thanks to its stocking caps (made of glass) hanging from the ceiling, curvy columns, and cave-like walls. Some of the world's top straight-ahead talent—Charlie Haden, Phil Woods, Abbey Lincoln, Ahmal Jamal—perform here regularly, but alas, the club's ambience does not match its whimsical decor. Prices are exceedingly steep and the staff can be rude. Still, the sound system and food are quite good.

Due to its location, the club attracts a mix of mostly well-heeled tourists and working musicians, who stop by here before or after their Lincoln Center shows. Guitar wizard Les Paul plays every Monday night, often to sell-out crowds; Pat Metheny and George Benson are among those who've stopped by to hear him perform.

Music: nightly. *Cover*: $$$$. *Food*: contemporary American.

Smoke, 2751 Broadway, bet. 105th and 106th St., 212–864–6662, www.smokejazz.com.

Small, cozy, and easy-going elegant, with candlelit tables, lots of dark wood, and heavy red curtains framing a tiny stage, Smoke is largely a haven for bebop—though more avant-garde types also play here. Thursdays are usually devoted to piano players, Fridays and Saturdays to quartets and quintets, Mondays to jam sessions, and Tuesdays to organ players—the latter as a tribute to the late Charles Earland. Earland was the one who first inspired Smoke's co-owner, West Berliner Paul Stache, to open a jazz club.

Among the many top musicians who've played here are Von Freeman, Lonnie Smith, Benny Golson, Freddie Hubbard, George Coleman, Leon Parker, Jackie Terrasin, and Jessie Davis. The club has good acoustics and sight lines, and attracts a mostly New York crowd. Cover prices are surprisingly reasonable.

Music: nightly. *Cover*: $$-$$$.

Also

Although primarily a Spanish language school, **El Taller** (2710 Broadway, at 104th St., 212–665–09460), often presents excellent Latin jazz on Friday and Saturday nights. The comfortable **Cleopatra's Needle** (2485 Broadway, at 94th St., 212–769–6969) is a seafood and Middle Eastern restaurant that has been featuring solid jazz performers every night of the week for years and years.

Since opening in February 2000, the **Rose Center for Earth and Space,** the state-of-the-art planetarium at the Museum of Natural History (Central Park West at 81st St., 212–769–5100, www.amnh.org) has produced a welcomed surprise: "Starry Nights," showcasing serious jazz. Nationally known musicians such as Jimmy Heath, Lou Donaldson, David "Fathead" Newman, or Steve Turre perform in the planetarium's soaring, all-glass atrium Fridays from 6–8 P.M.; tasty, albeit pricey, food and drink is for sale.

Museum admission, which includes the jazz concerts, is adults/$10, students and seniors/$7.50, and children/$6.

Harlem

St. Nick's Pub, 773 St. Nicholas Ave., at 149th St., 212–283–9728.

This small neighborhood joint, a few steps down from the street, has recently become one of the best places in the city in which to hear swinging jazz. Come on a Monday night when the Sugar Hill Quartet, run by sax player Patience Higgins, leads a smoking jam session showcasing top-notch vocal talent. Everyone from James Carter to Stevie Wonder has been known to stop by; "so many sweet faces in the house," the emcee calls out.

The narrow club, with its low stucco ceiling, features a bar to one side, a clutch of simple tables and chairs to another, and an informal step-up stage in back. Red lights glow from above the bar while three efficient bartenders bustle to and fro, one with a lit cigar hanging from his mouth.

The club is run by Ms. Alloway, a.k.a. Berta Indeed, who often shows up in the latter part of the evening. The audience is usually an equal mix of uptown New Yorkers, downtown New Yorkers, and foreign tourists, who arrive by the busload.

Music: W-M. *Cover/minimum*: $.

Lenox Lounge, 288 Lenox Ave., bet. 124th and 125th Sts., 212–427–0253.

The floors swirl with colored mosaic tiles, the walls sport elegant glass-finned lights, and the ceilings shine with dark polished leather. There's a Zebra Room in back, complete with black-and-white hide walls, and a bar in front, flanked by windows engraved with flowers and twirls.

Welcome to the Lenox Lounge, one of the classiest jazz rooms and the sole surviving Art Deco club interior in New York. The 1939 lounge was completed restored to the tune of $600,000 in early 2000, and now glows with the same spit, polish, and glamour that it did back in the days when Billie Holiday and Billy Eckstine were regulars here.

The bar is currently owned by Alvin Reed, Sr., a retired policeman who grew up in the neighborhood, and his son, Alvin Reed, Jr. Jazz is featured in the Zebra Room four nights a week, but unfortunately, it's often a formalized affair aimed at attracting downtowners and tourists (paying $5–15 covers), while the neighborhood clientele remains seated at the bar out front. On Mondays, there's a jazz jam run by trumpeter Roy Campbell, and on Thursdays, bands play blues and R&B to an often-packed house for no cover. Tuesdays are gay nights—the action then doesn't begin until midnight.

Music: Th-M. *Cover*: $-$$. *Food*: American.

Showman's, 375 W. 125th St., at St. Nicholas Ave., 212–864-8941.

With a history that dates back to 1942, Showman's has long been a mainstay of jazz in Harlem, as well as a gathering spot for the neighborhood's power elite. At one time, the club was located right next door to the Apollo and all the greats performing there used to stop by after the show: Count Basie, Lionel Hampton, Dizzy Gillespie, Nat "King" Cole.

Recently relocated once again, Showman's today is a neat, simple, congenial place presenting jazz most nights. Everyone knows everyone here, and there's a great sense of continuity in the air as the club fills up with musicians, tap dancers (the club was once home to the famed Copacetics), men and women relaxing after work, downtowners, and—once or twice a night—busloads of foreign tourists who stay for 45 minutes or so and then leave.

Regulars at the club include Jimmy "Preacher" Robins, Lonnie Youngblood, and Bobby Forrester. Come on a Thursday night when tap dancers and jazz musicians perform for an older crowd dressed in crisp dresses, three-piece suits, and fedoras.

Music: M-Sa. *Cover*: none, two-drink minimum.

The Sugar Shack, 2611 W 139th St., 212–491–4422.

Downtown meets uptown at the Sugar Shack, a Harlem club outfitted with a Soho-esque décor—overstuffed sofas and chairs, an open kitchen serving smothered chicken and candied yams, and a small stage flanked by kente cloth. Jazz musicians usually perform on Friday and Saturdays nights, while Wednesdays feature open-mike poetry readings.

Music: F-Sa. *Cover*: $. *Food*: Southern.

Gishen Café, 2150 Fifth Ave., at 132nd St., 212–283–7699.

Back in 1934, this site was the first black-owned bar to be issued a liquor license post-Prohibition. Sixty-odd years later, Fekadu Boressau has renovated the place into a tidy Ethiopian restaurant with exposed brick walls and lots of wood. Saxman David Murray inaugurated the club in August 1999, and it now offers jazz on Thursdays, Fridays, and some Saturdays in the earlier part of the evening, an Ethiopian band on Fridays and Saturdays at 1 A.M. But this schedule is subject to change—call ahead.

Music: Th-Su. *Cover*: none-$. *Food*: Ethiopian.

Cotton Club, 666 W. 125th St., between Broadway and Riverside Dr., 212–663–7980.

Dining and dancing, jazz, blues, and gospel, are mainstays at the Cotton Club, a nicely outfitted place complete with a cozy balcony overlooking the bandstand and portraits of jazz greats. The Cotton Club Allstars, a swing dance band, usually performs on Monday nights, while the Melvin Sparks Blues Band takes to the stage on Thursdays and Sundays, and jazz vocalist Ann Sinclair often performs on Fridays and Saturdays. A popular gospel brunch is featured on Sundays.

Throughout the week, expect to find lots of visitors arriving by tour bus here. Covers include an all-you-can-eat buffet.

Music: Th-M, Sa-Su gospel brunch. *Cover*: $$-$$$$. *Food*: American. Reservations recommended for brunch.

Also

Perk's Fine Cuisine (553 Manhattan Ave., at 123rd St., 212–666–8500) is a long and narrow restaurant with white tablecloths, attached to an equally long and narrow bar. On Wednesdays and Thursday, a jazz, R&B, and calypso band plays here; weekends feature a deejay.

The spare and elegant **Londel's Supper Club** (2620 Frederick Douglass Blvd., at 139th St., 212–234–6114) offers jazz along with fine dining on Fridays and Saturdays.

Brooklyn

Up Over Jazz Cafe, 351 Flatbush Ave., at Seventh Ave. (Park Slope), 718–398–5413, www.upoverjazz.com.

Many first-rate musicians play in this intimate, unassuming spot situated up a creaky flight of stairs above the Wing Wagon restaurant. Among them have been Freddie Hubbard, George Coleman, Billy Harper, and Hammiet Bluiett, making this Brooklyn's top club for jazz.

The friendly, sound-proofed cafe is simply laid out, with only a handful of blond-wood tables and chairs, a bar serving everything from herbal teas to mixed drinks, and a makeshift stage with a baby grand, framed by a deep green curtain. Proprietor Robert Myers, whose brother owns the restaurant downstairs, greets guests at the door while employees fetch orders of buffalo wings and chicken fingers for hungry patrons. Mondays are reserved for jazz jams led by Vincent Herring, while Thursdays usually feature vocalists.

Music: Th-M. *Cover*: $$-$$$. *Food*: buffalo wings, etc.

Also

In Bedford-Stuyvesant, find **Sista's Place** (456 Nostrand Ave., at Jefferson, 718–398–1766), a cozy, intimate spot that's both a coffeehouse and a cultural center. Jazz is featured on Saturday nights; among the regulars is trombonist Curtis Folks.

In Williamsburg, **Pete's Candy Store** (709 Lorimer St., bet. Richardson and Frost Sts., 718–302–3770) is a popular local hangout that sometimes features jazz. Among the regulars is the Howard Fishman Quartet, playing a combination of New Orleans jazz, blues, and swing.

Attached to Fort Greene's Brooklyn Academy of Music, world-renowned for its avant-garde theater productions, is the **BAM Café** (30 Lafayette Ave., at Ashland Pl., 718–636–4139, www.bam.org). The café presents live music, much of it jazz, Thursdays through Sundays for no cover with a $10 food/drink minimum; on Sundays, a gospel brunch is featured.

Not far from Sista's Place is **JAZZ 966** (966 Fulton St., bet. Grand Ave., and Cambridge Pl., 718–638–6910), which has been offering jazz dancing every Friday night over a decade. In Flatbush, find **Pumpkins** (1448 Nostrand Ave., 718–398–1766), presenting jazz seven days a week.

FOR BLUES

Chicago B.L.U.E.S., 73 Eighth Ave., bet. 13th and 14th Sts., 212–924–9755, www.chicagobluesnyc.com.

The city's premier blues club, Chicago B.L.U.E.S. presents an interesting mix of local, regional, and national acts. A long, dark, scruffy room usually packed with music fans, it features a wide, black bar to the front and a stage to the back, with seating areas oddly placed both in front and in back of the bands. The sound system is only mediocre and unless you're sitting directly in front of the stage, sight lines are poor. Still, this is the only club in the city where you'll hear everyone from New York–based Jimmy Vivino, Jon Paris, and David Johansen to touring acts such as Son Seals, James Cotton, and Otis Rush on a regular basis. On Monday nights, there's a blues jam, and Sundays feature swing bands (with dancing). Some rock-and-roll and funk is also presented here.

Music: nightly. *Cover*: $-$$$.

B. B. King Blues Club & Grill, 243 W. 42nd St., bet. 7th and 8th Aves., 212–997–4144, www.bbkingblues.com.

Posh, state-of-the-art, and all decked out in blue, B. B's sits smack in the heart of heavy-duty tourist territory. Nonetheless, against all odds, it's an enjoyable venue, thanks to its superb sound system, intimate stage, spacious seating arrangements, and excellent menu.

Located at the bottom of a wide, semi-circular staircase, B. B.'s is long and broad, with lots of big tables and chairs (seating capacity: 550), a spiffy mirrored bar that takes up the whole back wall, and a musical motif—notes carved into the chairs, guitar shapes swirling on the carpet. A lush red curtain frames the stage, while upstairs is a gift shop.

B. B. is part owner of the club, and plays several times each year. Otherwise, however, despite the club's namesake, blues acts come through here only a few times a month. Koko Taylor, Taj Mahal, Pinetop Perkins, and Robert Cray are among those who've appeared, but most nights feature more mainstream crowd-pleasers such as Roberta Flack, Little Feat, America, and Gregg Allman.

Music: nightly. *Cover*: $$$-$$$$. *Food:* contemporary American and continental.

Terra Blues, 149 Bleecker St., 212–777–7776.

Located deep in the heart of Bleecker Street madness (the thoroughfare is packed cheek-by-jowl on the weekends, with music blasting everywhere), Terra Blues nonetheless has its share of good blues bands. Most of those who perform are regional favorites such as Michael Powers or Moe Holmes, but better-known acts such as Mack "Guitar" Murphy or Big Jack Johnson also appear from time to time. Located upstairs, the room is all red and white, with a stuccoed ceiling, figureheads mounted on the walls, and picture windows overlooking the street.

Music: nightly. *Cover:* $.

Tribeca Blues, 16 Warren St., bet. Broadway and Church St., 212–766–1070, www.cumberlandproductions.com.

Long, high-ceilinged Tribeca Blues, complete with a big bar and tidy stage, has recently become a downtown center for blues. The New York Blues Society meets here on the first Wednesday of every month, while local favorites Kerry Kearney, Witness Protection, Jon Paris, and Poppa Chubby play the club on a regular basis. National acts such as George Porter and the Dirty Dozen Brass Band are also booked from time to time, and Wednesdays usually feature a blues jam led by Bobby Nathan.

Music: W-Sa. *Cover:* $-$$$.

Also

Numerous small bars and clubs in the city feature occasional blues shows and blues jams. The best way to find out what's happening where is to visit the **New York Blues Society** Web site at www.NYBluesSociety.org; or, call their hotline at 212–726-BLUE.

Blues very loosely defined, with a strong rock and some jazz and funk influences, comes to the **Baggot Inn** (82 W. Third St., bet. Thompson and Sullivan Sts., 212–477–0622, www.baggotinn.com) every Tuesday night, compliments of Dave Kolker and his Band, featuring the smoking saxman Isamu. An old-fashioned Greenwich Village club—of the kind now nearing extinction—the Baggot Inn is long, low-ceilinged, scruffy, and dark, with a friendly bar up front, a stage and tables in back.

Wetlands Preserve (161 Hudson St., at Laight St., 212–386–3600, www.wetlands-preserve.org) is an oddly earnest ecologically minded place offering scads of free PC literature along with acts ranging from ska and psychedelic rock to hip hop and blues. The New Orleans' Rebirth Brass Band sometimes performs here.

The rustic, peanut-shell-strewn **Rodeo Bar**, attached to the Albuquerque Restaurant (375 Third Ave., at 27th St., 212–683–6500) presents country, rock, and some blues; no cover. The hole-in-the-wall **Lakeside Lounge** (162 Ave. B, bet. 11th and 12th Sts., 212–529–8463) features mostly young rock bands but boasts a great blues jukebox.

Blues artists also occasionally perform at the **Blue Note, Village Underground, Bottom Line, S.O.B.'s, Joe's Pub, Birdland,** and **Cotton Club** (see "For Jazz," above).

Other Venues and Special Events

Jazz At Lincoln Center, 65th and Broadway, 212–258–9922 [events line] or 212–721–6500 [tickets], www.jazzatlincoln center.org.

The world's largest not-for-profit arts organization devoted exclusively to jazz, Jazz At Lincoln Center presents a whopping 450-plus jazz concerts, events, and broadcasts every year. Among them are performances at Alice Tully Hall by the Lincoln Center Jazz Orchestra, under the musical direction of Wynton Marsalis; concerts in an intimate candlelit penthouse featuring jazz piano masters; jazz films; jazz lectures; dance parties; jam sessions; a jazz series for young people, and master classes and workshops.

Scheduled to open in the autumn of 2003 is the Jazz At Lincoln Center's new home—$103-million Frederick P. Rose Hall, which will be the world's first performance, educational, and broadcast facility built exclusively for jazz. To be located at Columbus Circle (59th St. and Broadway) overlooking Central Park, the center will feature soaring 50-foot-high glass walls, a concert hall, performance atrium, jazz cafe, dance floor laid out beneath the stars, and classrooms.

St. Peter's Lutheran Church, 54th St. and Lexington Ave., 212–935–2200.

The Reverend John Garcia Gensel was pastor to the New York jazz community at St. Peter's, a big, modern sanctuary with towering ceilings and cubist colors, for over 25 years. Duke Ellington wrote a joyful tone poem in his honor, "The Shepherd Who Watches Over the Night Flock," and Billy Strayhorn donated his Steinway to the church. Musicians turned to Gensel in times of celebration and grief and he buried almost all the important jazz figures of the last few decades, including Thelonious Monk, John Coltrane, Eubie Blake, Alberta Hunter, and John Hammond. His funerals became legendary: like the New Orleans funerals of old, they were more like big musical celebrations than anything else.

The Reverend Gensel is no longer with us, but the many jazz events at St. Peter's continue, now under the leadership of the Reverend Dale Lind. Every Sunday afternoon at 5 P.M. there's jazz vespers, followed by a jazz concert at 7 P.M. Most Wednesdays September through June, 12:30 to 1:30 P.M., free jazz concerts are held in the Living Room; and every October, there's All-Nite Soul, a 12-hour jazz jam that runs from 5 P.M. Sunday to 5 A.M. Monday. All sorts of legends turn up for the All-Nite event, begun in 1970: Eubie Blake was there just before he turned 100, and Teddy Wilson appeared the year before he died.

Jazzmobile (154 W. 127th St., 212–866–4900) is a rolling bandstand, cofounded by jazz pianist-composer-educator Dr. Billy Taylor, that brings free jazz to the inner city every summer. Many of the 70-odd concerts, featuring greats such as

Jimmy Heath and Horace Silver, are held uptown, but some are presented in Midtown, Downtown, and in the other boroughs. The biggest concerts are held at Grant's Tomb (122nd St. and Riverside Dr., 212–666–1640).

Started up in 1973, **Highlights in Jazz** is the longest-running jazz concert series in the city. Now held at the Pace University Downtown Theatre (3 Spruce St., 212–346–1715; $$) September through May, the monthly event always features several first-class "official" performers and at least one surprise guest (Eubie Blake, Dizzy Gillespie, Branford Marsalis, Billy Taylor, and Stan Getz are but a few who have appeared over the years). "Sometimes I don't even know who's going to show up," says producer Jack Kleinsinger.

Major venues that frequently present jazz and blues concerts include **Town Hall** (123 W. 43rd St., bet. Sixth and Seventh Aves., 212–840–2824) and **Carnegie Hall** (154 W. 57th St., at Seventh Ave., 212–247–7800) (see "Landmarks and Legends," page 133), the **Beacon Theater** (2124 Broadway, at 74th St., 212–496–7070), **Aaron Davis Hall** at City College (138 Convent Ave., 212–650–6900), **Miller Theatre** at Columbia University (Broadway at 116th St., 212–854–7799), and **Merkin Concert Hall** (129 W. 67th St., bet. Broadway and Ninth Ave., 212–501–3330). The **Apollo Theatre** (253 W. 125th St., near Adam Clayton Powell Jr. Blvd., 212 749–5838) still offers a Wednesday "New Amateur Night at the Apollo," along with the occasional blues/R&B event (see "Landmarks and Legends," p. 127).

The **Schomburg Center for Research in Black Culture** (515 Malcolm X Blvd./Lenox Ave., at 135th St., 212–491–2200) presents frequent jazz concerts, films, and other events. The **Metropolitan Museum of Art** (Fifth Ave. and 82nd St., 212–535–7710) produces a first-rate jazz concert series every year. The **Brooklyn Museum of Art** (200 Eastern Pkwy., at Washington, 718–638–5000) hosts a variety of interesting music events, including some jazz and blues. Two churches known for their occasional jazz concerts are the **Cathedral of St. John the Divine** (1047 Amsterdam Ave., at 112th St., 212–662–2133) and **St. Mary's Episcopal Church** (521 W. 126th St., at Broadway, 212–864–4013).

The **New York Swing Dance Society** (212–696–9737) presents big-band dancing at Irving Plaza every Sunday night, 8 P.M.–midnight (17 Irving Pl., at 15th St., 212–777–6817; $$). A different band performs each week; among the regulars are George Gee & His Jump Jiving Wailers, the Roy Gerson Orchestra, and the Blue Saracens. A free hour of dance lessons is offered on the first Sunday of every month. Non-members welcome.

Giant Step (hotline: 212–714–8001, www.giantstep.net), where jazz meets rap and hip hop, is a traveling weekly event ($$), now over a decade old. As a deejay spins records, jazz musicians and rappers often take turns playing and improvising.

The **World Music Institute** (212–545–7536, www.HearThe World.org) presents a wide variety of imaginative bookings at various venues throughout the city. Since 1978, **Roulette** (228 W. Broadway at White St., 212–219–8242, www.roulette. org) has produced about 1,000 concerts by experimental composers and musicians, some of whom have been strongly influenced by jazz and blues; many of the events take place in the organization's intimate, no-frills, downtown setting. **Makor** (35 W. 67th St., 212–601–1000, www.makor.org), home to a cafe, lounge, and gallery, hosts major jazz and blues artists several times a month, along with films, lectures, classes, and events relating to Jewish culture; Sundays usually feature a jazz brunch.

Festivals

The **JVC Jazz Festival** and the **New York Jazz Festival** (produced by Knit Media/The Knitting Factory, with a corporate sponsor that changes each year) take place every June (see "Major Festivals," p. 458). The two-day **Charlie Parker Jazz Festival** (718–786–1379) is held in Tompkins Square Park in the East Village, where Parker once lived, every August. The **Village Jazz Festival** is an on-again, off-again event usually held in August; the **Central Brooklyn Jazz Festival** is a new fest that takes place in April. **SummerStage** (212–360–2777) presents many free concerts ranging from world music to jazz at the Central Park Band Shell each July through September. **Lincoln Center Out-of-Doors** (66th and Broadway, 212–875–5400) is a free performing arts festival that produces a little bit of everything, including some major players, such as Sonny Rollins. The **92nd Street Y** (1395 Lexington Ave., 212–996–1100) is known for its "Jazz in July" series. Throughout the summer, accomplished Juilliard School musicians perform free **Summergarden Concerts** at the Museum of Modern Art (11 W. 53rd St., bet. Fifth and Sixth Aves., 212–708–9480).

For more on these and many other special events—too numerous to mention—check the papers.

Record Stores

Among independent stores, the city's top shop for hard-to-find jazz records is the **Jazz Record Center** (236 W. 26th St.,

212–675–4480). The **Rainbow Music Shop** (102 W. 125ᵗʰ St., 212–864–52562) is the place to go for R&B and gospel. **Footlight Records** (113 E. 12ᵗʰ St., 212–533–1572) has a good used-CD section. **Casa Latina** (151 E. 116ᵗʰ St., 212–427–6062) is an excellent store for Latin jazz, or check out the motherlode of Latin recordings available via mail order through **Descarga** (718–693–2966, www.descarga.com).

Among chain stores, **Tower Records** (4ᵗʰ and Broadway, 212–505–1500; 66ᵗʰ and Broadway, 212–799–2500; 57ᵗʰ and Fifth, 212–838–8110), **HMV** (34ᵗʰ and Sixth, 212–629–0900; 46ᵗʰ and Fifth, 212–681–6700; 86ᵗʰ and Lexington, 212–348–0800; 125ᵗʰ and Frederick Douglass, 212–932–9616) and **Virgin Megastore** (14ᵗʰ and Broadway, 212–598–4666; 45ᵗʰ and Broadway, 212–921–1020) all have excellent selections.

Radio

WBGO/88.3 FM (973–624–8880). A 24-hour jazz station affiliated with NPR. Blues F afternoon, Sa A.M., Su night.
WKCR/89.9 FM (212–854–9290). Affiliated with Columbia University. Much jazz daily, some blues.
WQCD/101.9 FM (212–352–1019). Contemporary jazz station.

Other radio stations broadcasting some jazz and blues include **WBAI/99.5 FM, WBLS/107.5 FM, WNYC/93.9 FM,** and **WQXR/1560 AM**. Stations broadcasting big bands and nostalgia shows are **WRTN/93.5 FM, WLIM/1580 AM, WRIV/1390 AM,** and **WVNJ/1160 AM**.

Tours

Several companies offer tours of Harlem that include some of the sites described in this chapter. **Harlem Your Way!** (212–690–1687) offers daily walking tours of historic sites, as well as custom-made tours; prices start at $25. **Harlem Spirituals** (212–757–0425; www.harlemspirituals.com) specializes in visits to gospel services and soul food restaurants, but also has a night tour that includes dinner and a visit to a jazz club; prices start at $30. **Gray Line Tours** (212–397–2600; www.grayline.com) features Sunday morning gospel tours and tours of the Upper West Side, including Harlem.

Neighborhood historian Michael Henry Adams (212–281–5802) offers night tours of Harlem that begin with dinner and end with a jazz session. Val Ginter (212–496–6859), an urban historian and former jazz accordionist, conducts in-depth jazz tours of Harlem and other jazz-related neighborhoods for groups of six or more.

BOSTON

Updated by Fred Bouchard

While Boston has never been a major jazz or blues town, it has made a strong, steady contribution to the music. George Wein, the dean of festival producers (from the first Newport Festival in 1954 to a good dozen events around the country today), grew up here, attending Boston University and opening his famed Storyville in 1950, and Sonny Stitt, Dave Lambert, Serge Chaloff, and Roy Haynes were all born in Boston. Duke Ellington recruited two teenagers from the area, Johnny Hodges from Cambridge and Harry Carney from Roxbury. Others connected with the city include Pat Metheny, Paul Gonsalves, George Russell, Jaki Byard, Keith Jarrett, Cecil Taylor, and Dave McKenna, all of whom live or once lived in or near Boston. And the city is also home to the Berklee College of Music, famed for its jazz program, and the New England Conservatory of Music.

Like many other cities, Boston was red-hot during the late '40s and early '50s. At that time, the Massachusetts Avenue–Columbus Avenue area on the edge of Roxbury near the downtown was lined with six or seven different clubs, resembling a mini–52nd Street; the Hi Hat, the Savoy Café, the Big M, Wally's Paradise (now Wally's Café, see "Clubs, etc.," page 176), Estelle's, and the Pioneer. The Savoy Café at 410 Massachusetts Avenue was a short-term home to Sidney Bechet's New Orleans Rhythm Kings, who made a number of broadcasts from here in 1945, and the Hi Hat was the first club to offer bop to Boston. Charlie Parker played the Hi Hat in 1953, and sometimes, after work, he and a friend would wander around Boston Common until dawn, making birdcalls with little wooden gadgets from the Audubon Society.

The city's first major uptown club was George Wein's Storyville, which specialized in Dixieland and swing. Opening first in Kenmore Square, it later moved to the Copley Square Hotel and brought in many nationally known names, ranging in style from Wild Bill Davison and Pee Wee Russell to Count Basie and Duke Ellington.

Later, in the 1960s, there was Lennie's on the Turnpike (actually in Peabody, Mass.), which presented major artists such as Miles Davis, Charles Mingus, and Thelonious Monk; and Sandy's Jazz Revival in Beverly, which survived into the

'80s, presenting mostly mainstream acts such as Dexter Gordon, Zoot Sims, and Al Cohn. Another '60s institution was the two-sided Jazz Workshop/Paul's Mall, owned by Fred Taylor and Tony Mauriello. The Jazz Workshop was dedicated solely to serious jazz, while Paul's Mall offered up everything from soul to fusion. "We launched a lot of new artists who are superstars today," says Fred Taylor. "Herbie Hancock, Bruce Springsteen, Keith Jarrett—Keith was our house pianist when he was going to Berklee."

Also flourishing in the '60s was Club 47, a tiny Cambridge coffeehouse that was instrumental in bringing the urban blues to Middle America. Its owner, folksinger Jim Rooney, presented Muddy Waters, Howlin' Wolf, Junior Wells, Buddy Guy, and many others to a hitherto unexposed audience (along with some jazz artists) and the response was tremendous. Fans lined up around the block, and soon other coffeehouses in other cities were presenting the urban blues.

Boston—thanks in large part to nearby Providence, Rhode Island, which gave birth to Roomful of Blues and Duke Robillard, among others—continued to be known as a good blues town through the '70s and '80s. One especially legendary club, in operation up until the late '80s, was the 1369 Club in Cambridge (1369 Cambridge St.), which presented many major blues and jazz artists. A major, still-operating blues house in Providence is **Lupo's Heartbreak Hotel** (239 Westminster St., Providence, RI, 401–272–5876), which has been presenting blues and rock since the 1970s.

Sources

The weekly *Boston Phoenix* (617–536–5390, www.bostonphoenix.com) has excellent listings. Or, pick up the Thursday section of the *Boston Globe* (617–929–2000, www.globe.com/globe) or the Friday section of the *Boston Herald* (617–426–3000, www.bostonherald.com).

For maps and other information, contact the Greater Boston Convention and Visitor Bureau (617–536–4100, 1–888–SEE BOSTON, www.bostonusa.com) at Boston Common, near the State House (Park and Tremont streets), or at the Prudential Center, near the entrance to the Sheraton-Boston Hotel.

The Boston Blues Society and the New England Blues Society host Web sites at http://www.bostonblues.com and www.newenglandblues.com respectively. The Boston Blues Society also sponsors a Blues Hotline listing concert and club dates all over Eastern Massachusetts, from Newburyport to Nantucket: call 617–876–BLUE.

Monty Alexander's Yard Movement
plays Sculler's Lounge.

Fred Bouchard

A Note on Neighborhoods

Surrounded by island-studded Boston Harbor and other bays
and rivers, Boston, which was already 145 years old when the
Civil War began, can be a confusing place. Its downtown is a
jumble of crowded streets, historic buildings, and glittering
high-rises, while its outskirts are an equally confusing mass
of districts and suburban towns, all with seemingly interchangeable names. Two of these, mentioned below, are
Allston and Brookline, both located about 20 minutes west of
the harbor.

Driving in downtown Boston is difficult. There's much congestion, and parking is generally available only in expensive
lots. Two major arteries connecting almost everything are
Commonwealth Avenue, running east-west, and Massachusetts Avenue, called Mass. Ave. by locals, running north-south.

Cambridge, located on the north side of the Charles River,
is a short and easy bridge ride away from Boston proper.
Though best known for its students, who congregate around
Harvard Square, the city also houses large ethnic populations, many of whom live near Central Square. The heart of
the city's business district, Central Square is also a haven for
ex-hippies, free thinkers of all kinds, and the homeless.
Inman Square, once known for its jazz clubs (now only Ryles

is left) is just north of Central Square. Somerville is just north of that. All addresses in Cambridge are within 20 minutes of each other and street parking is usually available.

CLUBS, ETC.

Boston has two upscale hotel-based clubs that bring in national jazz (and occasional blues) talent: the **Regattabar** in the Charles Hotel and **Scullers** in the Guest Quarters Suite Hotel. **House of Blues** brings in national blues acts. Boston also has a large number of strong local clubs, and a blues jam can be found somewhere every night of the week.

Some of the top jazz musicians and bands playing in the Boston area today include vibraphonist Gary Burton; keyboard player Mark Rossi; trumpet player Tiger Okoshi and his group, Tiger's Baku; Frank Wilkins's Visions; pianists Bob Winter, Ray Santisi, and Dave McKenna; trumpet player Ruby Braff; vocalists Semenya McCord and Rebecca Parris; the Boston Jazz Orchestra; the Either/Orchestra; Orange Then Blue; the Boston Jazz Composers' Alliance; and the New Black Eagle Jazz Band. Some of the top blues artists are Roomful of Blues, Sugar Ray and the Bluetones, Luther "Guitar Junior" Johnson, Ronnie Earl and the Broadcasters, "Earring" George Mayweather, Joe Cook, and vocalist Shirley Lewis.

Generally speaking, clubs in the Boston area close at 2 A.M. though the music usually stops around 1 A.M.

Personal Choices

Best national jazz club: *Regattabar*
Best local jazz club: *Ryles*
Best historic jazz club: *Wally's*
Best national blues club: *House of Blues*
Best eclectic club: *Middle East*
Best neighborhood music bar: *Cantab Lounge*

FOR JAZZ

Regattabar, Charles Hotel, 1 Bennett St., Cambridge (Harvard Sq.), 617–864–1200, www.regattabar.com.

Housed in an upscale hotel in the heart of Cambridge, the classy Regattabar is the city's premier club for national acts. Mainstream jazz is what's usually featured (Benny Green, Ray Brown, Mark Cross), but fusion, blues, and traditional jazz are presented on occasion; top local stars appear in the early part of the week.

Located on the hotel's third floor, the Regattabar, best reached by a lighted, glass-walled elevator, is big but low-ceilinged, with lots of small, round, crowded tables. Sight lines are generally good, and the front rows are but an arm's length away from the players.

Music: Tu–Sa. *Cover:* $$–$$$. *Food:* light supper fare. Reservations recommended.

Ryles, 212 Hampshire St., Cambridge (Inman Sq.), 617–876–9330, www.rylesjazz.com.

The oldest jazz club in Cambridge and the second oldest in the Boston area, Ryles is known for its local talent. Many of the best Berklee students and professors perform here, and big names—Pat Metheny, Robben Ford, Grover Washington Jr.—make occasional surprise visits. Olga Roman, a popular local Latin vocalist who's since moved to Spain, got her start here, as did the 11-piece group, Heavy Metal Horns. Ryles presents most every kind of jazz, along with some blues and world beat, but shies away from the avant garde.

Once an Italian restaurant, Ryles is large and well lit with skinny pillars, plants, and a sea of battered wooden tables. There's a second room upstairs, smaller and windowless, that showcases somewhat lesser-known groups, while downstairs stands a great jazz jukebox, stocked with vintage 45's from the 1940s.

Currently, Ryles is presenting much Latin jazz; Wednesday is Brazilian night, and Thursday is devoted to salsa and merengue. On Sunday, there's a jazz brunch, 10 A.M.–3 P.M., and the Ryles Jazz Orchestra performs 4–7 P.M. The food's good, too.

Music: Tu–Su. *Cover:* $–$$. *Food:* American.

Wally's Café, 427 Mass. Ave., Boston (Back Bay), 617–424–1408, www.wallyscafe.com.

Wally's was there, back in the days when Mass. Ave.–Columbus Ave. was a happening thing. Originally housed in a large room across the street from its tiny current location, it was started up in 1947 by one Joseph Walcott, who used to drive a cab for Boston's Mayor Curley. The mayor helped Wally procure his first club, and soon thereafter, the young entrepreneur started presenting jazz, sometimes booking acts in conjunction with his old friend Eddie Smalls of Smalls' Paradise in New York (see "New York, Landmarks and Legends," page 122).

Once a mainstay in the African-American community, Wally's now draws a racially mixed crowd of older black neighborhood residents and fresh-faced Berklee students, who take to the stage most every night. The jazz is not always the best in town, but there's a great sense of tradition in the air. The club is a simple, brick-walled place—outfitted only with a bar and a few tables—that's now run by Wally's grandsons. A jazz jam is featured on Sunday afternoons, a blues jam on Mondays, Latin jazz on Thursdays, and bebop and modern jazz on Fridays and Saturdays.

Music: nightly. *No cover.*

Scullers, Guest Quarters Suite Hotel, 400 Soldiers Field Rd., Allston (where the Mass. Turnpike meets Storrow Drive), 617–779–4811 (jazz line) or 617–783–0090 (hotel), www.scullersjazz.com.

The Boston area's *other* major hotel club opened up in 1990, and it's a plush, cushiony affair with floral-patterned fabrics, small marble tables, mahogany walls, and a glorious view of the Charles River. The jazz is mainstream, and somewhat more sedate than that of the Regattabar: there's an emphasis on jazz legends and vocalists (Dakota Staton, Nancy Wilson, Mark Murphy, the Rippingtons), and horns are rarely heard. Local stars are presented in the early part of the week, and dinner packages are available in conjunction with the next-door Scullers restaurant, which serves international cuisine.

Music: Tu–Su. *Cover:* $$–$$$. Reservations recommended.

Middle East Restaurant, 472 and 480 Mass. Ave., Cambridge (Central Sq.), 617–497–0576, www.mideastclub. com.

A funky, well-lit restaurant with arched windows and lots of hanging plants, the storefront Middle East has been something of a community center for left-leaning Central Square for over three decades now. For the past fifteen or so years, it's also been known for an eclectic, often cutting-edge booking policy that presents everything from grunge rock and ethnic music to jazz and blues.

The Middle East has three music rooms, all of which operate most nights. Also on the ground floor is a back room equipped with long tables where smaller groups perform. Downstairs is a remodeled bowling alley that often hosts name acts, including some avant garde jazz and cross-over groups.

Music: nightly, some jazz and blues. *Cover:* $–$$. *Food:* Middle Eastern.

Les Zygomates, 129 South St., Boston, 617–542–5018, www.winebar.com.

This snazzy French bistro and wine bar, quixotically named for the facial muscles that help one smile, has featured jazz regularly since it opened in 1995. Small bands play on a cozy, raised dais, sometimes accompanied by a singer. Excellent wines are served by the glass, and every Tuesday there are wine tastings at 6 and 8 P.M. (cost: $25).

Music: M-Sa. *No cover. Food:* French bistro.

Wonder Bar, 186 Harvard St. (at Commonwealth Ave.), Allston, 617–351-COOL.

Sleek and sophisticated, this attractive bistro/jazz bar offers live music seven nights a week. "No sneakers or hats" is the door policy; candles flicker everywhere. A rotating roster of local jazz groups perform, including the Joe McMann Experience, the Wayne Escofry Trio, the Johnny Chronicle Chronicles, and the Rusty Scott Quartet. But the club's original tin roof, combined with a din of conversation, sometimes makes the music difficult to hear.

Music: nightly. *No cover. Food:* bistro French-American.

Ritz Roof, Ritz-Carlton Hotel, 15 Arlington St., Boston (Back Bay), 617–536–5700.

Prior to 1946, the "Ritz Roof" was known throughout Boston as an elegant eatery where one could dine and dance the night away while listening to the likes of Artie Shaw, Benny Goodman, and Tommy Dorsey. Then came World War II, when too many GI's were getting drunk on the rooftop to suit the Ritz-Carlton's taste and image, and on top of that the building was hit by a destructive hurricane. The restaurant was shut down, apparently for good.

In 1993, however, the "Ritz Roof" reopened and once again there is dining and dancing beneath the stars, compliments of local big bands. Note: The Roof may be closed for renovations during the summer of 2001.

Music: F–Sa, seasonal. *Cover:* $$. *Food:* New England, seafood.

Also

The Good Life (26 Kingston St., Boston, 617–451–2622) and **The Good Life Cambridge** (720 Massachusetts Ave., Cambridge, 617–868–8800) offer classic cocktails, tasty food, and easy-going jazz in snazzy, old-fashioned lounges.

The local jazz trio The Fringe plays Monday nights at the hip **Lizard Lounge** (1667 Mass. Ave., btwn. Harvard and Porter Sqs., Cambridge, 617–547–0759), complete with wooden church pews and dim red lights.

Bob the Chef's (604 Columbus Ave., Boston, 617–536–6204), a mellow bistro serving modern-style soul food, offers a jazz brunch on Sundays, and jazz duos, trios, and quartets Wednesdays through Saturdays.

Located on the 52nd floor of the Prudential Building, the **Top of the Hub** (800 Boylston St., Boston, 617–536–1775, www.topofthehub.com) is an old Boston standby offering great views of the city, along with small jazz combos that are often quite good. Singers are often featured, and there's also a full restaurant, good wine list, and small dance floor. Reservations recommended.

Cutting-edge jazz artists can be heard about once a month at **Johnny D's** (see "For Blues," below).

FOR BLUES

House of Blues, 96 Winthrop St., Cambridge (Harvard Sq.), 617–491-BLUE, www.livemusic.com.

Opened in 1992, this first of a now-national chain is housed in a historic wooden building which dates back to the 1800s. Painted blue and white on the outside and packed with blues memorabilia and Southern folk art on the inside, the House of Blues is a sort of upscale urban jukejoint, or "juke mansion," as its owners like to call it.

The ground floor is a restaurant, with rough-hewn wooden booths, blue-checked tablecloths, and video monitors describing various blues artists as their recordings come over the loudspeakers. Upstairs is the music room, with a state-of-the-art sound system, a peaked wooden ceiling, and more exquisite folk art (but few seats, a serious drawback when the place gets crowded). In the basement is a shop selling posters, books, T-shirts, and House of Blues leather jackets. You can bet Robert Johnson never saw anything like this.

The House of Blues was the brainchild of Isaac Tigrett, the man who started up the Hard Rock Café in London in 1971. Tigrett, who grew up in Memphis, has been a blues devotee ever since he worked as a chauffeur for Furry Lewis and Bukka White.

But the Boston House of Blues is more than just a club. It's also a foundation whose mission is to educate and raise cultural awareness. Groups of schoolkids are brought through here regularly to learn about the blues, African-American folk art, and Southern culture. And perhaps because of that, and its historic home, this venue has thus far evaded the irksome "corporate" feel of some of the chain's other locations.

The club usually features local and regional artists at the beginning of the week and national artists on the weekends. A gospel brunch is featured on Sundays.

Music: nightly. *Cover:* $–$$$. *Food:* Southern, American.

Cantab Lounge, 738 Massachusetts Ave., Cambridge (Central Sq.), 617–354–2685.

A worn and friendly neighborhood bar that attracts everyone from students to locals, Asian Americans to African Americans, the Cantab offers live music nightly, much of it compliments of veteran R&B/bluesman Joe Cook. Cook, who usually plays Thursdays through Saturdays, belts it out mean and good on local hits such as "Down at the Cantab" and "Sexy Lady from the Beauty Shop, You Make My Heart Go Bip-Ber-de-Bop." Wednesdays and Thursdays are blues jams, Monday is open-mike for folk music, and Tuesday is open mike for bluegrass. A variety of local bands are also booked into the club's downstairs room, the Third Rail.

Music: nightly. *Cover:* $-$$.

Midway Café, 3496 Washington St. (near Williams St.), Jamaica Plain, 617–524–9038.

A square-shaped neighborhood bar with scuffed wooden floors and a step-up stage, the Midway has an easy, laid-back, off-the-beaten-track feel. Located in a part of J. P. that's half blue-collar, half artists/writers/musicians, it features blues, R&B, or rock-a-billy most nights of the week. Tuesday is an open jam and Thursday is "Dyke Night." The bar dates back to 1934, when it catered to the workers of the Boston Gas Company, then situated across the street.

Music: Tu–Su. *Cover:* $.

The Plough & Stars, 912 Massachusetts Ave., Cambridge (bet. Central and Harvard squares), 617–492–9653.

Named after a play by Sean O'Casey, the Plough & Stars is a Cambridge institution, a small and well-lit Irish pub that's always packed to the bursting point with students and locals, professors and office workers, writers and would-be writers, talking, talking, talking. During the day, the place serves a stick-to-the-ribs pub lunch, while at night, music is featured. Most of it is rock-and-roll, but there's occasional blues as well. On weekend afternoons, soccer matches from England are shown. Madeline Hall & the Rhythm Hounds is the bar's regular blues act.

Music: W-Su, some blues. *No cover. Food:* pub fare.

Johnny D's Uptown Restaurant and Music Club, 17 Holland St., Somerville (Davis Sq.), 617–776–9667, www. johnnyds.com.

Run by a mother-daughter-son team, Johnny D's is a large and square-shaped neighborhood place, with a big dance floor and a step-up stage. Comfortable booths line some of the walls, and there's a friendly bar at the back.

National acts playing a wide variety of music—funk, Latin, country, rock, reggae, blues, jazz, folk—alternate with local bands playing the same. On Sundays there's a blues jam from 4:30 to 8:30 P.M.; cutting-edge jazz is featured about once a month.

Music: nightly, blues on Su. *Cover:* $–$$. *Food:* American.

Harper's Ferry, 158 Brighton Ave., Allston, 617–254–9743. Concert line: 617–254–7380.

When it comes to character, Harper's Ferry hasn't got it. A modern, cavernous place that feels more like a college cafeteria than a club, it's dominated by a huge rectangular bar and filled with young athletic-looking types on the make. The stage is stuck way down at one end, making the music seem like an afterthought, even though the musicians are often first-rate. Rick Russell, the Stovall Band, and Heavy Metal Horns are regulars.

Music: nightly. *Cover:* $–$$.

Redbones, 55 Chester St., Somerville (Davis Sq.), 617–628–2200.

Local blues, zydeco, and rock-a-billy acts play most nights at this loud, sometimes raucous restaurant serving barbecue and grilled foods. Upstairs is a Southern-style dining room and bar, downstairs is "Underbones," an often-teeming bar. Featured on the drink menu is a wide range of New England microbrews.

Music: nightly. *No cover. Food:* barbecue, etc.

Also

Blues can also be heard at the **Black Horse Tavern** in the Faneuil Hall Marketplace (340 Faneuil Hall, Boston, 617–227–2038), and in some of the jazz clubs mentioned above. Among them are **Les Zygomates**, **The Good Life** (especially the Cambridge location), **Regattabar**, and **Scullers**.

Other Venues and Special Events

The Berklee College of Music presents frequent faculty-student concerts at the **Berklee Performance Center** (136 Mass. Ave., Boston, 617–266–7455). The concerts are open to the public. The **New England Conservatory of Music** also presents some jazz at Jordan Hall (30 Gainsborough St., 617–536–2412).

Nationally known jazz and blues figures can occasionally be heard at **Symphony Hall** (301 Mass. Ave., Boston, 617–

266–1492), home of the Boston Symphony Orchestra. The **Charles Ballroom** at the Charles Hotel sometimes brings in big names, and tries to book them in some sort of meaningful conjunction with acts appearing in its Regattabar (Stan Getz and Astrud Gilberto, Gary Burton and Pat Metheny).

In addition to the **Boston Globe Jazz Festival** and the **Newport Jazz Festival** (see "Major Festivals," page 458), the Boston area hosts the **Bell Atlantic Jazz Festival**.

The **Museum of Fine Arts** (465 Huntington Ave., Boston, 617–267–9300) holds periodic jazz/blues concerts, in its Courtyard and Remis Auditorium. The **Isabella Stewart Gardner Museum** (2 Palace Rd., Boston, 617–566–1401), an exquisite Venetian palace, does the same, in its Renaissance music room.

For more information on these and other special music events, check the local papers.

Radio

WGBH/89.7 FM (617–300–2000). Affiliated with NPR. Jazz Su–Th, 7 P.M.–12 A.M. and 12–6 A.M. Blues F–Sa, 9 P.M.–2 A.M.
WHRB/95.3 FM (617–495–4818). On the Harvard University campus. Jazz weekdays, 6 A.M.–1 P.M.
WMBR/88.1 FM (617–253–4000). Affiliated with MIT. Jazz M–Th, 2–6 P.M. Blues Sa, 12–2 P.M.
WERS/88.9 FM (617–578–8890). Affiliated with Emerson College. Jazz M–F, 11 A.M.–2 P.M. Blues, Sa P.M.
WBUR/90.9 FM (617–353–2790). Affiliated with Boston University. Jazz F, 11 P.M.–5 A.M.

Record Stores

Most of the best jazz and blues music shops are located in liberal-minded, student-oriented Cambridge. **Stereo Jack's** (1686 Mass. Ave., Cambridge, 617–497–9447) specializes in jazz and blues, new and used, and has many well-informed radio hosts on staff. Two major chain stores, **HMV** (1 Brattle Sq., Cambridge, 617–868–9696) and **Tower** (360 Newbury St., Boston, 617–247–5900) both have extensive J&B departments.

There are scads of shops devoted to used recordings. Among the best are **Cheapo** (645 Mass. Ave., Cambridge, 617–354–4455), **Disc Diggers** (401 Highland Ave., Somerville, 617–776–7560), and **Looney Tunes** (1106 Boylston St., Boston, 617–247–2238; and 1001 Mass. Ave., Cambridge, 617–876–5624). **Skippy White's** (538 Mass. Ave., Cambridge, 617–491–3345) is especially good for blues and R&B.

PHILADELPHIA

Updated by James G. Spady

Philadelphia's musical roots—in gospel, in soul, in rock and especially in jazz—run strong and deep. Over the past 100 years, the city, which was home to one of the earliest pre–Civil War communities of free African Americans, has produced some of the finest jazz musicians in the world. Dizzy Gillespie lived here as a boy, John Coltrane as a young man, Bessie Smith as a mature artist. McCoy Tyner graduated from West Philadelphia High School; Archie Shepp and Stanley Clarke graduated from Germantown High School; David Amram spent his childhood in nearby Feasterville; and Lee Morgan grew up in North Philadelphia. Then there were the Heath brothers (Jimmy, Percy, and "Tootie"), Philly Joe Jones, Jimmy McGriff, Ethel Waters, Bill Doggett, Red Garland, Sunny Murray, Sonny Fortune, Benny Golson, Bobby Durham, Bobby Timmons, Kenny Barron, Jabbo Smith, Jimmy Oliver, Mickey Roker, Grover Washington Jr., Shirley Scott, Sun Ra, Trudy Pitts, Jamaladeen Tacuma, Gerald Veasley, Stanley Clarke, Monette Sudler, Leslie Burrs, Jymie Merritt, Mtume Heath (Jimmy Heath's son), Kevin Eubanks, Rosetta Tharpe, and many others, all of whom lived in the city at one time or continue to live there.

Sam Wooding was one of the first jazz musicians from Philadelphia to receive international acclaim. Born into a rich 19th-century cultural community in South Philadelphia (an area made famous through Dr. W. E. B. DuBois' classic sociological study, *The Philadelphia Negro*, 1899), Wooding evinced an early interest in the entertainment field. He became the first African-American musician to take a jazz orchestra out of the United States, the first American to make jazz records in Europe, the first to play jazz in the Soviet Union, and the first jazz artist to tour South America. Although jazz trumpeter Clifford Brown was Sam Wooding's best-known student, other musicians like Doc Cheatham, Jimmy Harrison, Sid Catlett, Bobby Martin, Willie Lewis, Percy Johnson, June Cole, and others played in his band.

Frankie Fairfax was a legendary figure in Philadelphia during the 1930s and '40s. Not only was he an active jazz musician, but he also succeeded in organizing the Black Musician's Union Local #274. The Black Musicians Union Hall was a central meeting place and job referral center in Philadelphia, just as it was in New Orleans, Chicago, and St. Louis.

During the 1920s and '30s, Philadelphia's African-American nightclubs centered around South Street (see "Landmarks and Legends," page 185). There were the Dunbar, the Lincoln, and the Standard, big theaters featuring name talent, along with numerous taverns and nightclubs. But it was from the '40s to the '60s that the city, along with New York, became one of the most significant centers for jazz in the country. Some of Philadelphia's most important clubs, including Pep's Musical Bar, the Blue Note, Watts Zanzibar, the Showboat, the Downbeat Club, the Red Rooster, and the Aqua Lounge were operating at that time, attracting musicians from all over the country.

Of these clubs, none played a greater role in fomenting the city's bop revolution than the North Philly club Watts Zanzibar (from which today's Zanzibar downtown takes its name), located at 1833 W. Columbia Ave. (now named Cecil B. Moore Avenue, in honor of the black attorney and 1960s Civil Rights leader). Watts Zanzibar was recognized as the bop spot and home of modern African-American culture. Sonically and sartorially hip, it both nurtured and reflected bop ethics and aesthetics. The very name reflected the old and the new: Africa and America. Two brothers, Richard and Robert Watts, served as proprietors of the club, which featured everyone from Slam Stewart, Illinois Jacquet, Philly Joe Jones, Ben Webster, Ike Quebec, and Charlie "Yardbird" Parker to Charlie Ventura, George Auld, and Arnett Cobb.

In the mid-'50s, Miles Davis came to Philadelphia to pick three of the four musicians (Philly Joe Jones, Red Garland, and John Coltrane) for his famed quintet, and during that same era, major musicians developing the "hard bop" style—Clifford Brown and Richie Powell among them—were living and working in town. Philadelphia is also known for its long line of great saxophonists, including John Coltrane, Jimmy Heath, Sonny Fortune, Archie Shepp, Odean Pope, and many others.

Sources

Both the *City Paper* (215–735–8444, www.cpcn.com) and the *Philadelphia Weekly* (215–563–7400, www.phillyweekly.com) have excellent listings. Other sources are the Friday sections of the *Philadelphia Inquirer* (215–854–2000, http://web. philly/content/inquirer), *Philadelphia Daily News* (215–854–2000, www.dailynews.philly.com), and *Philadelphia Tribune* (215–893–4050, www.phila-tribune.com).

The key Web site for jazz info in Philly is www.phillyjazz. org. WXPN deejay Jonny Meister hosts a blues Web site at www.bluesnet.com.

For maps and other information, contact the Philadelphia Visitors Center, 1525 John F. Kennedy Blvd. (215–636–1666, www.phillyvisitor.com).

A Note on Neighborhoods

With a population of 1.6 million, Philadelphia is the fifth largest city in America. Laid out in four quadrants, each with its own park, its heart is Old City Hall. Market Street divides the city into east and west, and Broad Street divides it into north and south.

The Old City is an historic neighborhood just north of Market Street, where Betsy Ross and Benjamin Franklin once lived; Northern Liberties is a former industrial neighborhood, now undergoing restoration, located just north of that. Society Hill, also near the downtown, is a restored cobblestoned area filled with fashionable restaurants and shops, while lower South Street is Philly's answer to Greenwich Village. Germantown is a residential neighborhood 20 minutes north of downtown.

Driving and parking in Philadelphia are difficult. Be prepared for much congestion and high parking fees.

Landmarks and Legends

(With the exception of the last two sites, all of the locations below are situated in or near the downtown and can be toured on foot.)

South Street, Tenth to 17th streets.

From the 1920s through the '50s, South Street was the main artery of black Philadelphia, and many of the city's most important theaters and nightclubs were located on or near it. Among the top spots were the Dunbar Theater, near 15th Street, where Sidney Bechet and Bessie Smith once starred together—and perhaps had a love affair—in a show called *How Come?;* Gibson's Standard Theater at 12th Street, where a then unknown Duke Ellington was playing just before he was hired by New York's Cotton Club; the Paradise Theater at Fitzwater and 16th streets; the Lincoln Theater and the Showboat at Broad and Lombard streets; and Pep's Musical Bar at Broad and South, where everyone from Dinah Washington to Yusef Lateef once performed. Of the above, only the Paradise Theater (now a housing project for the elderly) and the Showboat are still standing.

Showboat, 1409 Lombard St., near Broad St.

Back in the 1950s, this somber gray building was the site of the famous Showboat, where Coltrane, Dizzy, Monk, Jamal, Miles, Getz, and Rollins all performed. Across the street from the Showboat, in what is now a parking lot, was the Lincoln Theater, a major early 20th-century venue for African-American entertainers.

Kater Street

Bennie Moten wrote his "Kater Street Rag" about this tiny street that runs east-west, parallel to South Street, from the Delaware River to the Schuylkill. Ethel Waters lived here when it was a red-light district, and Bessie Smith purchased homes for her family here. Dizzy Gillespie also lived on Kater at one time.

Bessie Smith's family's home, 1147 Kater St.

Bessie Smith bought this now-abandoned house and the one nearby at 1143 Kater (no longer standing) for her family when she moved them up from Chattanooga, Tennessee, to Philadelphia in 1926. Her husband, Jack Gee, was reportedly not at all happy with the idea of having her family so close, but Bessie apparently appeased him by buying him a Cadillac for $5,000—an enormous sum at the time—for which she paid cash. She wanted her sisters and their children near her, partly, at least, to help her care for her adopted son, Jack, when she was out of town.

Academy of Music, Broad and Locust streets.

The opulent nineteenth-century Academy, styled after La Scala in Milan, is one of the finest theaters in Philadelphia. Built in the mid–1850s to the tune of $240,000, it stood roof-less for one year, exposed to the elements, so that its walls would "settle."

Concerts of all types are put on at the Academy, and it was here that, quite accidentally, Coltrane first heard Bird. He and Benny Golson had gone to the Academy to catch Dizzy Gillespie, as Golson recalls in *Chasin' the Trane,* when "this short, squat guy in a pin-stripe suit stepped on stage. The band took the break and he started playing alto while coming out of a crouch. John just sat there, taking it all in. . . . Imagine being a saxophonist and never having heard this kind of music before."

Stars honoring Philly musicians stud the Broad Street sidewalk outside the building. Among those so honored are John Coltrane, Dizzy Gillespie, Bessie Smith, Marian Anderson, and Pearl Bailey.

The Earle Theater, now demolished,
was to Philadelphia what the Apollo is
to New York.

Frank Driggs Collection

Earle Theater, SE corner of 11th and Market streets.

The famous old Earle Theater, where everyone from Jack Teagarden to Louis Armstrong performed, once stood at this corner, and it was here that Lucky Millinder, who had a propensity for firing people (see Crystal Caverns, page 221), gave Dizzy Gillespie two weeks notice. "He just fired me," Dizzy writes in his autobiography *To Be or Not to Bop,* "and I don't know what his actual reasons were. He didn't have a reason. . . . He just had this firing syndrome."

Dizzy didn't let his notice bother him. Instead, during his last week with the band, he played his heart out until Lucky, impressed, called him to his dressing room and said to forget about the firing, he'd like him to stay. Diz said he was sorry, but no, he already had another job lined up. Lucky promptly offered him a five-dollar-a-night raise. "That was unheard of, man!" Dizzy writes, "I already had a salary of eighteen dollars a night. . . ."

Another musician, jazz bassist Nelson Boyd, recalls: "There was a joint down on 11th Street in back of the Earle Theater between Chestnut and Market. The club was called the Downbeat. It was upstairs over a restaurant. That's where a lot of cats met. During that time Jimmy Golden, Jimmy Oliver, Charlie Rice and the lime cat called 'Shrimp Anderson' played bass. I was still in high school. Matt Sigel was the owner of the Downbeat. I went over there and played one night. Segal dug that I was into jazz. He was nice about it. He said, 'You can come in, but don't drink.' I used to go there every day."

Post Office and **Old Court House,** Ninth and Market streets.

A lovely Art Deco building with bas-relief sculptures depicting "Justice" and "The Law," the Old Courthouse now houses a rather sleepy-looking state superior court. Back in the 1940s, however, it was home to the intimidating federal courthouse, where Billie Holiday (who had just been playing the Earle Theater) was arraigned on May 27, 1947, for the concealment of narcotics.

Billie, broke and acting without a lawyer, pleaded guilty and was sentenced to a year and a day in the Federal Reformatory for Women at Alderson, West Virginia. The sentence was insignificant compared to what the verdict meant—that she could no longer work the New York clubs. A city regulation forbade the issuance of cabaret cards to anyone convicted of a felony. The press also treated her badly, and one leading radio station banned her records from the air.

Holiday found refuge at Sis Nottingham's, a safe house in South Philadelphia that drew many African-American musicians. The living room had a piano; Duke Ellington and others visited frequently.

John Coltrane's home, 1511 N. 33rd St. (20 min. NW of downtown).

This three-story red-and-brown wood framed house with dormer windows and a peaked roof was Coltrane's home throughout most of the '50s. Today, it's still the residence of his cousin, Mary Alexander, for whom he composed "Cousin Mary."

Coltrane moved to N. 33rd Street in 1951, following a stint on the road with Dizzy Gillespie. He had decided to spend a year at home with his family in order to attend music school and get the formal training he felt he lacked. Enrolling in the Granoff School of Music, he studied theory, saxophone, and classical music, taking weekend playing jobs whenever he could.

Today, Mary Alexander has established a children's music workshop in the building next door to number 1511. Eventually, she also hopes to raise enough funds to restore the house and open it to the public.

Bessie Smith's grave, Mt. Lawn Cemetery, 84th St. and Hook Rd., Sharon Hill (near the airport), 215–586–8220.

When Bessie Smith died in 1937, following a car accident in Clarksdale, Mississippi (see "Riverside Hotel," page 63), all of black Philadelphia turned out to pay her homage. Her days of prosperity were long over by then, but thanks to an insurance policy, she was buried in a grand metallic coffin trimmed in gold and lined with pink velvet. Her beloved adopted son was absent from the funeral because her estranged husband, Jack Gee, driving down from New York, had found no room for him in the car.

Bessie's funeral cost approximately $1,000 but her insurance policy did not cover the cost of a headstone, and her grave went unmarked for 33 years. During that time, Columbia Records made a handsome profit on her reissues, and the funds raised by two benefits held to finance a tombstone mysteriously disappeared (some said into the pockets of Jack Gee).

It took a Philadelphia housewife, Mrs. Barbara Muldow, writing a letter to the *Philadelphia Inquirer*'s Action Line in 1970, to make Bessie's headstone a reality. Reporter Frank Coffey followed up on Mrs. Muldow's letter by contacting Janis Joplin, an outspoken Bessie admirer, and Mrs. Juanita Green, a registered nurse and owner of two nursing homes who had worked for Bessie as a girl. Between the two of them, according to Chris Albertson in *Bessie*, the women pledged enough to buy a $500 tombstone.

Today, Bessie's stone, dark and solemn, sits proudly in a small African-American cemetery on the outskirts of Philadelphia. The epitaph reads: "The greatest blues singer in the world will never stop singing. Bessie Smith. 1895–1937."

Open: M–F, 9 A.M.–4 P.M., Sa, 9 A.M.–noon.

CLUBS, ETC.

For a grand old city of music, Philadelphia has very little in the way of jazz and blues clubs. Only two clubs present jazz full time: **Zanzibar,** the city's premier club for local and national acts, and **Ortlieb's,** which features mostly local artists. Two cultural organizations, the **Painted Bride** and the **Philadelphia Clef Club of Jazz and Performing Arts** also present national artists on occasion. The city's premiere blues club is **Warm Daddy's**.

Some of the best-known musicians living in Philadelphia today include pianist Shirley Scott; saxophonists Bootsie Barnes, Odean Pope, and Jimmy Oliver; drummer Mickey Roker, and blues great Sonny Rhodes. Other jazz players well worth catching include pianist Dave Burrell; keyboard player

Trudy Pitts; drummers George "Butch" Ballard and Ralph Peterson, Jr.; violinist John Blake; vibraharpist Khan Jamal; guitarists Jimmy Bruno and Monette Sudler; Bayard Lancaster, known by his friends as "Mr. Philadelphia Jazz" because of his love for the city; bagpipe player Rufus Harley; the pop-jazz-funk Posmontier Brothers; vocalist Evelyn Sims; and bass players Gerald Veasley, Jamaaladeen Tacuma and Jymie Merritt. Other blues players include Steve Guyger, the Dukes of Destiny, Little Red Rooster, Crosscut Saw, and Blues Deluxe.

Most bars and clubs remain open until 2 A.M.

Personal Choices

Best jazz club: *Zanzibar Blue*
Best jazz restaurant: *Prime Steak*
Best neighborhood club: *Bob & Barbara's*
Best jazz jams: *Natalie's, O'Hara's*
Best blues club: *Warm Daddy's*

FOR JAZZ

Zanzibar Blue, 200 S. Broad St., at Walnut (Center City), 215–732–4500, www.zanzibarblue.com.

A warm and lively upscale restaurant in the old Bellevue Stratford Hotel, Zanzibar is Philly's premier jazz club. A small place filled with mahogany wood, red tablecloths, and the club's signature cobalt-blue drinking glasses, it presents both first-rate local talent and national jazz stars. Among the artists who've performed here recently are David "Fathead" Newman, Hugh Masakela, Gerald Veasley, Norman Connors, Jean Cam, and Charles Fambrough. WJJZ, a smooth jazz station, broadcasts live from the club every Sunday, during a popular jazz brunch.

Music: nightly. *Cover*: $$-$$$$. *Food*: International.

Ortlieb's Jazz Haus, 847 N. Third St. (Northern Liberties), 215–922–1035.

Once the lunch hall of a large brewery, Ortlieb's still feels like an old-fashioned German gasthaus, complete with mounted animal heads, beer advertisements, rotating fans, and heavy wooden tables and chairs. The building itself is long and narrow, because before it was a lunch hall, it was a bowling alley.

Among the regulars here are Mickey Roker, Sid Simmons, Bootsie Barnes, Terell Stafford, and Orrin Evans, and there

Stanley Clarke
celebrates summer
at a Penn's Landing
Festival.

Leandre Jackson

are weekly jam sessions led by the "Haus" band. It's all a bit
predictable, but reliable as well, and sometimes known out-
of-towners (Sonny Rollins, Frank Morgan) playing the area
stop by. Ortlieb's is run by Pete Souders, a former Sun Oil
executive who also often plays sax with the band, and his
wife, Margaret, who was once a nurse.

Music: Tu–Su. *Cover:* none–$. *Food:* Cajun American.

Prime Rib, 1701 Locust St. (Center City), 215–772–1701,
www.theprimerib.com.

This popular restaurant, housed in the historic Warwick
Hotel, has a classic supper-club ambience, complete with black
lacquered walls, leopard-skin rugs, and black leather chairs.
With seating for about 220, it features a delightful jazz duo—
Kenny Gates on piano and the legendary Jymie Merritt on
bass—nightly. The restaurant was recently awarded the "Best
Steaks" prize in Philadelphia magazine's "Best of Philly" issue.

Music: nightly. *No cover. Food:* steaks, etc. Jackets
required after 5:00 P.M.

Chris' Jazz Cafe, 1421 Sansom St. (downtown, bet. Broad and 15th streets), 215–568–3131.

A friendly, wood-paneled bistro serving "Southwestern cuisine with an Oriental flavor," Chris' is home to a number of talented Philadelphia-based musicians, including Charles Fambrough and John Swana. The café is housed in an old three-room building all done up in green, with green tablecloths, walls, and ceilings.

Music: M-Sa. *Cover*: $-$$. *Food*: Southwestern, Oriental.

Bob & Barbara's, 1509 South St. (near downtown), 215–545–4511.

A vibrant neighborhood bar, Bob & Barbara's is long and narrow, dominated by a huge red-padded bar and lots of blinking Christmas-tree lights. The popular organist Nate Wiley plays here regularly, and many local jazz musicians stop by to jam with him on weekend nights. Their music, hot and bebop, bursts out into the deserted, sometimes not-so-safe streets, while inside, a bartender moves slowly to and fro below a lowered ceiling.

Music: M, F–Sa. *No cover.*

Natalie's Lounge, 4003 Market St. (University City), 215–222–8633.

Most Saturdays for close to two decades, Natalie's, a smallish, neighborhood club with lots of booths and tables and chairs, has been holding some of the best jam sessions in the city. Among the jazz artists who've played here recently are Carol Harris and Arpeggio Jazz Ensemble.

Music: Sa. *No cover.*

O'Hara's Fish House, 39th & Chestnut Sts., 215–349–9000.

In recent years, O'Hara's has gained a reputation for featuring jazz groups. Located near the University of Pennsylvania, it's a '50s-style place filled with comfortable booths and an easy-going ambience. A variety of local talent plays here on a rotating basis, and the house hosts frequent first-rate jazz jams.

Music: Th-Sa. *No cover. Food*: Seafood, burgers, etc.

Also

Not far from Bob & Barbara's, and similar to it in spirit, is **L2** (2201 South St., 215–732–7878), a neighborhood bar on historic South Street that presents much local jazz. There is no cover.

Philly has a number of restaurants that feature local jazz artists. Among them are **San Marzano** (1509 Walnut St.,

215–564–3562), a popular Italian restaurant downtown, and **Saint Jacks** (45 South 3rd St., 215–238–9353), a bar/restaurant in historic Old City Philadelphia that offers "global ethnic cuisine" and jazz bands on Monday nights. The **Meiji-En Restaurant** (Marine Ctr. and Columbus Blvd., downtown, 215–592–7100) is a Japanese restaurant that's especially known for good jazz. Regulars here include Trudy Pitts and Mr. C—long-time players on the local scene.

The lounge of the **Sofitel Hotel** (120 S. 17th St., 215–569–8300) presents jazz Thursdays through Sundays, often compliments of the consummate player Bill Meek, Jr. The **Swami Lounge** in the Four Seasons Hotel (1 Logan Sq., 215–963–1500) offers jazz on Fridays and Saturdays, often compliments of the Rosetta Washington Quartet.

Top Shelf (56th & Market Sts., West Philadelphia, 215–748–4245) is a neighborhood lounge that features live jazz on Saturdays from 5–9 P.M. Many top local groups are in the lineup; there is no cover charge.

Morgan's (17 E. Price St., Germantown, 215–844–6067), one of Philly most prestigious African-American clubs, no longer has the jazz lineup it once did, but still presents jazz on occasion. Housed in a 19th-century building surrounded by trees, the club features a long, handsome listening room lined with comfortable booths.

FOR BLUES

Warm Daddy's, 4 Front St., at Market (downtown), 215–627–8400, www.warmdaddys.com.

The premier club in the city for local, regional, and national blues acts, Warm Daddy's is an upscale restaurant-club that attracts a mix of Philly residents and tourists. Regulars include Georgie Bonds and Keisa Brown; national acts such as Koko Taylor, James Cotton, Easy Scott, and Big Jack Johnson come through about once a month. Every Tuesday night, there's an open blues jam.

Music: Tu-Su. *Cover*: $-$$. *Food*: Southern.

Tin Angel, 20 S. Second St. (downtown), 215–928–0770, www.tinangel.com.

Mostly a singer-songwriter haven presenting only acoustic musicians, the Tin Angel does feature blues musicians such as John Hammond on occasion. Long and narrow, the second-story club is equipped with a dropped tin ceiling, and tapestries and "pastel panels" on the walls. Tiny tin angels with wingspans of about 10 inches are suspended overhead.

Coffees and desserts are available at the candle-lit tables, while downstairs is Serrano restaurant, known for its international home cooking.

Music: Tu–Sa, occasional blues. *Cover:* $–$$.

Also

In Doylestown, about 45 minutes from Philadelphia, is **Cafe Classics** (812 N. Easton Rd. [Rt. 611N], 215–489–3535, www.cafeclassics.com). One of the best blues clubs in the area, it offers live music on Friday and Saturday nights.

Other Venues and Special Events

The **Painted Bride** (230 Vine St., 215–925–9914, www.paintedbride.org), now close to three decades old, is the place to go to hear players such as David Murray, the Sun Ra Arkestra, the Art Ensemble of Chicago, and Elvin Jones. Concerts are held about twice a month in the center's aesthetically spare but comfortable auditorium.

The **Philadelphia Clef Club of Jazz and Performing Arts** (736–38 S. Broad St., 215–893–9912) has a strong jazz education program headed by bandleader Lovett Hines. An outgrowth of the former Black Musician's Union, Local 274, the club also hosts frequent concerts by the likes of Benny Golson, Oliver Lake, Greg Osby, and Larry Ridley.

The **Plays and Players Theater** (1714 Delancey Pl., 215–735–0630), home to the Philadelphia Theater Company, also presents jazz concerts, usually by Philadelphia-based musicians. Recent performers here include Odean Pope, Khan Jamal, and High Zero.

The **Academy of Music** (Broad and Locust Sts., 215–893–1999) features jazz on occasion, as does **Irvine Auditorium** at the University of Pennsylvania (3401 Spruce St., 215–898–3900), which hosts a "Jazz At Penn Series," and the **Zellerbach Theater**, also at the University (3680 Walnut St., 215–898–3900). The **Keswick Theater** in nearby Glenside (Easton Rd. at Keswick Ave., 215–572–7650) is one of the finest concert venues in the Philadelphia area for jazz and blues.

In addition to the **Mellon Jazz Festival** held in the city each summer (see "Major Festivals," p. 458), **Penn's Landing/WRTI-RM** (215–636–1666, www.pennslandingcorp.com) presents a free summertime jazz series in the historic 37-acre park on the Delaware River where William Penn stepped ashore in 1682. Then there's the **Presidential Jazz Weekend** (215–636–6666), offering about 60 events (including concerts, club tours, and jazz for kids), which takes place every February. **Jam on the River** (215–636–1666), held over

Memorial Day weekend, features some jazz and blues, along with a wide variety of other musics. One of the largest blues fests in the area is the **Pocono Blues Festival** (www.pro-log.net), held at the Big Boulder Ski Resort (about 90 minutes from Philly) in late July/early August.

The **Philadelphia Blues Machine** (215–849–5465), a blues society, puts on two or three concerts a year featuring national acts. The Bucks County Blues Society (215–946–4794) hosts an annual **Bucks County Blues Picnic** that takes place in nearby Levittown in July.

Jazz vespers can be heard at the **Old Pine Street Presby-terian Church** in Society Hill (412 Pine St., 215–925–8051). The **Philadelphia Episcopal Cathedral Garden** (38th and Chestnut Sts., 215–386–0234) hosts a John Coltrane tribute every year.

Radio

WRTI/90.1 FM (215–204–8405). Affiliated with Temple University. Jazz 12 hours a day.

WXPN/88.9 FM (215–898–6677). University of Pennsylvania station. Some jazz. Blues, Sa 8–11 P.M. with Jonny Meister.

WJJZ/106. 1 FM (215–263–1106). Smooth jazz.

Record Stores

A good selection of jazz and blues recordings can be found at **Webb's Department Store** (2152 Ridge Ave., 215–765–9187), **Sounds of Market** (11th and Market Sts., 215–925–3152), **Sounds of Germantown** (5623 Germantown Ave., 215–843–2400), and the **Philadelphia Record Exchange** (618 S. 5th St., 215–922–2732).

PITTSBURGH

Updated by Mike Shanley

Some cities—New Orleans, Chicago, Kansas City—have a sound. Pittsburgh has an instrument: the piano. The number of world-class piano/keyboard players to have come out of this industrial city is truly phenomenal. They span many generations and many styles and include Earl Hines, Mary Lou Williams, Billy Strayhorn, Erroll Garner, Dodo Marmarosa, Ahmad Jamal, Horace Parlan, Shirley Scott, and Walt Harper.

Pittsburgh has produced more than its share of other jazz musicians as well. There are Ray Brown and Paul Chambers on bass, Kenny Clarke and Art Blakey on drums, George Benson on guitar, Roy Eldridge on trumpet, and Stanley Turrentine on sax—not to mention vocalists Billy Eckstine, Eddie Jefferson, Maxine Sullivan, and Dakota Staton. In addition, drummers Beaver Harris and Jeff "Tain" Watts were both born in Pittsburgh.

Surprisingly, for a city with so much talent, Pittsburgh has never had an especially strong jazz-club history. Musically speaking, it's always been a town to escape from, not to. Those historic clubs that did exist were primarily located in the Hill District, along Wylie and Centre avenues. Wylie Avenue was the site of the Leader House, where Earl Hines started out back in the 1920s, and of the Crawford Grill, where Stanley Turrentine and others played in the 1950s. Centre Avenue was the site of the Pythian Temple, the Savoy Ballroom, and the Bailey Hotel, once the finest African-American hotel in town.

Most of Pittsburgh's best-known musicians came out of three neighborhoods—East Liberty, Homewood, and the Hill District—and the young jazzmen and -women depended heavily on their high schools for their musical educations. Schenley and Westinghouse were particularly important. Both had and continue to have strong music programs, complete with top-quality bands.

Some musicians obtained an education of sorts through other routes as well. Mary Lou Williams, who was a child prodigy, once told a local deejay, "I used to play for the Mellons, you know, the very rich people. Their chauffeur would come and get me off the sidewalk to play at their parties. I was ten and known as the 'little piano girl.'"

Another child prodigy, George Benson, started his career at the age of 4 by singing and playing the ukelele on a street corner in the Hill District. By the time he was 8, he had switched to the guitar and was signing a record contract with RCA under the name "Little Georgie."

Sources

Listings can also be found in two free weeklies, *In Pittsburgh* (412–488–1212) and *City Paper* (412–316–3342). Other sources are the Friday sections of the *Pittsburgh Post-Gazette*

(412–263–1100) and the *Pittsburgh Tribune-Review* (412–391–3588). WDUQ/90.5 FM has music calendar listings throughout the day, Wednesdays through Fridays.

For maps and other information, contact the Visitor Information Center on Liberty Avenue near Point State Park (downtown, 412–281–9222) or 315 Grandview Ave. (in the Carnegie Library, 412–381–5134) or the Greater Pittsburgh Convention and Visitors Bureau (1–800–821–1888, www.pittsburgh-cvb.org).

For online information about Pittsburgh, visit Three Rivers Free-Net, www.trfn.clpgh.org, a Web resource for the Pittsburgh and Southwestern Pennsylvania community; http://pittsburgh.citysearch.com; or Pittsburgh.Net, www.pittsburgh.net/.

A Note on Neighborhoods

Pittsburgh, with a population of 1.5 million, may once have been the ugly, polluted steel capital of the Northeast, but times have changed. The steel industry has declined, *Fortune* 500 companies have moved in, and the environment has been cleaned up. Pittsburgh is now a surprisingly pretty place surrounded by glistening rivers and tree-covered mountains. Bridges seem to be everywhere.

The city's downtown is the Golden Triangle, so named because the Allegheny and Monongahela rivers come together here to form the Ohio River. Adjacent to the Triangle is the Strip District, a restored warehouse area now known for its nightlife. The Hill District is an historic African-American neighborhood just north and east of the downtown, while East Liberty and Homewood are two other important African-American neighborhoods located yet farther east. Between the Hill District and East Liberty is Oakland, home to the University of Pittsburgh and Carnegie Mellon University, and Shadyside, once known for its Bohemian atmosphere and now a trendy area filled with boutiques and restaurants. Duquesne University, nationally known for its fine music school, is sandwiched between Downtown and Uptown.

The North Side and the South Side are residential, predominantly working-class communities located across the Allegheny and Monongahela rivers respectively. Both are within ten minutes of the downtown.

Although the city has relatively little traffic, except in the Golden Triangle, driving is tricky. Hills and bridges pop up unexpectedly, and one wrong turn can send you over a river or into a neighborhood you never intended to visit.

Landmarks and Legends

(The route below starts in the Golden Triangle, proceeds to the Hill District and the University of Pittsburgh, and ends in Homewood. A car is necessary.)

The William Penn Hotel, now the Westin William Penn, 530 William Penn Place, 412–281–7100.

The William Penn, a sedate and luxurious landmark hotel in downtown Pittsburgh, had never had either an African-American patron or an African-American band when the then unknown Count Basie and his orchestra arrived there in 1936. The gig was an important one, according to John Hammond in *John Hammond on Record,* not only because the hotel had a network-radio wire, which would give the band national exposure, but also because it could lead to bookings in other William Penn–type establishments.

Alas, things did not go smoothly. First of all, though Basie tried to tone them down, the band couldn't help but swing. Second, the reviews (Hammond had invited several critics down from New York who had never heard the Basie band) were terrible.

Third, and potentially most disastrously, a major player went crazy one night after the show, attacking people in a local nightclub and knocking out two policemen. He was immediately taken to a nearby asylum, where he was placed in the violent ward, in a straitjacket, and allowed no visitors. He might have been lost in that institution were it not for the efforts of Hammond, who managed to talk the much more humane Neurological Institute of New York, which at that time did not treat African Americans, into accepting the musician. The man was found to have a secondary stage of syphilis (which, when combined with marijuana, can greatly disturb the nervous system), and three weeks later, following treatment, he was back with Basie, playing the Apollo.

Lower Wylie Avenue, now the Civic Arena, just south of the Hill District.

All of lower Wylie Avenue has been torn up and rebuilt, but back in the '20s and '30s, when Earl Hines was coming up, many major clubs and theaters were located here: the Collins Inn and the Grape Arbor, the Star Theatre and the Leader House.

Hines began playing at the Leader House regularly when he was still underage. Singer and house bandleader Lois Deppe, impressed with the boy's talent, convinced Hines Sr. to let his son join his band, and Earl moved in—literally—playing, eating, and sleeping at Leader's for the next two years. While there, he studied fellow piano players Jim Fellman, who had a "wonderful left hand" that stretched to make tenths, and Johnny Watters, who had a wonderful right hand that did the same.

Crawford Grill, 2141 Wylie Ave. (Hill District), 412–471–1565.

By the late '30s, lower Wylie Avenue had peaked. The action was now farther uptown, still on the avenue, but in the Hill District. A whole new generation of clubs emerged, including the Rhumba Theatre, the Bamboola, the Birdie, the Hurricane, and the Crawford Grill, number two (the Crawford Grill, number one, had been located on lower Wylie Avenue and was demolished for urban development).

Today, only the Crawford Grill, number two, is still standing. During its heyday in the '40s and '50s, it was a jazz mecca where all of the greats played—Charles Mingus, Clifford Brown, Nat King Cole, Maynard Ferguson, Thelonious Monk, and Max Roach. It was also here that three young Pittsburgh men got their start—George Benson, Stanley Turrentine, and Walt Harper, a household name in Pittsburgh circles.

During the '40s and '50s, the Crawford Grill was exploding with talent.

Janinalyce

After the riots of 1968, the Wylie Avenue community crumbled, to be replaced by abandoned buildings, drugs, and crime. Somehow, though, the Crawford Grill managed to survive, and even today, it operates as a neighborhood bar. A beautiful place—long, dark and cool—it's a sad oasis in the desperate streets around it. Exquisite African art is everywhere: masks and carvings line a shelf above the booths and there's a floor-to-ceiling totem pole in one corner.

The Grill is now run by Les Montgomery, and features music at least two nights a week, along with a jam session every Thursday.

Schenley High School, N. Bellefield and Centre avenues (near the Hill District).

Earl Hines attended Schenley High School back in the '20s, when he was living with his aunt, Sadie Phillips. Sadie performed in light opera and knew many of the name musicians of the day—Eubie Blake, Noble Sissle, Luckey Roberts—whom she'd invite over and make wait around until her nephew came home from school so that he could hear them play.

While at Schenley, Hines got his first taste of Wylie Avenue. An older cousin and a next-door neighbor dressed the 15-year-old up in long pants and a "big old diamond ring" and took him out for a night on the town to repay him for all the times he had entertained them and their girlfriends on the piano. "We were sitting in a restaurant," says Hines in *The World of Earl Hines*, "Eating big steaks like I'd never had before . . . when I heard this music upstairs. It had a beat and a rhythm to it that I'd never heard before. 'Oh,' I said, 'if only I could just get upstairs and see what they're doing—see what kind of music that is!'"

Art Blakey, Ray Brown, and Billy May, a big band leader who eventually did arrangements for Frank Sinatra, were three other Schenley High School graduates who went on to achieve fame.

International Academy of Jazz Hall of Fame, University of Pittsburgh, William Pitt Student Union, Fifth and Bigelow, 412–648–7815.

Founded in 1977, the Academy occupies approximately one fourth of the union's ground floor and is the oldest jazz hall of fame in the country. Plaques honoring notables such as Charlie Parker and Dizzy Gillespie line the walls, along with instruments donated by Sonny Rollins, Grover Washington, Jr., Clark Terry, and others.

Open: daily, 9 A.M.–11 P.M.

Westinghouse High School, 1104 N. Murtland St. (Homewood).

The list of great piano players who came out of this solid old high school is breathtakingly impressive: Mary Lou Williams, Ahmad Jamal (Fritzy Jones at the time), Errol Garner, Billy Strayhorn. Many studied with one teacher, Carl McVicker, Sr., a tall, refined, Anglo-Saxon trumpet player who came to Westinghouse in 1927. "Jazz was a dirty word then," McVicker told *Pittsburgh* magazine in 1979. "The people in the educational system thought it was dangerous to encourage jazz bands, but it was a way of interesting kids."

One of McVicker's finest, and most difficult, students was Erroll Garner. "The other teachers told me I was foolish to waste my time with him," he said. "They said that with his IQ, he was too stupid to get up to the microphone, much less do anything. . . . He was 12 or 13 and very small. He sat on two telephone books when he played. I could see how much talent he had, but he couldn't play in the band because he couldn't read music. Still he had perfect pitch and could memorize instantly. . . . He had his own style even then."

Cardwell Dawson School of Music, 7101 Apple St. (Homewood).

During the 1930s, pianist Mary Cardwell Dawson, founder of the National Negro Opera Company, ran a music school out of this now somewhat dilapidated 21-room house, equipped with a ballroom and servants quarters. Ahmad Jamal was one of her prize students, and for him and each of her other special students, she planted a tree in the front yard.

Dawson founded the National Negro Opera Company in Chicago in 1941 and soon thereafter established guilds in Pittsburgh, New York, and Washington, D.C. The National Negro Opera Company is the only opera company besides the Metropolitan Opera Company to have appeared at the Metropolitan Opera House in New York's Lincoln Center.

CLUBS, ETC.

Though Pittsburgh has no club that brings in national jazz artists on a regular basis, there are a number of fine, smaller clubs and restaurants that feature top local and regional talent most nights, and national artists on occasion. Among these are the **Club Café**, **Dowe's on 9th**, **Stolen Moments**, and **Ramsey's II**. The **Pittsburgh Jazz Society** and the **Manchester Craftsmen's Guild** also bring in national acts on a regular basis. National blues artists can most frequently be heard at **Moondog's**.

Some of the jazz artists and groups to watch out for include organist and local personality Walt Harper; veteran pianist Carl Arter; drummer Roger Humphries; saxophonists Don Aliquo, Sr., Scott Boni, Roby Edwards, and Eric DeFade; piano players Frank Cunimondo and Bobby Negri; guitar players Jimmy Ponder, Joe Negri, and Martin Ashby; violin player Rodney McCoy; trombone player Nelson Harrison; trumpet player Danny Kahn; vocalists Etta Cox and Maureen Budway; Dr. John Wilson's Big Band; the Balcony Big Band, and Trio Grande. Bassist Mark Perna and drummer John Schmidt play in several local jazz groups including the Art Ensemble of Valhalla and Perna, Madge, Schmidt & Sakash. The top blues singers and groups in town include Chismo Charles, Sandy Staley, Billy Price and the Swingtime Five, the Blues Orphans, the Blues Burners, and the Mystic Knights of the Sea.

Most clubs and bars in Pittsburgh close at 2 A.M.

Personal Choices

Best jazz restaurant-club: *Club Café*
Best historical/cultural center for jazz: *Crawford Grill, Manchester Craftsmen's Guild*
Best blues bar: *Moondog's*

FOR JAZZ

Club Café, 56–58 S. 12th St. (South Side), 412–381–3777.

Club Café features music of all types, seven nights a week, with jazz on two or three of them. The intimate room has excellent acoustics and a space-age supper club decor. Lighting from beneath the bar slowly shifts from green to pale orange. The white-glass screen immediately inside the door constantly broadcasts a series of slow moving images, like fish in a bowl or satellite transmissions of star clusters. Both tables and booths offer ample seating.

Opek 15, a large group made up of traditional and avant-garde musicians who play the music of Sun Ra, performs nearly once a month. Other regulars include Perna, Madge, Schmidt & Sakash—who explore the post-Coltrane musical landscape—and Margalit and the Liquidtones, led by a performance artist who sings torch songs.

Music: nightly, some jazz and blues. *Cover*: $-$$. *Food*: American.

Crawford Grill, 2141 Wylie Ave. (Hill District), 412–471–1565.

Pittsburgh's most fabled jazz club, a mecca for musicians is the '40s and '50s (see "Landmarks and Legends," p. 199) is now offering live music once again, usually courtesy of the Hardgroove Project, Gene Ludwig Organ Trio, or Real Silk Band. The club is a beautiful place, filled with much first-class African art, and one of the best jazz jams in the city takes place here on Thursday nights. Wednesdays are often reserved for poetry readings.

Music: Th-Sa. *Cover:* $.

Stolen Moments, 3239 Brighton Rd. (North Side), 412–766–4770.

Started up by veteran jazz pianist-composer Carl Arter, record producer Michael Frank, and bassist-physician Sunny Sunseri, Stolen Moments is a tiny, homey place that until recently was just a neighborhood bar. Now remodeled, with a small stage at the far end, a kitchen out back, and lots of vintage jazz posters on the wall, it aims at serving up serious music, as well as good food, until the wee hours of the morning. Arter usually plays two or three nights a week. "We wanted to feature Carl because we feel that he's one of the great, unrecognized jazz artists of Pittsburgh," says Frank, founder of Earwig Records.

Music: W–Sa. *No cover, except for special events. Food:* American.

Dowe's On 9th, 121 9th St. (downtown), 412–281–9225, www.doweson9th.com.

Once upon a time, downtown Pittsburgh had a bustling nightlife with movie and music theaters and clubs sprinkled throughout the area. While the area known as the "cultural district" is alive and well—courtesy of Heinz Hall, the Benedum and Byham Theaters—downtown nightclubs are in short supply. Trombonist Al Dowe aimed to revive the glory days of local jazz by opening his spacious club a few blocks from the theater district. With seating for over 200, Dowe's has the ambience of an upscale supper club, starting with its marble floor lobby and continuing through to its formal table seating, swank balcony, and dark purple walls. The stage and hardwood dance floor can be seen from all vantage points in the room.

Appearing weekly are the Al Dowe band with Etta Cox, the Dr. Zoot Swing Band, and the Roger Humphries Big Band. National acts, which have included Slide Hampton, Maynard Ferguson, and the Four Freshmen, also perform here.

Music: nightly. *Cover:* $-$$$. *Food:* American.

Segneri's Pasta Grill, 1500 Washington Rd. (Galleria), 412–561–7278.

Pianist Bobby Negri can be heard twice a week at this restaurant/club, known as much for its fine jazz as for its tasty home-cooked pasta. Negri plays both solo and with a trio that backs local "jazz diva" Sandy Staley. Co-owned by drummer Billy Kuhn, Segneri's features other local jazz musicians as well. Negri sometimes accompanies Danny Conn and Lou Schreiber, and Roger Humphries and Trio Grande appear regularly. Don Aliquo, Jr., also stops in from time to time.

Music: W, F-Sa. *No cover. Food*: Italian.

Cozumel, 5507 Walnut St. (Shadyside), 412–621–5100

Shadyside might not be the bohemian mecca it was a few decades ago, now that chain stores have replaced most of the small businesses that once lined Walnut Street. But Cozumel, located one flight up from the sidewalk, proves that this neighborhood has not completely abandoned live entertainment. On the weekends, performers run the gamut from the Scott Boni Quartet's straight-ahead jazz to Latin Impulse's salsa. Hill Jordan and the Hardgroove Project lead a jam session every Sunday.

Music: F-Su. *Food*: Mexican.

Valhalla Restaurant & Brewery, 1150 Smallman St. (Strip District), 412–434–1440.

Right over the main entrance of this restaurant, behind two gigantic boilers that brew beer, sits the bandstand. So, unless you're seated at one of the three tables in the balcony directly across from the band, you won't be able to see them. But Valhalla's split-level, high-ceiling design does help the music to travel without the need of a sound system. Although jazz often feels like an afterthought here, a band dubbed the Art Ensemble of Valhalla—featuring Don Aliquo, Sr.—nonetheless manages to turn in a creative session during their weekly gig. The Skip Peck Trio, the Latin-jazz group Salsamba, and variations of the Ensemble can be heard on other nights.

Music: W-Su. *No cover. Food:* American.

Foster's Bar & Grill, Holiday Inn at University Center, 100 Lytton Ave. (Oakland), 412–682–6200.

Home to the Pittsburgh Jazz Society (412–343–9555), which meets and presents concerts here every Sunday evening, Foster's features top local talent such as Trio Grande, the Wilson-Tomaro Jazz Orchestra, and Walt Harper & All That Jazz. Unfortunately, however, for all its good music, Foster's has little to offer in the way of atmosphere. The large window-lined lounge, which can seat up to 400, feels like what it is—a sterile room in a Holiday Inn. Adjacent to the lounge is a restaurant.

Music: F–Sa. *No cover. Food:* American.

Ramsey's II, 7310 Frankstown Ave. (Homewood), 412–371–3445.

With some of the best acoustics in the city for jazz, Ramsey's II is a sort of African-American cultural center that features jazz on the weekends; poetry, dramatic readings, fashion shows, and special events during the week. A number of fine local artists have appeared here (Jimmy Ponder, Bobby Jones), and the club has also sponsored some of the most unusual jazz events in the city, including a concert that paired a young Polish jazz orchestra with a young Pittsburgh jazz orchestra called the Kehonia Koncept, made up of 15- to 18-year-olds. Many "names," such as George Benson, Roy Ayers, and Mrs. Richard Wright (the wife of the former novelist; now living in Paris) stop by here when in town.

Ramsey's is run by John Brewer and his wife, Christina, who is both a fiber artist (her work is often displayed on the walls, along with that of other local artists) and the club's cook.

Music: F, Sa. *No cover, except for special events. Food:* Cajun, Jamaican, African.

James Street Restaurant, 422 Foreland St. (North Side), 412–323–2222.

For over a decade, James Street, once a sports bar, has been presenting some of the better-known names in Pittsburgh jazz, including Harold Betters, Rodney McCoy, Jimmy Sapienza and Five Guys Named Moe, Jimmy Ponder, and Roger Humphries, who hosts an open jam every Tuesday night. But no matter who's playing, James Street, housed in a 100-year-old building, remains primarily a restaurant. The upstairs, elegantly decorated with etched glass, mirrors, and wooden paneling, is devoted to dining only, while the music takes place on a makeshift stage in the equally pretty basement level.

Music: F–Sa. *No cover. Food:* New Orleans.

Too Sweet, 7101 Frankstown Ave. (Homewood), 412–731–5707.

A large modern club with a dance floor and portable stage that's brought out for the jazz shows, Too Sweet presents jazz on Friday nights. Usually performing is The Bottom Line with Flo Wilson.

Music: F. *Cover:* $. *Food:* simple American.

Coolpepper's Hothouse, 4324 Butler St. (Lawrenceville), 412–682–4001.

Normally a rock club, this neighborhood tavern hosts a rootsy jam session every Wednesday, where young and old players get together to swap ideas. Coolpepper's is indicative of Pittsburgh's unique landscape. Located in Lawrenceville, an historic neighborhood with classic storefronts begging for redevelopment, it's divided between two buildings. The first holds a bar stocked with pinball games and a pool table. The second resembles a rec room, with brick walls, an ample stage, and a few tables. Despite its working-class façade, Coolpepper's is also one of the few eateries in town that features Southwestern cuisine.

Up-and-coming musicians such as trumpet player Dean Alston and alto saxophonist Roby Edwards turn up regularly at the jam sessions, although players both known and unknown may drop by from week to week.

Music: W. *No cover. Food*: Southwestern.

FOR BLUES

Moondog's, 378 Freeport Rd. (Blawnox), 412–828–2040.

Moondog's is situated in Blawnox, a borough across the Allegheny River, which places it slightly off-the-beaten Pittsburgh track. But if you're looking for blues, it's worth the trip. Moondog's has become the premier place in town to hear national blues acts, along with local rock and blues performers.

Local institutions like the 8th Street Rox band and Gary Belloma & the Blues Bombers play Moondog's on a steady basis. Among the national acts that have performed here are Kenny Neal, Levon Helm Blues Band, and the Nighthawks.

Music: T, Th-Sa., some blues. *Cover*: $-$$$.

Blues Café, 19th and East Carson Sts. (South Side), 412–431–7080.

This South Side club has arguably the most unique set-up of any music venue in town. The bar sits in the center of the floor and extends almost the entire length of the room. With no space left for a stage, the musicians play on a balcony that looks down at the audience. The Café is also connected to one of the city's three Primanti Brothers' Sandwich Shops, famed locally for their unique sandwiches served with sides of both cole slaw and French fries piled between the slices of bread.

Blues Café caters almost exclusively to local blues acts, with music seven nights a week. Performers like Shari Richards, Tony Janflone, Chizmo Charles, and Glenn Pavone

& the Cyclones have weekly gigs, while a variety of different musicians appear on the weekends.

Music: nightly. *Cover*: $. *Food*: American.

Also

Blues can also be heard once or twice a week at **Roland's Iron Landing** (1904 Penn Ave., Strip District, 412–261–3401), **Excuses** (2526 East Carson, South Side. 412–431–4090), and **Trolls** (100 Waterfront Drive, Washington's Landing, 412–321–8765).

Other Venues and Special Events

Crafts and jazz don't usually go together, but then the **Manchester Craftsmen's Guild** (1815 Metropolitan St., 412–322–0800, www.mcgjazz.com) isn't a usual sort of place. Founded in 1968 to provide apprenticeships to inner-city high-school students in ceramics and photography, the school has since grown to include jazz. In addition, the Guild, which is housed in a modern brick building on the edge of town, is home to a fine state-of-the-art auditorium that brings in national talent. Max Roach has recorded an album here, and Ahmad Jamal picked out the stage piano. A free reception, complete with coffee and baked goods, follows each show. The Guild also puts on a **Winter Jazz Festival** during the third week of January.

Along with its Sunday-evening concerts at Foster's (see "For Jazz," page 204), the **Pittsburgh Jazz Society** (412–343–9555, pittsburghjazz.org), founded by WDUQ-FM deejay Tony Mowod, sponsors other, inexpensive jazz events around town, sometimes compliments of its Pittsburgh Jazz Society Big Band (composed of high school and college students). Watch the papers.

Heinz Hall (600 Penn Ave., 412–392–4800), where the Pittsburgh Symphony Orchestra performs, presents occasional jazz events, as do the **Civic Arena** (300 Auditorium Place, 412–333–7328) and the **I. C. Light Ampitheater** (1 Station Sq., 412–562–9900).

In addition to the **Mellon Jazz Festival** (see "Major Festivals," page 458), the 17-day **Three Rivers Arts Festival** (412–481–7040), one of the largest and oldest free festivals in the United States, is held in the city every June and features both national and local jazz and blues artists. The **South Side Summer Street Spectacular** (412–481–0651), the largest neighborhood festival in Pittsburgh, is a four-day event held in late July that features both jazz and blues. The **Shadyside**

Arts Festival (412–681–2809), which includes some jazz, is held the first weekend in August.

Radio

WDUQ/90.5 FM (412–434–6030). Affiliated with Duquesne University and NPR; jazz every midday and evening.
WYEP/91.3 FM (412–661–9100). An independent, listener-supported station. Blues and R&B all day Saturday.
WPTS/92.1 FM (412–383-WPTS). Affiliated with the University of Pittsburgh. Some jazz.
WRCT/88.3 FM (412–621-WRCT). Affiliated with Carnegie Mellon University. Some jazz.

Record Stores

Paul's Compact Discs (4526 Liberty Ave., Bloomfield, 412–621–3256) has a large collection of new jazz releases, including vinyl. **Jerry's Records** (2136 Murray Ave., Squirrel Hill, 412–421–4533) is a warehouse-sized used records store with a voluminous jazz section, including 10"s and 78s. **Off Minor Music** (5824 Forbes Ave., Squirrel Hill, 412–422–1077) sells new jazz and classical CDs.

BALTIMORE

Updated by Geoffrey Himes

Despite its small size, Baltimore has had its share of jazz history. For many years it served as a feeder line for musicians on their way to New York while at the same time developing a strong jazz environment of its own. Pennsylvania Avenue and the Royal Theatre were particularly popular spots, attracting talent from all over the country, many of whom took up residence for weeks. Local musicians tended to play on "the Block," a red-light district then located on Baltimore Street between Gay and Calvert streets.

Baltimore has also produced a number of legendary musicians, including Eubie Blake, Billie Holiday, and Chick Webb. Cab Calloway spent his boyhood in the city, while Blanche

Calloway, his sister and one of the nation's first women band-leaders, was born here. Later, there were guitarist Elmer Snowden, pianist Dick Katz, saxophonist Gary Bartz and vocalist Ethel Ennis, who once ran her own club on Cathedral Street and still resides in the area.

Many of Baltimore's earliest jazz musicians from the west side, Cab and Blanche Calloway among them, studied at Douglass High School under the tutelage of an earlier jazz and classical organist and cello player named William Llewellyn Wilson. Wilson was also the conductor of Baltimore's first African-American symphony orchestra.

More recent jazz artists to come out of the Baltimore area include Cyrus Chestnut, Antonio Hart, Greg Hatza, Gary Thomas, Rumba Club, Stuart Hart, Talib Kibwe, Dennis Chambers, Dontae Winslow, Greg Grainger, Gary Grainger, Elery Eskelin, George Colligan, Carl Filipiak, and Rodney "Skeets" Curtis. Blues musicians include the Nighthawks, Mark Brine, Linwood Taylor, the Hardway Connection, Big Jesse Yawn, Deanna Bogart, Gumbo Junkyard, Big Joe Maher, Steve Guyger, and Benjie Porecki.

Sources

The City Paper (410–523–2300, www.citypaper.com), the *Village Voice* of Baltimore, comes out on Wednesday and offers frequent jazz and blues coverage, in addition to the city's best listings. *The Baltimore Sun* (410–332–6000, www.sunspot.net) publishes a "Maryland Live" tabloid section every Thursday that has extensive listings and infrequent jazz and blues coverage. *Music Monthly* (410–494–0565), a free tabloid, comes out once a month and emphasizes the local music scene, including jazz and blues.

For maps and other information, contact the Baltimore Visitor Information Center, which is located at 300 Pratt St. in the Inner Harbor area; 410–837–4636, 800–282–6632, or 800–837-INFO, www.baltimore.org.

A Note on Neighborhoods

Over the past fifteen years or so, ever since the opening of the Rouse Company project Harborplace and the acclaimed National Aquarium, Baltimore has become a tourist destination. Its formerly decrepit and abandoned downtown is now filled with glittering restaurants, high-rise hotels, and expensive boutiques.

Once away from the Inner Harbor, however, Baltimore reverts back to its true self: a solid city of neighborhoods, divided into north and south by Baltimore Street, and into east and west by Charles Street. Fell's Point, lined with cobblestone streets and Colonial buildings, is a former shipbuilding and maritime center that dates back to the 1730s. Federal Hill is another cobblestone area near the downtown. Both are known for their nightlife.

Driving in Baltimore is easy. Traffic is light, and parking, except weekends in the Inner Harbor area and in Fell's Point, is plentiful.

Landmarks and Legends

(The sites below are best toured by car. Pennsylvania Avenue starts near the downtown; East Baltimore is about 15 minutes east of downtown; the Famous Ballroom and the Cab Calloway Room are to the north.)

Pennsylvania Avenue

From the 1920s through the 1950s, Pennsylvania Avenue, stretching 23 blocks from Franklin Avenue on the south to Fulton Avenue on the north, was *the* avenue of black Baltimore. Lined with shops, restaurants, schools, churches, theaters, nightclubs, taverns, and businesses, it provided the city's largest African-American community with everything it needed.

More than anything else, though, Pennsylvania Avenue was renowned for its entertainment. The first African-American-owned hotel in Baltimore, the Penn Hotel, was built here in 1921, and by 1945, in the 14 blocks between Biddle and Baker streets alone, there were 47 liquor licenses, most of them issued to nightclubs. Among these were the Comedy Club and Wendall's Tavern, Gamby's and Dreamland, the Ritz and the Sphinx Club. Live music was everywhere, and even the bars and taverns without formal stages had a solo piano or organ player.

Pennsylvania Avenue became a victim of urban renewal in the mid-seventies. The lower half or "the bottom," which stretched from Franklin to Dolphin Street, was completely demolished, to be replaced by an occasional dispirited church, apartment building, or school. The upper half fared a bit better, and though considerably more dangerous now than it once was, is still lined with a hodgepodge of dilapidated buildings.

Royal Theatre, 1329 Pennsylvania Ave.

Today, there's just an ugly 12-by–16-inch commemorative plaque standing on steel pipes in front of a fenced-in playing field, but the Royal Theatre was once one of the major stops on a black entertainment circuit that included the Apollo in New York, the Howard in Washington, the Earle in Philadelphia,

Fats Waller opened the Royal in 1925.

Courtesy Peale Museum

and the Regal in Chicago. It was here that Billie Holiday got booed by her own hometown (the Royal was reputedly even tougher than the cold-hearted Apollo; "They would throw anything," says one Baltimorean) and here that Pearl Bailey gave her first performances—as a chorus girl.

The Royal, which seated about 1,350 people, opened in 1921 as the Douglass Theater, the "finest colored theatre in America, owned and controlled by colored people." Four years later, however, it went bankrupt and reopened under white management as the Royal. The Royal's first performer was Fats Waller.

The theater was demolished in 1971.

The Sphinx Club, 2107 Pennsylvania Ave. (near downtown).

In operation until the early 1990s, the Sphinx was one of the oldest minority-owned clubs in the country, dating back to 1946 and the heyday of Pennsylvania Avenue. A well-known landmark in Baltimore's African-American community, it was founded by businessman Charles Phillip Tilghman and later run by his children.

Billie Holiday, Dinah Washington, and Sam Cooke were among the many who played the Sphinx, but the club never really had a true entertainment policy. Music was an informal thing. Anyone who wanted to play on the instruments lying around could, and often did. Today, the Sphinx has been replaced by a neighborhood bar.

Statue of Billie Holiday, Pennsylvania Ave., bet. Lanvale and Lafayette Streets.

She stands tall, strong, and lovely, this 8-foot-high bronze statue of Lady Day. A gardenia blooms in her hair; a long gown rustles to her feet; her face is filled with confidence and joy. The inscription on a nearby plaque reads: "I don't think I'm singing, I feel like I am playing a horn. I try to improvise. What comes out is what I feel."

The Eubie Blake National Museum and Cultural Center, 847 Howard St. (downtown), 410–625–3113.

Eubie Blake is one of Baltimore's most famous sons, born in 1883 to former slaves whose previous 10 children had all died at birth. He grew up an only child and his musical talent was first noticed when, at age six, he climbed up onto an organ stool in a local department store while shopping with his mother and began to pick out a melody. Mrs. Blake bought a $75 organ, paying a quarter a week, and Eubie took lessons from a next-door neighbor. Soon, much to his mother's consternation when she finally found out, he was sneaking out of his bedroom window at night to play ragtime at a nearby brothel.

Up until the summer of 1993, the Eubie Blake Museum was located in a beautiful white townhouse at 409 N. Charles St. Following a devastating fire, however, the museum moved several times before arriving at this large, four-story building, formerly a nursing school. Still in the process of getting set up, the museum expects to reopen again in early 2001, with exhibits not only about Eubie Blake, but also about Billie Holiday, Chick Webb, Cab Calloway, and Avon Long. Also in the building will be a gallery for emerging Baltimore artists (and occasional national shows), meeting rooms, a lounge, gift shop, and performance space, where the center hopes to present occasional jazz concerts.

Call for hours and admission fees.

East Baltimore, centering around N. Eden Street.

Chick Webb, Billie Holiday, and Eubie Blake all once lived in this working-class neighborhood located not far from downtown. Webb was born at 1313 Ashland Ave., while Blake lived for a time at 414 N. Eden St. and Holiday at 200 S. Durham St. Webb's home has been replaced by an attractive row house; Blake's house has also been torn down; Holiday's home is still standing, but is in dilapidated condition.

Today, in the center of East Baltimore, stands the well-worn Chick Webb Memorial Recreation Center (623 N. Eden St.), named after the legendary drummer whose life was the stuff that movies are made of. Born poor and hunchbacked in 1909, Webb became a cripple at the age of 5 after falling down the stairs. Nonetheless, four years later, he was out on the street selling newspapers so that he could buy his first set of drums.

Webb, who later led the house band at New York's Savoy Ballroom, was responsible for discovering Ella Fitzgerald. He first heard the then-shy girl sing at amateur night at the Apollo in 1934, and was so impressed that he hired her on the spot and brought her home to live with him and his wife.

Famous Ballroom, 1717 N. Charles St.

For years, Baltimore's Left Bank Jazz Society held weekly concerts presenting all the big names in jazz—John Coltrane, Count Basie, Duke Ellington—at this former downtown ballroom. The society recorded most of its events, for a total of 350 concerts between 1965 and 1980, and the tapes are a vast treasure-trove that has achieved legendary status among jazz fans. Nearly every conceivable name of the era was recorded: Dizzy Gillespie, Charles Mingus, Gary Bartz, Jimmy Heath, Blue Mitchell, Benny Golson, Archie Schepp, Sonny Stitt, Art Farmer, George Benson, Max Roach—and the list goes on and on.

Due to legal complications, the tapes lay dormant at Morgan State University for decades. But in 2000, Joel Dorn of Label M in New York began producing recordings from the Left's Bank's archives. As of this writing, he has put out CDs by Stan Getz and Sonny Stitt; many more are in the works.

The Left Bank, founded in 1964, scaled down its operations in 1980, because of escalating costs. The society still exists (see "Other Venues and Special Events," page 217), but it's less active and under different directorship.

Cab Calloway Room, Parlett L. Moore Library, Coppin State College, 2500 W. North Ave., 410–383–5926.

Although not born in Baltimore, Cab Calloway spent much of his boyhood here, and when it came time to decide how to dispose of his personal papers, he chose to donate them to this teacher training college, founded at the turn of the century. Some of the items on display in the Calloway Room, located in the college library, include a Hirshfeld caricature, the gold record received by the artist for his music for the movie *The Blues Brothers,* and his baton.

"Some artists make you think, others make you dream and still others like me want to entertain," reads a quote from the musician.

Open: M–F, 8 A.M.–5 P.M. or by appointment. *Admission:* free.

CLUBS, ETC.

Baltimore is a working city, which means people have to get up
early on weekdays and go to work. As a result, week nights are
tough propositions for local nightclubs, and because of that,
the live-music club scene is smaller than you might expect for
a city with a metropolitan-area population of two million.

That doesn't mean that there's a lack of great live music.
In addition to various neighborhood bars and restaurants, the
slack has been taken up by a proliferation of non-profit
groups, which play a larger role in Baltimore's music scene
than they do in almost any other city (see "Other Venues,
Non-Profit Groups, and Special Events," page 217).

Nationally known jazz and blues artists are occasionally
brought in by these non-profit groups, especially the **Left Bank
Jazz Society**, and by the **New Haven Lounge**. National blues
acts are also occasionally brought in by **Fletcher's** and **8X10**.

Some of the Baltimore-area players to watch out for
include jazz-blues singer Ethel Ennis; blues pianist Steve
Kramer; organist Sir Thomas Hurley; jazz guitarists Paul
Wingo and Carl Filipiak; saxmen Gary Thomas and Gary
Bartz (both ex-Baltimoreans now living in New York who still
play their hometown); Harold Adams and the Moon August
Band; bebop trumpeter Allen Houser; alto saxophonist
Thomas Whit Williams and his son, drummer Tom Williams;
bluesman Red Jones; and vocalists Sheila Ford and Aleta
Green. D.C.–based talent such as bluesmen Tom Principato
and Linwood Taylor, Big Joe & the Dynaflows, the Uptown
Rhythm Kings, and Deanna Bogart can also be heard in the
city regularly.

Most bars and clubs in Baltimore remain open until 2 A.M.

Personal Choices

Best jazz club: *New Haven Lounge*
Best non-profit jazz venues: *Left Bank Jazz Society, Jazz in
Cool Places*
Best jam session: *Sportsmen's Lounge*
Best club for the blues: *Bayou Blues*
Best neighborhood blues bars: *Full Moon, Café Tattoo*

FOR JAZZ

New Haven Lounge, 1552 Havenwood Rd. (Northwood Shopping Center, near Loch Raven Blvd., 15 min. NE of Downtown), 410–366–7416.

Though the New Haven only presents jazz three nights a week, it's currently the most serious club in town for straight-ahead sounds. Gary Bartz, Ralph Moore, Steve Wilson, Joey DeFrancesco, Paul Bollenback, and Sonny Fortune are among those who have appeared here.

Also a restaurant, the New Haven is housed in a smallish, high-ceilinged room that is part of one of the city's older shopping centers. Dark wood and comfortable booths line its walls, and candles light its tables.

Music: W, F, Sa. *Cover:* $. *Food:* American.

Bertha's, 734 S. Broadway (Fell's Point), 410–327–5795.

Bertha's is most famous for its mussels, which it serves up every which way: with garlic butter, with anchovies, with Spanish sauce. The building itself—long, thin, dark, and creaky—is as old as the neighborhood and, with its lanterns and round porthole windows, sometimes feels more like a ship than an edifice.

Despite its emphasis on food, music plays an integral role at Bertha's. Four nights a week, musicians crowd onto its tiny stage near the front door and play to a listening audience. Regulars include the Blue Flames, Jumping Hailstones, and Big Bertha's Rhythm Kings, a Dixieland band that somehow manages to squeeze itself onto the stage.

Music: Tu–Sa. *No cover. Food:* mussels, etc.

Cat's Eye Pub, 1730 Thames St. (Fell's Point), 410–276–9085, www.catseyepub.com.

Once best known for its Irish music, the Cat's Eye now devotes most of the week to jazz, blues, acoustic folk, and "'70s rock." Traditional jazz bands play once or twice a week, while Steve Kramer has been playing blues piano on Sunday afternoons for years.

The Cat's Eye, located on a cobblestone street on the edge of the harbor, is long and narrow and packed with enough "antiques" to keep anyone's grandmother happy. Maps and paintings hang on the walls, flags from the ceiling. The stage is rather oddly situated behind a big wooden partition that runs the length of the pub, and there's a second bar in the back.

Music: nightly, Sa–Su afternoons. *No cover.*

The Sportsmen's Lounge, 4723 Gwynn Oak Ave. (15 min. NW of Downtown), 410–664–1041.

Walter "Chappy" Chapman, a graphic artist, has been coming to this neighborhood club almost every night for over 30 years. A slight man who usually nurses one drink the entire evening, he sits in a corner and watches and listens. He has seen many of the greats come and go that way—Count Basie, Dexter Gordon, Sonny Stitt, Gene Ammons—and except for the time when he broke his leg, has never missed a jazz set. "I come here because it's a peaceful place," he says. "Everyone knows each other, it's like a family." He pauses. "And because the music's very meaningful."

The heyday of the Sportsmen's was the sixties, when it was owned by football player Lenny Moore and jazz in Baltimore was a happening thing. Those days are over, but the best jam session in the city still takes place here every Monday night.

Located in a quiet middle-class African-American neighborhood, the Sportsmen is simple-looking on the outside, but inside it's quite plush, with rows of mirrors, comfortable swivel chairs, and a big stage.

Music: M, F–Sa. *No cover.*

Also

Buddies Pub & Jazz Club, 313 N. Charles St., 410–332–4200, is a cozy downtown bar with live music on Fridays and Saturdays, compliments of its veteran house band.

FOR BLUES

Bayou Blues Cafe, 8133-A Honeygo Blvd (White Marsh Shopping Center), 410–931–2583, www.bayoubluescafe.com.

Though nestled in a shopping mall in the suburbs, this ordinary looking restaurant/bar boasts the best blues bookings in the area. On the music calendar is a mix of national acts (Big Jack Johnson, Tom Principato) and local bands. The menu is equally varied, ranging from Cajun cooking to vegetarian fare.

Music: Tu-Su. *Cover:* $. *Food:* varied American.

Full Moon Saloon, 1710 Aliceanna St. (Fell's Point), 410–558–2873.

The long, thin Full Moon, with its brick walls, scarred wooden bar and milky-white glass fixtures, dates back to the 1700s. It's a neighborhood bar with a neighborhood feel. A doctor sits next to a biker who sits next to a construction worker who orders a glass of milk. There's a moosehead mounted on the wall, a jar of pickled eggs on the counter, and a big white kitchen sink behind the bar.

Local and regional blues and R&B acts come to the Full Moon every night of the week as well as Saturday and Sunday late afternoons.

Music: nightly; Sa, Su, 4–8 P.M. *Cover:* $. *Food:* raw bar/seafood.

Café Tattoo, 4825 Belair Rd., 410–325-RIBS.

A friendly barbecue joint that's won all sorts of prizes for its sauces, chili, and beer (including the number two spot in the American Royal International Barbecue Sauce contest), Café Tattoo has local blues bands most nights of the week. Housed in a 1922 building, the club features a glass-brick front window, tin ceilings, tables along one wall, bar stools along another.

Music: Tu–Su. *Cover:* none. *Food:* barbecue, chili.

Also

Fletcher's Bar (701 S. Bond St., Fell's Point, 410–558–1889) is mostly a rock club but they do present occasional national and local blues acts. The same is true of the **8x10 Club** (10 E. Cross St., Federal Hill, 410–625–2000), a multi-roomed place housed in two side-by-side 19th-century buildings.

Other Venues, Non-Profit Groups, and Special Events

The granddaddy of Baltimore's non-profit music groups is the **Left Bank Jazz Society** (410–945–2266, www.baltimoremd. com/leftbank), which has been around since the '60s. Left Bank's concerts at the Famous Ballroom (see "Landmarks and Legends," page 214) were so legendary that Horace Silver once declared from the stage, "Everybody talks about what a great place Europe is for jazz; well, this is the Europe of America." The group has since cut back and moved, but they still present monthly concerts at a Teamsters Union Hall, with home-cooked food and top talent from the jazz mainstream (James Moody, Freddie Hubbard, Fathead Newman).

The new kid on the block is **Jazz in Cool Places** (410–235–9733), an innovative program that presents live jazz in Baltimore's most interesting architectural sites. Billy Harper played in a Stanford White–designed church; Matt Wilson played in a private club full of Tiffany windows.

Just as innovative is the **Roots Cafe**, sponsored by the Society for the Preservation of American Roots Music (410–880–3883). This series sponsors all-ages, smoke-free concert-dances in St. John's, an old stone church near the Johns Hopkins campus. It happens on the second and fourth Saturday of each month, Sept.-April. The bookings include jazz and blues, along with other roots music.

The Red Room is a refuge for free-music improvisers in the back room of **Normal's** (410–243–6888), one of the city's best used-record and used-book stores. The series mixes out-of-town artists (Joe McPhee, Evan Parker) with locals, and the Red Room also sponsors the High Zero Festival every fall. Another record store, **Dimensions in Music** (233 Park Ave., downtown, 410–752–7121), occasionally features live jazz shows and free food in its 60-seat, second-floor space.

The **Baltimore Blues Society** (410–679–2703, www. mojoworkin.com) hosts monthly concerts at the Rosedale American Legion Hall with artists such as Otis Rush and Joe Louis Walker, puts out one of the finest blues newsletters in the country, and hosts **Hot August Blues**, an outdoor blues-blowout picnic.

The **Chamber Jazz Society of Baltimore** (410–385–5888) presents four concerts by mainstream jazz artists (Charles Lloyd, Junior Mance) during the school year in the **Baltimore Museum of Art**'s auditorium. The BMA (410–396–7100) hosts its own jazz-concert series in its sculpture garden during the summer.

The **Potomac River Jazz Club** (410–799–0155 or 703–698–7752 [hotline], www.prjc.org) is the Baltimore-Washington area's top trad-jazz organization. The region is a hotbed of Dixieland revival bands, and those groups join out-of-towners for monthly concerts plus a daylong Jazz Picnic every September.

The **Montpelier Cultural Arts Center** (410–792–0664) is a non-profit arts venue in a restored mansion in Laurel, a town halfway between Baltimore and Washington. The center sponsors a Friday-night jazz series every fall and another every spring with national acts such as McCoy Tyner and Marcus Roberts sharing the schedule with locals such as Buck Hill and Keeter Betts.

Radio Stations

WEAA/88.9 FM (443–885–3564). Named major-market jazz station of the year by *Gavin Magazine* in 1999. Mainstream and contemporary jazz M–F, 6 A.M.–6 P.M.; specialty programs (avant-garde, Latin jazz, etc.) 9 P.M.–midnight; "Ballad Jazz" midnight–6 A.M.

WJHU/88.1 FM (410–516–9548). "Jazz with Andy Bienstock," emphasizing older, mainstream styles, M–F, 9 P.M.–midnight.

WTMD/89.7 FM (410–830–8936). Smooth jazz and New Age, M–Sa, 24 hours a day. Blues Su, 3–5 P.M.

WRNR/103.1 FM (410–269–7779). Much blues.

Other Nearby Locations

Annapolis, 45 minutes from Baltimore, is home to three music spots worth the trip. The **King of France Tavern** in the Maryland Inn (16 Church Circle, 410–216–6340) is a 1784 tavern with original stone walls, brick arches, and huge wooden beams; local jazz quartets, big bands, and blues groups play F–Su. The upscale **Rams Head Tavern** (33 West St., 410–268–4545) hosts blues and jazz performers (Maria Muldaur, Branford Marsalis, Jazz Is Dead) amid its regular line-up of singer-songwriters and roots-rockers. **The Ebb Tide** (985 Bay Bridge Rd., 410–269–1500), a club by the bridge that connects mainland Maryland to the Eastern Shore, hosts local blues acts on a regular basis.

WASHINGTON, D.C.

Updated by Eugene Holley, Jr.

With its proud African-American population, the nation's capital has always been an important jazz city. Duke Ellington, Mercer Ellington, Buck Hill, Jimmy Cobb, Claude Hopkins, Andy Razaf, Charlie Rouse, Ira Sullivan, Billy Taylor, Shirley Horn, Billy Hart, and Andrew White were all born here, while James Reese Europe, Jelly Roll Morton, Ben Webster, Benny Carter, Sonny Stitt, Stanley Turrentine, and Keeter Betts all lived here either as children or adults. Many other musicians also once used Washington as a sort of base of operations providing easy access to other cities on the "black entertainment" circuit—Philadelphia, New York, Baltimore, Atlanta—while at the same time frequenting the capitol's U Street area (see "Landmarks and Legends," page 221).

From the 1920s through the 1950s, U Street was the hub of black Washington's commercial, professional, and artistic worlds. The famous Howard Theater, the Lincoln Theater, the Majestic Theater, the Crystal Caverns (later the Bohemian Caverns), the Jungle Club, and the Club Bali were all located here in the northernmost section of the original city of Washington. "U Street was one of the best-kept secrets in the world," said the late Felix Grant, a longtime D.C. deejay, in an interview in 1990.

By the mid-sixties, U Street's activity had diminished considerably (the Bohemian Caverns was the only large club left), and after the race riots of '68, the area went into a steep decline. Jazz moved elsewhere, most notably Georgetown, where Blues Alley had been operating since 1965.

Yet today, history is once again reversing itself. With the extension of the city's METRO subway line to U Street in the mid-1990s, and the renovation of the Lincoln Theater, Bohemian Caverns, and other clubs, the historic district is quickly regaining its status as a hot entertainment district.

A number of blues artists are also associated with Washington, D.C. Among them are rock-bluesman Tom Principato, the acoustic blues team of John Cephas and Phil Wiggins, Jimmy Thackery and the Nighthawks, Big Chief Ellis, and the R&B group the Clovers.

Sources

The free weekly *City Paper* (202–628–6528, www.washington citypaper.com), D.C.'s version of New York's *Village Voice*, has the most comprehensive listings in town. Another good source is the Weekend section of the *Washington Post* (202–333–6000, www.washingtonpost.com), published on Fridays.

For maps and other information, contact the Washington, D.C., Convention and Visitors Association, 1212 New York Ave., NW, Suite 600, or the Washington, D.C., Visitor Center at 1455 Pennsylvania Ave., NW (202–789–7000; same number for both, www.washington.org).

A Note on Neighborhoods

Because so much of downtown Washington is devoted to government, there is little there in the way of entertainment—with a few exceptions, noted below. Georgetown has long been considered the place to go for nightlife in the capital, but in recent years, the historic area, known for its cobblestone streets and Federal-style buildings, has been overrun with college students, forcing older audiences to move elsewhere. The Adams Morgan neighborhood, centering on 18th Street and Columbia Road, NW, is a newer trendy favorite, as well as a multi-cultural mecca boasting many immigrants from El Salvador, Guatemala, Ethiopia, and Eritrea. U Street is now easily accessible by the METRO and safe for exploring on foot. Alexandria, Virginia, an historic area usually filled with tourists dressed in brilliant greens, yellows, and pinks, also boasts a few music spots.

Driving in Washington is difficult—diagonal streets and frequent traffic circles make the city confusing to navigate—and parking is limited, especially in the downtown area. You're often better off taking the METRO subway lines.

Blues Alley, D.C.'s best-known jazz
club, began as a Dixieland haunt.

Courtesy Blues Alley

Landmarks and Legends

(The following sites, most of which are located in northwest
Washington, near the downtown, are best toured by car.)

U Street, between Ninth and 17th streets, NW.

Throughout the '70s, '80s, and early '90s, the once-pros-
perous U Street area was sad, depressing, and dangerous,
empty except for a few idle men sitting on stoops or wandering
aimlessly about. This has all changed in the last five or six
years, however, with the resurrection of the Lincoln Theater
(1215–19 U St., NW; see "Other Venues and Special Events,"
below), the Crystal/Bohemian Caverns, and many other buildings and clubs.

Crystal Caverns (later Bohemian Caverns), SW corner of
11th and U streets, NW.

The Crystal Caverns was an important jazz spot from the
mid-twenties through the '60s. A basement club, it was decorated by Italian craftsmen to resemble a cave.

It was at the Crystal Caverns that blueswoman Ruth Brown got her first real break. She had come to Washington from Virginia with Lucky Millinder's band, and one night while in the capital, two of the musicians in the band asked her to bring them some Cokes. She obliged, and when Lucky saw her, he went wild, saying he had hired her as a vocalist, not a waitress, and since she couldn't sing anyway, he was firing her.

"I think I must have had about four dollars if I had a penny," Brown told Arnold Shaw, author of *Honkers and Shouters*. "I stood there in disbelief. . . . I was pretty close to home—about two hundred miles. But my Dad had said, and how could I forget those words: 'Once you leave, don't call back here for anything.'"

Luckily, Brown went on to find a job at the Crystal Caverns, then being managed by woman bandleader Blanche Calloway, who told her she could sing there for a week, long enough to earn her fare back home. During that week, Brown was noticed by a talent scout who eventually landed her a record contract with Atlantic. Even so, it took another year for her luck to turn: en route to the studio in New York, she was in a car crash that hospitalized her for 12 months.

After years of inactivity, the Bohemian Caverns reopened in 2000 and is once again a thriving club (see "For Jazz," page 229).

Jungle Club, 1200 block, U St., NW.

Just west of the Lincoln (on the right, when facing the box office) is the red-brick building that once housed Jelly Roll Morton's Jungle Club, also known at various points as the Music Box and the Blue Moon Inn. This was one of the last places where the musician played professionally before he went to the West Coast and died.

Jelly Roll (Ferdinand La Menthe) had come to Washington, D.C., in 1936 at the height of the Depression, leaving his wife, Mabel, behind in New York. He opened the club with his lover, Cordelia, and from the beginning the place brought him nothing but trouble. He and Cordelia fought constantly, patrons complained about the club's high prices, and the swing era was beginning, leaving Jelly Roll behind.

Then, for a while at least, his fortunes changed. Jazz fans, many of them white, discovered the club, and suddenly Jelly Roll was hot once more. He would play "by the hour . . . smiling, with the world again in a jug and the stopper in his hand," writes Alan Lomax in *Mister Jelly Roll*.

Alas, the era of plenty did not last. An angry patron stabbed Jelly Roll above the heart one night, and by the time he'd recovered, he'd decided to leave Washington. Nineteen thirty-nine found him in New York with a bad heart; in 1940, he was poverty-stricken on the West Coast. He died on May 1, 1941, in Los Angeles.

Howard Theater, 620 T St., NW.

The Howard, opened in 1915, was to Washington what the Apollo was to New York or the Royal to Baltimore. *Everyone* played here: Ethel Waters, Alberta Hunter, Duke Ellington, Pearl Bailey, Lena Horne, Billy Eckstine, Dinah Washington, Sammy Davis Jr. Ella Fitzgerald won an amateur contest here once; while a few white musicians, Woody Herman, Stan Kenton, and Artie Shaw among them, put on shows as well. There was a house orchestra, manned by musicians of many races and ethnicities—black, Cuban, and Puerto Rican—and a bouncer called "Big Dog."

"Back then, people would be lined up all the way down the blocks on both sides," says D.C.–based bass player Keter Betts. "When Pearl Bailey was performing, she would have tables out serving hot dogs and coffee. The place was completely alive. It was *the* corner of Washington."

By the late '50s and '60s, the golden age of jazz had ended and rock-and-roll took over the theater. The Howard closed its doors for good after the race riots of 1968.

Two sidemen from Lucky Millinder's band shoot the breeze on or near U Street, circa 1939.

Frank Driggs Collection

Corner of Seventh and T streets, NW.

Right around the corner from the Howard were three jazz joints—Gene Clores', the Offbeat, and the Club Harlem—located at numbers 1855, 1851, and 1849 Seventh St. All the musicians who performed at the Howard would come here to eat and jam after the show. On the opposite side of the street, now torn down, was a popular after-hours place called Old Rose's.

Also on the corner was the first of the *Waxie Maxie* record stores (later a chain in the D.C. area), owned by Max Silverman. Ahmet Ertegun, who would later found Atlantic Records, used to sleep on a cot in Max's backroom in his younger, poorer days, when he didn't feel like going home.

Duke Ellington's boyhood home, 1212 T St., NW.

Shortly after the Duke was born (given name, Edward Kennedy Ellington), his family moved to this lovely three-story turreted house in a quiet middle-class neighborhood. Ellington himself once wrote that he was "pampered and pampered, and spoiled rotten by all the women in the family." He attended the local Armstrong High School, got a job selling refreshments at a baseball park, and read all the mystery books he could get his hands on.

Ellington's musical talents took a while longer to assert themselves. His mother had signed him up for piano lessons with a local teacher named, all too appropriately, Mrs. Clinkscales, but he missed more lessons than he took. "At this point," he writes in his autobiography, *Music Is My Mistress,* "piano was not my recognized talent. Why, I thought, take it so seriously? After all, baseball, football, track and athletics were what the real he-men were identified with. . . ."

One summer, however, Ellington heard Harvey Brooks, a young piano player out of Philadelphia, and was so impressed that he decided he just *had* to learn how to play. Shortly thereafter he came up with his first piece, "Soda Fountain Rag," and at the next high-school party, an impressed "rather fancy" friend pushed him to the front of the room, saying that his buddy, "the Duke," would be happy to play for his classmates.

Thereafter, Ellington not only had a new nickname but also a new passion. "From then on," he writes, "I was invited to many parties, where I learned that when you were playing piano there was always a pretty girl standing down at the bass clef end of the piano. I ain't been no athlete since."

James Reese Europe's home, 1008 S. St., NW.

Just around the corner from the old Ellington residence is the former home of James Reese Europe. The Reese family moved here from Alabama in the early 1880s, and James and his sister, Mary Lorraine, a musician in her own right, grew up in this solid red-brick building with a garden full of flowers.

Europe was the nation's first African-American band-leader, and he is best remembered as the band master of the famous all-black 369th Regiment's Band in World War I, which was assigned to the French Army. (Noble Sissle was its drum major.) Reese played traditional band music, but he was the first to draw heavily on black musical styles: ragtime, jazz, blues, and spirituals.

Europe died tragically, stabbed to death by a member of his own band, a snare drummer who was known for his hot temper. It happened one night in 1919, when the band was appearing at the Mechanics' Hall in Boston. Europe had sent for the drummer to reprimand him over some small wrongdoing, and the man sprang at him, stabbing him in the neck with a penknife. Not realizing that he'd been seriously hurt, Reese calmly made arrangements for someone else to take over the band and then made his way to the hospital. He died a few hours later: his jugular vein had been severed.

Reese is buried in Arlington National Cemetery.

Charles Hotel, 1338 R St., NW.

"A man can leave home one morning and come home that night whistling and singing to find there ain't nobody there but him. I left two men like that," writes Billie Holiday in *Lady Sings the Blues.*

One of the men Billie left was Mr. John Levy, and they were staying at the Charles Hotel at the time. "There was snow up to your panties over the capital," she writes. Nonetheless, while Mr. Levy was out, she found her mink coat that he had hidden under the mattress, put her last few dollars in a bag (she had over $2,000 with her but Mr. Levy had locked them up in a safe downstairs), grabbed her dog, and walked down the fire escape in her stocking feet. A few hours later, she was in New York.

Duke Ellington's birthplace, 2129 Ward Pl., NW.

Now there's nothing here except a modern, sterile-looking post office building, but it was on this short street that Duke Ellington was born. A simple plaque marks the spot, while words above it read DUKE ELLINGTON BUILDING.

Even this much recognition for one of the greatest musicians of our time was hard-won: the late Felix Grant, a local deejay and the man responsible for the plaque's installation, worked on the project for 15 years before it became a reality.

Library of Congress, First St. near E. Capitol St., SE, 202–707–5000.

Into this impressive marble Italian Renaissance building—heralded as the largest and costliest library in the world when it was built in 1897—strode Mr. Jelly Roll Morton, musician and persona extraordinaire, in May 1938 to prove to the world that he and *not* W. C. Handy, as had been broadcast on a radio program, was the father of jazz. Morton came to the Library's Coolidge Auditorium to record for folklorist Alan Lomax, who describes the scene in *Mister Jelly Roll:* "With his long black Lincoln, his diamonds, and his high-class clothes, he scarcely looked like a good source for folklore. . . . Unimpressed by the austere setting of the most exclusive chamber-music recitals in the world, [he] tossed his expensive summer straw on the bench of the Steinway grand, raised the lid to stash away the bourbon bottle, and then fell to larruping away at *Alabama Bound.*. . . The plaster busts of Bach, Beethoven, and Brahms looked sternly down, but if Jelly noticed them, he probably figured they were learning a thing or two."

National Museum of American History, Smithsonian Institution, 14th St. & Constitution Ave., NW, 202–357–2700, www.sie.du.

Housed inside this branch of the venerable Smithsonian are several jazz-related archives, including the Duke Ellington Archives and the Jazz Oral History Project. The Smithsonian Jazz Masterworks Orchestra, led by Indiana University's David Baker, is also headquartered here, and the museum presents jazz concerts throughout the year.

Howard University, centered on Georgia Ave. and Sixth St., NW, 202–806–6100, www.howard.edu.

Established in 1867, Howard University is one of the oldest and best-known African-American universities in the country. Nicknamed "The Mecca," it boasts an incredible potpourri of talented graduates, including Ralph Bunche, Dr. Alain Locke, Debbie Allen, Thurgood Marshall, and Toni Morrison. The school did not have a jazz program until the mid-'70s, when Donald Byrd started one up, but many jazz stars, including Benny Golson, studied in its music department. Today, the university boasts a critically acclaimed jazz ensemble, which at various times has included Greg Osby, Steve Coleman, Wallace Roney, and Geri Allen.

CLUBS, ETC.

Washington's premier jazz club, especially since the much-lamented recent demise of the 30-year-old One Step Down, is **Blues Alley**. Two top spots for local and regional talent are **Twins** and **Takoma Station**, both of which have loyal patrons who like their music on the funky and down-home side. Newcomers **BET on Jazz Restaurant** and the rebuilt **Bohemian Caverns** offer jazz lovers good moves and grooves closer to downtown. **Zoo Bar** and **Las Vegas Lounge** are top choices for blues fans.

Jazz artists to watch out for in D.C. today include tenor saxophonists Buck Hill, Paul Carr, and Larry Seals; alto saxophonist Marshall Keys; bassists Steve Novosel, Keter Betts, and James King; guitarist Kenny Definis; pianist Rueben Brown; drummer Nasar Abadey, and vocalists Mary Jefferson, Sunny Sumpter, and Ronnie Wells. The Latin Five and Maria Rodriguez are two of D.C.'s top Latin jazz attractions.

D.C. doesn't have the kind of blues scene you'd find in Memphis or Chicago, but it does boast a decent selection of blues musicians. Tom Principato, Sedatrius Brown, John Cephas and Phil Wiggins, and Danny Gatton are among the more prominent artists. The Uptown Rhythm Kings, the Persuaders, and Saffire, The Uppity Blues Women are the standout ensembles.

Many clubs in D.C. stay open until 2 A.M. on weekdays and 3 P.M. on weekends.

Personal Choices

Best jazz club and jazz jam: *Twins*
Best jazz supper club: *Blues Alley*
Best blues club: *Zoo Blues*
Best soul-blues joint: *New Vegas Lounge*

FOR JAZZ

Blues Alley, 1073 Rear Wisconsin Ave., NW (Georgetown), 202–337–4141, www.bluesalley.com.

Ever since 1965, Blues Alley, the best-known club in Washington, has featured all the top names in jazz and then some. Located in a former carriage house opposite Georgetown Park Mall, the place is elegant, yet sturdy and low-slung, with exposed brick walls, lots of little tables covered with blue cloths, and vintage photos in the bar area. The seating capacity maxes out at 125 and that, coupled with the house piano, which is always kept in tune, makes for good sound. Many artists, including Wynton Marsalis, Dizzy Gillespie, Ahmad Jamal, Ramsey Lewis, and Charlie Byrd, have recorded albums here.

Despite its name, Blues Alley has always emphasized jazz, with blues being only an occasional thing. In fact, in the club's earliest days, it was primarily known for Dixieland. The club, is, however, located in an alley. Tobacco merchants once parked their buggies here when they came to the Georgetown wharf to buy and sell.

A second Blues Alley is located in Tokyo, Japan, and the club also sponsors several community outreach programs, including the Blues Alley Youth Orchestra, whose members are promising young musicians.

Music: nightly. *Cover/minimum:* $$–$$$$. *Food:* Creole. Reservations recommended.

Twin's Restaurant & Lounge, 5516 Colorado Ave., NW (at Longfellow, 20 min. from downtown), 202–882–2523.

For over 15 years, some of the hottest jazz in D.C. has been steaming out of this tiny Ethiopian-American restaurant located on a quiet street lined with trees. Run by the delightful twin sisters, Maze and Ellen Tesfaye, it's the best true jazz hang in the city. Dozens of jazz stars, from Randy Weston to Frank Morgan, play here regularly, and on Sunday nights, there's a jam that attracts top talent from all over the region.

Through it all, the two Tesfaye sisters move elegantly from table to table. They've put a great deal of care into their restaurant, and the place really feels more like a home than a commercial establishment. There are flowers and candles on the tables, baskets and neatly framed photos on the walls.

Music: Th–Sa. *Cover/minimum:* $. *Food:* Ethiopian-American.

Takoma Station Tavern, 6914 Fourth St., NW (20 min. from downtown), 202–829–1999. www.takomastation.com.

Remember that sit-com about a "buppie" club in D.C. called Linc's? Well, Linc's is based on Takoma Station Tavern, which is an even jazzier version of that show. Located just a stone's throw away from the Takoma Metro Station, this upbeat restaurant-club is a haven for hip African Americans. With a decent-sized bandstand contrasted by two large TVs book-ending the bar, the club is hectic and loud. Only some hard-driving music can cool out this crowd. Local superstars like Marshall Keys and Paul Carr are usually featured, but world stars like Wynton Marsalis have played here, and Stevie Wonder even showed up once to jam. Other fine local talent includes groups like Soul Patrol, poets, and jazz/spoken-word artists.

Music: nightly. *No cover,* except for big acts. *Food:* American.

BET on Jazz Supper Club, 730 11th Street, NW, 202–393–0975, www.bet.com.

Located in the downtown area across from the Grand Hyatt Hotel, this club is glamour all the way, with a dark lavender décor and art-deco motifs. Affiliated with Black Entertainment Television's BET on Jazz Channel, the venue sports an incredibly small bandstand, on which it presents both quiet-storm smooth jazz and mainstream sounds. Vocalists Pam Bricker and Sam Smith, and instrumentalists Walter Bell and Al Schulman, are frequent headliners.

Music: nightly. *Cover/Minimum:* $$$-$$$$. *Food:* American, New World Caribbean. Reservations recommended.

The Bohemian Caverns, 2001 11th Street, NW, 202–965–4900, www.bohemiancaverns.com.

The world first learned of the Bohemian Caverns via Ramsey Lewis' popular 1964 album, *Ramsey Lewis at the Bohemian Caverns.* Known originally as the Crystal Caverns, the club presented many jazz and blues greats from the 1920s on (see "Landmarks and Legends," page 221).

Only re-opened in July 2000, after many years of inactivity, the Bohemian Caverns is now poised to once again take Washington by storm. With giant-sized, black-and-white piano keys encircling the building's façade, the club offers music and dining on its first floor, dancing and dining on the floors above. Tuesday is usually blues night, Wednesday is often devoted to poetry, and Sunday is open mike. On Thursdays through Saturdays, high-profile mainstream jazz artists such as McCoy Tyner, Stanley Jordan, Sonny Fortune, and Sir Roland Hanna perform.

Music: Tu, Th-Su. *Cover:* none-$$$.

219 Restaurant/Basin Street Lounge/Bayou, 219 King St., Alexandria, Va., 703–549–1141.

On a first visit, this place is confusing, with a restaurant on the first two floors, a lounge on the third, and a ratskeller in the basement. Getting from one section to another is not easy—there's no telling where *this* staircase will lead—because number 219 was built as a mansion, not a commercial establishment.

In the end, though, it's the mansion atmosphere that gives the place its charm. Wonderfully Victorian, with elaborate floral wall-paper, antique furniture, and crystal chandeliers, it seems only appropriate that the local jazz featured here is usually light and frothy vocalese. Trios also perform regularly.

Music: W–Sa. *Cover:* $. *Food:* Southern provincial Creole.

Also

U-Topia (1418 U St., NW, 202–483–7669), is a cool, cozy bar and grill, owned by musician/businessman Jamal Sahri. Situated in the renovated U Street corridor, it has nice acoustics and usually features Brazilian jazz.

In Adams Morgan are a number of attractive jazz restaurants and bars. Among them are the spacious **Columbia Station**, (2325 18th St., NW, 202–462–6040), featuring jazz nightly compliments of the Charles Carlton Trio, Jerry Gordon and the Elite Quartet, and others; and **Felix** (2406 18th St., NW, 202–483–3549), a cabaret-style club/restaurant that hosts jazz vocalists most nights. **Mo Bay** (2437 18th St., NW, 202–745–1002), short for Jamaica's Montego Bay, has a colorful West Indian vibe, while the **Rumba Cafe** (2443 18th St., NW, 202–588–5501) and the tiny El Salvadoran **Latin Jazz Alley** (1721 Columbia Rd., NW, 202–328–6190) are good venues for Latin jazz. The racy, urban cowboy–type bar **Madam's Organ** (2461 18th St., NW, 202–667–5370), a raunchy word play on "Adams Morgan," features good-time jazz and blues.

In D.C.'s South West, the city's smallest quadrant, **Zanzibar on the Waterfront** (800 Water St., SW, 202–554–9100) is a prominent venue.

FOR BLUES

Zoo Bar, 3000 Connecticut Ave., NW, 202–232–4225, www.zoobardc.com.

Though its official name is the Oxford Tavern, everyone knows this small, well-worn, neighborhood watering hole— one of the oldest pubs in Washington—as the Zoo Bar. Located right across the street from the city's zoo, it's been attracting the same clientele for years and years. Everyone knows everyone here. Regular acts include Mike Baker, 6L6, and Joe Dicey and Jam Nation.

Music: W, Th, Sa. *Cover:* $. *Food:* burgers, pizza, quesadillas, etc.

New Vegas Lounge, 1415 P St., NW (near downtown), 202–483–3971.

Located on the corner of 14th Street, which back before the 1968 riots was known for its hole-in-the-wall blues clubs, the Vegas is the best place in the city to hear soul- and R&B-tinged blues. A small club that also serves up "Vegas burgers" and "Vegas soul ribs," it's managed by singer Dr. Blues, who once performed at the 14th Street clubs and still takes to the stage on occasion.

The club's mostly a word-of-mouth spot, but it has attracted its share of out-of-towners and Europeans. Rock musician Stephen Stills also comes by from time to time.

Music: Tu–Su. *Cover:* $. *Food:* burgers, ribs, etc.

Fat Tuesday's, 10673 Braddock Rd., Fairfax, Va. (15 min. from downtown D.C.), 703–385–5717.

A smallish place done up New Orleans style, with peanut shells on the floor and Mardi Gras paraphernalia (masks, beads, posters) on the walls, Fat Tuesday's presents a mix of local blues, progressive rock, and reggae, with blues featured about a third of the time. Every Sunday is blues, compliments of the Fat Tuesday Blues Band featuring Danny Morris of the Nighthawks and Kevin McKendree, who plays with Tom Principato.

Music: W–Su, some blues. *Cover:* $–$$. *Food:* Cajun.

Also

Three large predominantly rock venues that occasionally bring in national blues talent are the **9:30 Club** (930 F St., NW, 202–393–0930, www.930.com), one of D.C.'s oldest rock clubs; the **Roxy** (1214 18th St., NW, 202–296–9292); and the **Bayou** (3135 K St., NW [Georgetown], 202–333–2897), which was once one of the best places in town in which to hear big bands.

For more information on blues in the D.C. area, contact the **D.C. Blues Society** (P.O. Box 77315, Washington, D.C. 20013–7715; 202–828–3028). The Society puts on a monthly blues jam and occasionally sponsors other special events around town.

Other Venues and Special Events

Originally built in 1921 in the Georgian Revival style, the recently renovated **Lincoln Theater** (1215 U St., NW, 202–328–6000) on historic U Street hosts occasional jazz concerts. Among those who have performed here are Wynton Marsalis and the Mingus Big Band.

The **Thelonious Monk Institute of Jazz** (202–364–7272, www.monkinstitute.com), a non-profit educational organization, presents jazz competitions in the fall. The finals, which are open to the public, are held at the **Kennedy Center** (off Virginia Ave., near the intersection of F St. and New Hampshire Ave., NW, 202–416–8000, www.kennedycenter.org). Also an annual event is the engaging **Jazz at the Kennedy Center** series, hosted by pianist/educator Billy Taylor. The concerts are broadcast on National Public Radio (www.nprjazz.org). Every May, too, the Kennedy Center presents the **Mary Lou Williams Women in Jazz Festival**.

In the summer, the **Carter Barron Amphitheatre** (16th and Colorado Ave., NW, 202–426–6837) features blues and jazz artists. **Capital Jazzfest** (888–378-FEST, www.capitaljazz.com) brings in stars of contemporary jazz in June. The **Smithsonian Festival of American Folklife** (202–357–2700), which includes performances by numerous blues artists, is presented every June-July.

In suburban Vienna, Virginia, jazz and blues concerts can be heard at the **Wolf Trap Farm Park** (703–255–1900, www.wolf trap.org), a national park for the performing arts. Every June, the **Wolf Trap Jazz and Blues Festival**, showcasing some of the world's premier musicians, is also presented here. The **Montpelier Cultural Center** in Laurel, Maryland (301–953–1993), features a fine fall jazz series.

The **Potomac River Jazz Club**, based in Falls Church, Va., has been presenting traditional jazz for about three decades, and their hotline (703–698–7752) provides extensive information on what's going on, traditionally speaking, in the Washington-Baltimore area.

Radio

WPFW/89.3 FM (202–783–3100). Jazz and public affairs station, some blues.
WJZQ/105.9 FM (202–686–3100). Smooth jazz.

Record Stores

For outlets that feature new releases, **Tower Records** (2000 Pennsylvania Ave., NW, 202–331–2400, www.towerrecords. com) and **Olsson's Books and Records** (1239 Wisconsin Ave., NW, 202–338–6712, www.olssons.com) are your best bets. But for rare and out-of-print recordings, take a drive to **Orpheus Records** (3173 Wilson Blvd., Arlington, VA, 703–294–6774, www.orpheusrecords.com), the **Record Mart** (217 King St., Old Town Alexandria, VA, 703–683–4583, www.recordmart.com), or **Joe's Record Paradise** (1300 E. Gude Rd., Rockville, MD, 301–315–2235, www.joes-record-paradise.com).

A tribute to Louis and friends graces a wall outside Chicago's New Regal Theater.

CHICAGO

Updated by Mark Ruffin (jazz) and Bill Dahl (blues)

The first jazz musicians from New Orleans began arriving in Chicago in 1915, and by the mid-1920s, the city was packed with both jazzmen and clubs. King Oliver, Freddie Keppard, Jelly Roll Morton, Lil Hardin, Alberta Hunter, Johnny Dodds, Baby Dodds, and Tom Brown (heading what was probably the first white band to come North) were among the first to arrive. Among the early clubs were Lamb's Café, the Royal Gardens, the De Luxe Café, the Lincoln Gardens, the Pekin, and the Vendome. The musicians were only one small part of a huge African-American migration North that began around World War I and was due primarily to the economic draw of the munitions, auto, and meat-packing industries.

Joe Oliver was the undisputed king of the early Chicago jazz scene, and there was much excitement when a young Louis Armstrong, who had played with Oliver in New Orleans, arrived at the Illinois Central railroad station on July 8, 1922, to join his mentor. Among those who flocked to see Oliver and Armstrong over the coming months were the city's young white musicians: Jimmy McPartland, Bud Freeman, Benny Goodman, Hoagy Carmichael, Eddie Condon, and Bix Beiderbecke. McPartland, Freeman, and others later formed the Austin High School Gang, which came to epitomize the hard-edged sound of "Chicago jazz."

Most of Chicago's early African-American population settled into a narrow corridor along South State Street between 16th and 39th streets. East 35th became the city's black entertainment district, and it was lined with posh theaters and black-and-tan clubs—the Sunset, the Apex, the Plantation. The time was the Roarin' Twenties, an era of drinking, dancing, and abandonment; and there were constant clashes between the gangsters, who controlled many of the clubs, and the police. On December 25, 1926, for example, two South Side establishments run by the mob were raided by 40 policemen who arrested 500 blacks and whites for doing an "immoral" dance called "the black bottom."

In 1928, with the opening of the splendid Savoy Ballroom, "black Broadway" shifted from 35th to 47th Street, and soon that street was lined with a whole new generation of theaters and clubs, including the Regal Theater, Gerri's Palm Tavern, and the Dreamland Café. Forty-seventh Street remained a center for black nightlife until well into the '50s, but during the Depression, many of the clubs were closed down by a reformist government, popular interest in jazz declined, and, as Milt Hinton put it, "Chicago just went down."[1] By the 1930s, the center of jazz had moved to New York.

During the '40s and '50s, bebop flourished both on Chicago's South Side and in the downtown. The corner of 63rd Street and Cottage Grove was a particularly important spot, and then there were the Gate of Horn, the Sutherland Show Lounge, and the Bee Hive, where Charlie Parker played his last gig. In the mid-1960s, Chicago was again on the forefront of the music with the founding, by Muhal Richard Abrams, of the Association for the Advancement of Creative Musicians (AACM), an organization that has produced such cutting-edge artists as Roscoe Mitchell, Anthony Braxton, Henry Threadgill, and Ed Wilkerson.

Along with Chicago's earliest jazz musicians came its earliest blues musicians. By the time Lester Melrose began recording for RCA Victor and Columbia in the mid-1930s, the city was bursting with blues talent. Big Bill Broonzy, Tampa Red, Arthur "Big Boy" Crudup, John Lee "Sonny Boy" Williamson, Big Maceo, Memphis Minnie, and Lonnie Johnson were only a few of the many names that Melrose handled between 1934 and '51.

In the beginning, the Chicago blues had a simple, rhythmic country sound, but by the late '30s and '40s, things were taking on a distinct urban edge. There was a new intensity and excitement to the music, and a new sophisticated sound, most notably heard in the addition of the electric guitar, which first came to widespread attention through "Louisiana Blues," a hit recorded by Muddy Waters in 1950.

Early bluesmen arriving in Chicago usually headed for Maxwell Street (see "Landmarks and Legends," page 247), where they would meet other musicians and learn about Chicago's blues clubs, most of which were located on the South Side or along Lake and Madison streets on the West Side. Some of the best-known of these early clubs were Gatewood's Tavern, the Square Deal Club, and the 708 Club.

The Chicago blues scene reached its peak in the post–World War II years. All the top talent was living here then: Muddy Waters, Howlin' Wolf, Bo Diddley, Willie Dixon, James Cotton, and Sunnyland Slim; and Chess Records was recording prodigiously. It took a long time for the mainstream community to catch on, however, and as late as the early 1970s, it was still possible to hear such masters as Howlin' Wolf or James Cotton perform in a South or West Side club for as little as $2.

Sources

The best source is *The Reader* (312–828–0350, www.
chireader.com), a free weekly, which lists hundreds of clubs
all over the city. The Friday and Sunday sections of the
Chicago Tribune (312–222–3232, www.chicago.tribune.com)
and the *Chicago Sun-Times* (312–321–3000, www.suntimes.
com) also contain listings.

The Jazz Institute of Chicago runs a hotline at 312–427–
3300 and hosts a Web site at www.jazzinstituteofchicago.com.

For maps and other information, contact the Chicago
Tourism Council's Visitor Information Center at 78 E. Washington St. (also home of the Chicago Cultural Center) or 163
Pearson St., near the historic Water Tower, 312–744–2400,
www.choosechicago.com.

A Note on Neighborhoods

Chicago, city of ethnic neighborhoods, is spread along 29 miles
of gray-blue Lake Michigan shoreline. The downtown centers
on the Loop, Chicago's historic business district, which is still
encircled by the tracks of the elevated train, the El.

Lincoln Avenue, on the North Side, is the current center for
nightlife and it's always packed, especially on weekends,
when finding a parking space is a problem. Rush Street is a
somewhat older entertainment district, also on the North
Side. The South and West Sides are the city's oldest African-
American communities.

Because Chicago is so spread out, getting from one end to
another can take time, despite the city's efficient system of en-
circling highways. Finding parking downtown, except in expensive lots, is often difficult.

Landmarks and Legends

FOR JAZZ

South Side

(The following route starts at E. 14th Street and proceeds
south. A car is necessary.)

Coliseum, E. 14th St. and S. Wabash Ave. (now an empty lot).

The Coliseum was the site of the first jazz concert ever, organized by OKeh Records on February 27, 1926, for a crowd
of several thousand. "OKeh Race Records Artists Night" the

B.L.U.E.S., one of the best-known joints on the North Side, packs them in most every night.

advertisements read, and the event brought together an amazing roster of talent: Clarence Williams, Louis Armstrong, Sara Martin, Chippie Hill, Blanche Calloway, Sippie Wallace, Bennie Moten. Later that same year, on June 12, OKeh sponsored a second concert, this one an immense "battle of the bands" led by such notables as King Oliver, Louis Armstrong, Al Wynn, and Erskine Tate.

Sunset Café/Grand Terrace Ballroom, 315–17 E. 35th St. at S. Calumet Ave.

Now a hardware store, the Sunset Café, opened in 1921 under the control of Al Capone, was once one of the most popular black-and-tan clubs in Chicago. Louis Armstrong and Earl Hines were members of its house band, and Hines later became the club's musical director.

Open seven nights a week until 3:30 or 4 A.M., the Sunset was a major hangout for musicians, who would drop by after their gigs elsewhere were done. Benny Goodman would come with his clarinet in a sack, while Tommy Dorsey arrived with either a trumpet or a trombone, because he hadn't yet decided which one he wanted to play.

After the Sunset closed in 1937 it became the Grand Terrace, which had previously been located on the second floor of 3955 S. Parkway Blvd. (now Martin Luther King, Jr., Dr.—look for mock columns on the second floor). The Grand Terrace was also controlled by Al Capone, who would come into the club with his henchmen, order all the doors closed, and have the band play his requests. Everyone at the Grand Terrace, including the waiters, carried guns, and Earl Hines recalled a time when one gangster, shouting "the heat's on," tossed a package containing $12,000 into his lap and ran out the door. Hines, knowing that he would have to return the money eventually, hid it and was rewarded with $500 for his trouble.

When Count Basie first started playing at the Terrace, he was, according to record producer–music critic John Hammond, just awful. The ballroom, with its elaborate floor shows, demanded intricate musical arrangements, which Basie simply did not have at that time. Fletcher Henderson, in one of the more generous moves in music history, saved Basie's skin by allowing him to use half of his own arrangements.

Lil Hardin's home, 421 E. 44th St.

Lil Hardin, a piano player and Louis Armstrong's second wife, had a decisive influence on her husband's career. Without her help and encouragement, Armstrong, then a shy and unassertive young man, might never have gone beyond playing second cornet in King Oliver's band. It was Lil who prodded Louis into leaving Oliver, and Lil who encouraged him to go to New York.

Lil and Louis separated in 1931, and Lil remained in their home, this row house built of gray stone. She never remarried and, according to some, was in love with Louis all her life. She never took off the rings he had given her, and carefully preserved his old cornet, letters, and photographs.

Then, on August 27, 1971, in what must surely be one of the saddest ironies in jazz history, Lil suffered a massive heart attack while playing a memorial concert for Louis in Chicago. In the middle of her solo, she simply fell off the piano bench and died.

Gerri's Palm Tavern, 446 E. 47th St., 312–373–6292.

Back in the days when everyone was playing the Regal (see New Regal Theater, page 240), they all stopped in at Gerri's after the show. Louis "Scotty" Piper, the mayor of 47th Street, would be there, along with fighter Joe Louis and all the jazz and blues stars. "This was their home away from home," says Gerri Oliver, who has owned the tavern since 1957. "They would all leave messages here for their wives. It was a focal point for the community."

The Palm was a very elegant affair. Waiters dressed in tuxes and there was a big grand piano and a polished dance floor. Today, the club is still open for drinking, record spinning, and occasional live jazz.

Sutherland Show Lounge, Sutherland Hotel, E. 47th St., near Drexel.

During the late 1950s and 1960s, the Sutherland, which had a huge bar stretching from one end of the hotel's lobby to the other, featured performances by such greats as Cannonball Adderley, Nancy Wilson, Rahsaan Roland Kirk, and John Coltrane. In 1960, Miles Davis played to a packed audience so entranced, it didn't even budge when a fire broke out in the next room. "The firemen were outside the door putting out this fire," says Jimmy Cobb in *Miles Davis: A Biography,* by Ian Carr, "and nobody left! Smoke was all in the joint and nobody left. . . . Yeah, Miles was very popular."

Golden Lily, 309 E. 55th St. (also called Garfield Blvd.).

Now part of a store with iron grills across its front, the Golden Lily was once a second-floor Chinese restaurant known for its jazz. In the early 1930s, the Louisiana Stompers, led by drummer Francois Mosely with sidemen Teddy Wilson, Albert Ammons, and Punch Miller, played a long residency here; and in 1941, Coleman Hawkins packed the place (then called White's Emporium) with his immortal rendering of "Body and Soul."

Today, the only reminder of the building's earlier days is the vaguely Oriental white-and-yellow-tile trim that runs just beneath the roof.

Roberts Hotel, 301 E. 63rd St.

In 1959, comedian Dick Gregory called Roberts Show Club at 6222 South Parkway Blvd. (now MLK Drive) "the biggest Negro-owned nightclub in America." Owned by a former taxi-cab entrepreneur, Herman Roberts, who had turned his 55-cab garage into a social hall for his friends (shortly thereafter opening it to the public), it featured everyone from Dinah Washington to Count Basie.

Sammy Davis, Jr., appeared at the club for a five-day stint in the late '50s, and it was due to him that Roberts, tired of picking up the entertainer downtown, expanded into the hotel-motel business. The hotel is now abandoned, but the marquee is still there.

New Regal Theater, 1645 E. 79th St. (near Stony Island Ave.), 312–721–9301.

The old now demolished Regal Theater, which once stood at 4719 South Parkway Blvd., was at one time both a center for black nightlife in Chicago and a magnificent sight to behold. A 1928 edifice built in Moorish style, it could seat 3,500 and was opulently decorated with balconies, chandeliers, and velvet drapes. In its earliest days, it hosted variety acts by performers such as Josephine Baker, Buck and Bubbles, and the Mills Brothers; in the 1930s and '40s, it featured big bands and orchestras led by everyone from Duke Ellington to Woody Herman. Dinah Washington won an amateur contest there when she was 15, and in the 1950s and '60s, Miles Davis, Dizzy Gillespie, Wilson Pickett, and James Brown were featured entertainers. B. B. King's landmark album, *Live at the Regal*, was recorded at the theater.

The New Regal, which opened in 1987, has no real connection to the old. Nonetheless, its architecture is also opulent and Moorish, echoing its famous predecessor, and it features occasional jazz concerts by the likes of Bobby McFerrin.

West Side

Austin High School, 231 N. Pine Ave.

In 1921, a group of young white students would stop in after school at a place called the Spoon and Straw for ice cream and soda. The parlor was equipped with a Victrola and the teenagers would sit around listening to records. One day, there were some new Gennett records on the table. . . .

"They were by the New Orleans Rhythm Kings," says trumpet player Jimmy McPartland in *Hear Me Talkin' to Ya,* edited by Nat Shapiro and Nat Hentoff, "and I believe the first tune we played was 'Farewell Blues.' Boy, when we heard that—I'll tell you we went out of our minds. Everybody flipped. . . .

"We stayed there from about three in the afternoon until eight at night, just listening to those records one after another, over and over again. Right then and there we decided we would get a band and try to play like these guys."

That was the beginning of the famous Austin High School Gang, who came to epitomize the Chicago sound during the 1920s. Benny Goodman, Eddie Condon, Dave Tough, and others were also later affiliated with the group.

Today, Austin, a big yellow building still operating as a high school, is located in a rough, run-down section of town.

In or Near Downtown

Congress Hotel, 520 S. Michigan Ave.

In 1927, a young man named Francis "Cork" O'Keefe booked the Fletcher Henderson band into the prestigious Congress Hotel, much to the fury of the city's white musicians' union, which refused to accept the contract. An all-black band at a major hotel was still unheard of at that time. O'Keefe then threatened to take the contract to the black local, forcing the white local's hand, and that August, Henderson played an extended, and very successful, engagement.

The Congress, a magnificent hotel still in operation, witnessed a second racial breakthrough in 1935, when an interracial trio, led by Benny Goodman and including Gene Krupa and Teddy Wilson, played in a large commercial venue for the first time. The performance, sponsored by the Hot Club of Chicago, took place in the Urban Room at the corner of Michigan Avenue and Congress Parkway (now a cocktail lounge), and was so successful that Goodman (no crusader

The New Apartment Lounge once played host to everyone from Sonny Slitt to Clark Terry.

for civil rights; he had used Wilson purely for musical reasons) hired Wilson as a regular member of his organization.

Jane Addams's Hull-House Museum, 800 S. Halsted St. at Polk, 312–413–5353.

Jane Addams's settlement house once consisted of 13 buildings covering an entire city block. Immigrants then living in the area took classes here in sewing and cooking and theater, and some of the boys played in the settlement's Boys' Band. Among them were Benny Goodman, his brother Freddy Goodman, and Art Hodes.

"At Hull House we weren't playing jazz," Freddy Goodman says in *The World of Earl Hines.* "Most of the music was marches, small overtures, primer-type things. . . . The way we first heard jazz was when we'd be passing a ballroom. . . . We'd hear music. It would be real exciting, and we'd sneak in. . . . One time Benny just jumped up onstage, grabbed the guy's clarinet and started to play. He was a natural, that's all."

Today, only two of the original settlement buildings are left. Operated as a museum by the University of Illinois at Chicago, they are open for touring and often present special exhibits.

Open: M–F, 10 A.M.–4 P.M., Su, noon–5 P.M. *Free admission.*

Clark and Randolph Streets

Art Hodes's Chicagoans named a tune after this intersection, where the Lamb's Café and the Sherman Hotel (housing both the College Inn and the Panther Room) were once located. Three other pieces, Woody Herman's "Herman at the Sherman," Duke Ellington's "Sherman Shuffle," and Fats Waller's "Pantin' in the Panther Room," came out of this corner as well.

The Lamb's Café was one of Chicago's earliest venues for jazz. Tom Brown's Ragtime Band, probably the first white jazz band to appear in Chicago, was playing here before 1920. Later, the café featured Jabbo Smith and Johnny Dodds.

Both the College Inn and the Panther Room were important in the 1930s and '40s. Paul Whiteman's band was resident in the College Inn in 1933, and most of the big bands of the day played the Panther Room (decorated for its namesake), along with smaller groups led by artists such as Bud Freeman and Hot Lips Page. A young Bix Beiderbecke, sneaking out of Lake Forest Military Academy in Chicago's suburbs, sometimes visited the place. Says friend and fellow musician Sid Stewart in *Bix: Man and Legend,* "We sat there for hours and just listened. We thought it was wonderful . . . and it quickly became clear to me that Bix was destined for a career in professional music. It was as inevitable as death."

Civic Opera House and Theater, 20 N. Wacker Dr., 312–346–0270.

Built in 1929, the stunning Civic Opera House, which together with the Civic Theater takes up an entire city block, sometimes sponsors jazz concerts. In one especially historic 1946 event, Dizzy Gillespie, Sidney Bechet, Jimmy McPartland, Gene Sedric, and Bud Freeman all appeared together. The Chess brothers also rented space in the building in their early days, the results of which were their first recordings: "Union Man Blues" and "Bilbo's Dead" with vocalist Andrew Tibbs.

Grant Park, Soldier Field

It was near the Buckingham Fountain that Mezz Mezzrow and Frank Teschemacher once played late, late-night clarinet duets "in the style of Jimmy Noone and Doc Poston getting high on gauge and blowing until we were blue in the face." One night, a motorcycle cop approached and the twosome, already hounded elsewhere by the police, was sure it was the beginning of the end. Instead, the cop just nodded approvingly and motioned them to keep playing. "After that," writes Mezz Mezzrow in *Really the Blues*, ". . . night after night, Bud [Freeman], Dave [Tough], Tesch and as many others as could squeeze in my car would broom over to this hide-out in Grant Park and blow our tops under the twinklers, shooting riffs at the moon. . . ."

London House, 360 N. Michigan Ave.

This solid building was once the London House, an elegant dinner club that flourished in the 1950s and '60s. It was well known for its piano trios, and Oscar Peterson and George Shearing were regulars.

North Side

Aragon Ballroom, 1100 W. Lawrence Ave., 312–561–9500.

Once known as one of the best dance spots in town, the Aragon, still a beautiful and ornate if somewhat run-down building with a towering marquee, started presenting jazz in the mid-1920s. Wingy Manone and his band—including Art Hodes, Bud Freeman, Floyd O'Brien, and Gene Krupa—were the first jazz group to appear here, and during the swing era, performances of big bands were often broadcast live. Today, the Aragon is used for pop and rock concerts.

Webster Hotel, W. Webster Ave. and N. Lincoln Park West.

It was at the Webster Hotel, now a residential building located across the street from the Lincoln Park Zoo, that Jelly

Roll Morton and his Red Hot Peppers recorded for Victor Records in 1926. Despite being almost universally disliked among jazzmen (for his arrogance, for his lack of humor), Jelly Roll was apparently an agreeable musician to record with. Says Johnny St. Cyr, one of his sidemen, in *Mister Jelly Roll* by Alan Lomax, "He'd never give you any of your specialties, he'd leave it to your own judgment. . . . [He] was always open to suggestions."

FOR BLUES

Southside

(The following route starts near 21st Street, proceeds south to 35th Street and then east to Lakeland Avenue, before returning west to Indiana Avenue. A car is necessary.)

Chess Records, 2120 S. Michigan Ave.

Started by Phil and Leonard Chess, two young immigrant brothers from Poland, Chess Records recorded nearly all of the blues—and many of the jazz—musicians of note working the Midwest in the '50s and '60s. Among their most famous artists were Muddy Waters, Howlin' Wolf, Otis Rush, Bo Diddley, Willie Dixon, Little Walter, Chuck Berry, Gene Ammons, James Moody, Sonny Stitt, and Kenny Burrell.

From 1957 to 1966, Chess was located in this sturdy three-story building on Chicago's South Side, which has been designated a Chicago landmark. Later, the company moved to a huge factory building at 320 E. 21st St. where, amazingly enough, the chrome letters "Chess Recording Company" still adorn the façade.

The Chess brothers actually started out as nightclub owners of a place called the Macomba (39th Street and Cottage Grove), a popular neighborhood spot. They became involved with their first label, Aristocrat, in 1947, recording in the back of a street-level store, where they hung an open microphone in a tiny toilet to add echo. One of their first recording artists was Muddy Waters.

The brothers changed the name of their company to Chess in 1950, but it wasn't until 1955, when they released Chuck Berry's hit, "Maybellene," that they achieved any real success. Some eight years later, they bought a radio station called WVON ("Voice of the Negro").

Twice a year, Leonard Chess traveled down South, seeking new talent, and legend has it that he sometimes set up his tape recorder in a cotton field, running a long extension cord into the plantation house. Howlin' Wolf and Arthur "Big Boy"

Crudup were "discovered" on two such trips; another visit resulted in the acquisition of Jackie Brenston's "Rocket 88" from Sam Phillips.

Leonard Chess died in 1969, and Phil left the company shortly thereafter.

Site of John Lee "Sonny Boy" Williamson's death, S. Giles Ave. bet. 31st and 32nd Streets.

Somewhere on this block Sonny Boy Williamson was fatally stabbed on the morning of June 1, 1948. He had just left the Plantation Club on East 31st Street and was heading toward his home at 3226 South Giles Avenue (now torn down), when he was maliciously attacked, and his wallet, wristwatch, and harps were stolen. Bleeding from the head, he stumbled home to his wife, who, thinking he'd just been in a drunken brawl, didn't call the ambulance until 5 A.M. He was DOA at Michael Reese Hospital.

Smitty's Corner, NW Corner of 35th St. and Indiana Ave.

Though now completely remodeled and part of a liquor store, Smitty's Corner was Muddy Waters's home base throughout

The Checkerboard on the South Side has become so well known that it now has security parking.

the mid- and late 1950s. During those years, he left town only to do a regular Wednesday-night gig in Gary, Indiana.

All this changed in the fall of 1958, when, through an offer to tour with an English traditional jazz group led by Chris Barber, Muddy Waters became one of the first blues artists to break through to a white audience. Big Bill Broonzy, who was known for assisting younger artists, had helped pave the way by recommending Muddy for the job. (Broonzy had already made several trips to Europe himself, but by the late '50s he was in poor health).

Muddy Waters's Home, 4339 S. Lake Park Ave.

The small three-story building is still occupied, but there is plastic over its windows, and the screen door, which was once inscribed with Muddy's name, is gone. Muddy lived here during the '50s and '60s, until the death of his wife.

"This was the house of the blues in the fifties," says Muddy's son, Charles Morganfield, a quiet-spoken man who moved back to the house some time ago. "We got them all, down there in the basement—B. B., John Lee, Chuck Berry. I had to get out of bed one time to get Chuck Berry down to Chess just before he made 'Maybellene.'"

Muddy is buried in the Restvale Cemetery in Worth (117th St. and Laramie, just west of Cicero, 708–385–3506; open M–F, 8 A.M.–4 P.M., Sa, 8 A.M.–3 P.M.).

708 Club, 708 E. 47th St.

Bo Diddley played his first major gig at this small storefront club (now an abandoned shop, protected by an iron gate). Though originally from Mississippi, Diddley spent his youth in Chicago, playing the streets for about 12 years before appearing at the 708.

The 708 Club was a favorite among bluesmen in the '40s and '50s because its bandstand was located behind the bar, giving the musicians some protection from the club's wild audience. The South Side back then, writes Mike Rowe in *Chicago Breakdown,* was renowned for its "Saturday night tavern brawls, Sunday morning visits to the Provident Hospital emergency room and Monday morning appearances in the Fifth District Police Court at 48th and Wabash, 'the busiest police station in the world'."

Theresa's Tavern, 4801 S. Indiana Ave.

Formerly located in the basement of this brown corner building, "T's Basement," run by Theresa Needham, was once a South Side institution. "World-renowned Theresa's Tavern has more charisma or atmosphere than any other club in Chicago," reported *Living Blues* in 1973.

Opened in 1949 and closed in 1983–84, Theresa's started offering live music in 1953, much against the instincts of its owner, who once said she hated music. Buddy Guy was associated with the club for seven years, and Little Junior Wells for 18. Others who played here included Little Walter, James Cotton, Sunnyland Slim, and Otis Rush.

A "small, dark and generally cheerful" place with no special lights for the band and no dance floor, Theresa's was one of the first South Side clubs to start attracting a white audience in the early 1960s (many were college students from the nearby University of Chicago). The place was also famous for giving away food to the needy on Sundays. Each customer got pig feet and pig ears, two slices of bread, and hot sauce.

West Side

Maxwell Street, Between S. Halsted and S. Morgan Streets.

During its heyday in the early to mid-1900s, Maxwell Street (or "Jew Town") on a Sunday afternoon was a mile-long extravaganza of a bazaar filled with peddlers, pushcarts, and wooden stalls selling everything from spices and vegetables to clothes and appliances. Also to be seen everywhere, trying to attract passersby with their wares, were Gypsy fortune-tellers, dope dealers, and blues musicians.

For a newly arrived blues singer in Chicago, Maxwell Street was the primary meeting ground. Hound Dog Taylor played here, and so did Little Walter, Big Walter Horton, Honeyboy Edwards, Big Bill Broonzy, Floyd Jones, and Snooky Pryor. As Hound Dog Taylor tells Ira Berkow, author of *Maxwell Street*, "You used to get out on Maxwell Street on a Sunday morning and pick you out a good spot, babe. Dammit, we'd make more money than I ever looked at. Sometimes a hundred dollars, a hundred twenty dollars. Put you out a tub, you know, and put a pasteboard in there, like a newspaper? . . . When somebody throw a quarter or a nickel in there, can't nobody hear it. Otherwise, somebody come by, take the tub and cut out. . . ."[2]

Up until the mid-1990s, two blocks of Maxwell Street, between Halsted and Morgan, still functioned as a flea market on Sunday afternoons. Now, however, the area is being redeveloped by the University of Chicago.

1815 Club, 1815 W. Roosevelt Rd.

Once home base for Howlin' Wolf, and owned by his sax-man Eddie Shaw, the 1815 was a regular gig for innumerable West Side bluesmen, including Magic Sam and Otis Rush. Shaw, who had sold the place in the 1970s, bought it again in the early 1990s, hoping to resurrect his old club. Alas, the project did not take off and the building stands abandoned once more.

Before the 1815 was the 1815, it was the Club Apex, where the owner was killed in 1970 while trying to stop a knife fight between two women on the dance floor.

In the Suburbs

Howlin' Wolf's Grave, Oakridge Cemetery, Roosevelt Rd. and Oakridge Ave., Hillside (30 min. W of downtown), 708–344–5600.

In the early 1970s, Chester Burnett, then in his sixties, suffered a series of heart attacks. Then, in 1973, he was in an automobile accident that resulted in severe kidney injury. Still, he continued to play in public, even though he could "no longer make his trademark entrance: crawling on all fours with a wolflike gleam in his eyes."[3] He died on January 10, 1976, and is buried beneath a gravestone engraved with flowers and an electric guitar.

Open: M–Sa, 9 A.M.–4 P.M.; Su, 10 A.M.–4 P.M.

CLUBS, ETC.

Chicago has one premier room that brings in out-of-town jazz talent, the **Jazz Showcase,** and numerous other clubs that feature top-caliber area musicians. **Andy's** is a particularly good place to hear traditional and mainstream jazz, **Green Dolphin Street** is a jazz supper club in the best sense, and **Hothouse** and the **AACM**'s headquarters (see "Other Venues," p. 265) are top spots for progressive jazz. The **Green Mill** features both bebop and progressive, the **Cotton Club** is the city's premier African-American club and disco, and the historic **New Apartment Lounge** features first-rate jams.

Blues in Chicago is thriving. Its center has moved from the South Side to the North Side, and Lincoln Avenue especially is lined with one club after another, all offering music most nights. On the weekends, it's best to avoid the most famous clubs, **B.L.U.E.S.** and **Kingston Mines,** and head for lesser-knowns such as **Rosa's** and **Lilly's,** which also offer first-rate talent.

Although the blues joints on the South and West sides are not nearly as active as they once were, many still feature live entertainment at least once a week. Often the music, technically speaking, is not as good as that on the North Side (the top musicians are hired by the better-paying clubs), but the clubs' atmosphere—enthusiastic, friendly, and real in a way that a commercial place can never be—more than makes up for it.

Numerous top-caliber jazz and blues musicians play around Chicago today, and to select even a representative sampling is difficult, to say the least. Some of the top jazz musicians who appear most regularly, however, are veteran saxophonists Franz Jackson and Von Freeman, pianist Jodie Christian, violinist Johnny Frigo, bassist-multi-instrumentalist Malachi Favors, Mike Finnerty & the Heat Merchants, the Kimberly Gordon Trio, the Rob Parton Quartet, the Big Band of Chicago, vocalists Kurt Elling and Patricia Barber, saxmen Ken Vandermark and Fred Anderson, trumpet player Orbert Davis, guitarists Fareed Haque and George Freeman (Von's brother and Chico's uncle), pianist-vocalist Judy Roberts, percussionist Hamid Drake, and the Chicago Jazz Orchestra.

Among the many blues musicians with which Chicago abounds are A. C. Reed, Willie D. & the All-Stars, Jimmy Johnson, Eddie Campbell, Eddy Clearwater, Casey Jones, Koko Taylor, Buddy Guy, Junior Wells, Billy Branch, Joanna Connor, Jimmy Walker, Magic Slim & the Teardrops, Son Seals, Johnny B. Moore, Johnny Laws, Sugar Blue, and Willie Kent & the Gents.

Generally speaking, clubs have either 2 A.M. or 4 A.M. licenses.

Personal Choices

Best national jazz club: *Jazz Showcase*
Best jazz supper club: *Green Dolphin Street*
Best progressive jazz: *Hothouse*
Best North Side blues club: *B.L.U.E.S.*
Best South Side blues club: *Lee's Unleaded Blues*
Best historic clubs: *Green Mill, New Apartment Lounge*

FOR JAZZ

In or Near Downtown

Jazz Showcase, 59 W. Grand Ave., 312–670-BIRD (2473), www.jazz-showcase.com.

Joe Segal's internationally famous Jazz Showcase, located just off Ontario Street in the River North district, is *the* place to hear jazz in Chicago. Segal, who has been producing jazz concerts since 1947, has worked with all the greats (Max Roach, Dizzy Gillespie, Ira Sullivan, Dexter Gordon, Yusef

Lateef, Sun Ra, the Art Ensemble of Chicago) and he emphasizes much mainstream and straight-ahead.

Segal put on his first jazz sessions when he was still in college, studying at Roosevelt University on the G.I. Bill. Those sessions, which took place in a student lounge, continued for 10 years, and Segal never did graduate. In 1957, he moved the sessions—which he had dubbed the Jazz Showcase, based on his initials—to the Gate of Horn folk club, and in 1960, to the Sutherland Show Lounge on the South Side (see "Landmarks and Legends," p. 239). Later, the Showcase moved again and again to such now legendary spots as the Plugged Nickel, the Hungry Eye, the Happy Medium on Rush Street, and the historic Blackstone Hotel, before settling on Grand Avenue in 1995.

Today's Showcase is an acoustic gem, with a dark, sexy nightclub aura that harkens back to the club's days on Rush Street. There's a huge Duke Ellington portrait overlooking the stage and smaller historical pictures adorning the walls. There's not a bad seat in the split-level house and the sound is impeccable throughout.

The Showcase was the first jazz club in the country to institute a no smoking policy, and it's one of the few that actively welcomes children. (Su matinees only; those under 12 admitted free). Monday nights are usually dedicated to top local combos and big bands; nationally known names are often booked the rest of the week.

Music: M-Su, Su matinee. *Cover*: $$-$$$. Reservations recommended.

Andy's, 11 E. Hubbard St., 312–642–6805.

Back in 1978, Andy's started what has since become a Chicago tradition, "Jazz at Five." Every afternoon after work, middle-aged businesspeople and young professionals traipse down to this large old room, once frequented by newspaper pressmen, to relax with a drink and some of the finest traditional jazz and bebop around. Regulars include Von Freeman, Franz Jackson, and John Young.

Andy's is filled with lots of heavy wood, old-fashioned hanging lamps, silhouetted pictures of jazzmen, and revolving fans. An enormous rectangular bar is situated near the front of the club, while small tables, set with red plastic tablecloths and flickering candles, are placed near the back. Andy's also features a "Jazz At Noon" series for the lunchtime crowd, more jazz in the evening, and some blues on the weekend.

Music: M-Sa. *Cover*: $. *Food*: American.

The Aragon Ballroom was once one of the best swing dance spots in town.

Cotton Club, 1710 S. Michigan Ave., 312–341–9787.

The premier African-American club and disco in town, the Cotton Club—large, modern, and elegant—features jazz in the front room, and dancing in the back. An Art Deco–esque skyscraper adorns the façade, while inside, the décor is all black and white, exposed brick, and chrome.

Most of the jazz talent that appears here is high caliber and has as much an affinity for pop and funk as for mainstream jazz. Periodically, nationally known names such as Roy Ayers and Gerald Albright are booked.

Music: M-Sa. *Cover/minimum*: $-$$. Valet parking available.

Underground Wonder Bar, 10 E. Walton, 312–266–7761, undergroundwonderbar.com.

A dark, candle-lit basement club with mirrored walls, a low ceiling, and a handful of tables (equipped with paper and crayons for creative adults), the Underground is owned by Lonie Walker, a jazz and blues vocalist and piano player who has been performing in the Chicago area for over 20 years. Walker usually takes to the stage of her club about three nights a week, and she's often joined by members of her wait-staff—nearly everyone who works at the club is an aspiring musician or actor. The club's late night license also makes it a favorite haunt of musicians, who often lead spirited jam sessions until closing time. Regulars include the gifted pianist/vocalist Vince Willis and singer Joan Collaso.

Music: nightly. *Cover:* $.

Hothouse, 31 E. Balbo, 312–362–9707, www.hothouse.net.

This non-profit nightclub, right outside the south Loop, is the place for the progressive arts, both aural and visual. The art for sale on the walls is as diverse as the music, which ranges from local and national avant-garde and mainstream jazz acts to world music groups from Africa, the Caribbean, and South America. The clientele features a large international contingent, many Latin and African dancers, and poets and actors—who also perform here from time to time.

The sound is very good throughout the main music room, and the comfortable booths that ring much of the stage area are raised—a good thing when it gets crowded on the dance floor.

Music/events: nightly, mostly jazz. *Cover:* $-$$.

The Backroom, 1007 N. Rush St., 312–751–2433.

This aptly named room is one of the oldest nightspots in the city and perhaps the one least frequented by Chicago residents, as tourists and conventioneers are its dominant patrons. A long corridor leads about a quarter of a block off the street to the club's small, attractive space. The music is usually contemporary and in your face, played by musicians who are entertainers rather than technicians. There's also a unique balcony that hangs over the small stage but is hidden from the ground floor.

Music: nightly. *Cover/minimum:* $-$$. Reservations highly recommended.

Lush Life, 226 E. Ontario, 312–649–5874.

Located in a part of town called Streeterville, home to a few Asian restaurants, Lush Life is a softly lit room with a Japanese motif that's not nearly as complex as the beautiful song it is named after. However, the booking, done by owner and San Francisco guitarist Akio Sasajima, is top-notch and usually features a piano trio or sax quartet. The bands tend to be local, but there are periodic thematic gigs by international acts, usually from Japan (saxophonist Sadao Watanabe, pianist Makoto Ozone). The room is thin, with excellent sight lines and a wonderfully understated sound system.

Music: M-Sa. *Cover:* $. *Food:* Japanese appetizers and desserts.

Joe's Bebop Café & Jazz Emporium, 600 E. Grand St., 312–595–5299.

Because of its Navy Pier location and many tourists, not to mention its huge open patio and much early traditional jazz, Joe Segal's *other* place is the only jazz spot in Chicago that's reminiscent of a New Orleans' French Quarter nightclub. In fact, you could call this the *anti*-Jazz Showcase, as most of its acts are generic local folks, there is no cover, and customers are allowed to talk, eat, and smoke (any one of which would get them thrown out of the Showcase). By design, however, the atmosphere here is more festive and the service much more attentive than at the Showcase. The sound system is wonderful close to the stage, but tinny farther away from it. Sight lines are excellent whether you're sitting inside or outside at the patio bar overlooking Lake Michigan.

Music: nightly. *No cover. Food:* American, New Orleans.

North Side

Green Mill, 4802 N. Broadway, 773–878–5552.

The Green Mill is the oldest nightclub in Chicago, dating back to 1907. Once owned by Machine Gun Jack McGurn (one of Al Capone's henchmen, and the leader of the St. Valentine's Day massacre), it was home to singer Joe E. Louis for years. Then Louis, getting a better job offer, left the place. McGurn, outraged, had the singer's vocal chords slashed, and left him for dead. Louis survived, however, and went on to become a successful comedian.

At one time the Green Mill was a big complex, occupying nearly an entire city block. There were gardens, gazebos, a dance hall out back, and a green windmill (hence the name) on top. All the major swing bands played here, and then there were Billie Holiday, Anita O'Day, Jack Teagarden, and Claude Thornhill. The legendary Texas Guinan was once the Green Mill's hostess, and many movies were filmed here, including *Thief*, with James Caan. Hey Hey Humphrey, a great drummer down on his luck, froze to death in the club's basement.

Today, the Green Mill still feels like a creaky old-time speakeasy. The booths are covered with the original itchy horsehair and there are huge murky paintings on the walls. The jazz is top drawer and in recent years, the club has developed an international reputation as the Monday and Wednesday night home of singers Patricia Barber and Kurt

Elling respectively. A national act is usually booked two to three weekends a month, but most other nights feature the cream of the local scene, all of whom clamor to work at the Mill.

Music: nightly. *Cover:* $.

Green Dolphin Street, 2200 N. Ashland, 773–395–0066, www. jazzitup.com.

A winner of the Chicago Music Award's top jazz club honor, this big, airy, two-room place is a throwback to the jazz supper clubs of the '60s. Equipped with a wonderful outdoor patio on the banks of the Chicago River, the club is as beautiful as the song it's named after. The dining room offers only recorded music, but in the music room is a semi-auditorium that holds what may be the best stage of any jazz club in town. High enough for everyone to see, it is curtained off, giving the whole place a formal feel. Acoustic and electric jazz is served, along with a solid dose of Latin music and contemporary jazz. Top national acts are booked about once a month. Smoking, particularly of cigars, is not only encouraged here, but heavily indulged in—and sometimes annoyingly so, despite the elaborate air filter system.

Music: nightly. *Cover:* $-$$$. *Food:* Fine American.

Pops For Champagne, 2934 N. Sheffield, 773–472–1000.

Small acoustic groups are the rule at this long and narrow room, reminiscent of an English gentleman's club with lots of heavy wood and dark tones. The stage sits high behind the bar and provides excellent sight lines. Pops presents many well-known Chicago-based musicians, including Judy Roberts, Von Freeman, and Redd Holt. The club's real specialty, however is its champagne; over 150 varieties are available by the bottle, 12 by the glass. A jazz brunch is served on Sundays and Bastille Day is observed every year with a day-long music fest. Out back there's a garden that is open from late spring to fall, while a huge fireplace is stoked during the winter months. Connected to the music room is a bar offering recorded jazz for those more interested in socializing than listening.

Music: nightly. *Cover/minimum:* $-$$. *Food:* appetizers, desserts.

The Note, 1565 N. Milwaukee, 773–489–0011.

A hodge-podge kind of club presenting music that many purists wouldn't even consider jazz, the Note is perhaps the only place in Chicago where the full spectrum of contemporary electric jazz can be heard. The club is the unofficial home of Chicago acid-jazz, a music that mixes be-bop, avant-garde, and Hammond B–3 organ grooves with the funk and R&B

sounds of the '70s. Sometimes the audience—part college kids and part graying funk-a-teers—offers a mix that's just as striking as the music. Among the club's most popular acts are Fat Time and trumpeter Ron Haynes.

The décor of this long, dark room is black and neon. Sound and sight lines are decent but seats are a premium, even on weekdays.

Music: nightly. *Cover:* $.

Piano Man, 3001 N. Clark St., 773–472–2956.

This venerable Wrigleyville nightspot (near the famous ballpark where the Chicago Cubs play) recently resumed the music policy that it stopped more than 15 years ago. Back then, economic times forced the club's owners to crowd the stage into a small window space that it shared with the bar. But in our 21st-century prosperity, those same owners have knocked down some walls, absorbed the restaurant next door, and given the musicians a stage of their own in a room separate from the bar. On the music calendar is a mix of local mainstream jazz vocalists and instrumentalists.

Music: W-Sa. *Cover:* $. *Food:* American.

Davenport's Piano Bar & Cabaret, 1383 N. Milwaukee, 773–278–1830.

An alternative lifestyle is hardly needed to appreciate the fine singers who perform here, at this unabashedly gay club that's all that's left of Chicago's once-thriving cabaret scene. The royal blue face of this place makes it a bit conspicuous amid its drab storefront neighbors, and once inside, the serious music may take some seeking out, as the long attractive front room also has entertainment, including female impersonators. But a talented chanteuse or male crooner mixing tin pan alley with modern show tunes and a jazz sensibility works the cabaret room in back. A long comfortable couch runs the length of the wall opposite the stage and the room's rectangle shape results in great sight lines. There's also an impeccable sound system. With management committed to bringing in the best of the local scene, as well as singers from places like San Francisco and New York, Davenport's is one of the last bastions of cabaret in Chicago.

Music: M, W-Sa. *Cover:* $.

Also

There are many rock clubs that offer jazz weekly or periodically. The most famous is the **Empty Bottle** (1035 N. Western, 773–276–3600, www.emptybottle.com), where saxophonist Ken Vandermark produces his avant-garde series every Tuesday and Wednesday night, and from where he broadcasts a weekly show.

Chicago's acid-jazz scene is led by saxman Mars Williams and his very popular group Liquid Soul (featuring Nina Simone's daughter), and by the group Sumo, led by guitarist Gerey Johnson. Williams and his band play every Sunday night at the **Double Door** (1572 N. Milwaukee, 773–489–3160), while Sumo plays every Sunday night at the **Elbo Room** (2871 N. Lincoln, 773–549–5549).

Martyrs (3855 N. Lincoln, 773–404–9494) and **Schuba's** (3159 N. Southport, 773–525–2508) book national jazz acts from time to time. Jazz can also be heard at **Smoke Daddy's** (see "For Blues," below).

South Side

New Apartment Lounge, 504 E. 75th St., 773–483–7728.

Every Tuesday night for nearly 20 years, veteran saxman Von Freeman has been appearing at this small neighborhood club with its polished, sinuous bar, deep blue carpeting, and tiny colored lights. There's not an important young jazz star developed in Chicago in the last two decades who didn't woodshed here, from the late Art Porter and m-base jazz guru Steve Coleman to guitarist Fareed Haque and vocalist Kurt Elling (who still shows up often).

Though now somewhat sleepy and low-key, the New Apartment has an impressive earlier history as well. At one time, Sonny Stitt, Gene Ammons, Zoot Sims, Clark Terry, Sonny Criss, and Buddy Tate all played here, and the club was a popular stop for organ-based groups. Keyboardist Clarence Wheeler still performs here regularly.

Music: Tu-W. *Cover:* $.

Velvet Lounge, 2128 S. Indiana, 312–791–9050, www.velvet-lounge.net.

A funky little spot, housed in a cavernous old building, the Velvet Lounge is surrounded by growing gentrification. But for the moment at least, the club is the epicenter of the South Side's avant-garde and new music scene, and the main hang of local musical heroes such as guitarist Jeff Parker, drummer Hamid Drake, Japanese bassist Tatsu Aoki, and many members of the Association for the Advancement of Creative Musicians (AACM). McArthur fellow and international free jazz star Ken Vandermark also frequents the place, which is owned by saxophonist Fred Anderson, an AACM founder. With its fading striped wallpaper and awkward shape (resembling a "7," with the door at the bottom and the stage at the apex), the club is not the snazziest place in town, but it has one of the most hospitable staffs, as well as the best Miles Davis portrait in town. Velvet's is also very popular among college students and Chicago's growing Asian jazz community.

Music: W-Su. *Cover:* $.

Also

Jazz can sometimes be heard at the historic **Gerri's Palm Tavern** (see "Landmarks and Legends," p. 238) and at **Fitzgerald's** in the suburbs (see "For Blues," below).

FOR BLUES

North Side

B.L.U.E.S., 2519 N. Halsted St., 773–528–1012.

Still the nicest and most intimate live blues club to be found on Chicago's North Side, this venerable little room can't quite claim the non-stop, all-star talent line-up that it used to feature 365 nights a year. Too many luminaries, including the late piano patriarch Sunnyland Slim, who once performed here every Sunday, have passed away. But the tiny place itself hasn't changed much over the last two decades: decorated in time-honored, neighborhood-blues-club fashion, it's got a bar to the right, a few tables on a rise to the left, a few more tables up front, and black-and-white photos, LP covers, and strings of Christmas lights lining its slightly grimy walls.

Current regulars include veteran guitarists Jimmy Johnson, Eddie C. Campbell, and Eddy Clearwater; rock-solid bassist Willie Kent & the Gents, and sax wailer Eddie Shaw & the Wolf Gang.

Music: nightly. *Cover:* $–$$. Valet parking available.

Kingston Mines, 2548 N. Halsted St., 773–477–4646, www. kingston-mines.com.

Seemingly forever undergoing an expansion that's now increased its width to three full storefronts, the venerable Kingston Mines boasts one major advantage over the competition: it possesses a coveted 4 A.M. license (5 A.M. on Saturdays). Since all the other blues joints in town are required to lock their doors at 2 A.M. (3 A.M. on Saturdays), the night owls—and musicians—inevitably make tracks to the

Mines for two more hours of drinking and rowdy revelry. The Mines is usually at its most crowded during those final hours of business.

Billing itself as the "Playground to the Stars," the Mines has welcomed its share of visiting Hollywood luminaries and rock greats over the years (Bruce Willis, Mick Jagger, Bono of U2, Los Lobos, Chuck Berry). But it's live blues that brings tourists, conventioneers, suburbanites, and music aficionados alike through its doors—and the Mines delivers. Two separate stages offer non-stop blues; when the headlining band takes a break, the house combo on the adjoining stage immediately starts up—and patrons scramble to change seats.

Weekend bookings are solid if predictable. Eddy Clearwater, John Primer, harpist Billy Branch & Sons of Blues, or the lovably irascible saxman A. C. Reed alternate sets with longtime Mines mainstay J. W. Williams & the Chi-Town Hustlers. On Sunday nights, Casey Jones, Howard Scott, and Charlie Love usually perform.

Music: nightly. *Cover*: $$. *Food*: Ribs, seafood, chicken, sandwiches.

Lilly's, 2513 N. Lincoln Ave., 773–525–2422.

Though located in the heart of yuppified Lincoln Park, Lilly's has a decidedly West Side booking policy. Regulars include Jumpin' Willie Cobbs, Z. Z. Hill, Jr., and Little Howlin' Wolf—not exactly household names on the insulated, white-professional North Side.

Named after its longtime proprietress, Lilly's is awkwardly laid out, with weird corners, posts in odd places, and a curved bar that's practically on top of the tiny bandstand. The best plan is to head directly for the comfy balcony after scoring a drink; there you can relax, peer down at the bluesmen, and chuckle at the folks trying their best to squeeze past the crowded tables and down the twisting aisles.

Music: F-Sa. *Cover*: $.

Rosa's Lounge, 3420 W. Armitage Ave., 773–342–0452.

A blues bar run by Italians in a Latino neighborhood . . . hmm. At first, it's hard to know quite what to make of the concept, but as soon as owner Tony Manguillo starts to explain, things fall into place. It seems that when Tony was a teenager growing up in Italy, he got hooked on the blues. He went to every blues festival he could afford, and somewhere along the way, he met Junior Wells, who encouraged him to come to Chicago.

Soon thereafter, Manguillo, then in his twenties, arrived. "I felt like a Christian going to Jerusalem," he says. His first stop was the famous Theresa's on the South Side, and he liked it so much that he went back night after night for weeks.

Meanwhile, back in Italy, Mama Manguillo was getting worried. Finally she heard from her son. He had an extraordinary proposition: he wanted her to come to Chicago to help him open a blues bar. Then, Mama, who'd always wanted to come to America, did something even more extraordinary. She agreed.

Today, Rosa's—a spacious old club with wooden floors, a long bar, and a high stage—features blues nightly. Blues-rock guitarist Melvin Taylor plays frequently—perhaps too frequently. Tony himself sometimes sits in on drums, and also has the courage to occasionally book a comparatively obscure touring artist (such as soul/blues Memphis legend James Carr) who would otherwise never find a home in the Windy City.

Nominating itself as "Chicago's Friendliest Blues Lounge," the place undeniably sports an inviting feel, with Mama Rosa often tending bar. One word of warning: if you're traveling by taxi and the bar is packed, be sure to exit well before last call—Rosa's is cursed by its relatively distant location when it comes to late-night cabs.

Music: Tu-Su. *Cover*: $-$$.

Downtown/Near North Side/ Near South Side

Blue Chicago, 736 N. Clark St., 312–642–6261, www. bluechicago.com.

Though its address has changed since earlier editions of this guide, Blue Chicago's basic formula for success in trendy River North hasn't. Owner Gino Battaglia keeps a steady diet of female blues belters sashaying across his stage, creating a club identity that's clicked with the out-of-towners who comprise most of his constituency (some of the city's most opulent hotels are nearby).

The new Blue Chicago is far more attractive and better designed than its predecessor. The stage is situated at the back, and there are plenty of tables, several cozy booths, and a large oval bar. Vintage blues posters decorate the walls, along with specially commissioned blues-themed paintings that are available for sale as posters.

A female singer such as Big Time Sarah, Zora Young, Shirley Johnson, or Patricia Scott graces the bill most nights, usually accompanied by a local bandleader such as Willie Kent, Maurice John Vaughn, Willie Kent, or James Wheeler.

Music: M-Sa. *Cover*: $-$$.

Blue Chicago on Clark, 536 N. Clark St., 312–661–0100.

This smaller sister club to Blue Chicago is situated just two short blocks away and features the same distinctive entertainment policy: earthy female singers. Mainstays here include Mary Lane and Grana Louise, along with the aforementioned Sarah, Johnson, and Scott. Quite a few of the same illustrious bands turn up as well.

The second club is more intimate than the first, but the vibe is the same and chances are good that you'll hear the hoary "Sweet Home Chicago" no matter which site you choose. Next door to the smaller club is yet another Battaglia enterprise, a souvenir shop selling Chicago blues merchandise, with an all-ages performance venue in its basement. Live blues is showcased here every Saturday evening.

Music: Tu-Su. *Cover*: $-$$.

Buddy Guy's Legends, 754 S. Wabash Ave., 312–427–0333, www.buddyguys.com.

This is without a doubt the city's most commercially successful live blues venue—due largely to the hallowed presence of its owner, who inherited the mantle of Chicago blues king from the late Muddy Waters and shows no sign of letting it go. Unlike some of his peers who franchise out their names, Guy is a hands-on nightclub operator and if he's in town, he's likely to be sitting at the end of his bar, greeting fans and making sure everything is running right. During January, Guy also plays his club many nights (these shows are always sell-outs, so plan ahead), and he's been known to sit in with other outfits when the mood strikes him.

The room itself is nothing to write home about—it's wide and shallow, with below-average sight lines except at the tables directly in front of the sizable stage. Sound is equally inconsistent, except near the bathrooms in back. The color scheme is overwhelmingly blue, with some impressive memorabilia lining the walls; keep an eye out for Muddy Waters' credit cards on the north wall behind the pool tables.

Legends doesn't have an overly friendly feel—surly bouncers often order customers about—and the demographics can be unsettlingly young, male, and testosterone-ridden. But Legends recruits more touring blues artists than any other Chicago club—everyone from New Orleans guitarist Earl King to Bay Area mainstay Joe Louis Walker. Local guitar greats Lonnie Brooks and Otis Rush often headline as well, and Monday evenings are reserved for jam sessions.

Note: Legends will soon be moving to a new site one block north of the old club.

Music: nightly. *Cover*: $$-$$$. *Food*: Cajun, barbecue, burgers.

Koko Taylor's Celebrity, 1233 S. Wabash Ave., 312–566–0555 or 312–360–1558.

It's a little more than four blocks from Buddy Guy's Legends to Koko Taylor's recently inaugurated Celebrity. But it's a long, desolate stretch not blessed with a great deal of foot traffic. Nevertheless, the undisputed queen of Chicago blues is hanging tough so far.

Unlike during her previous ill-fated attempt to attract customers to a glitzy blues bar near Rush Street, Koko—along with her daughter Cookie—is closely involved with this club's day-to-day operations. An intriguing assortment of Koko memorabilia graces the club's vestibule, and the place is roomy enough to pitch a grand "Wang Dang Doodle" whenever the opportunity arises. Taylor and her band, the Blues Machine, occasionally perform, and on Sundays, there's a gospel buffet.

Music: W-Su. *Cover*: $-$$.

Smoke Daddy's, 1804 W. Division St., 773–772–6656.

Succulent sauce-soaked vittles and mellow music emphasizing both traditional blues and swinging jazz recommend this popular Wicker Park establishment. The bands play on a small stage up front, neatly divided in two by the entrance, and the walls are packed with an incredible vintage-photo collection of long-departed R&B, blues, and jazz greats. Blues is showcased five evenings a week; jazz on Tuesdays and Thursdays.

Music: nightly. *Cover*: none. *Food*: barbecue.

House of Blues Back Porch Stage, 329 N. Dearborn Ave., 312–527–2583 or 312–923–2000, www.hob.com.

Like most House of Blues clubs throughout the country, this Windy City outpost has principally distinguished itself by its utter lack of interest in booking blues. Instead, rock, rap, and hip-hop acts predominate in its expansive main room upstairs, while live blues carries on nightly on the minuscule Back Porch Stage in the restaurant downstairs. Occasionally, the club does spring for a blues artist of the caliber of Magic Slim or Eddie Shaw, but mostly lesser-known locals preside. On Sundays, there's an acclaimed if pricey gospel brunch, and live blues are featured daily at lunchtime from noon to 2 P.M.

Music: nightly. *Cover*: $. *Food*: southern-oriented cuisine.

Famous Dave's, 739 N. Clark St., 312–266–2400, www.famousdaves.com.

More of an upscale barbecue restaurant than a music room, this newcomer to Chicago's crowded near North Side blues circuit intermittently impresses by bringing in a worth-while touring act. Yet second-string locals are the norm.

To be fair, the stage is amply proportioned, attractively designed, and elevated enough so that everyone in the room can see. The sound system is also more than adequate. But unfortunately, the bar is awkwardly placed and the ambience leaves much to be desired. Despite a fair amount of prominently displayed music memorabilia, Famous Dave's looks more like Hollywood's idea of a blues-and-barbecue palace than the real deal. Among the worthwhile local musicians who gig here regularly are Little Smokey Smothers, Dave Specter & the Bluebirds, and Eddie C. Campbell.

Music: nightly. *Cover*: none-$$. *Food*: Barbecue.

Rooster Blues, 811 W. Lake St., 312–733–6577.

Chicago's newest blues club—unrelated to Jim O'Neal's record label of the same name—takes a page from the Mines' longstanding success story by boasting two stages alternating bands seven nights a week. The talent at this spacious club is mostly local, with veterans Carl Weathersby, Carlos Johnson, Billy Branch, Gwen Little, Sammy Fender, and Dion Payton among the regulars.

The club's kitchen—"Sonny's"—is a busy place, serving up lunches on weekdays and vittles for hungry blues fans at night, along with a Sunday brunch. Although the menu is dominated by barbecue, more exotic fare such as fried frog's legs with remoulade sauce, bayou bourbon shrimp, and chicken etouffee is also served.

Music: nightly, Su brunch. *Cover*: $-$$. *Food*: Barbecue, southern.

South and West Sides

Artis's, 1249 E. 87th St., 773–734–0491.

Harpist Billy Branch & Sons of Blues and bassist J. W. Williams & the Chi-Town Hustlers have called this classy club home for years. A large, horseshoe-shaped bar dominates the room as patrons enjoy the funky blues of Williams on Sundays and Branch on Mondays. There's also a Wednesday night jam.

Music: Su-M, W. *Cover*: none.

Celebrity Lounge, 4830 S. Cottage Grove Ave., 773–548–4812 or 773–285–8353.

Not to be confused with Koko Taylor's Celebrity, this relatively large—and considerably older—establishment features proprietor Fred Johnson and his band, the Checkmates, on Saturday nights. Sometimes the legendary ex–Muddy Waters guitarist Pee Wee Madison sits in with the combo as well. The Mississippi Raiders with singer Patricia Scott perform on Friday nights.

Music: F-Sa. *Cover*: none.

Checkerboard Lounge, 423 E. 43rd St., 773–624–3240.

Once upon a time, Buddy Guy co-owned this legendary blues joint. He's since moved onwards and upwards to operate his own outrageously successful South Loop club, but the Checkerboard perseveres without him as one of the South Side's leading blues meccas. These days, the crowd is a respectful mix of neighborhood regulars (often playing spirited games of bid whist), awed tourists (many of the overseas variety), and students from the nearby University of Chicago hell-bent on experiencing Chicago blues in a traditional setting.

The seating takes a little getting used to: long, thin tables flanked by chairs tightly arranged in rows. And during the winter, a massive heater in the rear blows with the ferocity of a propeller plane. But there's no questioning the proceedings whenever bandleaders Vance Kelly or Grady Freeman pound out their hard-hitting jams: this is meat-and-potatoes Chicago blues, shot through with tradition.

Music: M, Th-Sa. *Cover*: $.

East of the Ryan, 914 E. 79th St., 773–488–1000 or 773–874–1500.

Chicago's number one stop on the chitlin circuit, East of the Ryan is a large, venerable banquet hall. Master showmen like Bobby Rush, Little Milton, and Tyrone Davis pull out all the stops whenever they're top-billed here, performing their classic hits for appreciative fans (catered soul food is sometimes part of the presentation, too). Though some of these stars occasionally play up north, experiencing them on their home turf is a whole different journey. Since East of the Ryan does little advertising in the mainstream, you must call in order to find out about bookings—or listen to deejay Mr. A's wee-hours radio show on WNIB-FM.

Cover: $$-$$$.

Lee's Unleaded Blues, 7401 South Chicago Ave., 773–493–3477.

This is one red room. The furnishings are mostly red, the walls are lined with red carpet, and the lighting further contributes to an inviting rosy glow. Formerly renowned as the Queen Bee, the club is shaped like a slice of pie: a pair of lengthy bars line two of its walls, with a smattering of tables in between and a bandstand squeezed in one corner.

Lee's also happens to be one of the most comfortable and least pretentious blues clubs in Chicago. The yuppies and guitar-obsessed hordes don't venture out this far, and the music tends toward surging Tyrone Davis, Johnnie Taylor, and Bobby Bland R&B covers rather than the endless regurgitations of "Sweet Home Chicago." There's also a real sense of community here, with members of the audience poised to deliver guest numbers. Featured bandleaders include Johnny Drummer, Joe Barr, and Vance Kelly, all specializing in an attractive blues/soul sound.

Music: F-M. *Cover*: none.

Mr. G's, 1547 W. 87th St., 773–445–2020.

Chief rival to East of the Ryan for chitlin circuit superiority on the South Side, Mr. G's is just as amply constructed (capacity: about 500) and books the same exalted soul-singing stars, including Little Milton, Artie "Blues Boy" White, and Tyrone Davis. The place also has history—years ago, it was operated by the highly successful Windy City R&B record producer Carl Davis. As at East of the Ryan, bookings are sporadic; call ahead or get the official word from the aforementioned Mr. A.

Cover: $$-$$$.

Starlite, 605 S. Pulaski Rd., 773–826–5676.

Situated just south of the Eisenhower Expressway in the heart of the West Side, this little room conjures up an old-time juke joint ambiance every Sunday evening, when Jumpin' Willie Cobbs & the Fireballs hold court. Plenty of musical guests drop by as well, keeping things lively.

Music: Su. *Cover*: none.

290 Sports & Juice Bar, 3457 W. Harrison St., 773–533–9208.

Don't be misled by the name—you can order something considerably stronger than a cranberry juice cocktail at this friendly, modern West Side haunt. Veteran singer Willie D. & his All-Stars, sometimes accompanied by a snazzy horn section, provide an irresistible taste of soul-blues on Fridays and Sundays. The long, narrow club is also a good place to find out who's playing at other West Side nightspots (try though they might, the *Reader* doesn't list 'em all), as handbills are liberally passed out. The 290 is conveniently located near the aforementioned Starlite.

Music: F-Su. *Cover*: none.

Suburbs

Fitzgerald's, 6615 Roosevelt Rd., Berwyn (30 min. W of downtown), 708–788–2118.

An authentic roadhouse that dates back to 1917, Fitzgerald's is a large warm hall with maplewood floors, cypresswood paneling, and excellent sight lines. An eclectic mix of music is presented and the acts are often big names—Koko Taylor, the late Albert Collins, Tyrone Davis, the Count Basie band. Fitzgerald's may also be the most enjoyable venue in town; its stage is ample, its sound system is crisp, and its employees are genuinely polite.

Before Fitzgerald's was Fitzgerald's, it was the Deer Lodge and the Hunt Club, where Lil Hardin Armstrong once played. Al Capone ran the place during Prohibition; parts of the movie *The Color of Money*, with Paul Newman, were filmed here.

Music: Tu-Su. *Cover*: $-$$.

Also

Two upscale suburban blues restaurants/clubs presenting much fine local blues, as well as some national acts, are **Beale Street Blues Café** (1550 N. Rand Rd., Palatine, 847–776–9850) and **Chord On Blues** (106 S. 1st Ave., St. Charles, 630–513–0074).

Other Venues and Special Events

The **Association for the Advancement of Creative Musicians** (7047 S. Crandon, 312–752–2212, www.aacm chicago.com) presents several jazz concert series annually, featuring different faculty ensembles, at its School of Music and at other venues (museums, art galleries, etc.) around the city. The AACM's main focus, however, is its educational center, where volunteer faculty teach area youth in a tuition-free program.

In addition to the **Chicago Jazz Festival** and the **Chicago Blues Festival** (see "Major Festivals," page 458), two of the largest free jazz and blues festivals in the world, the **Annual Concerts in the Park Series** (773–294–2320) presents some free jazz and blues concerts during the summer. The **Ravinia Jazz In June Festival** and the **South Shore Jazz Festival** (773–734–2000) and the **African Festival of the Arts** (773–955–2787) are all also first-rate affairs, presenting big-name jazz (and some blues) entertainment. The **Jazz**

Institute of Chicago (773–427–1676) hosts an annual one-day **Jazz Fair**, during which a variety of different bands play, and a sort of "jazz midway," selling CDs, T-shirts, etc., is set up.

Concert venues sometimes presenting jazz or blues include the **Aire Crown Theatre** (2301 S. Lake Shore Dr., 773–791–6190) and the **New Regal Theater** (1647 E. 79th St., 773–721–9301). For others, check the local papers.

Record Stores

At 3,000 square feet, the **Jazz Record Mart** (11 W. Grand Ave., 312–222–1467) owned by Bob Koester, founder of Delmark Records, is an amazing place, billed as the "World's Largest Jazz and Blues Store." Koester also owns the **Collector's Record Mart** (4243 N. Lincoln, 312–528–8835), housed in the old Delmark Records building, which carries only LP's. Both locations are much more than just stores; they're joints where musicians hang out, jazz and blues films are occasionally screened (at the Lincoln St. address), and artists hold autograph parties.

Second Hand Tunes (2602 N. Clark St., 773–281–8813, and various other locations) is an excellent source for rare vinyl and classic CDs. The branch of **Tower Records** on Clark Street (2301 N. Clark, 312–477–5994) has a good jazz and blues selection.

Radio

WBEZ/91.5 FM (312–832–9150). NPR affiliate. Jazz weekday evenings, Sa and Su. Blues, Sa and Su early morning.
WNUR/89.3 FM (847–491–7101). Student-run station, affiliated with Northwestern University. Jazz weekday mornings, Su afternoons. Blues Su afternoon and evening.
WNIB/97.1 FM (312–633–9700). Blues weekdays, early morning.
WHPK/88.5 FM (773–702–8289). Affiliated with the University of Chicago. Jazz/blues some weekday evenings.
WDCB/90.9 FM. Public station affiliated with College of DuPage. Jazz weekdays.
WBEE/1570 AM. The oldest jazz station in Chicago, and one of the few commercial jazz stations left in the country. It primarily serves the South Side and south suburbs, as its signal can't be heard north of the Loop.

Other Nearby Locations

Davenport, Iowa

About three hours west of Chicago is the city of Davenport, Iowa, where Bix Beiderbecke was born. Davenport is situated on the banks of the Mississippi in the corner of the state, right next to Moline and Rock Island, Illinois, and Bettendorf, Iowa (the whole area is called the Quad Cities).

In the 1920s, Davenport was the turnaround and mooring point for the Streckfus riverboats coming up from New Orleans. Louis Armstrong was a player on one of those boats, and for decades Bix Beiderbecke fans have speculated about whether or not the two horn players met at that time.

Bix is not the only musician associated with the Quad Cities. Louie Bellson, born in Rock Falls, Illinois, was raised in Moline, at number 2515 Fifth Ave., a solid, two-story home. Bellson, the son of a music store owner, won a national Gene Krupa contest while still in high school, and later played drums with the Benny Goodman, Tommy Dorsey, and Duke Ellington bands. He was married to the late jazz singer, Pearl Bailey.

Davenport has done more to honor its most famous son than most cities. Several memorials are located throughout the town, and the Davenport Public Library (Fourth and Main streets) has a small Beiderbecke exhibit that includes his piano

Landmarks and Legends

Bix Beiderbecke's home, 1934 Grand Ave.

Leon "Bix" Beiderbecke was born in 1903 in this large white Victorian house set back from the road, and he went to school across the street at the Tyler Elementary School. He began playing the piano at about the age of 4 (a local paper called him a "boy music wonder"), and bought a cornet at 14, much to the consternation of his middle-class parents, who would never understand their son's attraction to jazz. On one dispiriting visit home, made years later when Beiderbecke was a renowned name in music circles, Bix found all the records he had proudly sent home to his parents in a closet, unopened.

Bix returned to his boyhood home periodically throughout his career, both to visit his family and to escape from an increasingly severe addiction to alcohol. It was during a 1924–25 visit that he wrote "Davenport Blues."

Bix Beiderbecke's grave, Oakdale Memorial Park, 2501 Eastern Ave., 319–324–5121.

Bix is buried in a large family plot in the cemetery where his brother worked up until the time of his own death at age 72. Near the gravesite is a garden dedicated to the musician. Once a small but lovely dancing figure playing a cornet stood here, but it was stolen a number of years ago.

Open: M–F, 8:30 A.M.–4:30 P.M.; Sa, 9 A.M.–noon.

Coliseum Ballroom, 1012 W. Fourth St.

A wonderful red-brick building with a rounded roof facade and white highlights, the Coliseum dates back to the 1920s. Some of the biggest names in jazz and blues, from Louis Armstrong to Jimi Hendrix, have played there, and national touring artists continue to be booked through.

Bix played the Coliseum on numerous occasions. He also appeared at Danceland, once located on the second story of 501 W. Fourth St. in downtown Davenport.

LeClaire Park, Beiderbecke Drive (near the Mississippi River).

Every year, during the last week of July, the four-day **Bix Beiderbecke Festival** is held in this charming, idyllic park by the riverside. A vintage bandshell stands at one end, next to a memorial honoring the cornet player. "He was a born genius, but they crowded him too much, with love," reads an inscription from Louis Armstrong.

The three-day **Mississippi Valley Blues Festival** with national and international talent is also held in the park every summer (see "Major Festivals," page 458).

KANSAS CITY, MISSOURI

Updated by Mike Metheny (jazz) and
Bill E. Williams (blues)

Today, Kansas City may look like just another low-key middle-American city, but during the late '20s and '30s, K.C., known for its blues-based, riff-oriented sound, was at the top of the jazz world. A wide-open, 24-hour town controlled by gangsters, it attracted musicians from all over the Mid- and Southwest. More than 160 nightclubs, dance halls, and vaudeville houses rocked the city from dusk until dawn, with jam sessions, a Kansas City specialty, lasting for hours upon hours as musicians came and went.

"Jam sessions in Kansas City?" says piano player Sam Price in *Hear Me Talkin' to Ya.* "I remember once at the Subway Club, on Eighteenth Street, I came by a session at about ten o'clock and then went home to clean up and change my clothes. I came back a little after one o'clock and they were still playing the same song."

Count Basie, originally known as Bill Basie, from Red Bank, N.J., got his start in K.C. So did Mary Lou Williams, Lester Young, Andy Kirk, Jay McShann, Joe Turner, Jimmy Rushing, Bennie Moten, George Lee, Julia Lee, Ben Webster, and Charlie Parker.

Kansas City has a strong blues tradition as well, to be heard not only in its blues-influenced jazz but also in the early sounds of such singers as Lottie Beaman ("the Kansas City Butterball") and Laura Rucker. As the westernmost stop on the TOBA circuit (Theatre Owners Booking Association, a string of black vaudeville theaters across the country) the city was always filled with blues talent, groups disbanding and then reforming in the city's many vaudeville houses.

The man who unwittingly spurred all this activity was Tom Pendergast, a corrupt political boss who allowed mobster Johnny Lazia to control the city. Throughout the Depression, Prohibition and closing hours were virtually ignored in K.C., and everything imaginable went down.

One of Kansas City's earliest jazz bands was the Bennie Moten orchestra, first formed in 1921. By 1929, Moten's group had grown to 12 pieces, and by 1932, it had acquired numerous members of Walter Page's Blue Devils, based in Oklahoma City, including Bill Basie, Jimmy Rushing, Oran "Hot Lips" Page, Eddie Durham, and finally, Walter Page, himself.

Most of K.C.'s clubs were located in and around 18th and Vine Streets (see "Landmarks and Legends," page 271). Preeminent among them was the Reno Club (12th Street, near Cherry, no longer standing), a long narrow place that attracted both blacks and whites, but kept them apart with a divider running down the middle. Bill Basie and his nine-piece band began playing at the Reno in 1935, broadcasting live on an experimental shortwave radio station, whose announcer, calling Bill a rather ordinary name, gave Basie his nickname. The Reno was also the band's ticket out of obscurity: record producer/music critic John Hammond, hearing the Reno broadcast one early morning in a parking lot in Chicago, drove all the way to K.C. to witness the band live, and then convinced the Music Corporation of America to sign them up.

Other well-known K.C. bands were Andy Kirk and his Clouds of Joy, featuring pianist Mary Lou Williams, one of the first women to penetrate the male-dominated jazz world, and the Jay McShann Orchestra, whose best-known musician was Charlie Parker. Parker, who grew up in Kansas City, hung around all the local clubs, and it was at the Reno that the legendary incident involving Jo Jones, who threw a cymbal at the then-too-cocky 15-year-old, occurred.

In 1938, Tom Pendergast was indicted for income-tax evasion and sentenced to 15 months in Leavenworth. In the same year, a reform movement swept the city and nightclubs everywhere were shut down. Many musicians left K.C. An era had ended.

More recent jazz artists to come out of K.C. include Bob Brookmeyer, Marilyn Maye, Carmell Jones, Pat Metheny, Bobby Watson, Karrin Allyson, and Kevin Mahogany.

Sources

Listings can be found in *Pitch Weekly* (816–561–6061, www.pitch.com), a free newspaper, and the Friday edition of the *Kansas City Star* (816–234–4141, www.kcstar.com). The *Kansas City Blues Society Newsletter*, which can be picked up at the Grand Emporium (see "Clubs, etc." page 280) is the best source for blues clubs listings. *JAM* is a free bi-monthly publication of the Kansas City Jazz Ambassadors (913–967–6767) and includes club listings.

For recorded information, call the Blues Hotline at 816–474–4774. The Kansas City Blues Society (816–737–0713) hosts a Web site at www.kcbluessociety.com, and the Jazz Ambassadors hosts a site at www.jazzkc.org.

The Convention and Visitors Bureau of Greater Kansas City is located at City Center Square, 1100 Main, Kansas City, MO 64105; 816–221–5242 or 800–767–7700; www.visitkc.com.

A Note on Neighborhoods

Kansas City, Missouri, not to be confused with Kansas City, Kansas, is bigger than it looks at first, with a downtown, located near the river, that then spreads south to Crown Center, midtown, and Country Club Plaza. Westport, located 10 minutes south of downtown, is a shopping district by day and a party district by night. On any given weekend, many thousands of revelers flood the four-block area, where perhaps 20 establishments have liquor licenses and many serve until 3 A.M.

Traditionally, Troost Avenue has been the dividing line between white and black Kansas City, and much of east K.C. is still predominantly black.

Driving in the city is a delight, as the traffic's usually light and free parking, plentiful.

Landmarks and Legends

18th and Vine Historic District

The neighborhood centered on 18th and Vine streets was once the premier African-American district in Kansas City. Numerous affluent black businesses, including the Winston Holmes Music Company, the Peoples Finance Corporation, and the Williams Photo Studio, had offices here.

During the peak of the Pendergast era, 18th and Vine, encompassing just six blocks, was home to an astounding 50 jazz clubs. Among the best-known of these were the aforementioned Reno, the Sunset, the Subway, the Cherry Blossom, Lucille's Band Box, the Hey Hay Club, the Hi Hat, and the Hole in the Wall. Except for a few core jazzmen hired by each club, musicians moved freely from joint to joint as the spirit moved them.

In addition to the Reno, one especially legendary club was the Sunset. Owned by a white man, Felix Payne, it was managed by a black man, Piney Brown, who was known throughout the city as the jazz musician's friend. The Subway also had a most unusual bartender, singer Joe Turner, who would turn the club's loud-speaker toward the main 12th Street–Highland Street intersection and begin to sing. His big blues voice attracted hundreds of patrons to the club.

Today, the 18th and Vine Historic District is alive and swinging again after a $26-million restoration project was christened in 1997. The area now includes the American Jazz Museum, a completely renovated Gem Theater, the Blue Room jazz club, the Negro Leagues Baseball Museum, and the Charlie Parker Memorial. More revitalization projects for the area are also in the works.

American Jazz Museum, 1616 E. 18th St., 816–474–8463.

This ultra-modern museum begins with an exhibit on Horace M. Peterson, founder of the Black Archives of Mid America, and proceeds with a showing of the film *Jazz Is . . .* , featuring Max Roach, Jay McShann, David Baker, and Shirley

Horn. Four large exhibits complete with listening stations, personal artifacts, and historical photographs are devoted to Louis Armstrong, Duke Ellington, Ella Fitzgerald, and Charlie Parker, and then comes an interactive glimpse of a working music studio.

Just west of the museum is the Charlie Parker Memorial, a 17-foot-high bronze figure of the sax player. The base of the statue simply reads "Bird Lives."

The museum stands on the site of what was once Bennie Moten's residence. In 1923, Moten and his orchestra made their first records, becoming only the third group in jazz history to do so. By 1929, Moten was known as "the most famous of the Kansas City bandleaders."

Nonetheless, times were often lean. In 1932, with the country in the midst of the Depression, the band, which by then included members of the Blue Devils band, traveled to Camden, N.J., for a long-awaited recording session. Recalls sideman Eddie Barefield: "We had to get to Camden to record, and along comes this little guy Archie with a raggedy old bus,

The ghosts of Basie, Joe Turner, and Bird still haunt the streets of 18th and Vine.

and he took us there. He got us a rabbit and four loaves of bread, and we cooked rabbit stew right on a pool table. That kept us from starving, and then we went on to make the records."[1]

Museum hours: Tu-Sa, 9 A.M.–6 P.M., Su noon–6 P.M. *Admission*: $$.

The Gem Theater, 1615 E. 18th St., 816–842–4538.

With the revitalization of the 18th and Vine Historic District in 1997 came a complete reconstruction of the legendary Gem Theater. The original facade remains, but inside, the theater is now a comfortable, state-of-the-art performance venue. At its '97 inauguration, jazz giants such as Tony Bennett, Al Jarreau, and Pat Metheny performed. Subsequent events have featured everyone from Billy Taylor, Marian McPartland, and Lionel Hampton to Dee Dee Bridgewater, Terence Blanchard, and Bobby Watson.

Subway Club, 1516 E. 18th St.

The Subway Club, like the Sunset, was operated by Felix Payne and Piney Brown, and it was especially popular during the mid-'30s, when it attracted more out-of-town jazzmen than any other K.C. club. Some of the many who were drawn to its all-night jam sessions were Benny Goodman, Gene Krupa, Chuck Berry, Coleman Hawkins, Roy Eldridge, and the Dorsey brothers.

Drummer Jesse Price performed a record feat at the Subway, now demolished, one morning. Challenged in a cutting contest by two drummers from out of town, he played 111 choruses of "Nagasaki." The solo went on for an incredible one hour and 15 minutes.

Count Basie residence, 1424 1/2 E. 18th St.

Basie lived at this address (no longer standing) for a short period after arriving in Kansas City in 1927. While here, he played the organ at the Eblon Theater (see page 274).

Lucille's Paradise Band Box, 1713 E. 18th St.

Recently demolished, number 1713 was once a club owned by a woman named Miss Lucille. Charles "Crook" Goodwin's band did radio broadcasts from here, Moten's "Band Box Shuffle" was named after the place, and Buster Smith's band played the club for a while. Smith was by that time a veteran alto player, and at his side was a 17-year-old neophyte, Charlie Parker.

"He used to call me his dad, and I called him my boy," Smith once said. "I couldn't get rid of him. He was always up under me. In my band, we'd split solos. If I took two, he'd take two; if I took three, he'd take three, and so forth. He always wanted me to take the first solo. I guess he thought he'd learn something that way. . . . But after a while, anything I could make on my horn, he could make, too—and make something better of it."[2]

Mutual Musicians Foundation, 1823 Highland Ave., 816–471–5212.

A pink-and-white duplex with musical notes on its facade, the Mutual Musicians Foundation, now a National Historic Landmark, was the African-American musicians' union hall during the '30s and '40s, when Kansas City jazz was at its height. All the legends—Basie, Moten, Bird, McShann, George and Julia Lee, Andy Kirk, Mary Lou Williams—congregated here back then, and it was the first place where Charlie Parker and Dizzy Gillespie played together, when Dizzy came through town in 1940 with Cab Calloway.

"Yes, I introduced them. . . ." trumpet player Buddy Anderson says in Dizzy Gillespie's *To Be or Not to Bop.* "[Dizzy and I] were talking and Charlie showed up, just outta the clear, showed up with his horn. . . . Dizzy wanted to hear us play. So we went over to the Musicians Local, 627. We went upstairs to the piano and Dizzy sat down at the piano; he played. He wanted to hear me play trumpet and Charlie play saxophone. So we went through several numbers. . . . [Dizzy] really didn't dig Bird, or me either, at that time. But it was a fine meeting."

Local 627 disbanded in 1958, when the city's white and black musicians' unions merged to form one integrated entity. The Mutual Musicians Foundation lived on, however, as a private organization for the perpetuation of Kansas City jazz, and today, the building is still a hangout for local jazzmen, who come here to rehearse or pass the time of day. Downstairs, there's a small clubroom with a big white piano, lots of old pictures, and a simple bar. Upstairs, there's a big, well-lit rehearsal hall equipped with two pianos, one out in the open, the other in a closet. The one in the closet—old and worn and painted blue, with no ivory on the keys—is the piano that all the greats, from Joplin to Basie, once played.

Visitors are welcome at the Foundation on the weekends, when jam sessions are held in the clubroom (see "Clubs, etc.," page 279). If the place looks familiar, it's because parts of the film *The Last of the Blue Devils* were filmed here.

Eblon Theatre/Cherry Blossom, 1822 Vine St.

Today just a facade standing exposed on all sides, the Eblon was once a movie theater where Count Basie, who traveled here from New Jersey with a vaudeville show, played accompaniment to silent films. Later, in 1933, the Eblon housed the Cherry Blossom, where what was probably the most famous cutting contest in all of jazz history took place on Dec. 18, 1933, between Coleman Hawkins, Ben Webster, Herschel Evans, and Lester Young.

Hawkins, then an established saxophonist playing with the Fletcher Henderson band, had heard about the prowess of the Kansas City saxmen in St. Louis and decided to stop by the Cherry Blossom to put them in their place. One half hour after his arrival, word of his presence had spread all over town, and sax players began arriving by the dozens, ready for a fight. By dawn, only Hawkins, Webster, Evans, and Young were left. Says Mary Lou Williams in *Hear Me Talkin' to Ya:*

> Around four A.M., I awoke to hear someone pecking on my screen. Opened the window on Ben Webster. He was saying, "Get up, pussycat, we're jamming and all the pianists are tired out now. . . ."
>
> Lester's style was light and . . . it took him maybe five choruses to warm up. But then he would really blow, then you couldn't handle him at a cutting session.
>
> That was how Hawkins got hung up. . . . When at last he gave up, he got straight in his car and drove to St. Louis. I heard he'd just bought a new Cadillac and that he burnt it out [getting there] . . . Yes, Hawkins was king until he met those crazy Kansas City tenor men.

Not only was the battle talked about by sidemen around the country for weeks, but it also led to a change in jazz style. The heavy vibrato sound of Hawkins was now "out"; the lighter, more melodic sound of Young, "in."

Note: This section of Vine Street was used in the filming of the 1996 movie *Kansas City*, directed by Robert Altman. The movie takes place in K.C. in the 1930s and includes scenes of the Eblon's famous cutting contests.

Elsewhere in the City

Kansas City Marriott Downtown 200 W. 12th St. (downtown), 816–421–6800.

The hotel's premier lounge, located on the main floor, right off the lobby, is a beautiful affair, with a huge mural around the tops of the walls depicting K.C.'s most famous jazz artists. Count Basie, Mary Lou Williams, Lester Young, and Charlie Parker—they're all here. The room, called the "12th Street Rag,"

The Charlie
Parker Memorial
at 18th and Vine.

Mike Metheny

was named after 12th Street, which it faces, and after the song of the same name written by Euday L. Bowman circa 1914.

Many of the hotel's meeting rooms are also named after K.C. jazzmen ("Yardbird Suite" seems particularly appropriate) and the sidewalk out front plays homage to the city's heritage, with stars embedded in the pavement honoring nine jazz artists.

Tom Pendergast's home, 200 W. 54th St. (20 min. from downtown).

Thomas J. Pendergast, the man who couldn't care less about jazz but nonetheless made it all happen, once lived in this large, attractive home on the north side of town. Pendergast, born in St. Joseph, Missouri, in 1872, started his Kansas City career working as a cashier in his brother's saloon; later, he was always in bed by 9 P.M. First elected to public office in 1896, he had a quick temper and a trademark derby that he wore cocked over one ear.

Charlie Parker's grave, Lincoln Cemetery, 8604 E. Truman Rd., near Blue Ridge Rd., 25 min. E of downtown. (On I–435 going north, exit on Truman Road and go right [east] about 300 yards. Take steep road on right to top of hill, bearing to the left.)

Getting here is a bit tricky, but the setting, on top of a secluded hill framed with trees, is beautiful. Far in the distance shimmers the Kansas City skyline, while overhead, wildlife chatters quietly to itself. Parker's grave is located near the front of the cemetery, on the right-hand side of the drive. Bird never wanted to be buried in Kansas City, but he lies near his mother, Addie, and their grave stones lie flat and enclosed by a four-inch-high wall. Half disintegrating reeds and tapes, left by fans, are often laid respectfully on the plot.

One of Bird's honorary pallbearers was the great blind piano player and teacher, Lennie Tristano. At one point in the ceremony, the actual pallbearers almost dropped the casket, but through some mysterious, intuitive knowledge, Tristano reached out and caught it.

On March 13, 1993, one day after the thirty-eighth anniversary of Charlie Parker's death, the *Kansas City Star*, in a front-page story, reported that the nameplate from his and his mother's grave had been stolen. In 1994, a new marker was unveiled, but not without controversy. What bears a striking resemblance to a tenor sax—Parker played *alto*—is engraved on the musician's new stone.

CLUBS, ETC.

Kansas City has several major clubs that feature first-rate local jazz talent. Among them are the **Blue Room** in the 18th and Vine District, the **Phoenix Piano Bar & Grill**, and **The Club at Plaza III**. Occasional national jazz acts and many national blues acts are brought in by the **Grand Emporium**, which was twice named the Number One Blues Club in America by the Blues Foundation. K.C. also boasts a large number of neighborhood blues joints with various blues jams throughout the week.

Some of the jazz artists to watch out for include veteran pianist-singer Jay McShann, who still performs on occasion; violinist Claude "Fiddler" Williams; bassists Bob Bowman and Milt Abel; guitarists Danny Embrey and Rod Fleeman; keyboard players Paul Smith, Joe Cartwright and Everette

DeVan; saxophonists Bobby Watson, Kim Park, and Jim Mair; trumpet players Mike Metheny, Gary Sivils, and Stan Kessler; pianist Tim Whitmer and his band, the K.C. Express; vocalists Lisa Henry, Julie Turner, and Angela Hagenbach; drummers Tommy Ruskin and Todd Strait; the McFadden Brothers; the Scamps (a 50-year-old vintage K.C. jazz group), and the River City Jazz Orchestra.

Among blues artists, there's Provine Little Hatch, a legendary harmonica player, the 360 Degree Band, the Dan Doran Band, the Full Blast band, jazz-blues vocalist Ida McBeth, blues-jazz guitarist Sonny Kenner, guitarist-vocalist Mileage Gilbert, Big John & the 39th St. Blues Band, Blues Notions, Cotton Candy & So Many Men, D. C. Bellamy, and John Paul & the Hellhounds.

In general, bars in K.C. remain open until 1 A.M., although some, especially those in Westport, serve liquor until 3 A.M.

Personal Choices

Best jazz clubs: *Phoenix, The Blue Room*
Best jazz restaurant-club: *The Club at Plaza III*
Best jazz jam: *210 at Fedora*
Best blues club: *Grand Emporium*
Best neighborhood blues club: *B. B.'s Lawnside*
Best after-hours jam: *Mutual Musicians Foundation*

FOR JAZZ

Phoenix Piano Bar & Grill, 302 W. 8th St., at Central (downtown), 816–472–0001.

One of the hottest jazz spots in town, the Phoenix presents music six nights a week. Tim Whitmer and the K.C. Express play most regularly, often in the early part of the evening, followed by other top K.C. names, including the Scamps, Joe Cartwright, Everette DeVan, Lisa Henry, Milt Abel, and Jim Mair.

Housed in a 100-year-old building in one of the city's older neighborhoods, the Phoenix has big picture windows, lots of dark wood, and dark green walls. There's just a handful of tables and chairs; the place only holds about 85, and is often packed with enthused music fans.

Music: M-Sa. *No cover. Food*: seafood, steaks, pasta, etc.

The Club at Plaza III, 4749 Pennsylvania Ave. (Country Club Plaza), 816–753–0000.

Upscale and sophisticated, the Club at Plaza III—formerly City Light—combines the best of two worlds; it's both a fine restaurant and a classy jazz club. Framed photographs of prominent jazz musicians hang discreetly on the walls, and elegant tables with flickering candles ring the room.

For years, the former City Light was Kansas City's only full-time jazz club, and the venue is still one of the best spots in town. On the music calendar are solo and duo artists mid-week, and larger ensembles on the weekends. Among the K.C. musicians who make regular appearances here are Claude "Fiddler" Williams, Dr. Ronnell Bright, and the Scamps.

Music: W-Sa. *Cover*: $. *Food*: contemporary American.

The Blue Room, 1616 E. 18th St., at Vine, 816–474–2929.

Though part of the American Jazz Museum by day, the Blue Room is transformed into a bona fide jazz club by night. All done up in 1930s decor, it features nine tables filled with jazz artifacts and a video jukebox with performances by jazz greats.

A jazz or blues jam usually takes place on Monday nights, while on Thursdays through Saturdays, a representative cross-section of top-notch K.C. talent performs. Bobby Watson, Inter-string, Ida McBeth, and the Dunn-Freeman Mix are among the many who have appeared here.

The Blue Room is named after what was once one of the hottest nightspots in the 18th and Vine District. Located in the now-long-demolished Street Hotel, it featured some of the biggest names in 1930s and '40s entertainment.

Music: M, Th-Sa. *Cover*: F-Sa only, $. No smoking allowed.

Mutual Musicians Foundation, 1823 Highland Ave. (18th and Vine District), 816–471–5212.

This small, historic clubroom (see "Landmarks and Legends," page 274) is simply laid out with a few tables, wooden chairs, and a makeshift stage, but on the weekend, the place is often filled with musicians from all over the city. Sometimes the music is great, sometimes it isn't, but there's always much potential here. The main after-hours jam begins about 11:00 P.M. on Saturday nights and sometimes lasts until the sun comes up.

Music: F–Sa. *Cover:* donation at the door.

Jardine's, 4536 Main (Country Club Plaza area), 816–561–6480.

Another prominent K.C. jazz restaurant/club, Jardine's has featured such local luminaries over the years as Karrin Allyson, Julie Turner, Stan Kessler, Paul Smith, and Mike Metheny. Dixieland, compliments of the New Red Onion Jazz Babies, and swing, compliments of Dave Stephens, is usually featured on week nights, while the weekends are devoted to much straight-ahead. Angela Hagenbach and Ida McBeth are among the artists who have performed in this intimate low-lit bistro, filled with photos and portraits of jazz musicians.

Music: Tu-Sa. *No cover. Food*: American.

210 at Fedora, 210 W. 47th (Country Club Plaza), 816–561–6565.

This upscale restaurant/bar on the Country Club Plaza features solo piano players on Mondays and Tuesdays, vocalists on Thursdays, and a mixed bag on the weekends that includes many of K.C.'s favorite jazz groups. On Saturday afternoons, the Tommy Ruskin jazz band takes to the stage, hosting a jam that features both new and established talent.

Music: M-Sa. *No cover. Food*: eclectic.

Also

Housed in a 1910 building that's on the National Register of Historic Places, the **Majestic Steak House** (931 Broadway, downtown, 816–471–8484) has high, pressed-tin ceilings, much fine food, and straight-ahead jazz seven nights a week. Regulars include vocalist Julie Turner and drummer Tommy Ruskin, the Billy Meynier Duo, and pianists Joe Cartwright and Bram Wijnands.

Jazz can also be heard at the **New Point Grille** (917 W. 44th, midtown 816–561–7600), an upscale steak and seafood restaurant with a cigar and wine bar; drummer-vocalist David Basse is often featured. At the **Canyon Cafe** (4626 Broadway, Country Club Plaza, 816–561–6111), a cheery Southwestern restaurant, the Latin jazz band Sons of Brasil play every Wednesday night. At **B. B.'s Lawnside Bar-B-Q**, the big band sounds of the River City Jazz Orchestra can be heard the first Wednesday of every month; jazz artists also occasionally perform at the **Grand Emporium** (see "For Blues," below).

FOR BLUES

The Grand Emporium, 3832 Main St. (midtown), 816–531–1504.

The premier blues and R&B club in Kansas City, the Grand Emporium is a long, big room with tin ceilings, revolving fans, and posters all around. Home to the Kansas City Blues Society, one of the most active blues societies in the United States, the club also brings in a fair amount of rock and reggae, and some jazz.

The Emporium's sound system is one of the best in town, and *everyone* has played here, including Buddy Guy, Bobby

Blue Bland, John Lee Hooker, Dr. John, Chick Corea, and Wynton and Branford Marsalis. Robert Cray and Stevie Ray Vaughan played the Grand Emporium before they hit it big; local harmonica phenomenon, teenage Brody Buster, performs during Friday happy hour.

The Grand Emporium has a lot of atmosphere, partly because the building has housed a bar since 1912. A hotel, now abandoned, was once located up above, and its patrons would come down here to drink and socialize.

Music: M–Sa, mostly blues, some jazz. *Cover:* $–$$. *Food:* barbecue and Creole.

B. B.'s Lawnside Bar-B-Q, 1205 E. 85th St. (20 min. from downtown; one block E of Stroud's), 816–822–7427.

Run by Lindsay Shannon, who hosts a blues show Sunday evenings on KCFX/101 FM, and his family, B. B.'s is a roadside barbecue restaurant, complete with a brick and wood front, beat-up wooden floors, an old-time smoker out back, and a new deck out front. The walls are hung with lots of blues and jazz posters, except for one wall in the dining room that's painted to look like the inside of an old blues joint. The Blues Society hosts its annual Acoustic Showcase under a big tent in B.B.'s parking lot in late August; in the past such legends as Snooky Pryor have performed.

Many first-rate Kansas City bluesmen and -women play here, including Little Hatch, the Lonnie Ray Blues Band, and John Paul & the Hellhounds. Regional acts such as Catfish Keith from Iowa and the Barbecue Bob Trio from Colorado are also occasionally featured.

Music: W–Su. *Cover:* $. *Food:* barbecue.

Harling's Upstairs, 3941-A Main St. (midtown), 816–531–0303.

A sprawling second-floor space with rooms and halls without doors, Harling's, located in an elegant-looking building with a white curlicue facade, has live music (rock, R&B, blues) most nights of the week. The best time to come, however, is on Saturday afternoons, when a huge blues jam attracts musicians from all over the city. The tradition, now seven years old, always packs the place.

Music: W–Sa, Sa afternoons. *Cover:* $, none for the jam.

Blayney's, 415 Westport Rd. (Westport), 816–561–3747, www.blayneys.com.

Located in a low-ceilinged basement, Blayney's is an informal Kansas City institution, complete with exposed rock walls and a crowd that includes both young locals and convention-business clientele (lots of hotels are nearby). Most of the music is a mix of the best local and regional blues, R&B, and rock. The club also began the first weekly R&B jam in K.C. over 20 years ago.

Jazz singer Kevin Mahogany got his start at Blayney's, first as a doorman, and then as a singer in the One-Two-Three band. After hearing him perform, owner Dick Schuelte advised him to return to being a doorman.

Music: M–Sa. *Cover:* $.

The Levee, 16 W. 43rd St. (midtown), 816–561–2821, www. thelevee.net.

A multilevel place with an upstairs deck looking out over a yardful of trees, the Levee presents blues with guitar player Sonny Kenner on Mondays and Tuesdays. The music room is located on the club's lower level, and it's a dark, comfortable place with walls of deep green.

Music: M-Tu. *Cover:* $. *Food:* American.

Club Paradox, 2006 N. 3rd St., Kansas City, KN, 913–281–1537.

The best reason to take a ride over to the Kansas City, Kansas, side of town, is the Club Paradox. This funky, friendly, neighborhood joint deep in blues territory is the real deal, with a serious blues jam every Monday night. Guitarist D. C. Bellamy often presides.

Music: M. *Cover:* $.

Mississippi Grace, 731 Minnesota, Kansas City, KN, 913–371–2600.

The second best reason to take a ride over to Kansas City, Kansas, is Mississippi Grace. A long and narrow store-front/concert hall, this club presents some big shows from time to time, including Little Milton and Bobby Rush. But the place is only open when a show is booked.

Music: varies. *Cover:* $-$$$.

Other Venues and Special Events

The historic **Folly Theater** (300 W. 12th St., 816–474–4444) in downtown Kansas City has a regular jazz concert series. The **University of Missouri–Kansas City Conservatory of Music** (4949 Cherry St., 816–235–2900), the **Music Hall** (13th & Wyandotte Streets, 816–931–3330), and the recently restored **Gem Theater** (1615 E. 18th St., 816–842–4538; see "Landmarks & Legends, page 273) also feature jazz and blues talent on occasion.

The **Kansas City Blues & Jazz Festival** (800–530-KCMO, seasonal; www.kcbluesjazz.org) has become a big affair, attracting crowds of over 100,000. Held the third weekend of July, it features blues, jazz, gospel, and zydeco. The **Kansas City Spirit Fest** (816–221–4444) is a three-day blues festival that takes place over Labor Day weekend.

On Fat Tuesday, the Kansas City Blues Society (816–737–0713) puts on the **Blues Society Mardi Gras Pub Crawl**. In June, the Kansas City Jazz Ambassadors (913–967–6767) sponsors the annual **Jazz Lover's Pub Crawl**®. Both "crawls" feature 15 clubs, 15 bands, and 15 buses to shuttle fans around town. A free **"Plaza Live! Summer Concert Series,"** presenting some jazz and blues, is sponsored by the Country Club Plaza Merchants every summer.

Started up by blues promoter Willie Cyrus in 1959, the **Thanksgiving Day Breakfast Dance** is a gala affair, drawing hundreds of folks dressed in formal attire who come to listen and dance to the blues. Now produced by Roger Naber, the owner of the Grand Emporium club, the event has featured such stars as Little Milton, Tyrone Davis, Johnny Taylor, and Bobby Bland. The dance is held in the Kansas City National Guard Armory from 10 A.M. to 2 P.M., and is usually sold out months in advance. Call 816–531–7557 for more information.

Radio

KCUR/89.3 FM (816–235–1551). An NPR affiliate. Jazz, weekday evenings and Su afternoons. Of special note: "Fish Fry," F, Sa evenings with Chuck Haddix.

KKFI/90.1 FM (816–931–5534). Jazz, noon to 2:00 P.M. weekdays, including "Lunch and Brunch" with the Jazz Disciple. Blues, 2–4:00 P.M. weekdays.

KCMW/90.9 FM (800–487–5269). Central Missouri State University station. Jazz daily, including "Dinner Jazz" weekday evenings featuring K.C. artists.

KANU/91.5 FM (785–864–4530). University of Kansas station. Jazz throughout the week and Saturday afternoon.

KPRS/103.3 FM (816–576–7103). "The Sunday Jazz Brunch," contemporary jazz.

KCIY/106.5 FM (816–576–7200). Smooth jazz.

Record Stores

The best stores in town for jazz and blues are the **Music Exchange** (4200 Broadway, 816–931–7560), **Streetside Records** (4128 Broadway, 816–561–1580, and 9200 Metcalf,

913–381–0292), and area outlets for **Borders Books & Music** and **Barnes & Noble** bookstores.

Other Nearby Events

Blues Masters at the Crossroads, 201 S. 8th, Salina, Kansas, 785–825–8609.

In Salina, Kansas, about 170 miles from K.C., entrepreneur Chad Kassem has developed a gem of blues events: Blues Masters at the Crossroads. Here, in a remodeled 80-year-old church complete with original stained glass windows, wooden pews, a performance space, and recording studio, Kassem presents a two-evening traditional blues event. Artists that have performed here include living legends Honeyboy Edwards, Jimmy Rogers, Robert Lockwood, Jr., Snooky Pryor, Henry Townsend, Hubert Sumlin, Wild Child Butler, Pinetop Perkins, and K.C. mainstay Bill Dye.

Located in north central Kansas, near the geographic center of the contiguous United States where I–70 and I–135 intersect, Blues Masters at the Crossroads is held in mid-October. Restaurants, watering holes, and hotels are nearby.

ST. LOUIS

Updated by Terry Perkins

> I hate to see the evening sun go down,
> Hate to see the evening sun go down,
> 'Cause my baby, he done left this town . . .
> —*W. C. Handy, "St. Louis Blues"*

The St. Louis blues go back to the beginning of the century, with African-American music in general a quintessential element in the city nightlife as early as the late nineteenth century. The famous ballad "Frankie and Johnny" is said to be about the murder and violence that were once an everyday occurrence in this then raw riverport town; the song "Staggerlee" is based on a real murder that took place in 1895 at a tavern on the corner of 11th and Morgan.

St. Louis is the city most frequently referred to as the birthplace of ragtime. Scott Joplin lived here for a number of years at the turn of the century, as did pioneer piano players Tom

A young Miles Davis (far right, back row) plays the Rhumboogie in 1944.

Frank Driggs Collection

Turpin and Louis Chauvin. The city's music was also strongly influenced by the New Orleans riverboat steamers bringing with them the sound of jazz.

From the 1910s through the 1930s, many jazz and blues musicians arriving from the South settled in "Deep Morgan" in St. Louis (now Delmar Blvd., between Tenth and 20th streets) or in the "Valley" in East St. Louis. Both neighborhoods have since been nearly completely torn down and rebuilt, but at one time, they were filled with drifters, hustlers, musicians, and the poor. East St. Louis in particular, located just across the river from St. Louis, in Illinois, was a notorious, ugly slum, and in 1917 it was the target of the most violent antiblack riots in U.S. history, from which some say it still has not recovered. Six thousand African-American workers who had been brought into the city by industrialists hoping to destroy a growing white unionization movement were burned out of their homes, and nearly two hundred died.

During the 1920s, St. Louis's largest jazz venue was the Arcadia Ballroom (first known as the Dreamland, and later called the Tune Town, after which Basie wrote the "Tune Town Shuffle"). Frank Trumbauer, Bix Beiderbecke, and Pee Wee Russell all played the Arcadia, once located at 3517

Olive St. Later, there was the Elks Club, where Clark Terry and Miles Davis struck up a friendship, and the Rhumboogie, where Tiny Bradshaw's orchestra, featuring Sonny Stitt, often played. All these venues have since been torn down.

Some of the early blues artists associated with St. Louis were the mythic Peetie Wheatstraw (a.k.a. "Devil's Son-in-Law," upon whom Ralph Ellison based a character in his novel *Invisible Man*), Lonnie Johnson, Roosevelt Sykes, James "Stump" Johnson, and Charlie "Specks" McFadden. The city has also been home to a long line of trumpet players, the best-known of which are Harold Baker, Clark Terry, Miles Davis, and Lester Bowie.

Other jazz/blues/R&B artists associated with St. Louis include Josephine Baker, who was living in East St. Louis at the time of the riots; Tina Turner, a native of the city, born Annie Mae Bullock; Ike Turner, who moved to St. Louis from Mississippi, married Annie Mae, and gave her her new name; Chuck Berry, who grew up in and still lives in the city; Oliver Sain, a saxophonist and music producer also still in the city; saxman David Sanborn, and vocalist Bobby McFerrin. As a jazz town, the city was particularly alive in the late '60s–early '70s, when Oliver Lake, Julius Hemphill, Hamiet Bluiett, Charles "Bobo" Shaw, and various other artists of various mediums formed the Black Artists Group, a collective modeled after the Association for the Advancement of Creative Musicians in Chicago. Talented jazz musicians who've come out of St. Louis in more recent years include Greg Osby, Marty Ehrlich, Eric Person, Russell Gunn, Jeremy Davenport, Chris Thomas, Peter Martin, and Marcus Baylor.

Sources

The best music source is *The Riverfront Times* (314–615–6666; www.rftstl.com), a free weekly with excellent listings. Another good source is the Thursday entertainment section of the *St. Louis Post-Dispatch* (314–340–8000; www.stlnet.com). *The Blues Letter*, published quarterly by the St. Louis Blues Society (314–241–BLUE), is available at about 70 drop-off points (clubs, CD stores, etc). Good blues Web sites are the St. Louis Blues Society site (www.stlblues.org) and News of the Blues (www.stlblues.net). For info on St. Louis jazz, visit Gateway 2 Jazz (www.gateway2jazz.com).

For general information, contact the St. Louis Convention and Visitors Commission, 10 S. Broadway, Suite 1000, 800–325–7962 or 314–421–1023, www.st-louis-cvc.com.

A Note on Neighborhoods

St. Louis, located on the western bank of the Mississippi River, is a flat sprawling city with a small downtown and lots of neighborhoods that merge into suburbs. East St. Louis, on the eastern bank of the Mississippi, also seems to stretch on for miles, but here, much of the cityscape is devastated and deserted.

In St. Louis, Laclede's Landing is a restored riverboat warehouse district located downtown and filled with cobblestone streets and wrought-iron street lamps. Soulard is another restored historic district, on the south side of town. Both are known for their nightlife. University City is located on Delmar Avenue, about 15 minutes west of St. Louis proper. The Central West End, another entertainment district, is also west of downtown. North St. Louis and East St. Louis, both about 15 minutes from downtown, are home to large African-American communities.

Driving in St. Louis is straightforward, as traffic is usually light, and free parking is plentiful.

Landmarks and Legends

(The first four sites are in St. Louis, the last three in East St. Louis. A car is necessary.)

The Scott Joplin House, 2658 Delmar Blvd. (5 min. NW of downtown).

Scott Joplin left his home in Texarkana, Texas, in 1882 at age 14 and spent years traveling around the Midwest, playing in small bands and nightspots here and there. Then, around the turn of the century, his composition "Maple Leaf Rag" was published and sold approximately 75,000 copies in six months; with his newfound "wealth" he gave up the itinerant life to settle down with his new bride. The Joplins lived on Delmar for less than three years (1900–1903), but the musician wrote some of his most famous compositions here, including "Elite Syncopations," "March Majestic," "The Ragtime Dance," and "The Entertainer."

The Joplins' former home, a Victorian row house where they occupied the upper east apartment, was declared a National Historic Landmark in 1976. Since then, the place has been renovated and part of it turned into a small museum. Items on display include sheet music, artifacts from the 1904 World's Fair (where Joplin was inspired to write "Cascade Blues," after viewing the fair's fountains and pools), and a player piano with rolls cut by Joplin.

Open: M–Sa, 10 A.M.–4 P.M.; Su, noon–5 P.M. *Free admission.*

St. Louis Walk of Fame, 6504 Delmar Ave. (University City).

Modeled after the Hollywood Walk of Fame, this stretch of sidewalk outside Blueberry Hill (see "For Blues," page 296) has approximately 40 stars embedded in it, complete with short bios. Scott Joplin, Tina Turner, and Chuck Berry are all honored.

Chuck Berry's home, 4319 Labadie (10 min. NW of downtown).

Chuck Berry's family moved to this white wooden duplex when he was in the fourth grade. With the country in the midst of the Depression, Berry's father was working only three days a week, and young Chuck helped him deliver vegetables in the early morning for extra income.

In high school, Berry made his first public musical appearance by singing a popular hit, "Confessin' the Blues," at a class show. "Without thought of how bold it would be, singing such a lowly blues in the rather sophisticated affair," he writes in his autobiography *Chuck Berry,* "I belted out the purple pleading tune with crooning cries. . . . 'How dare you?' showed on the faces of a couple of faculty members, [but] at the completion of my selection I was complimented with a tremendous ovation. . . . I bowed away and exited the stage backwards, watching my pathway through my legs. I feel satisfied that stage fright, if it ever lived within me, was murdered during that applause."

Oliver Sain's studio, 4521 Natural Bridge (10 min NW of downtown).

Oliver Sain, one of St. Louis's finest saxophonists as well as a songwriter and record producer, has recorded many an artist in this little windowless studio standing by itself on the side of a wide road. Fontella Bass, Barbara Carr, Bobby McClure, and Shirley Brown are among his most successful artists.

Lincoln High School, 1200 block of Bond Ave. (central East St. Louis).

A one-story red-brick building built in the 1950s, Lincoln High School (now closed) has produced some of our country's finest musicians, including Miles Davis. Even as late as the 1990s, the Lincoln High School band, under the directorship of Ron Carter, won repeatedly at festivals throughout the Midwest and was invited regularly to perform in Europe.

While at Lincoln High, Davis studied with trumpet player Elwood Buchanan, who had a tremendous influence both on his life and on his music. "One of the hippest things Mr.

Buchanan taught me was not to play with vibrato in my tone. . . ." Davis says in his autobiography *Miles*. "One day while I was playing in that style, with all this vibrato, Mr. Buchanan stopped the band and told me, 'Look here, Miles. . . . stop shaking all those notes and trembling them, because you gonna be shaking enough when you get old. Play straight, develop your *own* style, because you can do it. You got enough talent to be your own trumpet man.'"

Also at Lincoln, Davis met Irene Birth, who bore his first child, Cheryl, the year he graduated. Irene was the one who dared him—at age 17—to call up Eddie Randle of the Blue Devils band and ask for a job. Miles rose to the challenge and was hired.

Cosmopolitan Club, corner 17th St. and Bond Ave. (central East St. Louis).

It was at the Cosmopolitan Club, then a renovated supermarket, that Chuck Berry's career took "its first firm step" in 1953. Initially Berry was playing in a group called Johnnie Johnson's Sir John's Trio, but Berry proved to be so popular that the group soon renamed itself the Chuck Berryn Combo (an "n" was added to spare Berry Sr. any unnecessary embarrassment). Even so, Berry only earned about $21 for a weekend's worth of work, and so he volunteered to paint the place—in an elaborate design that included snow-capped mountains all around—for which he got paid $450.

Throughout the '50s and early '60s, the Cosmopolitan Club was one of the most important blues and R&B venues in the St. Louis area. Oliver Sain, Fontella Bass, Ike Turner, and Benny Sharp all played here. Today, alas, the club, though sturdy physically, is run-down and dispirited. There's no live music, and even in the middle of the afternoon, the place is filled with people down on their luck, drinking wordlessly at long thin tables while staring at the walls. Chuck Berry's snow-capped mountains are long gone.

Ike and Tina Turner's home, 3128 Virginia Pl. (south East St. Louis).

Ike and Tina Turner lived in this red-brick house with the large front porch from 1957 until 1961–1962. Their whole band lived with them, too. Ike was a dictatorial sort who liked to have the group nearby so he could rehearse whenever he wanted.

Virginia Place was once a prestigious East St. Louis address, with a grass median running down its center and gates at either end. The street still has a touch of grandeur, but it's seen better days.

CLUBS, ETC.

St. Louis has an enormous number of atmospheric bars and restaurants housed in historic buildings. Most of these are located in the Soulard or Laclede's Landing districts, and they're filled with heavy wooden bars, big mirrors, old gaslight fixtures, exposed brick walls, and revolving fans.

St. Louis also has an enormous number of blues artists, black and white. The blues, so long a part of the city's subterranean current, are suddenly exploding into public view. National blues acts are often booked into **Generations** and the **Broadway Oyster Bar**, and occasionally into **Off Broadway** and **Mississippi Nights**. The top spot for national jazz acts is **Jazz at the Bistro**.

Some of the many blues and R&B artists to watch out for in St. Louis include the legendary Henry Townsend, who has been performing ever since the 1920s; sax veteran Oliver Sain, who still plays occasionally; the world-famous Chuck Berry and his original pianist Johnnie Johnson; vocalists Fontella Bass, Clara McDaniel, and Larry Thurston; piano player Silvercloud; guitarists Bennie Smith, Ron Edwards, Leroy Pierson, Billy Peek, and Alvin Jett; and harp players Pops Porter, Eric McSpadden, and Keith Doder. Blues bands to watch out for include the Soulard Blues Band, Tommy Bankhead & Cryin' Shame, Marcell Strong & the Apostles, Patti Thomas & the Hitmen, and the River City Blues Band.

Among the top jazz artists in town are saxophonists Willie Akins, John Norment, Freddie Washington, Peanuts Whalum, Paul DeMarinis, and Chad Evans; pianists Ptah Williams, Jon Thomas, Kim Portnoy, Reggie Thomas, and CarolBeth True; drummers Gary Sykes, Kenny Rice, Kevin Gianino, and Jerome "Scrooge" Harris; vocalists Jeanne Trevor and Mardra Thomas; and guitarists Dave Black, Rob Block, Tom Byrne, Steve Schenkel, and Rick Hayden. Top jazz bands include the Dave Stone Trio with Eric Markowitz, the Modern Vintage Jazz Quartet, and the Sessions Big Band.

Generally speaking, bars in St. Louis remain open until 1 A.M., but some districts, most notably Laclede's Landing, have a 3 A.M. license.

Personal Choices

Best national jazz club: *Jazz at the Bistro*
Best neighborhood jazz joint: *Delmar Restaurant and Lounge*
Best national blues club: *Generations*
Best neighborhood blues joints: *BB's Jazz, Blues & Soups*
Best blues bar-hopping area: *Soulard*

FOR JAZZ

Jazz at the Bistro, 3536 Washington Ave, (midtown, near the Fox Theatre on Grand), 314–534–3663, www.jazzatthe-bistro.com.

The premier jazz venue in St. Louis since 1995, Jazz at the Bistro presents a mix of top-name national acts, up-and-coming musicians, and the best local jazz artists. Located adjoining the Bistro Europa restaurant, the club offers such known names such as Nicholas Payton, Ahmad Jamal, Dianne Reeves, Ray Brown, and Joey Defrancesco on alternating weeks September through May, with up-and-comers such as Russell Gunn, Mark Elf, or Eric Alexander featured during the weeks in-between.

The intimate, two-story club doesn't have a bad seat in the house, with seating for about 100 patrons, fine sight lines, and excellent acoustics. In between sets, the musicians usually head for the bar or a table in the back, so it's easy to strike up a conversation or get a favorite album or CD autographed. Bistro Europa, the restaurant that shares the site, offers an eclectic and tasty menu.

Music: W-Sa. *Cover/minimum*: $$-$$$. *Food*: contemporary American with a European accent.

Delmar Restaurant and Lounge, 6235 Delmar Ave. (University City Loop), 314–725 6505.

Located in the bustling Delmar Loop, this small club, all done up in dark reds, features top local musicians on the weekends. The tiny stage is crammed up front by the window overlooking the street, while cozy booths offer a choice of seating either right next to the musicians or in a quieter, more intimate setting in back.

The current lineup includes pianist Jon Thomas and Friends on Fridays, sax player John Norment's All Stars on Saturdays, and trombonist John Wolf's Quartet on Sundays. Norment is a fiery player who creates plenty of excitement, and Wolf is a former member of the nationally known Roomful of Blues.

Music: F-Su. *No cover*. *Food*: contemporary American.

Moose Lounge, 4571 Pope (north St. Louis), 314–385–5700.

Small and comfortable with a high stage surrounded by shimmering, shining walls, the Moose Lounge is a 20-plus-year-old club run by firefighter and jazz lover Tommy Gooch. "I've always loved the music," he says. "My brother is a jazz musician, it runs in the family." All the top local talent has played here at one time or another and big names just passing through—Sonny Stitt, David Sanborn (who grew up in St. Louis and played here when he was just starting out)—still put in surprise appearances. The neighborhood is not the best, which is why Gooch hires a security guard to stand watch over the streets and patrons' cars.

Music: F–Sa. *No cover.*

Gene Lynn's Cocktail Lounge, 348 N. Sarah St. (Central West End; in small shopping mall), 314–652–6242.

A glitzy, upscale cocktail lounge with shiny chandeliers, three prominent TVs, and jazz that even the owner Gene Lynn admits is frankly commercial, this place nonetheless attracts an interesting, racially and culturally diverse crowd. Bohemian types in exotic regalia sit cheek-by-jowl with stiff businessmen in dark suits.

Lynn, a large elegant man usually wearing a tux, is a veteran St. Louis jazz figure who once worked the Las Vegas–L.A. circuit. He is accompanied on Fridays by accomplished local pianist CarolBeth True, and plays with his band, the Trio Tres Bien, on Saturdays. On Wednesdays, Marty Abdullah and his popular Motown Revue perform.

Music: W–Sa. *No cover.*

Backstreet Jazz & Blues, 610 Westport Plaza (just north of intersection of Page Blvd. and I–270), 314–725–6565.

Opened only in 1999, the small and intimate Backstreet Jazz & Blues has already established itself as a favorite hangout for suburban music fans, who come to listen to top local jazz, and occasional blues, bands. You'll find none of the historic atmosphere of the riverfront here—this is cool, modern suburbia, after all—but you will find hot new bands such as Wild, Cool & Swinging. Local favorites also perform, including the sax-playing Bosman Twins, who've been a mainstay of the St. Louise jazz scene for over two decades now.

Music: W-Sa. *Cover:* $.

Also

Lafitte's Bar & Grill (809 N. 2nd St., 314–241–3202) in Laclede's Landing presents a mix of local jazz bands M-Th, with top players like Tom Byrne and John Norment holding down regular slots. At **Mangia Italiano** (3145 S. Grand Ave., 314–664–8585), a small restaurant in an eclectic, always interesting neighborhood, the Dave Stone Trio (recently named jazz band of the year by *Riverfront Times*) plays Th-Sa. **Turvey's on the Green** (255 Union Ave., 314–454–1667), just north of Forest Park in midtown, features exciting pianist Ptah Williams Th-F, and Eddie Randle, Jr., on Sundays. (Eddie is the son of Eddie Randle, Sr., who gave a teenage Miles Davis his first professional gig back in 1943).

Oliver Saln playing keyboards at BB's Jazz, Blues
& Soups.

Roscoe Crenshaw

Spruill's (2625 Stoddard St., 314–533–8050), off Jefferson
on the city's near north side, features Willie Akins, one of the
city's best tenor sax players, every Saturday in the early
evening. Jazz can also be heard regularly at **BB's Jazz, Blues
& Soups** (see "For Blues," below).

FOR BLUES

BB's Jazz, Blues & Soups, 700 S. Broadway (downtown),
314–436–5222, www.bbsjazzbluessoups.com.

The city's premier venue for local blues talent, BB's is
housed in a funky, three-story brick building that was once
home to everything from a transient hotel and boarding
house to a reception hall and house of ill repute. On
Monday nights, jazz is usually featured, with fine big bands
playing in the early evening, followed by hard bop groups.
But the rest of the week focuses on blues, and top performers like harp player Arthur Williams and blues guitarist
Bennie Smith appear weekly, along with many others. And
since the club stays open until 3 A.M., whenever a nationally

known artist hits St. Louis, he or she often shows up at BB's after the advertised gig to sit in and jam.

By the way, there's a whole lot more on the menu here than just soups, although it's tough to pass over the club's fine gumbo.

Music: nightly. *Cover*: $$. *Food*: Louisiana and St. Louis favorites.

Broadway Oyster Bar, 736 S. Broadway (downtown), 314–621–8811.

The Broadway is packed most nights, but fighting the crowds is worth the effort. In a city filled with unusual historic bars, this is one of the best. A narrow, crooked red-brick building standing by itself at the edge of town, the Broadway dates back to the nineteenth century. Inside, all is dark wood with a marble bar, stained-glass windows, a fireplace, and all sorts of paraphernalia (bottles, hurricane lights, piñatas) hanging from the ceiling and walls.

National blues, cajun, and zydeco bands appear here on a regular basis, along with local blues acts. Monday nights are especially fine, as the Soulard Blues Band usually turns the evening into a great jam session. The musicians crowd onto a stage near the front, a stage so small that it scarcely seems capable of holding three musicians, let alone the five or six who are usually there.

Music: M–Sa. *Cover:* $. *Food:* Cajun, Creole.

Molly's, 816 Geyer St. (Soulard), 314–436–0921.

Named after a dog who's "real old and kind of looks like a pig," Molly's is one of the most popular music bars in Soulard. Housed in a brick building that's all dark wood, with lots of antiques, old pictures, and brass instruments on the walls, it offers a mix of blues and rock acts six nights a week. Solo artists usually perform on weekend afternoons and there's an open mike night on Mondays. On one side of the club are three doors that open out onto a New Orleans–style courtyard.

Music: M–Sa. *Cover:* $.

Mike & Min's, Tenth and Geyer (Soulard), 314–421–1655.

Mike & Min's, an all-blues bar-restaurant, is a cheerful two-level affair with dining on the upper level, music on the lower. A comfortable, old-fashioned place with a boisterous crowd, the decor is pressed tin ceilings, revolving fans, huge mirrors, big wooden doors with lace curtains, and a semi-enclosed garden out back. Regulars include Alvin Jett & Hired Help and the Inner City Blues Band.

Music: W–Sa. *Cover:* $. *Food:* American.

Great Grizzly Bear, 1027 Geyer (Soulard), 314–231–0444.

Another historic Soulard bar with lots of character, the Great Grizzly features blues and R&B. Billy Peek, a guitar player who once played with Chuck Berry and Rod Stewart, is a regular here, as is the Soulard Blues Band. The place itself is owned by two brothers with a passion for bears (check out the collection behind the bar) and feels more like someone's casual living room than a bar. There's wood paneling all around, a huge mirror behind a heavy oak bar, and old-fashioned engraved light fixtures. Outside is, ahem, a bear garden, with its own giant bear.

Music: Th–Sa. *Cover:* $.

1860 Hard Shell Café & Bar, 1860 S. Ninth St. at Geyer (Soulard), 314–231–1860.

The 1860 Hard Shell Café & Bar, yet another blues bar in Soulard, has expanded over the past few years to include a fine Cajun-style restaurant complete with a brick fireplace and big picture windows. But the club's commitment to live blues remains as strong as it ever was, with top local groups playing every night. Regulars include Marcell Strong & the Apostles, Jimmy Lee, and the Sliders.

Music: W–Su. *Cover:* $. *Food:* American, Cajun.

Off Broadway, 3509 Lemp (near Soulard), 314–773–3363.

Run by a father-mother-and-son team, the Off Broadway has a different band almost every night of the week, some of which are local, some of which are from out of town (mostly Austin, California, and Chicago). About half of each month is devoted to roots rock, the other half to blues. Son Seals, Charmaine Neville, the Mannish Boys, A. C. Reed, Champion Jack Dupree, and James Harmon have all played here.

Unlike most clubs in town, the Off Broadway is large and spacious with a high ceiling, balcony area, carpeting, and exposed brick walls.

Music: M–Sa. *Cover:* $–$$.

Mississippi Nights, 914 N. First St. (Laclede's Landing), 314–421–3853.

A low red-brick building with an unassuming awning, Mississippi Nights brings in some of St. Louis's larger acts and is bigger inside than it looks. Up to 1,000 people can be accommodated at this comfortable nightclub, which features everything from heavy metal to reggae. Jazz and blues names from the past include Pat Metheny, Albert Collins, and Sonny Rollins, and every year Oliver Sain puts on a seven-hour "Soul Reunion," featuring some of the best musicians around. Note: Mississippi may close or move to a different address in 2001, as the area is slated for redevelopment; check with local sources.

Music: most nights. *Cover:* $–$$$.

Beulah's Red Velvet Lounge, 4769 Martin Luther King, Jr., Dr., near Walton (North St. Louis), 314–652–6154.

Most Saturday afternoons, the barbecue pit is lit up outside and the blues are turned on inside at this small, well-kept neighborhood club done up in red and white. As the hot sound of the blues drifts out the window, the sweet smell of the barbecue drifts in.

Music: Sa afternoons. *No cover.*

Blueberry Hill, 6504 Delmar Ave. (University City), 314–727–0880, www.blueberryhill.com.

A trendy music club, restaurant, funhouse, and museum all rolled into one, Blueberry Hill is a sort of Disneyland for vintage rock/blues fans. There is a lot of music memorabilia behind glass—a Chuck Berry guitar, a Chubby Checker album cover, Beatle dolls, a toothbrush adorned with Elvis's smiling face—to say nothing of a Pee Wee Herman collection, a comic-book collection, and a large assortment of baseball cards and beer bottles.

Downstairs, the Elvis Room (filled with memorabilia of the King) and the Duck Room, named after Chuck Berry's famous "duck walk," feature live music. Chuck Berry himself plays the Duck Room once a month, but tickets for his show must be purchased well in advance, as they sell out extremely quickly.

Music: Th–Sa, some blues. *Cover:* $. *Food:* burgers, etc.

Missouri Bar & Grille, 701 N. Tucker St. (downtown), 314–231–2234.

The main advantage of the Missouri is that it closes at 3 A.M., an hour after most other St. Louis bars, and serves food until 2:30 A.M. The main disadvantages are that the atmosphere is bland, especially compared to that of other clubs in town, and the full cover price is charged even at the end of the evening.

The bands, who play in a large, cold, recroom–like space off the bar, tend to be many in number, and they often slip in a little rock with their blues.

Music: F–Su. *Cover:* $. *Food:* American.

Generations Nightclub, Lindbergh Blvd. & Watson Rd. (Southwest St. Louis County), concert hotline: 314–516–9218, www.eliteconcerts.com.

At first glance, this suburban locale, housed in the Viking Conference Center complex just off I–44 in the city of Sunset Hills, seems like a highly unlikely location for a music club featuring national acts. But once you're inside Generations and the music starts, it's hard to imagine a more congenial place to hear the blues. The seats are comfortable, the management doesn't oversell the space, the sound system is excellent, and the multi-tier seating areas have excellent sight lines to the large elevated stage.

There's also lots of chrome fixtures and contemporary design, but the music is definitely the real deal, with acts such as Son Seals, Tinsley Ellis, Duke Robillard, Jimmy Thakery, Roomful of Blues, and Deborah Coleman performing on a regular basis.

Music: 3–4 nights weekly. *Cover*: $$$. *Food*: Complimentary pre-concert appetizer buffet.

Also

The list of blues clubs in St. Louis is extensive, and continues to grow. Just across the street from BB's Jazz, Blues & Soups is **Beale On Broadway** (701 S. Broadway, 314–621–7880), opened in fall 2000 with a lineup heavy on live blues; regulars include Billy Peek and Bennie Smith. **Hammerstone's** (2028 S. 9th, 314–773–5565), another Soulard club, features music nightly, along with a Sunday afternoon jam session. **Gino's Lounge** (6161 Natural Bridge, 314–385–4546) specializes in weekend afternoon sessions. The **St. Louis Brewery & Tap Room** (2100 Locust, 314–241–2337), best known for its microbrews, presents blues and roots music on weekends. The **Soulard Ale House** (1732 S. 9th, 314–436–7849) also showcases blues in its music mix.

Other Venues and Special Events

The **Crusaders for Jazz** (314–385–2380), a non-profit organization dedicated to promoting jazz and jazz education, sponsors monthly concerts featuring top local musicians at the Engineer's Club (4359 Lindell in mid-town); concerts take place on the last Friday of every month. The **Webster University Jazz Studies** department (314–968–7032) presents a series of Monday night concerts during the academic year at the Winifred Moore Auditorium (470 E. Lockwood in Webster Groves); performers include faculty members and local jazz musicians.

National jazz and blues artists occasionally appear at the historic **Fox Theatre** (527 N. Grand Blvd., 314–534–1111) and the **Sheldon Concert Hall** (3648 Washington Ave., 314–533–9900).

The free, annual **Big Muddy Blues Festival** is held over Labor Day weekend; local and national acts perform on stages scattered across the Laclede's Landing. A new music event, the **Clayton Jazz Festival**, debuts in 2001 in the mid-county suburb adjoining St. Louis city.

Radio

WSIE/88.7 FM (618–692–2228). A 24-hour jazz station affiliated with Southern Illinois University.
KDHX/88.1 FM (314–361–8870). Jazz and blues shows throughout the schedule.
KWMU/90.7 FM (314–553–5968). Affiliated with NPR. Jazz on Sunday evening.

Record Stores

The best stores for local jazz and blues are **Vintage Vinyl** (6362 Delmar Blvd., 314–721–4096), **Euclid Records** (4906 Laclede Blvd., 314–361–7353), and **Streetside Records** (various locations). The **Vinyl Shack** (7905 Big Bend Blvd., 314–961–8978) specializes in hard-to-find LPs, especially jazz.

DETROIT

Updated by Jim Dulzo

Detroit is best known for its Motown sound, but the city has also produced an enormous number of jazz musicians, many of whom later moved on to New York. During the bebop era, especially, the city was churning with talent: Betty Carter, Yusef Lateef, the Jones brothers (Thad, Hank, Elvin), Kenny Burrell, Donald Byrd, Alice Coltrane, Dorothy Ashby, Barry Harris, Tommy Flanagan, Sir Roland Hanna, Pepper Adams, Paul Chambers, Hugh Lawson, Billy Mitchell, Roy Brooks, and Charles McPherson.

From the late 1800s on, African-American musicians played an important role in the city's entertainment scene (dominating it almost completely to the exclusion of white performers in the

1920s), which perhaps helps account for the fact that Detroit's musicians' union has long been integrated. Most other cities maintained segregated locals until well into the '50s.

During the 1920s and '30s, Detroit was famous for first its society bands and then its big bands, the most important of which were Jean Goldkette's Victor Recording Orchestra and McKinney's Cotton Pickers. Don Redman, the chief arranger for the Fletcher Henderson orchestra, directed the McKinney band for four years, and under his leadership it became the foremost big jazz band in the Midwest.

Both the Goldkette and McKinney bands played at Detroit's most famous ballroom, the Graystone, a place of much legend and lore. One such tale has it that jazz violinist Joe Venuti, then with the Detroit Orchestra, was passing by the Graystone one day when he heard jazz for the first time and decided to throw over his classical career forever.

After-hours, the jazz musicians often went down to Paradise Valley, which was known both for its fancy black-and-tan clubs and its juke joints. The Valley was also home base for numerous blues artists such as Big Maceo, Bobo Jenkins, Tampa Red, and John Lee Hooker, and R&B artists such as Jackie Wilson and Hank Ballard and the Midnighters.

In the '50s, Detroit's jazz scene shifted to private sessions and music societies. Barry Harris held regular jams in his home, and after-hours sessions were held at the Rappa House in Paradise Valley and the West End Hotel in Delray. Then there was the New Music Society, the World Stage and the Bluebird Inn, all of which helped give birth to the golden era of bebop in Detroit.

Since then, Detroit has continued to produce bright, new, post-bop stars who have enlivened the international scene. The best recent examples include Geri Allen, Regina Carter, Kenny Garrett, and James Carter.

Sources

Excellent listings can be found in the Friday section of the *Detroit News* (313–222–2300, www.detroitnews.com) and in the *Metro Times* (313–961–4060, www.metrotimes.com), a free weekly. The *Detroit Free Press* (313–222–6400, www.freep. com) also carries very good listings and has an excellent jazz writer, Mark Stryker, who covers both the local and national scene with thoroughness and authority.

The Detroit Blues Society (313–582–5837) publishes its bi-monthly *Blues Review*, a free publication with a calendar and short articles that can be picked up at many clubs. The Detroit-based monthly *Big City Blues* (248–582–1544) covers

Detroit, Chicago, Memphis, and other blues towns; it covers clubs, festivals, and CD releases.

Jazz and blues radio station WEMU (89.1 FM) broadcasts a daily music calendar and runs a hotline at 734–487-WEMU.

For maps and other information, contact the Metropolitan Detroit Visitor Information Center, 100 Renaissance Center, Suite 1900, 313–202–1800 or 800-DETROIT, www.visitdetroit.com.

A Note on Neighborhoods

Of all the problem-ridden cities in the United States, Detroit has one of the worst reputations for crime, drugs, violence, and general decay. That's what makes visiting here such a surprise. The city is just a city after all—albeit a run-down one—and not some terrifying hellhole rotting away at the earth. In fact, thanks to an aggressive re-building program, the downtown has become much livelier and more user-friendly in recent years. Three new casinos, a wildly popular new baseball stadium, and a palpable feeling of forward momentum have brightened up the streets. People have begun moving back into rehabbed lofts, condos, and apartments in what were once some of the city's most desperate-looking areas.

The downtown is dominated by the Renaissance Center, six immense circular towers of dark glass surrounding the 73-floor Westin hotel. Small, revitalized historic neighborhoods—Bricktown, Greektown, Trappers Alley—surround the Renaissance and are connected by an elevated train called the "People Mover." Nearby is Eastern Market, the city's 11-acre farmers' market, also known for its restaurants and cafes.

Once outside the immediate downtown, the effects of Detroit's economic problems become more evident, but so do the city's increasingly successful comeback efforts. Many long-deserted streets and buildings are showing new signs of life, particularly as small businesses sprout in the city's extensive federal and state empowerment zones. Woodward Avenue is the city's main street, running roughly north and south; extensive apartment rehabbing and large new construction projects have generated a big increase in both street and foot traffic from the downtown all the way up to the New Center area. Theaters, clubs, and cultural institutions are located along this wide avenue.

The New Center is situated around the Fisher Building, about 10 minutes from the downtown. Hamtramck, once a Polish neighborhood 15 minutes to the northeast, retains its deep ethnicity but has also bloomed recently as a mini-Bohemia; many artists and musicians have flocked to its low-rent districts. Dearborn is home to a largely white population but is also the largest center of Arabic population and culture in the United States.

Ann Arbor, home to the University of Michigan, is about 45 minutes west of Detroit.

Traffic in Detroit is moderate during the day but often quite heavy at night, depending on which shows and sports teams are in town. Parking can also be difficult at night; those who are willing to park and walk a bit (the downtown is quite safe) or use the People Mover are at an advantage.

Landmarks and Legends

(The following route begins downtown, takes a brief detour east to St. Antoine Street, and then proceeds north up Woodward Avenue to Grand Avenue before heading to the west side. A car is necessary.)

Fox Theatre, 2211 Woodward Ave., 313–396–7600.

Once the largest movie theater in the nation, the 1928 Fox was recently restored to all of its sumptuous "Siamese Byzantine" splendour. Now, once again, its brilliant marquee illuminates Woodward Avenue at night.

Billie Holiday performed at the Fox while with the Count Basie Orchestra. "Detroit was between race riots then," she writes in *Lady Sings the Blues*, "and after three performances

Billie Holiday once played the Fox in "blackface."

the first day, the theater management went crazy." First, they made the white chorus girls dress in "blackface" and "mammy getups" because there'd been too many complaints about "all those Negro men up there on the stage with those bare-legged white girls." Then, they made Billie wear dark greasepaint because they thought she "was too yellow to sing with all the black men in [the] band."

Paradise Valley/Black Bottom/Hastings Street

Today, the area has been completely torn up by interstates, but the east side, centering around St. Antoine and Adams streets, was once the heart of Detroit's African-American entertainment district. Known as Paradise Valley or Black Bottom, it was home to countless clubs, including the Melody Club, the Club Harlem, the B&C Club, the Rhythm Club, the Band Box, El Sino, Club 666, and Henry's Swing Club. As in Harlem, the most exclusive spots, such as the Plantation and the Chocolate Bar, were black-and-tan clubs attracting primarily an upper-class white audience looking for "exotic" entertainment.

At the heart of Paradise Valley was Hastings Street, where Big Maceo had a regular gig at a place called Brown's Bar, and where John Lee Hooker, probably Detroit's best-known bluesman, played upon arriving in the city in 1943. Hooker performed along Hastings for five years while working a day job in a steel mill before he was "discovered," and his first hit song, "Boogie Chillen," describes walking down Hastings Street and dropping into Henry's Swing Club.

Today, the area is slated for demolition, as the second of Detroit's new stadiums is about to go up.

Detroit Symphony Orchestra Hall/Paradise Theater, 3711 Woodward Ave., 313–833–3700.

Originally built for the Detroit Symphony in 1919, Orchestra Hall was renamed Paradise Theater from the mid-'40s through the mid-'50s, when it was the Detroit venue of choice for many touring African-American jazz and big band stars. The hall closed down in the late '50s and was dormant until the late 1970s, when a bassoonist named Paul Ganson helped to save the place from the wrecking ball. The symphony returned in the mid-1980s, attracted by the hall's restored architectural splendor and its unsurpassed acoustics.

Charlie Parker, then with the Earl Hines band and renowned for missing shows, played one concert at the Paradise in his stocking feet and slept completely through another. Says Billy Eckstine in *Hear Me Talkin' to Ya:*

The Graystone Ballroom was once home base
for Jean Goldkette's band.

Graystone International Jazz Museum

One time . . . Bird says, "I ain't gonna miss no more. I'm
going to stay in the theater all night to make sure I'm
here."

We answered, "Okay. That's your business. Just
make the show, huh?"

Sure enough we come to work the next morning, we
get on the stand—no Bird. As usual. We think, So, he
said he was going to make the show and he didn't
make it.

This is the gospel truth. We played the whole show,
the curtains closed, and we're coming off the band cart,
when all of a sudden we hear a noise. We look under
the stand, and here come Bird out from underneath. He
had been under there asleep through the entire show!

Graystone Ballroom, 4237 Woodward Ave.

Demolished in 1980 (look for a big empty lot), the Graystone was once Detroit's most famous ballroom, built by the
bandleader Jean Goldkette in the 1920s. Goldkette also managed the place and directed the resident band, the Jean
Goldkette Victor Recording Orchestra. Among his sidemen

was Bix Beiderbecke, who often stayed around the corner from the ballroom at the still-standing Billinghurst Hotel (71 W. Willis).

In the 1930s, the Graystone was the only major ballroom in Detroit to employ black jazz bands, most notably the McKinney Synco Septet (better known as McKinney's Cotton Pickers, a name that Goldkette insisted the band adopt against their wishes). Racist attitudes prevailed in other ways as well, as African Americans were allowed to attend the ballroom on Monday nights only.

The 10-story Graystone was a grandiose terra-cotta affair, whose top three floors were never completed, owing to a lack of funds. The front hall was built of marble, while the second floor, reached via a magnificent red-carpeted staircase, was dominated by a tiled fountain lit with multicolored lights. No liquor was ever served at the Graystone.

Just before the Graystone was demolished, one James Jenkins, a retired bus driver and intensely devoted jazz lover, made a last-ditch effort to save it. His plan, which ultimately failed, was to transform the ballroom into a museum and entertainment center. "The Graystone was an enchanted place," he said. "It gave Detroit so much. It should still be here today."

Graystone International Jazz Museum, 1249 Washington Boulevard, Suite 201, 313–963–3813.

James Jenkins, who passed away in the late 1990s, was not only the last-minute protector of the Graystone Ballroom, but is also the founder of the Graystone International Jazz Museum, one of the only museums devoted to jazz in this country. The museum really has nothing to do with the Graystone, but was named after the ballroom in remembrance of good times.

Jenkins, who in addition to his work as a bus driver also once booked jazz talent for a local club, founded the museum in 1974, the year of Duke Ellington's death. He was driving down the highway, listening to the radio, when he learned that the great composer had died, and decided he just *had* to do something to honor the music he loved.

All of Jenkins's savings and much of his pension went into the museum, once a simple but moving affair filled with photographs, instruments, posters, records, and other memorabilia. Sadly, however, since the museum moved to its new location in this building several years ago, much of the exhibit is packed away in boxes. You can still visit the museum, but the display is very limited.

Open: Tu-F, 10 A.M.–4:30 P.M. *Admission:* $.

Motown Museum, 2648 W. Grand Blvd., 313–875–2264.

HITSVILLE U.S.A. reads the sign on the roof. YESTERDAY—TODAY—FOREVER reads the sign on the door.

Back in 1959, Berry Gordy, Jr., was an aspiring songwriter who had just quit his $85-a-week job with General Motors to pursue a writing and music management career. He bought this small, cheerful, turquoise abode as a base for his new operations, but before many years were up, he had become so successful that he also owned six other houses on the block.

From the very beginning, Motown (for "Motor City") functioned as a surrogate home for inner-city kids with musical ambitions—kids like an 11-year-old Stevie Wonder and the teenage Supremes. It was a place for them to play football, grab a sandwich, or simply hang out, while at the same time working on their music.

Today, a visit to the museum, which maintains a wonderfully simple, homespun feel, begins with a nine-minute video on the history of Motown. Next comes an escorted tour through the original recording studio, a small, wood-floored affair where everyone from the Four Tops to the Jackson Five once recorded. One of the highlights here is the toy piano that Diana Ross and the Supremes used in "I Hear a Symphony."

The rest of the museum is filled with photographs, album covers, sheet music, newspaper clippings, and gold and platinum records divided up into the Gordy Room, the International Room, the Black Forum Room, and others. The Michael Jackson Room contains a black hat and sequined glove, donated by the artist, who also contributed $125,000 to the museum.

Open: Tu–Sa, 10 A.M.–5 P.M.; M, noon–5 P.M., Su, 2 P.M.–5 P.M. *Admission:* $.

Bluebird Inn, 5021 Tireman Ave., 313–894–9539.

"I practically raised Tommy Flanagan and Barry Harris," said the late Clarence Eddins in 1989, owner of the Bluebird from 1953 to 1993. "I used to let them in through the backdoor and then when the music stopped, I put them back out."

During the '40s and '50s, all of the top names in jazz played the Bluebird. Some of the regulars back then included Billy Mitchell, Pepper Adams, Sonny Stitt, Donald Walden, Miles Davis (whom Eddins took under his wing while he was recovering from a long bout with drug addiction), Jimmy Smith ("He drove up here in a hearse," said Eddins, "and I thought, I done really made a mistake now"), and Gene Ammons ("He went to feeling the walls, I thought he was crazy. I didn't think nothing about acoustics back then").

The Bluebird, which opened shortly after Prohibition was repealed, was first known for its swing music, dining, and dancing, which drew customers from all over the city's African-American community. During World War II, a soldier in France even called the club to remind himself of home.

Ahmad Jamal was one of the last musicians to play at the Bluebird, in a gig that took place about 20 years ago. "I usually rebooked a musician right away," said Eddins, "but when I went to rebook Jamal, the agent raised the price $5,000. That was it for me. I couldn't afford it. [Later] I ran into Ahmad. He said, 'I'd play here for nothing.' . . . I never did take him up on it."

The Bluebird is now closed.

CLUBS, ETC.

Even more than most cities, Detroit has very few jazz clubs but very much jazz talent. Often the only way to hear the best players in town is through a concert series or festival (of which luckily, there are many; see "Other Venues and Special Events," page 311). Summers are far and away the best time for jazz in Detroit.

Among area clubs, only three offer mainstream jazz six or seven nights a week—**Baker's Keyboard Lounge** and, in Ann Arbor, **The Bird of Paradise** and **The Firefly Club.** Depending on the night, **Flood's** and **The Music Menu** are also good places to hear jazzy music in, respectively, more soul or blues-oriented grooves.

Blues clubs are in a healthier state, even though, comparatively speaking, the city's blues talent does not equal its jazz. Longtime deejay Famous Coachman and blues veteran Bobo Jenkins helped bring the music back to Detroit in the mid-1970s, and today the area boasts a number of steady blues clubs. Among them are **The Music Menu**, which offers several nights of top local blues weekly; **Cisco's On the Boulevard**, in the suburb of Taylor, which books both quality national acts and top local bands; **The Attic**, in Hamtramck, the area's most down-home blues joint; and the mildly upscale **Memphis Smoke**, in Royal Oak, which blends top local and occasional national blues acts with off-beat rock.

Preeminent among the area's jazz musicians are trumpet player Marcus Belgrave; drummer Roy Brooks; pianists Kenny Cox, Harold McKinney, and Bess Bonier; saxophonists Donald Walden, Charlie Gabriel, and Phil Lasley; the all-woman band Straight Ahead; Francisco Mora and his Latin band; the Sun Sounds Orchestra, and guitar player Ron English. There are also several very fine big bands, including the New Breed Bebop Society (led by Teddy Harris), the Graystone Big Band, and the Bird of Paradise Orchestra (in Ann Arbor).

Top blues–R&B artists include veteran piano player Jesse White; saxophonist Norma Jean Bell; guitarists-singers Johnnie Basset and the Blues Insurgents; the Butler Twins, Willie D. Warren, Rob Noll, and Eddie Burns; Harmonica Shah; vocalists Alberta Adams, Thornetta Davis and Ortheia Barnes; and the Detroit Blues Band, a rock-blues band.

Most clubs in Detroit close at 2 A.M.

Personal Choices

Best bebop and big bands: *Baker's Keyboard Lounge*
Best late-night jazz: *Bert's Marketplace*
Best neighborhood club: *Music Menu Café*
Best national blues club: *Cisco's on the Boulevard*
Best local blues club: *The Attic*
Best area jazz club: *Bird of Paradise (Ann Arbor)*

FOR JAZZ

Baker's Keyboard Lounge. 20510 Livernois Ave. at Eight Mile Rd. (30 min. from downtown), 313–345–6300.

On the Michigan State Historic Register, Baker's dates back to 1934. Art Tatum picked out the seven-foot-long piano here just before he died, and many greats from Sippie Wallace to John Coltrane, Charlie Parker to Yusef Lateef have passed through its doors.

Baker's closed down for a while in the mid-1990s, but re-opened about three years ago with a new owner—a former Detroit police officer—and a newly expanded kitchen. The club now concentrates on presenting the best "local" jazz artists, both new and veteran, as well as some awfully good soul food. The combination works like a charm, attracting young, old, black, white, diggin' all that bebop.

The 99-seat club is Art Deco inside and out and is fitted with a keyboard-shaped bar (which inspired Liberace to in-stall a piano-shaped pool in his Beverly Hills mansion), hand-painted murals, and tilted mirrors that allow the audience to see the pianist's hands. There's music every night, with high-lights including a Monday-night big band and mid-week jam sessions led by a variety of Detroit singers.

Eddie Jefferson, the musician credited with inventing vo-calese, was killed outside Baker's on May 9, 1979. He had just come out of the club following a performance and was about to enter a taxi when he was blown away by four blasts from a slowly passing Lincoln Continental. William Perryman, an unemployed factory worker whom Jefferson had allegedly discouraged from becoming a professional dancer, was charged with the murder (Jefferson himself had begun his career as a dancer), but beat the rap.

Music: M-Su. *No cover. Food*: Soul food.

Bert's Marketplace, 2027 Russell St. (Eastern Market), 313–567–2030.

One of Detroit's premier nightspots, Bert's is an especially fine place to visit on Saturday and Sunday mornings between midnight and 3 A.M. That's when all the top musicians in town come to jam after their gigs elsewhere are done. Earlier in the evening, bands led by Dwight Adams or the spectacular Larry Smith take to the stage with raw, vintage, Motor City bop.

Bert's is located in Eastern Market, an enormous farmer's market lined with Victorian-style sheds. Intimate and upscale, the restaurant-club is housed in an old refurbished building and is filled with black Formica tables, white tablecloths, and fresh flowers. Food is served at all hours.

Music: Tu–Su; F, Sa, after-hours. *Cover:* $. *Food:* American.

Bo-Mac's, 281 Gratiot Ave. (downtown), 313–961–5152.

What started out as a "traditional organ jazz joint" is now a hot spot for the more classic, soul side of jazz and R&B on Friday and Saturday nights. But jazz fans will most enjoy the Thursday night jam sessions. Hosted by the hilarious emcee and funky keyboard player Rudy Robinson, it's a come-what-may session that's at least as much about partyin' as it is about blowin'.

Bo-Mac's was opened in the late 1980s by a barber and a clothing salesman whose respective businesses had just closed down. The club, now twice its original size, is a warm and cozy place where the bartender heartily welcomes strangers and your lively hostess for the evening, Lotti the Body—a former shake dancer from the city's golden era—will greet you, seat you, and make you feel right at home, honey!

Music: W–Su. *No cover. Food:* soul food.

Magic Bag Theatre Café, 22918 Woodward (Ferndale, just N of Nine Mile Rd., 20 min. N of downtown), 313–544–3030.

A wonderful revamped 1925 theater with cabaret seating, a good sound system, and a lobby bar, the Magic Bag presents a little bit of everything: film, rock, alternative, jazz, blues. Touring talent also performs here regularly.

Music: most nights, jazz most F (call ahead). *Cover:* $–$$$.

The Music Menu, 511 Monroe, 313–964–6368.

Plunked down right in the middle of Detroit's lively Greektown, the Menu is either the jazziest blues or the bluesiest jazz club in Detroit. It feels just like Detroit in here— functional, unglamorous, a bit smoky, a bit on the loud side. Depending on the night, there's acid jazz, rockin' blues, classic r&b–flavored blues (this is the legendary Johnnie Bassett's home club when he's off the road), and some other groovy, stylistically ambiguous bands. Occasionally, a touring national act lands here, too. The food has a strong New Orleans twist, and the exceptionally friendly crowd is very mixed— black and white, young and old, hip and straight.

Music: nightly. *Cover:* $. *Food:* New Orleans and American.

Also

Flood's Bar & Grill (731 St. Antoine St., 313–963–1090) is a sophisticated downtown club-restaurant that offers nightly, high-quality, soulful and smooth jazz with a strong beat that quickly moves crowds onto the ad hoc dance floor. The **Serenigeti Ballroom** (2957 Woodward, 313–832–3010) opens its ancient doors for the occasional national act; the place is memorable for its unique, down-home art deco motif and home-made soul food. **Edison's** (220 Merrill, Birmingham, 248–645–2150) features pricey martinis, tons of cigar smoke, and an unbelievably noisy crowd of dressed-to-kill young suburban professionals who chat up a hurricane, often oblivious to the bluesy jazz band chugging away back in the corner.

FOR BLUES

Attic Bar, 11667 Joseph Campau (Hamtramck), 313–365–4194.

Creaky and cavernous, with a bar on one side and seating on the other, the Attic is home base for the superb veteran bluesman Jesse White. White, who plays both piano and harp, leads his own band on alternating Fridays; the equally old-fashioned and funky Butler Twins do the same on alternating Saturdays. On other nights, the neighborhood spot, with its pressed tin ceilings, "antique" collection (milk urns to beer ads), and basement party-room feel, offers a long, rotating list of Detroit blues bands that you will simply not hear anywhere else. A regular open blues jam is held on Thursdays.

Music: nightly. *Cover:* $. *No food.*

Memphis Smoke, 100 S. Main, Royal Oak, 248–543–4300.

This is a big, new suburban place with high ceilings, very good sight lines, a quality sound system, a curiously narrow, cramped stage, and decent if slightly timid barbecue. They serve up good blues, too—mostly quality local stuff and occasional national acts, along with bluesy hard rock bands. There was a line around the block the day the place opened, and although the lines are a little shorter now, you will still have to wait for a table on many weekend nights. The place has great potential, but thus far feels like a big restaurant that does a little blues, instead of the other way around. Be sure to note the hiply garbed pigs cavorting up on the roof.

Music: Tu-Su. *No cover. Food*: Southern-style barbecue with soulful sides.

Fifth Avenue Club, Fifth Ave. at Washington, Royal Oak, 248–542–9922.

This club may make most of its money on its fleet of pool tables, filling the entire first and half of the second floor, but its quality booking of home-grown blues, rock, and jazzy funk—along with an occasional national blues band—makes this place one to watch. Long-time regulars include Jazzhead and The Reefermen. The high ceilings, curvy bar, modest stage, and informal tables give the place an airy yet intimate feel; the crowd is the edgy side of suburban, mostly under 35, and dedicated to having a good time.

Music: Th-Tu. *Cover*: $-$$. *Food*: American.

Fifth Avenue Ballroom, 25750 Novi Road, Novi, 248–735–4011.

Sister club to the Fifth Avenue Club, the Ballroom is farther out in the 'burbs, and a little bigger and swankier, with a slightly more chic clientele and an upstairs outdoor patio. The seating is a bit more formalized, too, and there's more of a declared dance floor. But the booking policy is almost identical to the Club's.

Music: W-Sa. *Cover:* $-$$. *Food*: American.

Cisco's On the Boulevard, 5855 Monroe Blvd., Taylor, 313–278–5340.

This is a good, no-nonsense, straight-to-the-point blues bar. The place books nothing but sturdy local and nationally touring acts that most true blue fans will enjoy—even their "rockin' blues" bands are tastefully chosen. The stage really is a stage, with good lighting, sound and sight lines, and the seating ranges from tables in the center of the room to booths and barstools along the walls. Service is terrific; the food is expertly prepared pub grub. Perhaps it's the club's off-beat, down-river location, but the place does not get the respect it deserves. To reach Cisco's from downtown Detroit takes about 35 minutes, but it's definitely worth the drive.

Music: Th-Sa. *Cover*: $-$$. *Food*: American.

Also

The Music Menu, Bo-Mac's, and the **Magic Bag Theatre Café** (see "For Jazz," above) also present blues.

Other Venues and Special Events

The **Creative Arts Collective,** run by Spencer Barefield, presents a superb series of avant-garde jazz concerts, currently at the Harlequin Café (8047 Agnes, 313–331–0922). Both area artists (Spencer Barefield, Jaribu Shahid) and national talent (Oliver Lake, Richard Davis) are featured.

The **Graystone International Museum of Jazz** (313–963–3813) has an annual jazz concert series, usually in the summer months. For the past five years, the program has been called "Blue Monday" and has been presented at Hart Plaza on Mondays, 6–9 P.M. It's free.

In addition to the city's largest jazz fest, **Montreux Detroit Jazz** (see "Major Festivals," page 458), the three-day **Frog Island Festival** (313–487–2229), featuring jazz, blues, gospel, and zydeco, takes place every late June in an idyllic riverside setting. The **Ann Arbor Blues & Jazz Festival** (313–665–4755) is held in mid-September. Deejay Famous Coachman emcees a **Detroit Indoor Blues Festival** (313–571–2222) in the spring. **Flint's King Cobra Jazz Festival** takes place the last weekend of August. During the summer, the city of Detroit presents free outdoor concerts in **Chene Park** that include some jazz and blues.

Orchestra Hall (3711 Woodward Ave., 313–833–3700) has an excellent, extensive, and thriving jazz concert series. Touring acts can also be heard at the **Fox Theatre** (2211 Woodward Ave., 313–936–7600), and the **Majestic Theatre** (4140 Woodward Ave., 313–833–9700). The **University Musical Society in Ann Arbor** (734–764–2538) hosts an extensive concert series at a variety of venues on the University of Michigan campus throughout the fall and winter semesters, including some top-line national acts.

Radio

WEMU/89.1 FM (734–487–2229). A 24-hour news and jazz station. Affiliated with NPR and Eastern Michigan University, Ann Arbor.

WDET/101.9 FM (313–577–4146). Some jazz and blues daily. Of special note: straight-ahead bop M-F, 7–10 P.M., with Ed Love; avant-garde jazz Su, 7–10 P.M., with W. Kim Heron; blues & rhythm and blues Sa, 7–10 P.M., with Jim Dulzo.

WCBN/88.3 FM (734–763–3501). Student-run station affiliated with University of Michigan, Ann Arbor. Jazz weekday mornings, some evenings. Blues, Sa afternoons and M evenings.

WQBH/1400 AM. Blues weekday evenings.

WVMV/98.7 FM (313–298–7625). A 24-hour smooth jazz station.

Record Stores

Street Corner Music in Birmingham (17620 W. 13 Mile Rd., 644–4777), **Coachman's Records** (6340 Charlevoix, near Mt. Elliot, 571–2222)—a funky neighborhood place run by deejay Famous Coachman—and **Car City Classics** (21918 Harper, St. Clair Shores, 810–775–4770) are top area stores. Most **Borders Books & Music** stores also keep a good catalogue of jazz and blues.

    Schoolkids' Records in Exile (332 S. State St., downstairs, Ann Arbor, 734–663–7248) has an excellent jazz and blues selection.

Other Nearby Locations

Bird of Paradise, 312 South Main St., Ann Arbor, 734–662–8310.

    With over ten years on the scene as a full-line jazz club, the Bird continues to soar with a combination of top local and twice-monthly national jazz acts. The music is unremittingly mainstream bop, served up with an excellent sound system and a very good, in-tune piano. They do the music part right because the owner, Ron Brooks, also happens to be one of the area's best and most veteran bassists. The Bird offers slightly more seating, a lower ceiling, and a better functioning layout now that it's moved to its new downstairs digs on Main Street. Regular weekly highlights include the Bird of Paradise Orchestra on Monday nights and the Friday after-work trad jazz jam. There's good food, too.

    Music: nightly. *Cover*: $ to $$$. *Food*: healthy American.

The Firefly, 207 South Ashley, Ann Arbor, 734–665–9090.

When the Bird of Paradise pulled up stakes and moved to Main Street, the singer for the Bird of Paradise Orchestra, Susan Chastain, decided to start her own club in the Bird's old space. She rearranged the room and sharpened up the interior decorating. There are still some sight line problems, but use that as a spur to get herc early. The booking policy includes top local bop, swing, blues, and Dixie (for the Friday happy hour)—with Chastain at the microphone.

Music: nightly. *Cover*: $. *Food*: salads, light entrees.

The Cavern Club, 210 S. First St., Ann Arbor, 734–332–9900.

Here's a cool idea—restore the big tunnels beneath a 19th-century brewery; add an amazing array of antiques; build a bar, stage, and dance-floor, and hire blues-based bands dedicated to shaking your moneymaker. Want some private, intimate, dimly-lit conversation? Some boisterous boys-at-the-bar carrying on? A chance to dance your blues away? It's all down in The Cavern. Too bad it's only two nights a week, but the baby boomers who love it have responsible jobs throughout the week.

Music: F-S. *Cover*: $$.

INDIANAPOLIS

Updated by Matthew Socey

Indianapolis has had a long and proud jazz and blues history. One of the earliest jazz musicians, Noble Sissle, was born here in 1889, and others who have come out of the city include Freddie Hubbard, J. J. Johnson, Dave Baker, Leroy Vinnegar, Wes and Buddy Montgomery, James "Yank" Rachell, and Charlie Davis. Blues artists Leroy Carr and Francis "Scrapper" Blackwell also had a long association with the city, as has the Hampton family, several members of which (the Hampton Sisters and Pharez Whitted, the son of one of the sisters) still perform regularly around town.

Like other Midwestern cities, Indianapolis's African-American population grew enormously in the first part of the century—by 59 percent between 1910 and 1920 alone. Many of the new arrivals settled on Indiana Avenue, where most of the early jazz and blues clubs were also located (see "Land-marks and Legends," page 315).

During the 1930s and '40s, Indianapolis's reputation as a music center grew, and it attracted musicians from all over the Midwest, many of whom came to the Avenue to prove themselves. "You'd go from one jam session to another and stay out all night," said the late Thomas Parker, a former clar-inet player and city government official who once played the street. "And when you were out West and said you were from Indiana Avenue, you were respected."

Indianapolis was also the sort of place where musicians waited out the low periods in between gigs. Known as an in-expensive and hassle-free city, numerous groups disbanded and reformed themselves here.

Sources

The best periodicals to check the local scene include *NUVO Newsweekly* (317–254–2400, www.nuvo.net), a free weekly publication, and the Friday and Sunday entertainment sec-tions of the *Indianapolis Star* (317–624–4636, www.starnews.com). The *Indianapolis Recorder* (317–924–5143,www.indi-anapolisrecorder.com) is one of the oldest African-American newspapers in the country and has a weekly entertainment section.

A Note on Neighborhoods

Once sneered at as a placid cow-town, Indianapolis has re-cently earned the epithet, "Cinderella of the Rust Belt." A $1.8 billion downtown renaissance in the 1990s resulted in a whole host of new hotels, restaurants, and office buildings, and the place is still growing. The old Market Square Arena has been replaced by the Conseco Fieldhouse, home to the Indiana Pacers, and Union Station is currently in the midst of a complete facelift.

What's most striking to the visitor, however, is how safe the city seems. Indianapolis has the lowest crime rate of the 50 largest cities in the United States, and it's possible to venture absolutely anywhere without feeling threatened.

The city has a small blossoming downtown that's home to the vast Hoosier Dome and historic Indiana Avenue. Broad Ripple is a half Bohemian, half gentrified area filled with clap-board houses that have been turned into restaurants, bou-tiques, and clubs. It's located 20 minutes north of downtown.

Traffic in Indianapolis is relatively light.

Landmarks and Legends

(The locations below are located in or near the downtown area.)

Indiana Avenue

Before Indiana Avenue was Indiana Avenue, it was Front Street, an important thoroughfare in the then fledgling city of Indianapolis. Many of the town's most powerful early families had homes here, just north of White River.

Then came the malaria epidemic of 1821. It decimated the city's population, and the white settlers, suspecting the river as the source of the plague, fled in terror, leaving their homes behind. That left the Avenue open for newer immigrants coming in from Europe and for African Americans from the South, who began arriving in the city in the late nineteenth century. Doctors and lawyers, gardeners and laborers, all made their homes along the Avenue, which was also lined with restaurants, businesses, bars, and nightclubs. The Madame C. J. Walker Company opened up, as did the nearby Crispus Attucks High School, both now on the National Register of Historic Places.

But it was jazz that drew musicians from all over the country to the Avenue. By the '30s and on through the '40s and '50s, the street, especially the 400 block, was bursting with dozens of clubs, including the Sunset Terrace, Henri's, the Mitchell Inn, the British Lounge, the Place To Play, George's Bar, the Red Keg, and the Cotton Club.

No one club was predominant, but the Sunset Terrace, now a parking lot behind the Madame Walker Center, was especially popular. "It was a big dance hall with a balcony," said Thomas Parker. "I can remember hearing Billy Eckstine, Charlie Parker, Count Basie, Ella Fitzgerald. . . . Lots of white musicians came there for their education."

Local names who started out on the Avenue included Wes Montgomery, Earl Walker, Dave Baker, J. J. Johnson, The Inkspots, and Jimmy Coe. Members of big-name bands coming to perform at the Indiana Roof Ballroom or Circle Theater also often stopped in on the Avenue after the show.

Indiana Avenue began to decline in the late '50s with the advent of rock, the breakdown of color barriers, and the building of Interstate I–65, which cut the neighborhood in half. By the 1970s, except for a few liquor stores and pawnshops, the neighborhood was virtually dead. All the old jazz clubs were torn down.

Today, the area is being revitalized, with small businesses, restaurants, and shops gradually opening up.

Madame Walker Urban Life Center, 617 Indiana Ave., 317–236–2099 or –2088 (box office). www.mmewalkertheatre.org.

This triangular four-story building is a memorial to Madame C. J. Walker, America's first self-made African-American female millionaire. It is also the site of a lavish theater, where everyone from Noble Sissle to Dinah Washington once played.

Madame Walker, the daughter of impoverished ex-slaves, made her fortune by manufacturing hair-care products. Raised in Louisiana, she began by selling her products door to door, but when she moved to Indianapolis in 1910 she was already a wealthy businesswoman. Upon her arrival, she not only set up her company but also established a beauty school, became close friends with the leading artists and musicians of the day, and contributed generously to a wide variety of community projects.

The building itself was erected by Madame Walker's daughter in 1927 as both a tribute to her mother and a headquarters for the Madame C. J. Walker Manufacturing Co. Also in the center was a College of Beauty Culture; a salon, barber shop, and grocery store; the Coffee Pot Restaurant, a meeting place for African-American intellectuals; and a magnificent theater decorated with elaborate stucco sculptures and masks, elephant heads, spears, and brass fixtures.

Today, the building—one of the few surviving examples of the once popular Afro-Egyptian Art Deco architectural style—houses offices and community organizations, while its recently renovated theater puts on a variety of cultural events, including jazz and blues concerts. Among those who have performed here recently are Koko Taylor and Sonny Rollins. On the center's fourth floor is a small historical exhibit on Madame Walker, and the Casino Ballroom (see "Other Venues and Special Events," page 322), where jazz is presented on Friday nights.

Tours of the Center are available. Call for an appointment.

Indiana Roof Ballroom, 140 W. Washington St., 317–236–1870. www.indianaroof.com.

For nearly 50 years, the "Indiana Roof," built in 1927, was the center of elegant nightlife in Indianapolis. Women in ballgowns and men in tuxedos danced across its polished wooden floors—made up of one-inch pieces of wood laid out in an ever-widening spiral—while wispy clouds and stars drifted across the domed ceiling overhead.

Back then, it only cost 25 cents to get in, though once, a man who had been thrown out for misbehavior tried to offer an employee a $5,000 bribe. The employee turned him down;

the ballroom had rules, lots of rules, including those that banned liquor on the premises and blacks from the audience.

The ballroom, situated on the sixth floor, was closed for renovation during the '70s and '80s, but today, it's much the same as it ever was. The machine capable of creating clouds, bubbles, and fog is still here, and so are the strange, mock-villa facades that line the balconies. The dancing still exists too, with local big bands putting on nostalgic dance concerts about once a month (see "Other Venues and Special Events," page 322).

Of special interest is the room's "jazz door," preserved behind glass. It seems that during the '30s, two of the ballroom's lowlier employees, porter John M. Young and elevator operator Thomas Kelley, took it upon themselves to rate the bands coming through town. Cab Calloway got four stars, as did Noble Sissle, while Benny Goodman scored three. Though the twosome rated over 100 performers, they only gave out two five-star ratings—to themselves.

Indianapolis-born Noble Sissle (right) confers with Russell Smith

Courtesy Indiana Historical Society

CLUBS, ETC.

Indianapolis has no club that presents national-level jazz or blues artists on a regular basis, but the city has plenty of local talent and a number of small bars and restaurants that have music, including some national acts. Preeminent among these are the **Jazz Kitchen** and **Chatterbox Tavern**, which present jazz six nights a week, and the **Slippery Noodle Inn**, which presents local and regional blues six nights a week.

Among the many jazz musicians to watch out for in Indianapolis are veteran saxophonist Jimmy Coe; trombonist J. J. Johnson, who recently moved back to his hometown; cellist David Baker; the Hampton Sisters; trumpet player Pharez Whitted and his band, Decoy; piano players Claude Sifferlen, Steve Allee, Carl Hines, and Al Walton (also on organ); saxophonists Pookie Johnson, Mike Brown, and Kenny Washington; drummers Clem Tiggs, Dick Dickinson, "Mad" Harold Cardwell, Don Auston, and Larry Clark; trumpet players Clifford Ratliff and Michael Rodman; guitarist Steve Weakley; and vocalists Everette Green, Cherryl Hayes, Sam Gibson, and Vickie Daniel. Also, be sure to keep an eye out for talented musicians Tommy Mullinix, Greg Bacon, Cynthia Lane, and Monika Herzig.

Favorite local jazz bands include Cathy Morris & Collage, Tommy & the Tom Cats, Rob Swaynie's Moondance Trio, Larry Calland & Conga Jazz, Steve Corn Trio, Jack Gilfoy & His Naptown Quintet, the Indy All Stars Dixieland Band, the Michael Brown Quartet, the contemporary group Affinity, Dog Talk, and Jerry Jerome & The Stardusters.

Among blues artists are Duke Tumatoe, David Morgan, Chubby & the All-Stars, Harvey & The Bluetones, Governor Davis & The Blues Ambassadors, Gene Deer, Gordon Bonham, Red Beans & Rice, Mike Milligan & Steam Shovel, Cathi & Stuart Norton, Craig Brenner & the Crawdads, Tad Robinson, No Regrets, Jon Southern & The Blue Ghost Band, Dwight Edwards, and Webb, Stratyner, Webb & Stone.

Generally speaking, bars and clubs close at 2 or 3 A.M.

Personal Choices

Best jazz bar: *Jazz Kitchen*
Best blues bar: *Slippery Noodle*
Best jazz series: *Jazz on the Avenue at the Madame Walker Theatre*
Best jazz/blues/R&B/soul club: *Sherry's Nite Club*

FOR JAZZ

Jazz Kitchen, 5377 N. College Ave., 317–253–4900, www.thejazzkitchen.com.

A mix of local and touring jazz acts from across the country perform in this intimate, low-lit restaurant/club six nights a week. Recent national acts have included John Scofield, Kurt Elling, and Steve Turre, while local artists Frank Glover and his quartet, Steve Allee, and Clifford Ratliff and his quintet call the Kitchen home. On the menu is seafood, pasta, and chicken.

The club also hosts a Labor Day Street Fair every year, featuring local acts.

Music: M–Sa. *Cover:* $-$$. *Food:* American.

Chatterbox Tavern, 435 Massachusetts Ave. (midtown), 317–636–0584.

Surely this is the only place in the world where you'll find an autographed refrigerator—famous (Lou Rawls, John Hiatt) names only please—standing right next to the bar. Not that that's the best of what the Chatterbox, a small friendly neighborhood bar located in a 100-year-old building, has to offer. Some of the top jazz musicians in the city, playing everything from straight-ahead to progressive, can be found here. Regulars include Dick Dickinson, Claude Sifferlen, and Frank Glover. The club, which is done up with Christmas-tree lights and crazy sculptures created by area artists, is also one of the few places in town where musicians are welcome to sit in informally, anytime.

Music: M–Sa. *Cover:* $. *Food:* snacks.

Jazz Cooker, 925 E. Westfield Blvd. (Broad Ripple), 317–253–2883.

A Southern-style restaurant with as much seating out doors as in, the Jazz Cooker has presented the traditional Dick Laswell Trio for well over a decade, while blues acts and ragtime piano players take to the stage from time to time. The decor is pure New Orleans, with lots of posters and old instruments hanging from the walls.

Music: W–Su, Su brunch. *No cover. Food:* Creole, Cajun.

Also

Jazz can also be heard at **Sherry's Nite Club** (see "For Blues," below) and at various area restaurants. **Parrotheads** (5522 E. Fall Creek Pkwy., 317–543–0376), offers the Tommy Wills Trio on Wednesdays and a Dixieland band on Sundays; on the menu are steaks and seafood. **Malibu on Maryland** (4 W. Maryland St., 317–635–4334), best known for its seafood, features a piano player throughout the week and duos and trios on the weekends. Jazz trios play W-Sa at **Sullivan's Steakhouse** (3316 E. 86th St., 317–580–1280).

FOR BLUES

Slippery Noodle Inn, 372 S. Meridian St. (downtown), 317–631–6968.

The oldest bar in Indiana is also the best blues bar in Indianapolis, featuring local and regional acts most nights of the week, national acts on occasion. Blues Crew and Red Beans & Rice are among the regular locals; Lonnie Mack and Clarence Gatemouth Brown among the occasional nationals.

The Slippery Noodle, built in 1850, is on the National Register of Historic Places. Run by the Hal Yeagy family for about 30 years, it's a small funky place with a pressed-tin ceiling, hanging gaslight fixtures, and a beautiful wooden bar dating back to 1890. One side of the Noodle is for drinking and eating, the other side is for music, while downstairs is a quieter lounge for those who wish to talk. Next door is a second stage, housed in a building (adjacent to the first) that was once a stable. Most nights, two bands perform, and during special Indy events, such as the famed auto-racing weekends, the club also erects a tent in its parking lot, where yet a third band performs.

The Noodle's basement once was a haven for runaway slaves on the Underground Railroad; later, the inn's 16 upstairs rooms were converted into "a house of ill repute," where at least one murder took place. During the '30s and '40s, the bar was a haunt of gangsters "Diamond" Jim Brady and John Dillinger, and bullet holes can still be found in the walls.

Music: W–Sa. *Cover:* $–$$. *Food:* American.

Chubby's Club LaSalle, 3219 E. Michigan St. (near downtown), 317–632–6011.

A small neighborhood tavern with lots of atmosphere, Chubby's serves up simple food and much acoustic music. Sundays is an acoustic jam, Mondays is an electric and acoustic jam, and Tuesdays is blues night. Chubby's also hosts occasional touring acts like James Harman. A live CD was recently recorded at the club ("Live at Chubby's Club LaSalle"), featuring the Indy Blues Project, a collaboration of Indy blues players.

Music: nightly, blues T. *No cover. Food*: American.

Sherry's Nite Club, 2301 N. Meridian St, 317–926–4140.

For a mixture of blues, jazz, R&B, and soul, there's Sherry's Nite Club, a moderately sized indoor-outdoor venue. The club hosts live R&B/soul on the weekends, a jazz jam on Sundays, a Blues Monday (usually deejays), and deejays spinning R&B/soul the rest of the week. Most of the acts are local, but names such as Little Milton occasionally perform. The club is a throwback to the nightclubs of the '50s and '60s, with a mixed crowd of both old-schoolers and young folks who like to dress up and go out. Proper attire is required on the weekends, and a sign reads "No cursing or fighting."

Music: F-M, occasional other nights. *Cover/minimum:* $-$$$.

C. T. Peppers, 6283 N. College Ave. (Broad Ripple), 317–257–6277.

A large and modern glass-and-chrome club with a huge central bar, frosted-glass windows, and tall tiny tables, C. T.'s has a rotating roster of local blues talent, most of whom play for a week at a time. Paul Orta & the Kingpins and Bangkok Rooster are regulars, and regional acts such as Albert Washington are also brought in from time to time.

Music: W–Su. *Cover:* $. *Food:* American.

Also

While the Slippery Noodle is the only club in town with blues nightly, there are many other Indy clubs that present much local, and some touring, blues acts. **The Stone Mug Café** (6525 N. College Ave., 317–251–6985) is a blue-collar, after-work hangout that often hosts Harvey & the Bluetones and the Rev. Charlie Edmonds. **The Rathskeller** (401 E. Michigan St., 317–636–0396, www.rathskeller.com) is a downtown brewpub serving German food that attracts a mostly young crowd; regulars include Gene Deer and Gordon Bonham. **Ozzie's** (603 E. Market St., 317–631–3004), a hidden little tavern frequented by Indy's finest, presents acoustic blues on Tuesdays and live bands on the weekends. **Buckets** (9454 Haver Way, 317–575–8522), though located in a strip mall just north of I–465, hosts local favorites like No Regret and Mike Milligan once a week.

National blues and R&B acts can sometimes be heard at **The Vogue** (6259 N. College, 317–255–2828), a predominantly rock club. Among those that have performed here are Maceo Parker, Buckwheat Zydeco, Buddy Guy, and Robert Cray.

Other Venues and Special Events

A "Jazz on the Avenue" concert series, complete with a buffet, is held at the **Walker Center's Casino Ballroom** (617 Indiana Ave., 317–236–2099) every Friday evening. Every August the multiday **Indiana Avenue Jazz Festival** is also held here, as is the July "Women in Jazz Series."

The Indianapolis Artsgarden at the Circle Center Mall (317–681–8000) downtown presents a jazz or blues concert at least once a month, and sponsors **Blues in the Park** every August at White River State Park. Local acts such as Gordon Bonham and national names like Keb Mo play as the sun sets over Indy and the stars come out.

Inaugurated in 1999, **the Indy Jazz Fest** (800–635–2010, www.indyjazzfest.org) is a four-day event, spread out over multiple stages and venues, that has already presented some of the best in jazz (Herbie Hancock, Branford Marsalis, Cassandra Wilson), blues (B. B. King, Bobby Bland), and soul (Isaac Hayes, Al Green). The festival also features Indiana Avenue Revisited, a group of the old-school Indy players (Slide Hampton, Buddy Montgomery, Jimmy Coe, Mingo Jones) who used to jam on Indiana Avenue, and a Sunday Jazz Mass.

Indianapolis is home to the newly formed **Crossroads Blues Society** (formerly the Blues Society of Indiana) and the **Indianapolis Jazz Foundation**. Both sponsor events around town on occasion; watch the papers.

Record Stores

Indianapolis has a number of good record stores for jazz and blues. Among the best of its independents are **Vibes** (5975 E. 82nd St., 317–576–0404), **Luna Music** (1521 W. 86th St., 317–875–5862), and **Rockin' Billy's Records** (4435 N. Keystone Ave., 317–547–2582). Among the best of its chains are **Karma** (3540 W. 86th St., 38th & High School), and the **CD Warehouse** (6245 N. College Ave., 10030 E. Washington St., 7225 U.S. 31, and 1960 E. Stop 13 Rd.).

Radio and TV

WICR/88.7 FM (317–788–3280). Affiliated with University of Indianapolis. Jazz weekday afternoons, Sa evenings, Su afternoons. Blues Sa nights ("Beale Street Caravan," "Blues Before Dawn" with Ralph Adams).
WFYI/90.1 FM (317–636–2020). Affiliated with NPR. Blues Sa ("Nothing but the Blues" with Jay Zochowski) and Su ("Portraits in Blue").

WKLU/101.9 FM (317–239–1019). Blues Su ("Cool Blues Show" with Rich Hynes, "Blues Sunday" with Jimi Hurley). **WYJZ/100.9 FM** (317–293–9600). Smooth jazz.

"Circle City Jazz," an hour-long program featuring local jazz artists, can be seen on **WTBU** (channel 169) M at 10 P.M. and on **WFYI** (channel 20) Su at midnight.

CINCINNATI

Update and introduction by Larry Nager

Glittering casinos featuring top names in jazz and rhythm & blues; smoky juke joints where itinerant bluesmen stopped for nights of raw, gut-bucket music and bootleg whiskey; recording studios that churned out R&B hits; radio stations whose staff musicians were future jazz legends.

Nowadays, Cincinnati is a big Midwestern city made up of neat little neighborhoods nestled in the hills of the Ohio River Valley. It's a metropolis best-known as the corporate home of Procter & Gamble and the home office of Chiquita Banana. It has a conservative reputation and anti-porn stance immortalized in the film *The People Vs. Larry Flynt*.

But Cincinnati was once a thriving blues and jazz capital, a rough-and-ready river city where a trip across one of the bridges to Kentucky found illegal gambling and hot music all over the border towns of Newport and Covington.

The river brought jazz and blues to town early in the last century aboard the riverboats plying the Mississippi-Ohio River routes. In 1920, local girl Mamie Smith became the first African-American woman to record a blues song when she cut "Crazy Blues" for the OKeh label. The '20s saw the emergence of the Cincinnati Jug Band and such local bluesmen as Bob Coleman.

A gateway city from the South to the North, Cincinnati also became home, either temporarily or permanently, to thousands of Southern migrants heading to factory jobs. One of them was a young John Lee Hooker, who stopped in Cincinnati for a few years in the late '30s on his way up to Detroit.

More musicians came to town to work on the radio stations that turned Cincinnati into a broadcast center in the '30s.

Among them were Fats Waller and the Mills Brothers, both of whom broadcast over WLW, the Nation's Station, whose 500,000 clear-channel watts covered the U.S., Canada, and Mexico. Fats joined WLW in 1932, playing his trademark "stride" piano on "Fats Waller's Rhythm Club." He was allegedly fired a few years later for playing jazz on the station's pipe organ, "desecrating" the instrument that station founder Powel Crosley Jr. had installed in honor of his mother.

Outside of broadcasting, the steadiest work for musicians in those days was across the river. There, jazz bands and bluesmen played such posh nightspots as the Lookout House in Ft. Wright, Ky. (whites-only in those days), and the Copa Club, the top black nightspot in Newport. The latter was owned by the notorious Frank "Screw" Andrews, a white gangster who ran Newport's black numbers racket. The Copa featured former heavyweight champ Ezzard Charles as the doorman and presented such jazz heavyweights as the Duke Ellington Orchestra and Miles Davis' all-star sextet with John Coltrane, Cannonball Adderley, Wynton Kelly, Paul Chambers, and Jimmy Cobb. In the late '50s, suave blues singer/pianist Charles Brown found himself as a sort of indentured servant to Andrews, when the musician ran up a stiff gambling debt at the club. He wound up playing exclusively for him for years until the gangster's death (against all odds, in a cancer-related suicide, not a shooting).

Not all the jazz in the area was in Kentucky. Cincinnati's Cotton Club, in the Hotel Sterling at Sixth and Mound, presented such top big bands as Count Basie and Duke Ellington, as well as such popular "territory" bands as Tiny Bradshaw, who is buried here at Union Baptist Cemetery.

But Cincinnati's most important contribution to blues and jazz—and country, bluegrass, and funk as well—was King Records, arguably the most important independent label in the years just before rock 'n' roll. Founded by Sydney Nathan in 1943, King began as a country music label but soon expanded into rhythm & blues. King and its various subsidiaries released such seminal sides as Roy Brown's "Good Rocking Tonight" and Wynonie Harris' more successful version, inspirations for Elvis and the rock revolution to come.

King also recorded Little Willie John, Albert King, John Lee Hooker, the Five Royales, Bill Doggett, Earl Bostic, Freddie King, and jump blues bands such as Tiny Bradshaw. But it was James Brown whose King records forever changed popular music. His tenure with the label changed R&B from Sam Cooke's sweet gospel tones to the sweaty funk that has been JB's trademark for 35 years (see King Records, page 326).

Other jazz and blues artists associated with the city include George Russell, Frank Foster, Fred Hersch, Dave

Matthews, Michael Moore, Cal Collins, Amos Milburn, Charles Brown, Roosevelt Lee, tap dancer Marie Reynolds (who claimed that Louis Jordan wrote the song "Caldonia" about her), funk bassist Bootsy Collins, and the dean of jazz deejays, Oscar Treadwell (see "Radio," page 333).

Sources

The best entertainment listings can be found in the Friday edition of the *Cincinnati Enquirer* (513–721–2700, www. cincinnati.com), in the alternative weekly *CityBeat* (513–635–4700, www.citybeat.com) and in the Thursday edition of the *Cincinnati Post* (513–352–2000).

For maps and other information, contact the Greater Cincinnati Convention and Visitors Bureau, 3000 W. Sixth St., 513–621–2142 or 800–344–3445, www.cinyusa.com.

A Note on Neighborhoods

Cincinnati, sitting on the north bank of the Ohio River across from Kentucky, is an old Midwestern city with a solid Northeastern feel. Skyscraping hotels and office buildings dominate its small downtown, while its sidewalks are usually bustling with activity.

Historic Mt. Adams, located on a hill overlooking the city, is celebrated for its nightlife, but there are few jazz or blues clubs here. Corryville is a residential area that's home to the University of Cincinnati. Over-the-Rhine is a gentrifying area and entertainment district on the western edge of downtown. Mainstrasse Village is also an entertainment district, this one in downtown Covington, Ky. Walnut Hills and Bond Hill are districts with large African-American populations, while Roselawn is known as a "black-Jewish neighborhood." All of these areas are located within 20 minutes of downtown.

Cincinnatians pass over to Covington and Newport, Kentucky, located just a five-minute bridge-ride away, without giving it a second thought. Numerous clubs and restaurants are located here.

Traffic in Cincinnati is usually light and parking spaces are plentiful, except in the downtown during the day and in Mt. Adams at night.

Landmarks and Legends

Vocalstyle Music Roll Co., 412 E. Sixth St. (downtown).

Back in 1924, Jelly Roll Morton spent some time in Cincinnati, recording 13 piano rolls for the Vocalstyle Music Roll Co., which once had offices at this site. Only nine have been

The Blue Wisp is Cincinnati's oldest
and most beloved jazz club.

found, but they remain among the most important jazz piano
rolls ever made.

Moonlight Gardens Ballroom, Coney Island, 6201 Kellogg
Ave. (at I–275), 513–232–8230.

A big white beautiful building lined with white wrought-
iron balconies and sturdy green shutters, the Moonlight is located in an idyllic park on the banks of the Ohio River. At one
time all the big bands played here, and in 1936, Noble Sissle
and his group, which then included Sidney Bechet and Lena
Horne, were scheduled to appear. They were the first African-
American band to do so, but en route to the event, Sissle was
injured in an automobile accident, and Lena Horne, then only
19 years old, had to front the band.

Today, the Moonlight is part of Coney Island, a low-key
amusement park complete with a large pool, water rides,
miniature golf, restaurants, and gardens. Outdoor concerts
are occasionally presented.

Open: Memorial Day weekend through Labor Day, 10
A.M.–10 P.M.

King Records, 1540 Brewster St.

Founded by Syd Nathan, formerly of the furniture business, in 1943, King Records was known for its country-and-

western singers on the one hand and its R&B artists on the other (see chapter introduction). Most famous among them all was R&B-soulman James Brown.

Brown was signed to King on January 23, 1956, against the fierce objections of Nathan, who nonetheless let an employee talk him into it. At first, the public seemed to prove Nathan right, for Brown's records sold very poorly. Nathan was on the verge of letting him go when, in 1958, "Try Me" was released. It made No. 1 in R&B and the Top 50 in pop, and by the '60s, Brown was a legend. A publicity release from the time stated: "In an average month, he will give away some 5,000 autographed photos and 1,000 pairs of cuff links, will wear 120 freshly laundered shirts and more than 80 pairs of shoes, will change his performing costume 150 times, and will perform over 80 hours on the stage—singing, dancing, and also playing at least 960 songs on one or more of eight instruments."[1]

Today, all that's left of the record company, which once included a pressing plant and a warehouse, is a complex of brown buildings located near I-71.

Babe Baker's, 3128 Reading Rd., 513–751–9272.

Run by black real estate entrepreneur Babe Baker, this club, now a neighborhood bar called Babe's, was important from the mid-1950s through the 1960s. A long and narrow room, it brought in lots of name talent such as John Coltrane, Miles Davis, and McCoy Tyner, and featured a house band called the Jazz Disciples. "There'd be fast tempos all night long," recalls guitarist Cal Collins. "Lots of bebop, straight-ahead, Clifford Brown–type stuff."

CLUBS, ETC.

The most dependable jazz club in town is the **Blue Wisp**, famed for its Wednesday night gigs by the Blue Wisp Big Band and weekend gigs by regional and national jazz artists. The **Greenwich Tavern** is also a top spot, presenting both local and national acts.

Blues is everywhere, but one of the most distinctively "Cincinnati" clubs is **Lucille's Blues Club**, actually located across the river in Latonia, just outside Covington, Ky.; it combines the feel of a neighborhood bar with frequent national headliners. On the Cincinnati side, **Jefferson Hall** also regularly brings in national blues acts.

Some of the top jazz artists on the Cincinnati scene include guitarists Cal Collins, Wilbert Longmire, and Kenny Poole;

trumpeter Mike Wade; pianists Steve Schmidt (who also occasionally leads a killer organ trio), Ed Moss, Phil DeGreg, and Frank Vincent; drummers Art Gore and John Von Ohlen; bassists Mike Sharfe, Jim Anderson, and Steve Flora; and singers Ann Chamberlain, Mary Ellen Tanner, and Bill Chaffee. Giving the scene an international flavor is Latin X-Posure, a salsa/jazz group combining Latino singers and percussionists from Dayton with some of Cincinnati's top jazz players.

Current blues artists include boogie-woogie master Big Joe Duskin; blues-shouting wildman H-Bomb Ferguson; such fine bands as Sweet Alice & Unfinished Business, Sonny Hill & the Night Shift, and Greg Schaber & High Street; as well as a host of red-hot guitarslingers. including Sonny Moorman, Kelly Richey, and wunderkinds Scotty Bratcher and Noah Wotherspoon. The famed funk bassist Bootsy Collins also still lives in Cincinnati.

Most clubs in Cincinnati close at 2 A.M.

Personal Choices

Best jazz clubs: *Blue Wisp, Greenwich Tavern*
Best trad-jazz spots: *Dee Felice's, Kaldi's, Arnold's Bar & Grill*
Best blues clubs: *Lucille's, Mansion Hill, Jefferson Hall*
Best area club for national acts: *Gilly's (in Dayton)*

FOR JAZZ

Blue Wisp, 19 Garfield Pl. (downtown), 513–721–9801.

For 16 years, Marjean and Paul Wisby ran a jazz club in the O'Bryonville section of Cincinnati. It started as a whim—the couple had just bought a neighborhood bar and wanted to add entertainment—and ended up as a legend. The Blue Wisp is now Cincinnati's oldest and most beloved jazz club.

Relocated to the basement of a downtown office building over a decade ago now, the Wisp is filled with comfortable tables and chairs, and bathed in a dark blue light. The original Blue Wisp sign still flaunts its black magic above the stairs.

The best night to visit the club is Wednesday, when the Blue Wisp Big Band performs. Made up of the finest local musicians, many on the faculty of the University of Cincinnati College Conservatory of Music, the group swings hard, driven by the masterful John Von Ohlen on drums. That sexiest-man-alive George Clooney is sometimes in attendance, in town to visit his father Nick and Aunt Rosemary.

Weekends usually feature regional acts, but with the Phil DeGreg Trio as the house rhythm section, there's rarely a bad night at the Wisp.

Music: nightly. *Cover*: $-$$.

Greenwich Tavern, 2444 Gilbert Ave. (Walnut Hills), 513–221–1151.

The low-ceilinged Greenwich is an intimate neighborhood spot offering mostly straight-ahead jazz, an eclectic menu, and friendly, homey atmosphere. One of the most integrated clubs in town, it features both national players (Joshua Redman, Ahmad Jamal, Eddie Vinson, George Benson) and local and regional stars (including trumpet wiz Mike Wade). National blues artists such as Clarence "Gatemouth" Brown are also here from time to time.

The 90-plus-year-old restaurant/club sports a restaurant, lounge, and bar to one side, a music room to the other. The restaurant and lounge are decorated in an ancient Greek motif, complete with statuette replicas, while the music room has a contemporary feel, done up in pastels.

Music: F-Sa. *Cover*: $-$$. *Food*: eclectic.

Dee Felice Café, 529 Main St., Covington (Mainstrasse Village), 859–261–2365.

Heralded for its elegant dining, Dee's, as it's locally known, also offers up some fine piano trios, Dixieland, and traditional jazz with its excellent Creole menu. The restaurant is nicely laid out in four rooms with a rose-and-gray color scheme, frosted-glass windows, and pressed-tin ceilings. The stage, very long and narrow, is set up just above and behind a gleaming wooden bar, N'Awlins style.

Music: nightly. *No cover*. *Food*: Creole.

Kaldi's Coffeehouse & Bookstore, 1204 Main St. (Over-the-Rhine), 513–241–3070.

A wonderfully warm and cozy coffeehouse cum second-hand bookstore, Kaldi's presents jazz on Friday and Saturday nights, bluegrass on Tuesdays and Thursdays. A rotating roster of local jazz trios usually performs.

Kaldi's is housed in an atmospheric nineteenth-century building, complete with tin ceilings and wood floors. A simple menu ranging from vegetarian dishes to chicken entrees and burritos is served.

Music: Tu, Th-Su. *No cover*. *Food*: simple entrees, sandwiches, etc.

Sonny's Lounge, 1227 California Ave. (Bond Hill), 513–242–4579.

Owned by jazz-and-blues lover and two-time Ohio Golden Gloves champ Sonny Lewis, this is a down-home, neighborhood club that's famed for its Sunday-night jam sessions. Usually featured are a mix of music veterans and young students from the University of Cincinnati College Conservatory of Music.

Music: Su. *Cover:* $.

Also

Fringe jazz can be found at a variety of local clubs, from **Bogart's** (2621 Vine St., Corryville; Ticketmaster: 513–562–4949), a large, predominantly rock venue, to the **Barrelhouse Brewing Co**. (22 E. 12th St., downtown, 513–421–2337). **Arnold's Bar & Grill** (210 E. Eighth St., 513–421–6234), a well-lit checkered-tablecloth affair that's the oldest bar in Cincinnati, presents traditional jazz regularly.

FOR BLUES

Lucille's Blues Club, 3715 Winston Ave., Latonia, Ky., 859–431–8086.

The center of much of the blues activity in the area, Lucille's hosts the monthly meetings and jam sessions of the Greater Cincinnati Blues Society. Owners Patti and Greg Mebs (also a singer-guitarist in his own right) treat their customers like family, and that, combined with top-shelf blues acts, makes Lucille's the discerning jukologist's joint of choice.

Lucille's is housed in a turn-of-the-century building complete with pressed tin ceilings and an ornate mahogany back bar that dates back to 1893. Along most of the walls hang photos of blues greats, while to one side is a "signature guitar" signed by everyone from Walter Trout and Carl Weathersbey to Kenny Neal and Deborah Coleman—all of whom have played here.

National blues acts come through Lucille's about twice a month. Other nights are devoted to a variety of local and regional musicians; the house band is G. Miles & the Hitmen. When the national acts perform, a homemade buffet supper, usually pasta or a cookout, is served, and tickets are sold to only 105 lucky guests—all of whom get a seat.

Music: Tu-Sa, every other Su. *Cover*: $-$$. *Food*: simple entrees, for national acts only.

Jefferson Hall, 1150 Main St. (Over-the-Rhine), 513–723–9008.

A popular club located in the heart of the Main Street entertainment district, Jefferson Hall presents a steady mix of local, regional, and national acts. Among the top names in blues that have played here are Coco Montoya, Anson Funderburgh, Eddie Clearwater, Saffire, and Lil Ed & the Blues Imperials.

Music: nightly. *Cover*: $-$$.

Mansion Hill Tavern, 502 Washington St., Newport, Ky., 606-431–3538.

A neighborhood saloon that's been a bar for over 85 years, the Mansion is a dark and laid-back place with exposed brick walls, wood wainscot, lots of neon, boat paraphernalia, plants, and artwork. Blues come to the Mansion on weekend nights, and it's a favorite spot among the *cognoscenti*, drawing everyone, says one habitué, from "strippers to yuppies, blues aficionados to neighborhood people." Among the regulars who play here are guitarist Chris Carero's Trio and pianist Ricky Nye & the Red Hots. Every other Sunday there's a blues jam. During the day, the tavern is a popular lunch spot.

Music: F, Sa, every other Su. *Cover*: $. *Food*: simple entrees on F nights only.

Sonny's All Blues, 4040 Reading Rd., North Avondale, 513–281–0410.

Sister club to Sonny's Lounge (see "For Jazz," above) Sonny Lewis' *other* nightclub features blues every Sunday night, usually compliments of Uncle Russell & the Kinfolks. One Sunday a month, too, the club presents multi-act "festivals" featuring some of the area's top blues musicians. The neighborhood place is moderately sized, with a small dance floor, about 15 tables, several pool tables, and a back room.

Music: Su. *Cover*: none-$.

Allyn's Café, 3538 Columbia Parkway (5 min. N of downtown), 513–871–5779.

There's no dearth of odd memorabilia is this eclectic Cajun and Mexican restaurant, including more than 50 antique radios, a large collection of cuckoo clocks, and dozens of posters from Cincinnati's yearly Oktoberfest. The booths are all done up in Mexican pastels, and there's a patio out back.

Blues and blues-rock are also part of the scene, and the best night to come is Sundays, when the Blue Birds Big Band performs. This is an R&B revue, not a jazz band, and it comes with a full horn section, singer/guitarist Marc Sastre, and others playing some of the best music in town. Not bad for a $2 cover.

Music: most nights. *Cover:* $. *Food:* Tex-Mex, Cajun.

Burbank's Real Bar-B-Que in Sharonville, 11167 Dowlin Dr. (12 min. N of downtown), 513–771–1440.

This modern eatery, spread out over two large dining rooms with a bar in the middle, is owned by local radio legend Gary Burbank. A Memphis expatriate, Burbank was once the only white deejay on WDAI, Memphis' soul/blues/gospel powerhouse.

Burbank's, filled with lots of booths and aged wood, presents plenty of blues acts along with some of the best Southern-style barbecue in the area. Tuesday nights are open jams, and the rest of the week is devoted to a rotating roster of mostly local and regional bands.

Music: Tu-Sa. *No cover. Food:* barbecue.

Also

PJ's Lounge (2300 Reading Rd., Mount Auburn, 513–721–9444) is a down-home spot that presents blues on occasion. The annual Cincinnati Blues and Jazz Masters Summits, produced by local blues singer/promoter Keith Little, are often presented here.

The Blue Note (4520 W. Eighth St., Price Hill, 513–921–8898) is primarily a rock club, but whenever legendary blues-rock guitarist Lonnie Mack comes to town, he usually plays here. Back on his old stomping grounds, his sets usually include his autobiographical tune, "Cincinnati Jail."

Other Venues and Special Events

Southgate House (24 E. Third St., Newport, 859–431–2201) regularly presents such acoustic blues acts as Rory Block and Roy Bookbinder, and has presented electric bluesman Gatemouth Brown and a guitar lover's double-bill of Coco Montoya and Tommy Castro. Xavier University produces a series of jazz piano and guitar concerts featuring the likes of Mulgrew Miller, James Williams, and Bucky Pizzarelli; the series is currently held Sunday afternoons at the **Cincinnati Art Museum Theatre** (513–745–3161). The **University of Cincinnati College Conservatory of Music** (513–556–4183) produces concerts in its Corbett Auditorium featuring top local jazz players.

About a half-hour north of Cincinnati, Miami University's Hamilton Campus hosts a superb concert series in its **Parrish**

Auditorium (513–785–3000). Featured are jazz artists such as Diana Krall, Jim Hall, and Bill Frisell, as well as roots and blues musicians such as the Campbell Brothers.

The city's biggest annual musical event is the **Coors Light Festival** (513–621–2142), which despite being known as "the Jazz Fest," presents top old-school and new-school soul and R&B artists, including Bobby "Blue" Bland, Mary J. Blige, Patti LaBelle, and Frankie Beverly & Maze. Always held in late July, the three-day show usually also features some soul/jazz and crossover artists such as Chaka Khan and the late Grover Washington, Jr.

The **Greater Cincinnati Blues Society** (513–684–4227) produces an annual festival that is quickly gaining a national reputation. Known as the **Queen City Blues Fest**, held the second weekend in July, it fills the beautiful riverside park at Sawyer Point with top national, regional, and local acts. Past headliners have included Luther Allison, Billy Lee Riley, Johnnie Johnson, Lazy Lester, and Jimmie "Fast Fingers" Dawkins. What makes the event unique though is its Boogie Piano Stage which brings together players from around the world, such as Belgium's Renaud Patigny and England's Sonny Leyland, with local legends such as Big Joe Duskin and H-Bomb Ferguson.

Blues and jazz artists are featured throughout the year at other events, including the **Annual Midwest Black Family Reunion**, which takes place in August and has featured Little Milton. **WorldJam**, a new, free festival started up in 1999, has thus far presented Koko Taylor, the Funky Meters, and Chris Duarte, along with local blues favorite, Greg Schaber & High Street.

Record Stores

An excellent store for both new and used jazz and blues recordings is **Everybody's Records** (6106 Montgomery Rd. at Ridge, 513–531–4500).

Radio

Blues can be heard regularly on **WNKU/89.7 FM** and occasionally on **WAIF/88.3 FM** and **WVXU/91.7 FM**. Jazz, however, is currently having a hard time on Cincinnati radio. Other than nostalgic big-band shows, there's no one now regularly programming real jazz.

That's especially sad news because at one time, Cincinnati was home to esteemed jazz deejay Oscar Treadwell. Treadwell, for whom Bird wrote "An Oscar for Treadwell" and Monk wrote "Oska T.," was a young deejay at WDAS in Philadelphia when he first played Monk's "Misterioso" on the air. The station manager, listening, said that if the deejay ever played that work again, he'd be fired. Treadwell played it five more times and was thrown off. He was then invited to host a jazz show on the University of Cincinnati's WGUC, where he played whatever he liked for years and years.

Other Nearby Locations

Gilly's, Fifth and Jefferson Streets, Dayton (downtown), 937–228–8414.

Adjoining a bus station, about 45 miles north of Cincinnati on Interstate 75, is the premier club in the area. Gilly's, which seats about 250, has been presenting top talent for over 30 years, and it's a beautiful place, with an excellent sound system and superb sight lines. Among those who have performed here recently, in concerts produced by Dayton's CityFolk organization, are Mulgrew Miller, Kenny Barron, and the group Sphere. CityFolk (937–223–3655) also sponsors an annual music festival in downtown Dayton each June. Gilly's is closed if there's no music booked.

Music: most nights. *Cover*: $$-$$$.

MINNEAPOLIS/ST. PAUL

Updated by Tom Surowicz

The Twin Cities have played only a small role in jazz and blues history, but several major figures are connected with the area. Oscar Pettiford, the bassist of mixed black and Native American extraction who pioneered the use of the jazz cello, moved here from Oklahoma with his family's band during the 1930s and spent his youth in the cities. Lester Young also moved to Minneapolis with his family's band for a brief period in the 1920s and then returned as a young man in 1930. During his second stay, he played at the Nest Club with Frank Hines, Leroy White, and Eddie Barefield, and at the Cotton Club in the suburb of St. Louis Park.

According to Eddie Barefield, Minneapolis did have its share of jazz life in the late '20s and '30s, to be found mostly in speakeasies and back-street bars. The local radio stations also had their staff orchestras, and the hotels, their touring big bands. Peggy Lee, originally from North Dakota, took a big step in her career when she appeared at the Radisson Hotel with Sev Olson's band.

Later, there were the Prom Center ballroom in St. Paul and the Merigold ballroom in Minneapolis, along with a club called Freddie's, which had an NBC wire and featured major players such as Ella Fitzgerald and Teddy Wilson. Duke Ellington presented one of his rare sacred concerts at Minneapolis's Hennepin Avenue Baptist Church, and cornet player Paul "Doc" Evans was a regular at a traditional jazz joint called Mitch's. Also, pianist and songwriting great Dave Frishberg grew up in St. Paul, and still makes regular visits home—to play clubs, see family members, and check in with the inspiration for "My Attorney, Bernie."

Two major blues figures, Baby Doo Caston from Mississippi and Lazy Bill Lucas from Arkansas, also settled down in the Twin Cities area, while the '60s brought with them several significant white blues artists. Among these were the group Koerner, Ray, and Glover, an early John Lennon favorite, and the piano player Willie Murphy. Back then, the center of the Cities' music scene was the Triangle Bar at 1822 Riverside (still standing but no longer in use), where Bonnie Raitt and Bob Dylan also played. The Triangle was located on Minneapolis's rebellious West Bank near Cedar and Riverside, then called "the biomagnetic center of the universe." The West Bank is also one of the oldest districts in the Twin Cities; its bars date back to the early 1900s and were once watering holes for riverboat captains.

These days, teen blues-rock phenoms Jonny Lang and Shannon Curfman, and venerable acoustic guitar guru Leo Kottke are the big national names residing in town.

Sources

City Pages (612–375–1015), a free weekly, is a good source. So is *Freetime*, the wanna-be-a-weekly Friday section of the *Minneapolis Star Tribune* (612–673–4000). The Friday "Express" section of the *St. Paul Pioneer Press* (651–222–5011) and the Sunday "Arts & Entertainment" section of the *Star Tribune* also contain loads of listings.

The Twin Cities Jazz Society runs a hotline at 651–633–0329.

For maps and other information, contact the Greater Minneapolis Convention and Visitors Association at 4000 Multifoods Tower, 33 S. Sixth St., 612–0661–4700, and the

St. Paul Area Chamber of Commerce/St. Paul Convention & Visitor's Bureau at 55 East Fifth St., 651–223–5000/ 297–6985.

A Note on Neighborhoods

The Twin Cities, located about 10 minutes apart, like to enumerate their differences. Minneapolis is the newer, bigger, brasher of the two. St. Paul is older—more cultured but also somewhat stodgy.

To an outsider, however, the cities have much in common: lots of clean streets and city parks and big bearded men in winter parkas, numerous cultural institutions, little street crime, and relatively small ethnic populations. The restored Warehouse District, now filled with shops and restaurants, is in downtown Minneapolis; the West Bank, located near the University of Minnesota, is still a sort of "ex-hippie" district in east Minneapolis, and Seven Corners is a restaurant and theater district also in east Minneapolis.

Traffic in the Twin Cities is light and street parking is available almost everywhere.

Like most blues bars on the West Bank, the Viking once catered to Mississippi river-boat captains.

CLUBS, ETC.

The Twin Cities has two full-time, serious jazz clubs—both in St. Paul. The **Dakota** is a well-established and esteemed restaurant/club, while **The Artists' Quarter** focuses 100 per cent on music (though bartender Byron Nelson does make a mean sandwich—the club's only menu item). **The Times** and **Jitters**, two clubs in northeast Minneapolis, are also full-time jazz and occasional blues venues, but unlike the above showcases, don't regularly bring in any national acts. The area's top blues club is **Famous Dave's**, a large restaurant/bar that's just as well known for its barbecue. **Whiskey Junction** and **Brewbaker's** also bring in national blues acts with some regularity.

Area jazz artists to watch for include world-class bassist Anthony Cox; stride and trad piano mainstay Butch Thompson; octogenarian tenor saxophonist Irv Williams; sax stalwarts Eddie Berger and Dave Karr; former Buddy Rich Band pianist Bobby Peterson; avant players John Devine, Joe Smith, Donald Washington, Dean Granros, and George Cartwright (of Curlew renown); singers Esther Godinez, Debbie Duncan, Bruce Henry, Prudence Johnson, Connie Evingson, Carole Martin, and Charmin Michelle; organist Billy Holloman; drummers Phil Hey, Dave King, Eric Kamau Gravatt, Kenny Horst, and Jay Epstein; saxmen Pete Whitman, Morris Wilson, Brina Grivna, Kenny Holmen, Doug Little, and Gary Berg; trumpeters Bernie Edstrom, Gene Adams, and Jon Pemberton; vibists Dave Hagedorn, Marv Dahlgren, and Steve Yeager; piano players Peter Schimke, Bill Carrothers, Laura Caviani, Rick Carlson, and Mikkel Romstad; Prince's old horn section, The Hornheads; A.A.C.M. members Carei Thomas (piano, composition) and Douglas Ewart (reeds); guitarists Dean Magraw, Tim Sparks, and Dave Singley; bassists Billy Peterson, Tom Lewis, Terry Burns, and Gordy Johnson; the Cedar Ave. Big Band, Wolverines Big Band, JazzMn Big Band, and Bill Banfield's B-Magic Orchestra; fine post-boppers the Motion Poets and Departure Point; and arguably the most popular, electric, and aggressive combo in either town—Happy Apple.

Blues favorites include Big Walter Smith & the Groove Merchants; Ray & Glover; piano pounder, bassist, guitarist and bandleader Willie Murphy; the Butanes and the Butanes Soul Revue (a larger, more R&B oriented version of the same band); the veteran Lamont Cranston band (now into its fourth decade!); jump blues specialists, the Senders; harp man Joe T. Cook & the Long Shots; W. C. Handy award nominee/

singer Percy Strother; the Joel Johnson Band; pianist/singer John Beach; Rockin' Daddy & the Rough Cuts; the Big George Jackson Band; British-born bassist, Steve York, and the Hillbilly Voodoo Dolls.

Personal Choices

Best jazz restaurant: *Dakota Bar & Grill*
Best and most atmospheric jazz nightclub/listening room:
   Artists' Quarter
Best club for big bands: *O'Gara's*
Best blues clubs: *Famous Dave's, Arnellia's*
Best hole-in-the-wall blues club: *Viking Bar*

FOR JAZZ

Dakota Bar & Grill, Bandana Sq., 1021 Bandana Blvd., St. Paul (near downtown), 651–642–1442.

One of the more celebrated restaurants in town (critically acclaimed by even the *New York Times*), the Dakota is large and sprawling, filled with mauves, maroons, and blond wood. National artists come through on a very regular basis, usually playing multi-night stands in mid-week, while top local acts pack the room on weekends. McCoy Tyner has appeared here 12 times, and other very frequent visitors include Nicholas Payton, Roy Hargrove, Bobby Watson (who recorded a live CD at the Dakota), Ahmad Jamal, Elvin Jones, Geoff Keezer, and Karrin Allyson. The musical fare is mostly established legends, neo-bop young phenoms, and classy singers. But the occasional trad, fusion, or "outside" act sneaks in, with Steve Lacy making three amazing trio visits in recent years and Banu Gibson belting nicely for the swing and moldy fig set. Top local draws include Debbie Duncan, vocal group Moore By Four, charming Brazilian music specialist Esther Godinez, and the wacky jazz/rock horn band Bozo Allegro. Also, concert hall jazz acts—hello, Wynton—often come here to eat (then jam) after their shows.

Music: nightly. *Cover:* $-$$$. *Food:* American. Reservations recommended.

The Artists' Quarter, 366 Jackson St., St. Paul, 651–292–1359.

The only Twin Cities nightclub of any kind actually run by musicians, the AQ—as it is fondly known—is the domain of drummer Kenny Horst. He books talent, backs local and visiting hornmen, answers the phone, does some bartending, and often gets his whole family involved in the biz. This is a real jazz bar, with a classic Big Apple feel—but far cheaper prices. A dark and cozy basement space in a vintage downtown building, the AQ has pitch black walls and a high ceiling with black painted exposed fixtures. Heck, at this club there's no natural light difference between midday and midnight. The joint has a splendid sound and lighting system, and just about every seat in the place (capacity: 125) sports fine sightlines.

Whereas the Dakota usually books complete touring bands, the much more intimate AQ often pairs nationally-known visiting soloists with compatible Twin Cities rhythm sections. Lew Tabackin, Mose Allison, Tom Harrell, former Twin Citian Bob Rockwell, Ira Sullivan, JoAnne Brackeen, Dewey Redman, and Ben Sidran all make regular visits here. Legends such as Lee Konitz, Benny Golson, Roy Haynes, and the late Harry "Sweets" Edison have also appeared on some unforgettable nights. Top hometown draws include Happy Apple, Anthony Cox, Dave Karr, the Motion Poets, and Eddie Berger. Billy Holloman hosts a fun B–3 organ jam night every Tuesday.

The place has oodles of cool jazz art—photos, plaques, digital image blow-ups, framed album covers—adorning its ebony walls. Other nice touches include a hipster doorman named Davis Wilson who does swell tributes to Lord Buckley, and ace bartender/photographer Dyron Nelson, who loves and documents the music as it happens.

Music: Tu-Su. *Cover*: $-$$. *Food*: sandwiches.

The Times Bar & Cafe, 201 E. Hennepin Ave., Minneapolis (across the river from downtown), 612–617–8098.

Forced to move from its cramped digs on Nicollet Mall, the Times took some of its beautiful wood decor across the Mississippi—a nice touch that adds continuity and instant ambience to the bar's quite spacious and tony new digs. The club kept some of its local favorite artists, too. The Wolverines Trio still plays weekly, as do the venerable blues duo of Ray & Glover. However, Ray & Glover are now relegated to the club's basement space—**Jitters** (612–617–1111), a coffee and wine bar that sometimes also features jazz. One of the Times' best bets is its no-cover Sunday brunch, with classic American breakfast grub, and the excellent standards singer Judi Donaghy fronting a first-rate band.

Music: nightly. No cover. *Food*: American.

Jazzmine's, 123 N. 3rd St., M'polis. (downtown), 612–630–5299.

The only club in town catering to the "smooth jazz" crowd, this new hotspot also books classy singers, plus some blues,

R&B, and rock acts. Most of the artists are local, but at least a few national names of varying genres—Latin legend Eddie Palmieri, crossover sax guy Dave Koz, blueswoman Marcia Ball, singer-songwriter Karla Bonoff—show up each month. Top hometown draws here include fusion saxman Ronny Loew, Moore By Four singer Connie Evingson, and R&B vocal vet Maurice Jacox.

A quite small, very stylish room on the ground floor of a big old downtown office building, Jazzmine's has some definite sight-line problems. There are booth and table seats that don't face the stage, plus tables that are actually behind the stage. Crowds here also tend to be noisy, out for a good "hang," more than to see any particular act. But Jazzmine's decor is quite interesting, based on a club in Singapore that the owner used to frequent, and the food is nouvelle American cuisine at its lively best. The snappy sound system was installed by Steve Raitt, singer Bonnie's soundman brother.

Music: nightly. *Cover*: none–$$. *Food*: American.

Loring Bar, 1624 Harmon Pl. (downtown), M'polis. (Loring Park, downtown), 612–332–1617.

Housed in an atmospheric old building with a lot of mismatched furniture, the Loring is an eclectic restaurant-club that attracts a youngish, arts-oriented crowd. "More European than American," as one local fan describes it, it's located adjacent to a park overlooking a pond and offers both indoor and outdoor dining.

Music at the Loring runs the gamut, but it's always somewhat removed from the mainstream, and jazz is a regular feature. "Free jazz" saxmen John Devine, Bill Lang, Joe Smith, and Jimmy Wallace work here regularly, as do French *chanson* and *musette* groups, and arty, experimental rockers.

Music: nightly, jazz twice weekly. *No cover. Food:* innotative American.

Yvette, 600 Hwy. 169 S., at I–394 in the Interchange Tower, St. Louis Park (NW of Mpls.), 952–512–7200.

Occupying part of the ground floor of a suburban high-rise office complex, Yvette is a dark and woody lounge any businessman on an expense account could love. With a bar tucked away in the corner, this is a quite quiet, reasonably intimate dining room with a fine keyboard which attracts many of the area's best pianists, including Igmod and Concord Jazz recording artist Laura Caviani and Erroll Garner specialist/authority Tommy O'Donnell. The hometown duos and trios provide ambience aplenty, though most nights the crowd here just wants classy background sounds for their dining experience.

Yet at times, the room has brought in notable out-of-town luminaries, including the legendary Eartha Kitt, veteran Chicago guitarist/singer Frank D'Rone, singing star Karrin Allyson, and native son songwriter/pianist Dave Frishberg. It's well worth the drive to freeway-land on those special nights.

Music: nightly. *Cover*: none-$$$. *Food*: American.

O'Gara's Bar and Grill/O'Gara's Garage, 164 N. Snelling Ave., St. Paul (5 min. W of downtown), 651–644–3333.

Basically an old-time Irish bar and restaurant filled with green booths and frosted glass, O'Gara's has been presenting the great Cedar Avenue Big Band on Monday nights for years and years. Meanwhile, out back in O'Gara's Garage, a big spiffy place with lime-green lights and a black-and-chrome bar, blues bands such as the Hoopsnakes perform most weekends.

O'Gara's, which dates back to 1941, began as a restaurant that served food and liquor to factory workers who helped manufacture World War II munitions. Another historical tidbit: today's game room is housed in what used to be a barbershop that was run by Charles "Peanuts" Schulz's father.

Music: S–M, Th–Sa. *Cover:* $. *Food:* American.

Also

Club Ashe (322 N. 1st Ave., M'polis., 612–673–9694), a small cigar smoker's yuppie haunt, presents outstanding modern jazz sets on-the-cheap every Thursday. Motion Poets saxman Doug Little and other young post-bop heavyweights are usually on stand. The **Blue Nile Restaurant & Lounge** (2027 E. Franklin Ave., M'polis., 612–338–3000), a reggae and world-beat club, as well as a fine Ethiopian restaurant, has a jazz jam session with Morris Wilson every Monday. The **Fine Line Music Cafe** (318 1st Ave. N., M'polis., 612–338–8100), a semi-swanky, two-story downtown showcase room, books jazz acts (Patricia Barber, John Scofield) on rare occasions. **Sophia** (65 S.E. Main St., in Riverplace, M'polis., 612–379–1111), a fine dining spot overlooking the Mississippi, has a small and busy bar section where some of the premier singers in town (Debbie Duncan, Connie Evingson) turn up. With its "no cover" policy, Sophia is also a hangout for musicians on their nights off.

FOR BLUES

Famous Dave's, Calhoun Sq., 3001 Hennepin Ave., M'polis. (uptown), 612–822–9900.

The big flagship nightclub of a recently-founded, publicly-traded chain of mostly smaller and music-free barbecue "shacks," Famous Dave's is the best blues club in town, in spite of itself. It gets the hippest traveling acts, has the biggest stage and the nicest sound system, and charges the lowest cover—heck, the majority of the shows are free!

So what's wrong with this picture? Well, despite a major attempt to artificially provide ambience, Famous Dave's remains a rather sterile theme restaurant in a shopping mall location, with a headset-wearing staff that seems entirely immune to 12-bar music's charms. And most nights, the audience isn't much better. The bulk of the Famous Dave's patrons come for the passable, bland barbecue—ribs, chicken, cornbread, beans, etc.—which is reasonably priced, and doled out in whoppingly big portions.

But it's impossible to argue with "no cover" shows by the likes of Johnny Rawls, Alberta Adams, Johnnie Bassett, Chubby Carrier, Melvin Taylor, Sean Costello, and Rusty Zinn, as well as by out-of-town critics' favorites, underground legends, and hot up'n'comers. Toss in a blues happy hour, a weekend blues brunch, and some high quality local acts (Big John Dickerson, John Beach, Willie Murphy, Joe T. Cook) and this place adds up to a big boon to bluesers on a budget.

Music: nightly, plus happy hours and weekend brunches. *Cover*: none–$. *Food*: barbecue.

Whiskey Junction, 901 Cedar Ave. S., M'polis. (West Bank), 612–338–9550.

"We do the blues" is the motto of the most popular biker bar in the Twin Cities. On a nice summer night, the row of gleaming—and often roaring—Harleys in front of this joint is staggering to behold. A fairly large, two-roomed place with a long, long bar, Whiskey Junction has walls of exposed brick and a floor of black-and-white tile. The musicians crowd onto a medium-small stage at the far end, leaving plenty of room for dancing and drinking and yakking. The music is an all-indigo mix of fine local 12-bar acts and hard-touring, second-tier national blues names. On the right night, with the right visitors—say the always potent and hip Bel Airs, out of Missouri—this place can be big fun on-the-cheap.

Music: nightly. *Cover*: none–$. *Food*: pizza by-the-slice, plus blues breakfast.

Arnellia's, 1183 University Ave. (10 min. W of downtown, near M'polis.), St. Paul, 651–642–5975.

One of the few black-owned jazz venues in the Twin Cities, Arnellia's (named after its owner, Arnellia Alles) usually features music about five nights a week. A fairly large place with a bar to one side, tables and chairs to the other, the club is also a restaurant serving up good, old-fashioned American food such as meatloaf, roast chicken, and pork chops. Chitlin circuit R&B stars check in to Arnellia's with some regularity. Latimore, Marvin Sease, and that delightful senior citizen sex machine, Bobby Rush, have all packed the room. Arnellia's also features two R&B house bands, local blues acts, deejays, weekly gigs by organist Billy Holloman, and a Sunday night open jazz jam.

Music: five nights a week. *Cover:* $-$$. *Food:* American.

Brewbaker's, McKnight 36 Plaza, N. St. Paul (St. Paul suburbs), 651–779–0243.

A big club that seems like an overgrown game bar, Brewbaker's is an atmosphere-deficient haunt in a suburban shopping mall. What started out as a mostly blues, blues-rock, and boogie venue still books a fair amount of blue-wave bands, but they now compete with over-the-hill hard rockers such as Molly Hatchet and Night Ranger. A large stage and decent sound system are the strong suits of Brewbaker's, which otherwise has about as much color as a bingo hall. Some great old-school R&B road warriors appear here (Roomful of Blues, Paul Cebar & the Milwaukeeans), along with the occasional guitar star (Jeff Healey) or classic rock hero of yore (Leon Russell). Big Walter Smith and some other quality local faves get off-night gigs, but Brewbaker's is only worth the drive if the headliner's just right.

Music: nightly. *Cover:* $-$$$. *Food:* American.

The Cabooze, 917 Cedar Ave. S., M'polis. (West Bank), 612–338–6425.

From the outside the Cabooze looks small and narrow, like its namesake, but inside, it's a long and friendly atmospheric hall with crowds of people and a bandstand located way down at the other end. A large bar dominates the place, along with neon strips of blue and red and larger-than-life posters of artists such as Little Richard and Eddie Cochran.

The original Cabooze, founded in the early '70s, was a small locally renowned club that featured almost exclusively blues (Albert King, Junior Walker, Willie Dixon). Since then, it's become primarily a rock-and-roll club, but it does still present some local and national blues. Louisiana bluesman Tab Benoit is a house favorite.

Music: W-Su, occasional blues. *Cover:* $-$$.

Viking Bar, 1829 Riverside Ave. S., M'polis. (West Bank), 612–332–4259.

A West Bank bar that's been here since the 1920s, the Viking, long and narrow, is friendly and laid-back, soaked in the alcohol of time. Booths line one wall while a stained-glass sun pattern is splashed behind the bar. The Joel Johnson Band and the Front Porch Swingin' Liquor Pigs are mainstays here; KFAI-FM deejay Johnson also books the place. A long-running Monday afternoon "happy hour" jam attracts the cream of local blues talent, plus occasional out-of-town "heavies."

Music: Th–Su, and M 4–8 pm. *Cover:* none–$.

Blues Alley, 15 Glenwood Ave. N., M'polis. (10 min. N of downtown), 612–333–1327.

One of the oldest blues clubs in the city, Blues Alley is home to guitar ace Jimi "Primetime" Smith, among other veteran 12-bar acts.

Housed in an old building with exposed brick walls and ceiling fans, Blues Alley is divided into three small rooms. The stage is in the center room, and there's a wonderful big old bar up front. Until recently, the neighborhood around the club was considered to be somewhat rough, but since the construction of the Target Center Arena (home to the Timberwolves) across the street, the club and its neighborhood are prospering.

Music: F–Su. *Cover:* $. *Food:* burgers, etc.

First Avenue/Seventh Street Entry, 701 First Ave. N., M'polis. (Warehouse District), 612–332–1775.

Though mostly known as a rock, funk, and new music club made famous through Prince's 1984 movie *Purple Rain,* First Avenue, a rounded cinderblock building painted flat black, prides itself on offering all kinds of music, including *lots* of reggae, Afro-pop, and other world beat sounds, plus jazz, blues, and R&B. National acts who have played here include everyone from the Mighty Mighty Bosstones, NRBQ, and Burning Spear, to Joshua Redman and Dr. John.

First Avenue, which can accommodate 1,200, is actually housed in an old Greyhound bus terminal. There's a sunken dance floor flanked by large video screens, a game room, and a glassed-in mezzanine with another bar (this is where Prince used to sit, surrounded by bodyguards).

Ever since *Purple Rain*'s release, First Avenue has also become a tourist attraction. Never mind the fact that the movie is now nearly 20 years old—out-of-towners still come by occasionally, clicking their cameras.

Adjacent to First Avenue is the small, dark Seventh Street Entry, which is still a good place to catch local bands and up-and-coming talent. Tracy Chapman, Public Enemy, Soul Asylum, and Living Colour all played here before making it big.

Music: nightly, occasional blues and jazz. *Cover:* $-$$$.

Bunker's Music Bar & Grill, 761 Washington Ave. N., M'polis. (Warehouse District), 612–338–8188.

Once a dingy neighborhood bar with nothing but a wide-screen TV and a corny name (Archie's Bunker), Bunker's metamorphosed over a decade ago into a hot spot drawing both its old steady biker's crowd and a newer young, professional set, all of whom, curiously enough, seem to coexist peacefully. Acts in this big square-shaped club, newly decorated to fit its new image, are mostly local (Legendary Combo, Mick Sterling), but national artists (Koko Taylor, Junior Brown) come through from time to time.

Music: nightly. *Cover:* $, except for national acts. *Food:* burgers, etc.

The Minnesota Music Cafe, 499 Payne Ave., St. Paul (very near downtown), 651–776–4699.

A big, sprawling club with a really nifty display of Minnesota music memorabilia all over its walls, this bar rarely brings in out-of-town acts, despite having loads of room, an ample stage, and a good sound system. House bands rule the roost instead. Most of the weekly warriors—the Joe Juliano Band, The Good, The Bad & The Funky—play a very professional and potent mix of blues and R&B.

Music: nightly. *Cover:* $. *Food:* American.

Big Daddy's Old Kentucky Bar B Que, 214 E. 4th St., in Union Depot Place, St. Paul (downtown), 651–848–0788.

With its charming and hip location inside a huge converted downtown train station, Big Daddy's is worth a sightseeing and a culinary visit, if you don't mind barbecue that's yuppified. There's the usual ribs and chicken, and hey, that portobello mushroom burger looks mighty nice! Some all-pro blues players are usually always on hand to enhance your dining pleasure, including local slide guitar guru Lee Tedrow, John Beach, Joel Johnson, well-traveled harp man Tom Burns, and occasionally, the burly and splendid singer/harpist, Big George Jackson.

Music: nightly. *No cover.*

Also

There's lots of blues to be heard at the **Blues West Steak House** in otherwise sleepy Rockford, Minnesota (6030 Main St., 763–477–9355), including the rare visit from a touring act. Two great old "roots rock" venues with oodles of pre-WWII charm that occasionally book blues acts are **Lee's Liquor Bar** (11th & Glenwood, M'polis., 612–338–9491) and **Mayslack's**

(1428 4th St. N.E., M'polis., 612–789–9862), the latter in business in one form or another since 1887! Lee's is much more likely to feature national acts, while Mayslack's serves up regionally famous hot roast beef and horseradish sandwiches that are sensational. "Nobody beats Mayslack's meat" is their slogan.

Other Venues and Special Events

Both the **Fitzgerald Theater** (10 E. Exchange St., St. Paul, 651–290–1221) and the **Ordway Music Theatre** (345 Washington St., St. Paul, 651–224–4222) present jazz shows on occasion. The **Northrop Auditorium** and the **Ted Mann Theater**, both on the University of Minnesota campus (612–624–2345), and sometimes in conjunction with the **Walker Art Center** (725 Vineland Pl., M'polis., 612–375–7577), together have a terrific annual jazz series that often features more avant-garde sounds (Cecil Taylor, John Zorn's Masada, Joey Baron). All three institutions also occasionally present other jazz concerts, ranging from mainstream living legends (Sonny Rollins at the Northrop) to the cutting edge (Bill Frissell at the Walker). Meanwhile, **Orchestra Hall** (1111 Nicollet Mall, M'polis., 612–371–5656) always includes some jazz in its musical menu; trumpeter Doc Severinsen has been in charge of their "Summer Pops" series for several years.

A great venue for folk and world music sounds, the **Cedar Cultural Centre** (416 Cedar Ave., M'polis., 612–338–2674) also presents jazz and blues on occasion (Happy Apple, Toots Thielemans, Howard Levy, Honeyboy Edwards). A great resource/learning spot for drummers and percussionists, the **Cultural Center of Minnesota** (3013 Lyndale Ave. S., M'polis., 612–827–0771) sometimes features "avant" and Latin jazz heavyweights in its very intimate space. The talent roll call has included the Ethnic Heritage Ensemble, Poncho Sanchez, Andrew Cyrille, Roscoe Mitchell, Milton Cardona, and the center's own main man, Wallace Hill.

The **Twin Cities Jazz Society** (651–633–0329), one of the largest jazz societies in the U.S., runs an annual concert series. Sessions are held in rotating clubs, concert halls, and high school auditoriums, and nonmembers are welcome.

Numerous free concerts sponsored by the Twin Cities' Parks and Recreation Commissions are held throughout the summer months; watch the papers. The largest blues festival in the area is the **Bayfront Blues Festival** (800-4-DULUTH), a swell three-day event held in August in Duluth, Minn., approximately three hours away.

Radio

KBEM/88.5 FM (612–627–2833). A 24-hour jazz station. Licensed to the Minneapolis Public Schools.

KFAI/90.3 FM (612–341–3144). A real "hippy-dippy" throwback freeform radio station. Lefty public affairs programming, gay and lesbian shows, Hmong music hours, doo wop, reggae and ska, salsa and worldbeat, the best old-school R&B and Cajun/zydeco programs outside of the South, and LOADS of jazz and blues programs.

KNOW/91.1 FM (651–290–1500). Mostly news and public affairs. "The Jazz Image," Sa, 7 P.M., a much-beloved program hosted by local radio legend Leigh Kamman. The unstoppable, fluent, and florid Kamman's been on air—in either Minnesota or New York City—consistently for over 50 years. And in that time he's interviewed everybody of note in jazz, from Duke Ellington on down! Way back when, legendary bassist Oscar Pettiford recorded the blues, "Kamman's a Comin,'" in his honor.

Some jazz and blues can also be heard on **KMOJ/89.9 FM, WCAL/89.4 FM,** and **KLBB/1450 AM.**

Record Stores

Electric Fetus (2000 Fourth Ave. S., M'polis., 612–870–9300), a longtime head shop and a major record distributor for the seven-state area, has a great jazz-blues selection. Cold Wind Records, which records local blues artists such as Lamont Cranston, are sold here. Other good choices are **Hymie's Vintage Records** (3318 E. Lake St., M'polis., 612–729–8890), a top place for vinyl; and **Roadrunner Record Exchange** (4304 Nicollet Ave., M'polis., 612–822–0613), with its notable selection of "avant" music.

Deep Ellum once teemed with nightclubs,
theaters, and dance halls that rocked until
dawn.

TEXAS

"The Texas sound has more feeling, melodic syncopation and a different beat. . . . Anytime there's a Texas band, blues and jazz fit together."

So said Milton Larkin, speaking to Alan Govenar in *Meeting the Blues*. Larkin, a trombone/trumpet player and vocalist who died in Houston in 1996, was a territorial bandleader back in the 1930s when the Texas sound was first exploding into view. Some of the greatest Texas saxmen came up under his leadership: Arnett Cobb, Illinois Jacquet, Eddie "Cleanhead" Vinson.

Texas has made an enormous, yet often understated, contribution to jazz and blues. Scott Joplin was born in Texarkana in 1868 and two of the most seminal bluesmen, Huddie Ledbetter (better known as Leadbelly) and Blind Lemon Jefferson, were playing the streets of Dallas as early as 1912. In the 1920s and 1930s, the state was teeming not only with territorial jazz bands such as the one led by Larkin, but also with blues singers, small combos, and boogie-woogie piano players. Later there was Charlie Christian, bringing the electric guitar to jazz, and the big, blow-away sound of the sax, the instrument most frequently associated with Texas jazz and blues.

Texas has never had one dominant metropolis, and so many of its early jazz and blues men and women moved frequently between its cities. San Antonio, Houston, and Dallas were especially important. San Antonio was the city where Jack Teagarden, one of the most influential trombone players of all time, got his start. Houston was the site of numerous "battles of the bands" and home to Peck Kelley, a legendary piano player. Dallas was once the most important band town in Texas, launching the careers of innumerable first-rate musicians, including T-Bone Walker, Buster Smith, Charlie Christian, Oran Page, Herschel Evans, and Alphonso Trent.

Austin's primary contribution to the state's music took place a bit later. Gene Ramey and Teddy Wilson came out of the small tree-lined city in the 1940s, and in the '60s, '70s, and '80s, there were Stevie Ray Vaughan, Kim Wilson, Angela Strehli, and others.

HOUSTON

Updated by Roger Wood

One of the most famous of Houston's bluesmen is Lightnin' Hopkins; one of the most famous of its jazzmen is big-band leader Illinois Jacquet. Others associated with the sprawling coastal city include Beulah "Sippie" Wallace, who spent her childhood playing the organ in a local church; Willie Mae "Big Mama" Thornton, who moved here from Alabama in the hopes of furthering her career; Johnny Copeland, originally from Haynesville, Louisiana; Albert Collins, the unconventional electric guitarist known as "the Master of the Telecaster"; boogie-blues piano player and singer Katie Webster; saxophonists Arnett Cobb and Harold Land; saxophonist-vocalist Eddie "Cleanhead" Vinson; pianist Joe Sample and other founding members of The Crusaders; and bandleader Milton Larkin, whose band led many of the "battles of the bands" at the Harlem Square Club.

Then, too, there was the legendary Peck Kelley, who, despite many offers to join large prestigious bands on both coasts, spent most of his life playing in a Houston supper club and never recorded an album. Jack Teagarden often compared Peck to Art Tatum and once said of him, "If you didn't look at him, Peck would play ten choruses in a row. But it would get so great, you'd just have to look; then he'd get self-conscious and stop."[1]

Houston was once also home to the legendary Bronze Peacock Club, as well as Duke and Peacock Records, all owned by African-American businessman Don Robey. During the 1950s, Robey recorded everyone from Clarence "Gatemouth" Brown, Bobby "Blue" Bland, and Junior Parker to the Dixie Hummingbirds and the Five Blind Boys of Mississippi. Robey also recorded Johnny Ace, who met his untimely end in Houston's City Auditorium on Christmas Eve, 1954, (see "Landmarks and Legends," page 354).

Sources

Excellent listings can be found in the *Houston Press* (713–280–2444, www.houstonpress.com), a free weekly. The

Thursday edition of the *Houston Chronicle* (713–220–7171, www.houstonchronicle.com) also carries listings.

Maps and other information can be obtained from the Greater Houston Convention and Visitors Bureau (801 Congress, 713–227–3100 or 800–231–7799, www.houston-guide.com).

A Note on Neighborhoods

Houston is the fourth-largest city in the U.S., surrounded by immense expressways that are always teeming with traffic. Until recently, the downtown often felt empty; however, since the late '90s, the central business district has experienced a renaissance, fueled by the renovation and construction of many relatively upscale lofts and townhouses in the area. The emergence of the Bayou Place entertainment complex in the theater district on the western end of Texas Avenue, and of Enron Field (home to the Houston Astros) on the eastern end, has also triggered a boom of new restaurants, shops, and clubs.

Houston was originally laid out in a ward system of political boundaries arranged around the quadrants formed by Congress Avenue and Main Street. The northwest corner of the Congress-Main intersection was the First Ward, the northeast corner the Second, the southeast corner the Third, and the southwest corner the Fourth. As the city grew, more wards, eventually totaling nine, were added, with the African-American population settling into the Third, Fourth, and Fifth wards.

By the '20s and '30s, the ward system had lost its rigidity, and today the city is officially divided into council districts. People still refer to addresses by the old ward system, however. Other neighborhood names are also used. The Heights is an upper-middle-class area just northwest of downtown; Montrose is a young, somewhat Bohemian arts and theater area just west of downtown; the Galleria is an upscale district filled with shopping malls to the south of the city.

Despite the many intimidating highways surrounding the city, driving in Houston is relatively easy. Streets are well marked and parking is usually plentiful.

Landmarks and Legends

(The sites below are all located in or near the downtown, but are relatively far apart and should be viewed by car.)

The Third and Fourth wards, south of Congress Ave. (centering on Dowling St. between Gray and Elgin, and around West Dallas St. between downtown and Taft).

Most of Houston's African-American population once lived in the Third, Fourth, and Fifth wards, and the Third and Fourth wards were especially well known for their nightlife. The Eldorado Ballroom, along with the Lincoln Dance Hall, the Emancipation Park Dance Pavilion, the Lincoln Theater, and the Key Theater were all located here. Today, only the Eldorado remains standing, although Emancipation Park—sans dance pavilion—is still located across the street.

Dowling and West Dallas streets ran through the hearts of the Third and Fourth wards, respectively, and were home base for many bluesmen and -women. Lightnin' Hopkins used to play for change along the sidewalks of Dowling, while the Santa Fe group of barrelhouse piano players (a loose group of traveling men who once played the jukes along the Santa Fe railroad) played along West Dallas.

Eldorado Ballroom, corner of Elgin and Dowling streets.

Looking much the same on the outside today as it did back in the '50s, this large curved white building once housed one of the most famous dance halls in Texas. Nat "King" Cole and Ray Charles sang here, and Big Mama Thornton was discovered here by Don Robey, who immediately signed her up to an exclusive five-year contract. Two of Big Mama's most popular songs were "Hound Dog" and "Ball and Chain," which were later made into hits by Elvis Presley and Janis Joplin respectively. Presley and Joplin received much money and acclaim for their efforts, while Thornton's original versions went virtually unacknowledged.

The Eldorado, located on the building's second floor, was nicknamed "the house of happy feet." With a stage that could be pushed in and out of the wall as the occasion demanded, it attracted crowds of all ages. "In the afternoons," said Houston drummer George Haynes, "the young teenagers would come in. Admission was thirty-five or fifty cents, and then they'd go to the ice cream parlor for a triple dip. The older crowd would come in from eight to twelve, and then it was a brown-bag sort of situation."

Since 1999, the Eldorado has been owned and operated by Project Row Houses, Third Ward's nationally recognized public arts and community service organization. A variety of small businesses remain as tenants on the ground level of the building, including Caldwell Tailors, the base of operations for Booker T. Caldwell, who has created sartorial splendor for scores of famous musicians and entertainers over the last half century. By 2001, Project Row Houses will have completed its renovation of the building's second floor, which will serve as a performance venue for special concerts (jazz, blues, gospel, hip-hop), as well as a community meeting room and art exhibition space.

Club La Veek, 1511 Blodgett (Third Ward), 713–528–8267.

For nearly two decades, the La Veek, situated in a small rundown shopping strip, with cars pulled close to its brilliant graffiti'd facade, was the mainstay of Houston's jazz community. Arnett Cobb once led a house band here, and many jazz and blues greats—Little Milton, Buddy Rich, Jimmy Smith—passed through its doors. Today, the club operates as a neighborhood bar and social center only; there is no live music.

Old City Auditorium, since replaced by Jones Hall for the Performing Arts, 615 Louisiana St.

While sitting in his dressing room at the Old City waiting to go back on stage, blues singer Johnny Ace, who had once played piano in B. B. King's band, started fooling around with a gun. He liked to play with guns, and, feeling daring, dropped a bullet into the chamber. Then he spun the barrel and pointed the gun to his head—some say to impress a girl. He pulled the trigger and "his hair stood on end like horror movies. His brain oozed out of that little hole. . . ."[2] He was 26 years old.

Music Hall, 810 Bagby St. (demolished).

Recently torn down to make way for the Hobby Center for the Performing Arts, scheduled to open in 2002, Music Hall was the site of a controversial Jazz at the Philharmonic (JATP) concert produced by Norman Granz in 1955. JATP was a milestone in jazz history in that it gave first-class treatment to jazz musicians for the first time (see "Los Angeles," page 403). The musicians traveled first class all the way, and no segregation in the audience was allowed.

"The first thing I'd do," says Norman Granz in Gillespie's *To Be or Not To Bop*, "was rent the auditorium myself. Then I'd hire the ticket seller to sell tickets to my concert and tell him that there was to be no segregation whatsoever. . . . I removed the signs that said 'White toilets' and 'Negro toilets.' That was new. . . . The whole idea was to break all that shit open."

When JATP arrived in Houston, it was business as usual as far as Granz was concerned. But Houston had never had an integrated concert before, and the authorities were going to cause trouble one way or another. Dizzy Gillespie relates the story in his autobiography: "Between sets, we'd be in the back, shooting dice, playing cards, or whatever, and this time in Texas . . . the dressing room door burst open. The police came in and took us all to jail, including Ella Fitzgerald. They took us down, finger-printed us, and put us in jail. Norman put up a bond and got us out. He just wouldn't be intimidated by these people."

CLUBS, ETC.

Although Houston is home to a large number of first-class jazz musicians, it has only two full-time jazz clubs—**Scott Gertner's Sky Bar** and **Sambuca Jazz Café**—and no room that brings in national artists on a weekly basis. The best place to hear top local jazz talent is **Cezanne**. National blues artists occasionally appear at **Billy Blues** or the **Continental Club**, while the **Aerial Theatre at Bayou Place** books national acts of all types, including some jazz and blues.

The city's real treasures, however, are its many small neighborhood clubs, a few of which feature jazz, many of which feature blues, some of which feature both. The steadier of these small clubs are listed below.

Some of the jazz artists to look out for in Houston today include bandleader, composer, and saxophonist Conrad Johnson, now in his eighties, with his group the Big Blue Sound; vibraphonist Harry Sheppard; keyboard players Joe LoCascio and Paul English; pianist/vocalist Marsha Frazier; saxophonists Horace Young and David Caceres; saxman/flutist Gerald Stewart; trumpet players Dennis Dotson and Barry Lee Hall (when he's not on the road with the Duke Ellington Orchestra); bassist David Craig; flugelhorn player George Thomas, Jr.; vocalists Jewel Brown (who toured with Louis Armstrong in the 1960s) and Norma Zenteno, the city's Latin jazz queen; and drummers Malcolm Pinson, Sebastian Whittaker, Bubbha Thomas, Carl Lott, and G. T. Hogan (who once played with Bud Powell).

Creatively blurring the boundaries between jazz and blues is trumpeter and former B. B. King bandleader Calvin Owens. Some of the other notable blues artists in town include saxophonist Grady Gaines; guitarists Joe Hughes, Sherman Robertson, Rayfield "Guitar Slim" Jackson, Milton Hopkins, Pete Mayes, Texas Johnny Brown, I. J. Gosey, and Oscar Perry; piano player Earl Gilliam; and vocalists Trudy Lynn, Jimmy "T–99" Nelson, Gloria Edwards, and Carol Fran.

Most bars and clubs in Houston close at 2 A.M.

Personal Choices

Best jazz club: *Cezanne*
Best blues clubs: *The Big Easy*
Best hole-in-the-wall blues club: *Miss Ann's Playpen*
Best eclectic clubs: *Fabulous Satellite Lounge, Continental Club*
Best jam sessions: *Etta's Lounge, The Big Easy*

FOR JAZZ

Cezanne, 4100 Montrose Blvd. (at West Main), 713–522–9621.

Upstairs from the Black Labrador Restaurant (713–529–1199), Cezanne's is currently the steadiest place in town to hear straight-ahead jazz. A small room with a fine piano, the club features local artists most nights, touring guest soloists on occasion. Saxophonist Woody Witt books the place and performs regularly; others who have appeared here include Joe LoCasio, Harry Sheppard, David Craig, and Dennis Dotson.

Music: Th–Sa. *Cover:* $-$$. Seating is limited; early arrival recommended.

Scott Gertner's Sky Bar, 3400 Montrose Blvd. (at Hawthorne), 10th Fl., 713–520–9688.

Located atop an office building, the Sky Bar offers excellent views of the downtown and surrounding areas, best observed from its two outdoor terraces. The interior club (voted "Best Jazz Venue" in the 2000 *Houston Press* Music Awards) features good sightlines and effective acoustics in a roomy, relaxed atmosphere. Live music is typically a hybrid of soft jazz, adult pop, and light R&B. National touring acts are booked once or twice a month; among those who've performed here are Bob James, Acoustic Alchemy, Tito Puente, Chick Corea, and Tuck and Patti.

Club owner Scott Gertner is also a musician (bass and vocals) who has played in several notable Bayou City combos, including one featuring saxophonist Kirk Whalum and keyboardist Paul English. Gertner leads the Sky Bar house band and hosts a weekly amateur "Talent Search" contest ($100 cash prize), usually on Thursday nights. Mid-week evenings are often devoted to such themes as Big Band Night or Latin Jazz Night, and draw a variety of local players. Weekends are the best times to catch the more impressive regional stalwarts.

Music: usually M-Sa. *Cover:* $-$$. Reservations available.

Sambuca Jazz Café, 909 Texas Ave. (on the ground floor of the Rice Lofts building downtown), 713–224–5299, www.sambucajazzcafe.com.

The Houston link in a Dallas-based chain (which also includes an Atlanta location), the Sambuca Jazz Cafe is located in one of the most prestigious and historic residential buildings downtown (the former Rice Hotel). Though a trendy spot where the crush of "beautiful people" can detract from the live music experience, this club does offer a chance to hear top local/regional talent, as well as major national acts, who perform about once a month. Terence Blanchard, Larry Carlton, and Chuck Mangione are among those who've played here.

While the room is large, the performance space is small and difficult to see from many of the tables. And often, because of conversational din, the acoustics leave much to be desired. On the menu is what one local restaurant critic describes as "mass-market Mediterranean"; jazz varies from straight-ahead to smooth, big band swing to Latino.

Music: M–Su. *Cover*: $$$-$$$$, with two-drink minimum. Reservations recommended.

King Leo's, 4546 Griggs Rd. (15 min. SE of downtown), 713–741–5105.

Though it's currently featuring jazz only one night per week (contemporary R&B or DJs the rest of the time), this African-American-owned and operated establishment has housed some of the coolest out-of-the-way jams in the city over the past quarter century. These days the prime time to visit is Monday evenings, when trumpeter Leo Polk, a longtime presence on the local jazz scene, performs with his combo. Though his gig is not considered an open jam, Polk frequently accommodates his musician friends (such as the venerable Conrad Johnson) who happen to drop by. On the right night, the resulting improvisations can outshine anything else in town.

Music: jazz on M. *Cover:* none-$.

Ovations, 2536-B Times Blvd. at Kirby St. in the Rice University Village (near the Texas Medical Center), 713–522–9801.

Located in Houston's oldest shopping center, Ovations is an upscale three-tiered club with dramatic 25-foot-high ceilings that presents a mix of jazz, classical, and cabaret. Jazz vocalists usually perform on the weekends. Seating for about 125 is arranged around its stage, and many of the music majors and faculty from nearby Rice University and the University of Houston frequent the place.

Music: M–Sa, much jazz. *Cover:* $-$$.

Gallant Knight, 2337 W. Holcombe (near the Texas Medical Center), 713–665–9762.

Named after the English liqueur, this small, dark club, filled with nooks and crannies, has been offering jazz since the early 1980s. Located near Rice University, it attracts a well-integrated crowd that includes many students and academics. Candles flicker in wrought-iron chandeliers as owner

Monroe Wilkins greets his guests, many of whom have been coming here for years, at the door.

At one time, the music at the Gallant Knight was strictly jazz; now it tends more toward the "up-tempo and progressive."

Music: Th–Sa. *Cover:* $.

Also

Top local jazz artists often perform weekends at fine restaurants or area hotels. Among the more reliable of these venues are **River Cafe** (3615 Montrose Blvd., 713–529–0088), an upscale but casual Museum District eatery with a good-sized music room; the elegant **Terrace on Main** (5701 Main, in the historic Warwick Hotel, 713–526–1991), serving a variety of first-class foods along with jazz on Fridays and Saturdays; and the **Doubletree Hotel at Post Oak** (2001 Post Oak Rd., 713–961–9300). For Latin jazz and salsa, there's **Elvia's International Restaurant & Club** (2727 Fondren, 713–266–9631), which typically offers live music five nights per week.

FOR BLUES

The Big Easy Social and Pleasure Club, 5731 Kirby St. (near the Rice University Village), 713–523–9999.

A casual, anything-goes joint that attracts a diverse crowd (young and old, black and white, bikers and yuppies), The Big Easy has established itself as the most reliable and accessible place in town to hear high-quality blues. Since opening in 1994, free-spirited owner Tom "Yeah You Right" McLendon's establishment has won the "Best Blues Club" prize every single year in the *Houston Press* Music Awards. Though the bossman has named and decorated his place to reflect his love of New Orleans culture—complete with purple and gold paint—it's mainly straight Texas blues that resounds from the stage. The monthly gig calendar consistently reads like a "Who's Who" of the contemporary scene—from old-timers (Joe Hughes, Earl Gilliam, Pete Mayes) to relatively younger players (Mark May, Leonard "Low Down" Brown, Allison Fisher).

The Big Easy's two weekly jam sessions—on Tuesdays and Wednesdays—have served as catalysts for lots of fascinating musical interchanges, trumped only by the last-Thursday-of-the-month jam party sponsored by the Houston Blues Society. Sundays are reserved for zydeco and Mondays are "juke box appreciation night."

Music: Tu-Su. *No cover.*

Billy Blues, 6025 Richmond Ave., 713–266–9294, www.billy blues200.com.

It's hard to miss this club, thanks to the 62-foot-long blue saxophone lying at its entrance made up of Volkswagen parts, washtubs, empty kegs of beer, surfboards, and anything else that happened to be lying around at the time of its creation. Fact is, the saxophone was the subject of local controversy not long ago, with some arguing that it violated advertising codes, others arguing that it was art. Luckily for fans of the offbeat, the city council came down on the side of art.

Though it started out in the early '90s as part of a San Antonio–based chain, this Houston establishment is the sole remnant of that barbecue-and-blues-themed empire. As one local critic puts it, the club has a "touristy yuppie vibe but also tries to do right by the music." In the restaurant, there is an excellent display of historic photographs by Benny Joseph, which includes portraits of Lightnin' Hopkins, Clarence "Gatemouth" Brown, and Albert Collins. In the music room (where food is also served), there's a wide stage and seating for over 500. The quality of the booking varies widely, but the place has hosted some top national acts (Lonnie Brooks, Corey Harris, John Mayall). Otherwise, it features a steady roster of local and regional talent, ranging from the widely admired octogenarian singer Jimmy "T–99" Nelson to far less accomplished acts.

Music: Tu-Su. *Cover*: $-$$.

Harlon's Bayou Blues, 530 Texas Ave. (downtown, in the Bayou Place entertainment complex), 713–230–0111.

Primarily a cafeteria-style restaurant and bar, this establishment includes a small stage that usually features a rotating mix of blues, R&B, and light jazz on the weekends, with Texas Johnny Brown, now in his seventies, often gigging on Saturday nights. Harlon's kitchen consistently serves up good food, and it's reasonably priced (especially given its location in one of downtown's most popular nightlife districts).

Music: F-Sa. *No cover.*

Miss Ann's Playpen, 3710 Dowling St. (Third Ward), 713–520–9698.

Located two blocks south of the historic Eldorado Ballroom, this modest little club, distinguished by its bright blue awning over a red-brick storefront, is a favorite hangout for Third Warders. Owner and soul singer Bobby Lewis sometimes gigs with his own band, The Invaders, and leads a locally famous "Blue Monday" jam that attracts many of the top African-American players in town. They come for the music, the cheap beer, the free food, and the appreciative fans. The line-up on any given Monday can range from internationally known recording artists such as Sherman Robertson to obscure but often talented unknowns.

Music: F-Sa, M. *Cover*: $. BYOB for hard liquor, set-ups available.

Etta's Lounge & Restaurant, 5120 Scott St. (Third Ward, near University of Houston), 713–528–2611.

Grady Gaines is one of the best sax players you'll find in this city, and he blows what one local critic calls the "hottest, baddest blues to be found in Houston" every Sunday night at this small diner-type place with run-down booths and red gauze curtains. Owner Etta Coby, a nurse by day, started the place up about 20 years ago, and her jam sessions have since become legendary, attracting musicians from all over the city. "It's a home place," she says proudly. "We get people from all over. Yellow, purple, white—they're all welcome."

Music: Su. *Cover:* $.

Shakespeare Pub, 14129 Memorial Dr. (West Houston, between Kirkwood and Dairy-Ashford), 281–497–4625.

A comfortable neighborhood joint patterned after an English pub, with lots of wood and imported beer, Shakespeare's presents top local blues and zydeco acts most nights of the week. A horseshoe-shaped bar dominates the place, and there's a nook with two pool tables and a dart board in the back.

Music: Tu–Sa, much blues. *No cover.*

The Silver Slipper, 3717 Crane St. (Fifth Ward), 713–673–9004.

This down-home venue is the last of the legendary clubs in Frenchtown, a section of Fifth Ward settled by black Creoles in the early twentieth century. Owned and operated for four decades by the Cormier family, it offers a large room (built onto the original shotgun shack) and potent zydeco and blues. That musical double identity has been part of the club ever since the days when former neighborhood zydeco accordionist Clifton Chenier and his pal Lightnin' Hopkins traded licks on stage here.

Today, the Silver Slipper features real-deal zydeco on Fridays and Sundays, blues and R&B on Saturdays. The manager, Curly Cormier, is also a well-respected guitarist who usually plays the Saturday night gig with his band, The Gladiators.

Music: F-Su. *Cover*: $. BYOB for hard liquor, set-ups available.

C. Davis Bar-B-Q, 4833 Reed Rd. (20 min. S of downtown), 713–734–9051.

The parking lot is filled with pickup trucks; the club is filled with cowboy hats. Everywhere, inside and out, are people dining on beef brisket and sausage. Davis's, almost 30 years old, is a neighborhood place that's home to both blues and R&B, and it has a raw, rough, cowboy feel. Located in a working-class African-American community called Sunnyside, its two small rooms—the bar in the front, the music in the back—are run by the deceased founder's son and family, who do the cooking as well as the serving. Former Duke-Peacock session player I. J. Gosey—an exceptionally fluent, sweetly-toned guitarist—has been gigging here steadily since 1973.

Music: Tu, Su. *No cover*. BYOB for hard liquor, set-ups available.

Continental Club, 3700 Main St., 713–529–9899.

This new Houston branch of the venerable Austin club of the same name serves up high-quality live music seven nights a week. Most of it is homegrown Texas rock or national touring acts (including some neo-blues artists, such as Sue Foley or the North Mississippi All-Stars). But the happy hours on Wednesdays and Fridays (6:30–9 P.M.) are always devoted to traditional blues; regulars include pianist/vocalist Carol Fran and the I. J. Gosey Band.

Music: M-Su. *No cover* for happy hour (blues); otherwise, $-$$.

Dan Electro's Guitar Bar, 1031 East 24th St. (The Heights), 713–862–8707, www.danelectrosguitarbar.com.

When it comes to tasteful blues-rock fusion, this place consistently books some of the best local bands. But for hard-core blues fans, the right time to be here is Thursdays, when a weekly jam session attracts local African-American stalwarts of the idiom who creatively mix it up with some of the best white rock-weaned players in town.

Music: Th-Sa. *Cover*: $.

Also

Blues can sometimes be found at the swanky **Mercury Room** downtown (1008 Prairie, 713–225–MERC), the eccentric **Last Concert Cafe** in the warehouse/loft district on the northside (1403 Nance, 713–226–8563), and the futuristic **Fabulous Satellite Lounge** (3616 Washington Ave. near Heights Blvd., 713–869-COOL). **Fitzgerald's** (2706 White Oak Dr., 713–862–3838), a large, predominantly rock venue in a rambling two-story house in the Heights, also features occasional blues and R&B. A number of other small African-American neighborhood joints do, too, including **El Nedo Cafe** (3401 Ennis, Third Ward, 713–528–3524) and **Club Hole in the Wall** (10126 Jensen Dr., 713–697–8088).

In the northern suburban village of Humble, blues is regularly booked at **Cactus Moon** (7 W. Main St., 281–446–2202). Down in Galveston, the **Old Quarter** (413 20th St., 409–762–9199) features acoustic blues and roots music on weekends.

Other Venues and Special Events

August-Is-Jazz-Month in Houston and the celebration involves exhibits, films, concerts, and music at clubs all over the city, as well as an intensive four-day **Houston International Jazz Festival**. For information, call Jazz Education, Inc. at 713–227–8706. The **Houston International Festival** happens in mid-to-late April and features everything from jazz and blues to arts and crafts. The **Juneteenth Blues Festival**, formerly held the weekend near June 19 to commemorate the 1865 day when Texan African Americans first learned of the Emancipation Proclamation (it had been signed two years earlier), ceased production after the 1998 event, but various groups are hoping to resurrect it in 2001.

Jazz or blues concerts can sometimes be heard at the **Aerial Theater at Bayou Place** (520 Texas Ave., 713–230–1600), **Arena Theatre** (7326 Southwest Frwy., 713–988–1020), **Jones Hall for the Performing Arts** (615 Louisiana St., 713–227–3974), and the **Wortham Theater Center** (510 Preston Blvd., 713–237–1439).

Radio

KTSU/90.9 FM (713–527–7591). Student-run station affiliated with Texas Southern University. Jazz all day, M-Th; blues M nights.
KPFT/90.1 FM offers 12 straight hours of blues on Sundays (6 A.M.–6 P.M.) and jazz on Saturday evenings.
Jazz and blues can also sometimes be heard on **KTRU/91.7**.

Record Stores

Cactus Music & Video (2930 S. Shepherd, 713–526–9272) has a large collection of new and used jazz and blues records.
All Records (1960 W. Gray, 713–524–4900) also carries jazz.

Elsewhere in Southeast Texas

American Pop Culture Exhibit, Museum of the Gulf Coast, 700 Proctor St., Port Arthur (90 miles east of Houston), 409–982–7000.

Numerous musicians have come out of the southeast Texas–southwest Louisiana area, including Janis Joplin, Clarence "Gatemouth" Moore, Ivory Joe Hunter, Buddy Holly, and the Big Bopper; and the Museum of the Gulf Coast has set up an exhibit in their honor. Among the items on display are life-sized statues of Janis Joplin, Buddy Holly, Ritchie Valens, and the Big Bopper, and memorabilia from over 30 artists. Janis's corner includes pictures from her early childhood, a purple pantsuit with rhinestones, a slide-rule that she used in high school, "her personal Bible," and a reproduction of her psychedelic Porsche automobile, painted by the same artist who did the original back then.

Open: M–F, 9 A.M.–5 P.M.; Sun 1–5 P.M. *Admission:* $.

DALLAS

Updated by Malcolm Mayhew

In the 1920s, Dallas was a hotbed of both jazz and blues. The polished Alphonso Trent Orchestra was then playing to packed houses at the elegant Adolphus Hotel downtown, while out in Deep Ellum, along the abandoned railroad tracks, boogie-woogie piano players, blues singers, and small combos were rocking away until dawn and beyond.

One of the best-known musicians to come out of Deep Ellum was Blind Lemon Jefferson, who would walk the streets with a cane in one hand, a tin cup in another, and a guitar slung over his back. For a period, beginning in 1912, Blind Lemon was accompanied by Leadbelly, the singer later jailed for murder who eventually became the darling of New York City's folk-music scene. Leadbelly once said that when he and Lemon began to play, "The women would come running, Lawd have mercy! They'd hug and kiss us so much we could hardly play."

Another important musician to come out of Dallas in the '20s was Buster Smith, born just south of the city. Smith—

who would later join the Blue Devils, take Charlie Parker under his wing, and write Count Basie's signature song, "One O'Clock Jump," which he failed to copyright—began frequenting Deep Ellum as a young, serious student of music. He would watch the other clarinet players at work and pick up techniques from them.

Some of Dallas's most legendary nightspots—the Tip Top Club, Ella B. Moore's Park Theater, Fat Jack's Theater, the Green Parrot, and the Pythian Temple—were located in Deep Ellum. Later, in the 1940s, much of the area was destroyed by an expressway, and the jazz and blues scene moved elsewhere. The Rose Ballroom, later known as the Rose Room and then the Empire Room, was especially important, presenting everyone from T-Bone Walker, who later moved to the West Coast, to Zuzu Bollin, who, until his death in 1990, was one of the last surviving jump blues musicians.

Other musicians associated with the Dallas/Fort Worth area include Charlie Christian, who brought the electric guitar to jazz; boogie-woogie piano players Alex Moore and Sam Price; jazz pianists Red Garland and Cedar Walton; trumpeter-vocalist Oran "Hot Lips" Page; R&B singers Freddie King, Al Braggs, and Z. Z. Hill; the R&B band Anson Funderburgh and the Rockets; singer-songwriter Cal Valentine; saxophonist-composer Ornette Coleman; saxophonists James Clay, David "Fathead" Newman, and Julius Hemphill; and, more recently, trumpet player Roy Hargrove.

Sources

The *Dallas Observer* (214–757–9000; www.dallasobserver. com), a free weekly, has excellent listings. Other good sources are the Friday sections of the *Dallas Morning News* (214–977–8222; www.dallasnews.com) and the *Fort Worth Star Telegram* (817–390–7400; www.star-telegram.com). The Dallas Blues Society (http://homepages.go.com/~dallas-bluessociety) runs a Blues Hotline at 214–521–2583.

For maps and other information, visit the Dallas Visitors Center, 1303 Commerce St., or the Dallas Convention and Visitors Bureau, 1201 Elm St., Suite 2000, 214–571–1000 (www.dallascvb.com).

A Note on Neighborhoods

Filled with enormous, futuristic glass buildings and surrounded by superhighways, Dallas seems to have forgotten that it ever had a past. The city stretches out forever with trendy nightspots, expensive restaurants, and exclusive boutiques. Greenville Avenue Strip, stretching from downtown to

I–635, is where much of the city's nightlife is located. Lower Greenville is known for its small cafés and restaurants, Upper Greenville for its chrome, singles bars, and $50,000 cars. The West End, situated downtown, is a former factory and warehouse district now filled with restaurants, clubs, and shops. South Dallas is home to the city's largest African-American community.

Fort Worth is located approximately 40 minutes west of Dallas.

Landmarks and Legends

(The first four sites are located in or near the downtown and can be viewed on foot; the last three are in South Dallas and are best reached by car.)

Deep Ellum, centering on Elm Street, between Preston and Good Streets.

Located just east of the Central Expressway, Deep Ellum was first settled by free slaves after the Civil War; it was then

Blue Mondays at the Longhorn were once a Dallas institution.

called Freedman's Town. Elm Street was its main drag, and by the turn of the century, it was lined with shops and amusements of all kinds, including speakeasies, dance halls, nightclubs, and whorehouses. Medicine men staged shows on the corners, while bands and dancers performed for pennies in the streets. Love potions were for sale in back alleys, and there were stabbings and shootings almost every Saturday night.

In addition to Blind Lemon Jefferson, Leadbelly, and Buster Smith, some of the many musicians playing along the Central Tracks included Lonnie Johnson, Eddie Durham, Charlie Christian, Hot Lips Page, Herschel Evans, Alex Moore, and Sam Price. National stars such as Bessie Smith and Ma Rainey also played the area whenever they were in town. After World War II and the construction of the Central Expressway, businesses moved out of Deep Ellum. Today, however, the once gray, abandoned area is going through a revival, with art galleries, alternative music clubs, and small restaurants opening up left and right.

The Pythian Temple/Union Bankers Building, 2551 Elm St. (Deep Ellum).

A big gray stone building in the "eclectic Beaux Arts style," the 1915 Pythian was designed by William Sidney Pittman, the first black architect to practice in Dallas. The building, commissioned by a fraternal organization, the Knights of Pythian, had a big dance hall where musical events featuring the likes of Cab Calloway were presented. After the Depression, the imposing edifice was taken over by the Union Bankers Insurance Company.

Majestic Theatre, 1925 Elm St., 214–880–0137.

Looking as if it was sculpted out of candy, the five-story Beaux Arts Majestic was once one of the finest vaudeville/ movie houses in town. During the '20s and '30s, the plush theater, decorated in mirrors, gilt, and marble, hosted everyone from Harry Houdini to Mae West. Billing itself "a place where a man could bring his family without question," it featured the unusual "Land of Nod," a complete nursery with beds, trained nurses, and free milk and crackers, where patrons could leave their children during the show. The theater was renovated in 1979 and today is home to the Dallas Opera, the Dallas Black Dance Theatre, and others.

T-Bone Walker got one of his early breaks at the Majestic. He had just won first prize in an amateur concert sponsored there when Cab Calloway, also playing the theater, came through town. Cab invited T-Bone to join him in Houston and while there, T-Bone was approached by a Columbia Records representative. Shortly thereafter, he made his first record-ings—recordings that he did not hear until the 1980s (many early bluesmen had similar experiences; they were seldom notified when their records were released).

The Adolphus Hotel, 1321 Commerce St., 214–742–8200 (www.hoteladolphus.com).

Built by beer baron Adolphus Busch in 1912, the Adolphus Hotel is an opulent Dallas landmark, once called "the most beautiful building west of Venice." Completely restored in 1981 to the tune of $60 million, the 21-story neobaroque edi-fice featured jazz from the mid-1920s through the '50s. Alphonso Trent's orchestra played a long residency here in 1924, during which time shows were broadcast from the hotel on radio station WFAA.

The Alphonso Trent Orchestra was one of the most pol-ished and successful of the Texas territorial bands. Trent—a "small, wiry, durable, even-tempered" African American origi-nally from Arkansas—first brought his then six-piece band, the Synco Six, to the hotel for what was to be a two-week stand. Their shows proved to be so popular, however, that they were held over 18 months. They became the foremost music draw in Dallas and began touring the state, eventually earning so much money that the sidemen (making $150 per week, an enormous sum at that time), wore silk shirts, drove Cadillacs, and played gold-plated instruments.

Later, during the Swing Era, Artie Shaw, Benny Goodman, Harry James, Tommy and Jimmy Dorsey, and Glenn Miller all played the Adolphus.

American Woodmen's Hall, SW corner Oakland Ave. and Carpenter.

A solid yellow-brick building with maroon highlights, the Hall was once famous for its weekend jam sessions. "Everyone played there," said Dallas piano player Robert Clayton Sanders. "There were long picnic-type tables and you'd get your setups and sit down and groove to the music. There wasn't any noise—you just sat your ass down and listened, that was the jazz atti-tude." Some of the many musicians who played the Hall during its heyday in the late '50s were David Newman, Marchel Ivery, and Red Garland. The jam sessions were often led by saxo-phonist James Clay and keyboardist-saxophonist Claude Johnson.

Lincoln High School, 2826 Hatcher St. near Oakland Ave.

Many well-known Dallas jazz musicians once attended the old Lincoln (located in back of the newer building). Among them were Cedar Walton, Marchel Ivery, and David "Fathead"

Newman, who got his nickname here from a temperamental teacher who blew up at him after he'd flubbed an arpeggio.

CLUBS, ETC.

Dallas has no full-time jazz club, but a number of restaurants, most notably the twin **Sambucas**, feature first-class local artists on a regular basis, and the **Sammon Center for the Arts** hosts a unique and frequent jazz series. The largest club for national talent in the area is **Caravan of Dreams** in Fort Worth, which once presented almost exclusively jazz and now features a little bit of everything. National blues acts are sometimes booked into **Blue Cat Blues**, **J&J Blues Bar**, and **Poor David's Pub**, while the premier blues club in South Dallas is **Blues Palace**.

Some of the best jazz musicians playing in Dallas today include the fine Texas tenors Marchel Ivery and James Clay, drummer Herbie Cowens, Latin sax-flute player Vicho Vicencio, piano players Robert Clayton Sanders and Claude Johnson, vocalist Martha Burks, contemporary artist Tom Braxton, Peter Petersen and the Collection Jazz Orchestra, and the Dallas Jazz Orchestra. Among the top blues artists are Sam Myers, Big Al Dupree, Roger Boykin, Robert Ealey, Joe Jonas, Hash Brown, Smokin' Joe Kubek, Cookie McGee, Curly Barefoot Miller, Mike Morgan, R. L. Griffin, and Ernie Johnson.

Generally speaking, clubs in Dallas close at 2 A.M.

Personal Choices

Best jazz spots: *Sambuca (both locations)*
Best after-hours jazz: *Dan's Bar*
Best Deep Ellum blues: *Blue Cat Blues*
Best Fort Worth blues: *J&J Blues Bar*
Best South Dallas blues: *Blues Palace*
Best listening club: *Poor David's Pub*

FOR JAZZ

Sambuca Jazz Café, 2618 Elm St. (Deep Ellum), 214–744–0820, and 15207 Addison Rd. (Addison), 972–385–8455, www.sambucajazzcafe.com.

The best places in Dallas to hear straight-ahead jazz, the Sambucas are stylish restaurants that present many of the top musicians residing in the area, including Marchel Ivory, James Clay, Claude Johnson, Robert Sanders, and Smokin' Joe McBride. Latin jazz is also featured on occasion, and Roy Hargrove sometimes jams at one of the Sambucas when he's back in his hometown.

The Deep Ellum spot is located in a historic building and boasts exposed brick walls and leopard-skin booths. One room is enclosed glass, with a skylight; the other contains a long bar and the stage. The Addison offshoot, opened in 1993, is bigger, with multi-level eating areas, various theme bars, and a similar animal-inspired décor.

Music: nightly, at both locations. *Cover:* none, if having dinner (the only way to get a table 7–11 P.M.). *Minimum (at bar):* $$. *Food:* Mediterranean. Reservations taken Su-W only.

Caravan of Dreams, 312 Houston (downtown), Fort Worth, 817–877–3000, www.caravanofdreams.com.

The premier music club in the area, Caravan, which is financed by Edward Bass of the old Fort Worth Bass family, brings in a whole host of national talent. At one time, much of it was jazz. Ornette Coleman, a Fort Worth native, opened the place up 10 years ago, and Dizzy Gillespie, Herbie Hancock, Stanley Turrentine, Carmen McRae, and Billy Eckstine were among the many who played here.

Today the club's booking policy is much more eclectic. Everything from rock to Irish music can be heard, and the jazz that is presented tends toward the contemporary—Kirk Whalum, Grover Washington, Jr., and the like.

The club is a large sumptuous affair, made up to look like a plush sultan's tent, with a ceiling of silky fabric and a floor of red carpeting. Huge murals tracing the history of jazz cover one wall and the sound system is state of the art. On the second floor of the Caravan is a theater, and on the roof is the Grotto Bar, built to look like a cave. The view from up here is spectacular. And then there's the odd rooftop "Desert Dome," housing the "largest collection of cacti and succulents in Texas." So what if it's strange; this is Texas. Downstairs in the gift shop, cacti are for sale right next to record albums.

Music: nightly. *Cover:* $-$$$. *Food:* American.

Balcony Club, 1825 Abrams, 214–826–8104.

Both classy and a classic, the Balcony Club is a well-heeled but warm and cozy piano bar attached at the hip of the historic Lakewood Theater. Balcony mainstay pianist Al Dupree, whose hair is as white as the ice in his drink, plays old and new school jazz—both solo and with a two-piece backup band—Thursday through Saturday. Various locals such as the Arthur Riddles Trio and Rick Yost fill in the weekday slots. The bar up front can get rowdy, while the tables in the back suit those who'd rather disappear.

Music: nightly. *Cover:* $.

Winedale Tavern, 2110 Greenville Ave., 214–823–5018.

Trendy Greenville Avenue has lost most of its live music haunts to yup-scale danceterias and persnickety restaurants. Along with Poor David's and Muddy Waters (just down the street at 1518 Greenville Ave), this 20-year-old neighborhood bar is one of the last venues on the street to offer live jazz and blues. Don't go, though, if you don't want to get to know the person drinking next to you. At 30 feet wide and 80 feet long, this shotgun-style bar forces intimacy.

Music: nightly, jazz on Su. *Cover:* $.

Terilli's Restaurant, 2815 Greenville Ave., 214–827–3993, www.fiberscape.com/net/terillis/.

Located in the heart of trendy Lower Greenville Avenue, Terilli's, with large arched doorways, wood-framed booths and a lively outdoor patio, has a good dose of yuppie atmosphere. Nonetheless, decent jazz, ranging from straight-ahead to contemporary, is offered up six nights a week. Unfortunately, the stage is located near the bar, where it's often crowded and noisy, and the sound system is mediocre at best.

Music: Tu-Su. *No cover. Food:* Italian.

Dan's Bar, 119 S. Elm St., Denton, 940–891–1549.

With sepia-tone photos hanging from the walls and candles flickering on rustic tables, Dan's Bar looks more like an antique shop than a hipster restaurant that doubles as a live music venue. Squeezed into the back pocket of the downtown square of Denton, a cool college town 35 miles north of Dallas, Dan's often hosts local and national jazz and blues firebirds, along with rock and country acts. With the University of North Texas within spitting distance, Dan's is heavy on college kids, but not on frat-boys; these friendly, scruffy kids will buy ya a beer, and not expect a phone number in return.

Music: nightly. *Cover:* $-$$.

Also

Dallas Alley (Market St. at Munger, 214–880–7420) is a place to be avoided. With eight clubs under one roof (some of which claim to offer jazz and blues), it's a sort of horror show, complete with lots of neon and blow-dried hair.

Twenty-five miles northwest of Dallas is **Kirby's** (3305 E. Hwy. 114, South Lake, 817–410–2221), an upscale, sophisticated restaurant offering jazz that's as delicious as its food. Regulars include local favorites Larry Natwick and Dan Pitzer; music W-Su.

FOR BLUES

Blue Cat Blues, 2612 Commerce St. (Deep Ellum), 214–744–2293, www.bluecatblues.com.

Recently moved from the back half of a former warehouse to a stand-alone building, the Blue Cat offers up a solid mix of local, regional, and national blues. Smokin' Joe Kubek is a regular, and others who have played here include Lonnie Brooks, William Clark, Lucky Peterson, and the Kinsey Report.

The club's walls are lined with photos of blues greats, and most of the light in the place comes from the neon beer signs on the walls. Outside, there's a patio.

Music: W-Su; happy hour with blues recordings, M-F, 4:30–7 P.M. *Cover:* $-$$. *Food:* snacks.

The Bone, 2724 Elm St. (Deep Ellum), 214–744–2663, www.broadcast.com/thebone/archive.

Also housed in an atmospheric old building with exposed brick walls, high ceilings, and lazy ceiling fans, the Bone feels like a little bit of New Orleans set down in Dallas. A big wooden bar sits off to one side, while one room is filled with tables and chairs, another with three pool tables. Blues guitarist Hash Brown is a regular and he usually hosts a jam on Tuesday nights that attracts musicians from all over the city.

Music: Tu-Th. *No cover. Food:* New Orleans Cajun.

Poor David's Pub, 1924 Greenville Ave., 214–821–9891, www.poordavidspub.com.

Started up in the mid-1970s, Poor David's is the oldest continuously running club in town, and the second oldest continuously operating club in the state (Antone's in Austin is eight or nine months older). Long and thin and friendly with chairs and tables set in a semicircle, this is an eclectic club that's also a serious listening place. Everything from zydeco to R&B to folk to blues is featured, and blues regulars include John Lee Hooker, Buddy Guy, Junior Walker, and Delbert McClinton. Anson Funderburgh and the Rockets got their start here, playing every Monday night for 10 years, and they still perform on occasion.

Music: Tu-Sa, much blues and jazz. *Cover:* $-$$.

J&J Blues Bar, 937 Woodward, Fort Worth, 817–870–2337, www.jjbluesbar.com.

A fine, eclectic club, housed in a former machine shop by the banks of the Trinity River, behind the levee, J&J has been hosting top local and national talent for close to 20 years. Among the big names who've appeared here on nights past are Albert King, James Cotton, Koko Taylor, and Pinetop Perkins. Anson Funderburgh is a regular, and Wednesdays and Sundays are devoted to popular blues/R&B jams, hosted by a rotating roster of talented local bands.

Music: F-Su, occasional W-Th. *Cover:* $-$$.

Keys Lounge, 5677 Westcreek Dr., Fort Worth, 817–292–8627.

In North Texas, blues bars come and go as often as the groups that play them. But the Keys just celebrated its fourth birthday—a near-miracle of sorts. Part of what keeps the laid-back Keys going is its top-notch acts. Big-time locals like Hadden Sayers and Hash Brown are regulars, as are many of the Keys' patrons, a friendly bunch that greets strangers as if they were long-lost family. Best of all, this is one of the few blues clubs in North Texas that never has a cover.

Music: W-Su. *No cover.*

Blues Palace, 2715 Meadow St. (South Dallas, at Grand Ave.), 214–421–9867.

Owned and operated by blues singer R. L. Griffin, the Blues Palace is a large, 300-seat club located in the heart of South Dallas that sometimes presents famed blues and R&B artists such as Bobby "Blue" Bland, Denise LaSalle, and Tyrone Davis. Lots of local artists perform here as well, including Ernie Johnson, Charlie Roberson, and Griffin, and name talent touring the area often stop by here after their gigs elsewhere are done. The inside of the Blues Palace is all done up in red, with red walls, red tables, and red chairs.

Music: Th-Su. *Cover:* $.

Longhorn Ballroom, 216 Corinth (near downtown), 214–428–5900

Outside, the red-barn compound is lit up like a Christmas tree, with a huge painted cowboy, a mural of the gunfight at the O.K. Corral, and a blinding marquee below which stands an immense mock steer. Wind gusts through the place, leaving dust in its wake. A tall man in a cowboy hat walks slowly by.

The Longhorn Ballroom, which can seat 2,300, was built in 1949 for country-and-western swingman Bob Wills. Wills would play here five or six nights a week, leaving one night free for local African-American promoters, and soon the place became legendary for its Monday-night blues and R&B. Big Joe Turner, Nat King Cole, Lionel Hampton, Al Green, Bobby "Blue" Bland, B. B. King, Tyrone Davis, Millie Jackson, Little Johnny Taylor—everyone who was anyone played the Longhorn.

During the early 1950s, the Longhorn was managed by Jack Ruby, who went on to murder JFK's assassin, Lee Harvey Oswald. Today's manager, Willie Wren, has been here since 1964. "Back when I started," he says, "They had a rope down the middle with whites on one side, blacks on the other . . . People came from all over, and all the girls in the telephone company used to ask for Tuesdays off so they could stay out late."

Alas, blue Mondays at the Longhorn are no longer, but the hall does present big-name acts—rock, Latino, occasional blues—on the weekends. The hall—smelling of dust and time—stretches out forever, with lots of wooden folding chairs, checkered tablecloths, and revolving fans. A Texas flag hangs from the ceiling.

Music: F, Sa, some blues. *Cover:* $$-$$$.

Also

First-rate blues can also be heard regularly at **Dan's** and **Winedale** (see "For Jazz," above).

Other Venues and Special Events

The Sammon Center for the Arts (3630 Harry Hines Blvd. at Oak Lawn, 214–520–7788) sponsors a unique jazz series featuring the best of local talent at an historic three-storied water pumping station known as Turtle Creek. A low cover charge includes hors d'oeuvres, beer, and wine; valet parking is available.

The Dallas Museum of Art (1717 N. Harwood, 214–922–1200; www.dm-art.org) hosts a "Jazz Under the Stars" series every summer featuring internationally recognized artists. The Dallas Jazz Orchestra plays regularly around town and sometimes brings in national artists (hotline: 214–521–8816; www.djo.org).

Jazz and blues concerts can occasionally be heard at the **Smirnoff Music Center** (I–30 at Second, 214–421–1111; for tickets: www.ticketmaster.com) and the **Dallas Convention Center** (650 S. Griffin St., 214–939–2700; www.dallascc.com).

Radio

KNTU/88.1 FM (940–565–3688; www.kntu.fm). Jazz, 6 A.M.–
midnight M-F. Affiliated with the University of North Texas in
Denton.
KNON/89.3 FM (214–828–9500; www.knon.org). Blues 8 P.M.–
10 P.M. M-F.

Record Stores

Three top jazz and blues stores in the area are **Collectors
Records** (10616 Garland Rd., Dallas, 214–327–3313), **Record
Town** (3025 S. University, Fort Worth, 817–926–1331), and
Borders Books & Music (10720 Preston Rd., Dallas, 214–
363–1977; www.BordersStores.com).

Elsewhere in North Central Texas

Blind Lemon Jefferson's grave, off Highway 14, Wortham
(45 miles S of Dallas).

Blind Lemon Jefferson, who died tragically in a snowstorm
in Chicago just after an important recording session, is buried
here, the town of his birth, at the back of a small African-
American cemetery next to the spiffier, easier-to-find white
Wortham Cemetery. The grounds, though modest, are well
kept, and Blind Lemon's grave, an unmarked concrete slab, is
identified with a Texas State Historical Society plaque. Just
behind the grave, behind a barbed-wire fence, cows placidly
chew their cuds.

During the 1910s, when Lemon was living in Texas,
Wortham was a booming oil town, with hotels, bars, and
restaurants lining its railroad tracks. Now, it's a quiet,
windswept place, population 1,187. "We're not all convales-
cents," says one of today's residents, a large elderly black man
dressed in overalls and a big straw hat. "But we're all older.
We baby them baby boomers on up and ship them out of
here."

Jack Teagarden Exhibit, Red River Valley Museum, 4600
College Dr., Vernon (180 Miles NW of Dallas), 940–553–1848.

The musical Teagarden family, which included Charles on
trumpet, Clois on drums, Norma on piano, and Jack on trombone, originally came from Vernon, Texas. Their mother,
Helen Teagarden, was a ragtime piano player and a remarkable woman who encouraged her four children to become professional jazz musicians.

The small Jack Teagarden exhibit includes his desk, his
trombone, and his personal correspondence. There are also

lots of books, records, and newspaper clippings. The rest of the museum is dedicated to local history (ranching, cattle drives, the 530,000-acre Wagner Ranch, sculptress Electra Wagner Biggs), and natural history.

Open: Tu-Su, 1–5 P.M. *Free admission.*

SAN ANTONIO

Updated by Jim Beal Jr.

During the 1920s, San Antonio, then the largest city between New Orleans and Los Angeles, attracted musicians from all over Texas. Two major clubs were the Horn Palace Inn and the Shadowland Club. The Troy Floyd orchestra, a successful territorial band of the time, played a long residency at the Shadowland, while the Horn Palace was the site of Jack Teagarden's first professional gig.

Teagarden came to San Antonio from Vernon, Texas, in 1921, at the age of 16. At first his new job at the Shadowland delighted him, but then one night a gangland shooting occurred directly in front of the stage. The other, more experienced, musicians dove for cover, but Teagarden remained rooted to the spot—and when it came time for a trial, he was to be the prosecution's star witness.

That meant nothing but trouble. Gang members threatened to take his life. Then, providence intervened in the form of the great flood of 1921, which covered parts of San Antonio with 15 feet of water. Houses, businesses—and municipal records—were destroyed. All pending court cases were dismissed, and Teagarden lost no time in heading to Houston, where he joined Peck Kelley's band.

Another extraordinary musician associated with San Antonio is the enigmatic blues singer Robert Johnson, who recorded three of the only five sessions he ever did in a makeshift studio set up in the old Gunter Hotel (see "Landmarks and Legends," page 377). The three sessions took place in November 1936 and included some of his greatest songs, including "Terraplane Blues," "Walking Blues," and "Crossroad Blues."

Other jazz and blues musicians either from or associated with San Antonio include sax player Herschel Evans, who played with the Troy Floyd Orchestra; bandleader Don Albert,

At the Landing, the Jim Cullum
band plays some of the finest
traditional jazz in the country.

who came here from New Orleans; saxman Clifford Scott, who's played with Lionel Hampton and Ray Charles; the Cacares brothers; legendary tenor saxman Vernon "Spot" Barnett; Doug Sahm, who formed one of the city's first white R&B groups; and keyboard player Augie Meyers.

The city also has a strong Mexican-American jazz-blues tradition dating back to the '30s that continues to this day. During the '40s and '50s especially, a number of Mexican-American groups came out of San Antonio and the surrounding Rio Grande Valley. Most of these were known only to Texans, but one popular singer, Freddy Fender, achieved national recognition.

Sources

The best listings can be found in the Friday section of the *San Antonio Express-News* (210–225–7411; www.expressnews. com), called *The Weekender*, and in *The Current* (210–828–7660, www.sacurrent.com), a free weekly. Good Internet sources are the San Antonio Blues Society (www.sanantonioblues.com) and the informative site run by blues guitarist Damon "Sonny Boy" Lee (www.sonnyboylee.com). A transplant from Oregon who plays Chicago-style blues, Lee fronts the Sonny Boy Lee Blues Band.

For maps and other information, contact the San Antonio Convention and Visitors Bureau, 121 Alamo Plaza, 210–270–8700, www.sanantoniocvb.com.

A Note on Neighborhoods

San Antonio is a friendly, quirky city, over half of whose population is Mexican-American. River Walk (Paseo Del Rio), located 20 feet below street level, is a pedestrian walkway that follows the course of the San Antonio River. Lined with tropical plants, shops, restaurants, and music clubs, it's usually teeming with tourists. St. Mary's Street, or "The Strip," located about ten minutes north of the downtown, is another entertainment district, but it's down on its luck these days and home to only a handful of clubs.

Though easy to explore, San Antonio has its share of traffic problems. Parking downtown is a combination of high-rise and surface lots.

Landmarks and Legends

Gunter Hotel, 205 E. Houston St., at St. Mary's St. (downtown).

When Robert Johnson appeared one day in 1936 in the make-shift field studio of the American Record Corporation in the Gunter Hotel, he was a shy young man who had seldom been out of the Mississippi Delta. Slender and handsome, he only played for A&R man Don Law with his face turned toward the wall.

Later that night there was trouble. Law, who had found Johnson a room at the boarding house, was having dinner with his wife and friends when he was called to the phone. A policeman had picked Johnson up on a vagrancy charge. Law hurried down to the jail, where with some difficulty he had Johnson released; he had been worked over by the cops. Law took him back to the boarding house, gave him 45 cents for breakfast and told him not to go out again. Then he returned to his dinner, only to have Johnson call him on the phone. "I'm lonesome," Johnson said. "Lonesome?" Law asked. Johnson replied, "I'm lonesome and there's a lady here. She wants fifty cents and I lacks a nickel. . . ."

The Gunter is now the Sheraton Gunter, an upscale hostelry with 322 rooms.

(For years, some blues historians believed that it was the Blue Bonnet Hotel [at St. Mary's and Pecan Sts., now demolished] in which Johnson recorded, but more recent scholarship has pointed to the Gunter. A movement is underway to get a historical marker placed at the hotel.)

Cameo Theater, 1123 E. Commerce St., St. Paul Sq.

A pretty building in the Art Deco style, the renovated Cameo is located in the heart of St. Paul Square. During the '30s, '40s, and '50s, the square was the center of San Antonio's black entertainment district, jammed with nightclubs, restaurants, and the only hotels in town in which African Americans were allowed to stay overnight.

Most of the more famous clubs—the Avalon Grill and the Mona Lisa Club—are gone now, but the Cameo remains. Cab Calloway and Duke Ellington were among the greats who performed here.

St. Paul Square itself, which is lined with many other early twentieth-century buildings, has been declared a National Historic District and is in the process of restoration. The old Sunset Depot, a railroad station, has been transformed into a glitzy development, Sunset Station, whose upscale shops and restaurants threaten to one day take over the entire square.

The Cameo is currently in search of a tenant and is open only for special events.

Keyhole Inn, 1619 W. Poplar.

During the '50s and early '60s, this sturdy building, now a Spanish social club, was famous for blues and R&B. Clarence "Gatemouth" Brown got his start here just after being released from military service (San Antonio is the site of five military bases).

"The Keyhole could hold more than a thousand," says Nyolia Johnson, a blues singer born and bred in San Antonio who often plays with the Houserockers. "B. B., Big Joe Turner, Bobby 'Blue' Bland, they all played there. Miss Wiggles, the exotic dancer—she was there. It was a fancy and beautiful place."

CLUBS, ETC.

The Landing is the only club in town expressly designed for jazz, but there are a number of restaurants and unusual joints where some of the best music anywhere can be heard. San Antonians, especially those of Mexican-American heritage, carry on the Texas sax tradition in a big and serious way.

Some of the local jazz and blues players to watch out for include Jim Cullum's Jazz Band, one of the top traditional bands in the country, Randy Garibay and Cats Don't Sleep, the Regency Jazz Band, trumpet players Al Gomez and Charlie McBirney, saxmen Rocky Morales and Louie Bustos, trombonist Ron Wilkins, swing violinist Sebastian Campesi, bluesman Spot Barnett, trumpet player Curtis Calderon, the Richard Garcia & First Light jazz band, the Small World jazz band, Breakthrough, and blues vocalist Little Neesie. The town also has a number of fine, established blues bands, including the Houserockers featuring Nyolia Johnson, Bluesland, Damon "Sonny Boy" Lee Blues Band, Sauce & the West Side Sound, Eddie and the All-niters, River City Slim and the Rhythm Kings, Toat Lee Bluz, and the Smith Brothers.

Most bars and clubs in San Antonio close at 1 or 2 A.M.

Personal Choices

Best jazz spot: *The Landing*
Best jazz restaurant: *Dolores Del Rio*
Best blues jam: *Wings*
Best area dance hall: *Gruene Hall*

FOR JAZZ

The Landing, Hyatt Regency Hotel, 123 Losoya (River Walk), 210-222-1234 or 210-223-7266, www.landing.com.

Jim Cullum's Jazz Band, a traditional group with dozens of albums to its credit, call the Landing home. Their superb sound, always precise and energetic, offers a welcome respite from the commercial hubbub of River Walk.

The original Landing was founded in 1963 in another location by Jim Cullum's father, who was also a musician, and about 20 other jazz enthusiasts. Each put up $1,000 and then contributed time and energy to painting and restoring an old atmospheric basement club.

The new Landing, as its Hyatt address suggests, is a very different sort of place. Two-tiered and modern-elegant, with lots of little black tables and waitresses in evening clothes, it's usually packed (too packed) with a well-dressed crowd. There's also a bit of a fishbowl feel: the club has large windows and is located at the edge of a mall.

Still, the music's worth it. Cullum's seven-piece band puts on a terrific performance, and on Sundays, when he isn't playing, an expanded version of the top-caliber local jazz band Small World takes the stage. A public radio show, "River Walk," is taped here and broadcast to over 150 stations nationwide.

Music: nightly, also jazz duos on outside patio afternoons and F, Sa nights. *Cover:* $, none on the patio. *Food:* dinner, desserts; lunch served on the patio.

Dolores Del Rio, 106 River Walk, 210–223–0609.

Brought to you by the same people who ran the storied, now defunct, jazz and blues-heavy Nona's Restaurants, Dolores Del Rio is a small Italian restaurant nicely situated on a stretch of River Walk that's not overrun with tourists. On the weekends, the little joint offers jazz. There's also free wine for diners.

Music: F-Sa. *No cover. Food:* Italian.

Boardwalk Bistro, 4011 Broadway (10 min. N of downtown), 210–824–0100.

A casual indoor/outdoor restaurant, the Boardwalk Bistro features live music two nights a week, much of it jazz, some of it Celtic and folk music. Among the jazz acts that sometimes appear is the drum-bass duo version of the jazz band. The bistro-style restaurant also features a large beer and imported wine list, and there are lots of plants and artwork on the walls.

Music: W, Sa. *No cover. Food:* international.

Polo Lounge, 401 S. Alamo St., in the Fairmont Hotel (downtown), 210–224–8800.

Jazz and classic pop crooner Ken Slavin and his sharp band, which includes piano master Joe Piscatelle, roll back the musical years without coming across as camp. Polo's is a classy venue and the band and its music match the setting.

Music: F-Sa. *No cover.*

Dick's Last Resort, 406 Navarro St. (River Walk), 210–224–0026.

The place is a dump, filled with young beefy tourists downing "Love Cocktails" served with blown-up condoms, but the musicians are among the best in town. If you can stand the bright lights and the constant frat-house chatter, it's worth a short visit, but sit near the front, near the music. Some of the regulars include the house band Breakthrough and jazz-and-bluesman Bett Butler, who hosts the happy hours.

Dick's is one of a chain.

Music: nightly. *No cover. Food:* burgers, catfish, etc.

Niles Wine Bar, 7319 Broadway (15 min. N of downtown), 210–826–8463.

For some people it is indeed wine, and lots of it, that is the main attraction of this converted house in upscale Alamo Heights. But the folks who book music at Niles have an eclectic streak, so serious music fans also frequent the scene. On the calendar is some jazz and blues, along with much acoustic rock, singer/songwriters, and folk music. Jazz groups who've performed here recently include the straight-ahead Jazz Protagonists and Lara & Reyes, who play Latin and world jazz.

Music: Th-Sa. *Cover:* $. *Food:* cheese platters, etc., and a few entrees.

Also

The **Marbella Restaurant** in the Adams Mark Hotel (111 Pecan St., 210–354–2800) presents solo and duo jazz acts, along with occasional bands, that are a cut or two above the stereotypical hotel lounge/restaurant offerings; no cover.

FOR BLUES

Wings, 4904 West Ave. (15 min. E of downtown), 210–366–9464.

A plain, cinder-block, neighborhood bar, Wings is the most consistent blues joint in San Antonio, especially if your idea of blues runs to electric guitar slingers. Part biker bar, part rocking blues clubhouse, Wings features a blues jam on Wednesdays, bands on weekend nights, and occasional Sunday music benefits. Touring acts such as Mem Shannon & the Membership and Greg Piccolo & Heavy Juice are occasionally featured, but the calendar is heavily weighted toward local and area groups.

Music: W-Su. *Cover:* $

The Lucky Club, 255 Hobart St., at Acme Rd., 210–632–3791.

Owned and operated by a coalition of people that includes R&B tenor sax legend Vernon "Spot" Barnett and singer/songwriter/music publisher/attorney Lucky Tomblin, the Lucky Club—only open since Sept. 2000—is a music club first and foremost. On the outside, it looks like a stereotypical wood-frame roadhouse. On the inside, it's dominated by a huge stage. The house band is the Lucky 13 Orchestra, an R&B group that ventures into unique directions at times. Future plans call for live blues, R&B, and jazz most nights of the week. Barbecue is usually smoking on the outdoor pit.

Music: F-Su. *Cover:* $. *Food:* barbecue, etc.

Bayous Overlook, 517 N. Presa St. (River Walk), 210–223–6403.

Perched above the Bayous Restaurant, the Bayous Overlook features a variety of bands on the weekends. By far the best night to come, however, is Sunday, when Eddie & the All-Niters front and back what amounts to a casual, yet often all-star, blues jam.

Music: F-Su. *Cover:* none.

Carlsbad Tavern, 11407 West Ave. (20 min. E of downtown), 210–341–0716.

A neighborhood bar with an excellent stage and house P.A. system, Carlsbad features everything from local Top 40 bands to karaoke, folk rockers to blues, garage rock to zydeco. Occasionally, big acts such as Leon Russell and Mitch Ryder perform, but that's a rare deal. Most of the acts are local and area groups.

Music: F-Sa, with occasional midweek offerings. *Cover:* $.

Casbeers, 1719 Blanco Rd. (10 min. N of downtown), 210–732–3511.

This former enchilada joint, domino parlor, pool hall, and neighborhood bar was purchased in 1999 by Barbara Wolfe and Steve Silbas, a couple who love food, beer, sports, people, and live music. Though the duo didn't set out to turn the decades-old joint into a live music hangout, it's evolved that way. There's usually an acoustic jam on Tuesdays, singer/songwriters on Fridays, and bands on Saturdays, with an occasional Sunday show. Music ranges from folk to blues, rockabilly to garage rock, with local and area bands rubbing shoulders with touring acts such as the Blazers or Billy Bacon & the Forbidden Pigs. And the enchiladas and burgers are delicious.

Music: Tu, F-Sa. *Cover:* $. *Food:* simple American and Mexican-American.

Saluté, 2801 St. Mary's St., 210–732–5307.

A narrow, triangular-shaped room dominated by a large bar, Saluté is a casual neighborhood joint, popular among both Anglos and Latinos. With concrete walls painted bright colors and a small dance floor, the club features occasional blues and R&B, along with much Latin instrumental rock, *conjunto* music, rock, and alternative music.

Music: W–Sa. *No cover.*

Taco Land, 103 W. Grayson (10 min. N of downtown), 210–223–8406.

Made "famous" through a song recorded by the Dead Milkmen, Taco Land, located on a wooded lane somewhat off the beaten track, has been home to hundreds of young San Antonio musicians. Anyone, absolutely anyone, can play here, and lots of new groups, especially alternative music groups (as well as some blues, roots rock, punk, and variations thereof), do. "Some of the bands are great, some of them run my customers away," says owner Ram Ayala, now in his fifties. "But I don't care. As long as they get a chance to play."

Taco Land used to serve food, but that ended years ago. Now the tiny building with its suspended ceiling, and sparkling red vinyl booths is mostly a bar and pool room, while outside is a patio dominated by a centuries-old tree. The crowd, depending on the night, is usually either young and white, or middle-aged and Hispanic. Of special note: a wonderful bluesy tune on the jukebox called "Stop It, You're Killing Me" by local singer Little Neesie.

Music: W–Su. *Cover:* $.

Also

Sometimes, the little **P&M Lounge** (2310 Culebra St., 210–734–0605) is heavy on the oldies, but at other times, especially on Sunday evenings, it's home to the West Side R&B deluxe; no cover. **Wahooz** (9802 Colonnade St., 210–690–9100) is a Louisiana-themed restaurant that offers blues and blues/rock in its cocktail lounge on the weekends; no cover. Blues groups also occasionally perform at **Niles** (see "For Jazz," above).

Other Venues and Special Events

The **Carver Community Cultural Center** (226 N. Hackberry, 210–207–7211) has a concert series featuring national jazz talent. Jazz and blues can also sometimes be heard at the newly renovated **Majestic Theater** (230 E. Houston St., 210–226–3333), the **Laurie Auditorium** at Trinity University (210–736–8117), and the **Lila Cockrell Theatre** (Convention Center at Market near Bowie, 210–299–8500).

Jazz'SAlive is a free weekend festival held in Travis Park in September featuring local, regional, and national acts (210–299–8486). The **Carver Jazz Festival**, sponsored by the Carver Community Cultural Center, is an on-again, off-again festival usually held in August. **Holiday Saxophones**, a two-day gathering of the saxophone and jazz tribe, happens every December at the Guadalupe Theater. The four-day **Texas Folklife Festival** (210–558–2235), held every late summer since 1971, features 10 stages of live entertainment showcasing everything from Texas jazz to Celtic music.

Radio

KRTU/91.7 FM (210–736–8313). Jazz nightly.

KSYM/90.1 FM (210–733–2800). Jazz Sa 6 A.M.–2 P.M., blues Su 2–6 P.M. Third Coast Music Network, featuring much roots music, weekday afternoons and Su evenings.

Record Stores

A good source for blues and Texas music is **Hogwild Records and Tapes** (1824 N. Main St., 210–733–5354). Otherwise, the big chains, particularly **Borders** (225 E. Basse, 210–828–9496), have a good selection of blues and jazz. **CD Exchange** (5210 Walzem Rd, 210–650–3472), a used CD chain with a few San Antonio locations, also sometimes has a respectable selection of blues and jazz.

Other Nearby Locations

Gruene Hall, 1281 Gruene Rd., New Braunfels, 830–606–1281, www.gruenehall.com.

Gruene Hall, located half-way between San Antonio and Austin, is the oldest dance hall in Texas. A huge wooden building, half as long as a football field, with sawdust on the floor, chicken wire across the windows, and hundreds of burlap sacks hanging from the ceiling (for acoustical purposes), it opened in 1878 as a saloon and social hall for the area cotton farmers. Back then, the local residents, mostly Germans, used the hall for polkas and waltzes.

When the present owners took the place over in 1974, however, the dance floor hadn't been used in years. Only the bar up front was open, and, even worse, the tiny town of Gruene (pronounced "green") itself was a virtual ghost town.

Since then, Gruene Hall has been lovingly restored with the help of a longtime local resident and is back in full operation. Seven other buildings in town have also been restored, but although tourists now come to lunch in an old gristmill out back, the place has thus far escaped full-scale commercialization.

The hall, lined with advertisements from the turn of the century ("FEDERAL BANK LOANS, 4%", "FOR GOOD EATS AND DRINKS, BLUES SUGAR BOWL"), is open daily, but music is only featured at the end of the week. Most of the entertainment is roots music and country, with blues coming through regularly. Past performers include Bo Diddley, Marcia Ball, Omar and the

Howlers, Roomful of Blues, the Fabulous Thunderbirds, Buddy Guy, Koko Taylor, and Gatemouth Brown.

Music: Th–Su, some blues. *Cover:* $–$$$.

AUSTIN

Updated by David Courtney and John Spong

Largely because Austin did not have much of an African-American population, it was slower to develop a jazz-blues tradition than other Texas cities. The music could still be heard, however, along East 11th Street, the heart of the city's black community, as early as the 1920s, while the 1940s brought with them the founding of an important African-American music venue, the Victory Grill (see "Landmarks and Legends," page 387).

Also in the 1940s, Austin produced one of its most famous native sons, bassist Gene Ramey, who began his career at the age of 16 by playing the tuba in a local band. Ramey had a hard time getting anywhere in Austin, however, and soon moved on to Kansas City where he took up with Jay McShann's band. Austin's other 1940s star, pianist Teddy Wilson, moved as well, eventually landing in New York City, where he joined Benny Goodman.

Austin made its biggest contribution to music history in the 1960s and '70s, when the city's liberal reputation drew to it creative souls from all over the state. In the mid-1960s, there was Threadgill's, featuring a young new singer named Janis Joplin, and in the late '60s–early '70s, the Vulcan Gas Company and the Armadillo World Headquarters opened up. Both clubs presented white rock bands creating a new "Austin sound" and black bluesmen who had seldom performed before white audiences before.

Nineteen-seventy-five marked the opening of Antone's, Austin's most famous club, which has since become virtually a godfather of blues bars everywhere. In addition to featuring legends from all over the country, Antone's (now Antone's Billy Blues) has been instrumental in launching the careers of innumerable Texas bluesmen, including the late Stevie Ray Vaughan, Jimmie Vaughan, Angela Strehli, Marcia Ball, and Kim Wilson.

Other jazz and blues artists associated with Austin include trumpet player Kenny Dorham; blues guitarists Pee Wee Crayton and Mance Lipscomb; barrelhouse piano players Robert Shaw, Lavada Durst, and Grey Ghost; saxophonist Tomas Ramirez; and singer-songwriter Bill Neely.

Sources

The Austin Chronicle (512–454–5766, www.auschron.com), an alternative weekly, has excellent listings, as does the *Austin American-Statesman*'s weekly entertainment supplement "XLent" (512–445–3500, www.austin360.com/statesman/editions/thursday/xlent.html). Both are published on Thursdays and can be picked up free of charge at businesses throughout town. Online, www.austin.citysearch.com has decent listings, but nothing that compares with the *Chronicle* or "XLent."

Southwest Blues is a free monthly publication devoted to keeping the chitlin circuit alive, providing calendars and record reviews for blues, R&B, and soul acts in Texas and Oklahoma. But unless you have already made it into one of the clubs it touts, *Southwest Blues* can be hard to find. Send subscription inquiries to *Southwest Blues*, P.O. Box 710475, Dallas, Texas 75371.

For a map containing most music venues and other information, contact the Austin Conventions and Visitors Bureau, 201 E. Second St., 512–583–7235 or 800–926–2282.

KLBJ radio runs "The KLBJ Austintatious Entertainment Hotline," which includes information on music, at 512–832–4094.

A Note on Neighborhoods

Though small, Austin, the state capital, is quite spread out, sprawled over hills along the Colorado River. The city is filled with fine old homes and buildings, and is the site of the University of Texas, which with 50,000 students is one of the largest universities in the United States.

East Austin is the city's oldest African-American neighborhood. Sixth Street (Old Pecan Street) is an historic district that's recently been restored. Now squeaky-clean and lined with restaurants and second-rate music clubs (although there are exceptions, some of which are noted below), it attracts an estimated 40,000 to 50,000 people on the weekends, many of whom traipse endlessly up and down the street, in a never-ending quest for that elusive goal—fun.

Despite this, Austin still has a decidedly rebel feel. "Ex-hippies" and Texan freethinkers apparently gone straight pop up in the most unexpected of places with the most unexpected of opinions.

Landmarks and Legends

(The following route starts in East Austin, and proceeds west to the downtown and north to Manor Road and North Lamar. A car is necessary.)

East 11th Street, from I–35 to Rosewood Ave.

For 40 years, East 11th Street was the main thoroughfare for jazz and blues in Austin. During the '20s and '30s, there was the Cotton Club and the Paradise Club; during the '40s and '50s, the Victory Grill, Slim's, the Derby Lounge, and the Clock Lounge; during the '60s, Charlie's Playhouse and the IL Club.

Victory Grill, 1104 E. 11th St.

"I was responsible for booking B. B. King's first time in Texas," says Johnny Holmes, a tall man dressed in a light blue embroidered shirt, shiny patent leather shoes, and a big straw cowboy hat. "He came all the way out here from Tennessee for that show, and now look how big he is. We ate cheese and vanilla wafers in the car many times. We were just little country boys then. . . ."

Johnny Holmes and his Victory Grill are legendary names in Austin's music community. Holmes, now in his late eighties, brought them all to Austin—Clarence "Gatemouth" Brown, Little Johnny Taylor, James Brown, Ike and Tina Turner, and many, many more. He also booked talent into other venues all over the state.

The Grill, which can hold about 250 people, opened in 1945. In 1947, Bobby "Blue" Bland, then just an unknown soldier stationed at nearby Fort Hood, started playing at the club every weekend, dependably winning the weekly prize that the Grill offered to the best performer until Holmes made him stop.

Back then, 11th Street was teeming with clubs. "This whole street was like Little Harlem," says Holmes. "Business was bull. Some of the other clubs had trios or singers, but many didn't, because I had my place and it wasn't necessary."

The Grill's heyday lasted until the mid-1960s, when desegregation and changes in national music trends led black audiences to seek entertainment elsewhere. Holmes left for West Texas, leaving the club in the hands of his uncles, but when he returned 13 years later, he took over the Victory once again and continued to run it until a fire broke out in 1987. After a few attempts to get the club started again, Holmes retired, but the Victory Grill, now a state historical landmark, still hosts occasional shows and community events.

Charlie's Playhouse and **IL Club**, 1206 and 1124 E. 11 St.

When Holmes left for West Texas, business at the Grill died down and Charlie's Playhouse and the IL Club (both located on the north side of East 11th Street with a street running between them but both now deserted), stepped in to fill the void. Bobby "Blue" Bland, Freddie King, and Joe Tex all performed at Charlie's, along with the house band, Blues Boy Hubbard and the Jets, who were the city's premier local group in the '60s.

"Charlie's was always packed," says Clifford Antone of Antone's. "The crowd was half black, half college students. It was a beautiful scene."

Doris Miller Auditorium, corner of Rosewood and Chestnut avenues, near Rosewood Park.

The late Dr. Hepcat, a barrelhouse piano player and the first African-American deejay in Texas, once booked talent with Johnny Holmes into this small auditorium. The two brought in everyone from Louis Armstrong to Aretha Franklin, and often hired local talent for backup.

Later, Dr. Hepcat found religion and, as the Reverend Lavada Durst, refused to play in clubs, but did put in occasional appearances at festivals until his death in 1995.

Huston Tillotson College, 1820 E. Eighth St.

During the '50s and '60s, this African-American college, known for its jazz program, and Austin, known as the only liberal city in Texas, drew black musicians from all over the state. James Polk, Bobby Bradford, and Fred Smith all went to school at Huston Tillotson, and their Sunday-afternoon jam sessions, played at various venues throughout the city, became legendary.

Grey Ghost's home, 1914 E. 8th St.

By the time Grey Ghost turned 82 on Pearl Harbor Day, 1985, most people had forgotten all about him. A mythic barrelhouse piano player who had played the circuit from the '20s to the '60s, he hadn't performed in public since 1965. Then, in 1986, the Barker Texas History Center put on an exhibit called "From Lemon to Lightnin'," in which they featured Ghost's music and his photograph. Local blues fan Tary Owens, once a good friend of Janis Joplin's and founder of Catfish Records, recognized Ghost's face from the community work he did on 11th Street, and went to seek him out. At first, the older man was suspicious and surly, and refused to leave his house.

Owens kept going back, however, and back, and back, until finally Ghost agreed to accompany him to the exhibit.

"It's good to be recognized at my late date," he said around that time." I like to play. I don't like to play with no trumpet or singer. It's just me, myself, and I."

Soon after that, Ghost became nationally renowned, although he never left this small wooden house. He released his first album, "Grey Ghost," on Owens's Catfish label in 1992, and traveled to festivals around the country. He also recorded and played around town with Dr. Hepcat and Erbie Bowser (as the Piano Professors), and gigged every Wednesday afternoon at the Continental Club until his death in 1996.

Walk of the Stars, Sixth and Brazos streets.

Outside the elegant Driskill Hotel, an old cattlemen's establishment that is the second oldest hotel in Texas, there are stars embedded in the sidewalk. Willie Nelson was the first Austin musician to be so honored, and Janis Joplin and Kenneth Threadgill (see Threadgill's, page 390) among others, have since followed.

Vulcan Gas Company, 316 Congress Ave.

The W. B. Smith Building, now a sedate-looking office building, was once home to the Vulcan Gas Company, a locally infamous club that was more or less credited with starting the music scene in Austin. Opened in 1967—and named after an advertising sign found in an antique store—it was a sort of flagship rock club for local talent such as Shiva's Headband, Conqueroo, and Johnny Winter, as well as touring talent such as Moby Grape, Canned Heat, and the Velvet Underground. Once the club got off the ground, it also started booking blues acts—Sleepy John Estes, Lightnin' Hopkins, Muddy Waters, Big Mama Thornton—who had been touring through East Austin for years but had seldom crossed over into the white part of town.

Stephen F. Austin Hotel, 701 Congress Ave.

After a decade or so of dormancy, this grand old landmark reopened in May 2000 as the ritzy Intercontinental Stephen F. Austin Hotel. The only jazz here nowadays is the recorded smooth jazz playing in the overpriced lobby bar, but back in the 1930s, the hotel was a stop for swing bands. At that time, white Austin really wasn't ready for jazz yet, as Charlie Barnet, a popular bandleader of that time, relates in *Those Swinging Years:* "On arrival, I found we were all living in one big room, an unused banquet room, and that we played in the lobby of the hotel at noon every day and on Saturdays in the ballroom on the roof. We got twenty-five dollars a week besides our accommodations in the banquet room.

"It was a weird scene. The people would sit around the lobby and stare at us as we played. . . ."

Stevie Ray Vaughan Memorial (Auditorium Shores at Town Lake, just west of the South First Street Bridge, 2 min. S of downtown, near the new Threadgill's [see below]).

In a town filled with more than its share of internationally renowned names and carefully guarded local legends, Stevie Ray is something special—remembered, among other things, for his pure artistry on the guitar, his courage in working through his addictions, and the utter devotion of the people and players who helped him move his career along. This slightly larger-than-life statue was created by artist Ralph Helnick and unveiled in 1993, and not a day has gone by since then that fans haven't stopped by to leave flowers or guitar picks, or just sit and think. The statue is located near the site of some of Stevie's most memorable shows, on the city's outdoor Auditorium Shores stage, and it's impossible to look at it now and not picture him wailing away on his Stratocaster with the downtown city skyline all alight behind him.

Robert Shaw's store and home, 1917 Manor Rd.

Robert Shaw, the great barrelhouse piano player, started out as an itinerant musician riding the Santa Fe rails like many others of his time. He saw no future in it, however, and so moved back home where he opened up a small store and barbecue place, got married, and became involved in the church. He stopped playing the piano altogether and devoted himself to his business so completely that in 1964 he was voted the outstanding black businessman of the year.

Then along came Mack McCormick, a Houston music historian who helped Arhoolie Records founder Chris Strachwitz on his earliest recording trips. McCormick found Shaw through Dr. Hepcat (Shaw had been Hepcat's piano teacher), and persuaded him to return to music. Soon thereafter, Shaw was on the circuit once again, this time touring the United States and Europe.

Shaw died in 1985, and his long, low-slung store is now closed. His former home, a small white building, stands just behind the market.

Threadgill's, 6416 N. Lamar Blvd. (20 min. N of downtown), 512–451–5440, www.threadgills.com, and **Threadgill's World Headquarters**, 301 W. Riverside Drive (2 min. S of downtown), 512–472–9304.

Though never a true blues or jazz spot, Threadgill's was the club where Janis Joplin got her start. A picture of the star hangs on one side of the stage, a picture of onetime owner Kenneth Threadgill on the other, and there's a "History Room," lined with Joplin memorabilia in the center of the restaurant.

Threadgill was a former bootlegger and blues yodeler in the Jimmie Rodgers tradition. He opened his joint up in 1933, but for years, it wasn't a club at all, just a gas station and beer café. Then, in the late '40s, Threadgill started holding informal Wednesday-night jam sessions for local musicians.

The sessions were still a going concern by the time Joplin entered the University of Texas in 1962, the same year she was humiliated by being nominated for the university's "Ugly Man" contest. The first few times she performed at Threadgill's, she sang in a pure clear voice, but that soon changed.

Threadgill first recognized Joplin's talent when he heard her sing "Silver Thread and Golden Needles," and was extremely supportive of her throughout her career. She reciprocated his affection and when, in 1971, a birthday party was held in his honor, she canceled a concert in Hawaii to attend.

After Threadgill's death, the club was taken over by Eddie Wilson, who once ran the Armadillo World Headquarters. Today the multiroom place, filled with checkered tablecloths, is a restaurant serving great heaping plates of soul food. The music tradition continues through a revolving schedule of folk, bluegrass, and acoustic jazz players on Wednesday nights at the original location, and through country yodeler and local legend Don Walser at the new Threadgill's World Headquarters downtown.

Music: W. *No cover. Food:* Southern.

CLUBS, ETC.

Home to over 100 live music venues, Austin has a very eclectic music scene, with many clubs presenting blues, and sometimes jazz, once a week or so, along with other kinds of Texas music. The top full-time blues clubs in town is **Antone's**, a world-famous club that books both national and heavyweight local acts. The city's only real full-time jazz venue is the **Elephant Room.**

Top blues artists to watch out for while in town include the legendary Reverend Lavada Durst and Hosea Hargrove; Kim Wilson (who no longer lives in Austin but still plays here regularly), Blues Boy Hubbard, W. C. Clark, Alan Haynes, Lou Ann Barton, Marcia Ball, Jimmie Vaughan, the LeRoi

Brothers, Omar and the Howlers, "Guitar" Jake Andrews, and Clarence Pierce and the East Side Band.

Martin Banks, a veteran of the Apollo Theater house band and former member of both Duke Ellington's and Ray Charles's orchestras, is the dean of Austin's jazz scene, and can be found playing under his own billing and with CO2, JAMAD, and the Eastside Band.

Other jazz talent to watch for includes piano players James Polk, Floyd Domino, Rich Harney, and Bobby Doyle; saxman Tony Campise; vocalists Maryann Price, Carmen Bradford, and Chris O'Connell; piano player Margaret Wright; mandolin player Paul Glass; viola and guitar player Will Taylor; sax player Larry D. C. Williams; piano and violin player Danny Levin; guitarist Mitch Watkins; Beto y Los Fairlanes; the Creative Opportunity Orchestra (CO2); the Jazz Pharaohs; Tomas Ramirez's fusion band; Brew, also a fusion band; and 8 1/2 Souvenirs, a hot swing band in the Django/Grappelli mold. Swing/lounge acts, usually playing in upscale cigar/martini bars, have also become popular in recent years; among the best of these groups are Mr. Fabulous (playing standards), the Recliners (a tight, swinging big band playing familiar disco, metal, punk, and new wave songs), and Tosca (a tango orchestra performing original compositions, led by piano virtuoso Glover Gill).

Personal Choices

Best jazz clubs: *Elephant Room, Cedar Street*
Best downtown blues clubs: *Antone's, Joe's Generic Bar*
Best neighborhood blues club: *Eastside Lounge*

FOR JAZZ

Elephant Room, 315 Congress Ave. (downtown), 512–473–2279, www.natespace.com/elephant.htm.

An old brick basement with a smattering of tables, the subterranean Elephant Room presents jazz most nights of the week. Regulars include many of Austin's top jazz musicians—Tony Campise, Tomas Ramirez, Stanley Smith, Bobby Doyle, the Jazz Pharaohs—and trombonist Mike Mordecai hosts a jazz jam on Mondays. Touring acts are also brought through from time to time, and celebrities such as Clint Eastwood and Kevin Costner have occasionally stopped by.

The Elephant was once a storage room used to keep wine and, some say, old elephant bones (hence the name) warehoused here by the University of Texas.

Music: Th-M. *Cover:* $.

Cedar Street Courtyard, 208 W. Fourth St., 512–495–9669.

Billing itself as "King of the Gin Joints," the Cedar Street Courtyard—the anchor of Austin's burgeoning Warehouse District—is a popular playground for the many martini-drinking dot-commers who have recently moved to town. With a huge sunken courtyard that features a stage at one end and an indoor bar on either side, the club provides a beautiful setting—weather permitting—for its 6–8 P.M. jazz happy hours, when piano players are featured. Later in the night, there are full jazz bands. Look for the Tosca tango band, led by pianist/accordionist Glover Gill, as well as the Glover Gill Trio, the Brew, Robert Kraft Quartet, Blaze, and piano player Margaret Wright.

Music: nightly. *Cover:* $-$$.

Mercury at Jazz, 214 E. Sixth St., 512–478–6372.

With a recent move to new and roomier digs above Jazz: A Louisiana Kitchen (see below), the Mercury continues its tradition of showcasing local jazz/funk/hip-hop upstarts, along with occasional name touring acts. A few years back, hometown jazz/funk heroes Hot Buttered Rhythm found a home at the Mercury, and the band's founder and now-big-deal drummer Brannen Temple still returns to the club on occasion with his latest project, Blaze.

Presenting jazz on East Sixth Street—the mecca of party-happy college kids—is a bold move, but so far, the strategy has worked.

Music: M-Sa. *Cover:* $-$$.

Ringside at Sullivan's, 300 Colorado St., 512–474–1870.

Sophisticated, upscale Ringside at Sullivan's is a jazz lounge adjoining the swank Sullivan's Steakhouse. Look for top local names such as Tony Campise, Jon Blondell, Hank Hehmsoth, and Elias Haslanger to grace the raised corner stage that sits behind and above the room's sunken, semicircular bar.

As much a holding area for the steakhouse's waiting list as a true jazz venue, Ringside is equal parts meeting room and listening lounge. With the requisite cigar and martini, however, Ringside can still be enjoyed.

Music: M-Sa. *Cover:* $-$$. *Food:* appetizers and desserts.

Ritz Lounge, 320 E. Sixth St., 512–474–2270.

Enter through a side door to the Ritz Pool Hall—a converted movie theater—and proceed up the stairs to the converted balcony of said theater to one of Austin's grandest venues. With its box seating and stadium-style setup, there really isn't a bad seat in the house.

While not strictly speaking a jazz club, the Ritz does feature the lo-fi lounge jazz of Austin's popular and sometimes-tongue-in-cheek Recliners—probably the only jazz/swing band in the world to defile AC/DC's "Back in Black" by simply having it on the set list. The popular tango band Tosca also plays the Ritz regularly.

Music: Th-Sa. *Cover:* $.

Speakeasy, 412-D Congress Ave. (downtown), 512–476–8086.

Like the Ritz Lounge, the Speakeasy is not really a jazz venue. However, this monster of a martini bar does sometimes feature the soft jazz of such local favorites as the Recliners, Mr. Fabulous, and Casino Royale.

Music: nightly, some jazz. *Cover:* $-$$.

Buddy Guy gets down at Antone's

Susan Antone

Jazz: A Louisiana Kitchen, 214 E. 6ᵗʰ St., 512–479–0474.

Mostly a large, noisy, too-well-lit restaurant that presents jazz and blues acts during dinner, Jazz is well worth a visit on Thursday evenings when the Jazz Pharaohs play. Their music is '30s and '40s swing. Also a regular is Matthew Robinson's blues band, which plays every Friday. The theme through the restaurant is Louisiana, and there are lots of Mardi Gras masks, Mardi Gras beads, crocodiles, etc., everywhere.

Music: nightly. *No cover. Food:* Cajun.

Also

The **Sardine Rouge** (311 W. Sixth St., 512–473–8642), a restaurant, often features such top local talent as James Polk, Glover Gill, Marty Allen, and the incomparable Bobby Doyle. Jazz can also be heard at the **Continental Club** (see "For Blues," below).

FOR BLUES

Antone's, 213 Fifth St. (downtown), 512–474–5314.

For over 25 years, the four locations that have housed Antone's have been meccas for blues fans, mythic places that people in other parts of the world have talked about with awe. From its earliest incarnation as a backroom jam parlor behind a Sixth Street clothing store, through its present locale in a downtown warehouse, the house of blues that Clifford Antone built has hosted every major blues figure, from Muddy Waters to John Lee Hooker, and been a proving ground for any Austin guitar-slinger ready to prove his or her mettle.

A native of Port Arthur, Texas, Antone started up his club when he was just 25 years old. Clifton Chenier (also from Port Arthur and a friend from way back) played every night that first week, and for many years the Fabulous Thunderbirds were the house band. Little Walter was in the club logo, and Antone had a habit of honoring other departed blues musicians by staging festivals in their honor.

Over time, Antone's has not only featured almost all the living blues legends, but has also presented as many unknown Texas musicians as possible. Some, including Angela Strehli, Kim Wilson, and Stevie Ray Vaughan, went on to win international fame.

Blues is Antone's entire life. "I'm not anything," he says. "I'm just a guy who likes the blues. The musicians are the people. They're the ones who get on stage."

The club's long run has not been without its difficulties. A planned merger with San Antonio–based blues chain Billy Blues—intended to ease Antone's perennial cash-flow problems—fell through in the early '90s, and Clifford's own well-publicized trouble with the law (two busts for distributing marijuana) have landed him in the federal pen. These days, too, the club is as likely to be packed with college kids listening to rootsy singer-songwriters as it is with older blues fans. But on nights when the booking is right—like the anniversary celebrations held every July—there is no questioning Antone's status as Austin's Home of the Blues.

Music: nightly. *Cover:* $-$$$.

Joe's Generic Bar, 315 E. Sixth St., 512–480–0171.

"The Austin blues scene would collapse without Joe's," says John Conquest, editor of *Music City Texas*. This hole-in-the-wall joint—"the only dive on Sixth Street"—is the place to go to hear young musicians and up-and-coming bands. Some are genuine talent who go on to play much larger clubs, others are . . . well . . . umm . . . no comment.

The dark little room with its Elvis tapestries, Stevie Ray Vaughan posters, old advertising signs, and hodgepodge of mismatched tables and chairs has blues every night of the week. Come on a Wednesday, when the local favorite Tony Redman Band performs. No hard liquor is served; just beer and wine coolers.

Music: nightly. *No cover.*

311 Club, 311 E. Sixth St., 512–477–1630.

Two doors down from Joe's, just past the Midnight Cowboy massage parlor, sits the 311, a decidedly better-kept hangout that boasts jam sessions on Sundays and Tuesdays, and house band Joe Valentine and the Imperials on Wednesdays. The club also features a full bar and, believe it or not, carpeted floors. Legend has it that Brian Setzer once sat in with local guitar hero Rick Broussard here.

Music: nightly. *Cover:* none-$.

Babe's on Sixth Street, 208 E. Sixth St., 512–473–2035.

Home of Babe's Old Fashioned Hamburger, this restaurant-club is often a local band's next step after building a following at Joe's. Most of the music here is blues or blues-rock, with the biggest crowds coming in for Alan Haynes's Saturday shows. Babe's is housed in an old brick building with lots of stained wood, neon beer signs, and publicity stills of bands that presumably played here in years past. But the scorching playing of current regulars like Walter Higgs and John McVey make those other acts slip from the mind.

Music: nightly. *Cover:* $.

Continental Club, 1315 S. Congress Ave. (5 minutes from downtown), 512–441–2444, www.continentalclub.com.

A dark square room with vintage murals on the walls, the Continental dates back to the 1950s. Tommy Dorsey is said to have stopped by in his day, and the place has also played host to a topless bar and a red-neck hangout. Nowadays, the Continental presents mostly roots rock and rockabilly.

What makes the club interesting to blues fans, though, are its late weekday afternoons. On Fridays after work, the latest version of the Blues Specialists (the late T. D. Bell and Erbie Bowser band), now fronted by harp player Mel Harris, runs through a steady two-hour set of bona-fide East Austin blues that would make the old masters proud. And on Tuesdays, Miss Toni Price draws crowds as big as any weekender's to hear her impossibly soulful blues singing, backed by guitarists Scrappy Jud Newcombe and Casper Rawls.

Semi-regular bookings of out-of-town acts also keep jazz and blues fans happy. The Continental is Austin's headquarters for the Royal Crown Revue, a California jump swing band; Big Sandy & His Fly-rite Boys, hot Western swingers, also from California; Houston's Miss Lavelle White; and Oklahoma's Junior Brown. Avant-garde saxman Steve Lacy makes semi-annual trips to Austin that provide some of the Continental's most celebrated moments.

Music: roots most nights, much blues and jazz. *Cover:* $-$$ nights, none at happy hour.

Eastside Lounge, E. 12th St. just east of Comal St. (East Austin), 512–474–5005.

A small cinderblock building set back from the street, the Eastside is a neighborhood joint that features some of the best veteran blues talent around. Hosea Hargrove and the Enter City Band play on Sundays, while James Kuykendal and the Blues Express take most Fridays and Saturdays. But the real treat comes on Mondays and Thursdays, when house guitarist Clarence Pierce and the East Side Band host an old-fashioned "talent show" (read: jam session). Singers, piano players, harmonica players, and of course guitar players come from around the neighborhood, and even all over the world, to sit in and play in the last real juke joint left in Austin. The room is small and usually packed, mostly with a middle-aged crowd. Beer and setups are cheap.

Music: Th-M. *No cover.*

Also

Small and dark, the **Hole in the Wall** (2538 Guadalupe St., 512–472–5599) is one of Austin's oldest live music clubs. The late Stevie Ray Vaughan and Omar and the Howlers played here before making it big, but nowadays the club presents only occasional blues.

The singles bar **Ego's** (510 S. Congress St., 512–474–7091) presents Seth Walker's swing band on Tuesdays, Matt Powell's occasionally bluesy four-piece on Wednesdays, Guy Forsythe once a month, and Bobby Doyle on Fridays and Saturdays. And with Chet Baker and Nat King Cole on the juke box, the bar is always a good place to people-watch; scenes from the recent past include Dancin' Outlaw Jesco White tap-dancing near the stage and Quentin Tarantino eye-balling girls by the pool tables.

Other Venues and Special Events

The nationally syndicated TV show "Austin City Limits" is taped August–January at the University of Texas by public television station KLRU. Tickets are free, but getting them is tricky: local radio stations announce ticket availability at about 8 A.M. the morning of the event. For more information, call the KLRU hotline at 512–471–4812.

National jazz and blues acts can sometimes be heard at the **Paramount Theatre** (713 Congress Ave., 512–472–5411), and the **University of Texas Performing Arts Center** (E. 23rd St. at E. Campus Dr., 512–471–1444). The latter features a superb jazz series that in recent years has brought in many top names, including members of the Buena Vista Social Club, the Mingus Big Band, Wynton Marsalis's "Blood on the Fields" with the Lincoln Center Jazz Orchestra, and Marcus Roberts' Gershwin tribute, also with the Lincoln Center Jazz Orchestra.

The weekend-long **Longhorn Jazz Festival** is held at various spots on the University of Texas campus each April (512–475–8195 [info]; 512–477–6060 [tickets]). The **Zilker Park Fall Jazz Festival** takes place at the Hillside Theatre in Zilker Park (Barton Springs Rd. near downtown) every Labor Day weekend; the **Zilker Park Summer Jazz and Blues Series** features different players on Sundays in May and June. Admission to both Zilker festivals is free; call 512–440–1414 for info.

The **Austin Jazz and Arts Festival** books local and touring jazz and blues acts, along with world music and spoken word. The fest takes place in September in the lot next to the

Victory Grill. Antone's hosts the **Antone's Blues Festival** (512–474–5314) in Waterloo Park every May.

Radio

KAZI/88.7 FM (512–836–9544). Austin's African-American community radio station. Jazz and blues, Su-Th nights.

KUT/90.5 FM (512–471–1631). Affiliated with University of Texas. Jazz daily 2–3 P.M., and Tu-W, 8 P.M.–midnight. Blues M, 8–11 P.M.

KGSR/107.1 FM (512–390–5477). Jazz Su, 7 A.M.–noon; blues Tu, 11P.M.–midnight.

KOOP/91.7 FM (512–472–5667) and **KVRX/91.7 FM** (512–495–5879). These sister stations share the same frequency and freewheeling, outsider mindset. KOOP is community radio at its most basic, broadcast weekdays, 9 A.M.–7 P.M., and weekends, 9 A.M.–11 P.M. KVRX picks up the slack with a truly student-run station. Look for the jazz Sa, 9 A.M.–noon, and M, 9–10 P.M.; blues F, 10 A.M.–noon.

Record Stores

The best spot in town for blues and collectors is **Antone's Record Store** (2928 Guadalupe St., 512–322–0660), which stocks many local labels. **Waterloo Records** (Sixth St. and Lamar, 512-474-2500) gives similar emphasis to local labels and acts, and offers weekly in store performances by bands releasing new records. Waterloo's has also been selected "record store of the year" three times by the National Association of Recording Merchandisers and "best record store in Austin" by *The Austin Chronicle* 18 years in a row. **Jupiter Records** (1000 E. Red River, 512–454–5678; 5300 S. Mopac, 512–891–8765) carries all categories of new and used CDs and vinyl, but devotes more time and space to jazz than most. **Tower Records** (2402 Guadeloupe St., 512–478–5711) has a great imports section and knowledgeable staff.

Diz and Bird ignited the West Coast
bebop scene at Billy Berg's in 1945.

Frank Driggs Collection

West Coast

LOS ANGELES

Updated by Zan Stewart (jazz) and
Mary Katherine Aldin (blues)

"West Coast" jazz has come to connote a sort of light, airy
sound originated by a group of mostly white musicians working in the 1950s, but the term is misleading, because the
West Coast's contribution to the music is considerably older
and more complex than that. Jazz and blues in L.A. was
already well established by the 1940s at the latest, when
Central Avenue, a long straight street that runs from the
downtown to Watts, was filled with African-American clubs
and theaters of all kinds. Among the most famous of these
were the Club Alabam, an extravagant dance hall; the Down
Beat, where Charles Mingus and Buddy Collette led a septet;
the Brown Bomber, named after Joe Louis, the heavyweight
boxing champion; and the 331 Club, where Nat "King" Cole
got his start.

Somehow, though, Los Angeles' early contribution to jazz
and blues is often downplayed, perhaps because, like San
Francisco, it got a late start. The city had no sizable African-
American population until World War II, when the war industries and the Southern Pacific Railroad brought hundreds of
workers to the Coast from the Southern states.

Some of the many Los Angeles musicians who came of age
on Central Avenue included Dexter Gordon, Art Pepper,
Hampton Hawes, Charles Mingus, Chico Hamilton, Ernie
Andrews, Art Farmer, Teddy Edwards, and Sonny Criss.
Bluesmen Percy Mayfield, Jimmy Witherspoon, T-Bone
Walker, and Big Jay McNeely were also Avenue fixtures, as
was blind pianist Art Tatum, who played through the wee
morning hours at a breakfast club called Lovejoy's, and
Oakland artist Johnny Otis, whose big band swung away at
the Club Alabam.

Twenty miles away, Hollywood was also happening during
the '40s, with the famous Billy Berg's on Vine Street presenting Lee and Lester Young in 1941 and Benny Carter in 1943.
Charlie Parker (with Dizzy Gillespie) played Billy Berg's in
1945, igniting the local bebop scene while procuring heroin
from one Emry Byrd, a.k.a. "Moose the Mooche." Moose, a former honor student and athletic star at Jefferson High, who
became paralyzed through polio, ran a shoeshine stand on

Central Avenue that featured racks of records but actually sold dope.

Another significant 1940s development was Jazz at the Philharmonic (JATP). Started up in 1944 at the downtown Philharmonic Auditorium (since torn down) near Pershing Square by Norman Granz, a young film editor and jazz fan, it was the first concert series ever to give first-class treatment to jazz musicians. By the 1950s, JATP concerts, many featuring outstanding performances that are preserved on vinyl, were being produced at concert halls around the world, including Europe, Australia, and Japan. (The series was discontinued at the conservative Philharmonic in 1946 owing to "audience disturbances.")

"Cool" or "West Coast" jazz came to Los Angeles in the early 1950s, following the release of Miles Davis's influential *Birth of the Cool* album. Among its top L.A. proponents were Shelly Manne, Gerry Mulligan, Shorty Rogers, Lee Konitz, and Bud Shank, most of whom had actually come to the West Coast from elsewhere. The Lighthouse Café in Hermosa Beach, booked by Howard Rumsey, was the center of the new 1950s sound, although The Haig on Wilshire Boulevard and, later, Shelly's Manne-Hole in Hollywood were also important.

Some of the many other musicians associated with Los Angeles over the years include multi-instrumentalist Eric Dolphy, drummer Billy Higgins, trumpet players Chet Baker and Don Cherry, saxophonists Arthur Blythe and David Murray, and pianist Joanne Brackeen.

Sources

The *LA Weekly* (323–465–9909; www.laweekly.com) has superb listings that include everything from commercial spots to small neighborhood bars. The *Los Angeles Times* (213–237–5000; www.latimes.com) carries its most complete listings on Sundays, but also has briefer listings in its "Weekend" section on Thursdays. The *Los Angeles Daily News* (818–713–3000; www.dailynews.com) carries listings on Fridays. The weekly *New Times* (310–477–0403; www.new-timesla.com/) has both listings and critics' recommendations.

The *L. A. Jazz Scene* (818–505–2115, www.lajazzscene.com) is the city's only dedicated jazz newspaper. Published monthly, it has loads of info and reviews, and solid listings.

KLON-FM runs a concert hotline at (562) 597–9911.

For maps and other information, contact the Los Angeles Convention and Visitors Bureau, 213–689–8822, www.lacvb.com. The bureau's downtown office is located at 685 S. Figueroa St., its Hollywood office at 6541 Hollywood Blvd.

A Note on Neighborhoods

Los Angeles, population 8 million, is intimidating at first: all that sprawl, all that highway, all those districts (Hollywood, Santa Monica, Beverly Hills), or are they separate cities? Except during rush hour, however, the city is surprisingly painless to navigate, and addresses relatively easy to find as long as you're equipped with a detailed map. Parking downtown during the day and in Hollywood, day or night, is generally available only in paying lots; otherwise, street parking is plentiful.

Los Angeles' downtown is small and compact, and though it was once next to deserted after 5 P.M., it's now just beginning to exhibit a nightlife. Hollywood, to the northwest, has always had a reputation as an entertainment center, and Westwood, to the west, is home to UCLA. Venice and Santa Monica, about 20 minutes west of downtown, are on the beach. Venice is known as an arts community; Santa Monica, once a retirement community, as a thriving commercial and entertainment area. South Central L.A. is to the southwest of downtown, just below the Santa Monica Freeway, and many of the "Landmarks and Legends" situated there were untouched by the 1992 riots. The Leimert Park–Crenshaw District in South Central, also untouched by the riots, is a burgeoning artistic community complete with inexpensive shops, boutiques, and sidewalk vendors. Sherman Oaks and North Hollywood are in the San Fernando Valley, 40 minutes north of downtown; Compton is an African-American suburb, 20 minutes to the southwest.

Long Beach, a big, completely separate city, lies 40 minutes southwest of L.A.

Landmarks and Legends

(With the exception of the Lighthouse Café, all of the sites below are in or relatively near South Central L.A. and can easily be toured in an hour or two by car.)

Central Avenue, downtown to 103rd St.

"There was always something happening on Central Avenue," said flugelhorn and trumpet player Art Farmer. "One time, I was at the Down Beat, and Big Jay McNeely was playing across the street. He marched up and down the street playing his horn, he lay down on his back playing his horn, he came into the Down Beat playing his horn. Then the owner started shouting at us, 'Get a horn!, Get a horn!,' like it was some kind of duel, like his sax was a gun. [Central Avenue] was like a wild, wild Western show."

During its 1940s heyday, Central Avenue was somewhat of a mix between New York's 52nd Street and Harlem. Like 52nd Street, it was filled with dozens of small clubs and hundreds of musicians making the rounds from one spot to another (unlike 52nd Street, though, things were very spread out, stretching as they did for over 100 blocks). Like Harlem, it also had its share of classy theaters and dance halls that attracted not only African Americans of varying economic classes but also middle-class whites and Hollywood entertainers.

Central Avenue went into decline in the early 1950s when the economic boom of the war years was over, and the city's electric Red Car trolley system, the street's main form of public transportation, was disbanded. Today, much of the Avenue is dilapidated, boarded up, or torn down. Only a few reminders—the Hotel Dunbar, the Lincoln Theater—remain.

Hotel Dunbar, 4225 Central Ave., corner 42nd St.

From the 1920s through the 1940s, most of the top African-American entertainers passing through Los Angeles stayed at the Dunbar, which was the first hotel in the U.S. built specifically for blacks. A large solid brick building with arched doorways on the ground floor, it later stood unoccupied for many years except for one longtime resident, comedian Rudy Ray Moore. Moore did finally move out, in 1988, and the building is now an apartment house for senior citizens. A small museum with black entertainment memorabilia is on the ground floor.

Duke Ellington and his band sometimes stayed at the Dunbar, as Buck Clayton, who had an apartment there at one time, recalls in *Buck Clayton's Jazz World:*

> I'll never forget one day when I happened to be in a restaurant in the Dunbar and most of Duke's guys were in there too and they were all listening to the jukebox. It was the first time since leaving the East that they had heard their recording of *It don't mean a thing if it ain't got that swing,* and that restaurant was swinging like crazy. So much rhythm I'd never heard, as guys were beating on tables, instrument cases or anything else that they could beat on with knives, forks, rolled-up newspapers. . . . It was absolutely crazy. I found out one more thing about Duke's band being in a restaurant. If there is fifteen musicians that enter a restaurant they take up fifteen tables as everybody takes a table for himself. I never knew why, but everyone wanted and got his own table.

Club Alabam, Central Ave. near 42nd St.

Now a big vacant lot next door to the Hotel Dunbar, the opulent Club Alabam with its silk drapes, colored lights, and waitresses in scanty dress, was once the focal point of jazz on the Avenue. Founded in the '20s by drummer and bandleader Curtis Mosby (whose brother, Esvan, was elected mayor of Central Avenue), it featured dancing and entertainment nightly.

Among the many who showed up at the Club at one time or another were Andy Kirk, Fats Waller, Lena Horne, and Frank Sinatra, who came as a listener only but then sang a spontaneous number after the scheduled performers were done. Eddie Barefield's band played here in the '30s and Lee Young's (Lester Young's brother) during the war years. Among those who played with Young were Dexter Gordon, Art Pepper, and Charles Mingus.

Lincoln Theater, Central Ave. and 23rd St.

Now a somewhat run-down temple, the Lincoln Theater was popular during the '20s and '30s, when many of the local big bands and musicians performed here. Vocalist Ernie Andrews was once an usher at the Lincoln, and—rather ironically, given Central Avenue's current condition—the theater was once known for the benefits it sponsored for the poor.

5–4 Ballroom, 308 W. 54th St. at Broadway (South Central), 213–752–4933 or 291–3102.

First built in 1922 for whites who resided in South Central, the 5–4 became a cultural mecca for the city's black population around World War II, by which time the neighborhood's racial makeup had changed. All sorts of top African-American entertainers could be heard here back then, including Nat "King" Cole, B. B. King, Fats Domino, Dizzy Gillespie, and, later, Ornette Coleman. Ray Charles broadcast a TV program from here in the early 1960s, and the ballroom was still in operation as late as 1968.

Located on the second floor, with picture windows all around, the 5–4 was restored in the early 1990s as the 5–4 Blues Room, in the hopes that it would once again become a first-class South Central restaurant and club. Alas, however, the place was foreclosed by the bank in the late 1990s and now stands empty, except on those occasional evenings when it is rented out for private parties.

Western Avenue, 30th to 40th streets.

Following the demise of Central Avenue, much of the city's jazz activity moved westward, to clubs such as the **Tiki Room** (still standing at Western Ave. and 37th St.), the **Club Oasis** (also at 37th St. near Western), and the **California Club** (at

St. Andrew and Martin Luther King, near Western, now a lounge). Western Avenue was never able to recreate Central's old magic, however.

Thomas Jefferson High School, 1319 E. 41st St.

Many now well-known Los Angeles musicians once attended this stolid old high school, located just off Central Avenue. Among them were Dexter Gordon, Chico Hamilton, Big Jay McNeely, Sonny Criss, Ed Thigpen, Ernie Andrews, Horace Tapscott, Frank Morgan, Art and Addison Farmer, and Roy Ayers. All studied under one extraordinary teacher, Samuel Browne, who was the first African-American high school teacher hired by the Los Angeles school system. ("The oral exam committee," Browne said to Clint Rosemond of L.A.'s Jazz Heritage Foundation in 1983, "was concerned about what I would do if I had white students in my class; how would I handle it? I said, 'I'll just try to teach them, that's all; nothing special.'")

Browne, who was also known as the Count, was responsible for three school orchestras that performed around town for both public and private events. In addition to teaching music classes and running rehearsals, he also brought in many top musicians—Jimmie Lunceford, Nat "King" Cole, and Lionel Hampton—to perform and talk to his students.

Lighthouse Café, 30 Pier Ave., Hermosa Beach, 310–372–6911.

Still a handsome music club, now featuring mostly rock-and-roll, the legendary Lighthouse is in the laid-back beach community of Hermosa Beach. Owned by John Levine, and booked by Howard Rumsey starting in 1949, the Lighthouse was a jazz club for over 20 years. During the 1950s it was home base for Shorty Rogers, Shelly Manne, Teddy Edwards, Art Pepper, Sonny Criss, and Hampton Hawes, some of whom formed a recording group called the Lighthouse All Stars.

The Lighthouse was especially famous for its Sunday jam sessions, which began at two in the afternoon and lasted until two the following morning. "All those hours!" Shorty Rogers says in *Jazz West Coast* by Robert Gordon. "We'd start at two and I'd look out and there'd be people sitting in bathing suits, listening to the music. And then, just as I'd be about ready to collapse at two in the morning, I'd look again and they were still there—two in the morning in their bathing suits!"

Also

Ethel Waters once lived in a large Victorian home (1910 Harvard Blvd., near Washington Blvd.), now painted white with light green trim, in what was then known as the "Sugar

Hill" district of Los Angeles. **Nat "King" Cole** once lived in a beautiful brick house (401 Muirfield Rd. at Fourth St.), now draped with ivy and surrounded by landscaped gardens, in exclusive Hancock Park. When he died of lung cancer in 1965 at the age of 45, he was buried in the Forest Lawn Cemetery (1712 S. Glendale Ave., Glendale, 818–241–4151).

CLUBS, ETC.

Jazz in Los Angeles goes through cycles, and it's on a heady upswing now. Several recently opened venues, including **Steamers** in Fullerton, the **Jazz Spot** in the Los Feliz district, **Charlie O's** in the San Fernando Valley, and the **Knitting Factory** in Hollywood have added flair to the scene, which is based around such solidly established clubs as the **Catalina Bar & Grill** and **Jazz Bakery**. Lesser venues which are also important include the **Baked Potato** (both locations), the **World Stage, Jax, Lunaria,** and **Miceli's**.

National blues artists are booked into **B. B. King's Blues Club** and the **Blues Café**. Top spots for local artists include **Babe and Ricky's, Harvelle's,** and **Starboard Attitude**.

Among the many fine Los Angeles–based jazz musicians who regularly play the city are saxophonists Harold Land, Ralph Moore, Teddy Edwards, Doug Webb, Bob Sheppard, and Chuck Manning; trumpeters Sal Marquez, Jack Sheldon, and Bobby Bradford; pianists Billy Childs, Bill Cunliffe, Gerald Wiggins, and George Gaffney; guitarists Doug McDonald and John Pisano; bassists Dave Carpenter, Tony Dumas, Luther Hughes, and Bob Maize; and drummers Paul Kreibich, John Guerin, and Roy McCurdy. First-rate area big bands include Bill Holman's big band, the Clayton-Hamilton Jazz Orchestra, Gerald Wilson's Orchestra, Frank Capp's Juggernaut, Bob Florence's Limited Edition, and Chuck Flores' big band.

Blues and R&B talent worth looking out for include Guitar Shorty, Johnny Dyer, J. J. "Bad Boy" Jones and his Bad Boys, the Bernie Pearl Blues Band, Finis Tasby, South Side Slim, and Bill Clarke & the Mighty Balls of Fire.

Generally speaking, music in L.A. stops at 2 A.M.

Personal Choices

Best national jazz clubs: *Catalina's, Jazz Bakery*
Best sound: *Catalina's*
Best jazz surprise: *Charlie O's*
Best neighborhood jazz spots: *World Stage, Money Tree*

Best national blues club: *B. B. King's*
Best neighborhood blues club: *Babe and Ricky's*

FOR JAZZ

Catalina Bar & Grill, 1640 N. Cahuenga Blvd., Hollywood, 323–466–2210, www.catalinajazzclub.com.

Intimate and warm, the refurbished Catalina's has peach-colored walls adorned with jazz photography, sconce lighting, and a darn good sound system. All tables face the stage and there's good viewing from most spots. This is Los Angeles' premier jazz room: everyone from Art Blakey and McCoy Tyner to Tom Harrell and Hank Jones have played here. The policy of booking one touring band for six nights is not set in stone and sometimes such local artists as ace singer Barbara Morrison and Latin jazz advocate Bobby Matos get a weekend. There are a few seats at the back bar, but the tables offer the better listening experience.

Music: nightly. *Cover/minimum*: $$$-$$$$. *Food*: Continental. Reservations recommended.

Jazz Bakery, 3233 Helms Ave., Culver City, 310–271–9039, www.thejazzbakery.com.

More a small concert hall than a club, the Jazz Bakery is one of the best places in town to hear jazz. Located in a clean, well-lit, high-ceilinged space that was once part of the Helms Bakery garage, it's set up with rows of plastic patio chairs (seating 180), and there's no talking or smoking allowed. A small café in the lobby serves sandwiches and drinks, including mineral water, sodas, beer, wine, and espresso.

The Bakery is the brainchild of singer Ruth Price. Some of the many who have played here include Nicholas Payton, Tommy Flanagan, Abbey Lincoln, and Benny Golson.

Music: nightly. *Cover/minimum:* $$-$$$. *Food:* snack bar. Reservations recommended.

Charlie O's, 13725 Victory Blvd., Van Nuys, 818–994–3058.

Run by lifelong jazz fan Charlie Ottaviano, Charlie O's is a friendly restaurant that recently added music, becoming an intimate yet casual listening room like you might find in Manhattan or Chicago. The featured artists, all pretty much of the mainstream-minded variety and, so far, all deserving locals, have included bass great John Heard's trio, renowned drummer Earl Palmer, ex–Frank Sinatra guitarist Ron Anthony, and such saxophone aces as Pete Christlieb and Bill Perkins. L.A. has needed a good, no-nonsense, straight-ahead spot, and Charlie O's fits the bill perfectly.

Music: M, Sa. *Cover/minimum*: $-$$. *Food*: American. Reservations recommended.

Steamers Café, 138 W. Commonwealth Ave., Fullerton, 714–871–8800.

A lively, narrow club with the bandstand all the way at the back, Terrence Love's Steamers is a real jazz joint, and one that always seems to be packed. Good swinging sounds are on tap seven nights, with heavyweights like Joey DeFrancesco, Charles McPherson, Herb Geller, and Jeff Hamilton bolstering a line-up of local first-raters like Ron Eschete, Dewey Erney, Tom Ranier, and Susie Hansen. It's a very pleasant, engaging atmosphere in which to listen, and if you can't get inside, Love has a sound system that pipes the goods out into the street.

Music: nightly. *Cover/minimum*: $$-$$$. *Food*: Continental. Reservations recommended.

The Jazz Spot in the Los Feliz Restaurant, 2138 Hillhurst Ave., Los Feliz district, 323–666–8666.

This new club, located in a quiet room off a fine restaurant, is the dream child of Rick Clemente and Jim Britt, a singer and co-founder of the original Jazz Bakery (it was held in his studio). Behind glass-paneled doors that seal out almost all of the restaurant-bar's bubbly chatter are 70 seats in an open space facing a large stage. Since opening in early 2000, the Spot has been home to such talents as Bob Brookmeyer, Dave Frishberg, Bob Dorough, Ben Sidran, Ernie Andrews, Stephanie Haynes, and Jon Mayer. Sound is usually aces.

Music: Tu-Sa. *Cover*: $$-$$$. *Food*: California-Continental. Reservations recommended.

Baked Potato, 3787 Cahuenga Blvd., N. Hollywood, 818–980–1615, www.thebakedpotato.com.

Once a very famous contemporary club where Larry Carlton and Lee Ritenour started on their roads to fame, the Baked is more obscure these days but still presents a lot of very solid music. The atmosphere hasn't changed much: the place is small with tables close together, which means an intimate performance each time out, and the menu still offers large Idaho spuds with darn near everything you can think of stuffed inside them. The musical bill of fare is a mix of jazz/fusion and R&B/funk, with the occasional L.A. or even New York–based modern mainstream outfit featured (Chick Corea bassist Avishai Cohen, for one). Owner Don Randi's band Quest still plays several weekend nights a month.

Music: nightly. *Cover/minimum*: $$-$$$. *Food*: stuffed potatoes. Reservations recommended.

The Baked Potato Hollywood, 6266 1/2 Sunset Blvd., Hollywood, 323–461–6400.

This second Baked, owned by Don Randi's son, Justin, is like its predecessor, with the same spuds and a similar though slightly higher-marquee-value lineup. It's just a bit larger is all. Good for the edgy contemporary sound, with people like Bunny Brunel, Andy Summers, and Allan Holdsworth on tap.

Music: nightly. *Cover/minimum:* $$-$$$. *Food:* stuffed potatoes. Reservations recommended.

Knitting Factory, 7021 Hollywood Blvd., Hollywood, 323–463–0204, www.knittingfactory.com.

A classy, modern version of the original New York Knit, the Hollywood branch officially opened in September 2000. It has a large main stage with a beautiful wooden floor, metal appointments, and a high ceiling. It seats about 100, with standing room for another 100, and there's additional room on the second level. The Factory has played host to all manner of jazz folk, from avant-gardists like Dave Douglas, the Sun Ra Arkestra directed by Marshall Allen, and the Tin Hat Trio, to more mainstream purveyors like saxophonist Charles Lloyd. The small, adjacent AlterKnit Lounge can squeeze in maybe 75 people and presents such names as Art Davis and Sal Marquez.

Music: Tu-Su. *Cover/minimum:* $$-$$$. *Food:* varied. Reservations recommended.

Lunaria, 10351 Santa Monica Blvd. (between Beverly Hills and Venice), 310–282–8870, www.lunariajazzscene.com.

A large and sophisticated restaurant with a lounge that features jazz and other related musics, Lunaria, with its big open dining room, can be delightful. The French-based cuisine is first-rate and, often, so is the music. Such folks as Jack Sheldon, Conrad Janis, Sweet Baby Ja'I, and Linda Hopkins are regulars. The décor spotlights pastel colors and pleasing-to-the-eye lithographs.

Music: Tu.-Sa. *Cover/minimum:* $$-$$$. *Food:* French continental. Reservations recommended.

La Ve Lee, 12514 Ventura Blvd., Studio City, 818–980–8158.

This low-ceilinged, cozy, and hardly fancy joint mostly plays host to a variety of Latin sounds, from classic Afro-Cuban to Latin-funk and Brazilian. Occasionally, there's a steaming jazz/fusion band. Owner Eddie Arby has a feeling for the musicians and they seem to return it with often-stunning performances. Since it's small, the room guarantees intimacy; couples particularly enjoy the low-level lighting and candle-lit tables. Top-drawer musicians, from Poncho Sanchez and Frank Gambale to Dori Caymmi and Katia Moraes, hold forth here.

Music: Tu-Sa. *Cover/minimum*: $$-$$$. *Food*: Mediterranean. Reservations recommended.

World Stage, 4344 Degnan Blvd., Leimert Park–Crenshaw District, South Central, 323–293–2451.

A no-frills, community-based musicians' and poets' collective, the World Stage was started up in 1989 by drummer Billy Higgins, poet-writer Kamau Daa'ood, and organizer Dawan Muhammad. Since then, it has presented music workshops and performances by many jazz legends, including Elvin Jones, Barry Harris, Harold Land, Cedar Walton, and Max Roach, all of whom have donated their time to talk to the community and instruct its youth.

All workshops and concerts, usually held on the weekends, are open to the public for a nominal fee, and they're great opportunities to hear both big names and up-and-coming talent. The Stage is a small, friendly, and informal place, simply equipped with rows of yellow chairs and a raised stage. No food or drinks are served, and there's plenty of free and secure parking outside.

Music: F and Sa nights, Sa afternoons; call for other times. *Donation:* $.

The Money Tree, 10149 Riverside Dr., Toluca Lake, 818–752–8383.

This studio hangout—near Universal, Warner Brothers, and Disney—is back with a jazz policy on most nights. The room is noisy—the bar patrons chat it up pretty good—but the quality of the music tends to be high. Jack Sheldon and Ross Tompkins, trumpeter Stacy Rowles, and Paul Kreibich's Jazz Coop have appeared here recently.

Music: nightly. *Cover/minimum*: $. *Food*: Continental.

Monteleone's West, 19337 Ventura Blvd., Tarzana, 818–996–0662.

A genuine supper club tucked into the West San Fernando Valley, Monteleone's is run by Tom Monteleone, who insists that pianists keep their drinks off his shiny, in-tune baby grand, and that the singers and bands bring in a crowd. Usually, the latter policy works. The room is small and has good sound, perfect for the vocalists that are the major fare. Both jazz singers like Julie Kelly and Pamala Feener and pop-leaning vocalists are heard, and the renowned Pete Jolly Trio plays once a month.

Music: nightly. *Cover/minimum*: $$-$$$. *Food*: Continental. Reservations recommended.

Miceli's, 1646 N. Las Palmas Ave., Hollywood, 323–466–3438.

The bar area of this quaint but friendly Italian restaurant is given over to easy listening jazz seven nights a week. Nothing too heady goes on, but it's usually fun. The house pianist is Brian O'Rourke, who can definitely make the ivories come to life. Singer Jimmy Spencer is another regular.

Music: nightly. *Cover/minimum*: $-$$. *Food*: Italian.

The Living Room, 2636 Crenshaw Blvd. (South Central L.A.), 323–735–8748.

A cozy red room with red lights, a modern bar, and a small step-up stage, the Living Room is the kind of place that from the outside looks like just a place, but inside . . . ah, inside! Cornets and saxes overwhelm you with blasts of crazy notes circling through the air. An ultracool cat in a hat and dark gray suit wails away on alto sax, while a man with a wired flute blows in from far back near the bar. Everyone knows everyone at the Living Room, a neighborhood institution owned by Barbie Bostick. Jazz is usually featured about once a week, while on Sunday nights, Miss Mickey Champion holds down an open mike blues show.

Music: jazz varies, blues Su. *No cover.*

The Townhouse, 6835 La Tijera Blvd., Ladera Heights, 310–649–0091.

An upscale restaurant-club in a middle-class African-American neighborhood, the Townhouse is large, friendly, and multiroomed, with live music every night of the week. Vocalist Barbara Morrison is a regular, along with bluesman King Ernest. A jazz champagne brunch, followed by a jam session, is served on Sunday afternoons. Located only five minutes from LAX, the Townhouse is a favorite stopping-off spot among celebrities passing through town; Stevie Wonder, Chaka Khan, Don King, Daryl Strawberry, Nancy Wilson, and Dionne Warwick are among the many who have done so.

Music: nightly. *Cover:* $. *Food:* American.

Also

The **Cat & Fiddle Pub** (6530 Sunset Blvd., Hollywood, 323–468–3800) is a lively, rambling joint with an outside garden that features mainstream jazz on Sunday nights. The **Loew's Santa Monica Beach Hotel** (1700 Ocean Ave., 310–458–6700) features first-class musicians in its lobby lounge, while the **Cinegrill** in the grand Art Deco Hollywood Roosevelt Hotel (7000 Hollywood Blvd., 323–466–7000) also offers jazz on occasion. **La Louisanne** (5812 Overhill Dr., Ladera Heights, 323–293–5073) is an upscale African-American restaurant that presents jazz most weekends.

The **Bicycle Shop Café** (12217 Wilshire Blvd., West L.A., 310–826–7831) has jazz on Fridays and Saturdays. The **Atlas Supper Club** (3760 Wilshire Blvd., L.A., 213–380–8400) offers jazz on occasional nights. **Hal's Bar & Grill** (1349 Abbot Kinney Blvd., Venice, 310–396–3105) brings in solid bands Sundays and Mondays.

Located around the corner from the World Stage is **Fifth Street Dick's Coffee Company** (3335 W. 43rd Pl., Leimert Park, 323–296–3970), a long, neat, and narrow cafe with stools, paintings, posters, and a sidewalk patio. The place lost its founder when Richard Fulton passed away, but it still cooks. The schedule is erratic; call ahead.

Other decent jazz spots north and south of the city include **Jax** (339 Brand Blvd., Glendale, 818–504–1604), where straight-ahead is on tap a couple nights a week; **Hollywood Park Casino** (3883 Century Blvd., Inglewood, 310–330–2800), which hosts an "After Work Cool Down" with name artists on Tuesdays; **The Grapevine** (2110 W. Redondo Beach Blvd., Torrance, 310–366–6888), which hosts luminaries like John Heard, Sal Marquez, and the Littleton Brothers Thursdays through Saturdays; **M Bar/Grill** (213-A Pine Ave., Long Beach, 562–435–2525), home to avant-garde and experimental stuff as well as the occasional mainstream band; **Mr. B's Restaurant-Lounge** (1333 Hollywood Way, Burbank, 818–845–1800), where the occasional jazz act slips in between the pop and lounge folks; and **Geri's World Coffee House** (3425 W. Cahuenga Blvd., Universal City, 323–851–1350, ext. 127), where Friday night is jazz night.

Way north, about 240 miles to be exact, in Cambria, on the central California coast about 30 miles inland from San Luis Obispo, sits the **Hamlet Gardens at Moonstone Beach** (Hwy. One, Cambria, 805–927–3535). Here, vibist Charlie Shoemake and his wife, singer Sandi Shoemake, hold bi-weekly jazz Sundays, featuring a gang of name jazz players. Among them are Harold Land, Charles McPherson, Pete Christlieb, Joe Magnarelli, and Bruce Forman.

FOR BLUES

B. B. King's Blues Club, 1000 Universal Center Dr., Universal City, 818–6-BBKING.

It's a pity B. B.'s busy schedule doesn't allow him to play here more often than he does—his two or three stops each year are always standing room only. Because the club is located in the bustling Universal CityWalk, it shares parking facilities with sixteen movie theaters and the Universal Studios Tour, making parking something of a challenge. And largely because of the tourists who throng CityWalk day and night, B. B.'s rarely needs to worry about getting a good crowd. The three-story place seats between 250 and 400 (tall but small, as B. B. once said), and there isn't a bad seat in the house. On the menu is Southern soul food, and there are three bars, one on each floor. Weeknight bookings tend to be local bands, headliners come in on weekends, and Sundays feature a noon-time gospel brunch.

Music: nightly. *Cover*: $$$. *Food*: southern.

Babe and Ricky's, 4339 Leimert Blvd., Leimert Park, 323-295–9112.

Formerly located on famed Central Avenue, this landmark club owned by Miss Laura Gross was forced to move to Leimert Park after the "Rodney King riots" caused the area to become more dangerous and drug-ridden. The new venue contains many mementos of the old, with posters and photos adorning the walls, and Ms. Gross continues to be a second mother to many of South Central's younger players. There's a great juke box, and live music six nights a week. The bar serves beer and wine, and when the kitchen is open (always on weekends, sometimes on weeknights), the delicious smell of barbecue wafts through the small room as the tight house band, Bill Clark and the Mighty Balls of Fire, provides terrific back-up for whichever visiting musicians drop by.

Music: W-M. *Cover*: $. *Food*: barbecue.

Blue Cafe, 210 The Promenade, Long Beach, 562-983–7111.

Catering to a younger crowd, this beachfront club has helped put Long Beach on the blues map. Local bands are always on the bill, and touring national artists come in on the weekends. Unlike most area clubs, which are open only at night, this spot has blues bands playing from noon onward on weekends, and from 5:30 P.M. onward on weeknights. In addition to the music, they have thirteen pool tables and a large (and often loud) outdoor patio.

Music: nightly, Sa-Su afternoons. *Cover*: $$. *Food*: burgers, salads, etc.

Cafe Boogaloo, 1230 Hermosa Ave., Hermosa Beach, 310–318–2324.

This is an intimate, funky, and casual place, with live music five nights a week in the winter and nightly during the summer months. The menu is Louisiana-influenced, and dinner is served from 5–11 P.M. The musical fare is the usual mix of strong local talent on weeknights and somewhat bigger names on the weekends.

Music: most nights. *Cover*: $$. *Food*: Louisiana.

Harvelle's, 1432 Fourth St., Santa Monica, 310–395–1676.

A West Side music nightspot since 1931, this casual venue fitted with a heavy wooden bar and high ceiling fans became famous among local bands as the starting place for Keb' Mo', who played here (as Kevin Moore) every Tuesday night for several years until his big break came. The club's Monday night blues jam, hosted by L. J. & the Blues Factory, is one of the longest-running gigs in town. Come early on the weekends, as there can be long lines waiting to get in.

Music: nightly. *Cover*: $$.

Starboard Attitude, 202 The Pier, Redondo Beach, 310–379–5144.

As the South Bay's oldest blues club, in business since 1980, Starboard Attitude was home for over a decade to William Clarke & the Night Owls, which later became the William Clarke Band. Nowadays, a rotating roster of local blues players is featured, and there are four huge TV screens for sports fans. If you get there early enough, you'll catch beautiful views of the sun setting over the ocean.

Music: Tu-Su. *No cover.*

Cozy's Bar & Grill, 14058 Ventura Blvd., Sherman Oaks, 818–986–6000.

A haven for local acts, this club serves up a solid mix of blues and booze in a casual atmosphere.

Music: M-Sa. *Cover*: $$.

House of Blues Sunset Strip, 8430 Sunset Blvd., West Hollywood, 323–848–5100.

Despite its name, this link in a chain of national clubs almost never books any actual blues. Among the acts that have appeared here in recent months are Nancy Sinatra, Tom Jones, Duran Duran, King Crimson, The Tragically Hip . . . well, you get the idea. About once a month or so, a blues act will pop up in their ads; usually someone safe and sure, like Etta James, Bobby Bland, or Koko Taylor. Admission, food, and drink prices are astronomical, and the staff is either rude or indifferent. On Sundays, there's a gospel brunch.

Music: most nights, very occasional blues. *Cover*: $$$$. *Food*: American.

Also

At one time a jazz mecca, the **Lighthouse** (30 Pier Ave., Hermosa Beach, 310–372–6911) now tends to book mostly rock bands. However, there's usually an open blues jam one night a week (Tuesdays or Wednesdays).

A guitar store by day, **McCabe's** (3101 W. Pico Blvd., Santa Monica, 310–828–4497) is usually an acoustic folk room, but folk-based blues does occasionally sneak in. In the club's heyday, it booked Brownie McGhee & Sonny Terry, Memphis Slim, and Libba Cotten; more recently they've hosted Dave Van Ronk, John Hammond, Geoff Muldaur, and Doug Mac-Leod.

At one time an all-blues room, the **Mint** (6010 W. Pico Blvd., Mid City L.A., 323–954–9630) has shifted over almost exclusively to rock. But once in awhile you still get lucky; Alligator Records has hosted release parties here for Shemekia Copeland, among others.

The **Tea House** (25318 Crenshaw Blvd., Torrance, 310–326–5420) is a cozy restaurant offering local blues, R&B, and soul several nights a week. Blues can also be heard on Mondays in the **Living Room** (see "For Jazz," above).

Other Venues and Special Events

In addition to **Playboy Jazz Festival,** which is the biggest jazz fest in town (see "Major Festivals" page 458), there's the two-day **Simon Rodeo Music and Arts Festival,** held near Watts Towers at the end of July; the **Day of the Drum** festival, held in late September; the three-day **Long Beach Jazz Festival** (562–436–7794), held in August; the **Jazz Trax** fest held on Catalina Island in October (619–233–3722 or 800–866–TRAX); the two-day **Long Beach Blues Festival** (562–985–5566), held in September; and the one-day **Big Time Blues Festival** (562–426–0761), held every July in small, private Gemmrig Park in Long Beach. **Blues cruises** leave from Long Beach several times a year. For details on these and other special events, check the local papers.

The outdoor **Hollywood Bowl** (2301 N. Highland Ave., 323–851–2000), where the Playboy Jazz Festival takes place and where Art Tatum gave his last major performance, hosts a jazz series in the summer. Nationally known jazz and blues figures also occasionally appear at the **Greek Theater** in North Hollywood (2700 N. Vermont Ave., 323–665–1927).

Radio

KLON/88.1 FM (562–985–5566, WWW.klon.org). A 24-hour jazz station. Affiliated with California State University, Long Beach. Blues weekend afternoons.
KJAZ/1260 & 540 AM (310–478–5540). A 24-hour, mainstream, commercial jazz outlet.
KPFK/90.7FM (818–985–2711). L.A.'s Pacifica radio outlet. Blues, R&B, and jazz, M-F, 8–11 P.M.

Record Stores

Rhino Records (1720 Westwood Blvd., 310–474–8685) and **Poo Bah Records** (1101 E. Walnut, Pasadena, 626–449–3359) carry good selections of both jazz and blues, while the Sunset Strip branch of **Tower Records** (8801 W. Sunset Blvd., 310–657–7300) and **Aron's Record Shop** (1150 N. Highland, 323–469–4700) are good spots for jazz.

For used CDs and LPs, try **Atomic Records** (3818 W. Magnolia Blvd., Burbank, 818–848–7090), which has some of the best rare jazz LPs anywhere in the U.S., and **Record Surplus** (11609 W. Pico Blvd., West L.A., 310–478–4217), which specializes in variety and low prices.

SAN FRANCISCO/EAST BAY

Updated by Philip Elwood (jazz) and
Joseph Jordan (blues)

Prior to World War II, few people thought of San Francisco as either a jazz or blues town. Touring swing bands passed through the city's big hotels, major African-American entertainers appeared at Slim Jenkins's place in Oakland, and the Fillmore District boasted a few jazz-blues clubs (including what is now John Lee Hooker's Boom Boom Room, see page 429) but there was little home-grown talent, largely because San Francisco had virtually no black population.

Then came World War II, and the growth of the shipyards, and suddenly a tremendous influx of African-American workers arrived from Texas and the rural South. Many settled across the Bay in Oakland and Richmond (East Bay), and soon a black entertainment strip developed down the street from Slim Jenkins's Place. Jenkins continued to run the premier nightclub in town, attracting both blacks and whites to hear such stars as Dinah Washington, Earl Hines, and Ivory Joe Hunter (who wrote "Seventh Street Boogie" in its tribute), but now there were also smaller, rougher places offering a more raw, more mournful blues.

Lowell Fulson, Pee Wee Crayton, Jimmy McCracklin, and Jimmy Wilson were among the new arrivals, many of whom were eventually recorded by Bob Geddins, an African American also from Texas, who had started up a record company in Oakland in 1945. Geddins, who called his business Big Town Recordings, would scour the local clubs and churches looking for talent, and then record them on acetate disc in his garage-like shop at Eighth and Chestnut streets.

The Oakland blues scene peaked in the mid- to late-1960s. In the late '70s, however, according to East Bay blues writer Lee Hildebrand, the music again came to life through a new generation of artists: Sonny Rhodes, J. J. Malone, Troyce Key (see Eli's Mile High Club & Restaurant, page 430), Frankie Lee, and Bobby Murray. Clubs were packed once more, this time with young middle-class whites and blacks, as well as with the older black working class.

Jazz in the Bay Area took a somewhat different route. "San Francisco's biggest contribution to jazz is traditional jazz," says Philip Elwood, longtime critic for the *San Francisco Examiner.* He goes on to point to trombonist Turk Murphy and Lu Watters and his Yerba Buena Jazz Band, both of whom brought about the revival of the New Orleans sound in the 1940s. Traditional jazz continues to play a role in the Bay Area today: every Memorial Day weekend, the world's largest Dixieland and swing festival, the Sacramento Dixieland Jubilee, takes place near here, drawing over 100 bands (see "Major Festivals," page 458).

The '50s and '60s were also particularly fertile times for jazz in San Francisco. Small clubs were flourishing all over the city, including the Blackhawk, where Art Tatum played one of his last residencies; the Jazz Workshop, where Cannonball Adderley recorded with his quintet; the Club Hangover, where Earl Hines performed; Earthquake McGoon's, where Turk Murphy's trad-jazz band played for 20 years; and Bop City, where Dexter Gordon and Sonny Criss once played. Cool jazz proponents Dave Brubeck and Paul Desmond, and jazz/Latin/rock musician Carlos Santana were three of the best-known artists to emerge during this period, along with vibraphonist Cal Tjader, who was later known for his Latin jazz, and pianist-composer Vince Guaraldi.

A mural commemorates the jazz clubs that once packed San Francisco's North Beach.

The last of the legendary San Francisco jazz clubs was the Keystone Korner, which opened in 1972 and closed in the early '80s. Bay Area jazz fans still mention it with a sigh.

Sources

Excellent listings can be found in two free weeklies, the *San Francisco Bay Guardian* (415–255–3100, www.sfbayguardian.com) and the *San Francisco Weekly* (415–541–0700, www.sfweekly.com). The Sunday Datebook, or "Pink Section," of the *San Francisco Chronicle* (415–777–1111, www.sfgate.com/chronicle) and the *East Bay Express* (510–540–7400, www.eastbayexpress.com) also have superb listings.

Radio station KCSM runs a daily Jazzline at 415–808–5000, ext. 7855. Traditional jazz events are listed on the New Orleans Jazz Club of Northern California hotline, 415–398–NOJC or www.nojcnc.org.

For maps and other information, contact the San Francisco Visitor Information Center on the lower level of Hallidie Plaza, 900 Market St. at Powell St., 415–391–2000, www.sfvisitor.org.

A Note on Neighborhoods

Built on the hills of San Francisco Bay, San Francisco is a compact city of neighborhoods. Fisherman's Wharf is the famous tourist area on the waterfront to the north; North Beach is an old Italian neighborhood filled with cafés, restaurants, art galleries, and music clubs.

The Mission District, southwest of the Civic Center, is the center of the Latin community. It's filled with restaurants, cafes, saloons, clubs, and little theaters. The SOMA (South of Market St.) district, the fastest-redeveloping area of the city, has a dozen dance clubs (some private), some all-purpose rock/jazz rooms, a number of upscale restaurants, and the Pac Bell baseball park. The Embarcadero, or waterfront area, is also home to a number of restaurants and cafes, many of which feature music.

Across the Bay from San Francisco, connected by the Bay Bridge, are the East Bay communities, including Oakland, Richmond, Berkeley, and Emeryville. Oakland is the farthest south of the four; Richmond, the farthest north. Berkeley is the liberal community that's home to the University of California; Emeryville is a commercial district along the freeway. West Oakland and Richmond are home to large African-American communities.

Traveling across the bay, unless you're driving during rush hour, takes about 15 minutes. Driving in San Francisco can be tricky for those not accustomed to stopping on steep hills, and parking most anywhere in the city is often difficult. The city's BART (Bay Area Rapid Transit) transportation system, which extends to the East Bay, is excellent.

Landmarks and Legends

San Francisco

(With the exception of St. John's, the following sites can be toured on foot. The route starts downtown near the Civic Center and proceeds north, past Nob Hill to North Beach.)

Blackhawk, Turk and Hyde Sts. (near Civic Center).

The Blackhawk's big years were the '50s, when an astonishing number of the big names in jazz paraded through its "disreputable" quarters. Dave Brubeck's quartet, including drummer Cal Tjader, opened the joint (whose owner, Guido Caccienti, admitted was a "dump") in 1949. Red Norvo, with Charles Mingus, followed, and for the next decade, Miles Davis, Gerry Mulligan, Chet Baker, all the "West Coast Jazz" gang, Erroll Garner, Oscar Peterson, the Jazztet, Art Tatum, Anita O'Day, Johnny Hodges' band (with John Coltrane), and dozens of other greats played the room. Johnny Mathis was the entertainment during the Sunday-matinee, jam-session intermissions.

Dawn Club, 20 Annie St.

During the 1920s, 20 Annie St. was a notorious speakeasy, where ladies of the night picked their customers' pockets and hid their empty wallets in niches in the walls. When the building was renovated a number of years ago, workmen came across numerous samples of the ladies' spoils.

During the 1940s, number 20 became home base for Lu Watters and his Yerba Buena Jazz Band. Watters, who was also a professional chef, would cook out back and play his trumpet up front. As the music changed in the late '40s, however, he retired from performing for good and went to work as a cook for the Sonoma State Hospital.

Club Hangover, 729 Bush St. (downtown).

Now a gay moviehouse with a façade of mock gray stone, No. 729 once housed the Club Hangover, owned by Doc Dougherty. During the late '40s and early '50s, Marty Marsala, Turk Murphy, Ralph Sutton, George Lewis, Muggsy Spanier, Joe Sullivan, Jack Teagarden, and others played here regularly, and Louis Armstrong played a couple of one-nighters with his all stars, too. In 1952, Earl Hines was hired to front the house Dixieland band.

"When I got there," he says in *The World of Earl Hines,* "I saw all these elderly guys sitting around, and I said to the owner, 'Doc, when're you going to have the rehearsal? Where are the musicians?'

"'They're all here,' he said.

"'My goodness, what is this?' I thought as I looked at them."

Nonetheless, the arrangement worked out well, and Hines's initial eight-week engagement was extended first to three months and then to six. He moved his family out to San Francisco, bought a home in Oakland, and eventually ended up staying with the Hangover for seven years.

Grace Cathedral, 1051 Taylor St., near California St. (Nob Hill), 415–776–6611.

Duke Ellington presented his first concert of sacred music in the impressive Episcopal Grace Cathedral atop Nob Hill on September 16, 1965. Though he was filled with trepidation before-hand, the event met with widespread critical acclaim.

Two more Ellington concerts were later held here, and Turk Murphy's band played the cathedral every year. More recently, in 2000, Jim Cullum's band (from San Antonio) played a jazz mass here, and the San Francisco Jazz Festival has used the sanctuary for annual concerts since the early 1990s.

Jazz Workshop, 473 Broadway (North Beach).

During the 1950s and '60s, many bop and free-jazz musicians, including John Coltrane and Ornette Coleman, worked in this space, known at the turn of the century as the Hi-Ball, a club which also presented various bands. Cannonball Adderley and Charles Mingus both recorded albums here.

Keystone Korner, NW corner of Vallejo and Stockton Streets, next to the S.F. Police Dept.'s North Station (North Beach).

Now a Chinese mom-and-pop store, the Keystone was one of the most important jazz clubs around during the 1970s and early '80s, when it was known for its fine acoustics and appreciative audiences. A number of recordings were made here, including *In This Korner* by Art Blakey and his Jazz Messengers, and NPR broadcast a show from the club every New Year's Eve as part of its coast-to-coast celebration.

St. John's African Orthodox Church, 351 Divisadero St. (near Oak), 415–673–3572.

A small, storefront orthodox Catholic church, St. John's canonized John Coltrane about ten years ago. "Every Sunday, we take his music and put the liturgy on top of it," says Bishop F. W. King. "It's a beautiful, beautiful thing." One of St. John's priests, Father James Haven, is also a reedman, and the church has a small memorial band called Ohnedaruth that plays both during the services and at jam sessions around the city.

Services: Su, 11:45 A.M.

West Oakland

Seventh Street, from Wood to Broadway.

During the 1940s, Seventh Street was the center of African-American music in the Bay Area. Today, however, it is a sad and empty place, lined with nothing more than boarded-up storefronts and empty lots.

Esther's Breakfast Club, 1724 Seventh St., 415–451–5069.

One of the only remaining Seventh Street establishments is Esther's Breakfast Club, once located across the street from its present site and called at first Esther's Cocktail Lounge and then Esther's Orbit Room. Opened by Texan Esther Mabry in 1950, the lounge presented many of the greatest R&B and soul stars of the day: Lou Rawls, Joe Turner, Pee Wee Crayton, Lowell Fulson, Etta James, and Al Green.

Today Esther's no longer offers live music, but a deejay does sometimes spin records at the large, neat club on the weekends. Esther and/or her husband Bill are usually somewhere on the premises.

CLUBS, ETC.

San Francisco has a reputation for a lively jazz scene, but reality does not measure up to hearsay; as usual, jazz must be sought out. The blues scene, however, is considerably healthier, with a number of clubs featuring blues every night of the week.

The only area jazz clubs currently maintaining an all-jazz schedule are **Jazz At Pearl's** in San Francisco and **Yoshi's** in Oakland. Two world-class blues clubs, booking both national acts and top local talent, are **John Lee Hooker's Boom Boom Room** and **Biscuits and Blues**, winner of a W. C. Handy Award. Meanwhile, **Eli's Mile High Club** and **Bluesville** carry on the proud Oakland blues tradition.

Locally based jazz talent to watch out for include Bobby Hutcherson, John Handy, Larry Vuckovich, Eddie Marshall, Vince Lateano, Mark Levine, Bruce Forman, Ed Kelly, Jules Broussard, Allen Smith, Mel Martin, Harvey Wainapel, Dave Ellis, Will Bernard, and Ralph Carney. Top jazz singers include Denise Perrier, Kim Nalley, Paula West, and Faye Carrol; top jazz bands include Marcus Shelby and the Hot Club of San Francisco, and Lavay Smith & the Red Hot Skillet Lickers.

Blues talent to watch out for includes piano player-songwriter Jimmy McCracklin; singer-guitarists Joe Louis Walker (in the Robert Cray style) and Mark Hummel; vocalist Brenda Boykin; Eli's Mile High All Stars; Bobby Reed & Surprize; Maurice McKinnies & The Galaxy Band; Mark Naftalin; Johnny Nitro & the Doorslammers; Ron Hacker & the Hacksaws; Larry Holmes & Blues Express, and the Johnny Nocturne Band (with four saxes). Also keep an eye out for more recently minted stars Chris Cain, Rusty Zinn, Tommy Castro, Sy Klopps, Steve Freund, Sista Monica, and Alvin Youngblood Hart, a recent transplant from Mississippi. Superstars Bonnie Raitt, Charlie Musselwhite, and John Lee Hooker live in the area as well, and occasionally perform.

Generally speaking, clubs close at 2 A.M.

Personal Choices

Best jazz clubs: *Yoshi's, Jazz at Pearl's*
Best San Francisco blues clubs: *Biscuits and Blues, John Lee Hooker's Boom Boom Room*
Best Oakland blues joints: *Bluesville, Eli's Mile High Club*
Best soul-blues club: *Fifth Amendment*
Best one-of-a-kind concert room: *Bach Dancing & Dynamite Society*
Best eclectic clubs: *Café du Nord, Ashkenaz*

FOR JAZZ

San Francisco

Jazz at Pearl's, 256 Columbus Ave. (North Beach), 415–291–8255.

Pearl is Pearl Wong, who used to run a restaurant in Chinatown where musicians came to eat and jam after-hours after the famous Keystone Korner closed down. She's been at this favored location about ten years now and is still going strong, offering some of the best jazz in the city in an informal, wedge-shaped, basement club. Pearl's features primarily local jazz groups and soloists, with Mondays reserved for a star-packed big band, midweek nights for drummer Vince Lateano's trio and guests, and weekends for touring combos and soloists. The club is managed by Sonny Buxton, a TV and radio host/personality (now with KCSM).

Music: nightly. *No cover, $$ minimum*

Bruno's, 2389 Mission St. (Mission District), 415–648–7701.

A 1950s Italian restaurant and bar, with the décor to match, Bruno's has gradually evolved into a jazz hang-out, featuring both veteran and neophyte bands, soloists, and singers. It's crowded on the weeknights, jammed on the weekends, with young, vibrant audiences.

Music: M–Sa. *Cover:* none-$$. *Food:* Italian.

Café du Nord, 2170 Market St. (at Sanchez), 415–861–5016. www.cafedunord.com.

A hip cellar lounge, the Café du Nord attracts a young, boisterous crowd. Local talent ranging from jazz and blues to cabaret and rock-influenced acts perform nightly, and the club is home to Lavay Smith & the Red Hot Skillet Lickers. To one side is a long, often packed bar, to another a pool table. Excellent food is served.

Music: nightly. *Cover:* $.

Moose's, 1652 Stockton St. (North Beach), 415–989–7800.

Grand piano jazz can be found at this popular, upscale restaurant, in an area tucked between the crowded bar and dining room. Regulars include Jeanne Hoffman, Don Asher, Mike Lipskin, Mike Greensill, and Kevin Gibbs. Asher was the first "other room" pianist at the original hungry i—a famous club of the 1950s—and Hoffman's trio opened the Jazz Workshop at about the same time. Lipskin is nationally recognized for his stride piano styling; Greensill is a strong mainstream jazz pianist who sometimes accompanies his wife, singer Weslia Whitfield. During Moose's Sunday jazz matinees, even more fine piano jazz is presented, often compliments of such players as Lou Levy and Dave McKenna. Sometimes, though, the piano sounds are lost in the noise of the crowd.

Music: nightly, Su matinees. *No cover. Food*: American regional.

Also

What San Francisco lacks in bona fide jazz clubs, it makes up for (almost) in upscale restaurants, modest cafes, bistros, cabarets, and saloons presenting excellent jazz.

One of the country's best-known cabaret venues is the **Plush Room** (940 Sutter St., 415–885–2800), where some of the performers are jazz oriented; shows are often sold out. **The Blue Bar at the Black Cat** (501 Broadway, North Beach, 415–981–2233) is a popular restaurant-lounge with good local jazz acts, including singers, pianists, and combos.

Though its setting near the freeway, beneath 35-foot-high ceilings, is a bit weird, **Butterfly** (1710 Mission St., 415–864–5575, www.butterflysf.com) hosts some of the best Bay Area jazz musicians once a week. Cozy, friendly, off-the-beaten-track **Café Claude** (7 Claude Lane, downtown, 415–392–3515) presents piano trios and small combos in a bistro atmosphere.

Not far from the Black Cat and Pearl's is the popular **Enrico's** (504 Broadway, North Beach, 415–982–6223), a restaurant and saloon that squeezes a good cross-section of local jazz and pop acts into the small stage area against its back wall. A café extends out onto the sidewalk; this is about as San Francisco as you can get.

The comfortable **Jazz at 33** (Embarcadero at Pier 33, 415–788–4343) offers popular piano-based combos and singers in a wonderful waterfront setting. The friendly, noisy **Pier 23 Café** (Embarcadero at Pier 23, 415–362–5125) offers Sunday jazz brunches and Bay Area icon Ed Kelly's quartet on Thursdays, also in a waterfront setting.

Les Joullins Jazz Bistro (44 Ellis St., downtown, 415–397–5397) is a large room where you'll hear everything from excellent Dixie-swing to mainstream modern and bebop. Fine local combos play at **Shanghai 1930** (133 Stuart St., Embarcadero South, 415–896–5600), a very pleasant bar-lounge area in a rather elegant restaurant.

East Bay Communities

Yoshi's Restaurant & Jazz House, 510 Embarcadero West, Oakland, 510–238–9200, www.yoshis.com.

One of the finest jazz clubs in the nation, Yoshi's presents all the major jazz groups and solo stars by the week, for four-to-six night gigs. Meanwhile, early weeknights usually feature top Bay Area talent, often booked through Jazz in Flight, a nonprofit group that promotes local musicians.

Yoshi's sizeable stage looks out onto a semi-circular, tiered amphitheater area filled with tables and booths. Food service is available both in the Jazz House and in the main restaurant; on the menu is superb Japanese cuisine. Yoshi's is located in Jack London Square on the Oakland Estuary. Next door rises a large, five-story parking garage

Music: nightly. *Cover*: $$-$$$. *Food*: Japanese. Reservations essential for major acts.

Ashkenaz, 1317 San Pablo Ave., Berkeley, 510–525–5054, www.ashkenaz.com.

Originally established as a home-base for world-music dance enthusiasts and political mavericks (this is Berkeley, after all), Ashkenaz has since become a favorite venue for all kinds of fans for all kinds of music. It's a big place with a large dance floor that presents jazz, swing-jazz, Cuban bands, blues singers, R&B bands, African music of all types, Tex-Mex, Cajun, zydeco, and more. Often the crowd and dancehall atmosphere (to say nothing of the political tone of the place) seem as important as the music. Find a night when the music suits you, and come. You won't regret it. All ages welcome.

Music: Tu-Su. *Cover*: $$.

Freight & Salvage Coffee House, 1111 Addison St., Berkeley, 510–548–1761, www.thefreight.org.

The Freight began as a storefront folk music club about 1960, and although it moved to its current warehouse-like home years ago, it still has a coffee-tea-juice-cake-and-cookies atmosphere. The folk-music co-op often books string and swing jazz, local blues, and jazz legends, as well as contemporary folk. Large room, find sound, Berkeley-informal.

Music: nightly, some jazz and blues. *Cover:* $-$$$.

Kimball's East, 5800 Shellmound, EmeryBay Marketplace, Emeryville, 510–658–2555. www.kimballs.com.

What began as a fine upscale jazz supper club nearly went down the drain a few years ago, but recently, Kimball's, under new ownership, is showing signs of rebirth as an R&B, soul, occasional-jazz venue. In its heyday in the late '80s and early '90s, Kimball's headlined all the major jazz acts, from Herbie Hancock, Joe Henderson, Clark Terry, Illinois Jacquet, and Wayne Shorter to Nancy Wilson, Lou Rawls, and Nnenna Freelon. Dizzy Gillespie played his last notes at Kimball's East, collapsing on the stage in 1992. The club itself is an impressive place, with high ceilings, tiered seating for nearly 400, a dance floor, and a big concert stage. The fact that Emeryville has recently become a thriving commercial area— thanks to dot.com monies—has improved Kimball's chances of survival.

Music: Th-Su, some jazz and blues. *Cover:* $$$.

Bach Dancing and Dynamite Society, Douglas Beach House, Half Moon Bay, 650–726–4143 (22 miles south of San Francisco on Miramar Beach, in Half Moon Bay, off Highway 1).

"The best-kept secret in the world" is what Pete Douglas calls his Bach Dancing and Dynamite Society, and he could be right. Many Sunday afternoons for the past 30-plus years (though he's recently cut back to just a few concerts annually), Douglas has been presenting the best of jazz—both big name and local—in the best of settings—a high-ceilinged wood-paneled beach house overlooking the sea. As the musicians play on a stage up front surrounded by small stained glass windows, a fire crackles in the fireplace and waves lap the shore. No liquor is served, but there's always a buffet with wine before the show, and guests are welcome to bring their own picnics.

Douglas—a rugged white-haired man usually dressed in Levi's—lives in the dark wood beachhouse where he works, and he's put a lot of time and thought into his operation. Classical music is sometimes presented in his 95-seat concert hall as well.

The Dynamite Society began about 35 years ago, when Douglas and his friends used to hold musical beach parties on the sand, accompanied by food and considerable drink. At one such a gathering one Fourth of July, the group celebrated by igniting not fireworks, but a dynamite-like explosive—

much to the displeasure of local authorities. The gang then took the name "Dynamite Society" and moved their parties inside. Soon thereafter, in acknowledgment of Douglas' love for music, the "Bach Dancing and Dynamite Society" was born.

Music: some Su afternoons, call for schedule. *Cover:* $$.

The Baltic, 135 Park Place, Point Richmond, 510–235–2532.

Though not strictly a jazz club, the Baltic—currently in its 90th year—presents trad-jazz, jazz-blues, such bands as the Hot Club of San Francisco, and other exotic music on a fairly regular basis. This is a funky old place in a funky old town (essentially a suburb of Chevron's Richmond refinery) that is only gradually becoming part of the 21st century. A great place to hear music, too.

Music: some Su afternoons. *Cover:* $$. *Food:* simple buffet.

FOR BLUES

San Francisco

Biscuits and Blues, 401 Mason St. (at Geary), 415–292–2583.

Dynamic owner/booker Frank Klein has combined the best of down-home, Southern-style Delta cooking with a magnificent space in which to see nationally known musicians and the best of regional blues acts. The club's creative booking policy includes everything from "jam nights" and "acoustic blues weeks" to events that pay tribute to different instruments—"Guitar Masters Series," "Battle of the Harmonicas." Opened in 1995 in the heart of SF's renowned "Theater District," B&B is loud, cozy (capacity: 125), and below street level, with a dance floor directly in front of a wide but not-too-deep stage. Novena candles and unusual pieces of blues art adorn the walls inside; outside hang red shutters. The club is kid-friendly, though the music rarely starts before 9 P.M.

Music: nightly. *Cover:* $$. *Food:* Southern Delta.

John Lee Hooker's Boom Boom Room, 1601 Fillmore St. (at Geary), 415–673–8000. www.boomboomblues.com.

John Lee and his hard-working manager Alex Andreas have transformed the long-established drinking juke joint, Jack's Bar, into one of the most popular live music venues in the city. With good sounds seven nights a week, most of them blues and R&B, the Boom Boom Room is dark, small, and thoroughly enlivening. A small dance floor reigns in front of a tiny, red velvet-curtained stage, and the club features a full bar and fabulous black-and-white photos of blues greats. Big name touring acts are booked regularly and John Lee, the 80-plus-year-old patriarch of the Bay Area blues scene, has been known to play or at least sit in his permanently-reserved, best-seat-in-the-house, red leather booth adjacent to the dance floor.

Music: nightly. *Cover*: $$.

The Saloon, 1232 Grant Ave. (North Beach), 415–989–7666.

The oldest bar on record in San Francisco, the friendly, hole-in-the-wall Saloon features live music—mostly white R&B, with some blues, some rock—364 days of the year. It's closed on Christmas; everyone has to rest sometimes.

The original Saloon was called Wagner's Beer Hall and it was opened in 1861 by an Alsatian immigrant who also peddled beer in stone bottles on the street. Today, the Saloon, with its murky paintings, old wooden bar, and stained-glass windows, attracts an odd mix of long-haired, aging hipsters in leather and eager-faced tourists. The tiny dance floor is always densely packed, and there's usually a line out front on weekends waiting to get in.

Music: nightly; also Sa, Su, late afternoons. *Cover:* $.

Lou's Pier 47, 300 Jefferson St. (Fisherman's Wharf), 415–771–5687.

Though mostly a tourist spot, Lou's does present legitimate blues and R&B acts such as J. J. Malone and Mark Naftalin. Located on the second story of a long building with big windows overlooking the street, the room is filled with spiffy tables, chrome railings, and a sort of whitebread crowd. Downstairs is a restaurant serving everything from seafood to steak. Upstairs, appetizers are served.

Music: nightly, F–Su afternoons. *Cover:* $. *Food:* American.

East Bay Communities

Eli's Mile High Club & Restaurant, 3629 Martin Luther King, Jr., Way (near 36th St.), West Oakland, 510–655–6661.

A dark and creaky L-shaped place that was once just a neighborhood joint, Eli's now attracts visitors from around the world. Nonetheless, it's still the funkiest blues club in town, with a warm down-home feel and lots of great sounds. A SUBJECT TO SEARCH sign hangs on the wall; a pool table beckons up front.

Many greats have played Eli's, including Lowell Fulson, Jimmy McCracklin, and Charlie Musselwhite, and many "names" have stopped by, including Bruce Springsteen, Chuck

Berry, and Angela Davis. Up until his death about eight years ago, the owner, Troyce Key, a slim Southern gentleman usually given to wearing cream-colored suits, played most weekends; now the house band is Eli's Mile High All Stars, featuring vocalist Birdlegg and guitarist Steve Gannon. On Sundays, a reggae deejay dance night is featured, and on Mondays, there's a blues jam.

Music: F-M. *Cover:* $. *Food:* soul and health food.

Fifth Amendment, 3255 Lakeshore Ave., Oakland (near downtown), 510–832–3242.

Packed almost every night with an upscale African-American crowd, the friendly Fifth Amendment won the Bay Area Blues Society's Blues Club of the Year Award a number of years ago. Done up in muted orange and black, the place is really much more sophisticated than your average blues club, however, and its music is usually a jazz-blues-R&B mix. There's a long polished bar to one side, and a crowded dance floor to the front. The musicians, all local, put on a tight, hot show, and names such as B. B. King and Bobby "Blue" Bland have been known to stop by.

Music: nightly. *No cover.*

Bluesville, 131 Broadway, Oakland, 510–893–6215, www. bluesville-online.com.

This former funky restaurant, re opened in May of '99 as a blues club, features smokin' East Bay blues and R&B in the heart of revitalized Jack London Square on Oakland's waterfront. Run by the affable John Ivey, the club attracts a mixed crowd of old and young, black and white. The spacious venue (capacity: 225) offers several rooms, a great dance floor, pool tables, a full bar, and a complimentary buffet. Acts range from Joe Louis Walker to Texas transplant Kenny "Blue" Ray, playing behind Johnny Otis' vocalist Jackie Payne. The club's sound system leaves a lot to be desired, but all in good time, they say, at this highly welcomed addition to the Oakland scene.

Music: Th-Su. *Cover:* $$. *Food:* appetizers.

Jimmie's Cocktail Lounge & Nightclub, 1731 San Pablo Ave., Oakland, 510–268–8445.

A complex of several buildings built around a small outdoor patio, Jimmie's—capacity 600—brings in some of the biggest blues and R&B acts in the Bay Area. Many top names have appeared here, including Solomon Burke, Ike Turner, Denise LaSalle, and Frankie Lee. The club usually has a live blues or R&B band every Sunday and every other Friday, and deejays the other nights of the week.

Owned by a trio of old friends—"Sweet" Jimmie Ward, Irvin "Dusty" Williams, and Beret "Chief" Armstrong—Jimmie's is a modern, sophisticated club that attracts many of the city's top African-American professionals. Don't be put off by the strong-armed men in red satin jackets frisking people at the door—this is one safe club. It's frequented by a large number of off-duty cops, and security guards with walkie-talkies keep the parking lots under surveillance.

Music: F, Su. *Cover:* $-$$$.

Larry Blake's R&B Café, 2367 Telegraph Ave., Berkeley, 510–848–0888 (concert line) or 0886 (club).

A laid-back basement club in the heart of Berkeley, Larry Blake's caters to a mix of students and neighborhood folk. Equipped with rough thick pillars, heavy wooden tables, and black cement walls, the room was once a mainstay of the blues and R&B community, but now features blues just once a week—during its Monday Night Blues Jam. Now over 15 years old, the jam is run by ex-Brit Steve Gannon.

Music: blues on M. *Cover:* $. *Food:* American.

Also

Blues can be heard at **The Serenader** (504 Lake Park Ave., 510–832–2644), which is similar to (and near) the Fifth Amendment; and at **Sweetwater** (153 Throckmorton, Mill Valley, 415–388–2820), an eclectic club that features occasional national blues acts.

In Albany, about 20 minutes northwest of downtown Oakland, **Club Muse** (856 San Pablo Ave., 510–528–2878) and **The Ivy Room** (858 San Pablo Ave., 510–524–9220) offer blues and R&B five days and seven days a week respectively. **Everett & Jones** (126 Broadway, Oakland, 510–663–2350) is an Oakland barbecue joint featuring live blues every Saturday night.

Elsewhere in the Area

Ranch Nicasio Bar and Restaurant, On the Town Square, Nicasio, 415–662–2219, www.ranchonicasio.com.

Located off Highway 101 in woodsy, wealthy Marin County, about an hour north of San Francisco, the Ranch is run by Bob Brown and his blues-lady wife, Angela Strehli. An authentic roadhouse, just down the road apiece from ol' George Lucas' sprawling but hidden movie studio, "Skywalker Ranch," the club features primarily blues and roots music on Fridays and Saturdays. Sundays are devoted to pleasant, mid-day barbecues. A more-than-enjoyable venue with a friendly staff, roll-back prices, and a laid-back feel, the Ranch is well worth the trip across the Golden Gate.

Music: F-Su. *Cover*: $$. *Food*: American.

Moe's Alley Blues Club, 1535 Commercial Way, off Hwy. One, Santa Cruz, 831–479–1854, www.moesalley.com.

Only about 75 minutes south of San Francisco, Moe's Alley is one terrific blues bar. With its ample dance floor, a great sound system, an outdoor patio, and extra-friendly patrons and staff, Moe's is always a pleasure. The club features a full bar, intelligent booking, lots of national acts, and enthusiastic audiences nightly. It's owned and operated by the same guys that run the Santa Cruz Blues Festival.

Music: nightly. *Cover*: $$. *Food*: barbecue.

Other Venues

One of the most unusual and spirited churches in the country—named "The Church for the 21st Century" by *Life* magazine in 1997—is the **Glide Memorial Church** (331 Ellis St., at Taylor, San Francisco, 415–771–6300, www.glide.org). Located in the Tenderloin, just across from the San Francisco Hilton, the church holds "Celebrations" every Sunday morning at 9:00 A.M. and 11:00 A.M. With a seriously rockin' seven-piece R&B band called Change (led by former Sly and the Family Stone member John Turk) and a 150-voice modern gospel choir (The Glide Ensemble), this service is one you'll not soon forget. In attendance on various Sundays have been Bill and Chelsea Clinton, Sharon Stone, Robin Williams, and Maya Angelou. The church is co-pastored by Douglas Fitch and the legendary Methodist preacher Cecil Williams.

Though now primarily known for its arts-and-crafts programs for kids, the **Koncepts Kultural Gallery** (510–763–0682), a non-profit African-American arts organization, occasionally presents jazz at various venues around town.

In the 1960s and '70s, the grand, old-world **Great American Music Hall** (859 O'Farrell, 415–885–0750, www.musichallsf.com) was largely a jazz venue, with some folk, blues, and rock thrown in. Many of the greats, including Duke Ellington, performed here. Now, however, the European-style cabaret-theater presents jazz and blues only on occasion.

The **Herbst Theatre** in the Performing Arts Center (401 Van Ness Ave.), the setting of the city's first jazz festival in 1983, also presents occasional jazz concerts, as do the **Calvin Simmons Theater** in Oakland (Oak and Tenth Streets, 510–893–2082), **Davies Symphony Hall** in the San Francisco

Civic Center (Grove and Van Ness Ave., 415–431–5400), and **Bimbo's 365 Club** (1025 Columbus Ave., 415–474–0365), a San Francisco hall that's open for public lease.

Special Events

Two large music festivals, the **San Francisco Jazz Festival** and the **San Francisco Blues Festival** (see "Major Festivals," p. 458) are held every fall. A two-day **Jazz and All That Art** on Fillmore Fair takes place on Fillmore Street every July. A two-day **Concord Jazz Festival** has been held at the Concord Pavilion (800–7CONCORD) in Concord, Calif., every summer for over 30 years.

The East Bay hosts numerous festivals that feature much blues. Among them are the **Black Diamond Blues Festival**, held in Pittsburg the last weekend in May; the **Alameda County Fair**, held in Pleasanton in late June; and the **Hayward/Russell City Blues Festival**, held in early July. Oakland's **Home Grown Blues** takes place on late Wednesday afternoons starting in mid-July, and lasts for nine weeks. Vallejo's **Blues and Heritage Festival** is held on the Vallejo shoreline in mid-September. Oakland's **Blues and Heritage Festival**, sub-titled "The Blues They Played On 7th Street," shows up on Labor Day weekend. And then there's **Blues and Jazz at Dunsmuir House and Gardens**, held in Oakland in late September, and the **San Leandro Sausage and Suds Festival**, which takes place in early October and features three stages of music rife with blues and R&B. For information on any of these fests, call the **Bay Area Blues Society** at 510–836–2227.

The two-day **Santa Cruz Blues Festival**, www.santacruzbluesfestival.com, which takes place in stunning Aptos Village Park in late May, is one of the premier blues festivals in the country. So is the massive and hugely popular **Monterey Bay Blues Festival** (www.montereyblues.com), held at the Monterey County Fairgrounds for three days every June.

Radio

KCSM/91.1 FM (415–574–6427). A 24-hour jazz station.
KJAZ/92.7 FM (415–769–4800). A 24-hour jazz station.
KPOO/89.5 FM (415–346–5373). Some jazz and blues daily.
KPFA/94.1 FM (415–848–6767). Listener-supported radio. Blues Sa A.M., first with legendary musician Johnny Otis, then with San Francisco Blues Festival producer Tom Mazzolini.

Jazz and blues can also be heard occasionally on **KUSP/88.9 FM, KDIA/1310 AM, KALW/91.7 FM,** and **KKSF/103.7 FM.**

Record Stores

Called "The World's Greatest Record Store?" by *Rolling Stone* magazine, the **Amoeba** (2455 Telegraph Ave., Berkeley, 510–549–1125, and 1855 Haight St., San Francisco, 415–831–1200) has an almost overwhelming amount of new and used music posters, vinyl LPs and singles, CDs, cassettes, laser discs, DVDs, and VHS tapes.

Other good stores with excellent jazz and blues selections include **Village Music** in Mill Valley (9 E. Blythesdale Ave., 415–388–7400); **Down Home Music** in El Cerrito (10341 San Pablo Ave., 510–525–2129), a gold mine for blues lovers; **The Jazz Quarter** in San Francisco (1267 20th Ave., 415–661–2331), and **Jack's Record Cellar** (254 Scott St., 415–431–3047).

PORTLAND

Updated by George Fendel

Portland's contribution to jazz and blues history may be small, but the city can claim several important sons and daughters. Two premier, though not particularly well-known, women bebop artists emerged from the city in the 1940s: piano player Lorraine Geller, who had studied with Gene Confer, an influential Portland jazz educator, and trumpet player Norma Carson, who later played with Charlie Parker and others. Max Gordon, founder of New York's Village Vanguard, once lived in Portland and attended Reed College, and Ralph Towner and Glen Moore formed the nucleus of the group Oregon while studying at the University of Oregon in Eugene.

Also associated with the city are singer-pianist-songwriter Dave Frishberg, singer Rebecca Kilgore, and bass player David Friesen. Pianist Andrew Hill lived in Portland in the 1990s, as did the late baritone saxophonist Bill Hood. Upon his return to the U.S. after many years in Sweden, the late bassist Red Mitchell settled in the area, and another great bassist, Leroy Vinnegar, made Portland his home from 1985 until his death in 1999.

Like other West Coast cities, Portland had no African-American population to speak of until World War II, when the city's shipyards began attracting workers from Texas and the South. Most settled in Northeast Portland, and soon that area was thriving with music clubs and all-night jam sessions. Whenever major touring artists such as Nat Cole or Duke Ellington passed through town, they always stopped by Northeast Portland after the show.

Portland's most legendary club of all time was Sidney's (now a blues club called the Candlelight, see "For Blues," page 440), owned by pianist Sid Porter. At 6 feet 6 inches tall, Sid was both the club's host and its main performer, and during the 1950s and '60s, everyone from the mayor on down flocked down to the joint.

Sources

Willamette Week (503–243–2122), a free weekly, contains excellent listings, as does the Friday edition of *The Oregonian*, Portland's daily paper (503–221–8327). The most complete listings of jazz events can be found in *Jazzscene*, an excellent monthly magazine published by the Jazz Society of Oregon (503–234–1332). *Blues Notes* is a free monthly publication put out by the Cascade Blues Association that can be found in many of the clubs. The Jazz Society hosts an events Web site at www.jsojazzscene.org; the Cascade Blues Association hosts one at www.cascadeblues.org.

For maps and other information, contact the Portland, Oregon, Visitors Association at 26 SW Salmon St., 503–222–2223.

A Note on Neighborhoods

Portland is a friendly city divided into east and west by the Willamette River (the two sections are connected by 11 bridges) and into north and south by Burnside Street. Streets are named according to the quadrant they are in (SE, NE, etc.) which makes finding places very easy, especially since, in Portland, nothing is located too far apart.

CLUBS, ETC.

For a small city, Portland has considerably more than its share of first-rate jazz musicians, many of whom play the clubs on a rotating basis and have an enthusiastic following. To accommodate the consistent demand for live jazz, Portland boasts several clubs and hotel lounges that feature jazz on a near nightly basis: among them are **Atwater's**, **Brasserie Montmartre**, the **Heathman Hotel**, and **Jazz de Opus**. There is no regular venue for touring talent, however.

Portland also has a burgeoning blues and R&B scene, with several small clubs and restaurants featuring local artists five or six nights a week. Among them are **Candelight** and **Hopper's Pub**.

The city's top jazz artists include pianist-singer-song-writer Dave Frishberg; pianists Andrei Kitaev, Randy Porter, Darrell Grant, Geoff Lee, Steve Christofferson, and Tony Pacini; bass players Dave Friesen, Ed Bennett, Scott Steed, Andre St. James, and Phil Baker; drummers Mel Brown, Ron Steen, Alan Jones, and Donny Osborne; trumpet players Thara Memory and Paul Mazzio; saxophonists Lee Withenow and Warren Rand, and singers Rebecca Kilgore and Nancy King.

One of Portland's most popular blues acts—when they're back home from their heavy touring schedule—is Curtis Salgado & The Stilettos. Curtis is a veteran blues shouter on whom John Belushi and Dan Aykroyd patterned their Blues Brothers act while filming *Animal House* at the University of Oregon in Eugene. Other top blues and R&B talent includes the Paul Delay Blues Band, the Jim Mesi Band, the Norman Sylvester Band, Lloyd Jones, Terry Robb, Robbie Laws, Jessie Samsel, Aaron and Johnny Black, D. K. Stewart, Linda Hornbuckle, Jaybird Koder, The Essentials, the Power Band with Sonny Hess, Midnight Blue, Marquee, Andy Stokes, the Michael Henry Blues Project, Pin and Friends, Ellen Whyte, and Steve Bradley.

Personal Choices

Best jazz restaurant-bar: *Jazz de Opus*
Best jazz lounges: *Atwater's, Heathman Hotel*
Best blues restaurant-club: *Hopper's Pub*
Best historic blues club: *Candlelight Room*

FOR JAZZ

Brasserie Montmartre, 626 SW Park Ave. (downtown), 503–224–5552.

An elegant French restaurant located in the historic 1908 Calumet Hotel, the Brasserie is filled with all those charming continental accoutrements: tassled silk curtains, chandeliers, green velvet banquettes. This being Portland, however, and not Paris or New York, the atmosphere is laid back and relaxed, with items on the menu to suit every budget and taste—burgers to escargot.

Jazz by the best area musicians happens every night on the Brasserie's large central stage. But sight lines are only fair and the place can be noisy with talk, making it difficult to hear the music.

The Brasserie is a frequent stop for visiting celebrities, musicians off their own gigs, and party animals with late-night munchies. The kitchen remains open until 3 A.M. on Fridays and Saturdays; 1 A.M. the rest of the week.

Music: nightly. *No cover. Food*: French continental.

Jazz de Opus, 33 NW Second Ave. (downtown), 503–222–6077.

When Jazz de Opus first opened its doors in the early 1980s, it was a small beer and wine bar presenting such greats as Sonny Rollins, Nat Adderley, Roy Eldridge, and Oscar Peterson. Then, it added on a large restaurant with an open kitchen and for about six years stopped featuring music. Ever since the early '90s, however, to the delight of local music fans, the place has returned to its roots, making it the longest-running jazz club in the city.

The musicians play in a small, informal bar near the door, while the dinner patrons are seated in an adjacent area. Among the musicians appearing regularly are Nancy King and Steve Christofferson, the Ron Steen Quartet, and guitarist Dan Balmer.

Music: nightly. *Cover*: F-Sa only, $. *Food*: Steaks, seafood, pasta.

Atwater's, 111 SW Fifth Ave. (downtown), 503–275–3600.

Located high atop a downtown office building, with spectacular views of the city, Atwater's is one of the finest restaurants in Portland. Over the years, too, it has earned a reputation for presenting top-quality jazz.

Playing on the weekends is Atwater's Trio with Geoff Lee on piano, Andre St. James on bass, and Mel Brown on drums. The music takes place in a hushed, thick-carpeted lounge filled with plush sofas, peach-colored walls, and big picture windows. A light menu—eggplant sandwiches, wild mushroom and brie raviolis—is available, while next door is the main restaurant.

Music: Tu-Sa. *No cover. Food*: Contemporary American.

Heathman Hotel, 1001 SW Broadway (downtown), 503–241–4100.

The Heathman may be a modern hotel, but its high-ceilinged lobby lounge has a luxurious Old World feel, thanks to rich wood paneling, balconies all around, Persian rugs, and chandeliers. Candles flicker discreetly on small, round tables while couples and friends relax on brocade chairs, sipping brandy and cognac. The Heathman's most compelling performer is Russian-born pianist Andrei Kitaev, who plays on Wednesdays and Saturdays.

Music: Tu-Sa. *No cover. Food*: French cuisine with a Northwest flair.

Benson Hotel Lobby Court, 309 SW Broadway (downtown), 503–228–2000.

A Portland landmark, the Benson Hotel is generally considered to be the city's most elegant hotel. In this gorgeous setting, complete with a fireplace, heavy wood paneling, high ceilings, and sofas, some of Portland's finest jazz musicians perform. Among them are the Rebecca Kilgore Trio and pianists Jean Ronne and Tony Pacini.

Music: Tu-Sa. *No cover. Food*: light menu.

Also

Local and visiting jazz musicians take note: bring your axe over to **Produce Row Café** (204 SE Oak St., 503–232–8355), a ramshackle pub with a large beer-can collection and lots of dark booths. Veteran drummer Ron Steen hosts Portland's longest running jam session in this popular spot every Monday night.

Typhoon is a small bar in the Imperial Hotel (400 SW Broadway, 503–228–7221) that features pianists such as the exciting Darrell Grant, sometimes performing solo, sometimes in a duo or trio. Dave Frishberg and Rebecca Kilgore also occasionally perform, before an attentive listening audience.

Jimmy Mak's (300 NW 10th, 503–295–6542) is a neighborhood bar and restaurant with a varied music schedule. Renowned drummer Mel Brown, performing with a hard bop sextet, and trumpeter Thara Memory's Super Band are among the stalwarts here.

Sharkey's Grill (355 N. State Street, Lake Oswego, 503–699–3582), about 20 minutes from downtown Portland, boasts a grand piano that was once owned by Ramsey Lewis, and music six nights a week. Often heard here are longtime local favorite, pianist Eddie Wied; former Mel Torme drummer Donny Osborne; singer Marilyn Keller, and a Modern Jazz Quartet–inspired trio known as Tall Jazz.

FOR BLUES

Candlelight Room, 2032 SW Fifth Ave. (at Lincoln, near downtown), 503–222–3378.

Though at first glance a too clean and neat spiffed-up club with hanging plants, black tables, and dark blue carpets, the Candlelight nonetheless has atmosphere. Once an old whiskey bar and then a famous jazz club (Sidney's), good times and sweet sounds seem to hover in the air. A large square-shaped bar dominates the inside, while outside, the club's cement walls are painted baby blue. Regulars include D. K. Stewart, Linda Hornbuckle, Terry Robb, Norman Sylvester, and Jaybird Koder.

Music: nightly. *No cover*. *Food*: sandwiches, etc.

Hopper's Pub, 11121 SE Division St., 503–256–9521.

Cozy, comfortable, and down home, the high-energy Hopper's offers up live blues every night of the week. Also a restaurant serving Southern-style barbecue, the club features a mix of dining tables and overstuffed chairs. To one side is a dance floor, to another two pool tables and dartboards. Among the regulars are Robbie Laws, Jessie Samsel, and Aaron and Johnny Black. Jim Mesi and the Paul Delay Blues Band also play from time to time.

Music: nightly. *No cover*. *Food*: Southern.

M&M Lounge, 137 N. Main Street, Gresham (20 min. W of downtown), 503–665–2626.

A large and low-ceilinged lounge with mock leather arm-chairs, the M&M caters to everyone from young construction workers to middle-aged office workers. It's been a favorite neighborhood hangout for decades, and was once known for its country and western music.

Started up by two owners whose last names began with M, the club was originally a diner that gave away free packages of M&M's candies. More recently, it has undergone a total update, to now include a huge banquet room. Appearing here frequently are such local blues heroes as Jim Mesi, the Essentials, the Power Band with Sonny Hess, Midnight Blue, Marquee, and the Norman Sylvester Band.

Music: F-Sa. *No cover*. *Food*: American.

Billy Reed's Restaurant and Bar, 2808 NE Martin Luther King Blvd., 503–493–8127.

A large family restaurant that's also a music club, Billy Reed's presents music four nights a week, much of it blues, some of it jazz. On Wednesdays, Linda Hornbuckle and Janice Scroggins usually perform, while Sunday afternoons are devoted to the Albina Jazz Ensemble, playing a mix of jazz and blues.

Music: W-Su. *No cover*. *Food*: rustic American.

Also

The **Tillicum Lounge** (8585 SW Beaverton-Hillsdale Hwy., 503–292–1835) presents blues on a regular basis. Groups that have played here include the Michael Henry Blues Project, Pin and Friends, Ellen Whyte, Lloyd Jones, and Steve Bradley.

Smaller towns in the area also offer a number of good blues bars. About 20 minutes from downtown Portland is the **Gemini Bar and Grill** (456 N. State St., Lake Oswego, 503–636–9445), featuring live blues two, sometimes three, nights a week; regulars include Robbie Laws, Andy Stokes, and Linda Hornbuckle. About 30 minutes from downtown is the **Trail's End Saloon** (1320 Main Street, Oregon City, 503–656–3031); Paul Delay, Lloyd Jones, Robbie Laws, and Jim Mesi are among the top area musicians who perform here, Th-Su.

In Cascade, Washington, you'll find a clutch of busy blues clubs, including the **Cascade Tavern** (1500 S.E. Mill Plain Rd., 206–254–0749), which offers live music most nights of the week.

Other Venues and Special Events

Portland's largest annual event is the **Mt. Hood Jazz Festival,** held every August, which brings in nationally known jazz, pop-fusion, and blues acts (see "Major Festivals," page 458). The Jazz Society of Oregon (503–234–1332) presents **First Jazz**, an event that kicks off the New Year with performances by national, regional, and local artists in an intimate, friendly setting.

Diane Mitchell, wife of the late bassist Red Mitchell, hosts occasional solo piano concerts in her downtown Portland home. (Alas, they are usually word of mouth, but worth asking about while in town.) Among the many superb performers who have performed in her living room, with its terrific views of the city and Mt. Hood, have been Alan Broadbent, Bill Charlap, Bill Mays, Fred Hersch, Roger Kellaway, Mike Wofford, George Cables, Eric Reed, and Bill Mays.

The **Aladdin Theater** (3017 S.E. Milwaukie Ave., 503–233–1944) presents a varied year-round schedule of live music drawn mostly from the jazz, blues, folk, and ethnic arenas.

The largest blues bash in the region is the four-day **Waterfront Blues Festival** (503–282–0555; www.waterfront-bluesfest.com), held in Portland's Tom McCall Waterfront Park in July.

Radio

KMHD/89.1 FM (503–661–8900). Affiliated with Mt. Hood Community College. Jazz 24 hours most days; blues F afternoons and evenings.
KBOO/90.7 FM (503–231–8032). A spirited, eclectic, community-operated station featuring jazz and some blues most days.

Record Stores

The largest selection of new and used jazz can be found at **Everyday Music's Jazz and Classical** (1313 W. Burnside St., 503–274–1700), and its two outlets, (1931 NE Sandy Blvd., 503–239–7610; 3290 SW CedarHills Blvd., Beaverton, 503–350–0907). **Music Millennium** (3158 E. Burnside St., 503–231–8926; 801 NW 23rd, 503–248–0163) has a wide selection of new jazz and blues CDs, as well as smaller labels and collector's items.

At **Crossroads Music** (3130-B SE Hawthorne, 503–232–1767), a cooperative of approximately 25 music vendors, vinyl is king. **Django Records** (1111 SW Stark St., 503–227–4381) is one of Portland's oldest jazz record shops and is a favorite among collectors. A smaller, friendly shop specializing in jazz, classical, and blues is **Post Hip CDs Plus** (3570 SW Troy, 503–293–9125).

SEATTLE

Updated by Andrew Bartlett

Although there were few African Americans living in Seattle in the first decades of this century, the city already had integrated jazz bands as early as 1926. Soon thereafter, clubs—eventually numbering about 30—started springing up along Jackson Street, which was to remain the heart of the city's jazz scene until the 1950s. The most famous of these joints, which were mostly owned by African Americans and Chinese Americans, were the Rocking Horse Club, the Black & Tan Club (still standing at 1201 Jackson), Basin Street, and Club Maynard. These last two were best known for their blues, which could be heard in Seattle beginning in the 1940s.

Much of the reason why Seattle responded so quickly to jazz and blues, according to jazz historian Paul de Barros, was that the city was "completely corrupt." "Seattle was a speakeasy town even before Prohibition," de Barros said in an interview with *The Seattle Times/Seattle Post-Intelligencer.* "There was all the entertainment required by single male loggers and the city supported it. So although the black population was small in the beginning, it was very active musically and we had an underworld that supported jazz speakeasies."

One of the best-known musicians associated with Seattle is Jimi Hendrix. Born in Seattle and raised primarily by his father, Hendrix taught himself to play the guitar and joined a high school band called the Rocking Kings. The other members of the band were jealous of his popularity with girls, and he left the band after an intrigue with another member's girlfriend. Shortly thereafter, he also left Seattle, to become a paratrooper in the U.S. Army.

Hendrix, who fused jazz and blues into rock-and-roll, is considered by many to be one of the greatest guitarists of our time. He died at the age of 27 and is buried just south of the city in Greenwood Memorial Park (Fourth and Monroe streets, 255–1511; open 8:30 A.M.–5 P.M. daily) in the suburb of Renton.

Ray Charles is another major music figure connected with Seattle. Blind and alone in the world, he moved up to the city from Jacksonville, Florida, at the age of 17 with only one small suitcase and $600 to his name. "I had done as good in Florida as I was going to do . . . ," he writes in his autobiography, *Brother Ray: Ray Charles' Own Story.* "I didn't know anything about Seattle, I didn't know anyone living up there, and I hadn't heard a thing about the town. It just seemed like a reasonable place to go. All mystery and adventure."

Upon arrival, Charles, who had already gained much experience gigging around Florida, quickly picked up jobs along Jackson Street. He met Seattle resident Quincy Jones, who became a good friend; recorded his first record, "Confession Blues," and changed his named from Ray Charles Robinson to Ray Charles (to avoid confusion with Sugar Ray Robinson).

Other jazz and blues figures associated with Seattle include Ernestine Anderson, who now lives in the city; Larry Coryell, who grew up in Washington state and played some of his earliest gigs in Seattle; Robert Cray, who grew up in nearby Tacoma; Bing Crosby, who was born in Tacoma; Diane

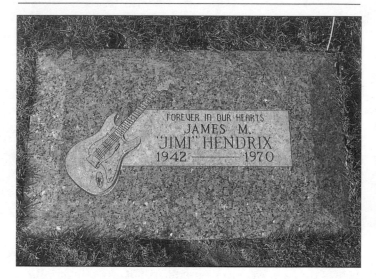

Jimi Hendrix is buried just south of Seattle.

Schuur, who grew up in Seattle; and Floyd Standifer, who still plays around town regularly.

Sources

The *Seattle Weekly* (206–441–5555) has excellent listings, as do the Friday editions of the *Seattle Post-Intelligencer* (206–448–8000, www.seattlep-i.nwsource.com) and the *Seattle Times* (206–464–2111, www.seattletimes.nwsource.com). *Earshot Jazz*, the monthly publication of the Earshot Jazz society (206–547–6763, www.earshot.org) and *BluesLetter*, the monthly publication of the Washington Blues Society (206–324–5491, www.wablues.org) also have extensive listings; both are free and can be picked up in most clubs.

The Tentacle (www.tentacle.org) has become the premier place for information on the edgier, avant-garde side of the Seattle jazz world, which is thriving. *The Stranger* (206–323–7101, www.thestranger.com) is a free alternative weekly with music coverage that spans genres, including occasional coverage of jazz and blues. *Blues To Do Monthly* (206–328–0662, www.bluestodo.com) is an extensive magazine devoted both to the local blues scene, its artists and venues, and to national artists.

The Seattle–King County Convention and Visitors Bureau is located at 800 Convention Place (206–461–5840, www.seeseattle.org). Two good general Web sites for information on Seattle arc www.citysearch.com and www.soundsofseattle.com.

A Note on Neighborhoods

Pioneer Square is a National Register Historic District located near the downtown. Filled with restored brick buildings dating back to the 1890s, it is the city's most popular entertainment district and is often packed on the weekends. Ballard, founded by Scandinavian fishermen and loggers, is located about 10 minutes north of the downtown (just over the Lake Washington Ship Canal), and is also known for its nightlife.

Landmarks and Legends

Experience Music Project, Fifth Ave. and Broad St., next to the Space Needle, 206–770–2700, www.emplive.com.

Few cities can boast a legend like Jimi Hendrix, and fewer still can boast having two of the world's wealthiest men living locally. Paul Allen, second to Bill Gates in wealth but not in ingenuity, funded the building of this gnarled, brightly painted postmodern Experience Music Project, which catches the eye from I–5, Seattle's main freeway. It's part of the Seattle Center and, while pricey to enter, contains some creative music memorabilia collections. As a monument to music in a town where the music business found just the right pair of bands (Nirvana and Pearl Jam) to turn alternative music into a marketing juggernaut, the EMP emphasizes rock and is rather light on jazz and blues. There are, however, spectacular music venues within the EMP, and in early 2001 the museum will go from hosting only occasional live music events to scheduling live music of all stripes in genre-specific festivals.

Open: Su-Th, 10 A.M.–6 P.M.; F-Sa, 10 A.M.–11 P.M. *Admission*: $$$.

CLUBS, ETC.

Seattle is home to one of the premier jazz clubs in the Northwest, **Dimitriou's Jazz Alley,** which brings in a wide variety of national artists. The **New Orleans Creole Restaurant,** which tends more toward mainstream acts, also presents some touring talent, along with top local musicians. More avant-garde sounds can be heard at the **OK Hotel.**

Several clubs feature local blues and R&B every night of the week. National blues artists are sometimes brought in by the **Ballard Firehouse**, **Jazz Alley**, or the **New Orleans Creole Restaurant**.

Jazz artists to look out for include veteran bass player Buddy Catlett; trombonist Julian Priester; trumpet player Floyd Standifer; vocalists Kendra Shank and Jay Clayton; guitarist Ralph Towner; recent ex–New Yorkers Bill Frisell and Wayne Horvitz; drummers Larry Jones and John Bishop; saxophone players Hadley Caliman and Bert Wilson; violinist Michael White; multi-instrumentalist Denney Goodhew; guitarist Brian Nova; pianists Marc Seales, Aaron Parks, and Jessica Williams; bass player Michael Bisio; the tireless bebopping Marriott Brothers, and trumpeter Jim Knapp's big band.

Top blues–R&B talent in the city includes singer-songwriter Tom McFarland; local favorite Isaac Scott; the David Brewer Band; vocalists Duffy Bishop, Kathi McDonald, Patti Allen, and Nora Michaels; drummers Chris Leighton and Leslie "Star Drums" Milton; slide guitarists Nick Vigarino and Henry Cooper; ex–B. B. King drummer Tony Coleman; Little Bill and the Blue Notes; harpman-keyboard player Dick Powell, and keyboard player-vocalist Norm Ballas. Several times every year, blues singer Kathy Hart organizes shows featuring seven to 13 "Seattle Women in Rhythm and Blues."

Many of the clubs in Pioneer Square, including the ones listed below, have a joint cover charge ($–$$) during the week and/or on the weekends. Five clubs join in this program Mondays–Wednesdays, six on Thursdays, and nine on Friday and Saturdays.

Music can often be heard as late as 1:30 or 2 A.M.

Personal Choices

Best jazz restaurant-clubs: *Jazz Alley, New Orleans Creole Restaurant*
Best progressive jazz: *OK Hotel*
Best jazz jam: *Tula's*
Best blues–R&B: *Pioneer Square bars, Scarlet Tree*

FOR JAZZ

Dimitriou's Jazz Alley, 2033 Sixth Ave. (at Lenora; entrance is in the back, just off Lenora), 206–441–9729, www.jazzalley.org.

A large and spacious club with excellent acoustics and sight lines, Jazz Alley presents virtually all the top touring jazz acts in the country. Max Roach, Eddie Palmieri, Charlie Byrd, and Ruth Brown are just a few of the many musicians who have appeared here.

For years, Jazz Alley booked artists for a week minimum. Then, in 1999, the club began featuring artists for one- or two-night stands in order to draw in top touring talent and to make its roster more versatile. As a result, Northwesterners like Bud Shank and Pearl Django (inspired by Django Reinhardt) now play here a few nights a week while major stars like Bobby "Blue" Bland, Ray Brown, Cyrus Chestnut, and Branford Marsalis still fetch longer stays.

Though usually quite full, the club never feels crowded, owing to its big, comfortable booths and tables. A wide balcony lines one wall, and large picture windows look out onto the street. Free parking is available in back.

Music: M–Sa. *Cover:* $$. *Food:* Italian-Mediterranean.

Tula's, 2214 Second Ave. (Belltown), 206–443–4221, www. tulas.com.

In the north end of Seattle's downtown, you'll find the musically thriving Belltown area, where rock clubs host major independent and alternative touring acts at venues like the Crocodile. Local jazz talent, largely those in the mainstream scene, gather at Tula's, a slightly crowded spot for folks who like their drinks stiff and the stage close up. Although it's a decidedly local venue, with big bands sometimes working on their charts during sets, Tula's is also a fine spot for touring artists like Patricia Barber, Jason Moran, and Steve Slagle. There's a full menu and a full bar—important in a town where many pubs serve only beer and wine.

Music: nightly. *Cover:* $. *Food:* American.

New Orleans Creole Restaurant, 114 First Ave. S. (Pioneer Square), 206–622–2563.

Big, long, and high-ceilinged, the New Orleans is all atmosphere, thanks to exposed brick walls, old wooden balconies, scuffed floors, and turn-of-the-century light fixtures. Once a stage-coach hotel used by men on their way to the Alaskan gold rush (rooms cost a mere 75 cents per night back then, as the sign outside still reads), it now serves Creole-Cajun food and jazz. Music styles range from traditional and bebop to contemporary, with some blues and zydeco thrown in. The great trumpet player Floyd Standifer has been playing here once a week for years and years, and national acts come through once or twice a month.

Music: nightly. *Cover:* $-$$. *Food:* Creole-Cajun.

OK Hotel, 212 Alaskan Way S. (behind Pioneer Square), 621–7903.

Under the viaduct behind Pioneer Square is Seattle's answer to the Knitting Factory in New York. A large, square, no-frills room, filled with rows of folding chairs, the OK presents everyone from former downtown New Yorkers Bill Frisell and Wayne Horvitz to the Baba Balkanettes ("Eastern Euro-soul music"). This is the place to go to hear the unexpected.

There's no drinking inside the OK's music room, but outside is a long and high-ceilinged café, lined with modern art and enormous dilapidated booths, where beer, wine, and food are served. To one side is a rickety, boarded-up staircase; this 1917 building was once a 300-room hotel and cat house, serving sailors and gold prospectors.

Music: W–Su, some jazz. *Cover:* $$. *Food:* American.

Also

The **700 Club** (700 Virginia Ave., 206–343–1255) caters to the crossroads between jazz and various other groove-heavy musics. Situated in the Belltown/Denny Regrade area in the heart of downtown, it has the feel of a slightly gritty urban club in a far bigger city. The music is eclectic, the full menu attractive, and the full bar magnetic.

Traditional jazzmen take to the stage of the **Latona Pub** (6423 Latona Ave., NE, 206–525–2238), a neighborhood café with aqua-blue walls and big picture windows, most weekend nights. Cabaret singer **Patti Summers** can often be found behind the piano of her namesake club, a dark, red-curtained place on the fringe of the city's adult entertainment district (94 Pike St., near First Ave., 206–621–8555). **Serafina** (2043 Eastlake Ave. E., 206–323–0807), which bills itself as a "rustic Euro-Italian restaurant and bar," features jazz on the weekends.

FOR BLUES

Larry's Blues Café, 209 First Ave. S. (Pioneer Square), 206–624–7665.

An often crowded but comfortable and laid-back bar and grill with brick walls, exposed beams, and a wooden floor, Larry's books top local R&B–blues bands every night of the week. The Scotty Harris Band plays here regularly, while bluesman Charles White leads a jam on Wednesday nights.

Larry's is owned and run by R&B fan and ex-musician Larry Culp and his brother, Charlie. The bar has been in their family for over 30 years, but it wasn't until they took over in 1986 that it started offering live blues.

Music: nightly. *Cover:* $-$$. *Food:* burgers, salads, etc.

The Central, 207 First Ave. S. (Pioneer Square), 206–622–0209.

The oldest saloon in Seattle, dating back to 1892, when it was also an employment office, post office, and gambling den for gold prospectors, the Central is a long, long, long room with a long, long, long bar (all dark wood, with enormous mirrors and old-fashioned light fixtures). Way down in the darkness at the end is a high stage where the musicians perform.

The lounge has had its share of history, new as well as old. In the late 1980s, the Central was the Central Tavern (what a difference a word makes), the spawning ground of Nirvana, Alice in Chains, and other grunge rock bands. For some years, the Central featured mostly R&B, but now they offer mostly rock, some R&B, and there's a barbecue smoker out back. The clientele ranges from biker types to preppies.

Music: nightly. *Cover:* $-$$. *Food:* smoked meats, chicken, ribs.

Old Timers' Café, 620 First Ave. (Pioneer Square), 206–623–9800.

Featuring mostly R&B, with salsa on the weekends, the atmospheric Old Timers' is a long, narrow, inviting place with heavy mirrored bars lining the walls and wrought-iron balconies all around. The patrons here often dance in the aisles and there's a patio area out front for the collective catching of breath. Regulars include saxmen Lonnie Williams and Fat James, and the Royals. The club also books national acts every once in a great while.

Music: nightly. *Cover:* $-$$. *Food:* American.

Scarlet Tree, 6521 Roosevelt (10 Min. N of downtown), 206–523–7153.

A dark and intimate neighborhood lounge with cushiony black and red seats and a well-mixed crowd (Hawaiian, Filipino, black, white), the Scarlet Tree offers R&B, with some blues mixed in, every night of the week. A rotating roster of eight to ten bands perform.

One side of the Scarlet Tree is a restaurant known for its breakfasts, the other is the bar and lounge. Carved wooden animals and dusty instruments hang above the informal, makeshift stage.

Music: nightly. *Cover:* $. *Food:* American (until 8 P.M. only).

Also

Although mostly a world music venue, the **Bohemian Café, Lounge, and Backstage** (111 Yesler Way, Pioneer Square,

206–447–1514) also hosts R&B acts about once a week and jazz on occasion. The **Tractor Tavern** (5213 Ballard Ave. N.W., 206–789–3599, http://tractortavern.citysearch.com/) and **Sunset Tavern** (5433 Ballard Ave. N.W., 206–784 4880), just down the street from each other in Ballard, both feature roots music that runs the gamut from whiskey-soaked alternative country to hard-driving electric blues. Most of what's showcased at both clubs is artists on tour, but you'll also hear locals who love to tear it up in these rustic, cozy settings.

Other Venues and Special Events

Touring jazz and blues artists sometimes appear at the Seattle Center's **Seattle Opera** (206–684–7200), the **Paramount Theater** (Ninth and Pine, 206–628–0888), and the University of Washington's **Meany Theater** (206–543–4880).

The **Rainbow** (722 NE 45th St., at I–5, 206–634–1761), a legendary venue just down from the equally legendary Blue Moon, began featuring live jazz shows in late 2000; most veer towards acid jazz, groove-heavy jam-band jazz, and further out. Though not a music club, the **Blue Moon** (712 NE 45th St., no phone) itself is also worth a stop. With its slogan, "Sorry, We're Open," the joint has been a central spot for drinkers, thinkers, and pool shooters ever since the 1930s. Poet Theodore Roethke, myriad lefty politicos, and virtually every Deadhead, post-'50s artist, and musician in the region has sat a spell here.

Earshot Jazz (206–547–6763, www.earshot.org), a nonprofit arts organization, produces a staggering number of concerts featuring local artists throughout the Seattle area during the course of the year. They also host the annual, two-week **Earshot Jazz Festival**, which has brought in the likes of Sonny Rollins, Cecil Taylor, Randy Weston, Dave Holland, Ornette Coleman, Charles Lloyd, and Kevin Eubanks.

City festivals featuring some jazz and blues include **Bumbershoot**, **The Seattle Arts Festival** (206–281–8111), which takes place over Labor Day weekend, and the **North West Fest** (206–542–9332), which takes place in late July. Other area events include the two-day **Port Townsend Blues Festival** in June (360385–3102), and the four-day **Jazz Port Townsend** (800–733–3608) in July.

Record Stores

Bud's Jazz Records (102 S. Jackson, 206–628–0445) is the city's top store for jazz and blues. **Wall of Sound** (2237 Second Ave., 206–441–9880) is a fantastic place in which to

discover new jazz and world music artists. **Repeat the Beat**
(7400 Greenwood Ave. N., 206–781–4870), in the Greenwood
neighborhood north of downtown, has a good selection of
used and new jazz LPs and CDs.

Bop Street Records (5512 20th St. N.W., 206–783–3009)
has a sign in the window that says "Probably the Only Place
in Seattle Not Serving Espresso"; instead the store serves up
a wide variety of LPs, tapes, and CDs. Run by one of the city's
well-known blues decjays, Bop Street has countless thousands of items—always haggle on prices here.

Radio

KPLU/88.5 FM (206–770–9820). A 24-hour jazz station.
Blues Sa, Su nights.
KBCS/91.3 FM (206–641–2424). Associated with Bellevue
Community college. Mostly jazz. Blues, Tu, Th, Sa nights.
K-LITE/95.7 FM (206–286–9536). Contemporary jazz station.

New York: *This* Birdland is not *that*
Birdland, but it's still got jazz.

A Brief History of Jazz and Blues

Although many scholars now believe that jazz, created primarily by African Americans in the early twentieth century, may have started developing in many parts of the country at once, New Orleans is generally credited as being the birthplace of the new music. In this sultry Southern town, with its brass-band traditions, French and Spanish influences, and outdoor marketplaces where African drumming was allowed (it was banned in many parts of the country as slave owners felt it led to rioting), the complex rhythms and harmonies of African musics, ragtime, and blues merged with Western melodies to create a new sound. Among the earliest of the New Orleans musicians were cornet player Buddy Bolden, who may have been the first jazzman ever; bandleader and cornet player Joseph "King" Oliver, who was Louis Armstrong's mentor; composer–piano player Jelly Roll Morton, a Creole who wore a 24-carat diamond in his front tooth; and soprano saxophonist-clarinet player Sidney Bechet, another Creole who was the first to take jazz to Europe. Jazz could be heard in many parts of New Orleans, but Storyville, a notorious red-light district with a dance hall or honky tonk on every corner, was especially known for the new sound.

Part of the reason that jazz first evolved in New Orleans was the existence there of the blues, an even earlier form of African-American music that probably first developed in the Mississippi Delta in the late nineteenth century. At first, the blues were heard only in the cotton fields and railroad work gangs, but by the early 1910s, a number of bluesmen, Charlie Patton and Tommy Johnson in the Delta, and Blind Lemon Jefferson and Leadbelly in Texas, were playing "professionally," for meager tips. W. C. Handy published the first formal blues in 1912, and in the early 1920s, a blues craze, honoring "classic" blues singers such as Alberta Hunter, Ma Rainey, and Bessie Smith, swept African-American communities throughout the country.

New Orleans remained the center of jazz until World War I, when a combination of elements—Mississippi riverboats, the closing of Storyville, and, especially, the economic pull of the

auto and munitions factories—led many musicians, along
with other African Americans, to head North. This migration
was to continue for decades, but already by the early 1920s,
Chicago was the new jazz capital and was teeming with talent,
including Jelly Roll Morton, Louis Armstrong, and King
Oliver. Pittsburgh piano player Earl Hines was also there,
along with pianist Lil Hardin, the first woman jazz instru-
mentalist and Armstrong's second wife; Bix Biederbecke, a
young, white cornet player from Davenport, Iowa, who was to
die of alcoholism at the age of 28; and the Austin High School
Gang, a group of native white Chicagoans, Jimmy McPartland
and Bud Freeman among them, who later came to epitomize
the hard-edged sound of "Chicago jazz." The time was the
Roarin' Twenties, an era of drinking, dancing, and abandonment, and there were constant clashes between the new jazz
clubs, many of which were controlled by gangsters, and the
police.

Chicago's heyday as the capital of jazz was short-lived,
however. In 1928, many of its illegal cabarets were shut down
by a reformist government, and by the 1930s, largely because
of the growing importance of the radio and recording industries, the center of jazz had shifted once again, this time to
New York, where it remains today.

The very first jazz recording ever had been made in New
York in 1917 by New Orleans's Original Dixieland Jazz Band.
Throughout the 1920s, the city was home to many early stride
piano players such as James P. Johnson, Willie "The Lion"
Smith, and Fats Waller (the stride style features a steady
"striding" left hand and an improvising right), and to numerous hot Harlem nightspots such as the Cotton Club—then
featuring the greatest of all jazz composers and bandleaders,
Duke Ellington—Connie's Inn, and Smalls' Paradise. All this
was nothing, however, compared to the 1930s, when New
York, along with the rest of the country, witnessed an
unprecedented rise in the popularity of jazz. As the big-band
era began in earnest, crowds black and white flocked to dance
halls and ballrooms all over the city to hear the then new
swing sounds of bands led by Fletcher Henderson, Chick
Webb, Lionel Hampton, Paul Whiteman, Benny Goodman,
Tommy Dorsey, and many others. "Battles of the bands," in
which two competitive big bands were pitted against each
other on opposite sides of a huge dance floor, became common.

Just prior to the big band era, Kansas City also played an
important role in the history of jazz. Then under the control of
a corrupt political boss, Tom Pendergast, K.C. was a wide-
open 24-hour town best known for its all-night jam sessions
and "cutting contests," in which musicians tried to outdo

each other by playing ever more complicated riffs and cho-ruses. Out of Kansas City during this period came many future stars, including alto saxophonist Charlie Parker, tenor saxophonist Lester Young, bandleaders Count Basie, Jay McShann and Bennie Moten, piano player Mary Lou Williams, and vocalist Joe Turner.

Meanwhile, the blues were flourishing throughout the South, with many musicians living itinerant lives that were taking them farther and farther from home. Bluesmen from the Delta tended to head first to Memphis and then on to Chicago and other points north, where they eventually set-tled, while bluesmen from Texas often congregated first in Dallas or Houston and then moved on to the West Coast. Among the many fine blues artists to emerge in the 1930s were Sonny Boy Williamson (Rice Miller) who later played har-monica on what was probably the most influential blues radio program ever, the "King Biscuit Time" on KFFA radio in Helena, Arkansas; Robert Johnson, the enigmatic singer-guitarist who reputedly sold his soul to the devil; T-Bone Walker, known for his lean, biting guitar licks; and Lightnin' Hopkins, a poetic blues minstrel from Houston.

The 1940s brought with them a major revolution in jazz: the advent of bebop or modern jazz, which was largely cre-ated by Charlie Parker on alto sax, Dizzy Gillespie on trumpet, Kenny Clarke on drums, and Thelonious Monk on piano in a small club in Harlem called Minton's. The first real avant-garde movement in jazz, bebop musicians turned the music around by experimenting with new chord progressions, har-monies, and rhythms. The innovative sound spread quickly, especially in New York (where it centered around 52nd Street), Detroit, and Philadelphia; simultaneously, sit-down jazz clubs intended for listening rather than dancing emerged for the first time. Among the many other artists associated with the new modern sound were drummer Max Roach; trumpet player Miles Davis; vocalists Billie Holiday, Sarah Vaughan, and Eddie Jefferson; and pianist Bud Powell. Charlie Christian, who brought the electric guitar to jazz, also played a seminal role in bebop's development.

Blues had changed considerably by the 1940s as well. Chicago, and not the Delta, was now the cutting edge of the music, and it was churning with bluesmen playing a grittier, more urban sound than their rural counterparts. Most impor-tant among the new city players were Muddy Waters, who later headed the first major electric blues band; Howlin' Wolf, the wild and passionate player who was Muddy's chief rival; and Willie Dixon, who composed dozens of blues hits. Others included Tampa Red, John Lee "Sonny Boy" Williamson, Lonnie Johnson, Memphis Minnie, Big Bill Broonzy, and Big

Maceo. Meanwhile, down in Memphis, a young B. B. King was hosting his first radio show, while out on the West Coast, a strong blues community nurturing such greats as Lowell Fulson was developing for the first time.

In the early 1950s, Miles Davis, who had started out in the bebop tradition, helped usher in the "cool school" of jazz through the release of his influential album, *The Birth of the Cool.* "Cool jazz," with its reflective, minimalist style, was soon heard in many parts of the United States, but it came to be especially closely associated with the West Coast, where Dave Brubeck and his quartet, which included Paul Desmond, were its most popular proponents. Other West Coast "cool" players, who were predominantly white, included drummer Shelly Manne, saxophonist Gerry Mulligan, and trumpet player Chet Baker. The Modern Jazz Quartet, pianist Lennie Tristano, and saxophonist Lee Konitz were also associated with the "cool" tradition.

After "cool jazz" came hard bop, which once again celebrated the more emotional roots of jazz. Drummer Art Blakey, bassist Charles Mingus, pianist Horace Silver, saxophonists Sonny Rollins and John Coltrane, and the Max Roach–Clifford Brown quintet came to the fore during this late-fifties period.

Yet other movements followed. The 1960s and early '70s saw the development of free jazz, which ignored the formal structures of more traditional jazz, and fusion, which combined elements of jazz and rock. Pianist-composer Cecil Taylor and saxophonists Ornette Coleman and John Coltrane were the names most frequently associated with early free jazz, while Miles Davis, Weather Report, and keyboard players Chick Corea and Herbie Hancock were those most frequently associated with early fusion. Later, whole new generations of players, including the Association for the Advancement of Creative Musicians, Sun Ra and his Arkestra, the Art Ensemble of Chicago, Anthony Braxton, and Lester Bowie brought yet more energy to the avant-garde sound.

Today's jazz and blues scene is extremely diverse. No longer does everyone seem to be searching for the "new." Traditional jazz has made a roaring comeback, thanks largely to the efforts of Wynton Marsalis and his disciples, while more experimental players such as John Zorn in New York and Ken Vandermark in Chicago have cadres of devoted followers. Meanwhile, the music's older masters like piano player Tommy Flanagan and trumpet player Clark Terry continue to attract enthusiastic audiences, as do bluesmen and women (B. B. King, Koko Taylor, John Lee Hooker, and Jimmie Vaughan, to name but a few) playing everything from acoustic blues to soul blues to R&B to blues-rock.

Major Festivals

The most complete listing of jazz festivals can be found in *Jazz Times* every April or May. The most complete listings of blues festivals can be found in *Living Blues* magazine every May/June, or in the semiannual *Living Blues Directory* (see "National Sources" page 13).

The events listed below are a selected list of major festivals only; some smaller citywide fests are also included under the city headings.

March

Sarasota Jazz Festival, Sarasota, Fla.
Contact: Sandra Lightfoot, Jazz Club of Sarasota, 290 Cocoanut Ave., Bldg. 3, Sarasota, Fla. 34236; 813–366–1552, www.jazzclubsarasota.com.
   Three to four days of indoor, ticketed events.

April

Pensacola Jazz Fest, Pensacola, Fla.
   Contact: WUWF Radio, University of West Florida, 11000 University Parkway, Pensacola, Fla. 32514; 904–474–2327 or 800–239-WUWF.
   A two- or three-day outdoor festival.

New Orleans Jazz and Heritage Festival, New Orleans, La.
   Contact: New Orleans Jazz and Heritage Foundation, P.O. Box 53407, New Orleans, La. 70153; 504–522–4786, www.insideneworleans.com/entertainment/nojazzfest.
   The premier music festival in the U.S. (see page 28). Ten days of music, food, and crafts, both indoors and out. Some events are free; most are not.

May

Sacramento Dixieland Jubilee, Sacramento, Calif.
Contact: Sacramento Traditional Jazz Society, 2787 Del Monte St., West Sacramento, Calif. 95691; 916–372–5277.
The largest traditional jazz fest in the U.S.; four days of music featuring over 100 bands.

Chicago Blues Festival, Chicago, Ill.
Contact: City of Chicago, Mayor's Office of Special Events, City Hall, Room 703, 121 N. LaSalle St., Chicago, Ill. 60602; 312–744–3315 or 800-ITS-CHGO.
One of the largest free blues festivals in the world. Three days of outdoor blues.

June

Mellon Jazz Festival, Pittsburgh, Pa.
Contact: Mellon Jazz Festival/Philadelphia, P.O. Box 1169, New York, N.Y. 10023, 212–501–1362, www.pajazz.org.
A 5-day festival featuring over 40 free and paid events, held indoors and out.

Central PA Mellon Jazz Festival, Harrisburg, Pa.
Contact: Central PA Friends of Jazz, PO Box 10738, Harrisburg, Pa. 17105, 717–540–1010.
Two days of festivities featuring national and local artists.

Playboy Jazz Festival, Los Angeles, Calif.
Contact: Playboy Jazz Festival, 9242 Beverly Blvd., Los Angeles, Calif. 90210; 310–246–4000.
One of the best outdoor jazz festivals. Two days of top talent.

Boston Globe Jazz Festival, Boston, Mass.
Contact: Public Affairs Dept., P.O. Box 2378, Boston Globe, Boston, Mass. 02107.
Seven days of concerts held throughout Boston.

Newport Jazz Festival, Saratoga Springs, N.Y.
Contact: Saratoga Performing Arts Center, Saratoga Springs, N.Y. 12866; 518–584–9330, www.jazzonthewater.com.
Two days of outdoor jazz, held in conjunction with the JVC Jazz Festival in New York City.

JVC Jazz Festival, New York, N.Y.

Contact: JVC Jazz Festival, P.O. Box 1169, New York, N.Y. 10023; 212–787–2020.

A descendant of the Newport Jazz Festival, the oldest jazz festival in the U.S. Held in New York since 1972; 8 to 10 days of ticketed events.

July

Mississippi Valley Blues Festival, Davenport, Iowa.

Contact: P.O. Box 2014, Davenport, Iowa 52809–2014; 319–32-BLUES.

A three-day festival put on by the Mississippi Valley Blues Society.

RiverBlues, Philadelphia, Pa.

Contact: Philadelphia Convention & Visitors Bureau, 1525 JFK Blvd., Philadelphia, Pa. 19102; 215–636–1666.

The biggest blues festival on the East Coast; two days of events.

The Texas Jazz Festival, Corpus Christi, Texas

Contact: Texas Jazz Festival Society, P.O. Box 424, Corpus Christi, Texas 78403; 512–883–4500, www.texas-jazzfest.org.

Five to seven days of music.

August

W. C. Handy Music Festival, Florence, Ala.

Contact: Music Preservation Society, P.O. Box 1827, Florence, Ala. 35631; 205–766–7642, www.wchandyfest.com.

A week-long fest featuring national and local artists (see page 66).

Mt. Hood Festival of Jazz, Gresham, Oregon

Contact: Mt. Hood Festival of Jazz Foundation, Inc., P.O. Box 2001, Gresham, Ore. 97030; 503–666–3810, www. mthoodjazz.com.

One of the best jazz festivals in the country; three days of music.

JVC Jazz Festival Newport, Newport, R.I.

Contact: JVC Jazz Festival Newport, P.O. Box 605, Newport, R.I. 02840; 401–847–3700, after June 1.

America's first jazz festival, begun in 1953. Three days of jazz in a glorious setting.

Chicago Jazz Festival, Chicago, Ill.

Contact: City of Chicago, Mayor's Office of Special Events, City Hall, Room 703, 121 N. LaSalle St., Chicago, Ill. 60602; 312–744–3315 or 800-ITS-CHGO.

Two to four days of outdoor jazz, and a jazz pub crawl.

River City/Bayou Blues Festival, Baton Rouge, La.

Contact: River City Festival Assn., 448 N. 11 St., Baton Rouge, La. 70802, or the Baton Rouge Visitors & Convention Bureau; 800–527–6843 or 504–383–1825.

Louisiana's *other* big festival. Two to three days of events.

September

Montreux Detroit Jazz, Detroit, Mich.

Contact: Detroit Renaissance Foundation, 100 Renaissance Center, Suite 1760, Detroit, Mich. 48243; 313–259–5400.

Five days of over 90 free open-air concerts, as well as some paid club events. Features international, national, and Detroit artists.

Mississippi Delta Blues Festival, Greenville, Miss.

Contact: MACE, 119 S. Theobald St., Greenville, Miss. 38701; 601–335–3523.

Only a one-day festival, but one of the best.

Russian River Jazz Festival, Guerneville, Calif.

Contact: Russian River Jazz Festival, P.O. Box 1913, Guerneville, Calif. 95446; 707–869–3940.

Two days of jazz on the banks of the Russian River, surrounded by redwoods.

Monterey Jazz Festival, Monterey, Calif.

Contact: P.O. Box JAZZ, Monterey, Calif. 93940; 408–373–3366, www.montereyjazzfestival.org.

Three days of ticketed concerts; no single-performance tickets available.

San Francisco Blues Festival, San Francisco, Calif.

Contact: Tom Mazzolini, 573 Hill St., San Francisco, Calif. 94114; 415–826–6837, www.sfblues.com.

The oldest blues festival in the U.S., begun in 1973. Two days of ticketed events that feature both Bay Area and national artists.

Notes

New Orleans

1. Whitney Balliett, *Such Sweet Thunder* (New York: Bobbs-Merrill, 1966), p. 235.

2. Jason Berry, Jonathan Foose, and Tad Jones, *Up from the Cradle of Jazz* (Athens, Ga.: University of Georgia Press, 1986), p. 21.

Mississippi

1. Robert Palmer, *Deep Blues* (New York: Penguin Books, 1981), p. 55.

2. Peter Guralnik, "Searching for Robert Johnson," *Living Blues,* Summer–Autumn 1982, p. 30.

Atlanta

1. Giles Oakley, *The Devil's Music: A History of the Blues* (New York: Taplinger, 1976), p. 136.

2. Albertson, *Bessie,* p. 27.

New York

1. Jim Haskins, *The Cotton Club* (New York: New American Library, 1977), p. 44.

2. Nat Shapiro and Nat Hentoff, eds., *Hear Me Talkin' to Ya* (New York: Dover, 1966), p. 354.

3. Samuel B. Charters and Leonard Kunstadt, *Jazz: A History of the New York Scene* (New York: Da Capo Press, 1981), p. 278.

4. Ellen Hopkins, "Where They Lived," *New York,* March 7, 1983, pp. 43–44.

5. Robert Reisner, *Bird: The Legend of Charlie Parker* (New York: Da Capo Press, 1975), p. 81.

6. John Chilton, *Billie's Blues: Billie Holiday's Story, 1933–59* (New York: Stein and Day, 1975), p. 57.

7. James Lincoln Collier, *Louis Armstrong: An American Genius* (New York: Oxford University Press, 1983), p. 331.

8. Hopkins, "Where They Lived," p. 50.

Chicago

1. Shapiro and Hentoff, *Hear Me Talkin'*, p. 135.
2. Palmer, *Deep Blues*, p. 144.
3. Arnold Shaw, *Honkers and Shouters* (New York: Collier Books, 1978), p. 306.

Kansas City

1. Ross Russell, *Jazz Style in Kansas City and the Southwest* (Los Angeles: University of California Press, 1971), p. 107.
2. *Ibid.*, p. 184.

Cincinnati

1. Peter Guralnick, *Sweet Soul Music: Rhythm and Blues and the Southern Dream of Freedom* (New York: Harper & Row, 1986), p. 234.

Houston

1. Russell, *Jazz Style*, p. 129.
2. Alan Govenar, *Meeting the Blues* (Dallas: Taylor, 1988), p. 99.

San Antonio

1. Frank Driggs, liner notes for *Robert Johnson, King of the Delta Blues Singers*, Columbia Records, No. CL1654.

Bibliography

Books

Albertson, Chris. *Bessie.* New York: Stein and Day, 1972.

Alleman, Richard. *The Movie Lover's Guide to New York.* New York: Harper & Row, 1988.

Armstrong, Louis. *Satchmo: My Life in New Orleans.* New York: Prentice-Hall, 1954.

Balliett, Whitney. *American Musicians: 56 Portraits in Jazz.* New York: Oxford University Press, 1986.

_____*Dinosaurs in the Morning.* New York: J. P. Lippincott, 1962.

_____*Ecstasy at the Onion.* New York: Bobbs-Merrill, 1971.

_____*Such Sweet Thunder.* New York: Bobbs-Merrill, 1966.

Barnet, Charlie, with Stanley Dance. *Those Swinging Years: The Autobiography of Charlie Barnet.* Baton Rouge: Louisiana State University Press, 1984.

Bechet, Sidney. *Treat It Gentle.* New York: Hill and Wang, 1960.

Berry, Chuck. *Chuck Berry: The Autobiography.* New York: Fireside Books, 1988.

Berry, Jason, Jonathan Foose, and Tad Jones. *Up from the Cradle of Jazz: New Orleans Music Since World War II.* Athens, Ga.: University of Georgia Press, 1986.

Bigard, Barney. *With Louis and the Duke: The Autobiography of a Jazz Clarinetist.* New York: Oxford University Press, 1986.

Britt, Stan. *Dexter Gordon: A Musical Biography.* New York: Da Capo Press, 1989.

Brown, Scott E. *James P. Johnson: A Case of Mistaken Identity.* Metuchen, N.J.: The Scarecrow Press and the Institute of Jazz Studies. Rutgers University, 1982.

Carr, Ian. *Miles Davis: A Biography.* New York: William Morrow, 1982.

Clayton, Buck, assisted by Nancy Miller Elliott. *Buck Clayton's Jazz World.* New York: Oxford University Press, 1987.

Center for Southern Folklore. *The Heritage of Black Music in Memphis.* Memphis: Center for Southern Folklore, 1986.

Charles, Ray, and David Ritz. *Brother Ray: Ray Charles' Own Story.* New York: Warner Books, 1979.

Charters, Samuel B., and Leonard Kunstadt. *Jazz: A History of the New York Scene.* New York: Da Capo Press, 1984.

Chilton, John. *Billie's Blues: Billie Holiday's Story, 1933–59.* New York: Stein and Day, 1975.

Collier, James Lincoln. *Louis Armstrong: An American Genius.* New York: Oxford University Press, 1983.

Dance, Helen Oakley. *Stormy Monday: The T-Bone Walker Story.* Baton Rouge: Louisiana State University Press, 1987.

Dance, Stanley. *The World of Earl Hines.* New York: Da Capo Press, 1983.

Davis, Miles, with Quincy Troupe. *Miles: The Autobiography.* New York: Simon & Schuster, 1989.

Ellington, Edward Kennedy. *Music Is My Mistress.* New York: Da Capo Press, 1976.

Feather, Leonard. *The Encyclopedia of Jazz.* New York: Horizon Press, 1960.

_____. *The Encyclopedia of Jazz in the '60s.* New York: Da Capo Press, 1986.

Feather, Leonard, and Ira Gitler. *The Encyclopedia of Jazz in the '70s.* New York: Da Capo Press, 1987.

Giddins, Gary. *Celebrating Bird: The Triumph of Charlie Parker.* New York: Beech Tree Books, 1987.

Gillespie, Dizzy, with Al Fraser. *To Be or Not to Bop.* New York: Da Capo Press, 1985.

Goldberg, Joe. *Jazz Masters of the Fifties.* New York: Da Capo Press, 1983.

Gordon, Max. *Live at the Village Vanguard.* New York: Da Capo Press, 1982.

Gordon, Robert. *Jazz West Coast.* New York: Quartet Books, 1986.

Govenar, Alan. *Meeting the Blues.* Dallas: Taylor, 1988.

Guralnick, Peter. *Lost Highway: Journeys and Arrivals of American Musicians.* New York: Vintage Books, 1982.

_____. *Sweet Soul Music: Rhythm and Blues and the Southern Dream of Freedom.* New York: Harper & Row, 1986.

Hammond, John, with Irving Townsend. *John Hammond on Record.* New York: Ridge Press, 1977.

Handy, W. C. *Father of the Blues: An Autobiography.* New York: Macmillan, 1941.

Harris, Sheldon. *Blues Who's Who.* New York: Da Capo Press, 1979.

Haskins, Jim. *The Cotton Club.* New York: New American Library, 1977.

Henderson, David. *'Scuse Me While I Kiss the Sky: The Life of Jimi Hendrix.* New York: Bantam Books, 1981.

Holiday, Billie, with William Dufty. *Lady Sings the Blues.* New York: Penguin Books, 1984.

Lewis, David Levering. *When Harlem Was in Vogue.* New York: Oxford University Press, 1979.

Lieb, Sandra. *Mother of the Blues: A Study of Ma Rainey.* Amherst, Mass.: University of Massachusetts Press, 1981.

Lomax, Alan. *Mister Jelly Roll.* London: Cassell & Co., 1952.

Marquis, Donald M. *In Search of Buddy Bolden: First Man of Jazz.* Baton Rouge: Louisiana State University Press, 1978.

McKee, Margaret, and Fred Chisenhall. *Beale Black and Blue: Life and Music on Black America's Main Street.* Baton Rouge: Louisiana State University Press, 1981.

Mezzrow, Milton, and Bernard Wolfe. *Really the Blues.* New York: Random House, 1946.

The New Grove Dictionary of Jazz. New York: Grove's Dictionaries of Music, 1988.

Oakley, Giles. *The Devil's Music: A History of the Blues.* New York: Taplinger, 1976.

Overbeck, Ruth Ann, et al. *D.C. "Blacks in the Arts."* 1987–1988 Completion Report of the Shaw School Urban Renewal Area, Washington, D.C.

Palmer, Robert. *Deep Blues.* New York: Penguin Books, 1982.

Pepper, Art, and Laurie Pepper. *Straight Life: The Story of Art Pepper.* New York: Schirmer Books, 1979.

Porter, Lewis. *Lester Young.* Boston: Twayne, 1985.

Priestley, Brian. *Mingus: A Critical Biography.* New York: Da Capo Press, 1983.

Reisner, Robert. *Bird: The Legend of Charlie Parker.* New York, Da Capo Press, 1977.

Rose, Al, and Eubie Blake. *Eubie Blake.* New York: Schirmer Books, 1979.

Rose, Al. *Storyville, New Orleans.* City University, Ala.: University of Alabama Press, 1974.

Rowe, Mike. *Chicago Blues: The City and the Music.* New York: Da Capo Press, 1981.

Russell, Ross. *Jazz Style in Kansas City and the Southwest.* Los Angeles: University of California Press, 1971.

Sales, Grover. *Jazz: America's Classical Music.* Englewood Cliffs, N.J.: Prentice-Hall, 1988.

Sawyer, Charles. *The Arrival of B. B. King: The Authorized Biography.* New York: Da Capo Press, 1980.

Shapiro, Nat, and Nat Hentoff, eds. *Hear Me Talkin' to Ya.* New York: Dover, 1966.

Shaw, Arnold. *52nd St.: The Street of Jazz.* New York: Da Capo Press, 1977.

———Honkers and Shouters: The Golden Years of Rhythm and Blues. New York: Collier Books, 1978.

———. *The Jazz Age.* New York: Oxford University Press, 1987.

Stearns, Marshall W. *The Story of Jazz.* New York: Oxford University Press, 1956.

Sudhalter, Richard M., Philip R. Evans, with William Dean-Myatt. *Bix: Man and Legend.* New Rochelle, N.Y.: Arlington House, 1974.

Taylor, Frank C., with Gerald Cook. *Alberta Hunter: A Celebration in Blues.* New York: McGraw-Hill, 1987.

Thomas, J. C. *Chasin' the Trane: The Music and Mystique of John Coltrane.* New York: Da Capo Press, 1976.

Titon, Jeff Todd. *Early Downhome Blues: A Musical and Cultural Analysis.* Chicago: University of Illinois Press, 1977.

Townley, Eric. *Tell Your Story.* Chigwell, England: Storyville Publications, 1976.

Travis, D. J. *An Autobiography of Black Jazz.* Chicago: Urban Research Institute, 1983.

Ulanov, Barry. *A History of Jazz in America.* New York: Viking Press, 1954.

Williams, Martin. *Jazz Masters in Transition, 1957–69.* New York: Da Capo Press, 1982.

Articles

For background material, I referred to back issues of *Living Blues, Down Beat* and *Jazz Times* and to local newspapers and magazines. The following articles are of particular relevance.

Bjorn, Lars. "Black Men in a White World: The Development of the Black Jazz Community in Detroit, 1917–1940." *Detroit in Perspective: A Journal of Regional History* (Fall 1980): 1–18.

"From Hastings Street to the Bluebird: The Blues and Jazz Tradition in Detroit." *Michigan Quarterly Review* (Spring 1986): 257–268.

Comiskey, Nancy L. "On the Avenue." *Indianapolis Monthly,* Feb. 1984, pp. 75–79.

Guralnick, Peter. "Searching for Robert Johnson." *Living Blues 53* (Summer–Autumn 1982): 27–41.

Hildebrand, Lee. "Oakland Blues: The Thrill Goes On." *Museum of California,* Sept.–Oct. 1982, pp. 5–7.

Hopkins, Ellen. "Where They Lived." *New York,* March 7, 1983, pp. 42–53.

Joseph, Frank. "We Got Jazz," *Pittsburgh,* Oct. 1979, pp. 31–52.

Marmorstein, Gary. "Jazz: The Men Who Won the West." *Los Angeles Herald Examiner,* Nov. 18, 1984, pp. 6–18.

Schuller, Tim. "Rebirth of a Bluesman." *D Magazine,* July 1989, pp. 34–36.

About the Contributors

Pedro Acevedo is a former calendar editor for the *Miami Herald*, where he also covered nightlife, before becoming a local reporter for the newspaper's Broward bureau. He has also worked as a senior assistant producer for Divina.com, a Web portal for Hispanic women.

Mary Katherine Aldin is a Grammy-nominated roots music reissue producer/annotator and music journalist. She is a regular contributor to *Living Blues* magazine, and writes the blues column for the *L.A. Weekly*.

Scott Barretta is the editor of *Living Blues* magazine, published by the University of Mississippi in Oxford, Mississippi. He previously edited the Swedish blues magazine *Jefferson*.

Andrew Bartlett is jazz editor for Amazon.com.

Jim Beal Jr. is an arts writer and music columnist for the *San Antonio Express-News*, and plays blues, zydeco, and etcetera bass in the San Antonio band Miss Neesie & the Ear Food Orchestra.

Fred Bouchard, a life-long Boston resident, has been *Down Beat* magazine's Boston correspondent since 1973.

David Courtney is a freelance writer living in Austin. He writes a music column for citysearch.com.

Chicago-based **Bill Dahl** is a veteran freelance blues and soul writer whose work has appeared in the *Reader, Living Blues, Goldmine*, and other publications; in 2000, he received the Blues Foundation's Keeping the Blues Alive Award in Journalism. He has also complied and annotated many CD reissues; in 1998, he was nominated for a Grammy for his liner notes contribution to the Ray Charles boxed set, *Genius & Soul—The 50th Anniversary Collection* (Rhino).

Jim Dulzo is a veteran Detroit-area jazz-and-blues broadcaster, journalist, and concert producer. He directed the Montreux Detroit Jazz Festival from 1994 to 1999.

Philip Elwood recently completed his 36th year as jazz critic for the *San Francisco Examiner*. In 1995 he retired after 45 years as a college teacher of American history, and in 1996 he left Pacifica Radio station KPFA after 44 continuous years of broadcasting the semi-weekly "Jazz Archives" and "Jazz Review" shows. He was born in Berkeley, where he still resides.

George Fendel hosts a jazz radio program, plays piano, and writes reviews and features for several publications and jazz CD liner notes. He may be reached at jazzfens@teleport.com.

Geoffrey Himes writes regularly for the *Washington Post, Baltimore City Paper, Oxford American, No Depression, Chicago Tribune*, and other publications. He has lived in Baltimore for 30 years.

Eugene Holley, Jr., is a freelance music journalist based in New York City. He has worked as a reporter/producer for National Public Radio in Washington, D.C., and served as program director for WCLK-FM in Atlanta, Georgia.

Joseph Jordan is a Bay Area–based blues journalist and author. He has been a contributing writer for *Blues Access, Blues Revue,* and *Southland Blues*. His Web site can be found at www.blueswriter.com.

Malcolm Mayhew was born and raised in Fort Worth, Texas. He has been a music critic at the *Fort Worth Star-Telegram* since 1992. He also writes reviews for *American Way* magazine.

Mike Metheny is a freelance jazz trumpet player in the Kansas City area, and the editor of *JAM*, the Jazz Ambassador Magazine.

Cincinnati Enquirer music critic **Larry Nager** has been writing about all forms of popular music since 1982. The former music editor for the *Memphis Commercial Appeal*, he documented that city's music history in his 1998 book, *Memphis Beat* (St. Martin's Press). He wrote and co-produced the acclaimed 1992 documentary film, *Bill Monroe, Father of Bluegrass* music and, in 1994, received the Blues Foundation's Keeping the Blues Alive Award for Journalism.

David Nelson was the editor of *Living Blues* magazine from 1992–1999. He lives in Snow Camp, North Carolina, and continues to write for *Living Blues*.

OffBeat is New Orleans' and Louisiana's music magazine, now celebrating its 13th year.

Terry Perkins writes about jazz and blues for the *St. Louis Post-Dispatch*, *The Riverfront Times*, and *Down Beat*. He is also a member of the Down Beat Critic's Poll.

From 1980 through 2000, **Mark Ruffin** was synonymous with jazz radio in Chicago, having worked at all the major jazz outlets during that time. He is now the jazz correspondent for the weekly television show "Artbeat Chicago" (WTTW-TV). Since 1985, he's been writing about Chicago nightlife as the jazz events editor of *Chicago Magazine*, and also contributes to Amazon.com, *Ndigo*, Jazzusa.com, *Jazziz*, downbeatjazz.com, the *Brazilian Music Review*, and many other publications.

Mike Shanley is the music editor of *In Pittsburgh Weekly*, an alternative news and arts weekly. A native of Pittsburgh, he has been part of the underground music scene for over 15 years, and owns what he considers to be too many records and CDs of all musical shapes and styles.

Matthew Socey is the blues columnist for *NUVO Newsweekly* and editor of the Crossroads Blues Society newsletter. His articles have appeared in *Down Beat*, *Blues Access*, and *Blues Revue*. He lives in Indianapolis.

American Book Award–winner **James G. Spady** is the author of *Georgie Woods: I'm Only A Man*, *Larry Neal and the Blues Streak of Mellow Wisdom*, *William L. Dawson: A Umum Tribute and A Marvelous Journey*, and a trilogy on rap music and hip hop culture: *Nation Conscious Rap* (1991), *Twisted Tales in the Hip Hop Streets of Philly* (1995), and *Street Conscious Rap* (1999). His forthcoming book, *360 Degreez of Sonia Sanchez, Hip Hop, Narrativity, Iqhawe and Public Spaces of Being* will be published in 2001. Spady was consultant and planner for the historic UMUM Black Music Seminar at Swarthmore College and the Philadelphia International Jazz Arts Conference, and is currently completing a study of Philly Joe Jones and the Philadelphia jazz scene.

John Spong is an assistant editor at *Texas Monthly*, based in Austin.

ASCAP–Deems Taylor recipient **Zan Stewart** has been covering the Los Angeles jazz community since the late 1970s. Stewart's affiliations have included the *Los Angeles Times* and the *L.A. Weekly*, as well as *Down Beat*, *Musician*, *Musica Jazz*, *Jazz Life*, and *Stereophile* magazines.

Tom Surowicz is a regular contributor to the *Minneapolis Star-Tribune*. His liner notes can be found on CDs by Jack McDuff, Tom Harrell, Joshua Breakstone, Carmen McRae, Dakota Staton, Big George Jackson, Joe T. Cook, and sundry other jazz and blues artists.

Bill E. Williams has been working in the television entertainment and public relations business for twenty years. He has served on the board of directors for both the Kansas City Blues Society and the Kansas City Jazz Ambassadors, and has booked much national, regional, and local talent for Kansas City events.

Roger Wood has written music features for *Living Blues*, the *Houston Press*, and the *Arkansas Review*, and is a contributor to the forthcoming book, *The History of Texas Music, From the Beginnings to 1950* (Texas A&M University Press).

Also contributing to the research of this book were **Felix Worhstein** in Chicago, and **John Ruskey** and **Euphus Ruth** in the Mississippi Delta.

Selected Index